MW00528955

LUCKY LOSER

that claim since Trump leaped to the front of a crowded Republican field earlier that year. Russ had reported on Trump's failures running casinos and golf courses, Susanne on his strained relationships with Wall Street and his hundreds of millions of dollars of debt. Then, days before the first debate, an anonymously addressed manila envelope arrived in Susanne's mailbox at the *Times*. She opened it to find what appeared to be a few pages from Trump's 1995 tax return. The line for total income showed a stunning figure, almost too jarring to seem plausible: negative $915,729,293.

The *Times* published our article, which we worked on with other colleagues, about Trump's nearly one-billion-dollar loss, the weekend after the first debate. It might have led some voters to think hard about whether Trump's business career indeed reflected the kind of thinking our country needed. Either way, six weeks later, enough voters in enough states chose Trump for him to become the forty-fifth president of the United States.

Political reporters in general were widely criticized for failing to recognize Trump's popularity and momentum. Fair enough. But it was also true that no major party candidate in the modern era had made it to Election Day with such a thin level of credential vetting. That, in our opinion, was a failure of equal proportion. But it was not for lack of will. It was largely due to the unique characteristics of Trump and his candidacy.

Nearly all candidates for president have lived in the public eye and occupied public office for decades. Their every move has been scrutinized. They have filed financial disclosure forms. Most have made little money outside public office, and their finances tend to be fairly simple. Trump was an anomaly on multiple levels.

He was perhaps the best-known businessperson in the country about whom almost nothing was known for certain. He had hovered for decades at the nexus of business and tabloid celebrity, often treated more as an entertaining sideshow than a man of consequence. He rose to national stature alongside the same media outlets that elevated the rich and successful to a new level of celebrity. Countless fawning profiles in more serious outlets, including in the *Times*, dutifully quoted him making assertions that could have been revealed as wildly false. The guiding journalistic principle seemed to be: What could it possibly matter if Donald Trump lies about himself? He was always available, working to charm journalists who could bring him the attention he needed more than water. And his bombast made for good copy and excellent television, boosting ratings and newsstand sales for decades. A portion of the nation happily went along for the ride, seemingly eager to believe a fantasy from a handsome rich man. None of it mattered. Until it did.

Trump had never run for public office but had publicly toyed with the idea, testing the waters in 1988, 2000, 2003, and 2013. The 2016 campaign began like another quixotic play, perhaps intended to generate attention that he could monetize.

Trump became the leading candidate too late to allow enough time to pry into his tightly held family operation. Chief executives of public corporations face a merciless grading period every 120 days, but only Trump graded Trump. The veracity of the claim that his business track record reflected the "kind of thinking" that would save America was buried in the records of a small company started by his father almost a century earlier.

We set out to find the truth. We began by gathering reams of public documents related to his father Fred's career, deeds, mortgages, court records, and congressional testimony. We closely analyzed the details of financial disclosure forms his sister had been required to file as a federal judge. We tracked down sources who had worked with Fred Trump and Donald Trump.

One court case in particular held great potential. After Fred's death, the adult children of Donald's deceased brother had accused their aunts and uncles of wrongfully cutting them out of Fred's estate. During the legal battle, some number of Fred's financial records had been turned over to Mary Trump and Fred Trump III, Donald's niece and nephew.

Our preliminary reporting suggested that Fred Trump III, known as Fritz, remained close and perhaps reliant on his aunts and uncles. Susanne took the lead in seeing whether Mary Trump might be interested in sharing the records she had received about her grandfather's finances. After rebuffing a few early contacts, Mary Trump opened her front door to Susanne. Soon after, we all—Mary, Susanne, Russ, and our *Times* colleague David Barstow—sat in Mary's living room and discussed the potential revelations locked away in her lawyer's file room. Mary did not know much about her grandfather's business, but she understood the importance of voters knowing more about her family history. She appreciated the risks she would be taking and decided to proceed anyway.

She surprised us with an unserious idea. She wanted all of us to go see the

LUCKY LOSER

HOW DONALD TRUMP SQUANDERED HIS FATHER'S FORTUNE AND CREATED THE ILLUSION OF SUCCESS

Russ Buettner *and* **Susanne Craig**

PENGUIN PRESS
NEW YORK
2024

PENGUIN PRESS
An imprint of Penguin Random House LLC
penguinrandomhouse.com

Image credits appear on page 501.

ISBN 9780593298640 (hardcover)
ISBN 9780593298657 (ebook)
ISBN 9780593834299 (international edition)

Printed in the United States of America
1st Printing

Designed by Amanda Dewey

FROM RUSS:

For Stacey, my love
And Emma, our light

FROM SUSANNE:

For Gary Park,
my first editor

CONTENTS

INTRODUCTION

THE WEEK BEFORE the 2016 presidential election, Donald J. Trump took a break from campaigning to attend the ceremonial opening of his new hotel a few blocks from the White House. Donald, his wife Melania, and his four grown children posed for photographers in their new Presidential Ballroom, clutching scissors at the edge of a long red ribbon bearing the Trump name.

Don Jr., Ivanka, and Eric, all in their thirties, were by then experienced ribbon cutters. They had each joined their father's business early in his star turn on *The Apprentice*, when his newfound fame made licensing the use of his name a core focus of the company. They had spent years traveling the world, posing with a shovel or pair of scissors and a developer paying to use the Trump name. The Trumps referred to those buildings as their "jobs." But the burdens of the work—the decision-making, overseeing construction, all the financial risk—fell to other companies.

This day represented a throwback to a time when the Trump name on a building signified that it had been built by Donald Trump. Back in 2012, the Trumps had won a bidding war to lease and redevelop the Old Post Office building, an ornate Romanesque revival building with a clock tower piercing the city's skyline. They committed to spending at least $200 million and paying base rent starting at $3 million a year. The Trump offer was so high that it gave a jolt to the government official overseeing the process and compelled other bidders, mostly major hotel chains, to protest that only a naïf could believe he would ever make a profit.

At the time, Trump acknowledged he was "paying too much for the Old Post Office." But now, standing in his new ballroom as the Republican nominee, he described his family's work on the hotel as the latest example of why he should be elected president.

"Today is a metaphor for what we can accomplish for this country," Trump said during the ceremony. "I've been very lucky, and I've led a great life," he added. "Now I want to give back to the country which I love so much and has been so good to me."

The truth of Trump's metaphor would remain hidden in his private records for years. What he had accomplished was to spend so much on the project that he would never make money running it. He would be forced to pump millions of dollars a year into the hotel's accounts to cover his losses. It was, by then, a defining pattern of his career, though one unknown to the outside world. He would eventually be forced to sell, and even that apparent windfall would not be what it seemed.

Throughout the campaign, Trump's most repeated argument for his candidacy leaned on his life in business, which he framed as one man's triumphant rise from modest beginnings. He typically mentioned his father, Fred C. Trump, a twentieth-century builder of tens of thousands of profitable homes and apartments, as a miniaturized contrast to his own enormity. During Trump's first debate with the Democratic nominee, Hillary Clinton, she pivoted from a question on economic policy to gently deride Trump as a child of wealth.

"Donald was very fortunate in his life, and that's all to his benefit," Clinton said.

Trump took no offense at Clinton mocking his economic policy as "trumped-up trickle-down." He could not, however, tolerate Clinton's suggestion that any factor other than his own genius made him rich enough to affix his name to golf courses, apartment buildings, casinos, hotels, and dress shirts.

"My father gave me a very small loan in 1975, and I built it into a company that's worth many, many billions of dollars, with some of the greatest assets in the world," Trump said. "And I say that only because that's the kind of thinking that our country needs."

The two of us—Susanne Craig and Russ Buettner of the investigative reporting team at *The New York Times*—had been exploring the moving parts of new Steven Spielberg film, *The Post*, which dramatized *The Washington Post*'s efforts to publish the Pentagon Papers, a secret history of U.S. involvement in Vietnam. The four of us met at a theater on Thirty-Fourth Street on a weeknight and proceeded to watch handsome renditions of newspaper reporters and editors sift through records, meet with confidential sources, and deal with external pressures.

After the movie, Mary asked us: Is that like what you guys will do?

We looked at one another for a beat. Pretty much, we said.

One drizzly fall evening not long after, Mary drove a rented van to her lawyer's office, filled it with boxes of records, and returned to her home on Long Island where we were waiting. We then transported those boxes back to a secret office at the *Times*, where we would spend most of the next year analyzing about one hundred thousand pages of audited financial statements, tax returns, bank records, general ledgers, and legal papers. The resulting story, published in October 2018, revealed for the first time that Donald Trump had received the equivalent of more than $400 million from his father, much of it through fraudulent tax evasion schemes. The story disproved Donald Trump's lifelong claim that his father gave him nothing more than a "small" $1 million loan. For our work exposing the true state of Trump's finances, we were honored with a Pulitzer Prize.

Mary Trump revealed her work with us in her bestselling book about her uncle, *Too Much and Never Enough*. As our reporting continued, we developed more sources from the Trump universe, many of whose names we cannot reveal. There were clandestine meetings in out-of-the-way places and chats on burner phones. During some of those meetings, sources provided us with Donald Trump's business and personal tax returns spanning several decades. That work resulted in several lengthy investigative articles in the *Times*.

Newspaper articles, though, rarely allow for the telling of a life story, a family story, a career, in the full breadth it deserves, especially a life as singular and consequential as Donald Trump's. And so we began work on this book. We have since spent three years building upon our prior reporting by conducting hundreds of new interviews and acquiring additional documents, including confidential correspondence, internal business records from *The Apprentice*, and unpublished memoirs.

The result offers unprecedented insights into the most central factor of Trump's identity: his money. By revealing the true sources behind his wealth, and the ways in which he lost so much of it, new details and larger truths emerged about the "kind of thinking" he has displayed in business and entertainment. For the first time, financial records set straight Donald Trump's chaotic onslaught of untruths and misdirection.

The sum of our work is an epic American tale, one set against a backdrop of broad economic and cultural changes that benefited Donald Trump perhaps more than anyone.

The family fortune that launched Donald Trump was built on government programs designed to ease the pain caused by the Great Depression and World War II, and to assist the veterans returning from that war. His father wrung millions of additional dollars from those programs by twisting the rules. When caught, he obsessed about his reputation, concerned that public mention of him making millions of dollars would damage his reputation as an honorable businessman.

That episode highlighted one of the many character traits that could make Fred and Donald seem like polar opposites. Fred viewed the perception of his wealth as threatening perceptions of his honor. Donald's viewed perceptions of his wealth as fueling perceptions of his honor.

Fred preferred to announce his projects once he had everything lined up—the land, the financing, the zoning approvals—and was ready to begin selling apartments or houses. Attention in pursuit of sales. Donald would announce dreams and fantasies as if they were a certainty before he had lined up anything. Attention in pursuit of attention.

Most often, the initial announcements came to nothing. But Donald Trump would get his headline and the glow of free publicity while building the impression he was everywhere. A day of reckoning, when reporters and the public might recognize that his announcements merely reflected the way he wanted things to be, rarely ever came.

There were more substantial differences in the business practices of the father and son. Fred forecasted the expenses and revenues of his projects to the dollar. He never missed. Donald early in his life decided that any project with his name above the door would bring enough revenue to cover whatever he spent. He missed often. Some of Donald's mistakes cost his father millions of dollars. Yet Fred never wavered in his support, one of the great enabling factors of Donald Trump's life.

Fred saw his rental empire as his legacy. He needed an heir to run it and grow it. The succession battle would be won by Donald almost by default. After ignoring his two daughters and feeling disappointed by his eldest son, Fred passed the reins, along with access to his financial and political connections, to a twenty-two-year-old Donald. Fred never questioned Donald's decisions, even as they went horribly wrong.

People who worked with the Trumps in the 1970s marveled to us about how Fred never scorned his son's efforts and ideas, which many saw as almost a tradition among self-made men with entitled heirs. Even when Donald falsely belittled his father's real estate empire to make it appear he had started with nothing, Fred did not object. "Everything he touches turns to gold," Fred began saying before Donald had touched much of anything.

Our reporting shows that the character traits that would become most identified with Donald Trump during his presidency were set in his early twenties through his relationship with his father. His instinct to fight everything without regard to cost or time or further reputational harm, to file lawsuits more like an angry trust funder than a businessman weighing risks and reward. His de facto definition of loyalty as a one-way street. His tendency to see himself as a victim of jealousy and unfairness. His belief that his instincts, which typically meant his desired reality, were superior to any reasoned analysis by experts. All of it emerges in his relationship with a doting, if cold, father.

No telling of Donald's Trump's life could be complete without occasionally marveling at the power of his innate and unique charisma. Across the decades, Donald Trump drew eyeballs, viewers, and everyday people who just wanted to touch his suit, all of which validated, at least in a cynical calculus, the decisions to give him ink and airtime.

The value America placed on this sort of charisma rose during Donald Trump's lifetime. Fred Trump developed some notoriety for his military-like precision in constructing sprawling apartment complexes. But mid-twentieth-century America provided few avenues for Fred to profit just from being well-known. By the time Donald Trump became a television celebrity, fame, detached from any other marketable talent or skill, had become a highly compensated vocation.

Mark Burnett, the television producer who made Trump a star, did not just hand him a fortune. In the editing bay, skilled hands created a version of Donald Trump—diligent, measured, polite but authoritative—that might have been nonexistent but was highly marketable. They hid the moments when he worked against the show's interest to squeeze out a few more dollars for himself on the side and the times his lack of focus or greed offended sponsors.

Fame from the show brought Trump hundreds of millions of dollars in endorsement and licensing deals that required little of him. We saw how his shortsighted lack of discipline, his concern only about the size of a check, led him into licensing deals that would collapse in failure, scandal, and lawsuits, risking the value of the brand name created by Burnett's editors and storytellers.

Sometimes, despite himself, Donald Trump received his fortune from those sources mostly outside of his ability to run a business. The secret of his life, one that emerges in hundreds of moments big and small, is that the less he has been involved in decision-making, the better his chances of financial success.

Donald Trump came to be imbued with a host of attributes that speak to how we confer admiration and status in modern America. Our awe of celebrity. Our tendency to conflate the trappings of wealth with expertise and ability. Our eagerness to believe people of apparent status will not lie to us. Our inability to distinguish the fruits of hard work from those of sheer luck.

That is the real work of this book. It is a story about Donald Trump, his family, his wealth, his failures. But it is also a story about this country, and how we've arrived at a moment when Donald Trump is a leading candidate for president for the third time.

Trump has clung to his hardscrabble fable. In his telling, his father created a "tiny, beautiful little company" and "didn't leave a great fortune" to pass on. His father's greatest contribution to his son was superior genes, knowledge, and a killer instinct. And from those humble beginnings he overcame a string of jealous scoundrels and scornful doubters. He has so completely hidden the truth, perhaps even from himself, that he can erase the lucky breaks from his extraordinarily lucky life.

"It has not been easy for me," Trump has said.

Part I

THE FATHER

Real estate cannot be lost or stolen, nor can it be carried away. Purchased with common sense, paid for in full, and managed with reasonable care, it is about the safest investment in the world.

—attributed to Franklin D. Roosevelt by real estate professionals since the 1940s

1

A NATURAL VIRGIN MARKET

In May 1923, a determined seventeen-year-old boy stared out from a page of *The Brooklyn Daily Eagle.* Above his thick blond hair ran the headline HELPS BUILD QUEENS. Two paragraphs announced to the world that this teenager, Fred C. Trump, envisioned "a big future in the building industry." He would become a "builder," he declared.

The borough of Queens was exploding with growth all around him. The population had roughly tripled since his birth and would double again by 1930. His alma mater—Richmond Hill High School—had been built for eight hundred students but was already jammed with two thousand teenagers. Classes were held on the front steps. Students waited in line for a desk in the study hall.

Outside, the streets teamed with new arrivals, mostly from Germany and Russia. The demand for housing was unyielding. It was a time when a paved street and a sewer line were luxuries notable enough to mention in an advertisement. Former farms and forests in Queens offered vast stretches of open land, newly within reach of Manhattan. After the Queensboro Bridge had connected the boroughs in 1909, train lines and trollies pushed farther and farther out. Real estate developers rushed to the site of each new train stop and advertised homes to Manhattan-bound commuters: "5-cent fare zone!"

Amid this epic building boom, Fred Trump worked incessantly to find his place. He ignored his school's extracurricular activities—the sports teams, the acting and singing troupes, the chapter of Arista, an honor society. Instead, he worked, earning money and learning how to build homes. He delivered building supplies to construction sites with a horse-drawn wagon. He took a job as an assistant foreman with a construction company. He eventually built a garage for a neighbor. He would come to believe that even his choice of childhood toys—blocks and erector sets—foretold his destiny.

In some measure, his interest in real estate tracked the unfulfilled dreams of his late father. His parents, Frederick and Elizabeth, had arrived from Germany during an earlier immigration wave, in the late 1800s. Frederick traveled to the western frontier, where he ran a restaurant that had once also operated as a brothel. He returned to New York City to manage a restaurant and pursue small real estate investments. He bought his young family a simple two-story house on a dirt road in the Woodhaven section of Queens, one block south of the bustling Jamaica Plank Road, then a key route packed with horse-drawn carriages making the journey to Manhattan from the farms of Long Island. Their neighbors mostly rented their homes and worked as janitors, house painters, store clerks, and in the shipyard.

Frederick's real estate career had just begun to gain momentum when he was struck down by the Spanish flu, the pandemic then ravaging the world. He died in 1918 at the age of forty-nine, leaving Elizabeth alone to raise their three children: Fred, twelve, John, ten, and Elizabeth, fourteen. They would not be destitute. Frederick left his wife an estate valued at $36,000, the equivalent of more than $800,000 today, mostly in the form of money due on loans he had made to builders and the value of a few vacant lots.

Elizabeth assumed the role of the family's business leader. While Fred was still in high school, his mother hired contractors and oversaw the building of homes on the vacant lots she owned. She had designs on creating a family real estate company with her three children. John, who had a way with figures and details, would become the architect. Elizabeth, her oldest, would run the office. And Fred would become the builder. She formed the first Trump family enterprise, E. Trump & Son, artfully masking her own gender and her two sons' youth.

Fred threw himself into the role. He took classes at a local YMCA in carpentry, and more classes to understand blueprints and engineering. He and his mother began buying undeveloped land. They did not borrow money to build. They would pay cash for a lot or two, Fred would work frantically to build a house, and they would offer it for sale before he had finished in hopes of using the proceeds to buy another piece of land. By the time Fred was in his early twenties, he and his mother regularly placed classified advertisements to sell homes under the E. Trump & Son name, offering easy terms for buyers.

By 1925, Elizabeth and her children moved a little farther out, to the neighborhood known as Jamaica, a name thought to be derived from the Native Americans known as Jameco, or Yamecah, who once lived there. The Trumps bought a house south of Hillside Avenue, the dividing line between the modest homes and tight lots of Jamaica to the south and a new world of wealth to the north, christened Jamaica Estates.

Jamaica Estates had been founded by an early generation of New York real estate royalty, nineteenth-century men with cookie-duster mustaches and formidable bearings. The best known of them was Felix Isman, considered to be worth $30 million in his early thirties and famous for having said a man could be correct about New York real estate only three quarters of the time and still make money.

Another Jamaica Estates founder, Michael J. Degnon, had been instrumental in construction of the Williamsburg Bridge over the East River, much of the new subway system under Manhattan, and a massive industrial park in Queens. Degnon himself bought the most prime swath of land in the area, a sixteen-acre plot atop the hill rising behind the owner's lodge. He commissioned a stone mansion surrounded by streams and forest. Newspapers articles of the time claimed that the highest ground in Jamaica Estates offered views of the Atlantic Ocean to the south and Long Island Sound to the north.

Isman, Degnon, and the other founders had modeled Jamaica Estates after an exclusive gated community in Orange County, north of New York City, known as Tuxedo Park. The black suits and ties with crisp, white shirts favored by the men of the community came to be known as tuxedos. Jamaica Estates would not have a gate, but it would have a stone gatehouse where Midland Parkway, conceived as the most exclusive address in the community, began its path north from Hillside Avenue. To the right of the entrance, the founders constructed a large Elizabethan-style lodge. They hired a famous landscape architect to incorporate the parklike qualities of the area into the street design, with roadways gently arcing around mature trees and hills. The founders gave streets names that evoked English estates—Cambridge, Devonshire, and Wexford Terrace. There would be tennis courts near the entrance, and a golf course on another neighborhood border.

For all their experience, the founders' vision to create an enclave of extreme wealth did not hold. The original partnership dissolved in discord. The neighborhood would remain a pocket of greater wealth than the working-class Jamaica all around it, but one of the mere professional classes. In one long weekend, two thousand lots in Jamaica Estates were sold off by Joseph P. Day, a famous real estate auctioneer of the early twentieth century. Weeks of advertisements and articles in the city's newspapers created a frenzy. More than fourteen hundred potential bidders showed up to sit under a large tent across Midland Parkway from the owner's lodge and buy multiple lots. If Fred and Elizabeth did not attend, they most certainly were aware of the spectacle.

From the bedroom where Fred Trump slept in his early twenties, he could walk three minutes north to Hillside Avenue and gaze up at the Degnon mansion, the estate of the legendary builder. He aimed his life toward earning a place in Jamaica Estates alongside the Ismans and Degnons of the world.

A year after he and his mother began regularly selling the homes he had built, they placed an advertisement in *The Chat*, a Brooklyn newspaper, that read "Builder will sell his own home," offering their six-room house just below Hillside Avenue for $9,250. Fred built them a house a few blocks north on Devonshire Road. He was not yet thirty years old. For the rest of his life, he would call Jamaica Estates his home.

Only Fred continued in the line of work about which his father had dreamed for himself and his mother had imagined for her children. His siblings went in different directions. John headed to college at the Polytechnic Institute, where he would be class valedictorian, and then to earn a doctorate from the Massachusetts Institute of Technology, where he became a respected professor and researcher. Their sister, Elizabeth, married a banker named William Walter, and they moved into one of Fred's early homes.

After several years of building modest houses in other neighborhoods, Fred set his sights on the wealthier buyers in Jamaica Estates. He built sixteen homes along both sides of Wareham Road, the next street over from the premiere addresses along Midland Parkway. Unlike his prior focus on utilitarian simplicity, these homes would feature architectural details and modern amenities. Most would be Tudor revivals, with multiple gabled rooflines and a mix of stone, brick, and wood-trimmed stucco. They featured landscaped yards and two-car garages. Then twenty-five years old, Fred spoke with a reporter about his experiences with discerning buyers during "my ten years in the building and developing field." He listed the homes at prices ranging from $17,500 to $30,000, multiples of anything he had built before.

"Stroll around this parklike section," urged his advertisement in *The Brooklyn Daily Eagle*. "You will wonder that this community, so like the aristocratic estates of Old England, is within the limits of New York, and but twenty minutes from Broadway.

"No detail has been spared that these homes might suit the individuality of the high type residents in this community."

At the bottom of the advertisement, there was no reference to his mother. Only one name appeared, offset by the job title that might have seemed like a distant dream just a few years earlier: "FRED C. TRUMP, Builder."

FRED TRUMP REMADE HIMSELF as a builder for the "high types" just as the national economy collapsed into the worst depression in the nation's history. Hundreds of thousands of properties were lost to foreclosure. Newspapers featured long lines of recently unemployed men waiting for food handouts. Nearly one quarter of Americans were out of work, with the construction industry particularly hard hit. Roughly half of all construction jobs had disappeared as home building slowed to a crawl.

As the economy hit its nadir, Fred returned to Woodhaven. He built a one-story box of a building near the house where he had grown up. He hung a sign outside—TRUMP MARKETS—and tried his hand at a new type of business, the supermarket, a reimagining of the grocery store with everything the modern homemaker needed under one roof, saving her separate trips to the butcher, the fishmonger, and the fruit stand. It was a concept created by a neighbor in Jamaica Estates, Michael J. Cullen, who had opened what was thought to be the first supermarket, King Kullen, several years earlier. After proudly advocating his aristocratic estates, Fred now peddled "genuine spring legs of lamb" for seventeen cents a pound, along with Chesterfield cigarettes, crab meat, cleaning supplies, dog food, and house paint.

Fred Trump, the grocer, would be a brief diversion. Months after he opened the market, an opportunity arose from the economic devastation. A decades-old financial house, J. Lehrenkrauss Corporation, crumbled in scandal. Fred bid in bankruptcy court for its mortgage-servicing business, eventually partnering with another bidder, a man named William Demm, to win the portfolio of failing mortgages and properties facing foreclosure. During the process, he became impressed with Demm's lawyer, William Hyman, an athletic-looking, blue-eyed son of Jewish immigrants from Europe. Fred soon parted ways with Demm, but he and Hyman formed a long-standing bond.

Nominally back in real estate, Fred sold his supermarket to Cullen and swore to himself he would never put his name on a business again. He focused his energies on selling the properties in the Lehrenkrauss portfolio. Cleaning up the mess in a failed lender's real estate portfolio, while a substantial endeavor for a young man finding his way through a horrible economy, was not how Fred had envisioned his career unfolding. But his fortunes were about to take a dramatic turn thanks to the federal government's efforts to deal with the economic calamity.

By 1934, Franklin Delano Roosevelt desperately wanted to get hammers back in the hands of construction workers. A year into his presidency, and with the nation locked in a deep depression, he was frustrated that the industry, a major driver of jobs in the 1920s, had not begun to turn around as quickly as others. He thought kick-starting home construction could also improve the "terrible conditions" of housing in much of the country, like the crowded tenement buildings on the Lower East Side of Manhattan, without sanitation or lighting.

But Roosevelt wrestled with how to accomplish those goals. During one confidential briefing with reporters, Roosevelt described the letters he had traded with his "very old friend" Joseph P. Day, the New York real estate man who had auctioned off lots in Jamaica Estates. Day told him that builders wanted the government to stay out of home building, insisting that "it is not the prerogative of government" and would be like the "terrible socialism" of some European states. Day admitted that private developers would not, on their own, see enough of a profit motive to build housing for millions of lower-income Americans, but he had faith that the market would "work itself out some way." Roosevelt was not willing to sit idly by and hope for the best, which he described as government and private enterprise throwing up their collective hands and saying, "We are licked."

"That is his answer, 'We are licked,'" Roosevelt told the reporters. "And if somebody asks the question, 'Is government going to consider itself licked in its effort to take care of people who cannot otherwise be taken care of?' The answer is, obviously, 'No!'"

That tension between government intervention and a purely free-market approach would shape the contours of federal housing programs for decades to come. The Roosevelt administration's first attempt to straddle those competing interests was the creation of the Federal Housing Administration.

Authorized by the National Housing Act of 1934, the FHA forever changed the economics of home buying in the country. Private lenders had historically been so worried about borrower defaults that they lent mostly only to people who did not need the money: loans had to be repaid within three to five years and would at most cover half of a home's value. The new rules would also allow for a repayment period of up to thirty years and loans of 80 percent of the home's value, easing payments for millions of homebuyers. The FHA would guarantee that homebuyers paid back their mortgages, opening a torrent of funding for construction by reducing the risk to the private sector.

Roosevelt recognized that millions of lower-income families would still be left out. And in practice, the FHA would refuse to insure mortgages to nearly all African Americans, under the notion that neighborhoods with "inharmonious groups"—or "people of [a] different race, color, nationality and culture"—led to "the destruction of value." As home ownership became the primary vehicle of wealth growth of most Americans, the FHA's practices set Black and white families on starkly different economic trajectories for the decades to come. The new agency soon issued rules for homes eligible for mortgage insurance, pages and pages of minimum construction and design standards. Fred Trump saw before him an opportunity to profitably build modest homes. He would never again aim for "high type" buyers of single-family houses that he had pursued in Jamaica Estates. He and a partner purchased lots to build more than four hundred homes on the former Barnum & Bailey circus grounds in Brooklyn, a bigger project than anything he had ever done. He posted signs that read TRUMP HOMES. Beyond them, as far as the eye could see down a long city block, hundreds of his masons and carpenters worked on fifty or more homes at a time, with a row of structures rising in unison. City newspapers began calling Fred "the Henry Ford of the building industry" for his assembly-line approach, a moniker Fred would use in advertisements. He would dig holes for the foundations of an entire block all at once, and then use high-speed mixers to pour the concrete. He set up long stretches of scaffolding so his brick masons could assemble a dozen homes at one time. Bricklaying for an entire block sometimes took only one week. The homes would sell for as little as $4,390, with loans backed by the FHA. When the model home for the circus grounds project opened in August 1936, the state FHA director, Thomas G. Grace, showed up to kick off the event. After the ceremony, there were so many potential buyers that Fred Trump installed floodlights to add a nighttime shift.

As HE WORKED around the clock in Brooklyn, according to family lore, Fred found time to go to a party attended by younger women from Scotland. Among them was Mary Anne MacLeod, a tall and lanky woman in her early twenties. As a teenager, she had left her rural village in Scotland, where her father was a fisherman and small-time farmer, to join two of her sisters in the Astoria section of Queens and find work as a maid. Mary, a native Gaelic speaker, spoke the English she had learned in school with a thick accent. Trump family lore does not explain how a recent immigrant living in Astoria and a workaholic young real estate developer living ten miles away in Jamaica Estates wound up at the same social function. Whatever the case, their courtship was a quick one.

Fred Trump, thirty, and Mary Anne MacLeod, twenty-three, married on January 11, 1936, at a Presbyterian church in Manhattan. Her hometown newspaper in Scotland, the *Stornoway Gazette*, reported that the bride wore a "princess gown of white satin and a tulle cap and veil" and carried a bouquet of white orchids and lilies of the valley. The ceremony was followed by a reception dinner for about twenty-five people at the Carlyle hotel, where guests were served a sit-down dinner of chicken au cresson and French Sauterne wine. After a brief trip to Atlantic City, Fred returned to work. His mother, Elizabeth, moved out of the house on Devonshire Road and into a small apartment nearby. The following year, Fred and Mary welcomed their first child, Maryanne, followed by a son, Fred Jr., in 1938.

Fred worked harder and longer days than ever, becoming one of the most prolific home builders in the country, all of it fueled by FHA-backed mortgages. He spent twelve hours a day on job sites, directing every task. He still controlled costs as if he were just starting out. He did not have an office and kept his financial records in his pocket. He did not borrow money—he boasted of writing five-figure checks to buy land and materials—and paid his workers and contractors in cash.

No expense was too small to reduce. He would turn off any lights that had been unnecessarily left on and water down paint. The story told over and over to capture Fred Trump's strict adherence to cost control is of him picking up unbent nails from the dust at construction sites and passing them on for one of his carpenters to use. Maybe the point of the practice was only to make a point. At the cost of nails in the late 1930s, Fred Trump would have had to scrounge up thirteen nails just to save one penny.

He delegated nothing of importance. He generally did not hire permanent employees until late in the 1930s, when he brought on Charles H. Luerssen Jr., the grandson of German immigrants, as his sales manager, and Luerssen's wife, Amy, the daughter of an Italian immigrant, as an executive assistant. Amy would remain Fred Trump's closest aide and favorite lunch companion for the rest of his life. Many would refer to her as Fred's secretary, but his family and insiders would come to see her as the chief operating officer, perhaps the only person outside the family whom Fred trusted completely.

His tight control of costs extended to his closest colleagues, even his longtime lawyer, William Hyman. Hyman's son, Milton, recalled decades later with a laugh, "He liked my pop a lot, but he never paid him much."

A feature article in *American Builder*, a trade magazine, said Fred was one of the few builders in the country to finish more than 150 homes a year. A photograph showed him sitting on a retaining wall at a construction site, surrounded by loose bricks, tossed lumber, and soil, wearing a long-sleeve shirt and tie with a straw fedora tilted back on his forehead. Lean and smiling broadly, he looked completely in his element, with a blueprint draped across his lap. The writer, Joseph B. Mason, then the East Coast editor of the journal and an advocate for the construction industry, marveled at Fred's ability to find undervalued sites and tailor his marketing to the predominant culture of the surrounding community, stressing the proximity to Catholic churches and parochial schools in one neighborhood, and synagogues and yeshivas in another.

The involvement of the FHA eased everything for Fred Trump and his buyers. Builders could readily obtain construction loans based on the total appraised value of their project by the FHA. For effective builders, there were cost savings from scale. Fred liked to say that a home of the size and quality of his row houses would rent for $75 a month, but could be bought for $43 a month, with just a $590 down payment. Buyers agreed. He held an open house in East Flatbush when he finished the first few of more than two hundred homes. So many potential buyers showed up that he had his crew build a makeshift gangplank to the front door of model homes so more people could take a look.

"When the big crowds arrived, I was dumbfounded," he said. "I never expected such a gathering, and I was not prepared to meet it."

He became a prominent promoter of home ownership in New York, though he could sound almost robotic with his nasally voice. He occasionally took awkward stabs at humor. After one of his new buyers welcomed a baby, Fred told a reporter for the *New York Daily News* that "even the stork endorses and approves of home ownership these days." At one point he hired a publicist to push his goals of increasing interest in home buying. He advocated for New York State to include a bossy motto on its license plates: "Own a Home." State officials instead went with "N.Y. World's Fair."

That was not far off message for Fred Trump. The 1939 World's Fair put Queens and modern home building at the center of the universe. The fair featured a mock neighborhood of twenty-one single-family homes billed as the "Town of Tomorrow." Fred sent five hundred of his craftsmen and sales staff to the fair and offered cash prizes to the workers who found the best ways to make homes he had under construction more modern and comfortable. The winner reported seeing an illuminated doorknob with a magnetic keyhole, easing nighttime entry into one's home.

Fred offered to cover the admission costs for up to five thousand people unable to afford tickets because of the Depression. With millions still relying on government aid or salaries from Roosevelt's Works Progress Administration, Fred said he and others who had become wealthy during the Depression should feel a responsibility to open the majestic event to all comers. "I refer to the vast number of people on relief and workers for the W.P.A., who, unless something is done along the lines suggested, will have to sadly admit for the rest of their lives that they missed the world's greatest pageant of education, history, amusement staged almost at their doorsteps, because they could not afford to go."

Thanks to the FHA, the Great Depression had turned into a Golden Age for home builders like Fred Trump, who had become one of the leading home builders of his generation. He continued to find large stretches of undeveloped land, even as the war in Europe cast doubt on the real estate market.

In April 1941, he purchased a fifty-five-acre plot in southern Brooklyn. It was bordered on one side by the new Bensonhurst Park and on another side by the recently completed Belt Parkway, which ran along the waterfront and offered the potential of a quick commute to Manhattan. The seller was Joseph P. Day, who had been unable to move forward with a plan to build apartment houses on the site for several years. Fred Trump was now doing business with a real estate titan of his childhood, and he vowed to outdo Day's performance. He would spend $500,000 in cash—the equivalent of more than $10 million today—to buy the land and install sewers. He expressed confidence that he would move quickly—not get stuck paying carrying costs as the prior owner had done.

"There is a natural virgin market for thousands of F.H.A. homes in this section of Bensonhurst," he said. "I do not believe in holding vacant property, and to assure its quick development, I have offered several other builders the opportunity of joining with me."

A writer for *The Brooklyn Daily Eagle* visited the construction site and used the language of military precision to praise Fred's deployment of his crews, how he directed "constantly advancing divisions of skilled craftsmen. Mr. Trump has achieved complete co-ordination between platoons of hustling masons, bricklayers, plasterers, carpenters, plumbers and a mobile column of giant cranes, tractors, steam shovels, mechanized mortars, ditch digging and finishing machines. The Trump system is a far cry from the days of the pick and shovel, wheel barrow and hand mixer."

Less than eight months after acquiring the property, Fred opened his first model homes on the site. Another 140 homes were under construction. Fred touted the value of the FHA homes—which he said would cost buyers as little as forty dollars a month for mortgage, taxes, and water—for "the finest location on which we have ever built homes."

That edition of the *Eagle* quoting an optimistic Fred Trump rolled off the presses on December 7, 1941, just as Japanese Zeros broke the morning silence over Pearl Harbor.

2

THE AMERICAN WAY OF LIFE

THE COASTAL AREA of Virginia known as Hampton Roads, where several rivers merge with the Chesapeake Bay and the Atlantic Ocean, has been one of America's most important ports since not long after English settlers arrived in 1607. The deep channels rarely freeze and are protected from rough seas by interlocking landmasses. The peninsula to the north, with the towns of Williamsburg, Newport News, and Hampton, juts down into the mouth of the James River. From the south, Willoughby Spit reaches up from Norfolk. And to the east, the Delmarva Peninsula stands sentry against the ocean. The resulting calm waters, making for smooth and speedy access to the Atlantic Ocean, gave the region its name: the "Road" is short for "roadstead," a nautical term for a waterway sheltered from rip currents and swells.

Tranquil as the waters may be, in the months after the attacks on Pearl Harbor thousands of newly drafted sailors and soldiers streamed into the naval installations and two nearby army bases, increasing the military population from 10,000 in 1939 to 168,500 in 1943. With destroyers, battleships, and aircraft carriers under construction at two shipyards, thousands of civilian men arrived to work in the newly frantic warship-building and repair industry. Hundreds of sailors at a time set ashore for temporary leave through the Hampton Roads Port of Embarkation.

They all jammed the streets and trolley cars, the bars, restaurants, and movie theaters. There were not enough teachers or doctors. The drinking-water system could not keep up. Garbage collection fell behind. The shortage of housing became so acute that there were reports of as many as twenty-five people stuffed into some houses. Landlords rented out bedrooms in two shifts for sleeping. Conditions were worse for African Americans, generally segregated to substandard housing. A city survey found as many as five Black people living in a single room, and as many as seventeen families sharing a single bathroom.

Disgusted by the living standards, five hundred workers a month at the Navy Yard simply packed up and went home, putting the warship-building effort at risk.

Washington responded with an amendment to the National Housing Act that added a new focus to the FHA's mission: incentivizing the construction of rental apartment buildings near military bases and factories important to the war effort.

Before the spring thaw in the Northeast, Fred Trump fired up his Cadillac in Jamaica Estates and drove four hundred miles down the Eastern Seaboard to Norfolk. His latest Brooklyn project was stalled, thanks to the federal government's limitations on the use of building materials for construction not vital to winning the war. Fred found a set of circumstances similar to what he had seen in the outreaches of Queens early in his career. Constant new arrivals. A housing shortage worsening every day. Thousands of men with money in their pockets. Empty land everywhere. And developers celebrated like the generals of a liberating army.

"Rents are still soaring in Norfolk, accommodations are scarce," Fred told a reporter. "One double bed often serves for four defense workers, two day workers by night and two night workers by day. The housing that we will provide, however, will help to alleviate this situation."

The rules of the new FHA program would unintentionally benefit builders with Fred Trump's strongest skill set: pushing down construction costs. The new program—known as Title VI, Section 608—offered low-interest loans that would cover 90 percent of estimated construction costs. The mortgage amounts would be based on cost estimates supplied by the builder. But the law did not require developers to later document how much had been spent, or to pay back any portion of the mortgage not spent on construction, leaving open the possibility of cash in the pocket for keeping costs down. Using little or none of their own cash, developers could build—and own—vast apartment complexes.

After years of basing his business model on building a home, or row of homes, and selling them once for his profit, Fred would now own large rental complexes on which he could collect rent every month. He once concluded an explanation of the program's potential upside with this dry sentence: "Dividends or rates of return are not limited."

First, he needed land. He had been beaten to that punch by another Queens builder named James Rosati, who had been buying land in the Hampton Roads area since before the attack on Pearl Harbor. Fred Trump partnered with Rosati on several projects. Fred's assembly-line process of overseeing construction was well suited to the mission. By the summer of 1942 he was hiring architects and contractors to build dozens of eight-family brick apartment buildings, two-story "garden apartments" separated by lawns, with a portico over the door as the sole architectural detail.

Fred occasionally stayed in Norfolk during the week and drove or flew home to Queens on weekends, but he soon tired of the commute and moved his growing family south. With the birth of Elizabeth in 1942, he and Mary had three children. They moved into a rental house near the shore in Virginia Beach, the next town over from Norfolk. Fred persuaded William Hyman to uproot his wife and two young boys and move the family to Virginia Beach. The Trump and Hyman kids would go to the beach some days, occasionally watching the navy practice amphibious landings. Bill Hyman returned from work in Norfolk most days with sailors who had wanted a ride to the beach hanging out the windows of his Chevy coupe.

Fred Trump formed other relationships in Hampton Roads that would remain important to his business prospects and his family life for years to come. He partnered on one project with W. Taylor Johnson, a born-and-bred local who lived just blocks from the shore in Virginia Beach. Taylor owned a successful insurance business but, seeing how lucrative the FHA war housing program could be, redirected his career. They were listed as partners on a four-hundred-unit apartment complex, funded with an FHA-backed mortgage, called the Southampton Apartments. The deal also included Rosati and George Alvin Massenburg, then a member of the Virginia legislature and the local commander of the Coast Guard Reserve.

Like Fred Trump, Taylor Johnson had a namesake son. The two boys were both around seven years old and formed a friendship that would endure into adulthood. Fred the father could be awkward around children. He occasionally pulled a novelty kaleidoscope from his suit pocket and told young Taylor to look through it. Taylor Jr. was shocked the first time he lifted it to his eye and did not see the typical swirl of shapes and colors but undulating young women in swimsuits.

Fred's relationships were nearly all based upon common professional interests. When he brought people from home to Virginia for a visit, it was associates from the Brooklyn Democratic Party who were important to his projects in New York. More than once he drove down with his two closest acquaintances from the patronage machine of the Madison Democratic Club: Abraham Beame, a schoolteacher and bookkeeper, and Abraham "Bunny" Lindenbaum, a lawyer and fundraiser for politicians. The three made for a striking study in physical contrast. At five foot two, Beame had to look up to see the knot in Fred's necktie. Lindenbaum, an affable charmer with a broad and rubbery grin, was distinguished as much for his roundness as Fred was for his lean height. But they had much in common. The three men were roughly the same age and the children of immigrant parents. Each of their livelihoods depended upon navigating government programs and proximity to political officeholders. During one drive south to Virginia, Fred became so engrossed explaining to Beame and Lindenbaum how the FHA mortgage program enabled him to build without investing a penny of his own money that he did not realize he was speeding, until a sheriff pulled him over.

By the end of the war in 1945, the housing crisis in Hampton Roads had eased, thanks to FHA-insured loans. Forty-two warships central to the United States' victory had been built in the area and hundreds more were repaired.

Fred Trump had built more than fourteen hundred apartments as part of the war effort, including a four-hundred-unit complex in Pennsylvania. As the federal government eased the wartime restrictions on construction, the growing Trump family returned to Jamaica Estates. Fred turned his attention once again toward the fifty-five-acre site he had left behind in Brooklyn, a project with the potential to create wealth for generations of Trumps to come.

IN THE EARLY SUMMER OF 1946, Fred Trump worked the phones nonstop, calling every nail supplier he knew. Call after call, he heard the same thing: no nails. There he was, in the middle of another housing shortage, looking out at some fifty-five acres of raw land in Brooklyn that he let people use as Victory gardens to grow vegetables during the war, and he could not buy a nail to save his life. "Nails are impossible to get," he complained to a reporter. "I've made 15 calls in the last few days without any luck." He was "going crazy" trying to find nails and "things are getting worse and worse."

Thousands of troops had returned home to the city. They were getting married, having babies, and searching for homes. A recent government study had estimated that more than 3.5 million veterans needed new housing. It was as if the demand Fred had seen in Hampton Roads during the war had overtaken the entire nation.

To support the building of homes for veterans, the new administration of President Harry S. Truman had altered the price-control system, but builders complained that they had inadvertently created incentives for manufacturers to divert raw materials away from building supplies. For Fred, that meant that a lot of metal was being used to make fence wire, not nails.

On June 14, 1946, Mary gave birth at Jamaica Hospital to their fourth child, a boy. They named him Donald John Trump. The family had by then moved to another house in Jamaica Estates, one of the smaller Tudor homes Fred had built for high types on Wareham Place just as the Depression took hold. Wedged between two driveways on a forty-foot-wide lot, the home now felt cramped for a family of six with a live-in maid. It was also no longer suitable for a man of Fred's station in the world. A neighbor, a jewelry maker named Edward Abel, who as president of the Jamaica Estates Association had sought to maintain the "high class restrictive character of the neighborhood," owned an empty hundred-foot-wide lot next door to his home on Midland Parkway, the most desirable street in the community.

Fred bought Abel's lot and began overseeing construction on a home of more than four thousand square feet, with nine bathrooms and bedrooms to spare, almost twice the size of the house on Wareham. It would be a Colonial Revival–style house, red brick with four thick white columns supporting a two-story portico over the entrance. Fred Trump, son of a restaurant owner who dreamed of a career in real estate, would now live one block north of the famous estate built in his youth by Michael Degnon, the legendary builder of the city's subways.

THE DELAYS THAT THE NAIL shortage caused Fred turned out to be the luckiest break of his life. Had he continued at his typical assembly-line pace to put up two-story row houses on his Bensonhurst land, he might have missed the most lucrative government construction program in American history, a source of almost free financing that put a far larger project within his reach.

Three weeks before Donald Trump was born, President Truman signed the Veterans' Emergency Housing Program, yet another amendment to the 1934 housing act, with the goal of "rapidly and adequately housing our veterans." Truman set the total amount of loans that the government would insure under the program at $3.8 billion, a monumental infusion of cash into the home-building industry.

The amendment sweetened the pot for developers even further, lowering interest rates to 4 percent. More significantly, the FHA had begun allowing developers to sidestep a $5 million cap on mortgages by applying for a separate mortgage on each distinct building in a project. Even buildings with a theoretical dividing line would be considered eligible for multiple $5 million mortgages.

To oversee that huge pot of money, the FHA put in charge Clyde Lilbon Powell, who had been born in Salem, Missouri, in 1896, and worked as a real estate broker before joining the FHA in 1934. He was a fireplug of a man, short and blocky, with a penchant for flashy suits and racehorses, who had also managed to keep a somewhat lengthy history of arrests—embezzlement, larceny, and passing bad checks in two states—hidden from his superiors.

Powell dispatched personnel across the country to enlist current and prospective real estate "promoters," anyone with the capacity to fill out a loan application and hire an architect and a construction manager. He crisscrossed the country himself to speak to groups of mortgage bankers, including nearly four hundred at the Waldorf-Astoria Hotel in Manhattan.

Knowing the program as well as Powell, Fred was ahead of the game. He threw out his plan for two-story attached homes at his Bensonhurst site. His old business model would be unlikely to produce the large profits now possible under Section 608, which created new incentives to pack far greater numbers of people on every acre. He came up with something far larger than anything he had built before.

He would call the project Shore Haven. It would be comprised of ten six-story elevator buildings with 1,344 apartments and a garage for seven hundred cars. Part of a new genre of "garden apartments" or "villages," Fred and other developers would market these sprawling complexes as a modern and convenient way of life. But the layout had one goal: to maximize the mortgage size the FHA would approve for the land. The result would be a collection of plain brick boxes separated by enough grass to keep the entire area from being cast into shadows all day. The 1946 changes to Section 608 unintentionally incentivized packing projects with apartments too small for most families. To maximize his loan amount, Fred designed Shore Haven so that 70 percent of the units would be studios or one-bedrooms. The development would be framed on one side by Bensonhurst Park and on another by several lanes of roadway running along Gravesend Bay.

Shore Haven was one of the first Section 608 projects in New York. Thomas G. Grace, the local FHA official who had approved every one of Fred's projects and appeared at ribbon cuttings with him for the prior decade, was now in charge of approving Section 608 mortgages in New York. Grace and Powell signed off on Fred's $9.125 million federally insured mortgage, which Grace said would be the largest private housing development ever in Brooklyn.

Fred's office soon received more than five thousand letters from prospective tenants seeking apartments in Shore Haven. *The Brooklyn Daily Eagle* ran a photograph of a female employee opening a pile of letters. By August, another three thousand applications had arrived, and Fred announced he would not accept any more. He made an impassioned plea for his brethren builders to join him to keep the federal government from building housing itself: "I believe that it is important that private industry wake up and deliver needed housing accommodations. Otherwise, there is a danger that public housing will step in and take over the industry." He warned that the government construction of housing would be a "calamity."

After spending the early part of his career publicly urging people to buy instead of rent, Fred announced he had shifted to rental housing, not because the veteran housing program offered him and his family untold riches, but as a service to the citizenry of his city. "I have now adopted the construction of rental housing only because I feel that I can give the home seeker a better break at present costs."

As he began construction of Shore Haven, Fred dispatched Hyman to buy several properties next to one another in the Brighton Beach neighborhood, about three miles from Shore Haven. A purchase in December 1947 finished the job. For less than $200,000, Fred had assembled a fifty-acre plot one mile from Coney Island Beach.

Fred called his second massive project Beach Haven, and it would borrow more from Shore Haven than a similar name. There would also be austere six-story brick buildings separated by grass and walkways, though this time farther from the shore. Beach Haven would hold 1,860 families, exceeding Shore Haven by more than five hundred apartments. Based on the cost estimates that Fred provided, Grace approved an initial mortgage amount of nearly $16 million to fund construction.

Grace and Powell, in Washington, allowed Fred to begin construction on Beach Haven before the financing had been finalized. The decision offered a massive potential gain for Fred. He would not have to start making mortgage payments until eighteen months after his loan was finalized. If he could finish before that date, he could collect rent for some months without having to pay his largest expense, a potential bonanza. But to execute the effort, he would need money to start construction before receiving anything from his mortgage.

To raise the construction money, Fred sold three of his projects, including the last apartments he had built in Virginia with his friend and insurance man, W. Taylor Johnson. He still did not feel comfortable putting up the full amount required to build for months before the mortgage cash began to flow, a total that would reach $1.9 million. So he took on a partner by the name of William V. Tomasello, whose company was then working for Fred laying thousands of bricks at Shore Haven. Tomasello's father, James Vincenzo Tomasello, had formed the company after arriving from Italy in the 1890s and went on to build apartment buildings on his own before his death in 1937. William, slender and a natty dresser like Fred, had access to cash. He would become a 25 percent partner in Beach Haven in exchange for contributing $500,000.

By the time the first $4.1 million payment on the mortgage closed, Tomasello's crews were almost finished with the brick exterior on the first building. Fred was set to receive a total of $25 million in cash from federally insured loans that he could use to build his two massive apartment complexes. He would deploy every cost-saving trick he knew—and invent a few more.

In the summer of 1948, as Fred spent long days in southern Brooklyn, Mary gave birth to their fifth child, Robert Stewart Trump. It was a difficult birth. Even after weeks resting in the new house on Midland Parkway, Mary did not recover with her typical vigor. Maryanne, only eleven years old, helped around the house, often by bathing her three younger siblings each evening.

Some months later, Maryanne awoke in the middle of the night and found her mother in a pool of blood on a bathroom floor. She ran for her father, who quickly called Jamaica Hospital, where all five children had been born and Fred was well connected. Mary was rushed to the hospital. Doctors performed an emergency hysterectomy. There were complications, as well as a second operation.

The road back to health for Mary Trump would not be smooth. She underwent two additional surgeries, a total of four, soon after. And there would be many more over the decades. The procedures led to osteoporosis, the long-term effect of which Maryanne came to describe more directly: "She broke every bone in her body." Mary would soon return to the kitchen in the big house on Midland Parkway, happily spending Sunday afternoons making dinners with soup and thick gravy. She would retain her outgoing demeanor, but her energy would never be quite the same. For Maryanne, the fear of those days would stick with her forever.

With his final child born, and only forty-three years old himself, Fred began the process of transferring his wealth to his children. He did so by creating a business artifice that served no business purpose whatsoever: making his children into his landlords at Shore Haven and Beach Haven. Even before he broke ground at Beach Haven, he transferred ownership of the two plots—more than one hundred acres in total—to a trust in his children's names and signed ninety-nine-year leases with them, with an option for his business to renew for another ninety-nine years. He would pay the trusts rent every month. He did the same thing with Shore Haven, and split the rent he paid there between trusts for his children and his mother, providing her a secure income.

The only cost to Fred or his children was a gift tax of $15,525. In exchange, his new young landlords would each receive $13,928 a year in rent, an amount that he would periodically increase in the decades ahead. Donald and his siblings did nothing for the money. It was a gift with the potential to keep giving forever, and with the added benefit that federal tax law allowed it to be taxed at the high gift-tax rate just once. Fred also began giving each of his children $6,000 as a gift each year at Christmas, the maximum at the time for a couple without facing a gift tax.

That roughly $20,000 a year paid to each of his children was the equivalent of about $265,000 in 2024. In postwar America, it was enough money to put each of the young Trump children in league with the wealthiest adults in the nation. At the time, only 3 percent of American families earned $10,000 or more a year. Physicians earned an average of $11,058.

The largest two-bedroom apartments at Shore Haven would soon rent for $1,260 a year; toddler Donald could easily have afforded four or five of them, and a new car. Had the rent money that Donald's father paid him been invested in a conservative stock fund each year, the total would have grown to $140 million by the time he campaigned for the U.S. presidency as a self-made billionaire.

EVERY WEEKDAY MORNING, two cars would leave the Trump house on Midland Parkway. One would whisk Fred Trump's school-age children the three miles to the private academy they attended, the Kew-Forest School. Another, Fred's chauffeur-driven Cadillac, would ferry the patriarch twenty miles to his job sites in southern Brooklyn. The Cadillac now bore a coveted new type of license plate showing only the initials "FCT."

Fred spent long days on both sites, expanding his management skills and construction knowledge as never before. Beach Haven sat on ground that had been reclaimed from the harbor and filled in with sand. Fred directed subcontractors to drive fifty-five-foot-long logs, treated with creosote to prevent decay, deep into the earth to support the new buildings. It was the largest project he had ever built, requiring 6.5 million feet of lumber and thirty-one elevators. He staggered tasks on buildings in various stages of construction, with welders, bricklayers, and carpenters directed like an orchestra, while as many as sixty families a week moved into neighboring buildings that had been completed.

He negotiated and renegotiated prices with his subcontractors to arrive at numbers far below the estimates he had provided to the FHA to receive his mortgage guarantees. FHA rules governing costs allowed for an architect's fee of about 5 percent of the total mortgage, which would be more than $1.3 million for the two projects. But Fred decided that the allowable rate included money for the architect to play a supervisory role during construction. Since Fred handled all supervision himself, he decided he could pay the architects a total of only $111,000 and keep the remaining $1.2 million.

By the time he finished construction at Shore Haven, Fred still had $1.5 million of the $10.4 million he had estimated as his costs and received through the Section 608 mortgage. In Fred's mind, that money was his, the result of nothing but the expertise he had developed cutting costs throughout his career. Before he could take the money out, an Internal Revenue auditor raised questions about his books on Shore Haven. But Clyde Powell, who had been signing off on Fred's projects for years, overruled the auditor, clearing Fred to write himself some massive checks.

Fred was still not satisfied. Federal income taxes could take as much as 70 percent of the total. In December 1950, Fred sent a politically connected Brooklyn lawyer named Richard P. Charles to meet with an official at the Internal Revenue Service. Charles requested an official ruling allowing Fred to pay a capital gains tax of 25 percent on his Shore Haven windfall instead of the regular income tax.

The next day, Charles wrote a letter to the IRS commissioner repeating his position: "All of the work in connection with the construction was performed by subcontractors and none of the stockholders performed any work in connection with the erection of the said buildings. Due to favorable agreements with the subcontractors, the corporation was able to complete the work for less than the mortgage proceeds."

It was a claim that was as audacious as it was absurd: after portraying himself as the hardest working man in construction for his entire life, Fred Trump asserted he had done no work on his signature accomplishment. It was, in this private telling, only an investment, and should be taxed as if he had simply bought and sold shares in General Motors. But it worked, at least initially.

Within one week, Fred received a response from high up in the agency. In a confidential letter dated December 29, 1950, E. I. McLarney, the deputy commissioner of the IRS, told Charles that Fred could declare any distributions he took from "the excess of the mortgage proceeds over the cost of the property" at the long-term capital gains rate, typically lower than the tax on income. The letter arrived on Saturday, December 30, just in time to close the books for the year. Fred wrote himself two checks from the Shore Haven corporations totaling $1 million. He had already taken out the other $500,000 the year before.

His estimates for Beach Haven would be off by even more—$4 million in total. A large chunk of that money came from the FHA allowing Fred to start construction before his loan was approved, which opened the door for him to collect $1.7 million in rent before he had to make a single mortgage payment. He and Tomasello used the proceeds to pay themselves back the cash they had injected up front. Fred Trump would own both massive projects without having any money invested. And the money Fred kept from the mortgage funds above his real costs totaled $5.5 million, making the Trump family extraordinarily wealthy even before the profits from running the buildings began flowing.

During construction of Fred Trump's two signature projects, Bill Hyman worked on the transfer of the land to Fred's children, filing the papers that would make young Donald and his siblings wealthy. Before he finished that task, Hyman suffered a fatal heart attack while climbing the stairs out of a subway station. He was forty-seven years old. He left behind his wife, Lillian, and their two sons, Milton, fourteen, and John, sixteen.

After hearing that Hyman had died, Fred telephoned Lillian to pay his respects. He of course knew the family well from their years together in Virginia Beach. He had his accountants settle up with Lillian, sending her a net of about $3,000. At some point, Fred learned that not long before his death Bill had promised Milton that if he got straight As that year, he would buy him a television. The father did not live to see the end of his son's school year.

"I wound up getting straight As that year," Milton Hyman recalled. "Fred heard about it and sent me a television."

Milton remembered the television gift fondly, though Fred's overall tightness with money was nonetheless something of a running joke in the Hyman family. The last punch line came a few years later when Milton, then a student at Cornell University, called Fred to see if he might need a strong kid like him for summer work. Fred hired him to do basic labor at his latest construction site. Milton was grateful, until he opened his first paycheck and realized that Fred had paid him half of the lowest union wage for a day laborer. He never went back.

"I went down to Atlantic Beach and got a job as a lifeguard," he recalled with a laugh.

Fred Trump finished construction at Shore Haven in one year, a remarkable accomplishment in efficiency. Each building filled with tenants as soon as his workers applied the last touch of paint.

He had spent nearly two decades working amid abrupt shifts in how America responded to emergencies. The Great Depression, World War II, and soldiers returning from war created three housing shortages of historic proportions. Each crisis tested the precepts of free market capitalism. Could the marketplace on its own generate housing for Americans hurt by economic forces beyond their control, or those brave souls who ran into the hellscape of war for their country? Two administrations and three sessions of Congress wrestled with those questions and chose a middle ground: providing generous incentives to private builders like Fred Trump.

That national dynamic enabled Fred to build and profit on a scope beyond anything he could have imagined and put him in league with the wealthiest Americans of his generation.

As he reflected on those accomplishments, Fred came to see himself not so much as a beneficiary of the nation's response to a crisis but as a hero of the crisis itself. He took out a full-page advertisement in several New York City newspapers with the headline "The American Way of Life" wrapped around a drawing of the Statue of Liberty. The ad, focused on a nearly fully rented Shore Haven, served no immediate business purpose. It was more of a victory lap, an homage to Fred Trump, by Fred Trump. He reframed the government's role as having "cooperated" with his financing rather than having conceived and enabled it, and he put his eighty-foot-tall brick boxes on par with the most iconic symbol of freedom in the world.

> For generations, the Statue of Liberty has greeted newcomers to the United States of America as the symbol of our basic freedom which has made possible the American Way of Life. And now a new community at the entrance of New York Harbor symbolizes this "American Way." Shore-Haven is one of the greatest housing projects ever erected by a private individual. It is a fitting greeting to all aboard the liners as they leave the ocean and steam up New York Harbor. Passengers may now look out on a panorama of modern American buildings at the spot where a little more than a year ago there was no sign of life . . . only sand dunes and tangled grass. . . .

> Shore-Haven is a new monument to the American spirit of free enterprise. The project was conceived, planned, executed by Fred C. Trump, acting as a free and rugged individualist to meet the basic need for human shelter.

Fred would sustain and cultivate that image of himself—not just as an effective builder but as an entrepreneurial patriot, a benevolent humanitarian—for a time. He would receive positive press for acts of generosity. He allowed the city schools to rent space in Beach Haven for one dollar a year. He provided free evening movies and dances for teenagers. He would be honored by a large Jewish philanthropy for raising support for its initiatives within the real estate sector and by the Women's Auxiliary of the Veterans of Foreign Wars for contributing to the social welfare of his tenants. He would even make a national Best Dressed list, along with entertainers and a new president, Dwight D. Eisenhower.

But the forces that would reveal a less flattering aspect of his accomplishments were already at work.

3

THEY JUST WENT WILD

By 1950, W. Taylor Johnson, Fred Trump's friend and occasional business partner, was considered a respected businessman and upstanding member of the Virginia Beach community. The insurance company bearing his name had reliably serviced the needs of the Hampton Roads region for three decades. He was a member of a local country club and lived a few blocks from the beach in an elegantly understated colonial revival house. Bespectacled and southern mannered, at fifty-eight years old he had a lovely wife, Foye, and three handsome children.

One summer day that year Taylor woke to find a different sort of man, a lump in a wrinkled suit, passed out in his basement recreation room. Clyde L. Powell, single and childless, had for years lived alone in a Washington, D.C., hotel. He had a penchant for gambling. He preferred racehorses but he would settle for gin rummy in a pinch. At fifty-four years old, his hair had turned white. He was short, with a bulbous nose, and favored flashy double-breasted suits and light-colored ties.

Clyde had come down to Virginia Beach the day before to help Taylor mark the near completion of his seminal real estate accomplishment, the Mayflower, a sixteen-story apartment tower one block from the glorious sands of Virginia Beach. It would be the tallest residential building in Virginia, and it was funded by Section 608, the federally insured mortgage program run by Clyde Powell.

Also there to mark the occasion was the lieutenant governor, the mayor of Virginia Beach, and Taylor's partner in the Mayflower, F. A. "Piggy" Van Patten, a former regional director for the FHA whom Taylor had lured away from government work to help him navigate Section 608 and Powell. They all posed for news cameras before adjourning to the Cavalier Beach and Cabana Club for a dignified luncheon, attended by about one hundred of Taylor's friends and associates. A smaller group then moved to Taylor's house for a dinner party, which was intended to mark the end of a long and memorable day. But at around midnight, Clyde announced that he wanted Piggy and Taylor to take him to the Dunes, a well-known illegal gambling hall a short walk from Taylor's home. Clyde was the man holding the nation's purse strings, so off the three men went into the night.

Upon their arrival, Clyde promptly took a seat at a craps table. He pulled out a roll of cash that looked to Piggy like about $2,000—intriguing, Piggy thought, for a guy whose federal salary totaled $10,000 a year. For several hours, Clyde displayed a fantastic knack for losing. When his cash disappeared, he asked the proprietor of the Dunes to advance him another $3,000. Taylor vouched for Clyde and the money was lent.

Clyde remained planted at that craps table, gambling and drinking cocktails, until well past sunrise, when the dealer scooped the last of his borrowed money from the felt. The three men walked back to Taylor's house, where Taylor mustered up breakfast. And then Clyde Powell, the man in charge of a $3.4 billion loan portfolio for the United States of America, passed out at a table in Taylor's basement recreation room.

And there he still was, at 4:00 p.m. the next day, a Saturday, folded all over himself in yesterday's suit, a plate of cold ham and eggs untouched in front of him. Clyde finally woke up, and the issue of him needing to repay $3,000 to the owners of the Dunes, and not having even one dollar, was addressed. Taylor, a man of his word, wrote Clyde a check, but the rumpled Washington bigwig did not care to leave a paper trail. He demanded cash. Finally fed up, Taylor picked up the phone and called Piggy, who was still half asleep when Taylor started hollering into the phone.

"Piggy, come over here and get this S.O.B. Clyde Powell and get him out of my house!" Taylor said. "I never want to see him again." He was doubly incensed that Powell had refused his check. "I had to send my yard boy down to the bank and get the cash to give it to him!"

Clyde Powell's sloppy excesses would soon draw attention to the sloppy excesses of the program he ran and the favors he had done, including for Fred Trump, over the years. Powell had not only waived off the FHA audit that might have prevented Fred from pulling money out of Shore Haven, but he had personally signed off on additional mortgage money when Fred said his costs had increased.

The excesses of the Section 608 program had become something of an open secret. Months before Powell's Virginia Beach gambling spree, the trade magazine *Architectural Forum* published a lengthy article itemizing the ways in which the cost estimates submitted by developers could game the system to pull millions of dollars out of their projects before the first veteran was handed an apartment key. The fees for an architect and a builder, typically approved at 10 percent of the total, need not be paid out. Builders could finish their projects early and start to collect rents months before they had to start making mortgage payments. They could drive down costs with suppliers and contractors and keep the gap between their actual costs and their original estimates. The original law required builders to cover at least 10 percent of construction costs, so they would have some investment in the buildings they would own, and then make their profit from rents. But oversight was so slight that millions of dollars poured through loopholes during construction. The magazine article quoted an anonymous consultant as saying the federal government left so much money on the table under Section 608 that no skills as a builder were required: "Give me any smart business man, and I can make him an apartment builder in three weeks."

THE WALLS WERE CLOSING in on Section 608 builders from all sides. In late 1951, President Truman appointed John B. Dunlap as commissioner of the Internal Revenue Service with a mandate to clean up and reorganize the agency after an unrelated scandal under the prior commissioner. The IRS soon reversed a position that had been beneficial to Fred: that Section 608 developers could pay the low capital gains rate on the money they collected because their estimates of construction costs exceeded the actual costs. Now, they would have to pay the higher tax rate for regular income.

Fred was among the first Section 608 developers alerted of the change. In 1952, he received notice from an IRS auditor saying that the taxes he had paid so far on the money he took out of Shore Haven would not be enough. The new policy would require him to pay an additional $280,000 in taxes, plus interest. Fred was livid. In correspondence not made public until now, he sent a letter to the IRS laced with all-caps outrage, saying the auditor had issued his decision "IN TOTAL DISREGARD OF THE RULING RECEIVED IN WRITING ON THE LETTERHEAD OF THE UNITED STATES TREASURY DEPARTMENT." When Fred's lawyer had asked for a ruling on one of the Shore Haven corporations, he had assumed it would cover payments to Fred from the other Shore Haven corporations. The new administration said it would respect the advantageous capital gains treatment for the one entity on which Fred had requested and received a written ruling, but not payments from the others. In his missive, Fred called the change "puzzling" and felt sure it would be "difficult for anyone to believe." He felt he was being taken advantage of because his lawyer had relied on a verbal assurance from the IRS.

"I find myself in the most embarrassing predicament of being called upon to pay several hundred thousands of dollars of additional taxes on a flimsy technicality, because someone failed to spend three cents for an extra sheet of paper. Although it is naturally not comparable to the entire United States Treasury Department, I run a substantial business involving the operation of many apartment houses. If one of my supervisory employees tells one of our tenants or a supplier or a contractor that we will do something, we do it, whether it is in writing or not."

As Fred complained, IRS agents were fast at work compiling a list of all the developers who had paid the lower capital gains tax on the money they made due to excessive cost estimates.

The IRS then sued George M. Gross, another New York City developer who built apartments with Section 608 loans, for back taxes, charging that he and his partners had wrongly reported the excess mortgage money as a capital gain to lower their taxes. T. Coleman Andrews, appointed commissioner of the Internal Revenue by President Eisenhower in early 1953, picked up where Dunlap left off. He called the Gross matter a test case that could lead the IRS to pursue similar actions against hundreds of developers who had done the same thing.

As the investigation progressed, Eisenhower ordered the impounding of files in all agency offices. Newspapers across the country carried news of the scandal, some showing photographs of chained and locked file cabinets in local FHA offices. FHA commissioner Guy T. O. Hollyday was the first to be fired. Hollyday had been in his post for less than a year since Eisenhower plucked him from a comfortable career in Baltimore as head of the national Mortgage Bankers Association. But his boss, Albert Cole, head of the Housing and Home Financing Agency, determined that the "fine Christian gentleman" had been aware of some of the problems "and did not act."

Cole hired William F. McKenna, a Los Angeles lawyer who had previously worked for a congressional committee investigating Teamsters boss Jimmy Hoffa, to delve into the causes and scope of the Section 608 scandal. McKenna and Cole quickly concluded that Clyde L. Powell, who had headed the Section 608 program for its entire history, was at the center of what had gone wrong.

They learned that the FBI had discovered in 1949 that Powell had a considerable criminal record prior to working at the FHA. He had been charged with embezzling from a St. Louis hotel where he worked, stealing from a guest room, passing bad checks in Philadelphia and Little Rock, and then was arrested again in St. Louis for driving without a license. But he had repeatedly written on employment forms that he had never been arrested or convicted. McKenna also discovered that the General Accounting Office had uncovered a pattern of developers giving gifts—televisions, watches, and bottles of liquor were quite popular choices—to the government officials approving their loans in Clyde's offices. A senator who had heard rumors of Clyde's night of debauchery with Taylor and Piggy had reported it to the FHA. The agency's lawyers dispatched investigators to speak with the owners of the Dunes. But the FHA had taken no action on any of it and did not refer the details to the Department of Justice for three years, which happened to coincide with the tolling of the statute of limitations on potential criminal charges.

On April 12, 1954, Cole summoned Clyde to his office, where he and McKenna awaited.

"There are certain allegations here with respect to your conduct which are of great concern to me," Cole told Powell. He ran through the key points and said he wanted to hear Clyde's side of the story.

"I believe I should see my lawyer," Clyde responded. "After I see him, I may return."

He did not return. A week later, Homer E. Capehart, a senator from Indiana who chaired the Banking and Currency Committee, launched hearings into what became known as the FHA Scandal. Capehart, a Republican, had become wealthy as a pioneer in the record player business before entering politics. When he appeared on a CBS show that week, Capehart said he was most offended by developers who had pocketed large sums based on inflated cost estimates.

"We certainly are going to stop what we know and think of as windfall profits. We're not going to permit that anymore. The American people don't want it, and I don't think the builders want it, that is, the honest builder."

Clyde Powell was among the first witnesses called before Capehart's committee. On April 19, 1954, he sat in a Senate hearing room wearing a double-breasted suit with a pocket handkerchief, his fingers interlocked on his lap, and a lawyer whispering in his ear. After stating his name for the record, Powell declined to provide his job titles at the FHA, citing his constitutional protection against being compelled to be a witness against himself. He provided the same answer to every question that followed.

Piggy Van Patten and Taylor Johnson testified later. They had since had a falling out. Piggy told the story of Powell's gambling with some glee. He added that Taylor had charged the $3,000 he gave Powell for his gambling debt as an expense to the Mayflower. The money to cover Clyde Powell's losses at the craps table had come straight out of the federal loan Powell had approved for Taylor and Piggy's project.

Taylor had explained the episode to senators in a closed executive session and was prickly when asked to do so again in a public hearing. He left the hearing room and suffered a heart attack soon after.

In the spring of 1954, the IRS turned over the tax records of 1,149 Section 608 developers who had taken cash out of their projects because the mortgage money they received exceeded the actual costs of construction. The preliminary findings of the investigation were released to newspapers across the country. On June 12, 1954, an article on the front page of *The Brooklyn Daily Eagle* led with a brutal sentence: "Federal investigators checking the housing loan scandals have accused Fred C. Trump, Jamaica (L.I.) builder, of pocketing a $4,047,900 windfall on the Beach Haven Apartments in Brooklyn." His tenants at Beach Haven read that the inflated cost estimates drove up the total mortgage amount, which had provided the basis for their rents, and began organizing to demand rent reductions. After decades of receiving a hero's welcome wherever he built, Fred Trump was now portrayed as a pariah feeding on government largesse and gouging his tenants.

Capehart scheduled a private interview with Fred for the following week. Fred entered the Capitol building and made his way to a small meeting room with his general counsel, Matthew Tosti, and extra firepower from Orrin G. Judd, a prominent New York lawyer who had served as the state's solicitor general. Fred repeatedly diverted from the questioning to make clear that he felt victimized by the investigation and the headlines. He referred to himself as "a builder with one of the best reputations in the City of New York." At another point, he said the whole thing "really louses up a good reputation." At yet another point, he said the investigation had done "a very bad thing" in damaging his reputation.

"I wish I had never seen a 608, because we would have made the same money, and without this smear business here," Fred protested later.

To bolster his point, he had brought along props—two large aerial photographs taken over Beach Haven. One photograph showed the empty Beach Haven lot on October 2, 1949, before he began construction, and a second about a year later when construction was nearly complete. In Fred's mind, those photographs demonstrated the exceptional accomplishment of finishing construction in only eleven months. And that exceptional ability, in his mind, was the only reason he had been able to come in under the original cost estimates. He brought out his photos three times during the ninety-minute interview to buttress his point.

"Part of it was due to our efficiency, as shown by these aerial photos," Fred told Capehart and William Simon, the chief counsel for the committee. Neither said anything in response.

Fred argued that his exceptional ability as a builder was also the reason that a bank had paid him a premium of 4 percent of the loan for the privilege of loaning him money for the project. In response, Simon said that "everybody" or at least "a great many" builders in New York at that time were offered 4 percent premiums for FHA-backed loans. Fred thought that impossible.

"This job got more mortgage premium than any other because due to its excellent location, due to its all-time long-term investment. We got more premium than most other builders."

Simon asked him: "Don't you think the premium resulted from the fact it was a government-guaranteed mortgage?"

"Partly," Trump said. "I can show you plenty of government-guaranteed mortgages that pay a point and a half."

"Can you show me any nongovernment mortgages of four percent?" Simon said.

"Premium? No," Trump conceded.

The private session ended with Simon requesting more records, including documents related to Fred giving the Beach Haven land to his children and making them his landlords.

Three weeks later, on a Friday afternoon in July, a subpoena arrived at the family house on Midland Parkway. Fred was ordered to return to Washington and appear before Capehart's committee on Monday for questioning in public. Newspapers had been following the hearings day after day, as builders and FHA officials were marched in to be asked in front of reporters about millions of dollars they received because of their exaggerated cost estimates and the lack of federal oversight.

Fred flew back to Washington with his lawyers Judd and Tosti. They took their seats in a public hearing room at the Senate Office Building. Capehart inquired about the gift to Donald and his siblings, noting that the government would have to pay the children $1.5 million if Fred defaulted on the loan. Fred was outraged at any suggestion he might default. But he again saved his greatest ire for the use of the word "windfall." The millions of dollars could not be a windfall, he insisted, because it was still sitting in the bank accounts of his Beach Haven corporations.

"That means I drew it out and put it in my pocket, and I have never drawn a salary the three years that Beach Haven has been operating." He added, "This is, I believe, very wrong and it hurts me. The only thing I am happy about is that it is not true."

Fred had, in fact, on several occasions temporarily borrowed from that surplus to buy other buildings and fund the shortfalls of still more, which he had acknowledged in the private session. Senator Herbert Henry Lehman, a Democrat from New York who had previous served as the state's governor, gently took Fred to task for suggesting there was a practical difference between money in his personal bank account and money in a corporate account that he alone controlled. "Well, Mr. Trump, without going into the merits or the justification for your having this so-called windfall of $4 million, isn't it a fact that that $4 million, while not paid out to you in the form of a windfall, is in the treasury of the company and could be paid out at any time?"

Fred stuck with his odd distinction: "I first have to take it out before I pocket it, Senator. Isn't that right?"

Lehman saw no reason to respond.

From there, Fred's line of reasoning took the shape of a circle. He repeatedly insisted that his cost estimates had not been padded, and then insisted that he was forced to pad the estimates because costs could increase during the six months it took the FHA to approve an application. "I had to allow for the risk of inflation," he said. He omitted the fact that when costs rose before construction was completed, builders were welcome to ask the FHA for an increase in the size of their mortgage, something Fred had done. The committee would eventually learn that all such increases were personally approved by Clyde Powell.

Fred argued repeatedly that he was entitled to the 10 percent of the expense earmarked for a builder's fee and an architect's fee because, in his view, he had performed the supervisory work those fees were intended to cover. He asserted that the 5 percent architect's fee was somehow mandated by FHA regulations, which was not true.

Finally, Tosti interrupted and broke down the math. It all came down to getting the maximum allowable mortgage of $8,100 per apartment: "Mr. Simon, the only thing that a builder, in signing one of these applications was interested in . . . He was building a project consisting of 391 apartments and he wanted $8,100 per apartment for it."

Fred had made the same point during the private session the week before, that he expected approval for the maximum $8,100 for each apartment: "You take that for granted."

And there was the heart of the matter. The cost estimates were all a cover, a phony math exercise to justify the per-apartment maximum of $8,100. What was intended to be the allowed maximum had become the expected minimum. And it made perfect sense to Fred and his lawyers.

The Department of Justice saw it differently. Warren Olney III, assistant attorney general in charge of the Criminal Division, told Capehart's committee that the estimates were "false and that they are lies" and that those responsible should be prosecuted. But his prosecutors had been thwarted by the FHA's surprising position that it did not rely on the estimates. "And that, Senator, is why it is impossible for the Department of Justice to prosecute on these Section 608 cases, because we cannot prove that the federal government was defrauded," Olney said. "So, they are in the position of saying that they weren't deceived or defrauded. They were just giving this stuff away."

Despite Fred's argument that his exceptional ability at controlling costs explained why he had millions of dollars left over after paying for construction, the committee found that Section 608's generous terms had generated similar mortgage surpluses for doctors and dentists and others with no experience in real estate, much as *Architectural Forum* had reported years earlier. In examining just a few hundred of more than seven thousand Section 608 projects, the investigation determined those developers had received $76 million above the actual construction costs.

"That is unpardonable and unconscionable," Capehart said to his Senate colleagues in explaining his committee's findings. "There was never any occasion for that. The FHA people just went wild."

It was repeatedly made clear during the hearings that the people who went wild were Clyde Powell and his associates. Powell's office and much of the executive staff that oversaw Section 608 was cleared out. In his final testimony to Capehart's committee, William McKenna said Clyde Powell was the "key man" at the center of the excessive mortgage problem. "In these cases where the windfall profits were greatest, there was a connection between Mr. Powell and the sponsors." He listed Fred Trump among the recipients of the largest windfall profits.

Witnesses had testified about Powell accepting bribes, asking for loans he did not repay, and his obsession with horse betting. His financial records showed cash moving in and out of his bank accounts far in excess of his federal salary, including payments that went to a bookie known as John "Black Jack" Keleher.

Powell spent most of his remaining years fending off federal prosecutors on various charges related to the scandal and potential tax fraud. In 1957, as the

IRS pursued taxes on his gambling winnings for years when he worked at the FHA, Powell testified that he was "ashamed of and embarrassed by" his years of gambling. He had not kept books but thought he had lost more than he won.

"It was a vice. It is something that I wish I hadn't done."

FRED RETURNED TO Jamaica Estates still angry with how he had been portrayed during the hearings. His two eldest children were old enough to be aware of what had happened. Maryanne later said the hearings felt like a cloud hanging over the family. Freddy joked to his high school pals that his father had stolen away to Cuba to avoid testifying.

Congress rewrote laws governing housing programs to require that private builders certify their costs after construction, return any unneeded mortgage funds, and invest an amount equal to 20 percent of the cost themselves. Fred saw those changes as "a radical reorganization" that began the day Clyde Powell was fired. He withdrew an application for mortgage insurance for another large apartment building in Brooklyn, this one on the site of a legendary Coney Island amusement park called Luna Park that had burned to the ground in 1944. When the FHA refused to refund his $32,000 application fee, he successfully sued the agency to get the money back and sold the land to the city at a small loss.

But a more serious threat was brewing than whatever reputational damage he had suffered during the hearings. President Eisenhower appointed Norman P. Mason, a lumber company executive from Massachusetts, to become the new FHA commissioner, with orders to clean up the mess left by Clyde Powell. Mason set out to exercise agency powers that Clyde had ignored.

The FHA had discovered it had legal authority to prevent the windfall payments that had been ignored by Clyde Powell. By regulation, the FHA was a preferred stockholder in each corporation that owned a Section 608 building. The stock was worth just one hundred dollars, but it came with considerable leverage. The founding documents of those corporations required that distributions to the developers come out of net earnings from running the buildings—not from a bureaucrat approving a bigger mortgage than was needed. FHA's stockholder status gave it grounds to demand the return of that money and take over the project if a builder did not comply. Mason launched takeover actions against Fred and sixteen other developers who had collected mortgage windfalls.

In July 1955, a full year after the hearings, Fred received a letter from Mason notifying him that Shore Haven was in default on its FHA-backed loan due to the money he had paid himself from the mortgage windfall. Mason demanded that Fred call a meeting of the preferred stockholders for the purpose of replacing the board of directors. Fred understood the plain meaning. FHA was the only preferred stockholder, and replacing the board meant replacing Fred. This was a standoff between the two men and their lawyers, with ownership of Fred's most valuable asset hanging in the balance.

In such a moment, anyone attached to Clyde Powell might have seemed too toxic to touch. But confidential correspondence that did not become public shows that is the universe to which Fred returned for help fending off the FHA's takeover threat. Two of Powell's former top aides, Thomas S. Gray and LeGrand W. Perce, both lawyers, had set up a consulting business leveraging their remaining connections at the FHA to help Section 608 developers fight the agency. Perce had frustrated senators during the hearings by testifying that he and Clyde Powell did not believe the FHA had any power to object to developers taking large distributions from excessive mortgages, including its power as a shareholder in the corporations. Now, he and Gray were profiting from telling developers that the agency did have that power, but that they could use their insider access with their former fellow employees to help lessen the blow. Gray and Perce typically required that their names be kept off public records and court documents. They impressed at least one other client by notifying him of the substance of a letter he would soon be receiving from the FHA.

To take the lead in most discussions with the FHA, Fred hired James Patrick McGranery, who had been the United States Attorney General for the last year of the Truman administration and a federal judge before that.

Gray and Perce quickly earned their fees. In September, Perce left a message with McGranery's office saying he had been in touch with people at the FHA and had good news: "The situation was not so bad as he had thought at first. Mr. Perce said he felt that this particular matter can be cleaned up fairly easily, perhaps with concessions on both sides."

After some back and forth, Gray left a message at McGranery's office that his contact at the FHA had presented an easy solution. Shore Haven had money in its accounts greater than the windfall distribution Fred had taken years earlier. All Fred had to do was commit to leaving that money in those accounts for a period of time. Gray added that he felt "there is a great deal of flexibility in the kind of terms Mr. Trump can make."

News of this agreement doesn't seem to have been made public. Other owners, without access to insider information on the FHA's goals or access to cash withdrawn years earlier, more acutely felt the pressure. The squeeze from the FHA was enough to incentivize them to bail out.

Their fear became Fred Trump's gain. When the FHA came after W. Taylor Johnson, Fred's old friend and business partner in Virginia Beach, Taylor asked Fred to bail him out. The FHA had demanded that he and his partners return the $244,700 from a mortgage windfall they had paid themselves from Ocean Air Apartments, a 468-unit project in the town of Hampton. At one point, Taylor thought he had worked out a deal with the FHA to put a smaller amount into the business. But someone at the FHA soured on accepting the reduced amount and sent Taylor and his wife, Foye, subpoenas to sit for depositions at the federal courthouse. Taylor called his old friend again. Fred asked McGranery to intervene. "Dear Judge: Taylor Johnson is upset and forwarded the enclosed papers to me," Fred wrote, with the subpoenas attached. He asked McGranery to get the deposition postponed or quickly finalize the deal with the FHA. Taylor wrote to McGranery expressing his concern: "I am fearful that unless prompt action is taken that the government might sue to recover the total amount claimed by them."

After negotiating with the agency over Fred's promise to spend about $66,000 on repairs, Fred took over Ocean Air. He paid Taylor and his partners the paltry sum of $27,000 and deposited $141,900 in the project's accounts, money he could take back after a few years. In exchange, he owned a building that had cost $2.85 million to build a decade earlier.

The source quoted by *Architectural Forum* back in 1950 had been proven correct by the federal investigations: the loosely written Section 608 law and Powell's looser oversight meant almost anyone could get a building constructed without losing money. But as the years wore on, the FHA and the real estate developers minted by Section 608 learned that running an apartment building—keeping it clean, fully occupied, and in good repair—was not a realm for dilettantes. The housing agency regularly foreclosed on and then auctioned off apartment buildings that had been poorly run and could not cover their mortgages. The FHA had taken over more than 250 Section 608 projects but did not want to be in the property management business.

As a result, Fred took over Section 608 buildings in Queens, Staten Island, Maryland, Ohio, and Virginia, sometimes by bidding in public auctions and sometimes with side deals smoothed by Gray and Perce. As Fred's efforts to take over a 608 project called Sinclair Farms, in Hampton, Virginia, reached a stalemate with the FHA, Gray handed him a piece of inside information: "Most confidentially," he wrote, "I expect the present Commissioner to resign at a fairly early date. Meanwhile, I am inclined to think his tendency will be to hold the status quo." Indeed, the commissioner's resignation became public about fifty days later, and Fred ultimately sealed the deal on Sinclair Farms.

His relationship with the agency grew increasingly contentious. The deal he struck to take over a Section 608 apartment building called Green Park Sussex—a ninety-six-unit building in Flushing, Queens, less than two miles from the home of the U.S. Open Tennis Championships—required Fred to, in essence, put $29,000 on deposit with the FHA until the mortgage was paid off. It was a tiny amount of money to own a building. But Fred waited more than two years to make the deposit and did so only when the FHA notified him that he was in default for not doing so.

A man of near robotic precision in construction and property management, Fred's negotiations occasionally revealed unusual thinking, an impulse to believe he had invented a clever tactic, while seemingly unaware that it was both conspicuously obvious and self-defeating.

A mostly innocuous example of that tendency occurred during his fight over Shore Haven. The FHA began requiring developers to provide new itemizations of what they had actually spent on construction, with a signature on the form. Failure to file the form was grounds for the FHA to foreclose. In confidential letters to his lawyers, Fred insisted that they type "VERIFICATION NOT REQUIRED BY FHA REGULATIONS" on the signature line. "It is Fred's idea," Tosti explained to McGranery, to avoid "the risk of being accused of deliberate falsification" if the FHA found errors. The FHA predictably objected, and Gray and Perce advised Tosti to sign as requested.

Another odd bit of Fred strategy had a greater negative impact. The FHA had foreclosed on a Philadelphia project that had been built by Dr. Daniel

Gevinson, a dentist in Washington, D.C., with no prior experience in real estate. Section 608 had increased his net worth from $50,000 to $2 million. But running his buildings turned out to be another matter. Gevinson sold the property in 1955, and it flipped again not long after. When the FHA finally foreclosed, the three-hundred-unit complex, which had been known as the Flamingo apartments, was about 25 percent vacant and in need of repair.

The FHA held an auction of the property with sealed bidding. Fred's bid did not include a precise minimum. He devised what he thought to be an ingenious ploy to ensure he won the bidding without any risk of overpaying: he offered $2.1 million, or $20,000 more than the next highest bidder, whichever was lower. The FHA saw through his gambit and notified him that it had accepted a bid for $1,836,000. Fred was incensed, sure that his strategy should have carried the day. He dashed off a telegram with a message for McGranery to pass on to the FHA: "As a taxpayer as well as the highest bidder with an unequaled record of performance with defaulted properties I strongly object to your unwarranted action in awarding property to a low bidder. I have directed my attorney to take proper and necessary action to correct his unfair decision."

He sent a memo to the lawyer expanding on his thoughts. He argued that his success turning around Taylor Johnson's Ocean Air Apartments in Hampton, Virginia, and the Grymes Hill Apartments on Staten Island made him "the best qualified of all bidders." And he seemed to threaten another public scandal for the agency, describing himself in the third person for use in McGranery's communications with the agency: "The rejection of Trump's bid would lead to severe criticism, as it is $20,000 higher than the next bidder. It could also lead to all kinds of questions which might have to be answered and all types of insinuations," Fred wrote, adding, "I would not want to open up a mountain of problems . . . You have the right man who could do it—I would not fuss around."

Fred sued to challenge the decision to ignore his crafty bid. The lawsuit was quickly dismissed. A federal judge agreed with the FHA's reasoning that Fred's tactic would "destroy the integrity of the bidding system." If every bid simply promised to pay a little more than any other possible bid, no firm winner would ever emerge. That seemed obvious to everyone involved, except Fred.

Even without the Philadelphia building, Fred Trump came to own more than 5,500 apartments funded under Section 608. Thanks in part to the excesses of that program, he had completely changed his business model. Before the war brought Section 608, he had efficiently built attached single-family homes, quickly sold them, and then needed to build more to make more money. The $5.5 million he made just from the excess mortgages on Shore Haven and Beach Haven most likely exceeded all his profits on the 2,500 homes he had built before the war.

Those large rental buildings were already enormously profitable. By the end of the decade, Beach Haven alone had amassed surplus profits of $4.5 million, the equivalent of about $60 million today. His partner, William Tomasello, sued to wrestle some of that money away.

Fred did not need that money to fund his lifestyle or further the growth of his business. His rental portfolio would generate hundreds of millions of dollars in profits for decades to come, providing a self-replenishing fortune for his family, even if he never picked up a loose nail again. Keeping that fortune in his family—away from the tax man, away from perceived gold-digging suitors of his children, and away even from his few business partners—would become the primary focus of Fred Trump's energies.

4

IN HIS FATHER'S SIGHTS

BY THE 1950S, signs of the Trumps' wealth stood out even in a neighborhood of wealthy families. It wasn't just that they lived in the biggest house on the best street in Jamaica Estates. It was the full-time help, the expensive new cars that arrived each year, and all the smaller novel comforts.

The Trump siblings would climb every morning into a chauffeured car for the brief ride to their private school. Mark Golding, a friend of Donald's, often caught a ride home in the Trump car. Mark and Donald would walk in the door of the Trump home and the lady who cooked and cleaned for the Trumps would make them hamburgers, served at the dining-room table. Sometimes they adjourned to the basement, where a wondrous model train scenescape awaited them. When they were both about ten years old, Fred bought a new color television, an expensive rarity at the time. Golding remembered being awed at the spectacle of watching the St. Patrick's Day Parade in living color.

Friends of Donald's older brother, Freddy, often entered through the garage, because they could take the stairs from there to the basement without being seen by his parents. If both parents were home, the large garage would be filled with his-and-hers Cadillac limousines. Mother Mary, a redhead, favored hers in red. Friends who were around long enough eventually realized that Fred replaced the Caddies every year with a brand-new model. At a time when such things were considered an advanced luxury technology, the garage door opened with the push of a button.

If Freddy and his friends stayed in the basement, the lady who cooked would bring them little sandwiches for snacks, typically with the crust cut from the edges. Mary rarely showed her face during those years and was very quiet when she did. Something had dimmed in her after Robert's birth and the painful surgeries that followed. But when Freddy's crew began heading out the door to walk down to the candy or record stores on Hillside Avenue, Mrs. Trump would buttonhole her eldest son and direct him to take along his little brother, Donald, eight years his junior. Freddy, tall and easy with a joke or a laugh, worried that the pipsqueak might hurt his image but did not put up much of an argument. His mom would seal the deal with enough cash for Freddy to buy a treat for the entire group.

"We'd go to some candy store or something and buy something," remembered Louis Droesch, who lived a few blocks from the Trumps and attended the Kew-Forest School with them. "And, you know, reluctantly, Fred would buy something for his brother. And it's not that he didn't like his brother or anything. He just, he was afraid that there was a social impact."

On some weekends, Droesch, who was in the same grade as Freddy, and his father would walk through Jamaica Estates, enjoying the meandering streets, large shade trees, and a father-son chat. Once, as they crossed Midland Parkway a few doors up from the Trumps' home, they saw Fred, the father, in front of his house loudly exchanging words with a big, burly man next to a flatbed truck. A sofa sat on the sidewalk near them. Droesch's father approached Fred and asked what all the commotion was about. Fred explained that he had called the man to come take away this old sofa, a job the man had accepted over the phone for five dollars. But when the man arrived, he said the sofa was larger than he had expected and wanted more money.

"We made a deal, and now he wants to break the deal, his word," Droesch recalls Fred saying. There was more discussion. But the man with the truck held firm. Fred went for a hard close: "Never mind, I'll get somebody else."

The man paused, and then relented. "All right, I'll take your damn couch for five bucks."

The Droeschs helped Fred and the reluctant buyer lift the sofa onto the flatbed. As the truck pulled away, Droesch's dad turned to Trump and said, "Fred, what are you doing? The poor guy . . ."

"Louie," Fred quipped back, "it's not the five bucks. It's the win."

Maybe there was something special to Fred about the five-dollar threshold. Donald once showed up for a friend's Bar Mitzvah reception in a flashy pinstripe jacket. He left the customary check, from his father, in an envelope. The boy's mother later dutifully logged the amount of each check so they could customize thank-you notes. Checks for one hundred dollars were not uncommon. The check in the name of Fred Trump, probably the richest father in the group, was just five dollars.

Fred's singular approach to money was a regular silent guest in the house on Midland Parkway. He would spend money on comforts and modest family vacations to Florida. He splurged on cars, and fur coats and jewelry for Mary. He did not blink an eye at tuition bills. He was a man of considerable wealth, modest tastes, and no expensive interests outside of his work.

He turned fifty the year after the FHA hearings and already had an eye toward picking a successor to keep his empire intact and within the family. His eldest child, Maryanne, recognized at a young age that she wasn't in the running. She had always been the strongest student in the family. But when she graduated from the Kew-Forest School in 1954, her parents expressed little interest in her higher education plans. They saw a woman's life as inevitably headed toward marriage and child-rearing. She considered attending the College of Home Economics at Cornell University "because I would be a better wife." Instead, she attended Mount Holyoke College, a small liberal arts school for women in South Hadley, Massachusetts, that she came to see as a "virtual nunnery" where classmates disappeared after getting pregnant.

The differences between how Fred saw his daughters and his sons became more apparent with each passing year. While he left both of his daughters at the small Kew-Forest School for their entire high school careers, he transferred all three of his sons to other schools.

For tenth grade, Freddy transferred to St. Paul's School, a private academy for boys just beyond the New York City border, in Garden City. The four-story building, surrounded by grass and athletic fields, was an architectural showpiece, a Victorian Gothic wonder of spires and slate, with dozens of windows framed by stone arches. It had been built in the 1880s by Alexander Turney Stewart, then one of the richest men in the nation's history. Stewart had created the first department stores in the country and built the leg of the Long Island Railroad that Freddy took to the school each day.

Freddy befriended four boys who took the same train to St. Paul's. They would flip one seat back, so that all five of them could face one another and pass the time playing an absurd twenty-five box version of tic-tac-toe. They fashioned themselves more as ironic intellectuals than jocks.

Their fathers were not poor: Homer Godwin's dad was a physician; and Jan VanHeiningen's father was maître d' at Toots Shor's, a Manhattan joint famous for celebrity clientele, from Charlie Chaplin to Joe DiMaggio. But the Trump house was by far the grandest of all their homes, and they regularly convened in its basement after school. It was the setting for their greatest pretend goal, forming a band comprised of a lousy trombone player (Homer Godwin), a lapsed clarinetist (James Nolan), and the unsteady rhythms emanating from a washboard (Freddy Trump), a triangle (Karl Walther), and a toilet plunger (Jan VanHeiningen).

"It was a total cacophony," Nolan said, laughing. "It usually deteriorated into a bunch of laughs."

It was during those years that Freddy acquired his first boat, a modest thing that he kept at Sheepshead Bay, about one mile from Beach Haven. During the warmer months, the boys would take the subway there for a pleasure cruise on the calm bay. Fred occasionally gave them a ride in one direction in his Cadillac limousine. They had to clear spots for themselves on the back seats, which were typically covered with Fred's work papers and blueprints. Fred would sit silently working for the thirty-minute drive with five teenage boys.

St. Paul's, owned by the Episcopal Diocese of Long Island, was run as a college preparatory academy from seventh grade through high school. Athletics were central to campus life, but not to Freddy's experience there. He played only one sport, soccer, for two years, during his sophomore and junior years. He joined the Sacristans Guild, a group of students who helped with the celebration of Holy Communion at 7:00 a.m. every day. But his largest presence was serving as business manager or treasurer for the yearbook and the student newspaper. VanHeiningen remembers thinking "that sort of made sense because we knew that his father wanted him to be the number one son."

Freddy possessed the sort of magnetic personality that made him popular. Tall and rail thin with thick blond hair and a smile that conveyed both warmth and mischief, he made an impression for his humor and outgoing nature. He liked to parrot one-liners made famous by (or misattributed to) W. C. Fields ("If you can't dazzle them with brilliance, baffle them with bullshit"). The school's yearbook when he was a senior in 1956 included a poll of what his classmates thought of themselves and one another. Freddy received no votes for "best informed" or "best athlete." But he was voted the "wittiest" member of the class and received thirty-five of forty votes cast for "best politician." Asked what they feared the most, one classmate wrote, "Trump's loud laugh." Freddy's likely vocation was listed as "millionaire."

The FHA hearings had drawn public attention to Fred's wealth. Freddy told his closest friends that he expected to join his father's business and take it over someday. "He certainly admired his father," Nolan recalled. "I think he knew his father was making a lot of money because of cutting corners. And I think he viewed that as him being a smart businessman."

Freddy did not strike his friends as a highly motivated student. Nolan, who went on to a career in college admissions, remembered that while teachers at St. Paul's gave almost no As, Freddy wound up with "a solid C" average. The two friends both applied to the University of Pennsylvania, home to a prestigious business school, and took a train together to Philadelphia for their admission interviews. Nolan was accepted. Freddy was not. He attended Lehigh University, a smaller institution in Bethlehem, Pennsylvania.

Freddy told his friends that his father was disappointed that he had not been accepted at Penn. Many of his friends came to see it as the first cut in the contest to take over the company. Maryanne would often say that she saw a "star quality" in Freddy. "He would walk into a room, and the room would light up. He charmed everybody." But it was always clear to her that Freddy's finest qualities were of little value to their father, who expressed no appreciation for something as ephemeral as a winning personality.

THE CAMPUS AT LEHIGH looked comfortably familiar to Freddy. It bore similarities to St. Paul's, but on a grander scale. Founded in 1865, the majestic stone buildings in the Collegiate Gothic architectural style sit on a hill above the Lehigh River, often described as one of the nation's most beautiful college campuses. Like St. Paul's, it was founded by a railroad titan, Asa Packer.

The eighteen-year-old Freddy Trump knew how to make an entrance. He rolled onto campus in a thirty-year-old Ford Model T, a car from his father's youth, sounding its nasally horn and waving to crowds of arriving students.

Like St. Paul's, Lehigh's undergraduate programs accepted only males. Fraternities held house parties that included women and formed the core of campus social life. Freddy found his way to Sigma Alpha Mu, which had been founded as a Jewish fraternity at the City College of New York. The Sammies, as they called themselves, had opened to all faiths a few years before Freddy arrived. Freddy nonetheless conjured up a story about an obscure Jewish relative—"grandmother, aunt, something like that," as one classmate recalled—for his interview at the house. His prospective brothers knew it was a ruse but did not care. It would be only the first of many times they would find themselves charmed by Freddy Trump. David Miller, a fraternity brother, saw in Freddy the personification of the old saying, "Hail, fellow! Well met!"

A wide porch spanned the front of the old fraternity house and was a favorite place to spend time. Some evenings that porch became Freddy's stage. In his big voice and loud laugh, he kept his fellow Sammies in stitches with his W. C. Fields schtick.

They all knew he had money, even though he rarely spoke of it directly. A smaller room on the second floor of the house was used as a communal closet. Most of the space was taken up by Freddy's collection of sport jackets. He was the only Sammy with a television in his room. A few friends regularly stayed up late in Freddy's room watching *Three Stooges* episodes and drinking beer. They struggled to make 8:00 classes the next morning.

It became a favorite parlor game after every spring break to sit on the porch and guess the color of the new Corvette their well-heeled brother would arrive in. It was the hottest car in America, the one they all wanted.

Sol Magrid, a fraternity brother, took one of Freddy's Corvettes for a spin. He parked it safely and thought, "Once was enough for me." During his junior year, Freddy lent his brand-new Corvette to another friend. The teenager took a turn at 100 miles per hour and crashed the car into a concrete abutment, ejecting his two passengers. All three survived, but the car was destroyed. Freddy soon had another new Corvette.

Early in his time at Lehigh, Freddy joined the college's flying club, founded by students to make learning to fly an affordable pursuit. He happened to arrive at Lehigh during the best four-year run in the club's history. It had existed before World War II, then been shut down during the war, then re-formed in

1946 by returning veterans, then shut down again after those veterans used the club's small planes to drop thousands of flyers over Lafayette College, Lehigh's archrival in football, before the annual big game. A new group of students relaunched the club in 1955, the year before Freddy arrived and bought a single-engine Aeronca Champion. Members could use a plane for four dollars an hour by themselves, or twice that amount with an instructor on board. Renting the plane for an entire weekend cost only thirty-two dollars.

Freddy applied for a student pilot license in October 1957, days after his nineteenth birthday. He listed his height as 6 feet and his weight as 137 pounds. Unlike in most team sports, his slight build was an asset in the small airplanes of the time. The Aeronca, a two-seater, could not get off the ground with much more than three hundred pounds and a full tank of fuel.

Flying small airplanes was a risky pursuit in those years. During the summer before Freddy's junior year, a club member crashed a plane in New Jersey. The student sustained compound fractures in both legs, eventually causing the amputation of his left leg below the knee. The plane was destroyed. Members acquired a replacement, a plane built by Taylorcraft, a few months later.

To hear Freddy's classmates tell it, he laughed at the danger. As he approached the grass airfield for a landing with his fraternity brother Stuart Oltchick in the passenger seat, Freddy pointed out the telephone wires strung about twenty-five feet above the ground near one end of the landing strip. He would say to Oltchick: "We have a decision to make . . . Should we go over those wires, or under them?" Freddy would pretend to be uncertain about the best choice until he saw fear in Oltchick's face, and then lift the plane's nose just above the wires.

Another time, with Freddy holding the plane level at about two thousand feet, Sol Magrid twisted in his seat to say something to his fraternity brother pilot. Somehow, the weight of his body popped open the plane door. Sol felt himself edge out into the wind. Freddy laughed loudly above the roar of the engine as Sol nervously struggled to get himself fully back in the plane. The episode left Sol thinking of Freddy as a bit of a daredevil.

When he was home for the summer before starting his junior year, Freddy and Billy Drake, a buddy from Jamaica Estates who was also excited about aviation, flew a small plane to the Bahamas. Freddy was still nineteen. During a stop en route, he met Linda Clapp, a girl from Fort Lauderdale with blond hair and a wide smile. She had competed in the new sport of synchronized swimming at Fort Lauderdale High School. Linda, whose father was a truck driver, fit right in with Billy Drake and Freddy Trump. She also dreamed of flying, hoping to see the world as a stewardess. Freddy was smitten.

Aside from that trip, Freddy spent much of his summer working for his father. He would leave behind his laughter and daring confidence in the sky for the stultifying underground warrens of an urban construction site.

His father was busy with the construction of the Southridge Apartments, an 1,800-unit cooperative apartment complex financed under another FHA program. He sent Freddy to the site every day to perform menial tasks. William Tomasello was again handling the brickwork and persuaded Fred to hire a nephew, Vincent Abramo, to work on the site. Abramo, a few years younger than Freddy and still in high school, practically tied himself to Freddy Trump.

By then, labor unions were ubiquitous in New York City construction, and Fred saw the unions as a nearly unavoidable challenge to his ability to manage costs. He particularly resented the rates charged by union painters for what seemed like easy and unskilled work. The union rules did not allow for the use of rollers, so even work on something as simple and unimportant as a laundry room floor had to be painted with a brush, extending the chargeable hours.

Fred saw in the two teenage boys a way to cut corners. During one summer hot spell, he ordered his son and Abramo to paint the floor of a basement laundry room using rollers. He insisted that they keep the doors to the room closed so no one from the union would see them.

Following orders, Freddy and Vincent closed the doors, scraped and swept the floors, opened the five-gallon bucket of oil-based gray paint, and put their rollers into action. The room was maybe fifteen feet long and half that wide, with two small windows ten feet above the floor. With the doors closed, the air felt stifling. The cement in the walls was still curing, which generated more heat. As they painted, a gasoline-like stench from the oil-based paint filled the room. Their eyes burned. They both began to feel faint. They finally flung open the steel doors and gasped for fresher air. After a few moments, they began applying a second coat. Then a voice boomed from the doorway.

"What the hell are you boys doing?"

It was the foreman for the painting company. He knew exactly what they were doing. Neither boy answered, and the foreman stalked off. Within a few minutes, the entire crew of forty painters walked off the site. The boys continued to do their work until Fred showed up. He was livid at Freddy for disobeying his orders and causing the work stoppage upstairs. Abramo was spared the older man's ire. His lasting impression from his three summers with the company was that "Freddy was always in Fred Trump's sights for something." Any risk to his son's health from the paint fumes was of no apparent concern. "It was all about time and money. How to squeeze a nickel at every opportunity."

5

TOY SOLDIER ACADEMY

By the time he turned ten, Donald became the dominant personality among the three Trump children still living at home. Elizabeth, four years older than Donald, was so quiet that visiting friends often wondered if she spoke at all. Robert was also quiet, and passive, compared to his older brother, who teased him incessantly. Donald and his mother have long told a story about Donald borrowing Robert's favorite toy, his wooden building blocks, and gluing them all together. Donald saw the story as evidence of his strength and determination, and, like his father recounting playing with erector sets and blocks as a boy, as a hint to his destiny.

He was the tallest among the sixteen fourth-grade students at Kew-Forest. His relative size was his greatest asset in sports. When the weather allowed, Donald and his friends would spend hours playing pickup games of baseball or soccer after school. On the soccer field, Donald and another tall classmate, Paul Onish, would create a formidable last line of defense as fullbacks, just in front of their goalie.

Unlike his siblings, young Donald developed a reputation for misbehaving. A neighbor said he once hurled a large rock through her window, damaging a wall in her room.

At the Atlantic Beach Club, a private club on the Long Beach barrier island fifteen miles south of Jamaica Estates, Donald would wait by the pool for arriving families to pass by in their street clothes and then soak them with a monster cannonball off the high diving board. "He always blamed everybody else for doing it, but, you know, I had seen him do it," recalled Sandy McIntosh, who was Donald's age and a member of the club in those years.

Fred Trump paid a premium for the largest beach cabana closest to the water. Donald would play canasta with the kids in a nearby tent, sometimes with Robert sitting silently near him. "He always treated Robert as if he were mentally deficient, and I just assumed that Robert had a problem," McIntosh said. Unlike most of the other fathers, Fred would never change out of his dark suit, and would often tip his hat toward women lounging in swimsuits as he passed.

At some point the Trumps stopped frequenting the club. McIntosh heard a rumor in those years that the family had been banned because of Donald's behavior. He never learned if it was true, but it struck many as believable. Unlike his slightly built brothers, the stockier Donald seemed to enjoy using his size to his advantage. "He was a bully," McIntosh said.

Donald's best friend during those years was Peter Brant, the son of an immigrant from Romania who became wealthy as the founder of a newsprint company. In seventh grade, Brant was president and Donald was vice president of their class of twelve boys and five girls. They shared a love for sports, especially baseball. When they weren't playing the game, they collected baseball cards and snuck transistor radios into school to listen to professional baseball games.

The school yearbook, which often included poems written by students during the year, featured one by sixth grader Donald in 1958, titled "Baseball":

> I like to see a baseball hit and the fielder catch it in his mit. I like to hear the crowd give cheers, so loud and noisy to my ears. When the score is five to five, I feel like I could cry.
>
> And when they get another run, I feel like I could die. Then the catcher makes an error, not a bit like Yogi Berra. The game is over and we say tomorrow is another day.

By the time they were in sixth or seventh grade, the two friends began taking the subway to Kew-Forest each day. They lived about twenty minutes from each other, on opposite sides of the school. But they became comfortable with the subways and began sneaking away to Manhattan, telling their parents they would be on a baseball field somewhere. They would ride the thirty minutes to the edge of Times Square, a bustling world of tall buildings and discount electronics stores, diners, and people watching unlike anything in their leafy semi-suburban lives. They found a magic store that sold smoke bombs and, enamored with the musical street fighting in *West Side Story*, eventually graduated to buying knives.

Toward the end of seventh grade, their fathers found out. Both boys were in trouble. But Fred had reached his limit with Donald. He sent him to a boarding school, a military academy north of the city. When Brant and Onish returned to Kew-Forest in the fall of 1959, Donald was nowhere to be found.

Onish noticed Trump's absence and asked his homeroom teacher. She had no idea where he'd gone, only that he would not be back. Onish heard rumors that the headmaster had suggested that Donald find another school, but no one knew for sure.

"That was it," Onish recalled. "Done gone."

A COUPLE OF MONTHS after his thirteenth birthday, Donald Trump rode in his father's Cadillac sixty miles north to rural Orange County, New York, just outside tiny Cornwall-on-Hudson. The car pulled into a narrow drive that led to the quadrangle of the New York Military Academy, a spread of grass about eighty yards long framed by three low-slung buildings: one for classes, one for sleeping, one for eating. That quad would be the center of his universe for the rest of his childhood. He would no longer be called a student; he was now a cadet. He was issued an M1 rifle with the firing pin removed, a set of military-like uniforms, and a single bed in Wright Hall, the smaller barracks for seventh- and eighth-grade boys. His parents left.

He would be allowed to leave those grounds overnight only for major holidays and summers. Fred and Mary made frequent trips north on weekends. They were allowed to take him off campus for a meal. During one visit, Mary cornered the mother of another student in his grade, George Michael Witek, who had easily transitioned to the academy from a strict Catholic school in Holyoke, Massachusetts. Donald's mother seemed distraught and begged Mrs. Witek for a magic solution to make her insolent son listen.

As a resident of Wright Hall, Donald fell under the command of Theodore Dobias, a stout man and avid boxer who had graduated from the academy, served with the U.S. Army in World War II, and then returned to Cornwall for the rest of his working life. Given the honorary rank of major, Dobias was known among the students as "the Maj." He lived in a house on campus with his wife and children and kept plaques on his office walls with motivational phrases like "Blame attitude for failure." From Dobias's perspective, young Donald, accustomed to a house with full-time help, did not know how to take care of himself. He was taught how to shine his shoes and make his bed to military boot-camp standards. When he failed to meet those standards, or stepped out of line, Dobias smacked him.

His days were ruled by rigid adherence to the clock. Loudspeakers blasted reveille at 6:00 a.m. The young boys of Wright Hall made their way to a communal bathroom in the basement, a tiled area with shower heads, toilets, and urinals, and no privacy partitions. After dressing in their uniforms, they would hustle outside to the quadrangle by 6:30 a.m., assembling in columns and grouped by platoon. The flag would be raised. They would march to the mess hall, and after eating, they would march back to their barracks to face a possible inspection. Then they would march to classes, mostly in the academic building, with its toy castle-like turrets rising at its corners and flanking its entrance. After classes, they would clean their neutered M1 rifles. On the open acres north of the quad, they would practice handling the weapon while marching, and then march some more. At about 3:00 p.m., everyone played sports, followed by showers and dinner in their uniforms. After eating, they marched back to the barracks for an enforced study period. The bugle would blow taps at 9:30 p.m. A census would be taken of cadets in their darkened rooms. Day was done.

Campus life had gone like that since the school was founded by a Civil War veteran in 1889. For generations, many boys, like Donald, had been sent to the academy because their parents felt they could not control them, or to pry them away from temptation. But the academy was not a reform school. Boys also arrived because their parents had divorced or died, or because they were planning for military careers. A dozen or so boys from wealthy Latin American families arrived each fall. The draw was the promise that these boys would learn self-discipline. A newspaper advertisement from 1906 described the academy's worldview:

> Conditions are such that in no city school can a boy receive proper training and influence. To get them he must go to a school in a quiet, out-of-town location, where he is never subject to questionable associations nor evil environment.
>
> The military life and discipline and the constant supervision of able instructors are powerful elements in making a boy's character what it should be.

If military veterans like Dobias set the emotional tone at the academy, the frontline management of younger cadets fell to the older students through a hierarchical military ranking structure. Power flowed downward from the first captain and his staff, beginning with the eight cadet captains who were each in charge of a company of thirty to forty students. Lieutenants, sergeants, and corporals carried out the wishes of the captains, and everyone else in the company was at the rank of private. Rank had privilege and power. The leadership teams were given broad authority to enforce standards—maintaining rooms, uniforms, weapons, displaying proper marching technique, standing crisply at attention when older cadets walked past—through inspections and punishments. The older students enforced "New Guy Rules," which essentially meant younger students were treated as lesser. When an older student passed in the hall, all the New Guys slammed their backs against a wall and shouted, "Sorry to be in your way, sir!" Failing to hit the wall hard enough could result in punishment.

To solidify control, the older children often relied on violence, or the perceived threat of violence. Whacks with a broomstick to a bare backside were a common tool. Kicks to the groin were not unusual.

Douglas Reichel, a classmate one year behind Donald, was thirteen the day he was issued an M1. It was a thing of wonder for him, even without a firing pin or ammunition. He had never held a firearm before, and he marveled at its long black barrel and heavy wooden stock. Outside in the quad, he raised the rifle above his shoulder and aimed at a tree. Just then, the captain of his company kicked him hard in the groin. He spent more than a week in the infirmary. In his mind, that first day set the tone for his five years at the academy. He would run away from school twice, only to be discovered and beaten upon his return. "There wasn't a day when I didn't want to be out of that school." He saw Donald and a few other cadets as favored nations, floating above the constant threat of taunting and beatings. In his mind, Donald lived "the life of a privileged kid."

The military training, such as it was, focused overwhelmingly on executing a precise definition of neatness. There were infrequent days when the firing pins were placed back in the M1s for target practice, or the cadets learned the proper use of a mortar launcher. Standing at perfect attention and marching in synchronicity occupied a tremendous amount of time. But no skills were more frequently drilled into cadets than polishing shoes and belt buckles, making beds to an exacting pattern, and folding laundry with crisp 90-degree angles, all while older children cast judgment and distributed abuse for minute failures or demonstrations of insubordination.

Donald excelled at the domestic hygiene requirements and demanded perfection in those skills from other cadets. He once lost his temper at the sight of a fellow cadet's halfheartedly made bed and ripped the sheets off in a fit of rage. The cadet, Theodore Levine, who was four foot eleven, grew angry and threw a boot at Donald, then took a swing at him with a stick. Donald charged at the smaller cadet and seemed to be trying to push him out a window when two other cadets intervened. The fight with Levine, who was more than a foot shorter than Donald, was the only example many of Donald's classmates could recall of him in a physical altercation.

All cadets were pushed to play on the school's sports teams, and it was through sports that Donald attained some status on campus. He played one year each of varsity football and soccer, and three years of varsity baseball, still his favorite sport. Dobias coached Donald during his time on the junior varsity team, and during his senior year Donald was named a cocaptain.

The academy, a small school with roughly ninety students in each grade, was not a standout in regional athletics. The baseball team played against other small private and parochial schools and won just five of its twelve games in Donald's senior year. Newspapers published box scores for five of those games. The results show Trump hit safely only once in eighteen at bats, a stunningly poor batting average of 0.55.

Because the academy's soccer team had at least ten players from Latin America during an era when the sport was not widely popular in the United States, many on campus perceived the soccer team to be the school's strongest. But that season did not go well either during Donald's varsity season: the soccer team won three of its eleven games.

Regardless of wins and losses or his personal performance, playing on two varsity teams in a school that overtly stressed athletics as a component of development granted Donald some standing in the barracks.

Donald returned to Jamaica Estates each summer. He would spend much of those months accompanying his father to work. Donald would follow his orders: Hose down a rubble pile on a construction site. Survey repairs of empty units. Paint a hallway. He was the small fish that everyone knew would soon be the big fish.

"He's got to learn while he's not in school," Fred told anyone who asked about the blond-haired scion holding a shovel.

During his junior year at the academy, Donald held the rank of supply sergeant in his company. He was put in charge of a storage room full of M1 rifles and made sure they were oiled and in good working order. Sandy McIntosh, who attended the military academy with Donald, saw the supply sergeant job as perfect for him because "he didn't have to deal with people."

Supply sergeant was not a rank that necessarily suggested a trajectory to the top of the heap. But then, in September of his final year, a surprise came from the administration: Donald Trump would be promoted to captain of Company A, putting him in one of the top leadership positions on campus.

McIntosh was one of twenty-nine "privates" who fell under his authority. They noticed that after dinner, Donald would adjourn to his barracks room and lock the door. He left discipline and evening bed checks to his underlings and paid no attention to what was going on outside during study hours, a favorite time for older cadets looking to harass their younger peers.

That detached leadership style came at a cost. During his first month as a company captain, one of Donald's sergeants shoved a freshman cadet named Lee Raoul Ains hard against a wall. Ains complained, and the school demoted the offending sergeant. The administration also reassigned Donald, and Dobias, long Trump's most stalwart defender from the academy, admitted he had been moved because he did not monitor his charges closely enough. Donald was allowed to keep the title of captain but now served as a training officer without a company directly under his command.

In his new role, Donald joined the central staff of Witek, the top-ranked student, whose mother Mary Trump had once asked for advice. Witek said he was told by the administration that another captain on his staff, William Specht, would take over Company A in order to get Trump "out of the barracks." Specht, who as a junior had been promoted to the second-highest rank of lieutenant, was disappointed but quickly got Company A under control. Still, Donald insisted that joining Witek's staff had been a promotion.

It was the first of several episodes that led Witek to believe Fred Trump held sway over the academy's administrators. "His father was rich, and he was protected," Witek recalled later. "They directly ordered me to stay away from Trump. Everybody knew Fred was pulling out his checkbook."

Soon after, the cadets were preparing to march in the annual Columbus Day Parade in Manhattan, as they had done in recent years. Witek was surprised when Anthony "Ace" Castellano, the assistant commandant of cadets, directed him to put Donald at the front of the parade. Witek assumed that Fred Trump had complained to the school about his son being pushed out of the prominent company leadership role.

Whatever the reason, on October 12, 1963, Donald led the specially assembled company of cadets down Fifth Avenue, past some of the premiere addresses in the city of his birth. Some of the cadets marching behind him wondered how it could be that Trump was in front and Witek, the highest-ranking cadet in the school and the senior class president, marched behind him. Trump arrived first at St. Patrick's Cathedral, where he met Cardinal Francis Spellman. Donald would always claim marching in the front of the parade was evidence of his "elite" status at the academy.

Back on campus, Witek assembled his staff for a yearbook photo. They met on the wide-open field behind the buildings surrounding the quad. They wore their finest dress uniforms: tar bucket parade hats with tall feather plumes and chin straps across their lower lips, waist-cut dark jackets with three columns of brass buttons, and white shoulder belts across their chests. As they marched side by side across an empty field, Witek shouted, "Draw . . . sabre." All except Trump followed the precise movement they had rehearsed for four years that ended with the blades coming to rest on the inside of their shoulders. Witek, facing forward, heard one of his captains tell Donald again to draw his sword. Again, he did not. The photographer snapped the photo. Donald was the only member of the senior staff shown in the yearbook photo with his sword still sheathed. Witek later heard that Trump pointed out the photograph to fellow cadets as a boast of his defiance.

If Donald resented taking orders from a contemporary like Witek, he still craved the tokens of status conferred by the system. Like most cadets, he had earned a few medals for good conduct and being neat and orderly. But his friend, Michael Scadron, had a full dozen by their senior year. On the day yearbook portraits were being taken, Donald showed up in Scadron's barracks room and asked to borrow his dress jacket with the medals attached. Donald wore those medals for the portrait, perplexing some of his fellow cadets. "He's wearing my medals on his uniform," Scadron recounted years later. "I didn't care one way or the other."

From Trump's perspective, Scadron came from another world. Scadron's father, Harold, had managed boxers in the 1930s and 1940s, most famously the fighter Bob Olin, who in 1934 won a light heavyweight championship in a fifteen-round match at Madison Square Garden. Scadron's mother, fifteen years younger than Harold, left him when Michael was young to pursue drinking and cavorting full-time in Los Angeles. Young Michael bounced between coasts for a few years before begging his father to send him to the military academy for some sense of stability.

Scadron, who learned to box from his father, found a home in the culture that valued such things. He could play by the rules at the academy, but he had a temper. One day in the spring of 1964, in Scadron's telling, he was holding a meeting with his squad when a younger cadet from a wealthy family called him "a dirty Jew bastard." Scadron, whose father was raised in the Jewish faith, lost it. "I decked him, and after I decked him, I kept on decking him." In his room, Scadron kept a two-foot-long wooden stick with a metal chain attached to one end. He had mostly used it as a theatrical prop, swinging it around like a movie villain in a dirty chariot race with Ben-Hur. But in a fit of rage that day, he used the crude device as a weapon: "I may have hit him with it, because when he called my father a dirty Jew bastard, all bets were off."

The culture of hazing at the school had become a liability. Scadron was expelled, and the superintendent of the academy and two other top administrators were forced to resign. The police were notified, but Scadron was not formally charged. He graduated from another high school and moved to Ohio to attend Kenyon College, where he had been accepted prior to the incident. His individual portrait was purged from the military academy yearbook, even though his medals made a cameo appearance on Donald Trump's chest. Scadron would lose track of nearly everyone else from those years except Donald Trump, who would hire him a decade later.

It was the first of many such relationships in Trump's life. He would be drawn to men who displayed a penchant for violence, and wax sentimentally about the days when, in his perception, society accepted resolving disputes with physical violence.

On a warm day in June 1964, hundreds of cadets and their families gathered in front of a stage on the quadrangle for the annual graduation commencement ceremony. Fred and Mary made the drive north. If they had been briefed by their son, they might have arrived expecting to see him endlessly feted. In Donald's mind, he was "a very elite person" and "top of the military heap" at the academy. The list of awards to be handed out to the top performers spanned five pages of the program. There were the top ten cadets—more than 10 percent of the entire class—graduating "with distinction." None was named Trump. There was the Head Boy Gold Medal, awarded for earning the highest marks in conduct, military, and scholastic work. The recipient was not named Trump. There were more than a dozen medals for accomplishment in individual subjects. The name Trump would not be mentioned.

For the top honor, the Achievement Alumni Award, the program noted that award would go to the graduating cadet who most excelled at the core values of the academy: "He shall be chosen for his strength of character, record of broad scholarship, athletic interest and ability, military proficiency and discipline, and for having done the most to increase and maintain the spirit and morale of the Corps during his life at the school." There were seven nominees selected by classmates, the headmaster, and the commandant. Donald Trump was not among them. The winner was George Witek. His name would be added to the list of prior winners on a large memorial near the flag in the quad, something approaching military academy immortality. During the commencement ceremony, Witek was called to the stage so many times that he barely had time to warm his chair. He received other top awards for military science proficiency, for school leadership, and for being a superior cadet.

Donald Trump received one distinction: like all fourteen captains, he was given an honorary saber.

When the yearbook was published, it listed the honors students had bestowed upon their classmates. Donald Trump's fellow students deemed him to be the "Ladies' Man" of their all-male campus. They picked Paul David Bekman, who went on to become a successful attorney in Maryland, as "Most Likely to Succeed." Not surprisingly, they crowned Witek the "Most Military" of the class.

No cadet took success at the academy more seriously than Witek. Yet his assessment of the school's military training would quickly diminish after he enlisted in the army. A few months in boot camp made his high school seem like a Toy Soldier Academy.

"When I got into basic training," Witek later said, "I realized very quickly that at the New York Military Academy we were just play-acting. What we had been taught was a sort of surface military thing."

With U.S. involvement in Vietnam escalating, many of Donald's classmates enlisted or were drafted. Witek and at least two other captains on his high school staff served in the military during the war. Specht, who took over Trump's leadership of Company A, entered the navy.

Donald Trump would never put his military education to the test. He obtained his first draft deferment shortly after graduation. But unlike Witek, Donald came to see his time in high school as superior to actual military service: "I always felt that I was in the military because I, in a way, had more training militarily than a lot of the guys that go into the military."

In the years to come, Donald would greatly exaggerate his high school athletic record. In Donald's telling, he was "always the best athlete" at the academy. In reality he was outbatted by several teammates, and often outplayed by Jim Toomey, the number-one pitcher and shortstop. Toomey also played quarterback for the football team and was a star in basketball. Toomey, not Donald, was named "Most Athletic." The school administrators agreed, giving Toomey the top award for athletic accomplishment.

Donald also claimed to be the best baseball player in New York at the time, but at least a dozen players in New York high schools during his senior year went on to play major league baseball. One was Ken Singleton, who was a year younger than Donald and played outfield at Mount Vernon High School. Singleton would be a first-round draft pick of the New York Mets in 1967, and during a fourteen-year major league career, mostly with the Baltimore Orioles, would be named an All-Star three times and win one World Series.

Donald regularly claimed to have been scouted by major league teams, and often directed reporters to call Dobias, who had been only his junior varsity coach, to serve as his witness. The Maj went along, but his accounts shifted over time. He once identified the scout as from the Chicago White Sox, and another time as from the Philadelphia Phillies, and a third time asserted there had been scouts from both the Boston Red Sox and the Phillies. In another interview, Dobias said "if he worked at it" Donald could have made it partway up the rung in the minor leagues.

Almost forty years after his graduation, Donald submitted an essay for publication in a book insisting that he had been invited to try out for professional baseball and decided against going pro:

> I was supposed to be a pro baseball player. . . . I was still thinking in high school that I had a shot at the Major Leagues until I attended a tryout with another young kid named Willie McCovey. I watched him hit the ball, and I said I really believe I will enjoy the real estate business for my entire life. I had always felt like the best player until I saw that man hit.

None of that could have happened. McCovey's pro tryout came in early 1955, when Donald Trump was a pudgy third grader in Queens. In 1959, McCovey made his major league debut with the San Francisco Giants and was named the National League's Rookie of the Year. Donald was then in eighth grade, learning to make his bed at the military academy.

Donald added that he decided against a career in professional baseball because the pay was too low. He singled out the $100,000 annual salary paid to Mickey Mantle, the star center fielder for the New York Yankees. While low by the standards of professional athletes in later decades, Mantle's salary then was the equivalent of more than $1 million a year today, not a level of compensation that would turn off most eighteen-year-olds.

Like his older brother, Freddy, Donald would disappoint his father by not attending the Wharton School of the University of Pennsylvania that fall. He would settle for Fordham University in the Bronx; his sister Maryanne would say privately she helped him get in. But as in high school, Donald Trump's performance in college would have no bearing on the direction of his life. And within four years, Donald's father would pay him more than the equivalent of Mickey Mantle's salary for demonstrating little more than a willingness to push his older brother out of his way.

6

MARCH THE LINE

In the summer of 1957, Fred Trump read in a city newspaper that a nonprofit group, United Housing Foundation, had won tentative approval from the city to build a six-thousand-unit cooperative apartment complex one mile south of Fred's Beach Haven apartments, about five hundred yards from the famed Coney Island beach and boardwalk. Following state laws to incentivize the building of housing for low- and middle-income families, the city comptroller had agreed to accept $250,000 in property taxes on the project, with the figure slowly increasing to a full level of about $2.5 million after twenty years.

Fred was enraged, and for years to come he would repeat the words that came to mind at that very moment: "Totally unfair!" He was paying a property tax bill of $1 million a year on Beach Haven and Shore Haven, which combined had just over half as many units as the planned project. He saw no public value in the government incentivizing new housing by allowing someone to pay lower property taxes than him. He didn't want "competition right across the way" paying lower taxes on "modern, fireproof apartments" that would be "in a better location, nearer transportation, and nearer the ocean."

It was a moment tailor made for the decades Fred Trump had spent building relationships within the Brooklyn Democratic Party. The Brooklyn borough president—who held the power to kill large-scale construction projects in the borough—was John Cashmore, who had spent most of his career in Fred's circle of influence.

Cashmore's best friend and closest associate also happened to be Richard P. Charles, Fred's lawyer for more than a decade. The three of them met for lunches at the Court Café, an unassuming restaurant on the ground floor below the Brooklyn Democratic Party headquarters. Fred and his two closest friends in the local party—Bunny Lindenbaum, the connected lawyer and fundraiser for politicians, and Abe Beame, the accountant, the two men he had taken for weekend getaways in Virginia during the war—had played central roles in events vital to any politician seeking prominence and voters in the borough. For a decade they had organized annual "Music Under the Stars" concerts, bringing national performers like Benny Goodman and Jimmy Durante to Ebbets Field in Brooklyn, to raise money for institutions in the new State of Israel. Cashmore had served as honorary chairman; Fred was treasurer. Beame would go on to become the city's budget director, the official to whom Cashmore would go with budget requests to fund road and sewer maintenance for a borough of more than two and a half million people.

Much of a borough president's power emanated from his seat on the city's Board of Estimate, which lorded over city government's biggest decisions and expenditures, including land use. By unwritten tradition, Board of Estimate members—three citywide elected officials and the five borough presidents—all deferred their judgment on individual real estate developments to the president of the affected borough.

After reading about the Coney Island project, Fred wrote a letter to Cashmore calling the tax abatement an unfair "giveaway." He followed up his letter with a private chat with Cashmore, and that same day spoke at a planning commission meeting, again calling the plan an "outright giveaway" and an unfair subsidy. The project stopped moving through the approval pipeline. Cashmore adopted Fred Trump's reasoning that tax breaks for new developments were unfair to private owners of existing apartments. Fred insisted he had no special pull with Cashmore, who had been borough president since 1940.

"I knew John Cashmore same as I've known a dozen other borough presidents," Fred said.

Cashmore, born the youngest of ten children to immigrants from England, had come to enjoy the finer things. He and his wife, Edythe, lived in a premiere apartment building near Prospect Park in Brooklyn and regularly took long cruises, including a nearly three-month sojourn on the Italian SS *Andrea Doria* to Europe in 1954. Though he was never charged with any crimes, he was known around Brooklyn as John Cashbox. His public positions and private life mixed and mingled to the benefit of both. When he failed to keep the Dodgers franchise in Brooklyn, he still spent time at the Dodgers' spring training camp in Vero Beach, Florida, while his wife flew to Havana with the team's royalty—including owner Walter O'Malley and longtime team announcer Vin Scully—on the team's private airplane. The details of their trip weren't known at the time, but a junket of that sort would have been scandalous in later years.

The founder of United Housing Foundation, Abraham E. Kazan, had also known Cashmore for years. In some ways, Kazan's career had unfolded on a parallel track to Fred Trump's. Both entered the field in the 1920s and considered themselves masters of containing costs. Both would oversee the construction of about twenty-five thousand housing units in their lifetimes. Where they diverged was on the final destination of the money. The money Fred Trump saved on expenses went to Fred Trump. The money United Housing saved on expenses went toward lowering costs for tenants.

Kazan had moved to New York from Kiev in 1904, when he was thirteen. He spent his teenage years in the overcrowding and filth of tenement buildings on the Lower East Side of Manhattan, where many buildings lacked indoor plumbing and adequate windows. Kazan came to see substandard housing as a threat to "the health, the morale, and the social outlook of its inhabitants" and made addressing that need his life's work.

Working for labor unions in his youth, Kazan developed ways to save members money through the cooperative purchase of costly staples. He led the International Ladies Garment Workers' Union to buy sugar and matzah at bulk discounts and sell the goods to its members at cost. In his thirties, while manager of the Amalgamated Clothing Workers Credit Union, he convinced the credit union to use its capital to build one of the nation's first cooperative apartment buildings, the Amalgamated Housing Cooperative in the Bronx. By keeping costs low, and taking no profit out of the building, the union sold individual units for a per-room down payment of five hundred dollars and carrying charges—the shared costs to maintain the building—of eleven dollars a month. Nelson Rockefeller, the New York governor, once said Kazan "could have gone into private business for himself and made a fortune," but chose a different path. Kazan responded that he was interested only in "building the cooperative commonwealth." A quiet man who *The New York Times* once described as resembling a sturdier version of Harry Truman, Kazan lived for decades in the

Amalgamated Houses as he went about building thousands more affordable apartments.

Kazan, considered the father of the cooperative housing movement, had built some of the largest and most successful middle-income apartment projects in the city. He met with Cashmore several times to make his case on the Coney Island proposal. "Friendliness didn't help in this case," Kazan would say. "All I know is that I did plead with the borough president to get approval, and we couldn't."

Kazan argued that the property tax abatement on the Coney Island project was needed to keep the monthly carrying costs of each apartment within reach of the target tenants: "The only way we can set rents at figures that can be afforded by the people in the greatest need of private housing is by getting partial property tax exemption for a limited period of time." By the time Cashmore stalled the project, more than three thousand families had already made down payments. The following summer, a thousand of them signed a petition asking Cashmore to let the project move along. They tried to deliver it to him in person at his office, but knowing they were coming he left to make "an inspection in the field."

Months went by, with newspapers regularly noting that the Board of Estimate had again delayed action. Finally, Fred Trump presented a solution—himself. He would take over construction of the project and pay the full property tax from the start. In Fred's recounting, he had won over the borough president. "John Cashmore was interested in receiving a fair return taxwise to hold down the tax rate in the borough of Brooklyn. And John Cashmore, I would say, was on my team when I offered to pay a million and a half dollars tax rather than a two-hundred-fifty-thousand-dollar-a-year offer, which the borough president had previously received from another outfit."

Kazan, and families hoping to move into the buildings, would continue to feel the pinch from Cashmore's delays while Fred Trump perfected his plans. Finally, after more than two years, Kazan and Trump were summoned to a back room at City Hall, where the Board of Estimate met for executive sessions. Kazan was told bluntly that his original plan of more than 6,000 units and a shopping center would be chopped in two, with a little more than half of the total units, and about three-quarters of the commercial space going to Fred Trump. With down payments from 2,500 buyers who needed homes, Kazan felt he had no more options. "We were in a very awkward position," he later recalled. "Here we had the people waiting all this time, and then Trump came in and took away the entire job from us. So, by way of compromise, we finally agreed to take the one half."

Cashmore never fully addressed his role in helping Fred Trump get what he wanted. One evening six months after he finally allowed the plan to pass through the Board of Estimate, Cashmore left a charity event at the Commodore Hotel in Manhattan and stepped into his city-owned limousine. On the drive to Brooklyn, his chauffeur noticed Cashmore slumped over in the back seat. He died of a heart attack that night at the age of sixty-five.

Fred, nearing sixty years old and thinking about which of his sons would take over his empire, prepared to break ground on this $60 million project, the biggest of his life, just as his eldest son returned from college. Fred had not put his name on any of his projects since his brief time owning Trump Market during the Great Depression. Someone convinced him to call this capstone achievement Trump Village. Initially reluctant, he went along because he decided that the project could become "something to remember the name Trump by."

"It took a long time to sell me on the idea," he said. "They told me it would be a monument to me, and most monuments I know are granite or marble."

Before he could break ground at Trump Village, Fred Trump faced one more major decision. Two state programs were available to fund construction, both of which offered a property tax abatement like the one he said had so offended him. One program would allow him unlimited profits. He could put every nickel he saved on costs straight into his pocket. But for that program, Fred would need a bank mortgage, which would come with higher interest rates. He had so far failed to find a willing lender. The other program, known as Mitchell-Lama, would award Fred a low-interest state mortgage, greatly cutting his costs and eliminating the need to convince a bank. But in exchange, he would be compelled to cap his profits at a little more than 7 percent of construction costs.

Fred solved that dilemma by picking the same path he had chosen with federal programs fifteen years earlier: deception. He took the government loan, agreed to limit his profits, and immediately began doing everything he could to get around that commitment.

He got started with the formation of a company called Boro Equipment

Corporation. It would be owned, indirectly, by one man, Fred Trump. And it would have only one customer, Fred Trump. Fred Trump would charge Fred Trump a fee for renting bulldozers and backhoes with a steep markup added for the benefit of one person. Fred Trump. And he would go out of his way to hide that relationship with himself from the state.

As soon as the plans for the area were approved, municipal lawyers began the work of condemning properties in the area. For decades, that section of Coney Island a few blocks from the beach had been called "the Gut," a collection of shanties and shacks once used for summer weekend getaways but now lived in year-round, in some cases by squatters. The city, which under Mitchell-Lama had the authority to condemn structures in the area, had also contracted with an outside relocation firm to find new homes for displaced people.

Fred knew the city was doing the work. He saw the results of the city's efforts as the months passed and he planned for construction. But still he directed some of the mortgage money—the proceeds of his inflated construction estimates—to Bunny Lindenbaum, the politically connected lawyer and ally, to ostensibly perform the same work. Lindenbaum had recently been forced to resign as a city planning commissioner after word leaked out that he had hosted a campaign fundraising luncheon for Mayor Robert F. Wagner Jr. with builders and real estate professionals, including Fred Trump.

As always, Fred had Matthew Tosti, by then his longest-serving and most trusted lawyer, working on Trump Village and the application materials. But just to be sure things ran smoothly, Fred paid $128,000 to the law firm of Senator MacNeil Mitchell, the Manhattan Republican who had cosponsored the Mitchell-Lama legislation.

As he focused on finalizing the architecture of his monument, Fred thought back to family vacations in Florida. He remembered being awed by the beautiful lobby of the Sans Souci, one of the many Miami-area hotels that bore the unique design sensibilities of architect Morris Lapidus. Fred called Lapidus and asked him to design the lobbies of the Trump Village buildings.

"I don't do lobbies!" Lapidus snapped back.

Well, Fred countered, how about designing the entire project? Lapidus knew that government-financed middle-income housing left little money for design flourishes. "They had to be plain boxes with punched windows," recalled Alan Lapidus, who had just started working with his father at the time.

But even if construction costs had to be tamped down, Morris Lapidus saw another attraction, his son recalled: "The generous fees for such bland and mindless work were irresistible."

What Lapidus saw as bland, Fred marketed as majestic. He told reporters through the preconstruction phase that Trump Village would "add a new dimension to the shorefront skyline" by bringing "the Lapidus touch of Miami Beach's svelte Fontainebleau, Eden Roc and Americana hotels to Brooklyn."

The building would, as Lapidus predicted, turn out to be a collection of plain boxes, with balconies. But the pricing and Fred's pronouncements drew crowds. Before the foundations were even poured, more than three hundred potential buyers had shown up over a weekend in July. Fred directed the real estate agency he had hired to expand the sales staff to fifteen people.

By the spring, the Trump Village site was ready for construction. On that cleared forty acres, a job more sprawling than anything in Fred Trump's long career, he would erect a mix of 7 cooperative and rental buildings, each towering 23 stories, the equivalent of a 161-story skyscraper.

As construction on the first buildings hit the fifteen-story mark, Fred began to feel out of his depth. His expertise was with buildings of six to eight stories. These taller buildings required structural work that was new to him. The state had demanded that he acquire bonding to guarantee he could pay all of his subcontractors, but he had been unable to obtain the bond. He turned to HRH Construction, one of the largest construction firms in the city, to take over construction and buy the payment and performance bond.

"I saw that this was growing beyond capacity which I wanted to undertake without assistance," he would later say.

DURING THE SUMMERS of 1962 and 1963, with Trump Village one of the largest construction sites in the city, Fred had both of his potential successors at his side on a near daily basis. Donald, home from the military academy for summer break, would be seen spraying water on debris piles to tamp down the dust.

Freddy was directed to focus on the mundane maintenance issues at his father's older buildings. He surveyed needed repairs and talked to building superintendents. Sometimes, his father would be at his side, and Freddy would learn the more subtle methods of keeping costs low, profits high. If tenants complained that Fred kept a building's heat too low during the winter, he would show up at their apartment, remove his suit jacket, and dramatically complain about the apartment being so hot.

When he exercised discretion, Freddy seemed to disappoint his father. At one older building, Freddy noticed the windows leaked, with tenants constantly complaining of drafts during the frigid Northeast winters. Freddy launched a window replacement project on his own initiative. His father heard about it later and belittled his eldest son's judgment in front of other employees.

Freddy sometimes joked about his grubby work to old friends and fraternity brothers from Lehigh. He would slip into his W. C. Fields impersonation to spin clumsy yarns. "One of the tenants called and complained to me, 'I got a leak in my sink.' I said to them, 'That's okay. Go right ahead. Everyone else does.'"

Freddy also told friends that his father was pushing him to build relationships with local politicians and judges. He respected his father's accomplishments, but those grittier aspects of how his dad did business bothered him. Sol Magrid remembers Freddy telling him that his father made him deliver envelopes filled with cash "to certain people."

"He had a difficult time with that," Magrid said.

Freddy never lived by his father's only-work-matters doctrine. Now a young man finished with school, he pursued interests that produced no earthly currency and made lasting friendships that did not benefit his job.

He remained close pals with Taylor Johnson Jr., the son of his father's friend and one time business partner from his days building military housing in Norfolk during the war. Freddy and Taylor Jr. had played together on the beach as small children and remained in touch through the years. The differences in their backgrounds were significant. Freddy grew up in Cadillacs and subways, moving with ease between the semisuburban serenity of Jamaica Estates and the urban street corners encroaching from all sides. Taylor grew up on the beaches and farms of a still-rural Virginia Beach. He learned to drive tractors and farm trucks by age twelve. He spoke with a southern accent and had a humble wonder at the ways of a big city.

Freddy periodically flew a small plane down to Virginia and brought Taylor back north with him. Taylor found himself playing man-of-the-city in Manhattan, with Freddy as his worldly ambassador planning days and nights and paying the tab at every meal.

Freddy's interest in boats had grown since his high school days floating on tranquil Sheepshead Bay. He bought a sport fishing boat with an elevated fly-bridge and a powerful engine. He entered himself and Taylor, who had grown up on the water, in shark-fishing contests off Long Island. Their memories would be more about the laughs than the victories. There was the time a shark they had caught lunged at Taylor's leg and took a bite out of the aluminum chair he was sitting in. There was the day Taylor noticed the boat laboring to get back to shore and discovered two feet of water had leaked through the new caulking around the exhaust pipes. They sat there slowly sinking, drinking beer, and telling stories for more than two hours until the U.S. Coast Guard finally arrived to give them a tow. Taylor mostly remembers having a great time while their big fishing plans went down the drink.

"It was a two-day tournament, and we didn't even get to fish the second day," Taylor recalled, still laughing decades later. "All the entrance money and everything for the tournament, ah, it wasn't any big deal to him. He says, 'The heck with it.'"

One day out of the blue, Linda Lee Clapp, the girl Freddy and Billy Drake had met on their flying trip to the Bahamas, called Freddy from Florida with news. She had just been hired as a stewardess by National Airlines to staff flights between New York and Florida. Flying was so glamorous that her hiring had been featured in the local newspaper, with a photo showing Linda smiling in the airline's uniform and pillbox hat. She wondered if Freddy could help her find an apartment. Not long after, she moved into one of Fred Trump's buildings, Saxony Hall in Jamaica Estates. Freddy proposed within the next year.

They were married on January 20, 1962, at All Saints Episcopal Church in Fort Lauderdale. Billy Drake stood as Freddy's best man. Taylor Johnson served as an usher. Fred and Mary attended but did not visibly warm to either Linda or her parents. Linda's father worked as a truck driver, and the family lived in a 1,700-square-foot, three-bedroom house about a ten-minute drive from the beach. The newlywed couple's friends saw the stress that Fred and Mary's disapproval placed on the new marriage.

"There was a real problem with Linda and Freddy's parents," recalled David Miller, a fraternity brother of Freddy who stayed close to him for years. "Maybe they felt she was a gold digger. Maybe they felt that she wasn't up to the Trump family standards." Annamaria Forcier, who lived near the Trumps in Jamaica Estates and began dating Billy Drake around that time, also picked up on the disapproval. "They just did not like her," Forcier recalled. "They thought she was from the wrong side of the tracks." From what Annamaria saw, Freddy's parents viewed his new wife as "a Florida cracker."

Even as he worked for his father, Freddy focused more than ever on becoming a professional pilot. He logged hundreds of hours in the air and continued to apply for upgrades to his pilot's license. He earned his rating to fly seaplanes, practicing taking off and landing on the water. He enrolled in a flight school on Long Island to earn his rating to fly under instrument-only conditions, spending hours essentially blindfolded to simulate zero-visibility conditions. He bought his first plane, a 1963 Piper PA-28-180 Cherokee Super Custom, for $17,500. By October 1963, he had acquired enough hours in the air and classroom to apply for his commercial pilot license. He took the test and passed.

Linda was expecting their first child within a month and wanted her husband to keep working for his father. She had quit the airline, because National Airlines in those years forced stewardesses to quit when they married. But during layovers she had seen enough hard drinking and philandering not to want her husband in that life.

Freddy remained determined. Taylor Johnson came up from Virginia Beach and could tell Freddy felt pressured. He alluded to "a rift" with his father, but Taylor did not pry. "His dad wanted him to take over," Taylor said, but Freddy did not want the job any longer. "He just wouldn't march the white line that Mr. Trump wanted him to, I guess."

He was soon accepted to the Trans World Airlines pilot training program. With the last buildings at Trump Village still under construction, Freddy quit his father's company and moved his young family to Marblehead, Massachusetts, a coastal town about twenty miles north of Boston. He left behind the mix of financial comfort and unhappiness that had set his course at his father's company.

Classmates in the training program noticed that he drank during the day. But his dream of flying professionally looked to be finally coming true, and at the same time his longtime flying buddy, Billy Drake, was also becoming a professional pilot. Billy married Annamaria Forcier and became a pilot for Pan Am. "It was very prestigious," Annamaria remembered. "TWA and Pan Am, that was the top bananas." And Freddy's pride in his accomplishment showed. "When he was a pilot, he was deliriously happy."

Around that time, Taylor Johnson Jr. proposed to a local woman in Virginia Beach. When he thought about whom he wanted as his best man, he thought of Freddy. For a region that has a special term for folks who are not locals—"come-a-here," as in, you're not from-a-here, you just come-a-here—Taylor's choice of a rich New York City boy bewildered and slightly insulted some of his local pals. But there was something in their friendship that made the choice seem obvious.

In May 1964, Freddy drove to Virginia Beach for the wedding. He and Linda arrived in a car Taylor would never forget, a convertible Jaguar XK-E, the sports car Enzo Ferrari is believed to have called the most beautiful automobile ever made, with long and low lines that curved as gracefully as an airplane wing. Fred and Mary, still friendly with Taylor's father, attended as well. Freddy seemed to be on top of the world, a commercial pilot at a time when the larger culture saw that life as equal parts romantic and heroic. He cut a dashing figure at the reception in Taylor's father's backyard, rail thin in his tailored suit, a martini in hand, framed by the flowering gardenia bushes and magnolia trees.

After he and Linda returned to Marblehead, Donald drove up in the Austin-Healey their father had given him as a high school graduation gift. Freddy took Donald fishing and introduced him to his new son, Frederick Crist Trump III. There is a photo Freddy took of Donald bent over a blue wading pool in Freddy's yard, smiling back at the camera as he helped his infant nephew stand in the pool. Robert Trump, barely a teenager, stands in the wading pool just behind them, clutching the baby's inflated Popeye punching bag. One evening during that visit, eighteen-year-old Donald communicated their father's view of his older brother. "Dad's right about you," Donald told him. "You're nothing but a glorified bus driver."

Freddy knew that his father did not approve of his career choice, but he kept trying. At the age of twenty-six he made it to the second seat as a pilot for TWA. But even in a work culture that embraced heavy drinking in off hours, Freddy's worsening problems with alcohol stood out. Decades later, the former president of the TWA Retired Pilots Association still remembered Freddy Trump's time as a pilot. "He had problems with the bottle," said Bob Kavula. "The problem was he couldn't get out of bed after consuming the alcohol."

Within weeks of his first flight, TWA encouraged Freddy to quit to avoid the airline taking an action that could result in him losing his pilot license. He would briefly fly with two smaller airlines, and both those jobs would also end quickly. He would never again fly professionally, and he increasingly drank like a condemned man. Taylor Johnson remembers fishing trips in Florida when Freddy started his day with vodka and orange juice. His weight plummeted. His friends worried.

He and Linda and baby Fred returned to Queens. They took an apartment in the Highlander, another of his father's buildings. He rented a small weekend place in Montauk, at the eastern tip of Long Island, and still lit up while fishing in the deep waters offshore with Taylor, Billy Drake, or his other friends. He would put up a movie screen outside and insist they watch W. C. Fields movies. But part of the spark, the happy-go-lucky personality, faded once he realized his flying career had slipped away. Annamaria looked at Freddy one weekend on Montauk and realized he had been broken. In her mind, he had "sort of lost his personality."

By the end of 1964 he returned to work for his father, aware that he had lost the older man's confidence forever.

On a frigid December day, Fred Trump and a collection of local Brooklyn businessmen held a small ceremony at the entrance to the first completed building at Trump Village. He stood there with his youngest daughter, Elizabeth, a quiet twenty-one-year-old, as a local florist handed out bouquets to the guests of honor: the first few families moving into Trump Village.

When applications were being accepted, a string of mostly Black and Jewish people from other parts of Brooklyn applied for their chance at a new apartment. But only Jews seemed to be moving in: the families of Louis Mendelson, Myron Armet, Abraham Koenigsburg, and Gerald Goldstein. Al Sinrod, the president of the Coney Island Board of Trade, told the new arrivals: "In this sub-freezing temperature, we extend our warm welcome to our community to you, and to the thousands who will follow you."

Even with construction still in full swing, Fred pushed forward with other acquisitions. That same month he opened another apartment building in Jamaica Estates, the 214-unit Wilshire, as well as a 190-unit apartment building, Ocean Terrace, across the street from his Beach Haven apartments.

He continued to scoop up projects built by other developers under the old FHA Section 608 program. "While we are basically a construction firm," he said at the time, "we have a reputation for curing ailing properties." He was the only bidder at an FHA auction of the 1,168-unit Swifton Village in Cincinnati. A few months later, he bought another money-losing apartment project, the 490-unit Patio Gardens in Flatbush, a Brooklyn neighborhood a few miles north of Trump Village.

Trump Village would be his capstone achievement, adding another 900 rental apartments to a portfolio that paid profitable levels of rent every month. Within just a few months in 1964, Fred took over or built a total of 5,700 apartments, a massive expansion of his empire. A decade after the congressional hearings over the FHA scandal put him in league with hacks and grifters, Fred Trump enjoyed a round of glowing publicity on a national scale. A profile in *The New York Times* ran under the headline DEVELOPMENT IN CONEY IS PEAK OF A 40-YEAR BUILDING CAREER. Another profile, by United Press International, ran in newspapers across the country. "I don't consider it work," Fred told the reporter. "There are irritations and disappointments. But generally speaking, I call it a hobby."

His operation though, in terms of personnel, was no larger than it had ever been. There were no trusted executives to whom he delegated important oversight. He still signed every check. He personally visited Virginia several times a year to check on his properties. He traveled to Maryland to check on Gregory Estates, the five-hundred-apartment complex he bought out of FHA foreclosure. And now, he began flying every Tuesday to Cincinnati to oversee the remodeling of Swifton Village. If he felt at all spread thin, he never let on. Asked in Ohio about his secret to success, Fred said only "Keep busy."

Fred was so busy that he did not notice the state auditor lurking around his construction site.

7

IT'S ALL OVER NOW

As the Trump Village towers rose higher and higher, the flags outside Steeplechase Park, a few blocks away on the famed Coney Island boardwalk, were lowered to half-mast. Frank Tilyou, the president of the company and the last surviving son of the founders, had just died. The family soon announced that the Steeplechase—the last of the three big amusement parks that gave Coney Island its reputation for fun, sun, and surf—would not reopen for the coming summer.

The closing inspired a wave of nostalgia. A piece of old New York had died. City newspapers ran sentimental retrospectives with photos showing throngs crowding the beach and boardwalk in earlier decades, when three amusement parks—Dreamland, Luna, and Steeplechase—drew a million visitors a day. Letters and stories waxed on about loves lost and won, adrenaline thrills, and feeling at one with the city's great mass of humanity.

The Tilyou family began entertaining offers to sell. By early 1965, it was clear they had a problem. The land was zoned for use as an amusement park, and the brokers and builders thought the site made business sense only if they could win a zoning change from the City Planning Commission to allow high-rise apartments. None of the potential buyers so far had thought that was a risk worth taking. James Onorato, who had managed the park for the Tilyou family for three decades, told the family why: "We know from the grapevine that the commission is set on no zone change."

With the city growing more crowded, public officials began to see value in preserving land for public use. Fred Trump, however, saw only a beautiful blank canvas. Twelve acres with an ocean view. Miami by the subway.

Fred offered the Tilyous $2.2 million, the equivalent today of more than $22 million, in the spring of 1965. He agreed to let the Tilyou family sell off the remaining rides, suggesting he had no interest running an amusement park. Marie Tilyou, the founder's daughter, quickly accepted.

On the morning of July 1, 1965, the parties and their lawyers all gathered for the formal closing in the Brooklyn Heights office of Wingate & Cullen, a century-old Brooklyn law firm that represented the Tilyou family. Seventeen people attended, including James Onorato and Marie Tilyou, two real estate brokers, and seven lawyers. Fred brought along his two lawyers—Matthew Tosti and Abe Lindenbaum—and a surprise guest: his middle son, Donald, who had just turned nineteen.

While Donald got to play like a dealmaker at the table, Freddy was charged with the grittier tasks to come. Over the months, as Onorato found problems with the fire sprinkler system and the natural gas lines, it was Freddy he briefed.

On the day of the closing, the Coney Island Chamber of Commerce made clear it would oppose rezoning the site for apartments. Freddy became the family's face for his father's unpopular plan. It was him, then twenty-eight years old, whom Fred directed to explain to reporters that the family would make every effort to reopen the site as an amusement park. "If we can make it pay as an amusement proposition, that's what it will be," Freddy said. "If not, it's going to have to go for senior-citizens housing."

If he was hoping for a boost from his old friend Abe Beame, it would not be coming. When Wagner retired as mayor after three terms, Beame ran to replace him—only to lose to John V. Lindsay, a moderate Republican congressman with whom Fred had no connections. Lindsay's incoming parks commissioner's first public comments that December included voicing his opposition to any effort by Fred Trump to build high-rise apartments at Steeplechase.

Fred announced that he had tried to convince three amusement park operators to take over Steeplechase, including Walt Disney. "They turned it down," Fred said, "all declaring that Coney Island had had its day." He remained committed to building an apartment tower of twenty to thirty stories, which he insisted, through Freddy, was necessary for him to save the neighborhood.

"The fact is that the whole of Coney Island needs redoing," Freddy told a reporter. "You and I wouldn't take our kids there. People are afraid to walk on Surf Ave. at night."

As his Steeplechase plans hit a wall, Fred began to slow down in the wake of a more personal experience.

On the evening of Monday, November 8, 1965, Fred missed a flight for his regular Tuesday survey of Swifton Village in Ohio. American Airlines Flight 383 took off at 5:38 p.m. from LaGuardia Airport without him. Passing through thick, low clouds from a thunderstorm during its descent into Greater Cincinnati Airport, the Boeing 727 crashed into a hillside about two miles short of the runway. The jet exploded shortly after impact, killing fifty-eight of the sixty-two people on board.

Fred told some family members that narrowly missing that ill-fated flight left him hesitant to fly. Already overtaxed by his far-flung empire, he would travel less frequently in the future to his out-of-state properties. His buildings in Maryland, Ohio, and Virginia would begin a long, slow slide into disrepair.

ROBERT STRAUSS, a field auditor for the state agency that financed Trump Village, visited the Trump Village construction site seven times. On each visit he made an entry in his notebook that he had witnessed heavy machinery bearing the name Boro Equipment Corporation moving dirt across the street, where Fred Trump was building a shopping center that he would own. He also spotted work crews, and the HRH construction bosses Fred had hired, working at the shopping center site. The evidence was clear: Fred Trump was using funds from a state program for affordable housing to build his shopping center.

"It should not be assumed that from the foregoing that these were the only occasions on which the events observed had taken place," Strauss wrote in his report.

The more Strauss dug, the worse it looked. He and his colleagues noticed that the rental rates Fred was paying Boro Equipment to rent bulldozers and backhoes were two and three times as much as it would have cost him to buy the equipment outright. And in an office full of people who spent their days around construction sites, no one had ever heard of Boro Equipment Corporation. They checked the form Fred Trump had filed with the state that required him to disclose all companies in which he had an interest. No mention of Boro Equipment.

Their frustration eventually found its way to the State Commission of Investigation, which had been created in part to help state agencies investigate corruption. A young investigator there, Joseph Fisch, uncovered a surprising truth: Boro Equipment was owned by none other than Fred Trump. Everything made sense to Fisch and the auditors now. The rental rates were so high because they were only a means for Fred Trump to line his pockets with more than the 6 percent profit to which he had committed. His tenants would pay the price.

As each of Trump Village's four sections were finished, state auditors and investigators scoured Fred's records, tolling the gap between his high estimated costs, the figures that provided the basis for his state-backed mortgage, and the low amounts that he actually spent. They saw what appeared to be evidence of fraud extending beyond Boro Equipment.

They found a second shell company that Fred created to evade the profit limits. From the state-supplied mortgage money, he paid Trump Village Operators, Inc., ostensibly a real estate brokerage, fifty dollars for each cooperative apartment sold. That entity then paid an outside broker twenty dollars to do the actual work. Fred pocketed thirty extra dollars on every apartment sold—for doing nothing.

Fred was summoned to a public hearing exploring the "windfall" builder's fee he generated through deception. On January 26, 1966, he walked into a state office building across from City Hall, in lower Manhattan, and took an elevator to the twenty-fifth-floor hearing room of the State Commission of Investigation.

Before Fred was sworn in, the four lawyers on the commission and their investigative staff questioned Leo Silverman, head of the audit division in the state housing agency. Silverman laid out the findings regarding the Boro Equipment rentals. One commissioner, Jacob B. Grumet, who as a federal and state prosecutor had brought mobsters and murderers to justice, called Fred's use of Boro Equipment "grasping and greedy."

During Fred's testimony, he bristled at all the attention to Boro Equipment. "This is peanuts, what you are talking about," Fred said. "Boro Equipment is peanuts compared to sixty million dollars."

Fred insisted that the rates he charged himself were what he would have had to pay an outside company for the same job. In Fred Trump's mind, if he did that work himself, he was entitled to whatever profit he decided that an outside company would have received. It was a rationale that would make sense in the purely private realm, where the marketplace would determine whether what he was selling was worth more than what he spent to make it. Fred, however, had chosen to operate with government support, a choice that came with benefits and limitations. And yet, he felt entitled to the best of both options. In his mind, even with the amount he had padded invoices to himself, he was still getting the work done cheaper than if he had paid an outside company to do it. He wanted the commissioners to take his word for what someone else would charge, and to thank him.

The state disagreed and demanded that he reduce the Boro Equipment bills by 25 percent to bring it a little more in line with typical charges. Fred had already agreed to do so. As the questions continued, Fred reverted to his defense from the FHA hearings a decade before: shock that anyone could be unhappy with a project that "has the finest reputation."

"Commissioner, I would like to say we knew nothing about a hearing this morning," Fred said. "We walked in here cold this afternoon, thought we had the finest job in the City of New York, the finest Mitchell-Lama, and never knew there was one blemish, or anyone who would say an unkind word about Trump Village."

Commissioner Grumet reminded Fred that he could only be unaware of the panel's findings through selective amnesia: He had sat for a private interview with the commission eight months earlier. Fred snapped back that he could not be expected to remember everything: "I have got forty-three corporations that I am a stockholder in, and these things escape my memory sometimes."

The commissioners drew an unflattering contrast between Fred's practices and those of Abraham Kazan. Kazan took only a 1 percent development fee—about $350,000—for United Housing Foundation to build the Amalgamated Warbasse Houses. Fred Trump collected ten times that much for his co-op buildings. Kazan told the commission that "ethically it would be wrong" for UHF to accept a higher fee because doing so would drive up costs to residents. With the savings, UHF spent $6 million to build a dedicated power-generation station. As a result, compared to Trump Village owners, Warbasse buyers paid 13 percent less in monthly carrying charges, and those lower charges included electricity and central air-conditioning. For their higher carrying charges, Trump Village residents paid for their electricity separately and were offered the opportunity to rent air conditioners from Fred Trump at an additional charge.

Auditors also discovered that Fred had spent more money building and appointing the rental apartments that would remain in his ownership than on the cooperatives he would sell. The rentals were larger and had finer appliances and features in the kitchens. Fred knew too well that over time it would be the rentals—just like at Shore Haven, Beach Haven, and his other large-scale projects—that would generate life-changing wealth for his family.

Silverman told the commissioners that Fred had collected a total of $4.8 million in fees and from that money paid $1 million to HRH for doing the actual work. He had inflated his cost estimates by $7.9 million, which artificially boosted his fee by $598,000. In addition, Fred had overestimated the cost of acquiring the land by $1.2 million. He used some of that money to buy the land for his private shopping center.

"In other words," a commissioner asked, Trump was "able to acquire the shopping and commercial areas without putting up a nickel of his own money?"

"Yes, sir," Silverman answered.

Fisch explained to the commissioners that Fred had clearly violated his contract with the state when he comingled money deposited by buyers as down payments with other money, then used that money to start construction before the state loan closed. Doing so allowed him to reduce his carrying costs and increase revenue by quickly finishing construction so he could sell off the co-ops and start collecting rents sooner. The state had agreed to allow Fred to start construction early, but only if he did so entirely with his own funds.

"And that agreement, of course, was violated by the use of these funds," Fisch said.

During the investigation, Fisch had grown incensed by the bills to the project submitted by Bunny Lindenbaum. Fisch knew the city had done all the legal work to condemn the properties and paid a relocation company to help residents find new homes. Bunny's bill claimed he and his associates—his own son, Samuel "Sandy" Lindenbaum, and Matthew Tosti—had performed that work and were due $520,000. Before the hearings began, Fisch obtained affidavits from the office of the city's lawyers and the president of the relocation company saying Bunny and his associates had not been involved in any of that work.

Once he was finished with Fred during the morning session, Fisch called Bunny to testify after lunch.

Fisch grilled Bunny about his ninety-nine-page bill, which included a list of tenants he had supposedly relocated or evicted and properties he had condemned. Fisch repeatedly asked Bunny who had made the list, and Bunny repeatedly answered that it "was made," a point that was never in doubt but did not address who had done the making. After a few more answers in the passive voice, Bunny said the list was made by the city, but insisted that his office had added the tenants' names. Then he shifted to claiming his office had worked with the relocation company to make the list. Fisch read from the affidavit of the president of the relocation company, who said Bunny had done nothing.

As he was dismissed, Bunny grasped for a narrow distinction: "You keep saying that I was to receive $520,000," he said to Fisch. "I, together with Mr. Tosti, were to receive that sum. It wasn't just for my firm alone."

That money would not come out of Fred's pocket. It would be charged directly to and spread among the buyers of the cooperative apartments in the form of a larger mortgage and higher monthly fees. Fred took care of his closest lawyer and political fixer without spending his own money.

Fisch was incensed. He referred the facts of what Fred Trump and Bunny Lindenbaum did to the Brooklyn District Attorney's Office. But with that office still controlled by the Brooklyn Democratic Party machine, nothing came of it. Fisch, who later became a prosecutor, a judge, and the state inspector general, always believed Fred's and Bunny's connections saved them.

"Today, prosecutors would fight a duel to get that type of stuff," he said.

The commissioners expressed frustration that the law did not allow any clear way for the state or the apartment buyers to make Fred Trump return the money he had deceptively taken from the project. Even aside from the tens of millions of dollars that Trump Village would produce for the Trump family in the coming decades, the proceeds of Fred Trump's deception would be worth nearly $20 million today.

Once again, news headlines focused attention on Fred Trump taking more profit out of a government-financed project than what he had agreed to accept. Once again, tenants accused Fred of fraudulently increasing their costs to line his own pocket.

In the hallway outside the hearing room, a television reporter politely asked Fred about the testimony earlier that he had used his influence over John Cashmore, the late Brooklyn borough president, to stall the project proposed by

Kazan and United Housing Foundation and ultimately take half the site. It was a point he had heard made for years and seen written in a stack of newspaper articles. Fred fixed his blue eyes on the reporter and answered calmly in his nasally voice.

"Never heard of that. First time I ever heard of a thing like that."

For the second summer that the Trumps owned Steeplechase, Fred wanted to generate revenue and draw attention. He had Freddy hire the operator of an animal show—including a family of otters, exhibits with baby minks and pigeons, and fifty thousand bees in an apiary—to fill the Pavilion of Fun. As he signed the contract, Freddy posed with a two-hundred-pound tiger breathing on his hand. By the end of June the animal show closed, having failed to draw a significant number of people.

As the summer wore on, it became clear that Fred had underestimated his problem. The City Planning Commission remained determined to "preserve as much of Coney Island as a recreation area as possible," a spokesman said at the time. Another planning official referred to the space near the boardwalk and beach as an important "safety valve" for residents stuck in small, hot apartments during the summer.

Fred came up with what looked like a hastily conceived plan. He proposed developing not just the 12 acres he owned, but a full 120 acres of beachfront, mostly owned by the city. He would build a 7-acre "Pleasure Dome"—which in Lapidus's sketch resembled a glass airplane hangar—that would include parking, retail, and amusements. There would be housing elsewhere, which the Trumps avoided saying would be on the land owned by the city. The Coney Island Chamber of Commerce saw through the dodge. "Mr. Trump is stuck with the present Steeplechase property, on which he cannot build housing because of the zoning," a spokesman for the Chamber of Commerce said at the time. "Under the plan he would exchange it for the city land. He's getting rid of a lemon." The chamber also complained that the plan did not include enough facilities for people just wanting to use the beach, like parking, lockers, and picnic areas. "The beach," the chamber declared, "would become a personal haven for people who lease apartments from Mr. Trump."

In a final act of petulance, Fred announced in September 1966 that he would host a demolition party. He promised that six young beauty contestants, one of whom had recently been crowned Miss New York, would be on-site in swimming suits to hurl bricks through the glass façade at the Pavilion of Fun.

Freddy was tasked with overseeing the unpleasant task. He showed up one day in the office of park manager James Onorato and told him of the demolition party, asking how to get the electricity shut off. A formal invitation arrived in the mail. "You are cordially invited as the guest of Fred C. Trump to attend a V.I.P. Farewell Ceremony marking the demolition of Steeplechase Park . . . as TV and news cameras record the end of a nostalgic era in Coney Island history." Onorato saw the event as crass and heartless.

Fred began demolition even before the party. Bulldozers arrived on September 15 and knocked down the pool office building, then went the bathhouses, the roller coaster, and the rest.

The day of the event, Fred smiled widely as he passed an axe up to young women in swimsuits standing atop a bulldozer. He encouraged guests to throw bricks at the glass front wall of the Pavilion of Fun. They seemed to aim for the smiling face of Tillie, the nineteenth-century caricature whose lips stretched literally ear to ear above and below Chiclet teeth. By the end of the day, Tillie's cartoon chin had been shattered.

The city eventually announced that the area would become a city park, with amenities for beachgoers, and paid Fred $3.7 million to take the property off his hands. The amount was $1.4 million more than his purchase price—enough to at least cover property taxes, security, and demolition, and a profit that Fred might have called peanuts.

He wrote a letter that was published in the *New York Daily News* urging, again, that the city throw out the park plan and allow the construction of housing to produce tax revenue: "Coney Island is highly ghettoized, and to put a park at Steeplechase is a disservice to the public interest."

As Fred's efforts at Steeplechase failed and the Trump Village hearings came to a close, he turned sixty-one. His mother, Elizabeth, who had enabled the start of his building career with her money and signature, died that June at the age of eighty-five.

Fred would never again pursue a large-scale project. The historical and economic forces central to his success had shifted, and federal funding for middle-income housing had tightened considerably, in no small part thanks to his own actions. He would never again build under the New York program that made Trump Village viable. The vast swaths of undeveloped land near subway stops that made his biggest projects possible were nearly gone. For most of his career the intense need for housing had afforded Fred not just access to money through government programs but also something approaching hero status with each new project. Now, in every corner of the city, something would have to be demolished to make room for something new. There would be people who wanted a neighborhood to stay the same. Everything would feel like a fight. Against tightened zoning regulations. Against preservationists. Against his own reputation.

He would mostly spend his days tending to the empire he had assembled, watching as increasingly large profits accumulated in his bank accounts, enough money to change the fortunes of his family for generations to come. Within twenty-five years after the Trump Village hearings ended, after he had sold all his properties outside of New York and nine within the state, the rental buildings assembled by Fred Trump would collect more than $65 million a year in rents. They would become increasingly profitable. Thanks to low-interest, government-backed loans, those buildings carried almost no debt, typically one of the largest expenses of rental buildings. He had invested very little of his own money and owned a portfolio of apartment buildings that would be worth nearly $1 billion in his lifetime.

He would make clear to his lawyers that he wanted that empire to stay intact and within his family, in perpetuity. That would require someone to take over, and that person would not be his eldest son. Freddy would never fully break from his father to pursue his own dreams, nor would he ever fully embrace his father's ways. He would slide deeper into alcoholic dysfunction and poor health, divorce Linda, and leave her to care for their two children. He would cast about for meaningful work, failing as the captain of a fishing boat in Florida and running his own employment agency, before returning to work for his father once again, this time as a low-level maintenance man.

Turning over the reins to one of his daughters never emerged as a possibility. Fred Trump never fully appreciated the abilities of his most independently accomplished child, his eldest daughter, Maryanne. She graduated with honors from Mount Holyoke College in 1958. She was pursuing a graduate degree in public law and government at Columbia University when she married David

Desmond, a somewhat rotund and hard-drinking Air Force veteran from Westchester County. They had a son, David Jr., and Maryanne decided to stay home with the baby after completing her master's degree. Desmond had graduated from a prep school and Columbia University and worked at a car dealership for a time, but his drinking continually cost him jobs. "My husband was a deadbeat, from day one, and a drunk," she told a relative. They lived in a Fred Trump apartment building in Jamaica Estates. Fred and Mary did not approve of Desmond, and she has said they withheld the financial support that could have made her life easier and her career path less bumpy. "They never knew how bad it was," she told the family member. "They knew it was bad. Or Mom did. Dad, you know, was clueless, just like the other men in the family."

From her mother, she was given access to one of the great, apparently tax-free, sources of cash in the family: coins from laundry rooms at the apartment buildings. The dimes and quarters from more than fifteen thousand apartments produced hundreds of thousands of dollars a year. Several family members—Fred's mother, Elizabeth; Fred's nephew, John Walter; and Fred's wife, Mary—collected coins from the laundry rooms. Maryanne has said she paid for food during those years with the laundry coins from her mother, delivered to her in Crisco cans. She broke up with Desmond, graduated from the Hofstra University School of Law, and eventually became a federal prosecutor and judge.

Her younger sister, Elizabeth, rarely displayed ambition. In the 1960s, she fell in love with a truck driver, only for her disapproving parents to chase the man away. Elizabeth took a job as a secretary at the bank where her father conducted most of his business. She would not marry for the next two decades.

Robert, the youngest of Fred Trump's children, would outperform his brother in college, at least in athletics. He became captain of the Boston University soccer team and its MVP during his senior year. Still, two years younger than Donald, Robert never seemed to be on his father's radar.

Fred Trump once said that no one other than Donald demonstrated an interest in the family business. It was not completely true; Fred Trump made it true.

8

ALL SHOW

IN 1964, Donald moved back into his parents' house. That summer, as his older brother fell from their father's favor, Donald occasionally flew with his father to Cincinnati on Tuesdays to help the grounds and maintenance crews. "He'd get in there and work with us," remembered Roy Knight, a member of the maintenance crew. "He wasn't skilled, but he'd do yard work and cleanup, whatever needed to be done."

In the fall, he began making a daily sixteen-mile commute to the northern Bronx campus of Fordham University. There, tree-shaded walkways wound between wide-open grassy fields and Gothic stone buildings, some of which dated back to when the campus served as a Catholic seminary. Founded by the Jesuits in 1841, when the grounds were surrounded by countryside, Fordham now stood apart from the rhythms of the urban neighborhood that now surrounded it.

The student body was still almost entirely white and male. The school had just opened the Thomas More College for women. After four years of wearing military-like garb around the clock, Donald would now be required to wear a suit jacket and tie. He enrolled in the business school, which was still new and quite small. On the Monday of orientation, the assistant dean of the business school, the Reverend J. Vincent Watson, took the entire incoming freshman class—sixteen men and five women—out to a dinner of spaghetti and meatballs at a local restaurant.

Donald formed a friendship with three other freshmen—Bob McMahon, John Malnati, and Roger Gedgard. The four of them regularly ate lunch together at a long table in the campus center. They talked about sports, mostly baseball. Donald did not generally dominate the conversation and could even seem reserved. He grew closest to Gedgard, who also lived in Queens and had played first base on his high school baseball team. The two of them began commuting together. Donald drove the Austin-Healey and Gedgard covered the twenty-five-cent bridge toll.

His three Fordham friends picked up quickly that his family was the wealthiest of the group. Gedgard showed up at the big house in Jamaica Estates one day, where Fred answered the doorbell. "Son, deliveries are made to the back," he said. Donald came to the door to straighten things out. "Dad, that is my buddy,' he said. "Let him in."

Despite his high school claims that he was talented enough for the major leagues, Donald did not play baseball at Fordham. He did join the school's unremarkable squash team. McMahon and Gedgard introduced their new friend to golf. When the days warmed, they would skip class and head off to a nearby public course. Donald fell in love with the game. He soon decided that the public course in the Bronx was too shabby. He told Malnati that he wanted to join a private country club, but his father would not let him. Malnati, who lived with his parents in Westchester County, just to the north of the Bronx, said the public courses there were much nicer. He encouraged the others to file applications for resident golf passes in Westchester using his parents' address. The passes soon arrived in the mail, and the Fordham foursome began making the longer drive to play on the Westchester golf courses.

By their own account, Trump and his Fordham friends were not academic overachievers. McMahon and Malnati have long said they all shared their report cards and all posted grades in the C-plus to B-minus range. Trump found a study partner in the small business college, a freshman named Georgette Pacia. Pacia quickly recognized Donald's unique way of learning. He would not take many notes in class, nor want to spend hours going over hers. He wanted her to talk him through her notes. Within that verbal exchange, he came to grasp the material. "He picked it up as quickly as I did," she said.

Pacia also learned to predict the days Donald would need help by looking out her window in the morning. Sunshine meant a late-day study session; rain meant she would see Donald in class. "He golfed every opportunity he had," she later recalled. "If it was a nice day, rest assured he didn't come" to class.

Donald's admiration for military life ended at Fordham. His friends remembered that he participated in Reserve Officers' Training Corps, or ROTC, during his freshman year, showing up to school each Wednesday in a military uniform. But with the United States' involvement in Vietnam escalating, he dropped out of ROTC in his sophomore year. The program at the time paid cadets forty dollars a month and required their participation in a summer training program. In exchange, cadets committed to assignment as commissioned officers upon graduation. That meant they could avoid the risk of being drafted as enlisted men, but it almost certainly meant a tour of duty in Vietnam. Donald did not need the money and would prove determined to avoid the draft.

An ancillary outcome of the growing draft was rising grades. To maintain their deferments, college students were required to perform well on a standardized test and to maintain high grades. Students at Fordham were told that falling into the bottom half of their class during freshman year, or the bottom third during sophomore year, would end their deferment unless they scored high on the test. A period of grade inflation began as professors felt the weight of sending young men to their deaths for mediocre scholarship. Pacia said Donald "had to do well or he probably would be drafted."

He may have needed to do well, but he did not excel. Donald did not make the dean's list in his first year, which required a grade-point average of 3.5, the equivalent of a solid B+. Though he hardly maximized the opportunities Fordham offered, Donald was restless. Early in his second year, he bumped into Steve Lesko, a fellow alumnus of New York Military Academy, who had just started classes at Fordham. After they spent a few moments catching up, Donald said he would be leaving Fordham to attend the Wharton School at the University of Pennsylvania. Lesko, still awestruck by the Fordham campus, asked why.

"Because where I'm going, I am going to make better contacts for my future," Donald answered.

Not long after, Donald's brother Freddy called his friend Jim Nolan, the lapsed clarinetist from their nominally musical basement band in high school. After graduating from the University of Pennsylvania, Nolan had taken a job in the admissions office there. Freddy requested a favor. Could Nolan schedule an interview to get his kid brother into the Wharton School of Finance and Commerce? Nolan did not remember Donald, but he agreed anyway. He had the impression that Freddy asked for the meeting at his father's direction. On the scheduled day, Donald and his father showed up in Nolan's office, in coats and ties. Nolan had spent countless hours during high school at the Trump house on Midland Parkway, but this was a different Fred Trump. "I think it was the first time the father ever spoke to me," Noland recalled later. "And of course, he's very gracious and very warm. But it was all show."

Nolan remembered the interview as unremarkable, and Donald's transfer application was processed. Looking back decades later, Nolan vaguely recalled that Trump's grades from Fordham were sufficient to meet the Wharton standards of that era. The school was not the highly selective elite program it became years later, he said.

"I would say we probably accepted thirty, forty percent of the people who applied," he said.

Later in his life, Donald would insist his admission to Wharton was evidence of his exceptional intelligence. "I got in quickly and easily," he would later say, "and it's one of the hardest schools to get into in the country—always has been."

He would very rarely mention that his college career began at Fordham, though years later he would describe an event during his first semester there that he found particularly educational. In his telling, he and his father attended the opening ceremony for the Verrazzano Bridge, which connects Brooklyn and Staten Island. Donald noticed that several politicians received rounds of applause, but the eighty-five-year-old engineer who designed the bridge, Othmar H. Ammann, stood quietly "and nobody even mentioned his name."

"I realized then and there," he told a reporter years later, "that if you let people treat you how they want, you'll be made a fool. I realized then and there something I would never forget: I don't want to be made anybody's sucker."

But Ammann's accomplishments hardly went unnoticed that day. He was introduced by Robert Moses, the powerful urban planner and master of ceremonies for the event, as "one of the significant great men of our time" and "the greatest living bridge engineer, perhaps the greatest of all time." Moses noted Ammann's importance to the city—he had also designed the George Washington Bridge and the bridges that young Donald crossed to get to school each day, among others. Moses asked Ammann to stand for a round of applause, and newspapers noted that the crowd obliged. Two days later, Ammann appeared at Donald's campus to accept an honorary doctorate from the dean of Fordham University, a moment captured on the front page of the school newspaper. And later that week, President Lyndon Baines Johnson announced that Ammann would receive the President's National Medal of Science during a White House ceremony.

All Donald remembered was that Moses forgot to say Ammann's name. His conviction that everyone was out to treat him like a sucker, and its corollary that anything less than comprehensive fawning represented an aggressive attack, would keep Trump on a verbal-war footing for his entire life.

As Fred Trump all but retired as a real estate developer, he turned his focus to transferring his wealth to his children. Back in the 1950s, he assigned their trust funds the land under Beach Haven and Shore Haven and arranged to pay them rent for their entire lives and beyond. He began giving them each $6,000 a year, the maximum cash gift then not subject to tax, the equivalent of about $60,000 today.

In 1962, he gave his children ownership of one of his buildings, Clyde Hall. And in the late 1960s, with his building days behind him, Fred formed Midland Associates, a corporation he named after the street in Jamaica Estates where he built the family mansion. With the use of that entity, he would give his children ownership in eight apartment buildings with more than a thousand apartments.

His tax returns showed little evidence of the transactions. He filed a gift-tax return on only one of the eight buildings, Sunnyside Towers, a 158-unit building in Queens. When he transferred that building to Midland Associates, he noted on a gift-tax return that each of his five children received a 15 percent share in the building, which he said was worth $1,301.21 to each child, a total of $6,516 for the 75 percent his five children now owned. That amount did not require Fred to pay a gift tax. Based on the amount of cash he put down, the total gift should have been listed at $93,750, which would have required payment of a gift tax.

Fred transferred the other buildings without a mention on his tax returns, typically shifting shares through a web of corporate entities to avoid gift and real estate transfer taxes. Any gift tax would have been, in Fred's words, peanuts. The real value came to his children over decades of watching the gift from their father grow in value and produce escalating income, while requiring nearly nothing of them. Fred managed all eight buildings, overseeing everything to keep them fully rented, maintained, and profitable.

Donald didn't do anything to acquire his percentage in those eight buildings, a portfolio he never publicly acknowledged and that would go on to produce $20 million for him, all hidden from public view.

When Donald Trump arrived for the fall 1966 semester, Wharton occupied one three-story building, Deitrick Hall, on the sprawling University of Pennsylvania campus in Philadelphia. Deitrick Hall's doors opened to Locust Walk, a pastoral pedestrian walkway lined by buildings dating back centuries and home to a statue of Benjamin Franklin, Penn's first president.

Walking in and out of Deitrick and onto the main pedestrian artery through campus, Donald Trump remained a ghost for most of his four semesters there. He enrolled in the real estate program, which had fewer than ten students, and disappeared in and out of classes. He did not linger to talk, and few of his classmates remember anything about him other than how rarely they saw him.

Bill Specht, who had graduated with Donald from the New York Military Academy and gone straight to Wharton, remembered occasionally crossing paths with him.

"Hi, Bill," Specht remembers Trump saying. "I'm buying apartments in Philadelphia, refurbishing them, and renting them to students."

"Oh, well," Specht would respond, "I'm going to the bar and having a beer."

Specht would look back later and realize, "It might not have even been true. He just told me that's what he was doing, and I just accepted the fact." Donald has long claimed that he began buying real estate during the months he spent at Penn, though scores of journalists have found no evidence, and Trump has provided none.

Trump didn't drink alcohol, and often used that as a reason for not spending time with classmates in the evenings. But even that cannot fully explain how remote he remained from campus life. He seemed to forge no lasting friendships. When the yearbook for his graduating class came out, there would be no photo of Donald Trump.

"I never saw him with another student," remembered Jim Nolan, Freddy's friend in the admissions office. "He was always alone."

Classmate Candice Bergen, the future actress, recalled Trump wearing a trendy burgundy suit and matching shoes on the otherwise tweedy campus. He did not stick around on weekends, telling classmates that he went home every weekend to help his father collect rent. "He was Fred's bill collector," remembered classmate Louis Calomaris, "and he would go to New York on Thursdays and Fridays—so I was told—and knock on doors and collect."

Trump himself would remember little from his Wharton experience. He claimed that a Wharton professor schooled him on the Laffer curve, the supply-side economics concept that Arthur Laffer first sketched on a napkin in 1974, six years after Trump graduated from Wharton. Arthur Laffer was to Trump's business education what Willie McCovey had been to his high school baseball career.

He also claimed for years to have graduated at the top of his class, but on May 20, 1968, when Fred and Mary attended Donald's graduation ceremony, they would have learned from the program that he hadn't even made the dean's list. It did not matter. Father and son smiled for a photo, Fred in his gray three-piece suit with a white shirt and pocket square, Donald in a black gown with gold draped around his neck. Donald Trump would not be applying for jobs with Fortune 500 companies or consulting firms. And Fred Trump would not be scouring the country for a seasoned and credentialed real estate executive to take over his company. He had his man.

There was just one more bit of business—avoiding the war in Vietnam. Donald had received two educational deferments from the draft while in college but now found himself fully exposed. Again, his father's influence kept him safe. Donald visited a podiatrist who leased office space from Fred Trump. That doctor found a problem that had not prevented Donald from playing sports but would be sufficient to shield him from the draft: bone spurs in his heels. That finding, possibly supported by a second podiatrist who also rented space from Fred Trump, provided the basis for a medical exemption from the draft. Donald would lie about the exemption for decades to come, claiming he had lucked out by receiving a high draft-lottery number, even though his medical exemption had come years before the draft lottery began.

In the luckiest stroke of a life filled with big breaks, Donald Trump finished college just as his father was prepared to begin passing along a business that would be worth a billion dollars. The position would offer almost endless collateral for loans, connections in banking and politics, and a reliable wellspring of cash to pursue dreams and fame.

Part II

THE SON

Real estate investing is a career rather than a one-time event; a marathon, not a sprint. Thus, if you want to be a successful real estate professional, patience and learning when to say "no" will be your greatest allies.

—*Peter Linneman, founding chairman of the Real Estate Department, Wharton School, University of Pennsylvania*

9

BY NO MEANS STANDING STILL

At twenty-two years old, Donald Trump was living year-round in the big house on Midland Parkway. He and his father commuted every day to a modest office on Avenue Z, where Fred Trump gave Donald impressive titles, naming him director or vice president of corporations that controlled thousands of rental apartments. He paid Donald a salary that would soon reach $100,000 a year and got him a Cadillac. Still, Donald was endlessly bored with the business, which entailed cajoling struggling tenants to pay rent on time, overseeing repairs of tar roofs and boilers, and hiring rental agents and superintendents.

He made his first imprint on the business almost in the shadows. Fred Trump occasionally placed classified advertisements in local newspapers, such as listing job openings or seeking to buy a dump truck and a tractor. The ad didn't include his name, just his office number—SH 3-4400, under New York's old exchange system—and his home number in Jamaica Estates—AX 7-7348.

In July 1968, just as Donald began working full-time at his father's office, a new ad ran in *The New York Times* seeking tenants for retail space—"Emphasis on BUTCHER, BAKER, CARD STORE"—at a building in Brooklyn. It listed a new contact: "Call MR. BARON SH 3-4400. SUNDAY. CALL AX 7-7348."

Donald Trump had coined a pseudonym for himself. The ads that directed interested parties to call this Mr. Baron—sometimes spelled "Barron"—showed up with increasing frequency. Donald used the name to sell his father's two-year-old Cadillac limousine—"All extras. Low mileage. Original owner."—as well as to find a building superintendent and tenants for apartments. He listed his brother Freddy's prized fishing boat for $32,500, calling the forty-foot boat "luxurious" and "meticulously maintained" with a tower, new twin engines, and tracking equipment.

He would use the name "John Baron" for decades to come, including in calls with reporters to insult foes or flatter himself. Whatever the reason he had for creating an alter ego, the young Donald Trump was clearly restless on Avenue Z.

In college he had contemplated a movie career and took half a step in that direction one afternoon in 1969, leaving the outer boroughs in the back of a chauffeured car for Manhattan. He rolled past the peep shows and pornographic film houses that crowded Times Square to the Palace Theatre, where David Black, a Broadway producer whose most recent play had just won a Tony Award, kept an office. Donald arrived without an appointment and dressed to the nines. He invited Black to lunch. He had a pitch to make, hoping that a taste of his father's money would buy him entry into a brighter life than he had found in Brooklyn.

The two men rode in Donald's limousine through Central Park to the Metropolitan Club, a formal members-only association that had been founded by J. P. Morgan in 1891 for newly rich titans of finance. The interior of the stately clubhouse on Fifth Avenue, in the heart of Manhattan's old-money Upper East Side, had been designed by a Parisian firm in the French baroque style, with elaborate ceiling paintings, golden relief panels, and red-velvet curtains.

David Black had spent his forty years toggling between art and commerce. He played violin as a boy, graduated from Harvard, worked as an opera singer, made a fortune selling mutual funds, then used that wealth to produce Broadway plays. With his bald head, glasses, and soft middle, he looked more the part of a workaholic banker than a raconteur, but he spent weekends competing in grueling cross-country equestrian jumping events. At that moment, Black had two shows nearing debut: *Salvation*, a modern rock and roll musical featuring a young Bette Midler; and *Paris Is Out!*, a light comedy about an older Jewish couple planning a European vacation.

Though Donald dreamed with the intensity of a young man, in restaurants and culture his tastes shuffled along with an older generation. As the two men dined in an ornate room of the Metropolitan Club, Donald said he had read about Black and *Paris Is Out!* in *Variety*. He hoped to try his hand as a Broadway producer. He asked Black to let him put up the money to coproduce the show. He peppered Black with questions about the business side of Broadway, asking how many performances it would take before he started making a profit. "He had done his homework, and that was unusual," Black later recalled. By the end of lunch, Black agreed to list Trump as a coproducer in exchange for an investment of $70,000, half the cost of the play. Donald put up the cash, the equivalent today of more than half a million dollars. The money came from Fred Trump, but Donald's name would appear on the marquee and inside the *Playbill* passed out to audience members.

To Black and the play's author, Richard Seff, Donald seemed earnestly interested in the show's success. He never meddled in the artistic side of the production. He showed up for early performances, watching from the back of the room, fretting over things like the placement of posters outside and why stagehands who only raised and lowered the curtain were paid for a full shift.

The show starred two stage veterans, Molly Picon, who gained fame in Yiddish theater and silent movies, and Sam Levene, a Russian-born star of stage and screen who grew up the son of a Jewish cantor on the Lower East Side of Manhattan. Black saw his play as a sentimental throwback, and opening night at the Brooks Atkinson Theatre arrived like a dispatch from a bygone era. Directly across the street at the Biltmore Theatre, the groundbreaking rock musical *Hair*—with its psychedelic anthem "Aquarius" and celebration of hippie counterculture and onstage nudity—was in the middle of a long and successful run.

Black expected most critics to hate the play, but hoped audiences might like it. He tried to protect the show's chances by staggering tickets for critics over the first few weeks. It did not work. Instead of a one-day tidal wave, negative reviews trickled out every few days: the *Times* called it "Trivial and silly"; "Embarrassingly bad," said *Newsday*; and *Variety*'s critic found it to be "Innocuous, if not entirely pointless."

The show closed in April 1970, after a run of about one hundred shows. Donald lost all of his father's money. The *Playbill* for *Paris Is Out!* noted that Black and Donald planned to coproduce a second show together. But Donald dropped out. Black suggested he stick to the family real estate business.

NOT LONG AFTER his play failed, Donald moved out of the family house in Jamaica Estates. Much as his father had seen promise of a better life in the mansions of nineteenth-century builders, Donald looked across the bridge to the titans of finance and industry, and their heirs, in uptown Manhattan. He took a small apartment on the seventeenth floor of a plain white-brick building on the Upper East Side, at Third Avenue and East Seventy-Fifth Street. Each morning, he left Manhattan for a twenty-mile reverse commute in his company Cadillac.

Even as they worked shoulder to shoulder, Donald began to erase his father from the company's public profile. For at least a decade, his father had referred to his company in news releases and advertisements as "the Fred Trump Organization." Donald rebranded the company as simply "The Trump Organization" and placed classified ads seeking to buy properties. The ads requested that financial details be sent to his attention—using his real name, not Mr. Baron—at the Beach Haven office. "All cash!" the ads screamed. It would be his father's cash, but Donald would make it increasingly clear that he was the Trump in the company name. His father would never object.

Fred still controlled the direction of the business, but he was more focused on protecting his wealth than taking risks to multiply it. He still occasionally bought existing buildings, including a two-hundred-unit apartment project in Queens, the sort of six-story brick shoebox that felt familiar. Taylor Johnson Jr., Freddy's friend and the son of Fred's buddy in Virginia, also helped Fred buy two towers overlooking the water in the Norfolk area.

Fred undertook one new project around this time, the stalled construction of an apartment building for low-income senior citizens in East Orange, New Jersey, about seventeen miles west of Manhattan. The original sponsor, an insurance company, had arranged government financing, commissioned plans, and hired a general contractor. But the insurance company dropped out when it determined the profits wouldn't be worth the effort. There was very little to do other than put up some cash and pick up where the insurance company had left off. Fred paid $862,752 to take ownership of what was to become an $8 million project.

The modest New Jersey building would mark the first time Fred didn't dole out his wealth evenly. He gave Donald 25 percent ownership in the new building. His siblings received no part of it.

To win the low-interest government loan, Fred had agreed to limit his profits. As he had with prior projects, he immediately set out to evade that limitation. This time, the excess profits would go to his chosen son.

After the building opened, Fred began paying about $48,000 a year to a company that Donald owned, ostensibly for managing the building. Donald did not have to cover the salaries of workers from that fee; employees on Fred's payroll did the work.

Once again, the Trumps offered air conditioners for rent to their low-income tenants. Fred let Donald keep that money too. The management job and air-conditioner fees added up. The drab building began annually kicking off for Donald Trump the equivalent of the money he had lost on Broadway the year before.

WITH FRED NOT TRAVELING much anymore, his far-flung properties began to languish, and he looked to sell. The first to go was Swifton Village, the large apartment complex in Cincinnati that he had bought from the FHA in 1964 after the original developer failed. A year later, he admitted defeat. "Cincinnati to us is a real disappointment," he told the *Cincinnati Enquirer*, adding that the property would always be a money loser. When a potential buyer expressed interest in 1972, Donald traveled to Ohio and gave the buyer a tour. Fred accepted the $6.75 million offer. It was mostly a wash, enough to cover the $6.2 million Fred had paid and invested in renovations and some of his operating losses over the years. But Donald would later make up bigger numbers to embellish the importance of his first deal.

Even in Fred's personal affairs, he had entered a period of contraction. In 1957, Fred had bought a house one mile from the beach in Westhampton, New York. It had four bedrooms, with a separate building for "servant quarters," sat on two acres. It was an hour drive from the Trump mansion in Jamaica Estates, a charming getaway just as he and Mary were welcoming grandchildren into their lives. Fred sold it in 1972.

The Trumps' block on Midland Parkway, with its stately houses and trees, remained unchanged. But a few blocks away, closer to Hillside Avenue, the elegant single-family homes had been replaced with larger apartment buildings. Muggings had grown so common that the neighborhood association had hired its own private security company. Some of the original country-estate features of the neighborhood had been picked away. To the north, the golf course created for residents had become the campus of St. John's University. The estate of Michael Degnon, the great builder of subway tunnels, had become a Catholic church and school. The north and south sections had been split by the Grand Central Parkway, a six-lane highway.

During his last rush of expansion through the 1960s, Fred Trump had built or bought ten apartment buildings, more than 1,300 units, in Jamaica Estates. Those buildings had become the housing for his children in times of need. Freddy lived alone in one. His wife, Linda, from whom he had separated, lived with their two children in another. Maryanne lived with her son in a third.

Fred had also bought the site once occupied by an emblem of the neighborhood's early-century grandeur, the Elizabethan lodge at the entrance to Jamaica Estates. At some point over the decades, the grand lodge had been razed. It now served as a parking lot for commuters using the nearby subway stop to Manhattan. Fred proposed building a nineteen-story building on the site, which would require a change in zoning.

In 1973, Donald attended a local community board meeting to promote the plan. A local state senator, Frank Padavan, told Donald that he saw any such proposal as dead on arrival: "I have a basic philosophy about high-rise apartments in Queens—I oppose them. We have exceeded our density limits in every area." Tenants and politicians, tired of the constant cramming of more bodies into the neighborhood, complained about the potential impact on the sewage system, on the drinking water supply, on already crowded subways and buses and schools.

The proposal failed. The Trumps would eventually lease part of the site to McDonald's. But unlike the blame Fred cast on Freddy for the failure at Steeplechase, Donald retained his father's unflinching support.

A FIFTEEN-MINUTE DRIVE from Fred's office at Beach Haven, the largest apartment construction project in Brooklyn had ground to a halt. United Housing Foundation, Fred's old foe at Trump Village, which had proposed a project to build six thousand apartments near the Shore Parkway and Jamaica Bay, hadn't been able to win approval for new streets and schools. The yearslong process caused such an increase in costs that United Housing backed out. The future of the project, known as Twin Pines, was in doubt.

Fred, a devoted reader of the real estate news in the city's newspapers, no doubt knew every turn the project had taken. It was the sort of project he might once have waged war to take over. But now that Fred was in his sixties, his days of taking off his jacket, rolling up his shirtsleeves, and searching through the mud for reusable nails were well behind him. He was now a man of wealth and status. And in that role, he would bring a different type of value to the stalled project.

Robert Olnick, a lawyer by trade, developed a plan with investment bankers to take over the Twin Pines project without having to put up the 10 percent equity stake—about $33 million—required to obtain the state loan. Working with Leonard Boxer, a young lawyer, Olnick decided to capitalize on recent tax law changes. They could raise the $33 million from wealthy people and then pass along to them the tax benefits of the biggest expenses—the cost of the buildings spread over time, known as depreciation, and interest on the loan. The apartment project would pay the costs, but through tax accounting magic allowed at the time, the IRS would allow the "investors" to reduce their taxable income by the same amount.

The state of New York approved the reformulated project at the end of July 1972, and the race to pull together the investors began. The investment was designed never to produce actual returns for the investors, only to shelter their other income from taxes. Lazard Freres, then one of the world's most prominent investment banks, looked to solicit families so rich that sheltering their millions from taxes was more important than making additional millions. "They weren't investing for gains," remembered Robert Rosenberg, a former housing official hired to run the apartment project. "They were doing it basically for tax shelter."

A dozen or so Lazard investment bankers put up almost 40 percent of the total needed. The remaining tax benefits went to fifteen of the wealthiest families in America. Malcom McLean, the inventor of shipping containers, put up $5 million. The heirs of General Motors cofounder Charles Stewart Mott bought in for $1.5 million. William S. Paley, who grew a small network of local radio stations into the CBS television network, signed on for $1 million.

One man invested more than any other: Fred Trump. He spent $5 million in his own name. And he recognized that he had already set up his grown children well enough—giving them eight buildings and the land under his biggest project—that they, too, would benefit from an expensive tax shelter. He invested another $1 million in the name of one company he had given to his children. It was an "investment" that put the Trumps in league with some of the wealthiest people in America.

Fred had purchased a minority share as a limited partner, with no input over construction or management. He could not even sell his stake without the approval of the general partners. Over the coming two decades, he would not collect a dime in profits from the project, now being called Starrett City, but the costs passed on to him through accounting magic would have wiped away his tax liability on $20 million of profits from his own businesses. It would do the same, on a smaller scale, for his wealthy grown children.

Donald Trump would take credit for his family's investment in Starrett City, saying he had heard about it during a holiday party at a law firm in Manhattan and called his father. "It's one of the best investments I ever made, and one of the first," he would say decades later. The other tax shelter investors—including Ahmet M. Ertegun and Jerry Wexler, the cofounders of Atlantic Records and future inductees into the Rock & Roll Hall of Fame—kept their involvement secret for decades. They certainly did not offer their tax shelter as proof that they were prominent real estate developers.

Fred never challenged Donald's claim of credit. And Donald would never acknowledge what spending millions of dollars on tax shelters said about his father's wealth, or about his own status as a rich heir.

As the years passed, Donald would recast his work for his father in these early years, puffing up each event to make it sound like a monumental or magnanimous achievement. He would call the New Jersey senior-citizens building project "our philanthropic endeavor," even though it had no charitable component. He would claim that he sold the Cincinnati project for $12 million, almost double the actual price of $6.75 million. He claimed that "we" had bought the Cincinnati project, and "we" straightened it out, all of which his father accomplished while he was in high school. The habit of Donald appropriating his father's accomplishments and wealth to inflate his own image had only begun.

On January 28, 1973, the front page of *The New York Times* announced that the war in Vietnam had ended with the signing of a peace accord in Paris. A separate story discussed how the end of the military draft would ease the minds of millions of young American men.

Donald Trump, having escaped the draft, had no such concern. Also inside that day's newspaper, on the front page of the Real Estate section, there appeared an article that could have served as a debutante's introduction to New

York real estate society. Under the headline A BUILDER LOOKS BACK—AND MOVES FORWARD, a photograph showed Donald and Fred Trump standing shoulder to shoulder on the roof of a building at Trump Village. Fred, looking all his sixty-seven years in a tall fedora hat and a polka-dot tie, stares blankly off to his left. At his right side, Donald gazes straight into the camera with a faint smirk, his blond hair draping over his collar and ears and dusting across his forehead.

The Trumps told the reporter that after decades of working in the boroughs, Fred Trump had made his first moves to build in Manhattan and was in the process of "buying a prime building site on the East Side for rental apartments." The biggest change at the company in recent years, the article asserted, had been the addition of Donald as its president, after he had graduated first in his class from Wharton. Donald was described as the only one of Fred Trump's five children to display an interest in real estate. It was Donald who offered evidence that the company was moving forward, including "our entry into the Manhattan field" and recently buying 20 percent of Starrett City. "It's a rental investment," he said. "We are by no means standing still."

Not much of what Donald told the reporter was true. He had graduated without honors. His brother Freddy had displayed an interest in the business and been pushed aside by their father. His brother Robert worked in finance after graduating from Boston University, but would soon join the family business. The Trumps had not bought land on the East Side of Manhattan for an apartment building and would not do so that decade. Contrary to what Donald said, the Starrett City tax shelter represented standing still by definition, tying up capital in a way designed to not grow.

The claims, fueled by Donald's drive, displayed a sharp demarcation from the way Fred had handled his affairs and image throughout his career. He had been the subject of hundreds of news articles over the decades. He could be immodest, grandiose even, describing his projects as patriotic. He alternated between advising working people to either buy or rent their homes in ways that could sound benevolent but inevitably tracked with whether he was currently selling or renting his latest project. But one would be hard-pressed to find a case in which Fred Trump said he was doing something that he was not, in fact, doing. This was a new day for the Trump name.

In these years, people in New York real estate noticed a difference in how

Fred Trump acted toward his favorite son versus how other prominent real estate tycoons interacted with their heirs apparent. Richard Kahan, who worked in and around real estate development in the city for decades, remembered how Samuel J. LeFrak, a contemporary of Fred, would take credit for everything, regardless of the contribution of Richard, his son.

"Fred was the opposite, which is an explanation for why Donald ended up with a high level of confidence," Kahan recalled. "Fred came up to me at dinners and would say, 'Isn't my Donny the greatest? Isn't my Donny the smartest?' He never pounded his own chest and said, 'Look what I built.' Never. It was a unique response coming from a real estate developer."

Fred would never fully explain why he allowed his young, inexperienced son so much leeway to set the future course of his company. But he made his faith in Donald clear. "Everything he touches turns to gold," Fred told the *Times* reporter in 1973, adding, "Donald is the smartest person I know."

From that day forward, Donald would not only serve as the public face of the company his father had built but would mold the company's direction by controlling the deployment of his father's reputation and fortune. And turning everything to gold would not prove to be a requirement of retaining his father's support.

10

SHADOWBOXING

On the morning of October 15, 1973, federal prosecutor Judith Wolf called Donald Trump to inform him that the United States Department of Justice had just filed a civil lawsuit against him and his father at the federal courthouse in Brooklyn. The suit alleged that the Trumps had long discriminated against prospective Black tenants. Wolf had already notified the office of Matt Tosti and Irwin Durben, Fred's longtime lawyers for trusts and real estate issues.

Following normal procedures, the Justice Department press office in Washington issued a brief release describing the lawsuit. By the end of the day, radio stations and newspapers were calling the Trumps for comment on the charges. Fred let Donald serve as the public voice of his company. "They are absolutely ridiculous," Donald told *The New York Times*. "We never have discriminated, and we never would."

The lawsuit could not have come as a surprise. Over the prior year, prosecutors had repeatedly updated Tosti and Fred's comptroller, Stuart Hyman, on their investigation into whether the Trumps' renting practices violated the Fair Housing Act of 1968. The investigation had begun after the Human Rights Commission of New York City passed along a complaint that the Trumps discouraged Black applicants.

The New York Urban League, a local civil rights group that, had launched an initiative to accelerate desegregation in the city, sent white and Black people to Trump buildings to inquire about available apartments. A trend emerged. Black applicants were told there were no vacancies or were steered to one specific Trump apartment project, Patio Gardens in the heart of Brooklyn; white applicants arriving moments later were told apartments were available. They reported the findings to federal prosecutors, who, along with FBI agents, began tracking down employees of the Trumps, some of whom said the company frowned upon leasing to Black tenants almost everywhere except Patio Gardens.

Fred Trump had been brushing off government inquiries for decades. He had paid connected lawyers to negotiate behind-the-scenes resolutions to the investigations of his windfall profits from the FHA in the 1950s, the audits of his taxes by the IRS, and the second windfall investigation by New York State in the 1960s. The lawyers he hired, and most of the steps they took on his behalf, never became widely known. For this new challenge, Fred first turned to his longtime friend and fixer, Abraham "Bunny" Lindenbaum, to make the case go away quickly and quietly.

Fred took Donald for a meeting with Bunny. The man who spent his life making trouble disappear advised them to settle the case. With no risk of being shut down or paying a penalty, dragging out the case would only generate growing legal bills and news articles repeating the allegation. The safe and expedient course would be to avoid further spectacle, as Samuel J. LeFrak had done not long before.

Within a couple of weeks after the suit was filed, Bunny let the prosecutors know that the Trumps were interested in signing a consent decree similar to what LeFrak had accepted. Bunny asked the prosecutors to send a copy of the LeFrak agreement. The prosecutors did just that, and let the Trumps know in a letter that if they signed a similar agreement saying that they would take steps to prevent future discrimination, they would not have to admit to discriminatory practices in the past. All things considered, pretty painless. But Donald's impulses were about to take the case in another direction.

AFTER RETURNING HOME from Brooklyn each day, Donald's social life centered around a sliver of the Upper East Side of Manhattan. He did not mix with the great masses of city life, or even people close to his age. Still in his midtwenties, he joined a members-only discotheque on East Fifty-Fifth Street called Le Club, a few blocks from his small apartment. Unlike the thumping bass and pulsating lights that were beginning to define the disco era, the mood at Le Club, considered to be one of the nation's first discotheques, was set by candles, a fireplace, and a large seventeenth-century Belgian tapestry hanging on a terra-cotta pink wall. The small room on the first floor of an apartment building could accommodate fewer than two hundred at a time. It had been founded in 1960 by Olivier Coquelin, a Frenchman who defined decadence as "a beautiful way of life, where everything is beautifully lazy, and all you have to do is raise your hand and you get service." But as other private discos cropped up, Le Club had been called "ancient history" by the *New York Daily News* and the "dowager queen of discos" by *The New York Times*.

The initial membership cost Donald only a few hundred dollars, but a board tightly controlled acceptance to maintain exclusivity, with a curated membership of eleven hundred. Le Club was a place where men from business mixed with men from politics and heiresses to fortunes. Where a newly widowed governor would bring an heiress of the Ford Motor Company fortune for not-so-secret dates, and where a brother-in-law of the late president John F. Kennedy would be arrested after skipping out on a taxi fare while drunk.

And one fall night in 1973, Le Club was where Donald Trump found himself seated at a table next to a powerful older man. Roy M. Cohn had earned a reputation by ruining the reputations of other people. The son of a judge, he graduated from law school at twenty, and soon after stretched the norms of his profession to win a death penalty sentence in the conviction of Julius and Ethel Rosenberg on charges they had spied for the Soviet Union. Cohn then served as chief counsel to Senator Joseph McCarthy in the ruthless hunt to tarnish U.S. citizens as communists. A small man who perfected a menacing dead-eyed glare, Cohn had by this night worked as a private lawyer in New York for more than a decade, leveraging threats and backroom connections to assist a growing list of prominent clients.

In Donald's telling, he arrived at Le Club angry that night. After being introduced to Cohn, he complained about the federal lawsuit and the suggestion from his father's longtime lawyer that they settle. "I'm just not built that way," Trump would say he told Cohn. "I'd rather fight than fold, because as soon as you fold once, you get the reputation of being a folder."

Trump asked Cohn for his opinion. Whether a kindred spirit or a man who could quickly spot a prospective client with more money than sense, Cohn agreed with Donald.

"My view is tell them to go to hell and fight the thing in court," Cohn said.

"And let them prove that you discriminated, which seems to me very difficult to do, in view of the fact that you have Black tenants."

As a private lawyer, Cohn specialized more in spectacle and prurient leaks to reporters than nuanced legal argument or marshaling evidence. Hiring Cohn would be a sharp departure from how Fred had navigated these sorts of problems throughout his life. But Fred let Donald take the lead, one of the first public signs that his favorite son's judgment and style were changing the direction of the company. Cohn had the job.

Less than two months later, Cohn filed a motion to dismiss the lawsuit, accusing the government of unfairly failing to divulge evidence of wrongdoing in its complaint.

The filing included an affidavit from Donald, complaining that he had been unaware of the allegations. "On the morning of October 15th while listening to the news on car radio, I was shocked to hear that the Government was bringing an action against me, my father, and Trump Management for bias in renting our apartments," Donald swore to the court. "The news report was all the more shocking inasmuch as I had not at that point received any formal communication from the government whatever, regarding the subject matter of the action. In fact, the first I heard about it was on my car radio the morning of the 15th."

Though it had no bearing on the case, the federal prosecutors would later recount to the judge the calls they made to both Donald Trump and to Tosti and Durben on the morning the case was filed. They noted that Donald did not mention the courtesy calls both he and his lawyers received within minutes of the filing from prosecutor Judith Wolf. Instead, he had relied on "the artful use of the phrase 'no formal communication'" to create the "foreseeable effect of misleading anyone who reads it."

Cohn also filed a countersuit against the federal government seeking $100 million in damages. The countersuit spanned all of four sentences, saying nothing more than prosecutors had knowingly provided false information to two newspapers about the Trumps.

The Trump team focused more time and energy on staging a news conference. In a meeting room at the New York Hilton Hotel, Donald told the assembled reporters that federal prosecutors were conspiring to force the Trumps and other landlords to take welfare recipients as tenants. "That would be reverse discrimination. The government is not going to experiment with our buildings to the detriment of ourselves and the thousands who live in them now."

Asked what evidence he had that the government was trying to force him to house welfare tenants, Donald said the LeFrak organization had been forced to sign a consent decree with that provision. He knew that it was not true. The consent decree sent to Bunny did not mention welfare. It showed that the LeFraks could continue their practice of requiring tenants' weekly income to equal 90 percent of the monthly rent, a threshold too high for welfare recipients to meet. Richard LeFrak told the *Times* that welfare recipients could not meet his company's income requirements "unless they have a rich uncle" willing to co-sign the lease, which would be fine with him.

In a related filing, prosecutors accused Cohn and Trump of engaging in "barristerial shadow boxing," hoping to get the case dismissed by inventing an imaginary enemy for the purpose of knocking him down. Instead, they asserted, the Trumps should address the evidence under oath.

Six weeks later, the judge on the case, Edward Neaher, threw out the Trumps' counterclaim. The filing of the counterclaim and its dismissal predictably generated more news stories about the Trumps' alleged racist practices. By dragging the case out, Donald had also opened the door to a deeper FBI investigation.

IN THE SPRING OF 1974, a young lawyer named Donna Fields Goldstein joined the case as a prosecutor. Unbeknownst to most, the lives of Goldstein and Donald Trump had played out on parallel tracks. She was one year younger than him and had grown up in Queens, one mile north of the Trump mansion in Jamaica Estates. But her childhood home had been an apartment in a simple redbrick row house. Like Donald, she was the grandchild of immigrants. Her paternal grandparents, Jacob and Millie Finkelstein, had arrived in New York from Russia in about 1907, escaping the pogroms of the era. They opened a laundry, and Goldstein's father would continue the family business. She graduated from Jamaica High School, the large public school that Donald would have attended had his father not sent him to private school. She went on to Beaver College, then a small women's college near Philadelphia, and Rutgers School of Law, in New Jersey, where a young Ruth Bader Ginsburg was a professor.

Goldstein's first job as a lawyer was with the Department of Justice's Civil

Rights Division. After being assigned to the small team prosecuting the lawsuit against Donald Trump and his father, she sent the FBI a list of former Trump company employees to interview about discriminatory practices and began scheduling interviews with some of those people herself.

One day that July, Goldstein scheduled an appointment with a former Trump building superintendent named Thomas Miranda, who had been interviewed once before by her predecessor. Miranda had said he was told by three Trump company employees, including the company comptroller, to mark applications from nonwhite applicants with a large "C"—code for "colored." He concluded his first interview by saying he feared Fred Trump would have him knocked off. By the time he spoke with Goldstein, his fear had grown more consuming. He told her he didn't want to be involved and again expressed concern that Fred Trump would come after him. But he invited Goldstein to stay for coffee and donuts. They chatted about Puerto Rico, where Miranda had grown up, and the problems Puerto Ricans faced in New York.

Within a day, Miranda visited the Trumps at the main office. He spoke with Donald for about ten minutes, telling him that he didn't want to be involved in this "lousy case." The Trumps had a brief affidavit written in Miranda's name saying he knew nothing of discriminatory practices and charging that Goldstein had intimidated and threatened him. The affidavit was notarized by William Preiss, a longtime employee of Fred Trump.

"I can no longer tolerate this persecution and am asking for the immediate cessation of any further dealings with Ms. Goldstein," the affidavit said. "Additionally, I would like to add that I am a Spanish speaking Puerto Rican hired directly by Mr. Donald Trump."

Ten days after Goldstein interviewed Miranda, Cohn filed a motion asking Judge Neaher to find Goldstein in contempt of court for "badgering and threatening" former employees. "Commencing with her entry upon the scene, the investigation, which had been conducted within the boundaries of legal propriety, turned into a gestapo-like interrogation," Cohn wrote in an affidavit. He said former employees had contacted the Trumps to complain that Miss Goldstein berated them with threats of jail, accusing them of "lying," and telling them they had been "taped" by the government. The motion also complained that Goldstein and student interns had "literally descended" upon Donald Trump's office.

Cohn did not explain how "literally descended" differed from "arrived." But even more aggressive was his use of the word "gestapo" to describe the actions of a young woman whose grandparents had fled Jew-murdering mobs in Russia. Though nonpracticing, Cohn was of Jewish descent himself. Goldstein's bosses worried that the allegations could damage her career if not addressed head-on. They requested a hearing to put the matter to rest. Cohn called only two witnesses. The first, Carol Falcone, who had left the Trump company to open her own sandwich shop, testified that she felt like "a criminal being held on a criminal charge" because FBI agents had been trying to reach her at odd hours.

Miranda said on the stand that he did not understand much of the wording in his affidavit, but he signed it anyway. He testified that when Goldstein interviewed him at his apartment, he felt threatened because she told him that if he did not speak with her, it was possible that "a higher authority" might ask to speak with him. He took that to mean an FBI agent. When Goldstein's colleagues questioned Miranda, his account of their conversation sounded quite pleasant. Miranda acknowledged inviting Goldstein to stay for coffee and donuts and telling her she would be welcome in his home anytime. "A nice girl, doing her job," he said.

Judge Neaher let the hearing go on for several hours. He gave Cohn one last chance to explain what this was all about. Cohn, who had terrorized scores of people as Joe McCarthy's chief counsel in the 1950s, finally cited what he saw as the major offense: "I think it is way out of line, in a civil rights' case, for agents to be at potential witnesses' homes."

The judge disagreed. Neaher reminded Cohn that the FBI is responsible for investigating both criminal and civil matters for the Department of Justice. "This is the first time it has ever been brought to my attention that anyone has charged an FBI agent or agents in a civil matter with some kind of conduct that could be described as storm trooper or Gestapo-type conduct," Neaher said. He threw out Cohn and Donald Trump's latest effort to engineer an end run around the evidence in the case, adding, "I have found no evidence in the record to sustain such a charge, and I think the charge is utterly without foundation."

After spending a year on a series of failed tactics, Cohn and the Trumps returned to negotiating a settlement, the posture Bunny Lindenbaum advocated from the start. They reached an agreement in January 1975, but the prosecutors could not pin down Cohn to arrange for it to be signed. That June, Goldstein and her boss, Frank E. Schwelb, the Justice Department lawyer who supervised all fair housing cases in the country, asked Judge Neaher to compel the Trumps to sign the settlement. They also turned the tables on Cohn, asking the judge to sanction him and the Trumps for delaying the inevitable by repeatedly breaking appointments during the prior six months.

Neaher scheduled a hearing for that week. Fred Trump stood up right away to reclaim control. He sounded like a man tired of the pointless delays, and legal bills, created by stretching this thing out. "Off the record, Judge, we can sign this this morning," Fred said on the record. "You call the shots. We change them, initial it." Judge Neaher started to say that the agreement seemed to be "final or so close to the edge" when Fred Trump interrupted again. "One hour, judge," Fred said. "We will be out of here."

But as they worked through the terms, a dispute over classified advertisements bogged down the hearing. The federal government had been requiring landlords who settled fair housing cases to agree to append three words to classified ads listing vacancies: "Equal Opportunity Housing." Fred took great offense at that requirement. "I think it is discriminatory against us," he told the judge. "It is expensive, and it makes us appear foolish, and we will be the laughingstock of the real estate industry."

Donald repeatedly complained that adding the line to every advertisement would be "very expensive." When asked, he did not say how much the additional line would cost the Trumps. *The New York Times*, in which the Trumps advertised vacancies, then charged about three dollars a line for real estate classified advertisements.

Goldstein tried to strike a conciliatory note by suggesting the line could be included in just half of their ads. Donald snapped back: "Will you pay for the expense, Donna?"

Throughout the long hearing, Donald and Fred repeatedly made clear they had forgotten why they were there. Goldstein reminded them, and the judge, that the Trumps were there because of "racial discrimination which has caused most Trump property in New York to be virtually all white."

"We deny that," Fred responded. Donald insisted that Goldstein should not "even be allowed to say that."

"We were not convicted," Fred complained at one point. "We would win this case if we fought it."

"Don't be too sure of that," Judge Neaher responded.

The judge had initially said that if Fred wanted to offer information, he should be sworn in and do so under oath. But Fred and Donald talked past that suggestion, and unbound by a potential perjury charge, they told a few whoppers. The Trumps wanted one of their Staten Island projects, Tysens Park, excluded in part because they insisted the project already had a high percentage of Black tenants. Fred insisted that Tysens was "over thirty percent" Black. Donald added, "I can attest to the fact that it is maybe in excess of thirty percent." But when the Trumps finally turned over the required demographic makeup of their tenants, their own figures showed that at the time Fred and Donald made those comments to the judge, only 11 percent of their tenants at Tysens were Black.

Finally, the judge proposed a plan. The Trumps would agree to place one ad a month that included the equal housing line. They were not required to admit guilt, only to promise not to discriminate in the future, just as the prosecutors had promised at the start of the case. The Trumps also agreed to send lists of vacancies to a civil rights group or to allow such a group first priority in providing applicants for apartments. After almost two years of Cohn's maneuvering, the Trumps agreed to a settlement that was slightly worse than the one originally offered to them.

The signing of the settlement generated another round of news coverage that repeated allegations that the Trumps had been racist when considering prospective tenants. Fred didn't engage with the press, and statements from the company came through Donald. He declared "full satisfaction" with the agreement because it did not include "any requirement that would compel the Trump Organization to accept persons on welfare as tenants unless as qualified as any other tenant." It was more shadowboxing, declaring victory over an enemy that did not exist—a habit that would persist throughout his life. Prosecutors never sought to require the Trumps to change Fred's long-standing practice of requiring tenants to prove their earnings in one week equaled the monthly rent, a threshold that generally excluded welfare recipients. Donald, though, would hang on for years to his victory over an imaginary enemy. He would repeat the claim more than a decade later in a draft of a book, again asserting that the LeFraks had been forced to accept welfare tenants. His publisher removed the claim from future editions after a lawyer for the LeFraks sent notice that Donald's claim was not true.

The lawsuit marked the transition of power from Fred to Donald, in style, substance, and direction. Fred Trump still owned his empire, except for the few pieces he had given to his grown children. But the decades when the name "Trump" meant Fred Trump had come to an end. Going forward, Fred would be Fred, and any mention of "Trump" would refer to Donald.

Donald's relationship with Cohn would remain strong, even as Cohn was later disbarred for deceiving and taking advantage of clients. Goldstein would go on to a distinguished legal career in law, including serving fifteen years as a judge in Los Angeles. Her older brother, Gerald Fields, earned his law degree from Yale University. Two decades after his sister battled Trump, he defended another major New York real estate owner, Leona Helmsley, against a lawsuit filed by Donald Trump. Fields described Trump's lawsuit as "utter horseshit . . . His claims are nothing but a transparent effort to make a pest of himself." A judge threw out the lawsuit, much the same as the judge had thrown out Trump's contempt motion against Fields's sister in the discrimination case. (Trump of Midland Parkway, 0, Finkelsteins of 174th Street, 2.)

While many have cited the federal discrimination case as evidence that Trump learned to fight from Cohn, it seems just as plausible that Trump found a stylistic brother in Cohn (who recognized he could profit handsomely from the combative impulses of the wealthy heir). If the case served as a learning experience for young Donald, he did not take away from it a lesson on how to avoid obvious and costly defeats. He did not come to see the wisdom underpinning his father's decades of success in such things, nor to appreciate Bunny Lindenbaum's methods for finding the easiest and cheapest path through trouble. He did not confront the cost of his youthful arrogance, his anger, or his impetuous decision-making. Instead of developing new tactical approaches, Donald Trump had lost this battle just as he would lose many more throughout his life. He would pursue litigation with no regard to his chances of victory or the costs involved. When he lost, he would invent a phony enemy, or assign a phony motive to a real enemy, and reframe it as a victory.

He gave full voice to his inner battle cry to the *Daily News* that year: "To make it in this city as a landlord, you've got to fight everything that's done, practically. This isn't the real estate business. This is combat. It's like being in the infantry."

Whether Cohn planted a tactical seed in Trump's mind or simply profited from his innate impulses is almost unimportant. What mattered was that Donald J. Trump, at the age of twenty-seven, was fully formed. And he had the force of his father's fortune at his disposal to pursue his vision of himself and settle scores as he saw fit.

11

WHATEVER THE TRUMPS WANT

On New Year's Day 1974, newly elected mayor Abraham Beame stood on the steps of City Hall in lower Manhattan delivering his inaugural speech. A young female aide stood at his side, towering over him as she contemplated two microphones arcing up to his forehead. As Beame, the shortest mayor in the city's history, continued to read his speech, the aide finally reached in front of him and sharply bent the microphones downward, aiming them toward his mouth.

Always affable but rarely inspiring, Beame continued to speak for eight minutes, without once being interrupted by applause from the crowd of about one thousand supporters. He alluded to the Watergate scandal then roiling national politics and threatening the presidency of Richard M. Nixon, mentioning that a "crisis of confidence has beset the nation, and every public official must face up to this." He said he wanted to bring safety, business, and pride back to New York City. And he hinted at the financial crisis beginning to threaten the city's ability to provide basic services: "We want to earn public respect for our governmental institutions by showing that we can provide high-quality services and that we can operate on a fiscally responsible basis."

Though the crowd may not have been audibly moved, one man had reason to feel elated. Fred Trump and Beame had been friends for decades. Now, after having attended countless fundraisers and dances for the Brooklyn Democratic Party, after years of contributing when asked and cultivating relationships, Fred Trump stood to personally benefit from his proximity to the city's political leadership more than at any other point in his life.

The new mayor's closest friend in the world, lawyer and fixer Bunny Lindenbaum, had also been Fred's lawyer and friend for three decades. Beame took the oath of office on a silver-bound Bible held by Nathan R. Sobel, a Brooklyn judge and another longtime friend of Fred Trump's. During World War II, Beame and Sobel had taken a long drive in Fred's Cadillac to Norfolk for a getaway and a tour of Fred's military housing projects.

Beame was aware he faced an uphill battle as mayor, as the worst of the problems the city faced had been known to him, even cultivated by him, during his years as budget director and city comptroller. With declining revenues and increased spending, the city had been financing basic operations with bond issues, essentially borrowing money just to keep the doors open at schools, police precincts, and fire departments. The coming crisis looked so bleak that Beame's predecessor, the tall and movie-star handsome John Lindsay, chose not to seek a third term, dodging a bullet he had helped shoot.

The national economy had entered a recession. Fuel shortages were causing long lines at gas stations and further hurting business profits. After years of population losses to the suburbs, and losses of manufacturing jobs to other parts of the country, New York City's best days seemed to have passed. Muggings and gang violence cast an air of menace over city streets and subways.

Even so, later that afternoon, Beame hosted a reception for about four thousand supporters at the Metropolitan Opera House. He drew the line at an open bar though; drinks were sold for $1.75 each.

The market for commercial and residential real estate had slumped into deep doldrums. Those with access to capital to buy or build hesitated to pursue new projects. Fred had millions of dollars in cash, properties that could serve as collateral for large loans, and now, friends in high places. But at the age of sixty-eight, he was no longer interested in pursuing large projects.

In the real estate world, it was a point in the city's history that would be perfect for someone impatient, or with something to prove, or willing to take extraordinary risks, or all of that. But also someone with powerful friends and a fortune for a tailwind. It was a moment tailor-made for Donald Trump.

NED EICHLER SPENT HIS DAYS that year coming to terms with a monumental task—how to sell off one of the largest real estate portfolios ever assembled, a disjointed collection of hotels, office buildings, and vacant land in cities across the country, a portfolio assembled by, of all things, two railroad companies.

The companies, New York Central and the Pennsylvania Railroad, had been drivers of American industrialization, connecting manufacturers to customers in cities across the Northeast and Midwest. But the railroads had since matured to the point of dysfunction, with too much debt, poor management, and a focus on paying returns to investors instead of maintaining equipment. Advancements in transportation brought competition. More than a century after the railroads wiped out operators of canal ferries and stagecoaches, large trucks and automobiles were now beating out railroads in the competition to move freight and people. In 1968, with both companies nearing complete failure, the two merged and became the Penn Central Transportation Company, creating the sixth-largest company in the nation, with the goal of saving the combined businesses through efficiencies.

The merger only made things worse. In 1970, Penn Central filed for bankruptcy, the largest bankruptcy in the nation's history, so massive that it put the investment bank Goldman Sachs at risk of collapse. In 1973, the bankruptcy court appointed Victor Palmieri to liquidate unnecessary assets. Palmieri, a dashing Stanford-educated lawyer who lived in Malibu, had founded a somewhat new business turning around bankrupt companies. He hired John Koskinen and Ned Eichler to handle the details.

Eichler and Koskinen made a formidable pair. Koskinen, the younger of the two at thirty-four, had grown up mostly in Kentucky before graduating with high honors from Duke University and Yale Law School. He had clerked for a federal judge and worked as a congressional staffer in Washington, D.C., and as a legislative assistant to Mayor Lindsay. Eichler, then about forty-three, had grown up the son of a prominent California real estate developer. His father's company, Eichler Homes, was a famous name in the San Francisco Bay Area. But Eichler had ventured out on his own after falling out with his father over the direction of the business.

The two set up shop in an office in Washington, D.C., a few blocks from the Capitol. They spent months creating a list of properties, because Penn Central did not even have reliable records of the real estate it owned. They decided to focus first on big-ticket items, including seventy-seven acres next to the Hudson River in Manhattan, the largest undeveloped tract of land on the island.

Known as the West Side Yards, the tangle of tracks and weeds had for decades served as a depot for transferring freight between larger trains coming into the city and smaller trains making the short trip to the manufacturing district downtown. The railroad companies operated under the assumption that their land was useful for one thing—railroad operations. Eichler and Koskinen calculated that with changes to how freight moved and the decay of manufacturing in lower Manhattan, a couple of guys with wheelbarrows could handle the load.

Eichler knew he faced a challenging task, given the national economy and the city's inability to fund basic services, let alone subsidize development. Few potential developers had the wherewithal for a large purchase and fewer still were in the mood to gamble on New York City. Months after he started work, Eichler was still formulating his plan when his office phone rang one day in late 1973. His receptionist told him someone named Donald Trump was on the line and wanted to speak with whoever could sell him the West Side Yards. Eichler had spent his entire forty-three years around real estate. He thought he knew every big name in the business. He could think of only one thing to say.

"Who the hell is Donald Trump?"

None of his colleagues within earshot knew the answer either. Curious, Eichler took the call. A pushy young man with a Queens accent began talking. "Are you the guy I talk to about buying the West Side Yards?" Eichler confirmed that he was that guy. "Good," Trump responded. "I want to buy them." He urged Eichler to visit him in New York and tour the 6,000-apartment project that he said he and his father were building in Brooklyn. Eichler said he had already planned to be in the city the following week and agreed to meet.

Sure enough, Donald Trump picked up Eichler in a limo and took him on a tour of his father's greatest accomplishments: Beach Haven, Shore Haven, and Trump Village. They drove through Starrett City, which Trump again claimed he and his father were building.

Eichler learned years later that the Trumps were not involved in building Starrett City, their passive tax-shelter investment. It would have been just as truthful for a General Motors stockholder to claim he was building Corvettes. But on that chilly January day in 1974, Eichler saw a young man crackling with energy, with his father's wealth and experience backing him up. And unlike many other would-be developers in the city at that time, the Trumps had no other projects in the works that might require attention or, worse, had stalled in the down economy. Donald Trump, Eichler thought, would be singularly focused on successfully developing the largest swath of bare land in Manhattan.

But even after feeling dazzled during the tour with Donald, Eichler became increasingly concerned that such a young and inexperienced man might not be able to navigate the complicated process of winning a zoning change for the land. During a meeting in an office not long after their day together, Eichler raised that point with Donald.

"I guess you should ask the mayor," Trump told him.

Eichler thought Trump might be playing games. He said he would not expect the mayor of New York City to answer a call from a stranger.

"I can get him to see you," Donald said. "When do you want to do it?"

Still suspecting Trump was bluffing, Eichler said, "Tomorrow afternoon?"

Trump made a show of making a quick phone call, then turned back to Eichler. "The limo will pick you up in front of your office at 1:30 tomorrow to take you to his office. I'll meet you there." Eichler was stunned. He was a little surprised again when the limousine showed up on time. During the ride downtown, Eichler realized that Fred Trump and Abe Beame had probably known each other from their years in Brooklyn. He had no idea how well they knew each other.

As the car arrived at City Hall, Eichler was ushered directly to the mayor's expansive office. Abe Beame, Donald, and Fred were waiting for him. Beame's new city planning commissioner, John Zuccotti, also attended. Beame stood between Fred and Donald, the two of them towering over him like turrets abutting a castle entrance. "What do you want?" Beame asked. Eichler told the mayor that he and Donald were close to a deal on the West Side Yards, but he was not sure Donald could navigate the maze of city requirements needed to complete a large-scale project. Beame offered an immediate response.

"Whatever the Trumps want in this city, they get," the new mayor said.

There would never again be a time in Donald Trump's life when he could say "Go ask the mayor about me" and be certain of a positive result. But on that day, given his father's three-decade friendship with the mayor and the mayor's best friend, he had a winning hand.

Eichler could also see in Donald a more theatrical version of himself, had he enjoyed his own father's support. As he stood outside City Hall with Fred and Donald after the meeting with Mayor Beame, he could not help but notice how Fred willingly took a back seat to his son. "Many very successful fathers, self-made men, as I understood Donald's father to be—as my father was—are rather ambivalent about their sons at a very young age becoming big figures and successful," he said later. "But it seemed clear to me that this was a very unusual relationship, that his father seemed totally supportive that this was Donald's project."

Eichler and Koskinen soon moved to New York City and took space in an office building owned by the railroad. Donald would frequently drop by to iron out details. He continually offered to take Eichler and Koskinen to expensive events in the city—the U.S. Open tennis tournament, New York Knicks basketball games, a Frank Sinatra concert. He sent Eichler a television. Eichler and Koskinen rejected each offer to avoid the appearance of impropriety.

One day, Eichler and Trump walked through Central Park, and Donald looked up at the surrounding buildings. Not yet thirty years old, he grew wistful and struck a personal note. "I don't drink or smoke. I am not married and will stay that way. In five years, I will be the biggest developer in this city. And in ten years, I will be dead."

For all his dramatic certainty, no part of Donald's telling of his own fortunes that day would prove correct. But Eichler and Koskinen were sold. They had come to believe Donald's line that he had extensive experience in the construction of large apartment buildings with his father, even though all those projects were completed before he finished school. They were convinced that Donald, with his father's support, could deliver a big project on the West Side Yards.

As Donald became the public face of his father's company, he began making more pronouncements of things he would do. Big things, grand things, but mostly, things that would never happen. It was a sharp demarcation from his father's practices over the decades. Fred Trump had announced projects when he owned the land, had the financing lined up, and had a fully formed plan in his hands. Donald felt no need to abide by such restrictions. Fred Trump's announcements served as advertisements to potential renters and buyers of soon-to-be-available new homes. Donald Trump's announcements served as advertisements of Donald Trump.

Late that July, Donald announced that he would buy the West Side Yards for at least $100 million, and as much as $150 million. In reality, he had offered to buy an option to buy the sites that, if executed, would require him to pay $62 million. He said he would build twenty-six thousand apartment units on the site, surpassing his father's lifetime of work in one swoop. But it was all still a dream. He needed the approval of the bankruptcy trustee and the shareholders in the railroad bankruptcy case even to acquire the option. And to break ground, he would need an actual development plan, financing, and approvals for a zoning change from the community and the city. *The New York Times* called Donald "a major New York builder," even though he had not yet built anything in New York.

He also told reporters that the Trump Organization had paid $15 million for one hundred acres along the Brooklyn shore, about one mile from his father's Shore Haven Apartments. Donald said he and his father planned to build either apartment buildings or a shopping center on the land, and he claimed that several department store companies had expressed interest.

Property records, which were not so easy to track down in those years, showed a different story. The Trumps had not bought the property. Fred had paid $100,000 for an option to buy it, with an undisclosed remaining balance due eight months later. The land, which had been underwater until it was filled with dirt from the construction of the Verrazzano Bridge, was zoned for neither use. The article may have served as a wonderful free advertisement to draw potential tenants, but the Trumps never took over the site. They gave up the $100,000 and walked away without anyone noticing.

Three months later, the city announced it would explore replacing the decrepit terminal in lower Manhattan where thousands of commuters arrived and departed every day on ferries bound for Staten Island. Donald seized the opportunity to draw attention. He quickly announced that he could build a new terminal on the Manhattan side for $55 million. The *New York Daily News* referred to him as "Donald C. Trump, president of the Trump Organization," and "a Brooklyn developer." Donald added that he could include a seventy-story office tower on the site. While he admitted that he hadn't lined up financing for the proposal and did not own any of the land, the *Daily News*'s editorial page, then a highly influential driver of city affairs, insisted that the proposal by "Brooklyn builder-developer Donald Trump" deserved a "serious, searching study."

Thanks to his father's wealth and reputation, newspapers conferred an air of credibility on Donald's every utterance. Those stories, and those that followed, began to establish an image of Donald Trump as a man of consequence and big ideas, and few took notice that most of his proposals went nowhere.

Regardless of what he claimed publicly, Donald still faced two remaining obstacles when it came to the West Side Yards. Eichler expected that the lawyer representing the shareholders would object, as he had to previous offers. And another bidder, the Starrett Housing Company, had submitted a last-minute bid. The federal judge overseeing the Penn Central bankruptcy case, John P. Fullam, scheduled a hearing on Trump's offer for November. With the date fast approaching, Donald took matters into his own hands.

First, he scheduled a private meeting in Philadelphia with David Berger, a prominent lawyer who represented shareholders of the railroad's stock. Berger's general response to the sale of assets had been to put up a fight for at least a while. Donald called Eichler one evening and told him to meet him at Berger's office in Philadelphia the next day. When Eichler arrived at Berger's four-story brownstone mansion, he found that Donald had beat him there. With some minor changes to the contract, Berger had promised not to oppose the deal at the upcoming hearing. "I've done your job for you," Berger said to Eichler. "I should get part of your fee." Eichler felt shocked that Berger had so easily acquiesced, but he never learned of any evidence that something untoward had taken place.

Not long after, Donald paid a visit to Robert Olnick, the chairman of Starrett Housing Company. Olnick soon withdrew his offer without explanation. Trump would claim he had persuaded Olnick by mentioning his father's investment in Starrett City, but in reality, Trump had no meaningful leverage over Olnick, at least not related to Starrett City. Like the other tax shelter investors in the project, Fred Trump had signed a partnership agreement that gave him no input on operations and required him to get approval of the general partners even to sell his own shares. As Donald said about Starrett during the fair housing case: "We are limited partners in that. Really nothing to do with it."

During those weeks, Donald's persuasive abilities, his skills at gaining people's confidence, appeared to be in full force. When the hearing arrived, Donald made a principled and effective argument, and Fullam seemed to be on board. But not long before the hearing, another bidder had emerged: HRH Construction, the company that Fred Trump had hired to complete Trump Village. Fullam thought it warranted consideration.

Eichler, who remained confident in Donald's ability to obtain financing and win the needed zoning changes, took care of that last roadblock. He filed an analysis with the judge arguing that Trump's offer would be marginally better for the railroad company and its suffering creditors over the long term. Although the HRH bid appeared to offer more up front, Eichler concluded that Trump's proposal offered greater promise once the development was completed.

Eichler raised what he called one more "major factor"—how much, if any, cash the company received "will be dependent upon the performance of the developer." He again turned what could have been seen as Donald Trump's greatest weakness—that he had no projects in the pipeline—into a strength, arguing that it made him less likely to be distracted by the needs of a neighboring construction site. "Trump has no projects in the New York area under construction or completed with rental difficulties. Even more important, Trump has no project in direct competition with the West Side properties." Eichler omitted from his analysis a related point: Donald Trump had no projects in the pipeline because he had not been in this line of work long enough to have launched anything.

More months passed. Finally, in March 1975, Fullam approved granting the option to Trump. The deal required no cash up front. If he ever built anything there, Trump would pay at least $62 million and Penn Central would be a 25 percent partner. In his decision, Fullam noted that everyone involved considered the yards to be "a wasting asset," a stretch of barren land declining in value, producing no income yet requiring "vast outlays" for maintenance and taxes. Trump might have taken that to heart. Instead, it became a risk he adopted.

Though winning approval for the option generated another round of news articles describing Donald Trump as a major developer, it would be an empty victory if he could not build a profitable development plan. Eichler had picked his horse in part based on the observation that he seemed undistracted by other projects. By then, Donald Trump was already in the process of distracting himself.

12

EVERYTHING HE TOUCHES

After opening in 1919, the Commodore Hotel became one of the city's most desirable locations for conventions and stylish functions. It rose some twenty-six stories above street level. The first few floors filled an entire city block, with a large lobby surrounded by potted palm trees and arches evoking an Italian courtyard. The tower rose skyward with cutouts in the middle, giving the building an H shape from above. It held more than two thousand rooms, each with their own bathroom—a noteworthy feature at the time it was built. Its kitchens and ballrooms were billed as the largest in the world, with the capacity to seat five thousand and serve ten thousand meals a day. *The New York Times Magazine* described the new Commodore as "one of the most colossal structures of the kind in town."

The hotel was built by a division of the New York Central Railroad and named in honor of the company's late owner, Cornelius "Commodore" Vanderbilt, the nation's original railroad tycoon and the driving force behind the creation of Grand Central. And now, almost sixty years later, Eichler and Koskinen were stuck with what was left of the great man's namesake.

More than half the rooms were uninhabitable. Homeless people and giant rats had taken up residence in the boiler room, which was accessible from the train terminal. Squatters and prostitutes claimed some empty rooms. One store space was occupied by a massage parlor operating as what the *New York Daily News* called a "flossy sex emporium." It felt like the seediness of Times Square, with its peep shows and open prostitution and drug dealing, was swelling and swallowing the area around Grand Central.

Eichler and Koskinen's office was around the corner from Grand Central.

The assets on their list of Penn Central's properties included four once grand hotels in midtown Manhattan that had fallen into various states of neglect, but the Commodore presented the biggest challenge.

Eichler obtained an appraisal of the Commodore, which came back at $10 million. In a vacuum, that number could sound like a shockingly good deal, given that the hotel had cost $6 million to build almost sixty years earlier. But in the dingy world of mid-1970s Manhattan, Eichler knew the number still defied common sense. Every real estate professional in town was aware that the iconic Chrysler Building, just across Lexington Avenue from the Commodore with its art deco stainless-steel peak shimmering in the skyline, had lost so many tenants that it faced foreclosure. If the Chrysler Building could fail, what chance could the decrepit Commodore possibly have?

Still, Eichler pitched the Commodore to several developers. He heard the level of interest he expected. "You guys should pay me to take this turkey off your hands," one responded. He also mentioned the hotel to Donald Trump, who initially showed no sign of interest. But unlike more experienced developers, Donald did not let the idea go.

CLAUDE SHOSTAL AND MIKE BAILKIN had the same problems as Eichler and Koskinen. They had been appointed by Beame to run the Mayor's Office of Lower Manhattan Development, with Shostal as the director and Bailkin as counsel. But with no more development going on in lower Manhattan than in any other part of Manhattan, the experienced developers were sitting on the sidelines with their cash, waiting for the city's fortunes to shift.

Enter Donald Trump, who kept showing up, unsolicited, to pitch them his latest ideas, though never making much of an impression. Donald would insist on driving them around in the chauffeured limo, asking about various lots, and offering ideas. He would occasionally excuse himself to supposedly speak on his car phone with Hugh Carey, the new governor of New York. The end of the conversations sounded so much like a bad comedy routine—"Yeah, right. Yeah, no. I'll do that. I'll get back to you."—that they suspected it was a ruse.

Shostal told Bailkin not to waste his time. "This twerp is never going to do anything. He's never going to build anything."

"You know, you're probably right," Bailkin answered. "But John has told me to work with him."

John was John Zuccotti, who had been in Beame's office on the day the mayor told Eichler that the Trumps got whatever they wanted in the city. Zuccotti had since been promoted to deputy mayor, the second-highest office in the city, and made clear to Bailkin that Donald Trump had favored-son status. So Bailkin dutifully listened. He even went to lunch with Donald, though he refused Donald's offer to pay at the 21 Club. Not a good look for a city official, he thought.

Trump also often arrived with Samuel "Sandy" Lindenbaum, Bunny's son. Sandy, about a decade older than Donald, had earned his law degree from Harvard in 1959 and was by then a powerful real estate lawyer in his own right. Bringing him along, which meant paying him, made an impression on Shostal and Bailkin. And Sandy's connections to the mayor via his father served as another reason not to send the young Donald Trump packing.

One day, Donald showed up at Bailkin's office with a prop, a picture of the Commodore Hotel. "Hey, you got to help me on this," Trump said. Bailkin was quite familiar with the giant old hotel. He knew that the Commodore was in horrible shape, that it could close at any moment, and that closing it could further grind down the important commercial district around Grand Central. Trump told him that he had an agreement with Penn Central to redevelop the hotel. Bailkin thought for a moment. He recognized that despite Trump's lack of experience, the city now had no choice except to deal with him. He controlled the site.

In truth, Trump did not have even an informal commitment with Eichler or Koskinen. He was bluffing, trading on the impression that his father's wealth and accomplishments made it believable that at twenty-eight years old and with no résumé to speak of he probably did just commit millions of dollars to buy a broken-down hotel.

With that bluff sold, Trump shared with Bailkin that banks would not loan him the $70 million he estimated he needed unless he could convince the city to eliminate property taxes on the hotel. He thought he had that nailed at the state level, thanks to his relationship with the governor, but it had fallen through because of the financial crisis in New York. Now he wanted the city to step in and waive the property taxes. That was the only way the banks would believe he had a shot at being profitable and making his loan payments. It was a bold request. The city's municipal budget survives on property taxes. Every commercial property owner complains about the size of their tax bills, generally one of their largest expenses. How would the city government, with its own finances collapsing, justify giving a connected first-time developer such a competitive edge?

Trump told Bailkin that "his father was going to back it, that he was going to put some money into the deal" and persuade Mayor Beame to go along. For as much as Bailkin knew about the plight of the hotel, he also knew that his own efforts to woo developers and businesses willing to expand in the city had yielded exactly no one. He put aside pondering whether Trump was the right person to turn around a decrepit hotel. What mattered was that this young man had control of the site and his father's approval to gamble with part of the family fortune.

On the fly, Bailkin proposed a plan. Instead of the city waiving taxes outright, Trump would give the hotel to a government agency, removing it from the tax rolls in the process, and Trump would lease it back from the agency at a rate based on his profits. Making the property taxes contingent on profits would lessen the risk that Trump could not repay the loan. Trump thought the idea sounded interesting and asked Bailkin to speak with Sandy Lindenbaum about it.

Lindenbaum and Bailkin got the city comptroller's office to sign off on the legality of the maneuver before presenting it to the mayor. Beame, still not entirely sure this was all a good idea, summoned both Donald and Fred Trump to his office at City Hall. Fred and Donald arrived together. They set out to sell Beame on the importance of saving the hotel and its fourteen hundred jobs, while also halting the deterioration of an important part of Manhattan. Fred made clear to his old friend that his young son would not be using the project as an apprenticeship. "I'm going to watch the construction and provide financial credibility," Fred said to Beame. The mayor was persuaded. He finally turned to Bailkin and said, "I want to take a shot on this. I believe in Fred Trump."

City officials wanted to make sure they would wind up with a stable and high-quality hotel, one suitable for conventions. They made it a condition of the deal that Trump had to partner with a first-rate hotel operator. Just a couple of months before those discussions began, *The New York Times Magazine* published a lengthy profile of the Pritzker family of Chicago. Their flagship company, Hyatt Hotels, had expanded from one hotel in 1957 to more than forty, including a dozen overseas. But the company had no hotels in New York City. Trump cold-called Joseph Amoroso, the Hyatt executive vice president who headed up development from the company's Southern California headquarters. Amoroso had been looking for a chance to open a Hyatt hotel in Manhattan, but as he listened to Donald Trump fast-talk through the phone, one word came to his mind: "kook." Still, Amoroso's job was finding new opportunities, so he did not completely dismiss the idea. On a trip to New York, he met with Trump. The young man showed him a rough drawing of his plan, which suggested not being ready for the big time. Amoroso thought he might be done. Then Trump mentioned his tax abatement, words that sounded like music to Amoroso's ears.

Separately, an associate of Fred Trump's reached out to Jay Pritzker, the family patriarch. Henry Benach, the head of Starrett Housing Corporation, set up a meeting with Pritzker, Fred, and Donald, and a deal was struck. Pritzker's company and the Trumps would form a partnership.

BY NOW, Eichler and Koskinen had become students of Donald Trump. They came to suspect that his boisterous nature might be holding him back. Donald constantly mentioned his age to lenders, apparently hoping to impress. "You know, you got to quit saying you're twenty-nine," Koskinen told Trump one day. "Nobody wants to loan that much money to a twenty-nine-year-old."

Trump was also eager to boast that he had more than enough cash in the bank to pay the $10 million asking price. Koskinen and Eichler understood that it was Fred, not Donald, who had more than $10 million in cash.

Inside the Beame administration, there was still concern that the tax abatement could look like a giveaway to a friend at a time of economic strife. With New York City on the verge of bankruptcy, Beame had traveled to Washington, D.C., to plead with the U.S. Senate for a federal bailout in the form of a loan. President Gerald R. Ford, who had replaced Nixon after Watergate, announced that he would kill any such effort. The moment inspired one of the greatest front-page headlines in the history of New York City tabloids. The front page of the *Daily News* screamed: FORD TO CITY: DROP DEAD.

Looking to close the deal with his friend without making it look like a special deal, Beame framed the idea Bailkin had devised for Trump as the first award in what would be a broad new program. He offered few parameters, or even a consistent name, other than the goal of incentivizing projects that might not otherwise be profitable enough to attract interest. Harry Helmsley, a prominent developer, complained that "maybe too much is being given" to Trump. The city hotel owners' association complained that the Trump deal, as part of a program or not, put other hotel operators at a competitive disadvantage and suggested that maybe owners who had stuck around through the hard years should receive an incentive. A managing director of the nearby New York Hilton said granting Trump a forty-year tax break went far past the level required to help the hotel become established: "Give them ten years' incentive, and then let's compete."

Instead of paying $4 million a year in property taxes, Trump would pay "rent" of $250,000, an annual amount that would slowly increase to $2.775 million after forty years. Trump's purchase price of $10 million would go to the city to pay back taxes, which had gone unpaid since Penn Central declared bankruptcy in 1970. The Trump-Hyatt partnership would also be required to pay the city a share of its profits. When news of the abatement became public, *The Wall Street Journal* called it "the tax deal of the century."

With a key vote on the project nearing and opposition mounting, the Palmieri firm announced that the hotel was on pace to lose $4.6 million for the year. He had been warning that the hotel could not survive the year. Now he said it would close within days. Officials worried about the five hundred employees who would be laid off, and that boarding up one more building could push the Grand Central area over the edge. Koskinen insisted the announcement was not timed to help Trump. Either way, the special tax abatement for the Trumps won approval of the city's Board of Estimate days later.

Donald Trump still did not actually hold a signed option to redevelop the hotel, and he still did not have financing. Koskinen and Eichler stuck with him because no other developer had come forward with an offer. They continued to be impressed by his endless energy and his ability to hire expensive consultants.

In addition to Sandy Lindenbaum, considered to be the most effective lawyer at winning changes to zoning in the city, Trump had hired Louise Sunshine, the political consultant most responsible for Hugh Carey becoming governor. They became friendly during Carey's 1974 campaign, when Sunshine ran his fundraising operation and Fred and Donald Trump emerged as Carey's second-biggest contributors, just behind the governor's own brother. Once

Carey won and installed Sunshine in a few official posts, Donald called in a favor. He rang her one day asking for help obtaining a prize he had coveted since childhood: a personalized license plate bearing his initials, just like Dad's. He had been thwarted because another New Yorker already possessed a "DJT" plate. Sunshine made a call to put his name on a waiting list, and by luck the other DJT moved soon after and returned the plates. She made the boy from Jamaica Estates very happy. "He was this spoiled kid," Sunshine later recalled. "After I had obtained the plates for Donald, I became even more important in his eyes, and I became somebody who could accomplish great things, even though it was really just a matter of fate that I obtained those plates."

As he tried to push projects through city and state agencies, Trump convinced Sunshine to pack up her Rolodex and come to work for him. Sunshine, a grandchild of the founder of the Barneys New York luxury department stores, grew up wealthy on Park Avenue and spoke comfortably with the wealthy and powerful New Yorkers who often shunned outer-borough strivers like Donald Trump. Before entering professional politics, she had graduated from Brandeis University, married a physician, and focused her life on raising three children. She would be the no-nonsense voice in Donald Trump's ear as he sought to make a name for himself separate from his father, even as his father paid her salary.

Donald also hired Howard Rubenstein, the city's biggest name in public relations. Rubenstein, the son of a newspaper reporter, had been close to Mayor Beame and Bunny Lindenbaum since the 1950s. He represented the New York Jets, the New York Yankees, and Rupert Murdoch. Neither Sunshine nor Rubenstein came cheap, though Donald was not paying with his own money. In her first year, the Trumps paid Sunshine a salary of $20,000 and a bonus of $250,000.

Even to Koskinen and Eichler, two men new to the people and ways of New York City, the names of Lindenbaum, Sunshine, and Rubenstein had an impact. "I knew their reputations and was intrigued with the amount of money he had to be paying all of them while the projects were in the planning and development stage and not producing any income," Koskinen later recalled. "It was clear that this was all part of his strategy to present himself as a major player in Manhattan. And, of course, the three of them were very experienced and influential people who could help him work through the various power structures, so he was getting something for the money."

The gamble of going years without revenue while working to win approval for the Commodore project broke in Donald Trump's favor. The city's hotel business had begun to turn around. The city drew more visitors and conventions in 1976 than it had in a decade.

THOUGH DONALD HADN'T YET GENERATED any significant revenue for his father's business, his lifestyle continued to improve. He moved into a one-bedroom penthouse apartment in the Phoenix, a newer building in the monied heart of the Upper East Side, on East Sixty-Fifth Street near Lexington Avenue, and handed down his first apartment to his younger brother, Robert. He held season tickets to the New York Knicks basketball and Rangers hockey games, and became a member at the Winged Foot Golf Club in Mamaroneck, north of the city. He spent his evenings in the most expensive and exclusive nightlife locations on the Upper East Side. His favorite spots were still Le Club, where he had met Roy Cohn, and Maxwell's Plum, a lavish dinner-and-drink hangout a few long blocks from his new apartment. Its interior design of red velvet wallpaper, stained-glass ceiling, and large chandeliers matched his preference for opulent formality.

At thirty years old, he had not shown much interest in long-term relationships. Eichler remembered Donald saying he was unlikely ever to get married. Bailkin recalls Donald speaking of attractive women as billboards for his own supremacy more than potential soul mates. He believed, as Bailkin recalled, that having the most attractive woman on his arm served as "a clear mark of success" and a sign of his dominance.

Then, one summer evening at Maxwell's Plum in 1976, Trump spotted a group of tall and slender young women looking impatient near the maître d' stand. One in particular captured his attention. She had long blond hair and was wearing a very short red dress and high heels. Trump strode across the room and touched her gently on the arm. Having been on the receiving end of too many unwanted advances, she spun around and cast a death stare in his direction. Trump did not miss a beat. He introduced himself and offered to help her: "I noticed that you and your friends are waiting for a table. I know the manager, and I can get you one fast."

The woman found something charming, something all-American, in this tall young man with blond hair and blue eyes. She told him her name. Ivana Zelníčková. Then twenty-seven years old, she had been born in Czechoslovakia and now worked as a model based in Canada. In her thick accent, she accepted his offer of help. And sure enough, he quickly procured a table. He also took it upon himself to sit down with the eight models. He kept quiet, listened politely, and ate a hamburger while they dined on low-calorie fare. As the women finished, he disappeared without saying goodbye. Strange, Ivana thought. But when they asked for their check, the waiter told them that the four-hundred-dollar tab had already been paid.

They walked out of Maxwell's to see a long Cadillac limousine parked at the curb. Behind the wheel sat their new friend and benefactor. Donald and Ivana looked at each other and both laughed. They accepted his offer of a ride to their hotel. When Ivana stepped from the limo, she leaned into the driver's-side window and gave him a polite good-night kiss on the cheek.

The next day, one hundred roses arrived at her hotel. He called to invite her to dinner that night at Le Club. The day after that dinner, he took her to lunch at the 21 Club, the third of his favorite spots, a place with a string of thirty-five jockey statues above the entrance and a menu that included the 21 Burger for $8.50, which would buy about fifteen gallons of gas at the time.

Ivana, a child of the deprivations of the old Soviet Union, saw herself as different from the trivial beauties she encountered in America. She prided herself on not being a pushover. Donald found her enthralling. After lunch at the 21 Club, he said goodbye with a kiss to the back of her hand. She caught a flight back to Montreal, where she was living with another man.

Within months, she had left her boyfriend in Canada and moved to Manhattan. As Donald worked days to get his first project going, he spent nights courting Ivana in expensive and trendy Manhattan restaurants. One evening, he called Jeffrey Walker, an old friend from their high school days at the military academy, and suggested they double date at Maxwell's Plum. Walker had last seen Donald in 1973, when Donald showed up unexpectedly at the funeral of Walker's father. Walker's father had been chief executive of the American Tobacco Company, and his death, including the funeral details, had been reported in the *Times*. Trump and Walker hadn't been in touch since high school, but Trump had driven more than an hour north of the city to a waspy Episcopalian church in Darien, Connecticut, wearing his flashy burgundy suit. Walker still fondly remembered the gesture. He accepted Trump's dinner invitation. But that night at Maxwell's Plum he saw a new and different side of Donald

Trump in full bloom, talking nonstop about himself and all his amazing accomplishments. When the tab arrived, Donald waved around a thick roll of cash. As they left, Walker's wife told him, "I don't ever want to go out with him again."

Ivana began regularly accompanying Donald to meals with his family, a lunch at Tavern on the Green in Central Park, weekly lunches at the big house in Jamaica Estates, and dinners at Fred's favorite restaurant, Peter Luger Steak House in Brooklyn. Fred's five grown children struck her like planets caught in the gravitational pull of their father. Donald always sat at his father's side, and all five followed Fred's lead. Whatever he ordered, they ordered. Fred did not drink alcohol, so neither did his grown children.

Dinners at Peter Luger would remain a family tradition for years to come, and the restaurant could not be more different from the posh and pretentious establishments favored by Donald. Since 1887, the steakhouse had occupied the ground floor of a simple four-story brick building in Brooklyn near the rumble of the Williamsburg Bridge to Manhattan. It was an old-time ode to rare beef, famous for being the most spartanly decorated of the city's most expensive restaurants. Wood panels painted black, bare, worn wood floors, simple wooden chairs. Tabs typically ran $25 per person, the equivalent of about $135 today, and Peter Luger took no credit cards. Fred Trump had a house account. Waiters delivered signature slabs of steak on the bone, large enough for several people, typically dripping with blood. The waiter pressed each piece onto a sizzling platter to, ostensibly, complete the cooking process. Not much else was offered beyond home fries, creamed spinach, tomato-and-onion salad, and simple desserts. At the end of a meal, with all the blood and bone, tables could invoke visions of a wolf attack on a cattle ranch. The Trumps' table would also be littered with more than a dozen empty Coke bottles.

In her telling, Ivana resisted the expectation to follow Fred in all things, including his conservative 1940s idea of female fashion that left Maryanne and Elizabeth resembling off-duty nuns. But Fred welcomed her into the family. On New Year's Eve, during a ski trip to Aspen five months after they met, she accepted Donald's proposal to marry.

Around that time, Donald took a *New York Times* reporter on a tour of what he described as his typical day. They met outside the Upper East Side apartment building where he lived. He wore what had become his signature three-piece burgundy suit, with matching patent-leather shoes and a white shirt with his initials sewn on the cuffs in burgundy thread. His silver Cadillac limousine pulled up, the one with a rare custom license plate bearing his initials. They climbed in the back and were driven away by Donald's full-time chauffeur and bodyguard, a former city cop who had been laid off by Mayor Beame.

They toured what Donald called "his jobs," which included two Manhattan locations—the West Side Yards and the Commodore Hotel—and the apartment buildings that his father had built. Donald professed his love of "architectural creativeness" to explain why he entered real estate. "And I like the financial creativeness too. There's a beauty in putting together a financial package that really works, whether it be through tax credits, or a mortgage financing arrangement, or a leaseback arrangement.

"Of course, the gamble is an exciting part, too," he said, grinning. "But so far, I've never made a bad deal."

If the *Times* profile of Fred and Donald in 1973 had served as the son's debutante introduction to New York real estate society, this new article painted Donald Trump as a cultural phenomenon. "He is tall, lean and blond, with dazzling white teeth, and he looks ever so much like Robert Redford," the article began. "He dates slinky fashion models, belongs to the most elegant clubs and, at only 30 years of age, estimates that he is worth 'more than $200 million.'"

The article cited "three imaginative" projects he had "in the works": a convention center in Manhattan; 14,500 federally subsidized apartments at the West Side Yards; and redevelopment of the Commodore. What was not made clear was that Trump had not yet begun construction on any of those projects. For two of them, he never would.

The Commodore was the furthest along, but he had not yet acquired the option or financing, only the verbal approval from Koskinen on behalf of the railroad. His housing plan for the uptown portion of the West Side Yards had gone nowhere. On the downtown portion, he had dumped his initial plan for housing and, at Koskinen's suggestion, proposed to build a convention center there. But that pitch had stalled as well.

He continued to convince reporters to describe him as a "major developer" without having developed anything, trading on the implication that his father's achievements were his own. He had recently announced a proposal to build a convention center in Washington, D.C. "It can be the most lucrative of all convention centers in the U.S.," he said at the time. "Washington is going to have to have a convention center or people will stop coming here." He showed up to a planning meeting with a simple model on a board and got no further. "This is ridiculous," he sniped. "That's why Washington doesn't have a convention center."

Donald Trump did not publicize the smaller-scale work he occasionally continued to do for his father. He especially went out of his way to distance himself from anything not big, not new, and not in Manhattan. He had recently used his pseudonym, Mr. Baron, in classified ads seeking to hire an air-conditioning mechanic and to rent out office space in his father's buildings—"PRIME FLUSHING LOCATION . . . BARGAIN RENT . . . Call Mr. Baron." As Mr. Baron, he also advertised for a rental manager and then a superintendent for two luxury apartment towers Fred had bought in Norfolk.

The help did not arrive soon enough. Tenants at the Pembroke and Hague Towers blamed the Trumps for infestations of cockroaches and mice, a broken air-conditioning system, elevators that did not work, a lack of hot water, and an unusable swimming pool. They staged what they called a white-collar tenants' strike, threatening to put their rent payments in escrow accounts. Fred made the trip south to hear them out. He blamed his two on-site managers for not making the repairs or informing him of the problems, but he insisted everything would be fixed. Wearing a light-colored suit and tie, he stood before the angry crowd with his arms outstretched and hands turned upward like a bewildered Jesus.

"You have a gorgeous building here," he said.

The crowd erupted in boos.

"This has never happened to us before," Fred responded.

The tenants sued. Fred fired the air-conditioning repairman and two resident property managers. He hired a local property management company to take over the buildings and vowed to make all needed repairs. The tenants dropped their suit. The following week, Donald Trump traveled south and made what would become his default promise in the decades to come.

"We are going to make something here like Virginia has not seen yet," he told a crowd of assembled residents. "We want to make these the finest buildings in Virginia." Tenants tentatively believed him. Donald left for home. At 8:00 p.m. that evening, a pipe burst between the second and third floors, sending water gushing into the laundry room, the beauty shop, storage areas, and then down the stairwell and into the lobby. "We're going to have the first aquarium in downtown Norfolk," one resident joked.

Fred Trump would sell Pembroke and Hague within a few years, continuing his retreat from buildings outside of New York City.

Another apartment project outside New York was also in trouble. Years earlier, Fred had taken over Gregory Estates, a 504-unit complex in Prince George's County, Maryland, from the FHA for one dollar after the original developer failed. By the mid-1970s, it had fallen into disrepair and amassed a stack of housing code violations. Unable to get the Trumps to respond, local officials finally did not renew the license for the Trumps to fill vacancies. Months later, Fred scheduled a meeting with officials at the apartments hoping to resolve the impasse. Instead, he was arrested and taken to the local jail. The local chief of housing code enforcement told *The Washington Post* that Fred had been "a little upset, to put it mildly." Fred, then seventy years old, posted a $1,000 bond and went home to New York. After a hearing in which local officials again refused to renew the license allowing the Trumps to fill what had become forty-five vacancies, Donald called it a "terrible situation" and vowed to challenge the decision in court. But Fred pled no contest to five misdemeanor charges, paid a $3,640 fine, and gave away the project.

None of that out-of-state unpleasantness received attention in New York, and none of it was mentioned in the *Times* profile of the exciting young developer. In the article, Donald's claim of being worth "more than $200 million" was no truer than his assertion to the reporter that he was Swedish. Everything Fred owned was then worth about $200 million.

Donald also claimed he had "probably made $14 million" during the last two years buying and selling land in California and owned a house in Beverly Hills. If he did any business in California in that era, it has been lost to time. What has remained knowable is that for all of Donald's talk of extreme wealth and great deals, his father paid him about $100,000 that year, and he received a little more income from his trusts and from renting air conditioners to senior citizens at the New Jersey apartment building. For that year, during which he picked up tabs at expensive restaurants, dressed in expensive suits, and was chauffeured in a personal limousine, Donald Trump reported taxable income of $24,594. The figure was lowered by the Starrett City tax shelter his father had bought for him. As 1976 ended, Fred Trump gave Donald another $1 million in a new trust fund, an amount Donald was not required to report on his income tax form.

Donald used the article to make clear that he was now completely in control of the company's direction, and to mark the end of the deliberate path that had made his family enormously wealthy. "It was psychology," he told the reporter. "My father knew Brooklyn very well, and he knew Queens very well. But now, that psychology is ended."

Fred once again betrayed no hint of taking offense. "Donald is the smartest person I know," he said, repeating the exact comment he had made to the *Times* three years earlier.

IN EARLY APRIL 1977, Donald and Ivana were wed in a ceremony at Marble Collegiate Church on Fifth Avenue, four blocks south of the Empire State Building. The church had been built in 1854, designed in the Neo-Romanesque Gothic style from white marble quarried north of the city. Dr. Norman Vincent Peale, senior minister since 1932, officiated the Trump ceremony. Peale was a religious celebrity of his time, a radio personality with a syndicated newspaper column and bestselling books, most notably *The Power of Positive Thinking*. Donald's mother, Mary, had long been a devotee of the Peale doctrine, which viewed mindset as the key to success and happiness.

Donald's older brother, Fred Jr., now gaunt from drinking, traveled north from Florida, where he was working as a fishing boat captain, to serve as best man. Robert was an usher. Ivana had Donald's sisters, Maryanne and Elizabeth, stand as her bridesmaids. Her father traveled from Czechoslovakia, accompanied by an aunt because her mother had come down with something and could not make the trip. Four of her girlfriends from Montreal attended. She knew almost no one else among the several hundred people who attended. The original mahogany pews filled that day with business associates from Fred Trump's long career, many of whom were now working to help his son Donald with the Commodore Hotel. Mayor Beame and key members of his administration attended. Bunny Lindenbaum, Fred's friend, fixer, and lawyer, was there, and so was his son, Sandy. Roy Cohn attended; his contribution to the blessed event had been convincing Donald to demand a prenuptial agreement, shielding his inheritance and future earnings from his betrothed. Michael Bailkin, the city official who invented the tax abatement that made Donald's deal for the Commodore possible, was seated near the front, even though he did not consider Donald anything more than a business acquaintance. "This was a political event," Bailkin later recalled. "I think that's one of the reasons I got invited. Anybody that had been doing business with him, was important to him, or who he could use in the future, was invited to that wedding."

The ceremony had been bookended by events at Donald's favorite haunts, a bachelor party at Maxwell's Plum and a reception at the 21 Club. The newlyweds headed to Acapulco for a honeymoon, but returned after just two days so Donald could complete details on the lease agreement for the Commodore with city and state officials. Donald made his new wife his first hire for the job, naming her vice president of interior design. She had no background in interior design, or even any professional résumé, but he liked her taste. And she was already pregnant with their first child.

It would take another year to borrow the $70 million for construction. When the day finally arrived, Donald did not sign the documents alone. Manufacturers Hanover, a bank with long ties to Fred Trump, agreed to loan the money with one significant condition: Fred Trump and Jay Pritzker would coguarantee that construction would be completed, and each would contribute about $2 million up front.

Much like his father in the 1930s and 1940s, Donald Trump had benefited from government responses to economic downturns. But unlike his father, Donald did not need to start small. His father gave him access to large loans and powerful officials, as well as a presumption of competency no first-time developer could reasonably expect. Even having not yet put a shovel in the ground, he had carved a place for himself in the public life of the nation's biggest city.

13

THE LATEST JEWEL

By the time Donald Trump broke ground for the Commodore, Mayor Abe Beame, who had been central to winning approval for the project, had lost his reelection bid. Voters were tired of growing crime, reduced services, and the constant threat of the city going bankrupt. The victor, Ed Koch, a charismatic and gregarious congressman, ran as a "liberal with sanity" on a law-and-order platform.

Donald invited Beame to the ceremonial groundbreaking, as well as Koch and Governor Carey. Before the news crews covering the event, Koch theatrically sold his hard hat to a television cameraman and promised to donate the fifteen dollars to the strapped city coffers. Carey, following Koch's lead, gave his hard hat away for nothing. Beame was not given a hard hat and disappeared alone into the crowded city streets.

As work began, Donald spent hours in the back seat of his idling Cadillac, making calls on his car phone, or at a desk in the offices of architects or designers he had contracted for the job. One architect, Ralph Steinglass, frequently arrived at his office on Broadway, across from the Ed Sullivan Theater, at 9:00 a.m. to find Donald already badgering lower-level employees about his construction budget. Steinglass had been hired by the firm Gruzen Samton at the request of Hyatt, having just completed work on the new Hyatt in Washington, D.C. He eventually told Donald not to bother anyone until he arrived.

Trump's inexperience became an immediate issue. He would defer to architects and construction experts on everything except matters of taste and cost. He struck Steinglass as "kind of fumbly" and seeming to believe "he could bluster his way through" this complex project.

While trying to negotiate the deal with the city and Hyatt, Trump had said he would take the entire structure down to its steel beams, doing away with the old dull brown brick-and-limestone façade. But everyone else involved recognized that the $37 million construction contract with HRH would not support a gut renovation. The tension between Trump's vision and his budget became a stubborn problem.

Some of his architects and architectural critics hoped the new hotel would blend in with the early twentieth-century details and masonry of the surrounding buildings. They at least hoped Trump would select granite for the lower levels, which would match the adjoining granite on the front of Grand Central Station. Hyatt had supported the idea. Trump would have none of it. "I hate granite!" he blurted out one day to Peter Samton, a lead architect on the project. Donald envisioned a new and modern look, entirely distinct from its older neighbors, one of polished metal and mirrored glass.

Samton suggested sheathing the building in mirrored glass, a sort of clamped-on second skin. "You would save a ton of money," Samton told him. Trump jumped at the idea.

Another architect had Donald's ear—and a piece of his budget. Donald had found a kindred spirit in Der Scutt, a prominent advocate of shimmery glass towers. Born Donald Clark Scutt in Pennsylvania, he had changed his name to the German rendition of "the Scutt." They had met after Donald saw the apartment of a golf buddy that had been decorated by Scutt. He invited Scutt to his apartment, and after Scutt pushed most of Donald's fussy furniture into the hall, the two went out to dinner at Maxwell's Plum, where Scutt drew some ideas for the Commodore on a menu. Though the Gruzen Samton firm remained the primary architects, Donald kept Scutt on as a consultant. He would call Scutt as many as fifteen times a day.

Steinglass and Samton saw trouble on the horizon. Trump had commissioned general artist renderings to sell the project, but now the specifics had to line up with the money, and everyone involved thought Trump had set the budget too low.

THE ENTIRETY OF Donald Trump's staff—four people in all—fit into what is known in the construction trades as a shanty, on the top floor of the hotel. There were two men, both serving as the eyes and ears of Trump and the Pritzkers, and two women focused on clerical duties. Hyatt had selected Phil Wolf, a seasoned construction professional, to serve as the owner's representative for its partnership with Trump. And Trump offered the job of looking out for his interests to Jeffrey Walker, his old friend from the New York Military Academy. Walker easily forgot about the bad double date with Donald a few years earlier and accepted. Beyond those four people, all other work and oversight would be handled by outside contractors.

Before demolition began, Wolf and Walker hired a company to hold the largest tag sale in history. People lined up for weeks for a chance to buy silverware, televisions, bedding, and furnishings, some from a room where President Dwight D. Eisenhower had once slept, others from rooms where more recently prostitutes and their clients had not slept. Even though the hotel had been closed for two years, there were still long-term tenants living in some rooms and retail tenants on the ground floor, including a sketchy electronics store and the massage parlor. Walker spent months "helping" tenants find new quarters. He felt good about some of it, but in other cases, he used tactics he would prefer never to discuss.

Donald did not generally want to know either. It was a management style that emerged early and endeared Trump to Walker. He would direct Walker to get it done, and let Walker figure out how. He did not want to be bothered with the details. If things went badly, there would be hell to pay. But Walker appreciated the trust and felt he thrived under the freedom.

The actual construction would be performed by HRH Construction, the large firm that Fred had hired to finish Trump Village when it became too much for him. Irving Fischer, the company's president, put a great deal of faith in a young female construction executive named Barbara Res. She was only six years out of college, where she had earned an engineering degree, and had just finished working on another tall midtown building. She was typically the only woman on her construction sites. She had grown up in working-class neighborhoods of Brooklyn and Queens and felt she knew how to handle crude men.

Everyone involved knew that this would be Donald Trump's first construction job, and that even his experienced father had never handled anything like gutting and rebuilding an old twenty-six-story building.

During her first day on the job site, Res saw her boss, Fischer, quickly walking in her direction with a fist full of papers. "Read this, memorize it," Fischer told her, holding out the company's contract with Trump. "Write down everything that happens on this job, and make sure it is covered in this contract." Fisher worried that Trump's inexperience would blow up the $37 million construction budget, and he did not want to get stuck covering the overages. The banks that lent money to the Trumps and the Pritzker family also planned to keep a close eye on Donald for the same reason.

Donald came up with a plan that echoed the lore of his father picking up nails dropped by carpenters and watering down paint. Rather than gutting the interior, plumbing, electrical, and duct work, Donald told Res to save as much of the old material as possible. Res suspected that would mean saving money on some building supplies, but it would massively increase labor costs. It meant doing demolition with a scalpel instead of a sledgehammer. It meant navigating new ducts and pipes around old ducts and pipes, and there would be a lot of that because the old hotel rooms were so small that the plan called for combining every three rooms into two. Res began with a coloring assignment for the burly men on the job. She told them to spray-paint color-coded marks on everything to show whether it would be ripped out or remain.

The change orders came fast. Every wall and ceiling cracked open created an unforeseen dilemma. Donald initially told Res to keep all of the steel framing, but much of it turned out to be corroded and had to be removed later at a higher cost. Trump insisted on keeping all the old wooden doors, each of which had to be sandblasted to remove decades of paint and grime, adding another big labor expense. When an expensive piece of ductwork from the kitchen had to be remade, the head "tin knocker," a mountain of a man who stood a foot taller than Res, grew so incensed that he told her to "Go fuck yourself!" and tried to get her fired.

The general roughness of construction sites and the violence of the city encroached on the project, though Donald was rarely on-site to experience it. During a brawl, one worker stabbed another. Walker wound up riding in the back seat of a police cruiser with the victim, pressing his hand into the bloody wound until they arrived at a hospital. The IBM Selectric typewriter, which had cost more than $1,000, went missing from the shanty, until an electrician who claimed not to be the thief offered to sell it back to Walker at a discount.

When Walker and Wolf presented the expense for Donald's approval, he grew animated. "You're dealing with a crook!" he shouted. But he paid the tab after Wolf presented the real-world options.

Hyatt's in-house architect, John Nicolls, found out after the project was complete that Trump had cut costs in ways that created problems later. Rather than installing the typical metal ductwork to draw air from the guests' bathrooms up to the roof, Trump had shafts built of drywall, which leaked and made balancing the system impossible. He also didn't fully replace the old cooling system, which had to be fixed years later. "There were a number of issues like that, most of which stem from trying to do the project fast and cheap," Nicolls said.

Eventually, there were too many extra costs to track. HRH demanded that Trump alter its contract to make obtaining reimbursement for the extra costs easier. Steinglass said that in meetings with architects and HRH when costs came up, Trump was easy to read. "He would sit down to negotiate with HRH about how much things should cost," Steinglass recalled. "They would throw out a number, and he would cut it in half. And pretty soon they figured him out. So they would quote twice as much as they needed. And they would settle on half."

IVANA, WHO WAS PREGNANT, regularly visited the construction site, but she grew increasingly worried about going into labor in a building without elevators, with no one but plumbers and electricians around. She finally called her obstetrician in December. The doctor induced labor on New Year's Eve, the one-year anniversary of their engagement and not quite nine months after their wedding. She would later say that when she told her husband the boy's name would be Donald J. Trump Jr., his response was, "What if he's a loser?" Ivana told him that the name was her decision because she had carried the baby.

Donald's work associates wondered whether the timing of the induced birth was pure luck or soulless tax planning. He could now claim a dependent tax deduction as if he had been a parent for twelve months when it had been true for only about six hours.

They were still living in Donald's second bachelor apartment, a two-bedroom unit in Olympic Tower, at East Fifty-First Street and Fifth Avenue, but decided it was too small with a baby. They rented a larger apartment a few blocks north on Fifth Avenue, near the southeast corner of Central Park, with huge windows looking out over the park and the Plaza Hotel. Ivana set out to redecorate their new home. She hired an interior decorator named Barbara Greene to create a modern and monotone feel, with beige wall-to-wall carpet and beige velvet upholstered furniture in the living room. A rarely used hammock hung in front of a large window. The entryway centered around a galleria table made in Italy from bone. Dining tables were covered with goatskin. They were so pleased with the results that Ivana brought Barbara into the Commodore project.

The Hyatt felt no particular need for help with interior design. The Pritzkers had been buying, building, and renovating hotels for decades, and they had established relationships and standards. The ballroom, the lobby, the restaurants, and final say over the rooms would all remain under Hyatt's control. Ivana, with Barbara Greene at her side, would design a few model guest rooms. They developed reputations for ordering work, not liking the results, and then ordering that it be redone. They were costly mistakes. Barbara Res remembers that the workers loved Ivana, because an order for more work from the boss's wife was sure to be fully paid.

Wolf, Hyatt's representative on the site, held weekly construction meetings that could run long and focus on an excruciating level of detail. Donald rarely attended. But to the occasional horror of the architects and building professionals who did, Ivana began showing up every week. She occasionally made good suggestions, but she also regularly chimed in on subjects about which she knew nothing. In her mind, Donald had given her tremendous authority. "Every single decision, big or small—from the towels to the flooring, who to hire and fire, the completion timeline—was up to me," she would later write in a memoir. "I was a natural at making quick, smart decisions."

Donald's attempts to save as much of the old works of the building as possible continued to cause costs to rise. Res became convinced they were spending "so much money going around things, and fixing things, that a complete gut would have been cheaper and faster." Donald also wanted all the finishes to look expensive, and they often were. All of it added up to an approach that struck Steinglass as "grandiose."

It was around this time that the very first casino opened in Atlantic City. Donald obsessively followed the news coverage, reading about the money to be made in gambling, and the talk of legalizing gambling in New York. One fact especially stuck in his head: the Hilton hotel chain made most of its profits from just two hotels that had casinos. One day, as Donald chatted with John Koskinen, the man who helped him win control of the Commodore from the bankrupt railroad, he began talking excitedly about casinos. "If you can make $25 million with a hotel casino, why would you build just a hotel?" he asked. Koskinen thought it was an interesting thought from a guy who was at that moment focused on building "just a hotel." Shortly after, Donald expanded the plan for the public spaces at the hotel to make sure they would be large enough to accommodate a casino, should gambling be legalized in New York. The extra costs to complete the first three floors—the ballroom and restaurants and lobbies—added further strain to the budget.

The construction budget that began at $37 million had more than doubled. As word reached Chicago of the continuing overruns, Jay Pritzker was not pleased that he would have to come up with the extra money and worried that Donald might not have access to cover his share. Donald once again turned to his rich father.

Though it was not known at the time, Fred Trump gave Donald a personal line of credit during the Hyatt construction. Donald received as many as four checks a month, with the total coming to $4.7 million. Fred loaned Donald another $8.8 million during that period, with no specific date for repayment.

Fred also connected Donald with Conrad Stephenson, his personal banker at Chase Manhattan. Stephenson arranged a $35 million personal line of credit for Donald. The Trump name was so trusted, thanks to Fred, that the bank gave Donald access to that massive amount of cash without making him sign a written agreement or secure payback with any collateral. The costs of his decision-making would be alleviated, at least for now, by his father.

THE COMMODORE REQUIRED his attention, but Donald spread himself in as many directions as he could imagine. He entered a new and frenzied phase of his life, a period of unbridled confidence and boundless energy. If he could read about something in a newspaper, if he could see it on the streets, if he knew another wealthy person or multinational company had done it, then Donald Trump had complete certainty that he could buy it, build it, and run it. His father would never hold him back or try to dissuade him, to rein him in, tell him to finish one thing or master one line of business before beginning another.

With no real estate or financial staff at his disposal, Donald's assessment of a potential opportunity started and stopped at the end of his nose. There would be no deliberative planning and very little in the way of an analysis of risks or potential return on investment. Every entrepreneur relies at some level on instinct, typically after running the numbers. Donald Trump went straight to instinct. The only brakes on this endless energy train would be whether he could leverage his father's wealth to borrow tens of millions of dollars. In essence, he left the analysis of whether a plan would work, whether he could repay a loan, to a bank or a lending partner, much like a first-time homebuyer with poor credit might lean on a mortgage officer to tell him what he can afford.

His public announcements continued to be geared toward maximizing attention. In the fall of 1978, newspaper articles noted that executives of a German bank had met with Peter Goldmark, the executive director of the Port Authority of New York and New Jersey, to discuss buying the World Trade Center. No price for the two iconic towers had been discussed. The meeting ended without either side committing to anything.

Soon after, Goldmark received a call from Louise Sunshine. Goldmark knew that Sunshine had been the political adviser to one of his two bosses, Governor Carey of New York, so he took the call. Sunshine had a message. Her new employer, Donald Trump, had seen the stories and wanted to discuss buying the towers himself. It was moxie on a monumental scale. The towers had been completed five years earlier at a cost of almost $1 billion, and any offer would have to be much higher to motivate the agency to sell. Still, Goldmark agreed to take a meeting with this very connected, but very unproven, developer.

He hosted Donald for lunch at the Port Authority's executive dining room in the Trade Center. Donald made a pitch that sounded to Goldmark somewhere between not well thought out and not quite legal. When Goldmark made clear that he did not think much of Donald's conceptualization of such a massive transaction, Donald threatened to call Carey and get him fired. It was a misread of the civics. Firing the executive director of the bistate agency takes two governors. Goldmark told Donald to leave.

The Port Authority kept the buildings, and Goldmark stayed in his job. But a day after their lunch, articles appeared in newspapers saying Donald Trump was interested in buying the towers. The offerless meeting led the *Chicago Tribune* to run a profile of Donald. "I don't like to talk about a deal until it happens," Donald told the paper, while talking about the deal. Still not having finished his first project, he had conjured up a national public image as a man in league with international banks pursuing billion-dollar properties.

Not long after, newspapers in New York announced that the New York Mets professional baseball franchise was up for sale. Baseball was Donald Trump's first love in the sports world. He bid $19 million for the team and came in third. The winning bid of $21.1 million came from a consortium led by Nelson Doubleday Jr., then head of the publishing company Doubleday & Company, founded by his grandfather. Under Doubleday, the Mets roared back to success and won the World Series in 1986.

When Donald read a magazine article about a bankrupt department store chain, Bonwit Teller, which had its flagship store on Fifth Avenue next to Tiffany & Co., he saw an opportunity similar to what he had found in the Penn Central bankruptcy. He set up a meeting with the firm handling the sale of the company's assets, but nothing came of it. Louise Sunshine then called a friend of hers who happened to be a large stockholder in the company that owned Bonwit. She came through again. Sunshine's friend committed to helping Donald buy the building, so long as Donald could find the financing for $25 million. Donald called his father's banker, Conrad Stephenson at Chase Manhattan, and quickly acquired a letter of credit. The details would take months to resolve. While Donald's costs on the Commodore grew, he made plans for his first original building, a skyscraper with a mix of apartments, offices, and retail shops.

DONALD HADN'T FORGOTTEN what he had read about the impact a casino operation could have on hotel profits. On a cold day in February 1980, he and Ivana traveled to Atlantic City, took in a Frank Sinatra show, and strolled the boardwalk with a real estate broker.

By mid-July, the broker had assembled a collection of lots, some with multiple owners. More than one hundred people—owners and partners and lawyers—assembled in an Atlantic City law office to sign the closing documents. As the last of the sellers signed, a limousine arrived. Out stepped Donald Trump, followed by the man whose signature was needed to make sure someone could pay for all this: Fred Trump.

Fred, then seventy-four, came up to the law office. He signed some documents and went back out to his car. A panic ensued because he had missed several lines where his signature was needed. Calls were placed to his car, and he returned to finish. Finally, it was all committed to paper. Donald agreed to begin making payments on leases, which he would cover with the Chase line of credit he had obtained from his father's banker. But he could not build until he acquired a license from the New Jersey gaming authorities. That might mean years of expenses without revenue. And there was no guarantee he would ever obtain a license.

With all of that going on, he acquired the right to develop another piece of prime Manhattan real estate, a city block across the street from Bloomingdale's on the Upper East Side. He didn't buy the property outright. The family that owned the site didn't want to sell. Instead, he took over what is known as a "ground lease" of the site, meaning he would pay the owners rent every month for ninety-nine years. It was a term Donald knew well. When he was a toddler, his father had similarly given him and his siblings the land under his two biggest apartment complexes, Shore Haven and Beach Haven, and committed to paying rent to their trust funds for ninety-nine years. With this new Manhattan lease, Donald could build on the land, but he would have to start making lease payments no later than 1983. The clock was ticking.

He was a company of one man who had just committed to three large acquisitions, each generating monthly bills and no revenue. And he still had a major construction project blowing its budget. Something had to give.

That something would be the West Side Yards, the massive swath of land that first made Donald Trump appear consequential in his own right. He had already abandoned his plan to build housing on the downtown portion of the site, and shifted to lobbying for the construction of a convention center.

Business leaders and politicians favored other sites for a convention center, and so Trump deployed Louise Sunshine again to win support. Mayor Beame and Governor Carey supported the choice, and Sunshine convinced businessmen who had contributed to Carey's campaigns. After Mayor Koch took office, he flirted with another site before deciding in April 1979 to go with the land that Donald Trump controlled. Already overwhelmed, Donald agreed to let another builder handle construction. But under the terms of his agreement with the railroad, he still stood to collect a $500,000 commission. Some city officials suggested that Trump forgo his commission to help his cash-strapped city. It was not out of spirit for the times. The biggest real estate families in New York City had come up with a plan to prepay hundreds of millions of dollars in property taxes, giving up the liquidity and returns on that money to help the city through the fiscal crisis. But Donald, who had spent nothing so far to control the option, called the suggestion "a bit unfair."

A few months later, Donald told the city he would waive his commission if the city put his surname on the convention center. He was displeased his name would not be on the completed Hyatt hotel, and was now willing to give up half a million dollars to see those five letters on a large convention center. He framed it as a flash of magnanimity. "The city really needs the center and having it named after my family would be a nice thing. From an economic standpoint for me, it's a foolish thing." Koch shot him down: "You don't buy a name, at least in this administration."

The uptown portion of the yards went next. The neighborhood had pushed back against Donald's general proposal to build almost fifteen thousand apartments there. John Koskinen, who with Eichler had pushed for Donald to acquire the yards, saw that Donald had a bit more on his plate than he could chew. At the end of 1979, rather than make a $100,000 payment to keep the option alive, Donald relinquished control. The loss would haunt him for years to come.

In midtown Manhattan, his efforts to rezone the Bonwit Teller site met with some initial opposition. The economic doldrums that had stalled construction in the city had lifted, and more than twenty tall buildings were under construction or proposed in that neighborhood. Residents and prominent businessmen worried the area could be forever cast into shadows and burdened with overcrowded streets. During a city hearing, speaker after speaker came to the microphone to oppose Donald's plan. He sat in the back of the room quietly complaining that he was being unfairly singled out. "Anyone else proposing this building would get it through in a minute. Because it's me, there's trouble.

For some reason—maybe it's because of the success of my developments—people look at my projects more closely. If I proposed a park on Fifth Avenue, some people would oppose it just because of *me*."

While he lamented the perceived difficulties of his life, a platoon of expensive lawyers bankrolled by his father marshaled representatives from major retailers in the area, including Tiffany's, to speak on his behalf. One month later, a city agency approved his rezoning request, at four stories lower than he sought. He had prevailed, but the view of himself as persecuted would weave like a thread throughout his life.

In late September 1980, Donald and Ivana briefly danced together across the Grand Hyatt's new atrium lobby as hundreds of prominent New Yorkers looked on. Harry Helmsley, a contemporary of Fred's who then owned a vast real estate portfolio that included the Empire State Building, spun and twirled his wife, Leona, through the room. Blond waitresses fanned out, offering champagne and escargots en brioche. There were touches that revealed Donald's unique sense of glamour, the style choices that would bring him quiet mockery from old-money Manhattan, like the shiny gold tablecloths, the gold-leafed lion's heads, and the sculpture of brass rods hanging from a mirrored ceiling. A waterfall, shiny bronze columns, and thick slabs of Paradiso Italian marble at the entrance foyer all communicated the sleek modern look Donald had demanded.

Ivana, glamorous in a white satin Galanos gown sparkling with rhinestones, spent much of the evening at their table with Donald's bankers. She told people she was exhausted from working eighteen months at the construction site, with no days off, all to ensure her husband's every wish would be fulfilled. He giddily worked the room, huddling with Roy Cohn and politicians he had befriended with campaign contributions, like Andrew Stein, the Manhattan borough president, and Governor Carey.

He paid his respects to his father, Fred Trump, who made the entire project possible but happily stayed in the wings as his son put himself at the center of the event. Mayor Ed Koch said Donald had "taken a sow's ear and turned it into a silk purse." Governor Carey called the hotel "the latest jewel" in the crown of New York City. The crowd regularly erupted in applause when Donald Trump's name was mentioned.

As the evening wound down, Donald and Ivana approached Barbara Res and her husband, Pete, both slightly out of place in a room of major Manhattan movers. After an introduction, Donald turned to Pete. "Barbara is a terrific gal," Donald said. "She's going to work for me." He turned back to Barbara and told her to make an appointment with Ivana to meet them at their apartment. Res felt overwhelmed by the turn her life seemed to have just taken.

In the coming weeks, Donald took a victory lap through a series of interviews and appearances. He talked about an "inclination to do something very big" in philanthropy. He said he had been in such demand that he was turning down "great little deals, cute little deals." He was thirty-four years old and said he felt almost paralyzed by the magnitude of his early success. "It's tough," he told a UPI reporter. "You do the Grand Hyatt Hotel, the New York City Convention Center, it's very hard to get into another deal, psychologically."

He began taking credit for turning around the Grand Central area. If he forgot to mention the point, someone from Howard Rubenstein's public relations team would chime in: "When you went into the area, it was a terrible area. You brought it back. You started a renaissance in the area."

The realities were more complicated. During the four years that the hotel remained closed after the city approved Trump's tax abatement, the blocks around Grand Central had staged a healthy comeback. Fears that the neighborhood would collapse if the Commodore closed, a fear that had motivated quick action by the city, turned out to be unwarranted. The tide of companies leaving midtown had stemmed. Mobil Oil had decided to remain on Forty-Second Street. Philip Morris was developing a building at Park Avenue and Forty-Second Street. The owner of the Chrysler Building, which had been approaching foreclosure as Donald negotiated on the Commodore, had embarked on a $23 million refurbishment, one of the largest in the world for a single building.

During those four years, there had been a hotel building boom. Koskinen had sold Penn Central's other three Manhattan hotels—the Barclay, the Biltmore, and the Roosevelt—for $45 million to the Loews Corporation. Harry Helmsley had just opened a fifty-one-story hotel, bigger and with higher room rates than the Grand Hyatt, nine blocks uptown from the Commodore, and he was finishing a second hotel, the Harley of New York, one block east of the Commodore. In 1979, hotel occupancy rates in New York reached a thirty-year high of 81.4 percent.

The final construction expense on the Commodore came in at twice Donald's original budget. But he was saved by the turnaround in hotel revenues and the Grand Central area. In the first year of operations, the Grand Hyatt's room rates and vacancy levels totaled about 50 percent higher than what Trump and Hyatt had forecast in the doldrums of 1975.

Koskinen, who paid attention to Donald's business activities in the decades to come, would say, "I think it may be the best deal he ever made."

By the time the hotel opened, Donald's unique PR approach had paid a more valuable dividend, one that differentiated him from the silent royalty of New York real estate families—seldom-heard names like Rudin, Durst, Tishman, and Rose. Those families never saw the upside in publicly talking about themselves or their projects, at least until they had vacancies to fill. But Donald, after years of seeking attention for things that never happened—massive residential numbers at the West Side Yards, convention centers in New York and Washington, buying the World Trade Center—had created a reputation that far outweighed the reality. Whether he had executed a masterful plot or compulsively fed an insatiable hunger, his attention seeking made it easy to forget he had just one building under his belt. Now, after years of seeming to be everywhere at once, he became a national figure, a thirty-four-year-old man whose thoughts on macroeconomics and world affairs had value.

Within a month of the Grand Hyatt opening, he taped two interviews for national news programs. On NBC, Tom Brokaw solicited Trump's "advice to people who are interested in real estate investment" and inquired, "What's left in your life?" In an extended interview, Rona Barrett, also of NBC, asked Trump how he would make America perfect and whether he would consider running for president. "You've accomplished a great deal, even though you are only thirty-four," she said. "I know there's a lot of things that you possibly can do in the years ahead. Why wouldn't you dedicate yourself to public service?"

"Because I think it's a very mean life," Donald answered. "I would love, and I would dedicate my life to this country, but I see it as being a mean life. And I also see it in somebody with strong views, and somebody with the kind of views that are maybe a little bit unpopular, which may be right, but may be unpopular, wouldn't necessarily have a chance of getting elected against somebody with no great brain but a big smile. That's a sad commentary for the political process."

He was certainly aided by a media landscape that, partially thanks to his father's accomplishments and wealth, rarely revisited his claims and afforded credibility to everything he said. Barrett said Trump's assets were "considered to be over a billion dollars." That may have been true of Fred Trump's assets, but those buildings still belonged entirely to Fred.

For 1979, the year before the hotel opened, Donald Trump reported taxable income of negative $3.4 million and paid no income taxes. His projects had generated expenses but no significant revenue until the Grand Hyatt opened. Yet he lived, thanks to his father, a life that bore the hallmarks of extreme wealth and success, now including a ski house in Aspen and a rented summer house in the Hamptons.

His father had provided the financial support and the connections that made the Grand Hyatt viable. He had bankrolled his son, paying for expensive lawyers and consultants and architects, cosigning bank loans, and giving him millions of dollars in supposed loans to cover operating costs and budget overages. About the time that the Grand Hyatt opened, Donald leased his own office in Manhattan, and Fred paid for that as well. Unknown for decades, we discovered that Donald would never repay at least $15 million of the money he borrowed from his father in those years. In essence, his father had given him the capital to launch a business and not received equity in those businesses. In the language of the tax code, Fred had given his son taxable gifts masquerading as loans, a likely tax fraud that went unnoticed.

There was one aspect of the Grand Hyatt project that Donald did not want to repeat: someone else's name appeared over the front door. As the hotel opened, he came up with a temporary remedy. A large banner appeared on the scaffolding outside of Grand Central, facing Park Avenue, in full view of approaching cars and pedestrians, and bearing only five large block letters: TRUMP.

"That was my idea, 100 percent," Donald told a *New York Daily News* gossip columnist. He had convinced the city to let him skip paying sales tax on building materials during construction and instead to use that money later to pay for a cleaning crew to remove decades worth of soot and pigeon poop from the exterior of Grand Central. As a cleaning contractor worked, Donald had the sign hung, and now made it sound like he was performing a greater civic service than just paying his taxes. "Nobody else has ever restored Grand Central," he told the *Daily News*. "Because of the magnitude of the project, it becomes a major sort of event. It signifies that we're on the job."

City workers eventually showed up and pulled down the banner, giving it to Walker, Trump's man on the site. Dumb choice, Walker thought. The next day, someone using Trump's favorite pseudonym, Mr. John Baron, called the *Daily News* on behalf of the Trump Organization to report that the banner had been stolen but would soon be replaced. Indeed, Walker and a couple of men climbed to the top of the scaffolding and rehung the banner. And there the name TRUMP stayed until the cleaning crew finished. It would be the last time that those five letters did not appear outside a Donald Trump project.

14

MR. BARON'S TOWER

In late 1979, Donald walked past Tiffany's, around the corner of East Fifty-Seventh Street and Fifth Avenue, to where the Bonwit Teller company was renovating a smaller building to replace the larger building he was about to tear down. Still boyish with blond hair over his collar at thirty-three years old, he stood out among the sweaty and dirty workers. He paused to chat with the foreman, who told him that he and his employees came from Poland. They were known as the Polish Brigade and worked for five dollars an hour, or less, far cheaper than union members, and they did not have legal immigration status. As the foreman remembered it, Donald surveyed the crew and said, "Those Polish guys are good, hard workers."

The Polish Brigade typically operated under the name Interstate Window Cleaning Company. The owner, William Kaszycki, had taken a big leap trying his hand at this interior demolition project. But Donald heard a ticking clock in his head. If he did not get the Bonwit Teller building demolished by the following September, he would have to begin paying an expensive property tax bill.

Within weeks, he signed Kaszycki's Polish Brigade for the biggest job in its history, the complete demolition of the twelve-story Bonwit Teller store on one of the busiest urban street corners in America. Donald agreed to pay Kaszycki's company $775,000 for the job, and $25,000 more if he finished on time. Kaszycki changed his company's name to Kaszycki & Sons Contractors, Inc., because, he later recalled, "It didn't sound good for a window cleaning company to do demolition work."

This would become Donald's standard method of hiring companies and people. Rather than broadly researching and interviewing, checking references and performing due diligence, he often hired the person who most recently crossed his path. Many times, the job he was hiring them for was far greater than anything they had done. The practice came with an upside, engendering the sort of unquestioning loyalty that mattered most to Donald. But it also carried substantial risk.

While planning to close the Bonwit Teller store, Donald had grown fond of a young man named Thomas Macari, who worked as Bonwit's building engineer, a job focused on tasks like arranging repairs for air-conditioning systems and elevators and flooring. Donald named Macari a company vice president of the Trump Organization and put him in charge of overseeing a potentially dangerous demolition job, even though Macari was unfamiliar with large demolition projects.

The Polish Brigade began slugging away at the interior of the Bonwit Teller building within days, months before anyone obtained the building permit required for the job. Kaszycki kept no records and did not withhold Social Security or income tax payments from the men's pay. Thirty to forty men labored long days, and another wave of greater numbers showed up to work all night. Often working without hard hats or other safety equipment, they wielded sledgehammers and blowtorches to break down walls and floors, rip out electrical wires and pipes, and haul the dusty debris in wheelbarrows to trucks waiting on the busy streets below.

By mid-March, Kaszycki was in over his head. He fell further behind every week, ran short of money, and stopped regularly paying his men. The workers staged several stoppages. Six of the workers enlisted the help of a Queens lawyer, John Szabo, who called Macari for the first time in late March 1980 for help getting the men paid. After pressuring Kaszycki failed to improve the situation, Macari set up a bank account with Kaszycki that required both their signatures for every expenditure, an extreme measure to make sure Kaszycki did not misdirect funds. The bank signature card listed Macari as a vice president of Kaszycki & Sons, a position he never held.

But even with Macari overseeing the finances directly, problems persisted. The union responsible for such work at the time, the House Wreckers Union Local 95, had seemed mostly unaware of the job. But after an article in *The New York Times* described the ongoing demolition work that March, the union showed up and demanded jobs. Kaszycki complied but also kept his Polish workers on the job, still paying them far less than their union counterparts and not making payments to the union pension and welfare fund on their behalf.

FROM THE WINDOWS of his art gallery across Fifth Avenue, Robert Miller watched with trepidation as demolition workers labored on the Bonwit Teller building. For as long as he had been there, he had admired the two limestone bas-relief sculptures of vaguely nude female forms, their legs striding in powerful athleticism, their arms arched and aimed as if they might be firing invisible arrows, with carved scarves geometrically arching around their angular forms. A perfect example of art deco sculpture, he thought, right there on the ninth floor of a department store, the sort of unnecessarily beautiful detail that had fallen out of fashion in modern architecture.

As the demolition crew began work on the exterior, Miller contacted Penelope Hunter-Stiebel, an associate curator in charge of Twentieth Century Decorative Arts at the nearby Metropolitan Museum of Art. She had not long before acquired a wall of glass panels painted in the art deco style that had once adorned the Grand Salon of the Normandie, a luxury ocean liner. After Miller called, she discussed the sculptures with her superior, Ashton Hawkins, who for more than a decade had been driving the most aggressive period of acquisitions in the museum's history. Hawkins agreed with her that the Met should pursue the naked ladies of Bonwit Teller.

Soon after, Hunter-Stiebel and Miller spoke with Donald Trump and convinced him to promise he would donate the sculptures, along with a decorative iron grille above the main entrance, to the museum. In the weeks that followed, a pattern developed. She would call his office to inquire about the commitment letter and someone in the office would tell her that the letter would soon be in the mail. By late February 1980, she grew tired of being put off and showed up unannounced. Finally, she was handed a letter signed by Donald Trump. Trump wrote that "it is our pleasure to donate the two stone sculptures and the iron grille work that are on the front of 721 Fifth Avenue." He added that his contractor "has been instructed to save these artifacts" but that the donation "must be subject to their successful removal and their appraised value." He promised to contact the museum "as soon as we begin the removal."

Hunter-Stiebel stayed on the case. She called at least weekly to check on progress. But it was not enough. In April, someone from Donald's office called to inform her that the Polish Brigade, apparently acting on their own on a Sunday, had dismantled the iron grille, which then went missing. Disappointed, she redoubled her efforts to make sure the sculptures met a better fate.

Then, on June 5, Robert Miller looked again out of his gallery's windows. This time, he saw men in hard hats standing on the scaffolding in front of one of the sculptures. A jackhammer came into focus. He dialed Penelope Hunter-Stiebel's number at the Met as quickly as he could. "Get down here right away!" he said. "They're jackhammering the sculptures." Nine months pregnant, she ran out of the museum and hailed a taxi. When the cab got stuck in traffic, she leaped out and ran the last ten blocks as best she could.

Miller did not wait for her to arrive. He hurried out of his building, across the avenue, and buttonholed a worker. He would pay, he told the worker, if they could just briefly pause the demolition. He was told that the man in charge had ordered them to demolish both statues. By the time Hunter-Stiebel arrived, only the ladies' legs remained. "It was one of the worst days of my life," she would later recall.

Outrage soon spread among the city's art and historic preservation circles. *The New York Times* was notified. Hawkins told a reporter about Donald's prior promise and expressed his disappointment. "Architectural sculpture of this quality is rare and would have made definite sense in our collections," he said. Miller described watching the destruction. "It was just tragic. They were very much in the Art Deco style, very beautiful and very gracious."

A reporter called Trump's office for a response. Donald chose to hide behind his alter ego, John Baron, who claimed to be a vice president of the Trump Organization and said the company had decided that the "merit of these stones was not great enough to justify the effort to save them." He said an appraiser had found the sculptures to be "without artistic merit," a dramatic departure from experts with the Metropolitan.

On the fourth day of news stories expressing shock that Trump had broken his promise, he finally emerged from behind his John Baron shield. Donald was quoted saying he had been out of town, and that this Baron fellow had it wrong. The $32,000 cost of removing the sculptures was not an issue. "I contribute that much every month to painters and artists—that's nothing," he said, which appears to have been entirely untrue. The issue, Donald said, was that the delay would have cost him hundreds of thousands of dollars. But really, he insisted, he was only thinking of everyone except himself. "My biggest concern was the safety of people on the street below," he told the *Times*. "If one of those stones had slipped, people would have been killed. To me, it could not have been worth that kind of risk."

THAT SUMMER, Donald Trump moved into his first official office in Manhattan, paid for by his father. One of Fred's corporations, Trump Village Construction Corp., subleased space on the second floor of an office building at Fifth Avenue and East Fifty-Seventh Street, just across Fifth Avenue from the Bonwit demolition site. Fred's company spent $107,471.35 remodeling and outfitting the space and wrote off the expense to reduce his taxes. Donald took the corner office, decorated with simple blinds and a plant, with a desk he and Ivana bought made of Brazilian rosewood and imported from Italy. Louise Sunshine, who had left politics to join him years earlier, took the large office next to his. Harvey Freeman, the lawyer Donald had hired to handle his efforts to build a casino in Atlantic City, moved into another office in the suite. Donald hired an executive secretary named Norma Foerderer, a fifty-year-old college graduate who had worked as a secretary for the U.S. ambassadors in Tunis and Uganda. Norma sat in the open area between the offices, four of which were empty, leaving space to grow. In those first months in his new office, Donald typically arrived at 7:00 a.m., unlocked the doors, and answered the phone himself for two hours until Norma arrived.

From his office he could look across Fifth Avenue to see the ongoing demolition of Bonwit Teller. As the pay problems with the Polish Brigade continued, Donald at least once sent Macari across the street with a wad of cash to pay the men. Over the months, he paid $425,740 in expenses that the Kaszycki Corporation should have paid, in addition to the $742,000 he paid under the original demolition agreement. The cost of his first major hiring decision was rising.

Still, even with all that, Kaszycki's disputes with the Polish Brigade festered, with the September deadline to begin paying property taxes bearing down. That summer, Szabo, the lawyer helping the Polish workers, placed liens of about $100,000 on the project for back wages, a legal maneuver that threatened to freeze all work. During one phone conversation with Macari, Szabo grew frustrated and asked to speak with someone higher up at the Trump Organization.

Within an hour, Szabo received a call from a man who identified himself as John Baron, a lawyer with the Trump Organization. Twelve years after Donald had begun using the name John Baron in classified ads, he had given his alter ego a law degree and promotion to in-house attorney. This John Baron threatened Szabo with a $100 million lawsuit, an amount that had been Donald Trump's go-to threat ever since his failed $100 million lawsuit against the federal government during the discrimination case in 1973.

Two weeks later, Szabo received another threatening call, this one from a man who identified himself as Irwin Durben and said he was a lawyer and John Baron's boss at the Trump Organization. This Irwin Durben said Donald Trump would not pay the back wages and threatened to produce more than one hundred members of the House Wreckers Union as witnesses to testify that there were no Polish men working the job. The caller also threatened to report all the Poles to immigration authorities for deportation.

There was, indeed, a lawyer named Irwin Durben, who had worked with Fred Trump for decades. But the real Mr. Durben handled tax and finance issues for Fred Trump. He was the trustee on Donald's trust funds. The real Irwin Durben later said that he did not recall ever speaking with a man named Szabo. "I suspect whoever spoke to Szabo may have used my name. I don't go around threatening people. As far as being an immigration lawyer, I never handled an immigration case in my life."

Szabo dropped the liens and reported the matter to the federal labor department, which set in motion several legal disputes that would linger for fifteen years. Donald eventually paid $1.375 million to settle a claim for unpaid health and pension funds on behalf of the Polish workers. But he successfully fought to keep the terms of the settlement secret for decades and continued to claim he never settled lawsuits.

One day in the fall of 1980, Barbara Res sat down on the white sofa in Donald and Ivana's all-white apartment, with bright light beaming through large windows high above Central Park. Res had grown accustomed to the filth and filthy mouths of major construction sites. A designer might describe it as biege; Res saw only white. The carpet. The furniture. The curtains. Ivana's hair. All pure and pristine, even with a toddler boy in the next room.

Donald wasted no time on small talk. "I want you to build Trump Tower for me," he said. Unlike her smaller role at the Grand Hyatt project, he told her to handle the project as if it were her own. The words landed in Barbara's ears like a jackhammer on a steel plate. At thirty-one years old, she had never been fully in charge of any construction site. He was taking a gamble on her. She knew it, appreciated it, and was a little freighted by it. After their short meeting, still feeling disoriented, she told her husband, Peter, about the offer. He convinced her she would rise to the occasion, just like always. She quit her job at HRH, the city's most prominent construction company.

Donald said he would pay her $55,000 a year, almost double what she had been making at HRH. But he had to choreograph an accounting dance to make it happen. Res's salary would be paid by Fred Trump, and Donald told Barbara that his father would not approve any salary above $50,0000 because that's what he paid his top person in Brooklyn. So he would pay her a salary of $49,000 and another $6,000 as reimbursement for fictional expenses. Donald did not mention that structuring her pay that way meant that payroll taxes—income taxes and Social Security contributions—would not be deducted from her bogus expense reimbursements, a form of tax fraud that Donald would continue to engage in until prosecutors discovered it decades later.

Donald found other ways to circumvent his father's pay limits. He called Res into his office one day to tell her that he had been impressed by something he had seen the night before at the semifinal match at the U.S. Open tennis championships. He watched in disgust from his seat as two young men in the top deck began shouting during serves, "Come on, Chris!" or "Come on, Martina!" Match play stopped as the crowd pointed to the two hecklers and security guards rushed up the steps. Donald focused on one particularly burly guard, surrounded by as many as a dozen colleagues and police officers. The biggest security guard knocked the two around and shoved them toward an exit. Donald got the security guard's name and directed Res to find him and offer him a job. But he told her that his dad would not cover the salary of anyone else, so the guard would need to go, at least for a while, on the payroll of HRH, his construction contractor.

Res tracked down the guard: Matthew Calamari, a twenty-five-year-old from Long Island who had been working part-time in security since injuring his knee as a football player at New York Institute of Technology. Donald already had a bodyguard on the payroll, a former city police officer who had been laid off during the city's 1970s fiscal crisis. Matt was hired as Donald's director of security, though what that meant was not yet clear. He would report to Res, who liked his generally easygoing disposition. Calamari, who had not found a career path since finishing college, was instantly grateful and fiercely loyal to Donald.

Barbara picked the second-biggest office in Donald's new office suite. As she looked across the street to the hole left by the Polish Brigade, she still did not know what a Trump Tower would look like. The way Donald explained it to her, Trump Tower would be nearly seventy stories tall and the "most important project in the world." Like Olympic Tower, he said, but better.

Olympic Tower had been developed by Aristotle Onassis, the Greek shipping magnate, and Arthur G. Cohen, a prominent New York real estate developer. It was located a few blocks south on Fifth Avenue and topped out at 51 stories, with 230 condominium apartments, 19 floors of offices, 2 floors of stores, and a 3-story atrium open to all comers. When it opened in 1975, Olympic Tower ushered in a new era of luxury apartment buildings.

The building's height and mix of residential and commercial uses came out of government programs created to alter the course of challenging economic and social trends. By the early 1970s, the glitzy stores of Fifth Avenue's past were being replaced by mundane bank branches and travel agencies. The buzz of street life had diminished as a migration to the suburbs continued. A new zoning regulation allowed developers to add stories to their buildings in exchange for including extra room for stores. Including a space open to the public, either an indoor atrium or an outdoor plaza, allowed even more height.

Donald, who had lived in Olympic Tower as a bachelor and a newlywed, set out to copy its model. Donald's favorite architect, Der Scutt, sketched out what would be a standard dark glass rectangle except for a signature set of features on one corner. On that edge, the lower floors top out in twenty-one cube-shaped terraces at staggered heights. Above them, set back on a diagonal, a series of 90-degree angles jut up to create what has been described as a "sawtooth" effect. Der Scutt soon exhausted the partners at his firm, Swanke Hayden Connell, and leading the job fell to John Peter Barie. Barie's team focused on maximizing the height bonuses by including an indoor atrium, additional retail space, and even five small outdoor terraces near the top of the atrium. "It was all legal, and it was all encouraged by the City of New York," Barie later recalled.

To go even higher, Donald needed to acquire the air rights—the unused vertical space between a building's height and the height allowed in zoning regulations—from Tiffany's next door. Again, he turned to his father for help. Fred Trump knew Walter Hoving, the Tiffany chairman.

Together, they hashed out a deal and arranged a meeting at Hoving's office to finalize the details, with Donald and lawyers for both sides present. Walter and Fred agreed on $5 million and shook hands. They were about to leave when Hoving's lawyer interrupted to ask Fred to sign a contract. As George Ross, Donald's longtime lawyer remembers it, Hoving, a proudly formal and dignified man in his early eighties, chided his own lawyer.

"Young man, you may be a good lawyer, but you have a lot to learn about dealing with people," Hoving said. "When Fred Trump makes a deal, his word is good enough, and there's no need for a written document."

There was one final piece to the Olympic Tower business model: a property tax abatement that had been created in 1971 to stem the tide of residents moving from New York City to the suburbs by incentivizing new apartment buildings. The lawmakers who created the program had envisioned it being used to build housing for regular New Yorkers. Olympic Tower was the first luxury building to receive the benefit. Donald believed he would be entitled to that abatement, a benefit that could net him as much as $50 million over a decade. But the rules would not allow him to apply until he had construction significantly underway.

WITH COSTS MOUNTING and the threat of property tax bills approaching, Barie's team had yet to finish the design of all floors. A choice was made to fast-track construction, which meant building a floor as soon as the design was approved.

To speed things up, the architects advised Donald to build with reinforced concrete instead of steel. With concrete, he could build each floor as the plan for that floor was finalized. The plan had been to let HRH pick the concrete contractor, but Fred Trump, who had until then happily stayed on the sidelines, watching and supporting the son he invariably called the smartest person he knew, made an objection. He had made clear that he had never mastered steel-frame construction, or tall buildings, or any building with twenty-eight sides. But he felt confident that he knew the concrete business in New York City. He insisted that his own longtime concrete contractor, Joe DePaola of DIC Concrete Corporation, be allowed to bid.

Res took the brunt of Fred's objections. She always suspected that he did not believe a woman should be in charge of a major construction site. Now this seventy-five-year-old man with a nasally Queens accent and absurdly bushy eyebrows kept yelling at her in the office. "No, no!" he would scream at her, "That's no good!" She saw other signs that he had lost a step, or at least seemed quirkily out of touch. He sometimes carried a pocketful of silver dollars that he passed out as a token for a job well done. He also insisted that his simple 1950s contract was superior to the more sophisticated contract that HRH's lawyers had developed over the decades. One day, Res decided she could take no more and stormed into Donald's office.

"You gotta take him off my back," she said.

Donald knowingly smirked. "I put up with him," he told Res, "and you have to put up with him too."

Fred might have been off about the wording of the contract and nutty about the dollar coins, but he was on to something in recommending DIC Concrete Corporation. Joe DePaola would be credited with inventing, back in 1950, the two-day work schedule that first made concrete construction much faster than building around steel beams. His two-day schedule sounds simple in concept: prep one day, pour the next. As the concrete sets on the floor just poured, prep the next floor up, and so on. In execution, it required choreographing a brutal ballet in the sky, with tons of wood, metal, and wet concrete dangerously twirling high above the nation's most crowded sidewalks and streets. Prepping a floor involved building wood forms that shape the concrete, and laying rebar reinforcements, electrical conduits, and plumbing pipes. On pour days, trucks left concrete plants outside of Manhattan early in the morning. Within ninety minutes before the concrete begins to turn hard, the trucks navigate city traffic, pour their cargo into buckets on hoists, workers wait for the buckets to rise, then empty the bucket into the forms, where, finally, teams of masons level and shape the concrete.

DePaola's process would be central to Donald's need for construction to move quickly, and all of it spoke to how different the start of Fred Trump's career had been from Donald's launch. Fred had started small with garages, expanded to row houses as his abilities grew, and hired HRH when the needs of a large job exceeded his hands-on skills. On the back of his father's wealth and connections, a young Donald Trump had leapfrogged straight to that last step.

In the fall of 1980, DePaola's crews began filling in the pit left by demolition. The first few floors, built around the high-ceilinged atrium lobby and retail space, required the most difficult and detailed concrete work. But with the foundation in place, Donald Trump's first tower was underway, and he was finally free to apply for the same property tax abatement that Aristotle Onassis had received on Olympic Tower.

WITHIN DAYS AFTER he filed his application for the abatement, Donald heard that the city's housing commissioner was likely to turn him down. He had fewer places to turn for help now, with his father's friend Abe Beame out as mayor. He called Andrew Stein, the borough president of Manhattan, with whom he had cultivated a relationship by making large campaign contributions with his father's money.

"I don't understand it," Donald told Stein. "Everybody else got it. Onassis got it for Olympic Tower."

The two shared some common ground. They were both roughly the same age and both the chosen heirs to a family fortune. Andrew's father had founded the *New York Law Journal* and other publications. *New York* magazine wrote that he was widely seen as the "*enfant horrible* of New York politics, the spoiled little rich boy who had bought his way into office." Even when he did well, insiders still saw him as "an incompetent who had the luck and money to hire an excellent staff," a complaint that might have felt personal to Donald Trump. Both he and Donald paid great attention to their appearance, especially their hair. Andrew, who wore the most infamous toupee in New York City politics, was said to have once stood on a Hamptons beach pointing helplessly at his wig in response to his date screaming to be rescued from a dangerous undertow. Whether true or apocryphal, the tale seemed to track with the widely shared perception of Stein's vanity.

Stein took an unusually accommodating step on Donald's behalf. He personally called the city's housing commissioner, Anthony Gliedman, and suggested he come to Stein's apartment for a private meeting with Donald Trump. "Trump requested to see you," Stein said. "He heard you're going to turn him down. He wants to know what you want."

Within a week, Gliedman found himself in Stein's gracious apartment on Park Avenue, the sort of place that greatly exceeded the purchasing power of Stein's government salary. They were three men of a similar age, all in their midthirties. But where Donald and Andrew were thin and well dressed, Tony was quite heavy and did not do much to hide his receding hairline. He had focused much of his one year as housing commissioner on the Bronx, where property owners had been abandoning and burning their buildings out of desperation, reducing vast stretches to rubble. But here he was being pushed to waive most of the property tax bill for luxury apartments expected to start at $407,000 for a one-bedroom.

During the meeting, Donald rested his argument on one pillar: he was entitled to the same break that Onassis received. Gliedman, whom everyone called Tony, explained what should have been obvious. After Onassis completed Olympic Tower, the city issued new guidelines to tighten eligibility. The original law defined eligible projects as those replacing a property that was "underutilized" on the day in 1971 when the law went into effect. That squishy term had opened the door for nearly every applicant. The newer guidelines instead required that the existing property be "functionally obsolete." Stein ended the meeting in his apartment by suggesting Donald file additional evidence that the Bonwit Teller building met that definition. Tony agreed to look at anything Donald filed, and he left.

Gliedman was not one to simply roll over. The son of a judge, he had graduated from Amherst College and Columbia Law School before joining the Koch administration. One week after the meeting at Stein's apartment, at 4:30 on a Friday afternoon, he called Donald and gave him the bad news: he was denying the application because the Bonwit Teller building had not been functionally obsolete in 1971, when the store recorded sales of $30 million.

The call ended without any fireworks. But ninety minutes later, Donald called back, and he was furious. "I don't know whether it's still possible for you to change your decision or not," Donald said, "but I want you to know that I am a very rich and powerful person in this town, and there is a reason I got that way. I will never forget what you did."

Gliedman said nothing to ease his fury, and so Donald went to his boss, Mayor Koch. He told Koch that Gliedman had committed a "miscarriage of justice" in denying his abatement application. "I am entitled to the exemption!" Donald said, as Koch recalled.

Koch refused to intervene and suggested that if Donald felt wronged, he should file a lawsuit. Three days later, Roy Cohn did just that. Donald's lawsuit challenging the denial of the abatement would wind through state courts for several years. Along the way, he would repeatedly portray himself as a victim, underappreciated and singled out for retribution by city officials, while ignoring the material differences between his project and others that had received the abatement.

He won an interim victory that summer, when a judge, while expressing sympathy for the city's position that the abatement was intended to encourage lower-income housing, noted that the legislature had not included that language in the law. Donald told *The New York Times* that denying him the abatement was "the most discriminatory thing I've seen in my life." In his telling, the dispute was not over a narrow legal question in the public interest but about people being out to get him. He expanded on that theme to the *New York Daily News*, saying, "I was treated very unfairly. I was singled out. Aristotle Onassis was allowed a tax abatement for Olympic Tower, but Donald Trump wasn't allowed a tax abatement for Trump Tower."

The next day, he filed a separate lawsuit in federal court seeking $138 million in damages, including $10 million from Tony Gliedman personally. The lawsuit would die a quick death.

He saved a particularly personal level of vitriol for Tony. In private, Donald had begun to refer to Tony only as "the Fat Fuck." He was not much more subtle in his public remarks. One reporter wrote that Donald called Tony a name that implied that he would be most at home "having some grain thrown into his pen."

"This 350-pound commissioner tells me I'm not gonna get my tax abatement," Donald told the reporter. "I said, 'You've gotta be kidding.' I've given more than I've gotten. I've given them a hotel, the Grand Hyatt. It was a craphouse five years ago. . . . I built a beautiful hotel and I have 1,500 people working there." He mentioned his efforts to get the city to build the convention center on the land on which he held an option, for which he received a $500,000 commission and framed it as an act of generosity. "They were gonna build the convention center over the water. The piles might go all the way to China before it hit something. Instead, I've given them a better location farther downtown and they'll have a better facility. All I did was save them 150 to 200 million dollars. All of this, and nobody has ever said, 'Thank you, Donald.' Instead, they make me look like an idiot."

Three weeks later, news broke that the city approved an abatement on a plan for another luxury building, this one planned by a British developer. Gliedman explained that the luxury tower would replace one- and two-story buildings that met any reasonable interpretation of "underutilized," unlike a twelve-story department store doing millions of dollars in business every year. Donald felt his wound open anew. He wrote a private letter to Mayor Koch. "It does seem sad that someone who has worked long and hard for New York City has to use the legal process to obtain that to which he is legally entitled, while foreigners of questionable reputation seem to do so well so effortlessly."

The city continued to pursue appeals. When one decision broke the city's way, the Associated Press received a comment from Donald's alter ego, John Baron. "It seems incredible that a ten-story building replaced by a 68-story building was an underutilization," John Baron told the paper, creating a fictional height for the old twelve-story building. "We will be appealing."

The case twice went up to New York's highest court, which each time ruled in Donald's favor. The judges determined that the city's narrowed definition of qualified buildings was not in the law as written, and that there was also nothing in the law to support limiting the abatement to low- or middle-income housing.

In the end, the Koch administration could not overcome the impact of a badly written law, and Donald was positioned to see his expenses on Trump Tower drop by $50 million over the first decade.

Now all he had to do was build it.

15

SO MUCH HOOPLA

Freddy Trump quietly came undone in the house where he grew up. His health had been bad for years, his spirits worse. Having lost his father's respect and his dream of becoming a commercial pilot, having given up on his consolation plan of working as a fishing boat captain, his drinking escalated. At one point, his closest high school friends visited him in the hospital. They found him still jovial, except for a sentence that he kept repeating: "I have got to get off the sauce." Doctors later diagnosed a heart condition, and he underwent a complicated surgery. Freddy moved back home to his parents' house in Jamaica Estates, and took a job for his father overseeing a maintenance crew. He continued to drink. During the summer of 1981, his aunt Maryanne found him a spot in an inpatient addiction treatment program in New Jersey. But he began drinking as soon as he returned to the austere room with a cot and a portable radio in his parents' house.

On September 26, 1981, either Fred or Mary called for an ambulance and notified their other four children that Freddy might not recover this time. Donald came to the house briefly, went to see a movie with his sister Elizabeth, and returned to Manhattan for the night. Not long after he left, at 9:20 that evening, Fred Crist Trump Jr. died at the age of forty-two.

The Trumps did not widely announce his death. Some of Freddy's old friends did not learn of his passing for several years. Word spread among Freddy's fraternity pals from Lehigh University, and many attended the services in Queens.

Mary, his now sixteen-year-old daughter, received little comfort from her father's family. She would remember that her brother gave the only eulogy. Elizabeth, the meekest of the siblings, sobbed uncontrollably and collapsed near the coffin. As the family left the funeral, Mary begged her grandfather to please allow her father's ashes to be spread in the water off Montauk, the scene of many of his happiest moments: deep-sea fishing, flying his plane, and cracking up Linda and his friends with a W. C. Fields impersonation. "That's not going to happen," Fred Trump answered.

Not long after, Mary and her brother, Fred III, who had just turned nineteen and was known as Fritz, met with Irwin Durben, the mild-mannered lawyer who handled estate issues for Fred Trump. Paperwork filed in court with their father's will showed that he left them a total of $746.81 in two bank accounts and a $250,000 life insurance policy. The rest of his money was tied up in the trusts created by their grandfather, Fred, and their great-grandmother, Elizabeth. These were the trusts created to avoid gift and estate taxes, each a little confection, invented by accountants and attorneys to make Fred's children look like his miniature business partners. Durben told Fritz and Mary that they would not be able to withdraw money from the trusts on their own until they turned thirty. Until then, Durben and their aunts and uncles would need to approve any distributions. And following their grandfather's overarching confidence in his middle son, Donald would have the ultimate vote.

Mary understood little about what Durben told them. He also mentioned something complicated about an income tax issue. The transfer between generations could generate an estate tax bill, then a steep 55 percent of the value of whatever went to the kids.

But the Trumps found a way to minimize that hit, a tool that would become central to passing Fred's enormous wealth on to his children, especially Donald. The tactic would hinge on hiring a friendly property appraiser. Robert Von Ancken, a well-known and respected appraiser in the city, valued seven of the eight buildings Fred Trump had given his children at a total of $13.2 million, about $13,000 for each apartment. Though it all went unnoticed for decades, we discovered years later that Donald and his siblings had filed documents during the same time span in which they certified that the buildings were worth seven times that figure.

After Freddy's death, Fred began overseeing the conversion of those buildings from rentals to cooperatives that would be sold to tenants, all for the benefit of his grown children. State laws required the family to file documents showing the value of the buildings before offering them for sale to tenant-owners. Those documents showed the Trumps valued the buildings at a total of $90.4 million. That figure would have generated a federal estate tax bill of about $10 million, whereas Von Ancken's low appraisal kept the federal tax bill at just $737,861. When we spoke to Von Ancken decades later, he said he no longer had his working papers for the Trump appraisals, but felt certain those documents would support his conclusion. For years to come, Von Ancken would serve as the family's primary appraiser when seeking to minimize a tax bill. And Donald's handling of his brother's estate was the earliest example of a dubious maneuver that would become central to Donald Trump's business life: declare a low value when dealing with tax authorities and a high value when trying to extract money from banks and buyers.

Over the course of their lives, Fritz and Mary would receive several million dollars from the family trusts, but little more. Soon after their father's death, Fred Trump wrote them out of his will and spread their father's share among Donald and his siblings, increasing their eventual inheritance. Mary and Fritz did not become aware of the change for years to come. Mary would later be told, by way of an explanation, that her grandfather never approved of her mother and that her father was worth "a whole lot of nothing" when he died.

The contrast would be most stark in comparison to the treatment of Donald's children, who stood to enter life far wealthier than any of their cousins.

And Donald's family was growing. A month after Freddy died, Donald and Ivana welcomed a new addition, a girl they named Ivanka.

Even as his father's chosen successor and the child who benefited the most from his father's wealth, Donald accelerated his long effort to erase his father's accomplishments from the public consciousness in service of artificially inflating his own.

In October 1980, nationally syndicated columnist Jack O'Brian described Donald Trump as a "kid billionaire" and asserted that "Trump owns a billion and a half in N.Y. real estate alone," with no mention of his father. In 1981, *New York Daily News* gossip columnist Claudia Cohen, who counted the

Trumps as friends for years, also stated as fact that Donald alone possessed a "billion-dollar real estate empire."

A few months later, Rona Barrett, an entertainment reporter, hosted a television special during which she also stated Donald's massive wealth as a near fact: "Your assets are considered to be over a billion dollars," she said. Donald made no attempt to correct her, or to give credit to his father. Barrett followed up by asking Donald how he had mustered "the incentive" to become a billionaire by age thirty-four. "I really enjoy what I'm doing," Donald responded. "I look at it as being somewhat creative."

The source of such an audacious assertion wasn't divulged. But in 1982, Jonathan Greenberg, then a twenty-five-year-old business reporter for *Forbes*, ran up against its accuracy. Greenberg had been assigned to work on the magazine's first list of the four hundred wealthiest Americans. The wealth of privately held real estate companies proved the hardest to measure, with none of the documentation created by publicly held corporations.

Many of the wealthiest people asked to be left off the list. Donald took the opposite tack. He invited Greenberg to his office and argued that the Trump company was worth more than $900 million. He insisted that the Trump portfolio included 23,000 apartments in New York City and that he personally owned 80 percent of those units.

Both assertions were not true. Fred Trump's financial records, which we obtained decades later, showed that he still controlled the vast bulk of his empire. And that empire included about ten thousand apartment units in the city, still a large number, but less than half of what Donald claimed. The only portion of his father's empire that Donald owned was his share of the 1,598 units his father had given to him and his siblings when he was still in high school.

Trump told Greenberg those fictitious 23,000 units were worth $40,000 each, forming the basis of his claim of being worth more than $900 million. Greenberg pushed back on the per-unit valuation. Trump shrugged in acquiescence. "Okay, then $20,000 each," he said. In reality, Fred Trump gave Donald access to cash and collateral, but Donald had no more legal claim to his father's assets than his siblings. Even using Donald's round and rosy valuations, each sibling's share of what Fred had put in the trusts totaled between $8 million and $16 million.

Greenberg and his colleagues ended up writing that Fred and Donald "Share fortune estimated at over $200 million. Donald claims $500 million." The item described Fred as "self-made" but otherwise focused on Donald, including a quote on his zero-sum world view: "Man is the most vicious of all animals, and life is a series of battles ending in victory or defeat."

Whatever the accuracy, the *Forbes* listing gave Donald credibility. Other journalists were left to either accept or disprove the prominent business publication.

The adult Donald Trump and the *Forbes* list arrived holding hands at the dawn of a broad cultural shift in America. The syndicated television show *Lifestyles of the Rich and Famous* would soon debut, ushering in an era of "wealth porn," a voyeuristic celebration of money and its trappings. Whatever taboo had existed against seeming boastful of one's wealth, at least among "old money" Americans, melted away. It was a moment tailor-made for Donald Trump. Handsome and telegenic, able to conjure charm for short periods and willing to clear his calendar for a television camera, he embraced the guiding ethos of the moment: great wealth, or at least the appearance of great wealth, means supremacy in all things. Donald would be among the supposedly rich and famous interviewed by host Robin Leach during an early two-hour special edition of *Lifestyles*, along with Lady Diana, Cher, and David Hasselhoff.

THE UNTRUTH UNDERLYING EVERYTHING Donald Trump said about his wealth that year sat mostly unexamined in a little-known office in Atlantic City, New Jersey. As part of the review for Donald's license to operate a casino, he had turned over tax returns, banking records, and financial statements to auditors from the New Jersey Attorney General's Office, Division of Gaming Enforcement. The division issued a report in March 1982 that did not paint the picture of independent wealth that Donald had claimed.

Over the prior five years, he had been surviving, and funding his business ventures, from his father's wealth and from money he had borrowed thanks to his father. His father had paid him $500,000 in salary and let him collect another $463,500 in commissions for selling some of Fred's tax-shelter investments in Starrett City. His father's company still paid for the lease on Donald's Cadillac limousine.

His father had also loaned him $8.5 million, with no specific repayment date. Donald used the $35 million line of credit from Chase—received with his father's involvement and with no required collateral—to finish the Hyatt and get going in Atlantic City.

He had received $1 million as a commission for lining up the Hyatt deal, and the same amount for negotiating a new lease for Bonwit Teller in the building he had acquired around the corner from the site of Trump Tower. But that was not enough to cover his costs.

The final tally on his tax returns showed negative income in 1978 and 1979 totaling $3.8 million. As a result, he paid no income tax for those years. The report said the losses were primarily attributable to "cash disbursements" on properties he had purchased and interest on his loans. Donald Trump was still losing money as a businessman.

Before *Forbes* published its first list, Roy Cohn had called the reporter to insist that Donald had $500 million in cash on hand. "He's worth more than any of those other guys in this town!" Cohn insisted. The New Jersey investigators discovered that Donald held no stocks in public companies and had little cash on hand. What wealth he had remained tied up in his father's businesses and his trusts.

Donald had for years claimed that he made $30 million trading gold in the late 1970s. "My best deals aren't even in real estate," he would say. New Jersey investigators found no trace in his bank or tax records of such a windfall.

Donald continued to tilt his lifestyle far away from his parents' financially conservative existence. He and Ivana had for several years rented a house in the Hamptons for getaways on summer weekends, but to reach the Long Island beaches they faced brutally slow traffic. Jeff Walker, who had always lived in Connecticut, suggested they would be happier near the water there. Ivana asked him to arrange a tour.

Walker hired a helicopter pilot who had flown in the Vietnam War. The veteran took them on a white-knuckle tour, diving and darting a few dozen feet above the Greenwich shoreline on Long Island Sound. As Walker remembers it, they were so low at one point that he recognized a *Vogue* magazine sitting on a table in one house. Ivana kept focused on the mission. She saw something she liked in the stately houses, especially one near the end of a peninsula on an inlet called Indian Harbor. "Let me check on it," Walker said.

After the flight, Walker discovered that the house, 21 Vista Drive, was for sale. Donald took a little persuading, but the Trumps bought the eight-bedroom house, surrounded by nearly six acres, for $3.7 million. Donald's new second home was orders of magnitude larger and grander than the dream house Fred Trump had built for his family in Jamaica Estates. From the backyard, near the pool, Donald and Ivana could gaze out at the water to a horizon dotted with nothing but the masts of anchored sailboats. They added a few Trumpian décor touches to the old white colonial not likely to meet Greenwich society's dictates for a blue-blooded manor. In the grand two-story foyer just inside the front door, they had mirrors installed on the curving walls along the double staircases.

WHILE RES, BARIE, AND WALKER served as Donald's eyes and ears on the Trump Tower construction site, he focused on new deals. He still had a tiny staff, without experience handling more than one project at a time. But he seemed unable to say no. And in an era of increasingly easy lending, bankers rarely said no to him.

Louise Sunshine caught wind that another old Manhattan hotel might be available for sale. This one, the Barbizon Plaza, on Central Park South and a couple of blocks west of the Trump Tower construction site. The deal included a building next door filled with rent-controlled apartments, which greatly suppressed its value because the rents could not be increased, and tenants could not be easily evicted. Donald paid $65 million. He borrowed $50 million from Chase Manhattan, where Conrad Stephenson served as personal banker to Fred and Donald, and took over the seller's mortgage for the remainder. He dispatched Macari, the former Bonwit Teller building engineer who had cajoled and intimidated the Polish Brigade into compliance, to cajole and intimidate his new rent-controlled tenants into moving out.

Donald borrowed another $35 million from Manufacturers Hanover to build a thirty-six-story apartment building that he would call Trump Plaza on the land a few blocks north of the Trump Tower construction site. He hired HRH to begin work there before Trump Tower was complete.

He met resistance, though, trying to find loans to build a casino in Atlantic City. Everything else was lined up. He had signed a lease for land on the boardwalk. The New Jersey Casino Control Commission had granted him a license to run a gambling hall. He had spent countless hours traveling to Atlantic City to meet with government agencies to win approval for the design, often with his architect, Alan Lapidus, son of the famous architect who had designed Trump Village for Fred in the 1960s. Donald figured that he needed some $200 million. He had already spent about $20 million, and the total was growing each month.

Donald and Lapidus pitched several banks. Lapidus, typically wearing his favorite "architect uniform" of a black turtleneck sweater and tweed sport jacket, wooed the bankers with the splendor of his thirty-nine-story and six-hundred-plus-room design. Donald, increasingly famous, spoke of how his involvement guaranteed success. They were repeatedly shut down by bankers uneasy with Donald's lack of experience running hotels and casinos, and by the fact that he had only completed one construction project.

Growing desperate, Donald traveled to Los Angeles to meet with Michael Milken, the junk bond king, to explore the possibility of a very high-interest bond offering. He paid a visit to Bob Guccione, the owner of the adult magazine *Penthouse*, whose own casino plans had failed, to measure his interest in loaning him the money. After many meetings and hours planning, he had only a commitment from a smaller California bank to try to find investors. Donald warned Lapidus that he may have to pull the plug on the project.

Then a savior arrived in the form of a six-foot-six-inch-tall Ohio native with a voice like a bass guitar. Michael D. Rose had recently been named chief executive and chairman of Holiday Inns Inc., with a mandate to expand. The company owned Harrah's casinos, including the Harrah's Marina Hotel and Casino in Atlantic City, and Rose saw potential in adding a second location on Donald's parcel at the beach and boardwalk. He flew to New York and made an offer similar to Donald's deal with the Pritzkers on the Grand Hyatt: you build it, we'll run it. The two agreed on the broad outlines of a deal for a casino to be named Harrah's Boardwalk. Harrah's would put up $50 million in cash, which included covering the $20 million Donald had spent so far, and they would split the profits. Ultimately, Harrah's would wind up guaranteeing a loan of $170 million.

Donald was on the verge of a great deal, one that would also get him out of a bind. Before leaving, Rose told Donald that his board of directors would want to see with their own eyes that construction was underway, evidence that this young builder could make this happen. Donald kept the truth to himself. He did not have things underway because he did not have the money. He directed his construction supervisor to hire every piece of earth-moving machinery he could find. The day the Holiday Inn board visited, dozens of bulldozers and backhoes pointlessly pushed mounds of earth around the 2.6-acre site in an elaborate ruse with no purpose other than to fool his new business partner.

Phil Satre, a top executive with the Harrah's division, flew from Reno to New York to iron out the details with Donald. Satre was a West Coast guy. He had been to the city only once before, when, as a football player at Stanford, he had passed through en route to a game at West Point. He had never heard the name Donald Trump.

He spent the night at the Grand Hyatt and in the morning made his way to the Trump Tower construction site. Even though workers were still busy on the building, Trump had opened a sales office on a lower floor and invited Satre to meet him there. A television in the office had a sales video for the apartments running on an endless loop. Satre, who ran a sizable division of a public corporation, sat staring at the screen while he waited.

Finally, Donald arrived and introduced himself with a line that Satre would never forget: "I think I'm probably the most successful person my age in the United States." He made small talk for a few minutes, giving Satre unwanted advice, telling him the best place to meet aspiring actresses and models in New York City was the Port Authority bus station. Satre, married with children, asked Donald if they could discuss the deal. Donald made his new concern very clear. "I want my name on it," he said.

Trump had come to believe that his own fame had grown to the point that the building should bear his name, not the Harrah's brand. He argued that he was very well known in the New York area and drawing customers to Atlantic City from the area would be important to the casino's eventual success.

Satre thought this was all silly. The primary rationale for their partnership was that Harrah's operational expertise and stature in the casino business would draw customers. Trump brought value as a construction manager. Satre was not accustomed to business partners so quickly reneging on an agreement. But after a lengthy negotiation, they settled on a new name, Harrah's at Trump Plaza.

Satre left Trump Tower that day wondering whether this partnership would last.

Barbara Res woke up at 5:30 a.m. to the sound of her ringing phone. She picked up the receiver and heard Ivana Trump's voice. "The building is on fire, come here immediately," Ivana said. Piles of dry wood on the highest floor under construction at Trump Tower had somehow burst into flames. The entire twenty-eighth floor glowed and flickered in orange and yellow for more than an hour, with burning embers and bits of concrete crashing down to the sidewalk.

More than two hundred firefighters had responded and calmed the flames by setting up a water cannon on the roof of a tall building across the street. It was the second fire on the job in two months. Res's first thought was: This thing was intentionally set by the mob-controlled concrete cartel as retribution for the job going to Fred Trump's concrete guy, Joe DePaola. Whether intentional or not, the fire appeared to have been started by kerosene-fueled space heaters near the wood.

The fire collapsed the twenty-eighth floor, a significant setback. By the late spring, concrete men and HRH's crews were back on DePaola's alternating schedule. Once the structure rose past the twentieth story, the floor plans remained the same all the way up, speeding up the work. That summer, they added a new floor every two days, building thirty floors in just over two months, reaching the top floor by the end of June. Eddie Bispo, the concrete superintendent for DePaola, worked at least six days a week from 6:00 a.m. to whenever the last of his 150 workers called it a day, sometimes just shy of midnight. He didn't take a vacation during his three years building Trump Tower. "It was hard to work this way," he said later. "It didn't give anybody enough time."

By tradition, finishing structural work on the top floor of a Manhattan skyscraper is cause for celebration, a "topping out" party for workers and tradesmen to celebrate their accomplishment—and their survival. They were typically low-key events with beer and good cheer. Donald Trump had something else in mind. He hired a prominent event planner. He ordered commemorative coffee cups and ashtrays in black with gold lettering, thousands of helium balloons, and a band to play swing jazz. The event would be catered, with champagne and fine food. He let Res know he was not keen to have all the workers show up. But he extended invitations to Andrew Stein, Mayor Koch, and Governor Carey, and seven hundred other guests. There were some thirty other tall buildings under construction in Manhattan at the time, one of the greatest building booms in the city's history, and New York's top public officials did not typically attend developers' celebrations of themselves. But on the morning of July 26, 1982, the state's leaders made a pilgrimage to Fifth Avenue and East Fifty-Sixth Street.

Koch's car crashed on the way uptown, somehow making an otherwise news-free event into national news. When he finally arrived, the mayor took the construction elevator to the top floor, 654 feet above the street, to a windswept concrete deck with rough wood construction ramps and scaffolding. He stood next to Fred and Donald and read a three-line toast wishing happiness to all who would dwell within. A reporter asked Koch how apartments too expensive for most New Yorkers would help "the common man." Koch, gamely hiding his displeasure with Donald receiving a property tax break, said the rich residents would pay taxes that would help fund essential services for everyone. "There's nothing wrong with being rich," the mayor said. "I wish there were more rich people."

Koch patted Fred on the back and called Donald "a chip off the old block." Fred stood beaming from under a large white hard hat bearing his three initials. He looked equal parts elated and bewildered, like the aged version of a little boy touring a construction site. Approaching his seventy-seventh birthday, his dense mustache dyed chestnut brown, he spoke briefly with a television reporter. "It's a very happy day," Fred said, while smiling awkwardly and gesturing with his hands. "The completion of the tallest concrete building in the city of New York." The reporter asked Fred how the apartment sales were going. "Ah, well, I have nothing to do with sales. But I hear they're going excellent . . . fantastic . . . unbelievable."

They all adjourned to the seventeenth floor, still only bare concrete and dangling electrical wire with no finishings or glass in the window openings. The jazz band played from a corner as the guests sipped champagne. Donald let everyone know that his employees would release ten thousand balloons from the base of the building just after noon. "So have a good time," he said.

"I've never been to a topping-off party so elaborate," one plumber quipped. "The guy's got money to burn."

Res was a little chaffed that her workers had not been the focus of the party. She still had more than a year's worth of work ahead of her. Installing bronze glass all the way up the exterior. Finishing out the apartments. But her first priority was completing the atrium and retail area so Donald could begin collecting those rent checks.

Tom Balsley sat in Donald Trump's office nervously waiting for his turn to pitch his design for a waterwall inside the atrium of Trump Tower. He watched as a prospective designer of another element of the lobby bombed out, and Donald abrasively ordered him to leave. That might be me in about one minute, he thought.

A few years earlier, during the dead construction years of the 1970s, Balsley had made ends meet by running an underground all-night dance club. As things picked up for him in design, he quickly developed a reputation for creatively weaving natural elements into urban life. Now about forty years old, he looked like a former college football star, with a square jaw and shoulders, but spoke like a philosopher-artist.

Balsley had never met Donald Trump, having been hired on the recommendation of the lead architect, John Barie. But he was built for these situations. When his moment arrived, he let some slick design rap fly, gesturing toward his renderings on the wall as he evoked visions of the granite, light, and flowing water all uniting to create a transcendent, Zen-like experience.

"Stop, stop, stop," Donald said.

That's it for me, Balsley thought. But Donald surprised him. "Don't change a thing," he said.

And that was it. The design was locked.

Donald Trump had expressed little interest in how things worked in the construction of Trump Tower beyond the cost and time involved. But as the building neared completion, he focused intensely on how things would look, and he completely trusted his immediate response, positive or negative. At that point, Res and others around him appreciated his decisiveness. Nothing ever slowed down because the boss was uncertain or ambivalent.

Only sometimes, when he saw what he had approved, he would change directions in a fit of anger. A few months later, during another meeting of the design team, Donald arrived unexpectedly. "Ivana wants the wall to be marble," he said. Now they hated Balsley's choice of granite, just as they had hated the suggestion of granite at the Grand Hyatt. Everything would be shiny. The dull and rough texture of granite, the way it would cause the water to bounce and move instead of looking like a clear curtain on a shiny surface, held no allure for the Trumps. Barbara Res, John Barie, and Ivana soon boarded a plane for Italy to shop for marble at a finishing plant in Carrara.

After more than one thousand marble rectangles were hung from the wall, reaching five stories into the atrium, Balsley prepared to test the aerators included in his design. They would cause the water to bubble and foam as it poured from between the marble slabs, which Balsley thought would make the water more alive and noticeable. Donald watched as the aerators were turned on for the first time. They spit and sputtered, spraying streams of water in odd directions. Balsley was not surprised. He had expected adjustments would be needed. But Donald saw that first test and angrily blurted out something to the effect of "turn those goddamn things off." He made clear he did not ever want to hear another word about the aerators, which had cost thousands of dollars to install. The water would fall in a clear shiny sheet across a shiny sheet of marble.

Another change, of course, would be more expensive. The design for the atrium that the city had approved, in exchange for Donald building extra stories, called for the installation of five substantial natural trees. Balsley made several trips to Florida looking for the best option. He went with Jeff Walker, because Walker had previously worked in landscaping. They crisscrossed the state looking for the biggest and most beautiful trees they could find, working to match the lush urban forest look that Donald had approved of from Balsley's design renderings. They bought five ficus trees that would reach twenty- to twenty-five feet, leaving them in a "shade house" to acclimate them to their future home. In the atrium, crews dug deep planter pits in the floor.

Balsley and Walker were told that by the time the trees were moved up north they would have lost many of their leaves, giving the branches an open and feathery look. But then the schedule, and the sense of urgency, picked up. With full and thick canopies, the five ficus trees were placed in heated trailer trucks and shipped north at significant expense. The trucks arrived on a very cold day in January. Walker and Res directed crews to build a temporary heated tunnel from the truck parking area to the front door, and a custom elevator to lower the trees into the pits.

That night, Balsley received an urgent call from Donald's assistant: Get to Trump Tower right away. He arrived to find Donald fuming on the second-floor balcony. From there, he could not see any of the retail storefronts through all the leaves. Walker and Res had been called to the woodshed as well. Donald lit into the group: "Get them out! Get them out! I don't want them. This looks terrible!" He had seen the rendering, but said something to the effect of "What the hell are you doing?"

Walker, his longest-standing acquaintance in the group, urged patience. They will shed their leaves, he said, and then everything will look better. Balsley made the same point. Donald would have none of it. "Get rid of them!" he shouted again. Walker and Balsley teamed up once more, hoping to reach a compromise. They suggested a little pruning. Cut some branches out and see how it looks.

Donald stormed off. Walker gathered a crew, found a chain saw, and began overseeing an aggressive prune. The next day, they called Donald back to the atrium to see the results. He went nuts all over again. He had brought his bodyguard with him, who stood between Donald and Balsley as Donald grew more animated. "God damnit! Get 'em out of here! They look terrible!"

The crew with the chain saws was still on the atrium main level below them. Recognizing Donald would not wait for the leaves to drop, Walker and Balsley suggested chopping down one tree and gauging the effect. Down went one tree. Donald was not assuaged. Down went another. Walker looked at one of the workers he had hired from Italy and noticed he began to weep as more trees came down. With just one left standing, Res took her shot. "Donald, it's one tree," she said. "Just leave the last one."

"No, no, no!" Donald said. "Take it down. Get rid of it!"

And down it came. Within a few days, the planting pits were filled and covered with more marble. The trees had cost about $500,000 to buy, transport, and install. But that did not concern Donald.

His crew of managers came to believe he made the right decision, given that he was designing the atrium to function as a high-end shopping mall. Removing the trees certainly created more visibility for the stores. But Donald, in exchange for receiving approval to add floors beyond what zoning regulations allowed, had promised to plant and maintain those trees.

It took the city awhile to catch on. A City Planning department lawyer eventually wrote to Donald announcing he had learned that the trees had been removed. The lawyer warned Donald that the trees "must be replaced immediately," per the original agreement.

When Donald responded, he did not admit or defend his decision. He hid behind a lie and an empty promise. "The original trees died due to the enclosed environment," he wrote in a letter to the City Planning department. "The missing trees in the lobby will be reinstalled within the next week." He never replaced the trees. And the city never enforced the requirement.

His screaming and blaming others would become an unpleasant recurring memory for many who would work on Donald Trump projects. Balsley, who went on to become recognized as the premiere landscape designer of these sorts of public spaces in the city, took no offense to Donald changing course. "It's his tower," Balsley thought. "It's his money. And if that's what he wants, then so be it."

TRUMP TOWER OFFICIALLY OPENED on Valentine's Day in 1983. Two doormen on Fifth Avenue wore tall black fur grenadier caps and red uniforms, a grand touch chosen by Ivana to evoke the formality of Buckingham Palace. After passing under the polished brass "Trump Tower" nameplate above the revolving doors, visitors were greeted with show tunes and pop songs echoing from a violinist and a pianist. The names of high-end stores surrounded the escalators going up six stories. Asprey of London, Harry Winston, Charles Jourdan, Buccellati, and Cartier. Tilted brass double-T statues served as floral podiums. Highly polished brass reflected from everywhere, especially the escalators crisscrossing five stories toward the pitched skylight ceiling. The eye traveled across wall-mounted mirrors and polished rose-and-peach-colored marble, an unending visual feedback loop of shine.

Trump had worked incessantly to generate publicity for his first new building. He and Louise Sunshine boasted that throngs of internationally famous people would be seen in the lobby. Using his fake name, John Baron, he planted bogus stories that Prince Charles and Lady Diana would be taking up residence at Trump Tower. Res marveled that a likeness of Trump Tower appeared on the cover of French *Vogue. The New York Times* architectural review of Trump Tower began by asking, "What New York building has been surrounded by so much hoopla?"

All that publicity had an unintended consequence. His first creation became a magnet for those of modest means drawn to peer into the lives of the wealthy, many hoping to spot a celebrity or just see how rich people lived. The Trump Tower atrium joined a key Manhattan tourist stroll, situated midway on a ten-block walk from Rockefeller Center, with its Christmas tree and skating rink, and the glorious St. Patrick's Cathedral, uptown to the Plaza Hotel, Central Park, and F.A.O. Schwartz. Sightseers from around the world took respite in the atrium, cooling themselves on muggy summer days and warming up during cold winters. They filled the escalators, craning their necks to take it all in, making it seem that more people were taking pictures than shopping. They spread out at the tables at the base of the waterwall and the benches elsewhere in the atrium, spending nothing but time. Some store owners, trying to cover their high rents, hoped that as more apartments sold the traffic might shift more toward their desired wealthy demographic.

Trump could not ask people to leave. He had committed to keeping the atrium open to the public, an indoor park in his temple to exclusivity. Homeless souls took to napping on the marble benches. One of the first assignments Donald gave Matt Calamari, the former security guard at the U.S. Open, was to have workers place large planters on the benches to keep homeless people off, remove the planters when city officials complained he was breaking his agreement, and replace them after city officials left.

Upstairs, many of the 263 apartments were undergoing extensive remodels. Donald had cut his costs at the end by using cheap finishings, reasoning that buyers would rip out everything and start over anyway. One interior designer, Ross MacTaggart, kept busy for years with renovations of brand-new Trump Tower apartments, replacing the cheap cabinets, Formica countertops, fake marble, parquet floor tiles, and low-end kitchen appliances. His clients had bought before the building was completed, based on the sales presentation in Trump's office, and they "were horrified" to see the final product in a $750,000 two-bedroom apartment. "They expected to just move in and decorate," he recalled later. "They didn't expect that they would have to tear everything out. Even the doors were cheap."

Donald and Ivana were in the process of spending lavishly on their own apartment, a triplex on the topmost floors. They hired a prominent interior designer to undertake a build-out that would take two years to complete. The building would become his home and base of operations for decades to come. Donald vacated his first office across the street and moved his small staff into a sprawling office on the twenty-sixth floor of Trump Tower. He added a conference room with a long table and chairs and views of Central Park. He joked about almost calling it the boardroom, until he realized that he was the only member of the board.

The construction of his first building had been a sometimes messy process that revealed, to those close to him at least, elements of his personality that would not become part of his public image for many more years. His propensity to threaten legal action and file losing lawsuits just to inflict discomfort, regardless of the costs to himself. Seeing himself, a wealthy heir, as the victim, or underappreciated. Lying about what he had done, or even who he was, in telephone calls to get his way. Insulting the appearance of people who did not bow to his desires. A combination of a lack of attention to detail in the planning stage followed by a raging disapproval and blame of others when he saw the finished product.

But it was a major accomplishment. He had brought the project across the finish line with just a few loyal aides overseeing large contractors. Even with the budget blown by changes, a rising market all but ensured financial success. As his partner, Equitable, had forecast, the apartment sales covered the cost of construction, and the retail and commercial spaces began producing profits. When we obtained his tax records decades later, the Trump Tower commercial and retail space stood out as the most reliably profitable asset that he had ever created.

One of several lengthy newspaper and magazine profiles marking the opening of Trump Tower quoted Francis L. Bryant Jr., a senior vice president of Manufacturers Hanover Trust, one of Donald's lenders, as saying that while Donald "appears to be a wild man," he actually "sticks to what he knows."

The same article hinted that Donald had already begun the departure from the business he knew. It mentioned that he was interested in the communications and sports industries. He was drawn to the "merger game" and undaunted by the idea of taking over companies in other fields. "The day we opened we knew we had a smash," he told another reporter. "There was talent and luck involved. I don't suspect there is much more I can do in real estate."

Part III

THE EVERYTHING MAN

Young men starting in life should avoid running into debt. There is scarcely anything that drags a person down like debt.

—P. T. Barnum

16

ALMOST RATIONAL

David Dixon spent his working years dreaming of ways to turn his passions—art, sports, and his beloved hometown of New Orleans—into businesses. By 1961, he had built a prosperous life as an art dealer. As he looked at the landscape of professional football, with its short fall season and relatively small number of cities with teams, he saw an opening for a new league that would play in the spring. He hired a market research firm, which found support among football fans for spring ball. Armed with data, Dixon traveled the country pitching wealthy men on the merits of spending money to start a league and own a team.

A convincing salesman, Dixon had great success signing potential owners. But he hit a wall trying to secure a broadcast contract with any of the three national networks, so he dropped his plan for spring football. In the coming years, Dixon helped secure an NFL expansion slot for the New Orleans Saints, served as a leading figure in the construction of the Louisiana Superdome, and co-founded the World Championship Tennis tour.

Then, in 1979, he saw a new opportunity for his old idea. The introduction of cable television created scores of new stations, including a twenty-four-hour sports channel called ESPN. Dixon went on the road again, convincing wealthy men to buy a team for $6 million each. His travels led him to the doorstep of a young developer who, although he was then working on his first new building in Manhattan, had been identified in New York newspapers and on television as extremely rich. Donald Trump attended several meetings with other prospective owners. But he backed out. He was in the middle of trying to buy the

Baltimore Colts of the NFL. Dixon hired a media broker, who secured a contract with ABC to broadcast seventeen games in each of the first two spring seasons for a total of $18 million. ESPN soon followed with an $11 million deal. Those figures looked tiny compared to the $2 billion deal the NFL had just signed with the networks. But the numbers were big enough to schedule opening day in the spring of 1983.

Dixon advocated a slow and steady buildup, with teams keeping salaries in check as revenues increased. The owner of the New Jersey Generals franchise, Oklahoma oilman J. Walter Duncan, did not completely abide to that guidance. He pushed the Generals ahead of many teams in signing a three-year, $5 million contract with Herschel Walker, the running back who had won the Heisman Trophy at the University of Georgia and still had one year remaining of college eligibility.

In the league's first season, television ratings and ticket sales exceeded expectations. Teams fielded talented players, most of whom had been overlooked by the NFL. A style of freewheeling play emerged, with spontaneous lateral passes and bombs that lent shock and more excitement to a game that had grown predictably precise in the NFL.

But for Duncan, that first season proved too demanding. He grew weary of traveling from Oklahoma to a different city every week, so he asked Jimmy Gould, a young man who had worked with several teams during the league's formation, for help finding someone to buy the New Jersey Generals.

Gould turned immediately to the guy everyone said was rich but who had refused to buy a team in the first year. Donald Trump by then had been rebuffed by the Colts, as he had by the Dallas Cowboys and other major sports teams. Gould eventually reached Trump on the phone and made his pitch: become the owner of the New Jersey Generals for only $8.5 million. A cheap way to get into the game.

"Get to New York," Gould remembered Trump telling him.

On a September day in 1983, a crowd of several dozen reporters and photographers assembled in the atrium of the new Trump Tower, waiting for what had been billed as a major press conference. An aide passed out biographical information about the proprietor to reporters. All eyes veered upward as Donald Trump, wearing a dark blue suit, a blue-and-white striped shirt, and a dark tie, appeared at the top of the escalator for a smooth glide down to his shiny marble-and-brass lobby. He walked to a podium in the shape of a T and announced what everyone there already knew: he had purchased the New Jersey Generals of the United States Football League. He had committed to pay about $10 million for a team that had lost $3 million the year before and said he would spend whatever it took to make the team the winner. "We're really not doing this as an economic venture," he told reporters. "I would really like to be an exciting owner."

With the purchase, Donald left behind the self-restraint and personal and financial discipline that had been the hallmarks of his father's career. He entered a period of frenzied acquisitions, assembling an eclectic conglomerate untethered from any core competency. He had completed just a couple of successful projects, both with more experienced partners, in the profession that had been the focus of his entire life. Almost overnight he saw himself as capable of running any type of business.

"What I like is for people to tell me that something can't be done, when I think it can," he told *The New York Times*.

"They read that the Grand Hyatt would never be built, but it was," he told *Sports Illustrated*. "They read that Trump Tower would never be built, but it was. Now they see me buy a football team. They're gonna believe.

"When I want something, I want victory, completeness, results," he added.

Three months after buying the Generals, Trump appeared on a panel for major New York–area sports team owners. He sat on the dais with Fred Wilpon, who had won the bidding for the New York Mets that Trump had lost, and George Steinbrenner, the owner of the New York Yankees and most recognized sports team owner of his era. Steinbrenner's face and latest comments regularly graced the sports pages of the city's newspapers, most recently for firing his manager, Billy Martin, for the third time. During the panel discussion, Trump described his league as at war with the NFL and said he welcomed a coming "bloodbath" over players. That position was too provocative for even a famous provocateur like Steinbrenner. "War is not a good thing," Steinbrenner said in response. "I'd worry about getting this thing together."

Trump's purchase of the team spawned a wave of profiles in major newspapers and magazines and on television shows. He began appearing as a commentator during broadcasts before NFL games. He generated more media attention by offering Don Shula, the legendary Miami Dolphins coach, a $1 million contract, which Shula rejected. He publicly vowed to lure Lawrence Taylor, the All-Pro linebacker, away from the New York Giants, which never happened either.

George Young, the Giants general manager, described Trump's promises as more like "what he'd like to do as opposed to what he's doing." Young presented a test to news organizations that most would fail for years to come. "Donald Trump can say what he wants to say. It's up to you [the media] to decide how credible he is."

Breaking with Dixon's plan to keep costs down while building a following for the league, Trump signed several NFL players at greater salaries than the NFL was willing to pay, most notably Gary Barbaro, the safety for the Kansas City Chiefs with three Pro Bowl appearances, and Brian Sipe, the onetime MVP quarterback for the Cleveland Browns. Sipe's new two-year contract would pay him $1.9 million, about double the Browns' offer. Before the year ended, Donald had signed four other NFL players, as well as Walt Michaels, the former coach of the New York Jets, to a three-year deal worth $500,000.

He quickly set the upstart league on a collision course with the NFL. On January 17, 1984, four months after he bought the Generals, he wrote a letter to his fellow owners saying that the USFL would be "foolish" to keep playing in the spring. He revealed what some owners began calling his grand plan to trick the NFL into converting their lesser teams into full NFL franchises through a merger. "If we expect the networks to pay us a great deal of money for a period where there is a small television audience, then we are being foolish," he wrote. "The N.F.L. knows this and are just waiting. Their only fear is a switch of our league to the winter—an event which will either lead to a merger, or, in the alternative, a common draft with a first-class, traditional league.

"I did not come into this league to be second rate," he continued. "We are sitting on something much bigger and better than most people realize. We had better get smart and take advantage of it."

The more direct interpretation might have been that there was a smaller television audience for spring football not because of some inalienable seasonal limitation but because it was a new idea with mostly unknown and unproven players. There was never any evidence that the NFL, with its massive television contracts and control of stadiums in major cities, was cowering at a clearly second-tier league. It had fended off two other alternative leagues in the prior two decades.

The letter did encapsulate what became Donald Trump's three-step rhetorical style, a pattern so predictable and unique it could be branded "Trump Logic." First, he confidently makes an assertion that often oversimplifies or ignores the truth of the matter. He builds upon that soft foundation with an act of clairvoyance, claiming to know what large groups of people fear, or at whom they laugh, as proof that his original assertion was true. Finally, he closes the deal by making clear that disagreeing with his un-facts or his psychic vision is prima facie evidence of stupidity.

The day after Trump sent his letter to fellow owners, they all assembled in New Orleans for a league meeting. In a conference room at the Hyatt Regency Hotel, Trump set out to persuade everyone to move their schedule to the fall and go head-to-head with the NFL. "People don't want to watch spring football," he told them, a bald-faced assertion for which he provided no evidence. He assured the assembled owners that he could singlehandedly control the business of sports broadcasting.

"I guarantee you folks in this room that I will produce CBS, and I will produce NBC, and that I will produce ABC, guaranteed and for a hell of a lot more money than the horseshit you're getting right now," he told the football executives. He pitched the outcome of the war he wanted to wage as sealing the inevitable legacy of every owner, especially himself. "I don't want to be a loser. I've never been a loser before. And if we're losers in this, fellas, I will tell you what, it's going to haunt us . . . Every time there's an article written about you, it's going to be you owned this goddamn team which failed . . . and I'm not going to be a failure."

As HE HAD with his prior project, Donald gave Ivana a visual design role with the football team: uniforms for the cheerleaders. She worked with a fashion designer to come up with an outfit she described as "partly Star Wars, partly military type." The top bore three bars of color across the front, epaulets on the shoulders, braided rope, and cowgirl boots.

Ivana was also traveling to Atlantic City periodically to review interior-design choices for the coming Trump casino in partnership with Harrah's. And she was nine months pregnant with their third child. She scheduled an appointment to induce labor late on a Friday, hoping to miss as little work as possible. A boy, whom they named Eric, was born in the early evening of January 6, 1984.

She missed only five workdays. On the Sunday nine days after Eric's birth, she and Donald appeared together in the lobby at Trump Tower at a private event staged to bring attention to the football team. A panel of judges would select thirty young women from a group of finalists to become the Generals' cheerleading squad, a job that paid thirty-five dollars per home game. The young women who tried out wore tiny and tight red leotards with sashes bearing the team's name and danced to a playlist heavy with Michael Jackson songs. The judges added to the surreal atmosphere: LeRoy Neiman, the famous painter of the sports world with a mustache as subtle as a warthog's tusk. Joey Adams, the seventy-three-year-old comedian who got his start in vaudeville. And, as if to make the whole thing seem like an absurdist commentary on the links between celebrity and culture, the artist Andy Warhol judged the unknown fame seekers through his bush of white straw bangs.

Waiters served caviar sandwiches on silver platters. An eight-foot-long floral football, covered in red carnations and white daisies, rested on a podium. A man wearing a kilt played a bagpipe from the top of an escalator.

"This is a natural place for the tryouts," Ivana said during the event. "We have a lot of charity dinners and other parties here." It was true that the Trumps frequently closed the atrium for private events. And each time they did, the cheerleader tryouts included, they broke the agreement Donald had signed with the city. The atrium was a public space that Donald used as a private banquet facility.

Trump Tower had become not just his base of operations but his place for everything. He lived on the top three floors and commuted to his office on the twenty-sixth floor. He frequently ate at the restaurant in the lobby. His parents, Fred and Mary, came in from Queens for lunch and a visit at the restaurant. Trump gave his parents an apartment in the building, should they want to stay in Manhattan after a visit, which they said they never did.

Ivana and the influential interior designer they hired, Angelo Donghia, had just completed work on their seven-bedroom apartment. The look reflected Donghia's signature mix of understated elegance and comfort. Donald described it as "warm modern" and told *Architectural Digest* that they "wanted it decorated as an important apartment." The shimmer and shine of the tower's public spaces could be found in the residence as well. The living room featured a marble fireplace and windows nearly twenty feet high, leading up to a gold-leafed ceiling. Some pieces were upholstered in understated neutral tones, others in gold-painted fabric. The stairwell was lined with bronze mirrored panels and brass handrails. Their bedroom was bathed in the "feminine" feeling Ivana requested, with peach-pink mirrors and peach-colored suede walls. On the top of the three floors there were bedrooms for each of their three children, along with a second kitchen and dining room. There was a separate bedroom for their two nannies, both Irish-born women who worked alternating shifts.

Millions of dollars had been spent on the renovation. Donald publicly spoke of the importance of the design. He had gone along with the decisions as they were presented to him on paper. But in the end, he did not like what he saw. He would soon order a complete redo on the décor, which he came to see as insufficiently glitzy.

While Ivana worked to win his approval for her design savvy and substance as a businessperson, there were signs that Donald had soured on the marriage. Out of public view, he ordered changes to the prenuptial agreement that Roy Cohn had crafted prior to their wedding. Now, should they split, he would be the sole owner of the triplex, and she would own the mansion in Greenwich. Ivana would also receive a lump sum of $2.5 million.

The evening of the cheerleader finals, Donald and Ivana were featured on the second special of *Lifestyles of the Rich and Famous*, hosted by Robin Leach. The opening sequence presented the show's signposts of extravagance: a country estate, a yacht, a helicopter, and a jet, and young women in bikinis. The five-minute segment on the Trumps began by introducing him with the wrong middle initial: "Rome wasn't built in a day," an unidentified announcer said. "But it might have been, and at a handsome profit, if this man lived there. Donald S. Trump, head of a billion-dollar real estate empire." The scene cut to Donald, sitting at his desk in Trump Tower with a window behind revealing treetops across Central Park. He earnestly introduced himself to viewers using a phrase similar to the one he had used two years earlier to introduce himself to his new business partners at Harrah's: "At an age of thirty-seven, I don't believe anyone's really ever built more things than we have, in terms of the business that I'm in."

Donald would make recurring appearances on the show. Leellen Patchen, a director on *Lifestyles* for its entire run, later recalled that Trump, unlike most people they approached in the business world, could always be relied upon to open his life to the show's prying cameras and say things that would make viewers' heads snap. "Trump made great TV," she said. "Great TV to me is something people will watch and go, Oh, my gosh, did that really just happen? Or, did he just really say that? Or, does he just really have that? You know, it's excesses."

During that first appearance, Donald described a business philosophy that the show dubbed "Trump's Money-No-Object Motto." He posited that any amount he spent to create a business would generate an even larger increase in revenue. "I believe in spending extra money," he said. "I believe in expending maybe more money than other people would think almost rational. Because in the long run you're talking about a very small difference in terms of the money spent, but you're almost guaranteeing success."

One USFL team owner emerged as the leading foil to Donald's plan. John Bassett, owner of the USFL's Tampa Bay Bandits, believed in David Dixon's model of growing expenses only as revenue increased. Bassett had owned a team in the World Football League, which had failed in the 1970s in large part because it could not compete with the NFL for television contracts, and he was not looking to repeat that failure by rushing things. The payroll of his entire team was less than Herschel Walker's contract.

Bassett had always been passionate about sports, having played four sports in college and been a local squash champion in Ontario. He had been born to wealth, the son of a Canadian media mogul and sports team owner, but never hid that fact. He went on to produce films and own a cable television network, along with several other professional sports teams in Canada. But he came away from those experiences with an entirely different approach to business, and publicity, than Donald Trump.

In October 1983, he wrote a letter to his fellow owners warning that salary escalation had reached "a point where our biggest market could not break even if it sold out every seat." It was a business "structure that strangled us financially and took our fate out of our own hands."

Bassett was not alone in that view. Another owner, Tad Taube of the Oakland Invaders, also warned that inflated spending on salaries threatened the league's existence. "If we are not successful in establishing player caps," Taube wrote in a letter to other owners, "I can guarantee that there will not be a USFL within three years, irrespective of improved television revenue." He concluded by saying, "We have sighted the enemy, and they are us!"

As frustrated as he grew with what he saw as Donald's undisciplined approach, Bassett became just as exasperated with the news organizations that broadcast his every utterance. As a young man, Bassett had worked at a newspaper owned by his father, becoming the third-generation newspaperman in his family. He read *The New York Times* with a mix of awe and anger on April 15, 1984. An article on the front page of the sports section quoted an unidentified league executive who announced that "people who control the league" had made "an executive decision" to move the USFL to a fall schedule. Bassett, identified in the article as a member of this amorphous grouping, knew it was entirely untrue.

"*The New York Times* is supposed to be the most respected newspaper in the world and all they listen to is Donald Trump, who has duped them," Bassett told *The Sporting News*. "[The story] is absolute nonsense. I hate to see [the *Times*] used by a con man. It upsets the hell out of me. Donald Trump is trying to manage the news and browbeat the rest of the owners in this league. In the end, his philosophical view may be correct, but his tactics stink. At this point there is absolutely no basis to [the story] whatsoever."

"We haven't even come close to considering something like that," Myles Tanenbaum, owner of the Philadelphia Stars, told *The Sporting News*. "It's not even responsible to talk about it. The guy who came up with the idea is wonderful. He never lets himself become encumbered by facts."

Around that time, Trump rented a room at the Pierre hotel in Manhattan, four blocks uptown from Trump Tower, for a meeting with Pete Rozelle, the commissioner of the NFL. The meeting remained a secret for several years. Rozelle, who took notes, said Trump issued a passive threat to file an antitrust lawsuit against the NFL unless he was granted an expansion NFL team in New York. If that happened, Trump said he would "find some stiff" to buy the Generals and drop any lawsuit plans.

When asked about the meeting later, Trump presented an opposite account. It was Rozelle who offered a sort of bribe: keep the USFL on a spring schedule, drop the lawsuit plans, and I'll get you an NFL franchise. Trump's account did not comport with the agreed-upon facts: it was Trump who set up the meeting; and Rozelle did not have the power to award an NFL franchise. That would have required approval of twenty-one of the twenty-eight team owners. The two did not reach an accord.

Despite what Trump had told the *Times*, less than half of the owners supported his plan. The USFL hired McKinsey & Company, a leading management consulting firm, to explore the potential risks and rewards of moving to the fall. It was the type of standard business process, consulting with experts, that Donald Trump increasingly did not respect.

In August 1984, after the end of Donald's first season as an owner, Sharon Patrick of McKinsey presented the findings to the league owners during a meeting at the Hyatt Regency Hotel in Chicago. She urged a measured path, keeping costs in line with revenues and the schedule in the spring, through at least the 1986 season, and not considering a major change to the fall until at least then. She added that the market research study had found that the public disputes between the owners over when to play and spending on players had created doubts in the minds of fans about the league's long-term prospects. Taking on the NFL, she said, would spell near certain death for the league.

Once Patrick left the room, Trump told the owners that the McKinsey report was "bullshit." Move to the fall now, he said, or he would likely bail out and take all the attention with him. He assured them again that rich television contracts were a sure thing. Several, including John Bassett, thought McKinsey's cautious plan made sense. But with several clubs in financial trouble after spending money on players to keep up with Trump, enough owners bought into Trump's mix of threats and promises to vote in favor of moving to the fall in 1986.

Despite Trump's promises, the television networks vowed only to take a look when, and if, the USFL finalized its plans for a fall schedule. ABC made clear that the move would jeopardize its contract with the league. "We don't think it makes sense to go head-to-head with the NFL on Sunday afternoons," Jim Spence, the ABC Sports senior vice president, told the *Times*.

Trump pushed for one final move, hiring Roy Cohn to file an antitrust lawsuit against the NFL and perhaps the three national television networks. It was not a novel idea. The NFL had been sued, unsuccessfully, under antitrust laws by the upstart American Football League in 1960 and the new World Football League in 1979. Both lawsuits failed. Trump was sure this time would be different.

Cohn called a news conference to announce the lawsuit at the Upper East Side townhouse that served as both his home and his office. He and Trump both wore red-and-white-striped shirts and sat next to each other on a sofa while speaking to reporters. Cohn, his sun-leathered skin taut around squinty eyes, accused the NFL of operating a "secret" committee "created exclusively for the purpose of combating the USFL." Extracting the menace from those words left the plain meaning that the NFL was running a competitive business. Trump told reporters he was sure that the NFL was "petrified."

"If you are going to play football in the spring, you cannot get the monies necessary to make it an economic, to make it a viable, a really viable enterprise," Trump told the assembled reporters. "So, we have to go into the fall. We go into the fall and what do we find? We find the NFL is on all three networks."

Trump could have discovered that fact by buying a copy of *TV Guide* instead of a football team. Yet he continued to spend without any apparent concern about the need for increased television revenue. After being knocked out of the 1984 playoffs in the first round with Brian Sipe as quarterback, Trump pursued an even bigger deal with Doug Flutie, who had become a national sensation in his senior year at Boston College with a Hail Mary pass in a nationally televised game. At five foot ten, Flutie was generally considered too small for the modern NFL. But Trump signed him to an $8.2 million contract over six years, with the first two guaranteed.

In the 1985 season, Flutie struggled in his early games. A reporter from UPI received an unsolicited call from one John Baron, Donald's alter ego, complaining that other USFL owners had not come through on a verbal promise they had made to cover part of the cost of Flutie's contract. "When a guy goes out and spends more money than a player is worth, he expects to get partial reimbursement from the other owners," Baron said. "Everybody asked Trump to go out and sign Flutie . . . for the good of the league."

The wire story ran in newspapers across the country. Other owners scoffed at the idea and said they had never been asked to cover Trump's costs, and they would not have agreed if they had been. Flutie, for his part, was not pleased at being called overpaid. Donald called reporters again, this time in his own name, to complain that his man John Baron had been misquoted: Donald wanted the money from the other owners, but he had not overpaid for Flutie.

Following up on the Flutie stories, Bob Sansevere of the Minneapolis *Star Tribune* called Trump's office and asked to speak with John Baron. He noticed that Baron's voice was "shockingly similar to Trump's." He called back to check the basic facts and was given three different spellings of the name Baron. One secretary told him Baron had only recently been hired and another said he had been with the company "a long time" and "absolutely" exists. Sansevere wrote a brief story pointing out that no beat reporters had ever seen Baron and suspected the name was "an alias Trump uses." But the local story received no national coverage. It caused no moment of shame for Donald, no moment of reputational reckoning. He would continue hiding behind the name for years to come with impunity.

The league was now running with Donald Trump's playbook. The lawsuit, Trump's final gambit, would need to produce a win before the league spent itself into oblivion.

As he pushed to change professional football, construction on the casino neared completion. He had signed off quickly on the design by Alan Lapidus, a design that broke with tradition by locating the casino on the second floor, making it not the first thing arriving guests would see. The silhouette of the casino resembled a white shoebox with a narrow thirty-nine-story hotel tower rising at one end. On the boardwalk side, the windowed walls tilted back at staggered angles, creating a glass pyramid for the first few floors. The tower had a saw toothed design similar to Trump Tower to maximize ocean views from the 614 hotel rooms. The day he first saw the sketches in Lapidus's office, Donald quickly blurted out what was becoming a signature phrase: "Don't change anything."

His company's payroll, overseen by his father's accountant in Brooklyn, would remain small even as he took on another large-scale project. He chose a big construction company, Perini Corporation, to build the casino, and then hired a dozen temporary construction managers to watch over Perini. He relied heavily on his brother, Robert, to be a regular presence at the site. As at Trump

Tower, Ivana would be involved with interior-design choices. And the gaming floor and lobby would be dominated by shiny surfaces. Harrah's executives began referring to the Trump aesthetic as "brass, glass and class."

Harrah's booked big-name entertainers, including Sammy Davis Jr. and Bob Hope, for the 750-seat showroom to fill the casino in the first couple of weeks. An enclosed catwalk had been built connecting the gambling hall to the giant old Atlantic City Convention Center next door. For the grand opening in June, Harrah's rented the convention center for three nights and booked Neil Diamond, the singer-songwriter whose eight prior albums had each gone platinum. The 17,000-seat arena sold out for all three nights, guaranteeing a rush of potential gamblers.

Diamond had enough hits in his pocket to bring down the house—"Sweet Caroline," "Cracklin' Rosie," "Forever in Blue Jeans." He opened with "America," a pean to immigrants:

Far,
We've been traveling far,
Without a home,
But not without a star

Holmes Hendricksen, Harrah's director of entertainment, looked out across the floor of the barrel-roofed hall, thumping from the power of Diamond's voice and his eight-member band. He saw thousands of fans singing and dancing along. A success, he thought. He expected that Harrah's partner, Donald Trump, who would receive half the profits without performing any further work, would be pleased as well. But when he found Donald and Ivana watching the performance, Donald's face was knotted in a scowl.

"How much is this fucking guy costing me?" Trump shouted above the music.

Trump had expressed anger with his partners over the last month. The casino's soft opening in mid-May, tightly controlled by casino regulators, revealed problems with the operation of slot machines. Regulators would not let all 1,734 slots open for nearly a month, resulting in the loss of millions in potential revenues. The opening of large casinos rarely came off perfectly, but Donald used the blip to attack Harrah's management abilities and set the stage for a potential breakup.

Though he was willing to spend any amount to bring attention to his football team, and described almost irrational spending as his business model on *Lifestyles*, Donald would object to almost all spending by his partners on the Plaza casino. Satre, Harrah's gaming executive, pushed Donald to meet his commitment to build a parking garage with thirty-two hundred spaces on land Trump controlled across the street from the casino. The Plaza was intended to attract higher-end gamblers, and Harrah's had the lower-end bus crowd covered at their other Atlantic City casino, in the marina area about one mile away.

Just as with the McKinsey report on the USFL, Donald showed contempt for Harrah's market research. Darrell Luery, Harrah's general manager at the Plaza casino, regularly showed Donald the company's research. Harrah's knew their customers' net worth, how many minutes they were likely to spend gambling, even the intervals at which they would take bathroom breaks. "We would get into a certain amount of detail, and he would dismiss it," Luery remembered years later. Donald would say, "Never mind that crap," and change the subject.

Under the partnership agreement, Donald and Robert had no voice in operational matters other than the approval of budgets. From Harrah's perspective, there was no reason for them to be on-site once construction was completed. But they were both there. And Donald complained. A lot. He would even complain when he learned a gambler had been on a winning streak. In his mind, that represented lost money, not the cost of running a casino. He complained because eighty-five suites built with amenities aimed at high rollers were often sitting empty, but he refused to build the parking lot that might help fill those rooms. He complained about Harrah's plans to spend more on services to make the casino stand out in a marketplace that had quickly grown competitive. The Plaza was the city's tenth casino, and three more were under construction.

Donald grew increasingly frustrated with the Plaza casino barely breaking even month after month, while he read that Harrah's Marina was recording significant profits. He began demanding that Harrah's somehow push their Marina customers to instead go play at the Plaza. Satre made clear that would not happen. "That caused a lot of, how do I put it, angry responses from him and disagreements over how the properties should be run," Satre later recalled. "He didn't want to do what was necessary in order to be competitive, and from a standpoint of both wages, but also product and the customer's experience."

Robert periodically tried to smooth things over. Luery met with Robert Trump at least weekly and considered him "a lot more calm and reasonable" and "a joy" to be around. Unlike his brother, Robert saw the value in the extensive research that a large public corporation can pull together about the marketplace and its customers. But, ultimately, Robert answered to his brother. During one lunch at the casino, Robert suggested that Donald deserved as much attention from the Holiday corporation as the company devoted to all its other shareholders combined.

In October 1984, Harrah's agreed to rechristen the casino without its name, as Trump Plaza Hotel and Casino, ostensibly to help eliminate any possible confusion among customers between the Plaza and the Harrah's Marina casino a mile away. Some confusion would remain. The original $500,000 sign that read "Harrah's at Trump Plaza" would stay atop the building for months. The slot machines would carry the Harrah's name, though the cocktail napkins would bear only the Trump brand. None of it would assuage Donald. He repeatedly accused Harrah's, considered to be one of the best-run casino companies in the industry, of tarnishing his name, which he had for several years been referring to as something that added value to everything it touched. Someone identified only as an "associate of Trump" told *The Philadelphia Inquirer*: "He built them a Lamborghini and they didn't know how to turn the key. And his name was on it. And his success is his name."

Satre and other Harrah's executives came to believe that Trump, who had once recognized that he needed their expertise to get the casino up and running, now wanted to become a major casino figure on his own, something he thought would not be possible as a second to Harrah's. So he began undermining the partnership as soon as construction ended.

Satre traveled to New Jersey for a meeting with Trump at the new casino. With staff members watching, things quickly devolved into a "vicious argument" about money. Both wanted the Plaza positioned as a higher-end casino, but Trump loudly refused to approve any expenditures. He still refused to build the parking garage.

As Trump battled with his partners at Harrah's, the Hilton corporation was putting the finishing touches on another Atlantic City casino and hotel directly across the street from Harrah's casino in the marina district. But the Hilton corporation, one of the country's premiere hotel companies, was having trouble obtaining a license to operate. The Casino Control Commission, which was created to keep the mob out of Atlantic City, raised questions about Hilton's thirteen-year business relationship with Sidney Korshak, a lawyer, on labor issues. Government reports had described Korshak as a senior adviser to organized crime groups in several states, though he was never formally charged with any crime.

After examining the relationship, the commission's investigative arm, the state's Division of Gaming Enforcement within the Attorney General's Office, recommended that the commission grant Hilton's application, and the commission's chairman followed suit. But two commissioners refused to go along, and in February 1985 the Hilton application was denied, just as the company's $308 million casino neared completion. In the history of the commission, it was the only time that it had denied a license to a publicly traded corporation.

It was a tremendously lucky break for Donald Trump. Hilton needed to sell its new casino, and quickly. Donald's license to operate in Atlantic City meant he was one of the few people in the world who could buy a casino without risk of being denied. Some other casino operators were slowing down out of concern that it was not clear how many more casinos Atlantic City could support. Donald sped up.

The Hilton company and Donald negotiated a deal in ten days. Trump agreed to pay $320 million. He put in no cash of his own. He funded the purchase with $351.8 million in bonds, which brought him only $300 million after the expenses of issuing the bonds. He put everything else he owned up as collateral. Another $50 million from a bank loan covered the rest of the purchase price and other preopening expenses. The high interest rate of 13.75 percent on the bonds meant interest payments of $40 million a year, plus interest on the bank loan—big bills to cover. And that problem would grow in 1990, when Trump would also have to start paying back the principal on the bonds.

Satre called Donald, concerned about what this new hotel would mean for their partnership at the Plaza. He asked Donald what he intended to call the new hotel, and he warned Donald that placing the Trump name on the hotel would violate his partnership contract with Harrah's.

"I wouldn't do that to our partnership," Satre later remembered Trump saying.

But he did just that. He soon announced that he would call the new casino Trump Castle. He wrote Satre a letter striking a very different note than he had on the phone. "The Trump name has been so badly bloodied by your management of the facility," Trump wrote, "that hopefully Trump's Castle Casino Hotel can do something to bring it back."

On the day the Castle opened in June 1985, Trump's partners at Harrah's sued him for breaching a noncompete clause. Satre complained that Harrah's had already spent $8 million promoting the Trump name in Atlantic City, and now Trump was opening a casino that would compete with Trump Plaza, in addition to their Marina casino across the street. Trump countersued, arguing that the problems with the slot machines at the Plaza opening, and a small outbreak of salmonella poisoning among customers, threatened to damage his name. He now spoke of his name as a product of great worth, portable to any sort of business.

"I have created the value that exists in my name by investing an enormous amount of skill, time, energy, effort and resources in developing highly successful and highly publicized real estate and other business ventures that have made the name Trump famous and synonymous with me," he wrote in an affidavit.

He increasingly saw no value in working with partners, or in heeding the advice of others, whether prominent business consultants, experienced sports team owners, or executives with one of the best-run hotel and casino companies in the world.

A year after finishing construction on the Plaza casino, and having never run a casino on his own, he had taken on enormous and expensive debt in buying the Castle. If he prevailed in the lawsuit with Harrah's, he would have to come up with hundreds of millions of dollars more to buy them out, a further gamble on his unproven operational abilities. And none of that had very much to do with developing real estate, his primary area of expertise.

17

RISK AND REWARD

Barbara Res was bored. She had played a major role in the renovation of the Grand Hyatt and led construction of Trump Tower for Donald. But the Trump Organization had not started any new construction for more than two years and had nothing on the horizon. Res wanted to build more skyscrapers, but she had been reduced to helping office tenants in Trump Tower complete their interior renovations. She reluctantly found another job, this one overseeing construction of a headquarters for Hartz Mountain Industries, a manufacturer of pet foods and owner and developer of millions of square feet of real estate in New Jersey. Trump graciously asked her to stay and threw her a going-away party in the office when she declined. He gave her a Cartier bracelet engraved with the words "Towers of Thanks, Love, Donald." She thought she might someday return.

Trump had hoped to be building something in the city by now, but all his efforts had failed or stalled. Three years after he had bought the building just south of Central Park, he still had not been able to evict more than one hundred tenants protected by rent regulation laws, a predictable outcome to those familiar with rent regulations in New York. He had filed lawsuits, not maintained the building, had windows covered in foil to make the building look shabby, reduced security, even turned off heat and hot water. Trump insisted, with no evidence, that the tenants were "millionaires who send their limousines to pick up their lawyers" while claiming to be middle class. He called it an "injustice" committed upon himself.

He had also failed to build an apartment building he would have called Trump Castle, with glass turrets and a moat, on the Upper East Side. His partner, Prudential, dropped out after concluding that Donald's plan to put up a building that required selling apartments for $1.5 million each was out of touch with the realities of the marketplace.

He had paid an architect to draw up plans for the world's tallest building and pitched city officials on letting him develop it on a filled-in section of the river near Wall Street. The respected architecture critic for the *Chicago Tribune* commissioned his own sketch of what Trump's 150-story tower might look like in proportion to its surroundings and concluded that "the world's tallest tower would be one of the silliest things anyone could inflict on New York or any other city." The critic, Paul Gapp, added that the building would be so narrow on the upper floors that it would be "economically inefficient . . . because so much space in their interior cores must be devoted to elevator shafts, fire stairs, and a myriad of mechanical entrails." Trump sued Gapp and the newspaper for $500 million. A judge tossed out the lawsuit almost as quickly as Trump's proposal for the building failed.

He had also proposed, in early 1985, a massive 130-story tower near Central Park in Manhattan but lost out in the bidding. Trump blamed the same demons that he believed had vexed him six years earlier, when his plan for Trump Tower faced a momentary bump in the city approval process. In his mind, he was being singled out, persecuted. "It was easier for me 10 years ago," he told the *Los Angeles Times*. "Nobody knew who I was, and nobody cared. Then, I wasn't the guy everyone was trying to stop."

There was stronger evidence that, as a city official noted at the time, Donald's best ally in those early projects had been the business cycle. Winning approval for zoning changes and tax abatements came easier in a down economy, and by the time he finished, the market had risen to make the project more profitable. Now, during a building boom and with the economy up, approvals came harder, and any delay meant a project could reach completion just as everything turned south.

THERE WAS ONE PIECE of property that Donald had never forgotten—the former rail yards on the West Side of Manhattan, the seventy-two acres on which he had let his option to buy expire in 1979. The current holder of the option, an Argentinian developer, Francesco Macri, had paid architects to design a huge project: nineteen buildings, with ten million square feet of indoor space, including forty-three hundred apartments. He had won city approval, but made big promises in exchange, including a commitment to contribute $33 million toward the rebuilding of a nearby subway stop to handle the tide of new residents. Macri had been unable to obtain financing for the $1 billion project. He had taken out a $75 million loan from Chase Manhattan for seed money, and it just so happened that his banker at Chase was Conrad Stephenson, Fred Trump's primary banker who had helped Donald obtain financing for the Grand Hyatt and Trump Tower. In mid-1984, Stephenson foreclosed on Macri's loan, putting pressure on the Argentinian to quickly line up financing elsewhere or risk losing everything.

Around that time, Norman Levin's phone started ringing. After growing up in South Africa, where he earned a master's degree in urban planning and designed squatters' camps, Levin moved to New York City to pursue bigger urban projects and wound up at Macri's firm working on the West Side project. The word inside Macri's company was that Stephenson was pushing Macri out because he wanted to force a transfer to Donald Trump. And now Trump was calling Levin.

"He had started to call me quietly behind the scenes, asking me my view on the project, what I thought about it, what the pricing was going to be, whether it was a viable operation," Levin later recalled. He would answer Trump's questions, and then brief his colleagues at Macri about the call.

Later that year, city officials added to the pressure on Macri by setting a deadline of February 1985 for him to obtain financing or lose approval for his project. Macri had been pushed into a corner. He agreed to let Stephenson, who had confidence that Trump could navigate the approval and construction process, hand the project to Trump. Trump took over Macri's loan and added another $40 million to the tab. Donald assumed a $115 million mortgage and responsibility for property taxes, and finally owned the largest undeveloped swath of land in Manhattan.

Before the deal was even announced, Donald showed up one day at Macri's offices in midtown Manhattan. He arrived alone and asked all the employees to meet with him. They gathered in a conference room with renderings on a wall showing the Macri plan, a design by Rafael Viñoly, a Uruguayan-born architect whose New York–based firm designed major buildings around the world. After a few moments of discussing the plan, Donald interrupted. He shocked the people in the room, who had battled and compromised to win approval for the project, by saying he thought it was too small. Given the commitment to pay for improvements to the subway, Donald did not think the scope of the project as approved for Macri was sufficient to cover costs. He intended to nearly triple its size, even filling some space that Macri had left clear to preserve the view of an existing apartment building. Trump said something to the effect of "I'm going to build in front of these guys, they don't own the view," as Levin recalled.

It was a colossal gamble, throwing out a plan that had barely made it through the city's now very difficult approval process and pushing for something three times as big. Levin told him that he didn't think a bigger project would fly with the community groups, but Donald was confident that he could make it happen.

Trump announced that he had hired Helmut Jahn, a German-born architect then known for his involvement in some of the tallest buildings planned in the world. Jahn, a short man with long flowing hair, favored wide-brimmed hats and flashy double-breasted striped suits. At forty-five years old, his Chicago-based firm was working on skyscrapers in Houston, Philadelphia, Chicago, and Frankfurt, Germany.

"I like big better than small," he once told a reporter. To Trump, it sounded like a match made in architecture heaven. In announcing that he had hired Jahn, Donald said, "I wanted the ultimate in architecture for the job and, therefore, the ultimate architect."

Donald also stole Levin away from the Macri firm. Levin took an office on the twenty-sixth floor at Trump Tower, joining the very small staff of a couple secretaries and family members—Ivana and Robert both had offices—along with the lawyer, Harvey Freeman, Louise Sunshine, and a leasing agent. Levin would handle everything to do with the rail yards that Donald did not do himself, keeping tabs on the outside lawyers, consultants, and architects working toward developing a new plan, finding financing, and winning city approval. At first, he answered to Robert and Harvey, but they were still occupied with the new casino. He asked them if he could report directly to Donald, which he guessed would be better for his career as well as the project. Robert and Harvey both grinned, as if they knew something that Levin had not yet figured out, and let him do as he wished.

Levin had a few pleasant exchanges with Donald, simple updates on next steps, before he encountered a different version of the man. One morning, Trump greeted him by screaming insults. He had heard that people were walking through the deserted rail yards unimpeded. "Why hasn't the site been fenced off?" Trump screamed. "Anybody can walk on there! This has got to be closed down! You're not doing your job!"

Levin was about Donald's age. He had been in the working world for fifteen years. But he had never seen anyone erupt with the unhinged hostility Donald displayed that day. "That explosion absolutely unnerved me," he recalled decades later. But he would soon come to expect more. "Pretty much everybody in the office had to experience this explosion from time to time."

Trump arranged for a cyclone fence to surround the property, peppered with large blue signs bearing his signature and this command: "Respect this land . . . They're not making any more of it."

WITHIN MONTHS, Jahn's design came together. Its most striking feature and centerpiece would be the one Donald cared about the most: The world's tallest building, a 150-story colossus piercing the skyline. Jahn's design called for six other towers, all skyscrapers in their own right at 76 stories and lined up in a row. He proposed dealing with the challenging terrain—the elevated West Side Highway along the western edge and uneven slopes between it and the river—by covering the entire plot with a gigantic platform that would cut off much of the surrounding neighborhoods from the waterfront.

Some of the staff and consultants around Donald tried to talk him down from the scope of the project, especially the central tower. Levin told him the amount of people he planned to funnel into that neighborhood through the Upper West Side would create massive problems and put community approval in jeopardy. Even the Federal Aviation Administration would now have to sign off, with this structure piercing crucial flight paths. There were concerns about the economic viability of such a tall building. Der Scutt, Trump's friend and occasional favorite architect, would say, "The only reason you would want to build a one-hundred-fifty-story tower is for status, economically it is insane." But Levin remembers the internal pushback being fairly tame. Robert went along with everything. And the rest of the group, given Donald's success with winning local approval on the Grand Hyatt, Trump Tower, and his casino, relied on Donald.

"I think people were mesmerized by him," Levin later recalled. "He had this extraordinary charisma that anything he said was like gospel." But Levin saw trouble in Donald's inability, or unwillingness, to respect honest and clear-eyed analyses. He trusted his instinct, which became a proxy for his ego. "He's not reviewing the pros and cons," Levin thought at the time. "He's not balancing the risk-reward. He's not looking at the technical viability. He's looking at how does he look good. And I knew that there's very little we could do to sway him because as long as his ego was on the line, his sense of self-importance was on the line, that that was the primary thing. None of the facts and figures that we presented made any difference."

As Jahn finished models of his design, NBC announced that it might look to leave its historic headquarters in Rockefeller Center as its leases expired in the coming years. Donald directed Jahn to add space for a modern television studio on the site. He reached out to NBC and leaked items to gossip columnists that he might snag the network. An anchor tenant of that magnitude would greatly improve his chances of obtaining financing for the project. He would call it Television City. Just as he had seemed brazenly confident that he could "produce" television networks to write massive checks to the USFL, Donald now seemed completely confident that he could produce the network to anchor his largest project ever.

As the announcement approached, Fred Trump visited his son's offices at Trump Tower. He had turned eighty and lost a step. Earlier that year, while accepting an award that honors Americans whose lives reflected a "rags-to-riches" story, Fred had misattributed his own father's favorite saying—"Never follow an empty wagon, because nothing ever falls off"—to Shakespeare. As he spoke the words "empty wagon" he tapped his forehead and said "up here" to precisely define the metaphor. A cancer scare had also altered his appearance. A lump on his neck, along with part of his jaw, had been surgically removed, leaving a pronounced indentation in front of his right ear.

In his son's office that day, Fred marveled at Jahn's model of Television City. Levin was struck by the older man's lack of airs, how he could have been any older gent on the street while no doubt being the richest man Levin had ever met. Fred asked Levin what he thought of the project. Would it be successful? As Levin answered, Donald entered the room and took over, narrating a tour of the model for his father. After Fred left, Donald turned to Levin and said, "My father, he could never do something like this."

What Fred had done was build a family fortune, one that Donald diminished when he described it, while at the same time lying that it was all his. When the fourth annual Forbes 400 list came out that October, it dropped Fred from the list under the false claim that "full control apparently belongs to flamboyant son, Donald." The listing for Donald, the first in which all his father's wealth was attributed to him, said he "took over 1976" after "they amassed 20,000 NYC apts" and that Donald's "net worth should exceed $600 million." It was a step beyond the exaggerations he told the magazine in 1982, and still not true. Fred stubbornly retained complete ownership of his empire, a fact becoming a source of strife within the family. Should Fred have died before transferring his assets through a trust, Donald and his siblings would likely have been forced to sell off much of it to cover the estate tax bill. By then, Fred's properties carried almost no debt and were kicking off millions of dollars annually in pure profit, swelling his cash on hand every year. By contrast, Donald had buried his businesses under mountains of debt.

But Fred, so determined to find immortality in his son's accomplishments, never seemed to question why Donald lied about him to elevate his own stature. He never wavered in his support, even as Donald broke the fundamental rules of business that had been central to Fred's success. Careful planning and financial forecasting. A hesitancy to take on large debts, and never with a personal guarantee. Fred's eternal and unquestioning support came to define Donald's idea of loyalty, his baseline expectation for anyone wishing to remain in his good graces. It also became a level of grace he extended to no one.

TRUMP AND HOWARD RUBENSTEIN's public relations firm scheduled a news conference to announce his plans for the rail yards, including the world's tallest building. Newspapers across the country carried wire-service articles teasing the announcement for Monday morning, November 19, 1985, in a ballroom at the Grand Hyatt, the site of Donald's first success.

The revered CBS news program *60 Minutes* had been working on a profile of Donald. A producer on the show later recalled that segment came about organically from the simple observation that Donald Trump seemed to be everywhere. But whether due to serendipity or careful scheduling by Rubenstein and Trump, the show aired nationally the evening before Donald's big announcement. Known for his tough scrutiny of subjects, correspondent Mike Wallace opened the segment by lending his voice to Donald Trump's favorite version of himself. "In a world where mere millionaires have become a dime a dozen," Wallace said, "there's a new billionaire in town. Trump's the name. Donald Trump."

The most serious news program on national television had just crowned Donald Trump a billionaire, nearly double the level of wealth that *Forbes* assigned to him based on his lies. Wallace asked one question that went to the segment's reason for being—Trump's penchant for putting his name on everything.

"It sells, Mike," Donald answered. "It has nothing to do with the ego. All I know is it sells."

The piece showed Wallace and Donald walking through the weedy rail yards, with Trump promising "magnificent marinas, shopping, restaurants, everything, all over the Hudson River." Wallace briefly asked Donald about potential obstacles he might face from the community and the city. Trump brushed them aside, again framing his life as a triumphant struggle against those who oppose him. "I've had trouble all my life, as far as that's concerned," he answered. But, Wallace responded, "you want tax abatements, you want special treatment, and by and large you've gotten special treatment and tax abatements."

"That's correct," Donald answered.

As the segment ended, Wallace told viewers: "Tomorrow morning Donald Trump will reveal his plans to build the tallest building on Manhattan Island."

The table was set, the appetite whetted. The next morning, the Empire Ballroom at the Grand Hyatt filled with reporters and Donald's supporters and contractors. He stood on a dais in front of nine photographic blowups of Jahn's model forming a panorama behind him that spanned more than twenty feet. Sitting off to the side were his mother and father, his brother Robert, Jahn the architect, and Levin.

Donald described the 7,900 apartments, 1.7 million square feet of retail space, and 3 million square feet of offices, all surrounded by 40 acres of parks. He described the need for NBC to have modern television studio space and said he would name the project Television City, a brief departure from his habit of calling everything "Trump." And he spoke with passion about the 150-story centerpiece, more than 200 feet taller than the Sears Tower in Chicago, then the world's tallest building.

"The world's tallest building belongs in New York," he told the crowd. "The New York City dream is having this development, and we plan to build it."

That night, Donald and his advisers, including Levin and Jahn, made a presentation in a college auditorium to the local community board whose approval he would need. "Prepare yourself for one hell of a fight, Mr. Trump," chided resident Dora Friedman, to an eruption of cheers. She asked him how he expected an already crowded neighborhood to absorb another forty-five thousand people. "What are you going to do, Mr. Trump? Helicopter them in and drop them into the area?"

"It looks like the quintessential phallic symbol," Jan Levy, who lived nearby, told him. She looked at all his tall buildings lined up and said he had a lot of work to do. "You can start by chopping a lot of them off."

For most of his father's career, these citizen bodies had no role in zoning changes. The rules were revamped in the early 1960s as an attempt to end the sort of backroom deals that had allowed Fred Trump to grab the development rights for Trump Village away from a nonprofit organization. Donald Trump now walked into an Upper West Side where residents liked no place more on earth than the Upper West Side, as it existed, with few buildings taller than fifteen stories along the north-south avenues and mostly smaller four- or five-story buildings along the side streets.

Rather than respond in a combative note, Donald tried to make light of the brushback: "Of all the neighborhoods in New York, this is the one I get, right?"

Donald had succeeded again at winning national attention for a plan well before any aspect of it was a sure thing. But whether he could get it off the drawing board remained unclear. He was spending tens of millions of dollars a year on his loan and property taxes. He had bet it all on the belief that Macri's plan had failed because it was too small, and he could overcome community opposition with a much larger project.

He ran the risk, a tremendous risk in this case, of feeding the most ravenous money-eating predator in real estate: time. Though he often dismissed his father's expertise, he might have taken to heart a lesson Fred said he had tried to impart to his favorite son: "I always told Donald, 'If you dawdle, you lose your shirt. You pay interest 365 days a year.'"

18

ALL OF LIFE IS A STAGE

In the 1920s, as a young Fred Trump built his first few houses in Queens, the titans of an earlier era were growing restless with the level of comfort and glamour they found while wintering on a barrier island on the east coast of Florida. Many stayed for months at the Breakers, a 1,100-room luxury hotel with bungalows next to the Atlantic Ocean. It had been built in 1890 by Henry Flagler, a cofounder, with John D. Rockefeller, of Standard Oil. Flagler had founded the town of Palm Beach, the country's first answer to the Mediterranean riviera.

But Flagler's wealthy fellow industrialists came to feel that the well-appointed rooms and bungalows at the Breakers no longer provided everything they required for a pleasing three-month winter season. With untaxed fortunes from the Gilded Age, the booming years following the Civil War, they bought up large tracts of sand and scrub that spanned the narrow island between the Atlantic Ocean and Lake Worth. They commissioned the grandest estates in American history, matching in scope and detail what would have been considered castles in another era. With Spanish and Italian influences, the Mediterranean palaces featured grand rising towers, rows of arches and columns, and lavish tile work.

Steel magnate Henry Phipps built Casa Bendita (Blessed House) on twenty-eight acres. Joshua Cosden, who made his fortune in the oil fields of Oklahoma, built Playa Riente (Laughing Beach), a seventy-room mansion on twenty-seven acres. Eva Stotesbury, whose husband Edward Townsend "Ned" Stotesbury was a prominent investment banker, built El Mirasol (The Sunflower), a forty-room mansion, on forty-two acres.

And Marjorie Merriweather Post, who inherited the General Foods Corporation, bought seventeen acres and commissioned one of the larger mansions of the era: fifty-eight bedrooms, thirty-three bathrooms with gold-plated fixtures, and a massive living room with forty-two-foot-high ceilings. She called it Mar-a-Lago (Sea to Lake).

By the 1950s, as the original industrialists lost their fortunes or died, the astronomical costs of maintaining their beach palaces became too much for their heirs to bear. One by one, wrecking balls knocked them down to the sand, clearing the way for subdivisions of smaller, though still exclusive, retreats.

Mar-a-Lago was the one that survived, though barely. Post had wished for the mansion to serve as a winter White House for U.S. presidents, so Mar-a-Lago was given to the federal government after her death in 1973. President Richard M. Nixon made a surprise visit in a helicopter. But, as with the other Gilded Age beach mansions, the costs were too high, even for the U.S. government, which returned the property to the Post family foundation in 1980. The foundation, not wanting to cover the costs, listed the house for sale in 1981. Four brokers, including Sotheby's, marketed the property. Articles appeared in newspapers across the country, including the *New York Daily News* and *The New York Times*, announcing that the mansion could be purchased for upward of $15 million or $20 million. Newspapers reported on interest from a developer in Pittsburgh and a sheik from Saudi Arabia.

But Donald Trump remained in the dark, he would say, until he and Ivana vacationed at the Breakers during the winter of 1982–83. During a taxi ride, Donald asked the driver, "What's good around here that's for sale," he would later testify in a court deposition.

"Well, maybe Mar-a-Lago is for sale," the cabdriver said, according to Donald.

Months later, Donald bid $9 million, with a goal of subdividing the property into fourteen houses. The Post foundation rejected the offer because it did not believe he had a chance to win approval from the town. Other bidders emerged. The Marriott Corporation explored converting it into a resort. Two other groups of prospective buyers, at least one of whom planned to subdivide the property, backed out.

None of the serious potential buyers considered owning the property as a private residence. Then, in the fall of 1985, as he prepared to announce what would have been the largest development of his life on the West Side of Manhattan, Donald bid $8 million for the estate and its contents, plus another $2 million for a four-hundred-foot strip of beach across Ocean Boulevard from the mansion.

One last time, Conrad Stephenson, as he was about to retire from Chase, directed the bank to issue Donald a loan. The money was not secured by the property, only by a personal guarantee from Donald. Trump persuaded Chase that his personal guarantee meant the loan was not a mortgage and need not be filed with the local county government, the usual procedure for a mortgage. As a result, many news articles reported he had paid cash. But Trump could not have paid for a used Chevy Malibu with the money he put down. For the $10 million note, the bank only required a down payment of $2,812.

For those first few months, the Trumps flew back and forth between Florida and New York most weekends. Donald and Ivana engaged with the local old-money crowd, but at arm's length. They allowed Mar-a-Lago to be the site of a fundraiser for the local landmark preservation charity, but they relegated the black-tied and formal-gowned guests to an outdoor tent. They broke the staid local norms by letting *Lifestyles of the Rich and Famous* film the event as part of another profile of Donald Trump's wealth.

"Trump heads a two-billion-dollar-plus real estate empire," host Robin Leach said, a figure double what *60 Minutes* had said when it doubled what *Forbes* had incorrectly said. Leach promised viewers that learning what Trump had been up to would "shock, surprise, and delight you."

"He's bought a winter house! But not any winter house. This Trump castle is the number-one home in America," Leach said as a helicopter camera shot zoomed across the beach toward the estate's red-tile roofs. "It's the nation's largest and most expensive private residence. You're about to tour this incredible estate—all one hundred twenty-eight rooms!"

The scene eventually cut to Donald Trump, sitting in his newly acquired estate wearing a dark pinstripe suit, crisp white shirt, and red tie. "Other people wanted to buy Mar-a-Lago," he said. "Many, many other people. But they had different ideas. They wanted to condo it. They wanted to make it into a hotel. They wanted to do all, in my opinion, the wrong things with Mar-a-Lago. This is a treasure. This is a U.S. treasure. And it had to be preserved."

Ivana told Leach that they employed a staff of twenty-one, and it took four months for them to wax the furniture. Trump was soon spending more than $1.5 million a year to maintain his third home.

Leach worked in a moment to allow Trump to position himself as a thinker on world affairs. Apropos of nothing, he said to Donald: "You care very much about peace in the world" and asked Trump if he harbored any broader aspirations. "No political aspiration," Trump answered. "But I think we have a big problem. And I will tell you, as sure as we're sitting here, that if something isn't done about nuclear weaponry, and I mean quickly, your peace doesn't mean a damn thing, Robin, because all of the beauty of Mar-a-Lago, and all of the great people of the world, and of this country, and of other great countries, they're not going to be here to really enjoy what we were all trying to preserve."

WITH HIS DEBT MOUNTING and monthly expenses on a steep incline, Trump accelerated his spending. One day that year, as he looked across Lake Worth from Mar-a-Lago, he spotted two white thirty-two-story towers and wondered whether he might buy them. The towers had been mentioned in newspaper articles for years, especially after the bank foreclosed on the property the same month Donald bought Mar-a-Lago. But Donald Trump apparently did not know. He dispatched Bill Fugazy, a golfing buddy who owned a limousine company in New York City. Not shockingly, Fugazy learned the buildings could be bought.

Soon after, Trump bought the 221-apartment condominium project, except for the twelve units that had been sold, for $43 million. He took on a $60 million mortgage on the property. He paid Fugazy a $400,000 finder's fee and promised him up to $400,000 more if the deal became profitable. Sales of apartments in the towers, which backed up to a lower-income section of West Palm Beach, had been slow. More broadly, condominium sales across the state had cooled. The purchase would be a real-world test of whether Trump had the foresight to navigate his way through a down market, as well as of his long-held beliefs that anything with his name on it would sell. As a first step, he renamed the project Trump Plaza of the Palm Beaches.

"We changed the name," he told the *Miami Herald*, "because we have had such a tremendous success in New York with Trump Tower. Trump Tower is probably the most successful building in the country. This really has nothing to do with ego. It has become a tremendous selling tool. It's a name that represents quality, real quality."

He announced that he would have a big-name partner in the project: Lee Iacocca, the former head of the Chrysler Corporation who had become a celebrity in his own right after the publication of his business memoir. Trump made Iacocca a 50 percent owner in the project in exchange for Iacocca loaning the partnership $200,000 and guaranteeing about $20 million of the loan. Trump later said he had expected Iacocca to send potential buyers his way, though Iacocca never seemed clear about his role. "People think that I'm thinking about becoming a real estate tycoon," Iacocca said at the time. "I'm not. I'm in the car business. I've always believed that you are born for one business. I'm Donald Trump's partner, and real estate is his business."

Around the same time, Donald also bought the thirty-eight-story Hotel St. Moritz from Harry Helmsley for $73.2 million. Built in 1930 during a large-scale building boom along Central Park South, the hotel had been designed by Emery Roth, the architect who also designed some of the most iconic apartment buildings around Central Park, including the El Dorado, the Beresford, and the San Remo. The rooms had grown dowdy, but the upper floors offered stunning views of the park. Trump did not pay any cash. Bankers Trust issued him a mortgage for almost $6 million more than he paid, putting money in his pocket. But he was paying interest on another $80 million in borrowed money, for a hotel that had been underperforming for years. He said he would continue to run it as a hotel until he came up with a plan.

Not long after, he bought the New York Foundling Hospital on the Upper East Side of Manhattan from the Catholic Archdiocese of New York for $60 million, and obtained a mortgage for exactly that amount from Citibank. He announced that he planned to tear down the hospital and build a new apartment building in its place but would rent the building to the church until he came up with firm plans.

At the same time Donald pursued all these acquisitions and projects in 1985 and 1986—the world's tallest building on the West Side, Mar-a-Lago, the West Palm Beach condo building, the old Foundling Hospital, the old St. Moritz hotel, while still trying to develop the old Barbizon Plaza hotel and its rent-controlled neighbor—he was also busy learning how to run a casino and pushing an upstart football league into a head-on collision with the NFL.

It might have seemed prudent to let a sure thing in his heavily leveraged portfolio continue unruffled for a period of time. His partnership with Harrah's at what was now called Trump Plaza Casino and Hotel gave Trump 50 percent of all profit, with Harrah's covering any losses for the first five years. But Trump wanted complete control. Their competing lawsuits and recriminations continued for a year. The Harrah's executives who had brought Trump in to handle construction realized there would be no going back to a happy working arrangement. Though Donald owned a minority share, by insulating him from any losses Harrah's had taken away his incentive not to damage the casino's bottom line as a tactic to force them out. Harrah's executives came to believe he was doing just that, including by using the Trump Plaza customer list to draw players to the Castle, which he owned alone. In the spring of 1986, they settled for basically what they had put into the casino just to get away.

Donald took on yet another expensive loan load to buy out his partner. On his behalf, Bear Stearns issued bonds totaling $250 million at the high interest rate of almost 13 percent. He would have to start making interest payments twice a year. Donald also agreed to pay another $17 million to Harrah's over the next seven years, at a 10 percent interest rate.

Described as a real estate developer wunderkind, he was about to turn forty years old and had completed a total of two new buildings in Manhattan and one casino in Atlantic City. He had excelled at convincing lenders to fund a remarkable number of large acquisitions without requiring him to put in any of his own money. He was now making payments on $362 million in loans and paying real estate taxes on properties that were not producing any revenue. In all, he had taken on, in less than four years, more than $1 billion in debt, much of it at high interest rates and personally guaranteed by him.

Though small by comparison, he still owed his father $15 million from a decade earlier. Donald had leveraged his father's stature, connections, and wealth to acquire his own empire in record time. But it was a borrowed empire, and whether he could cover those debts and earn a profit by running his businesses effectively remained an uncertainty.

For Donald's fortieth birthday, on June 14, 1986, there were no plans for a lavish party. He spent the day in Manhattan toggling between a series of meetings with no common theme other than his presence. He met architects who were drawing up plans for his conversion of the Barbizon hotel into condominium apartments. He met with lawyers in preparation for his testimony in the lawsuit against the NFL that he had spearheaded. And he met with a television director about playing himself in a miniseries adaptation of Judith Krantz's titillating novel *I'll Take Manhattan*, which featured a brief appearance by a rich and benevolent Donald Trump.

When a reporter showed up to witness filming, Krantz asked: "Who else could play Donald? He's a bigger-than-life character playing a bigger-than-life character." The star of the series, Valerie Bertinelli, agreed. "The man is beautiful!" she gushed. "He could pass for an actor any day."

"I guess all of life is a stage, when you get right down to it," Donald told a reporter during filming. "And because of that, acting shouldn't be that different."

Through a string of heavily leveraged purchases, scores of plans that went nowhere, and battles with partners and officials, all reliably, if not breathlessly, covered by news organizations, Trump had been transformed from a real estate developer into a national celebrity. People stopped him on the streets of Manhattan for an autograph. Some asked to touch him for good luck, as if he were a Blarney Stone in pinstripes. He may not have had a glitzy birthday party, but he had been included, along with three entertainers, in a segment on the *Today* show, the highly rated national morning show on NBC, about the first baby boomers reaching the age of forty. His name appeared in newspapers every day, sometimes in multiple places in the same paper. He had become so well-known that "Donald Trump" was now its own simile and metaphor, shorthand for success and prominence. In the few weeks before his birthday, one article in *The New York Times* included the phrase "big time real estate entrepreneurs such as Donald Trump" and another invoked "the nation's firmament of big developers—the Donald Trumps." The *Times* name-checked him as among prominent businesspeople—along with the heads of American Express, General Electric, and Citicorp—who belonged to golf country clubs. He was listed by the dean of the Wharton School, his alma mater, as evidence the school did not only produce people who worked in finance: "We're also damn good at turning out entrepreneurs—the Donald Trumps, the Michael Milkens, the Saul Steinbergs."

Just as he benefited from pop culture and people's growing interest in the lives of the rich and famous, he also benefited from an explosive trend in book publishing. Four years earlier, there had been no biographies, memoirs, or autobiographies on *The New York Times* hardcover bestseller list. But the week

Donald Trump turned forty, those categories comprised more than half of the nonfiction bestsellers. And the longest-running title on the nonfiction list remained *Iacocca: An Autobiography.* The book chronicled Lee Iacocca's rise from child of Italian immigrants in Pennsylvania to leading the Chrysler Corporation back from the brink of collapse in the early 1980s. It became the bestselling nonfiction book of 1984 and 1985, made Iacocca into a new sort of celebrity chief executive, and spawned, as the *Times* put it in a headline, THE RUSH TO WRITE 'SON OF IACOCCA.' That *Times* article quoted Julian Bach, a literary agent, describing the genre as suddenly "more important now than ever because you have a star system in which big names in business, politics and the arts have an exposure the likes of which we have never had before." Phyllis Grann, publisher of G. P. Putnam's Sons, christened the larger trend in terms that could just as appropriately have been used to describe Donald Trump's place in the world at that moment. "People want household names associated with glamour, high living and excitement," she said.

As publishers searched for the next bestselling business memoir, S. I. Newhouse, owner of the Condé Nast magazine empire and Random House, recalled a cover article on Donald Trump from the May 1984 edition of his *GQ* magazine that had sold very well. He persuaded Trump to sign a book contract with a $500,000 advance. Trump hired Tony Schwartz, a magazine writer, to do the actual writing, and agreed to split the advance and royalties with him. Schwartz, who had written a critical article about Trump for *New York* magazine, told Trump that he was still too young to write an autobiography. He suggested *The Art of the Deal* as a framework, part how-to and part day-in-the-life of a high-living business celebrity.

The book-in-progress was announced by Liz Smith, then one of the most prominent gossip columnists in the country, as the lead item in her nationally syndicated column, which ended with this line: "This book could very well out-Iacocca Lee Iacocca's smashing best seller!"

Schwartz quickly grew frustrated trying to get Trump to concentrate for more than an hour at a time. He gave up on interviewing him and switched his approach to serving as a fly on the wall, watching Trump take calls and plot in his Trump Tower office. Schwartz kept a journal. He wrote that Trump struck him as driven by an unending need for public attention. "All he is is 'stomp, stomp, stomp'—recognition from outside, bigger, more, a whole series of things that go nowhere in particular," he wrote. Schwartz, who had earned a reputation as a substantial and careful journalist, wrote a note to himself that a truthful rendition of his subject could make Trump seem "just hateful or, worse yet, a one-dimensional blowhard." But he recognized that crafting Trump into a "sympathetic character—even weirdly sympathetic," would be vital to the book's success.

A TEST OF DONALD TRUMP's tactical and analytical abilities came about a week after his fortieth birthday, when he entered the witness box in a federal courtroom in lower Manhattan. He had put himself at the front of the USFL's lawsuit against the NFL. The legal strategy centered around presenting the NFL as willing to do anything to squeeze the USFL out of existence. And providing direct testimony of that effort fell mostly to Trump. He testified that during his meeting with Pete Rozelle, the NFL commissioner, in a room at the Pierre, Rozelle had offered him his own franchise if he would drop plans to file an antitrust lawsuit.

A couple of weeks later, Rozelle testified that he made no such offer and attended at Trump's request. Rozelle had taken notes at the meeting, including noting that Trump said he would "get some stiff" to buy the Generals if Rozelle got him an NFL team. Trump took no notes but did not dispute that he had requested the meeting and rented the hotel room.

As the trial progressed, the NFL lawyers set out to make Trump the face of the USFL. They argued that Trump and a few of his fellow owners spent themselves into oblivion, ignoring warnings from John Bassett and other owners to be more prudent. In his closing arguments, Frank Rothman, one of the NFL lawyers, accused Trump of using the lawsuit to find a cheap back door into the NFL. He said the USFL would frame the case as David versus Goliath, "while I suggest it is Donald versus Goliath." And he quoted Bassett, who said, "We did it to ourselves. We have nobody to blame except ourselves."

Roy Cohn had filed the case for Trump but had since become deathly ill from the virus that causes AIDS. He was also disbarred shortly before the trial began for mishandling clients' funds and tricking a senile client into appointing him coexecutor of his estate. Trump picked Harvey Myerson, an attorney he had worked with before, to represent the USFL. Whereas Rothman was lean, reserved, and logical, Myerson was short, round, and bombastic, flamboyant even, with thick and curly long, dark hair. He began his summation by loudly telling the jury, "Nail them! That's what this country is looking for you to do.

"Without damages," Myerson continued, "you know this league is dead, and it is a signal that every other league that tries to compete is dead." He concluded with a sort of prayer: "Please, God, find for us."

In his instructions to the jurors, Judge Peter K. Leisure undermined the argument Trump had been making since the day he announced the lawsuit from Roy Cohn's couch two years before—that he realized the NFL was an evil monopoly when he discovered they had contracts with three networks. The mere fact that the NFL had contracts with networks to broadcast games, Judge Leisure said, does not mean they had done something illegal or were required to help "the newcomer to compete with it.

"Thus, you should infer no anticompetitive intent or effect from the mere existence of these contracts," Leisure said to the jury. He added that they could simply award one dollar if they could not distinguish between USFL losses attributable to poor management and those caused by the NFL's monopolistic practices.

After deliberating for four days, the six jurors reached a verdict. The courtroom refilled with reporters and the parties. Trump stood in the back with his arms folded as the jurors entered. A court clerk read through dozens of technical questions related to the verdict before getting to the first one everyone in the room cared about: Did some NFL teams conspire "with the specific intent to acquire or maintain monopoly power."

"Yes," replied Patricia McCabe, the jury forewoman and a computer technician from a suburb north of the city.

There was a gasp in the courtroom. It seemed that the USFL had prevailed. For about one beat. Then the court clerk asked whether the NFL teams had taken any "overt action" to acquire or maintain their monopoly power.

"No," answered McCabe.

Heads snapped. The jurors found that the NFL enjoyed a monopoly but did not do anything untoward to eliminate competitors. The court clerk then asked, "What total damages, if any, have the USFL and all its member clubs incurred?"

"One dollar," McCabe said.

And that would be the final value of Donald Trump's yearslong effort to push his way into the NFL and recruit his fellow USFL owners into his win-or-die mission. One dollar, plus interest.

Trump's spend-and-they-will-come business philosophy had led the league to spend itself into oblivion before making sure it had the revenue to cover those expenses. He said in court papers that he had lost $22 million on the league. He still owed several million dollars to Flutie and Walker, whose salaries he had personally guaranteed, though he would dispatch an aide to renege on the promise.

The USFL had played its last game, its players cast to the wind. And Trump had burned any chance he had for the foreseeable future of persuading NFL owners to approve him for an expansion team.

One minor victory for the USFL came after the trial. Because the jury had ruled partially in the USFL's favor, Judge Leisure ordered the NFL to pay the USFL's legal fees, which totaled $5.5 million. For his part, Trump at the time called the verdict "a great moral victory." Decades later, when Michael Tollin, a former USFL employee, made a documentary about how Trump led the league to ruin, Trump dismissed the entire episode as involving too little money to matter to him.

"It was small potatoes," he said.

For all the mentions of Trump as a giant of entrepreneurial America, his operation still did not have an accounting or payroll department. Those functions were handled, and paid for, by his father, at his tiny office on the ground floor of the old Beach Haven apartment complex in Brooklyn. Employees saw the evidence. In 1986, when Barbara Res received a tax form for a small payment the prior year, it listed the payer as "Donald J. Trump, 2611 West 2nd Street, Brooklyn, N.Y.," with his personal social security number.

That form had been prepared by Allen Weisselberg, a forty-year-old accountant who had worked for Fred Trump since 1973, not long after he graduated from Pace University. Weisselberg dealt with Fred's outside tax accountants, balanced the books on ten thousand apartment units, and filed reports to the federal housing agency on some of the buildings. In 1986, the year Donald turned forty and his debt-driven acquisition phase reached breakneck pace, Fred turned Weisselberg over to Donald. Weisselberg, a portly bald man with a thick mustache and a face that infrequently formed an expression, set up an accounts payable operation, a payroll operation, and handled the finances overall, moving cash among the businesses to cover shortfalls. Donald did not own the apartments in Trump Tower or Trump Plaza, but he still had management contracts to maintain the public areas of those buildings. He typically lost money on those businesses, but he considered it important to protecting his company's image. Weisselberg created the monthly reports to the board of owners at those buildings. He also handled Donald's personal finances, including providing records to Donald's outside accountants and lawyers. Weisselberg, at Trump's direction, created glowing "statements of financial condition" that bore no resemblance to Trump's actual state of affairs. Those documents, and Trump's constant insistence that he was worth billions, independent of his father, fueled Trump's image as an icon of wealth and accomplishment.

All of that made Allen Weisselberg the only person at Trump Organization headquarters who knew the overall state of Donald Trump's finances, most critically whether all the businesses combined turned a profit. Weisselberg was the first person to see the shocking figures on the tax returns that Donald Trump filed for the year that he turned forty, the year that he was working on a book about his exceptional dealmaking skills, the year that he bought a grand mansion and a second casino, the years that *Forbes* reported he was worth a net of $700 million after debts and other news reports regularly declared him to be a billionaire.

The figures on those tax returns remained a tightly held secret for more than thirty years. In 2019, as part of our work for *The New York Times*, we obtained Trump's tax transcripts for those years. We finally saw what Trump and Weisselberg and his outside tax accountants had long known: Even when Trump appeared to be at his best, he was failing.

Because his businesses were organized as partnerships, the results all flowed directly to his personal tax return. For 1986, Trump reported income from his core businesses of negative $68.7 million. It was not an anomaly. He carried over another $42.4 million in losses from the prior year. He reported $2.7 million in wages, a salary he had paid himself.

When we asked Trump about those staggering losses, he attributed the red ink to depreciation, a provision in the tax code that can allow owners of real estate to reduce their taxable income over time by the amount they spent on a building, excluding the cost of the land. But Trump had not spent enough on buildings he owned to generate that much of a deduction for depreciation. The truth was that Trump was hemorrhaging cash, largely from massive interest payments. But it was all other people's cash. His entire operation, and his lifestyle, was a float. He was living, and creating a phony image, on borrowed money. And he was only warming up.

19

ENTERTAINER-IMPRESARIO

By the mid-1980s, newspaper business pages regularly mentioned Wall Street rumors involving a new breed of financier—some with cartoon villain names like Carl Icahn or T. Boone Pickens—who came to be known as corporate raiders. Rumors that they were buying shares in a company could cause a sharp rise in its stock price and lead the company's executives to take costly measures to block the takeover threat. Another man, Michael Milken, became synonymous with new financial devices, junk bonds and dark pools of money, that could raise enough capital to make it conceivable for the raiders to buy a majority of the shares of a large public corporation. Sometimes they targeted companies with assets more valuable than the total value of the outstanding stock shares, and a raider would pulverize his quarry into cash, selling off the assets and laying off workers across the country. Sometimes the raiders sold as the stocks rose. Other times, they weren't there at all, just boogeymen under the bed. Whatever the case, the fear and excitement created by the mere possibility of a well-financed hostile takeover still drove up a stock's price.

The filmmaker Oliver Stone developed a movie, *Wall Street*, that became a cultural touchstone of the era. His lead actor, Michael Douglas, playing a raider named Gordon Gekko, with hair greased back and suspenders pulled tight, uttered the phrase that defined the stock market's place in the life of the country at that point: "Greed, for lack of a better word, is good."

As much as Icahn, Pickens, and Gekko, Dan Dorfman was built for the moment. Dorfman had worked his way up from copyboy at fashion publications to writing the Heard on the Street column for *The Wall Street Journal* in the late 1960s and early 1970s. He lost that job after being caught buying a new investment product through a source.

In 1976, as Dorfman worked to rebuild his reputation, he connected with a young developer working on his first project. Donald Trump was upset because he had heard that a prominent businessman, Preston Robert Tisch, had privately questioned the merits of the proposed tax abatement for the Grand Hyatt. In an article for *New York* magazine, Dorfman elevated the twenty-nine-year-old Trump's gossipy complaint into "a serious rift . . . that could have negative implications for the economic health of the city."

"It's a damned outrage," he quoted Trump saying.

A decade later, with the corporate raiders in full bloom, Dorfman had become the reporter who, above all others, possessed the power to move stock prices. He wrote a regular column on the stock market for *USA Today* that was syndicated to newspapers across the country. He prided himself on breaking stories with every column, beating his competition to the punch. If Dorfman had one rule for himself, it was "Do not come in second." Born with a personage well suited for newspaper work—with squirrel-tail eyebrows, the body of a lawn gnome, and a nasally voice spitting rapid-fire Brooklynese—Dorfman became an unlikely television expert, regularly dishing broad market advice and highlighting individual stocks on national networks. His pronouncements in print and on television so predictably drove stock prices that the Chicago Stock Exchange created a "Dorfman rule" that briefly suspended small-order computerized trading of any stock he mentioned.

Trump's anger with his former partners at Harrah's, meanwhile, had not been quite mollified, even after he bought them out. And so, a decade after Dorfman first wrote about Donald Trump, their paths crossed again.

In early September 1986, Dorfman pushed his column out a day earlier than normal due to the urgency of its news: Donald Trump had acquired 2.5 percent of the outstanding stock in Harrah's parent company, Holiday Corporation, "and may seek control of the company." Dorfman wrote that Trump controlled real estate worth $3 billion, a fantastical exaggeration that made Trump's takeover of Holiday seem plausible. He wrote that Trump was unavailable, but an unnamed source communicated a thinly veiled threat. "The Holiday stake is an investment for Donald that's unlikely to remain just an investment for long."

"The source said Trump, an avowed empire builder who is estimated to have a personal net worth of more than $1 billion, believes that Holiday's management is 'sleepy' and that he could turn Holiday Corp. into a far more productive and profitable operation."

This was a new world for Trump. As recently as one year before he had told New Jersey casino regulators that he held no stocks in public companies. Though it was not known at the time, Trump had his own generous supplier of cash. To buy his stocks, he dealt directly with Alan "Ace" Greenberg, the chief executive of Wall Street investment bank Bear Stearns. Greenberg, serving as Trump's personal stockbroker, opened two margin accounts for Trump, allowing stock to be purchased while only requiring him to put up half the money. For the other half, Trump still did not reach into his own bank account. He borrowed that money also, using his credit lines at three banks.

Within a month, Trump had bought $69 million of Holiday stock without putting in any of his own money. That amounted to about 4.4 percent of all outstanding shares. Taking a majority of shares in Holiday would have required far more—something on the order of $750 million—but the coverage of Donald Trump as being worth billions of dollars created the impression that he could afford such a play, that he might just be in league with the Icahns and Pickens of the era.

Mike Rose, the chairman and chief executive of Holiday, thought he had been done with Donald Trump when he let Trump takeover the Plaza casino. Now here he was again, causing trouble for Holiday.

One day that week, Trump called Rose at Holiday headquarters in Memphis. He told Rose he had bought the stock only as an investment. Rose was inclined to believe him. He did not think Trump had the ability to run a large public company, and probably not the interest. But Rose knew that the increased value of the company's real estate assets made it attractive for someone, even if that someone was not named Trump, to wage a hostile takeover. He met with investment bankers at Goldman Sachs and Michael Milken's firm, Drexel Burnham. He quickly came to believe that he had no choice other than to weigh down his profitable company with $2.4 billion in junk bonds, enough debt to make a takeover unlikely and appease shareholders with a $65-per-share dividend. The challenge had been averted, but the balance sheet was now broken. Spending money to upgrade Harrah's Marina casino to better compete with Trump's casino across the street would be out of the question for the near future. Not quite four weeks after the original Dorfman column, *The Wall Street Journal* reported that Trump appeared to be still interested in a takeover, and the market continued to respond. Holiday's shares had risen from $63.25 the day Dorfman's column first appeared to $71.50. An earlier *Journal* article had quoted a Drexel Burnham analyst throwing water on the idea of a Trump takeover. This one quoted an anonymous trader saying he was still buying on the news of Trump's possible takeover. "At the very best, he'll make a bid for perhaps in the $75-to-$80 range. At the very least, he'll force the company to reorganize."

Trump sold his stocks that November, about ninety days after he started buying with borrowed money. Casino regulators with access to his financial records would later report that after covering $6 million in commission and interest to Bear Stearns, he had pocketed $12.6 million.

As Trump sold his shares in Holiday, analysts noted that trading accelerated in shares of another company that owned casinos in Atlantic City and Nevada, Bally Manufacturing. Because controlling companies that own casinos required a license from that state, the universe of potential buyers was small. Trump already had a license in New Jersey and had applied for one in Nevada while buying Holiday's stock. Suspicion spread on Wall Street that Trump was making a run on that company, possibly with the aim of taking it over. Bally executives had no clue who had bought up two million shares in one day.

Trump did not make any public comments on the rumors for one week, while he continued to buy shares. When he finally did speak, he said only that he saw the company as a "good place to park my money." As it turned out, it was mostly not Trump's money that got parked. Using the profits from his Holiday play and tens of millions more advanced to him by Bear Stearns and banks, Ace Greenberg executed more than $61 million in Bally trades stock for Trump. Within a week after the rumors broke, the stock's price had risen from $17 a share to $21.65. By then, Trump controlled just under 10 percent of the outstanding Bally stock.

Paul Bible had seen enough. A lawyer finishing up his term as chairman of the Nevada Gaming Commission, Bible worried that Trump was playing games with Bally as he had seemed to have done with Holiday, and doing so in ways that could cripple the companies for years to come. He took what was for him, a lawyer who could never tear himself away from the laid-back life in Reno and Lake Tahoe, an unusually bold step. He called a reporter for the *Reno Gazette Journal*, the paper he had delivered as a boy, and raised the possibility that Donald Trump, a bigshot from New York City, was a greenmailer. "Greenmailer" is a term for a suit-and-tie version of a blackmailer, someone who buys a large chunk of a company's stock and holds it hostage, implicitly or explicitly threatening a hostile takeover, until the company's executives pay a ransom to ward off the attack, buying back the stock at inflated prices. Bible told the reporter that Trump had hobbled Holiday with a bluff and now looked to be heading in the same direction with Bally.

"It appears what Donald Trump is doing is using his resources and his New Jersey gaming license to extort greenmail from these two companies," Bible told the reporter. "And I'm concerned that if he does get bought out of Bally, he will look to another company to do the same." He went on to say that the companies would be forced to spend money "to pay off the greenmailer" instead of strengthening their companies. "If he is making his investment as a legitimate investor, or is legitimately interested in Bally, then that's fine. But if the only purpose in the investment is to become a greenmailer, then he's got a serious problem in getting a license."

Trump took Bible's accusations seriously enough to plan a quick trip to Nevada. A little more than a week later, he visited Bally's casinos in Las Vegas and Reno, met with the governor, and spoke with reporters from the *Reno Gazette Journal.* He played good-Trump, bad-Trump on the tour. He charmed Governor Richard Bryan, who said he found Trump to be "a very personable gentleman—very bright and very articulate." And he laid Bally's managers and Paul Bible out in filth. He said that Bally's top executives were paid too much and were fighting him to protect their undeserved large salaries, and that their casinos looked shabby. All of which sounded like someone threatening to take over the company and fire its leadership. And he went after Bible's ethics. He pointed out that Bible's father, retired U.S. senator Alan Bible, had once sat on the Holiday board of directors and that Paul Bible's former law firm once represented Bally. Trump did not mention that Paul Bible had left the law firm three years earlier and his father had left his position on the Bally board two years prior to that. He invoked his favorite anonymous "some people" to elevate his complaint beyond himself. "I was very surprised—some people were shocked—that a person in the regulatory business and without any knowledge as to the facts can make a statement as to greenmailing.

"Greenmailing—the term sounds so bad," he said. "I didn't greenmail anybody. I bought the stock in Holiday Inn, and I sold it to the public."

Bally responded as if Trump were a greenmailer, and he went along. In late February, the company agreed to buy most of Trump's shares for $24 each, and the rest at $33 a share, and pay him an additional $6.2 million not to buy any of its voting stock or try to influence its management for the next decade. In another ninety days using borrowed money and his high public profile, Trump stood to gain at least $21 million, after paying Bear Stearns' expenses.

He would later say in sworn testimony that neither he nor anyone working for him did any "great studies" of the Bally company. "I just felt instinctively—when I do research on things, they never work out very well. I just felt instinctively that it was a low price."

The federal government eventually sued Trump, charging that he had failed to comply with federal regulations requiring him to notify the federal Department of Justice and Federal Trade Commission of his plans to make such large stock buys and then let a sixty-day waiting period expire before buying the stock. The regulation allowed only a maximum fine of $10,000 for each day out of compliance, and prosecutors alleged that Trump was in violation of the act on 149 days in late 1986 and early 1987. Trump split the difference in a settlement, agreeing to pay a fine of $750,000. He said he had acted under the guidance of the "most respected lawyers in the business" and Bear Stearns. "I assume Bear Stearns will reimburse me for this expense." He also eventually agreed to pay $2.25 million to Bally shareholders to settle their lawsuit. But given the numbers involved, the fine and the settlement could be seen only as a slap on the wrist.

Two weeks after Trump closed out the Bally payoff, *The Wall Street Journal* cited unnamed sources saying that he had been buying shares in United Airlines, once again through Bear Stearns. One source was familiar enough with his thinking to tell the reporter that it was "pure investment." The rumor sent the stock price soaring.

Some analysts already suspected Trump was not serious about taking over a large company. "In real estate he's very successful," one told *The New York*

Donald Trump fishing on a boat belonging to his older brother, Freddy, off Montauk, Long Island, in the early 1960s. Their relationships with each other and their father would profoundly impact both of their lives.

Freddy and Linda Trump with their son, Fred Trump III, also known as Fritz, in 1963 in front of Freddy's first plane. Flying became Freddy's passion, but his father did not approve.

Freddy and Linda in 1964, shortly after Freddy finished a pilot training course in Kansas City with Trans World Airlines.

Trump and his brother Robert playing with their nephew on a visit to Freddy's home in Marblehead, Massachusetts, in the summer of 1964. One evening during that visit, Donald told Freddy that their father did not approve of his chosen career. "Dad's right about you," Donald said. "You're nothing but a glorified bus driver." Freddy's brief flying career would be cut short by drinking problems. Donald would win his father's unquestioning support.

Fred Trump with Freddy in the 1970s at North Hills Country Club, in Manhasset, New York, where Fred was a member.

Trump received a massive tax abatement from New York City in the 1970s to renovate the old Commodore Hotel in Manhattan. He partnered with Hyatt Hotels on the renovation. Fred Trump's political connections and financial support were central to Trump's success with the project.

Trump and Roy Cohn together at Le Club in 1979, celebrating Trump's thirty-third birthday. In the early 1970s Cohn encouraged Trump 's desire to fight a lawsuit the Justice Department brought against Donald, Fred, and Trump Management. Cohn would be by his side in other contentious legal battles for years to come.

In 1983, Trump bought the New Jersey Generals football team of the upstart United States Football League. Ivana Trump is seen here at Trump Tower with finalists for the Generals's cheerleading squad. Trump would push his fellow team owners to sue the NFL, a decision that led to the league's demise.

Trump in 1985 with a model of Television City, a fantastical project that never materialized. His plan included 8,000 apartments, 1.7 million square feet of retail space, more than 3 million square feet of offices, and the world's tallest building.

Fred Trump chatting with Abraham Beame in 1985 during Fred and Mary Trump's fiftieth wedding anniversary celebration at the Plaza Hotel in Manhattan. Beame was one of Fred Trump's closest friends and the mayor of New York City for four years in the 1970s. "Whatever the Trumps want in this city, they get," he once said.

Donald and Fred Trump at a party in 1987 to celebrate the release of Trump's first book, *The Art of the Deal.* Trump's finances were already deep in the red. He recorded $42.2 million in core business losses that year.

Trump at the opening of the Trump Taj Mahal Hotel and Casino in April 1990. He saddled the casino with hundreds of millions of dollars in high-interest debt. The Taj Mahal drew customers from his other Atlantic City casinos and never turned a profit.

Trump and Marla Maples were married in December 1993. In 1997, he announced they had separated. Their prenuptial agreement showed Marla would receive $1 million thirty days after she vacated all of Trump's properties, and another $1 million to buy her own home.

Trump with Mark Burnett and Allen Weisselberg, Trump's longtime chief financial officer. Burnett, a television producer, created *The Apprentice* and recruited Trump as his star. Burnett and his team edited into existence a version of Donald Trump—diligent, measured, and successful—that was highly marketable. Trump would go on to make more than $400 million from the show and licensing and endorsement deals.

As Trump's popularity surged after *The Apprentice*'s debut, his rush of endorsement money included $1.1 million to promote laundry detergent. The ad campaign ran with the slogan "Softness fit for a Trump."

Donald Trump Jr. speaking in 2006 at a news conference announcing the launch of Trump Mortgage. "This one's really my baby," he told *Forbes*. The company was soon caught up in controversy and shut down in 2007.

Trump with Eric, Ivanka, and Donald Jr. in 2007 at Trump International Hotel and Tower in Chicago. In 2008, Trump told the IRS that his investment in the tower was worthless. He lost about $100 million of his own money, did not repay more than $270 million in loans, and never declared a profit on the tower through at least 2020.

In 2008, Trump visited his mother's childhood home on the Isle of Lewis in Scotland, accompanied by his sister, Maryanne. The trip was designed to win over skeptics who opposed his plans to build a golf course in the country. Trump said he selected Scotland because his mother was "Scotch."

Mark Burnett publicly distanced himself from Trump during the 2016 election. "I am not now and have never been a supporter of Donald Trump's candidacy," he said just weeks before Trump was first elected. Yet months later Burnett joined the team that organized Trump's inauguration. The two men are seen here in January 2017 at a preinauguration dinner at Union Station in Washington, D.C.

Times. "On Wall Street he's now considered not a buyer of companies, but a guy who's looking to make a buck for himself." But United's stock kept rising.

Trump personally called Richard Ferris, the chief executive of United Airlines, at his office in Chicago. He just wanted to let Ferris know that he thought the company's stock was a good investment, though he did not tell Ferris whether he had bought any stock in the company. And Trump gave Ferris no hint whether he would wage a takeover attempt. But he almost immediately began making public statements that sounded, in his unique way, like someone interested in taking over the company. He said the company's new name—Allegis—would be "better suited to the next world-class disease." To fend off an earlier takeover attempt, the company had acquired part of Pan American World Airways, Hertz, and Hilton International, and now Trump said, "I totally disagree with the integration of the company."

"I totally disagree with the way the company is being run," he added.

The suspicion that Trump might wage a hostile takeover led United's airline pilots' union to make a $4.5 billion offer to take the company private. United rejected the offer because it would saddle the company with too much debt. The perception of Trump as endlessly wealthy and able to obtain limitless loans fueled speculation that he might be able to pull together a better deal and know how to run a corporation with operating revenues approaching $10 billion a year and seventy-six thousand employees in businesses with which he had no experience.

It would be hard to reconcile that scenario with the realities on the twenty-sixth floor of Trump Tower, where about ten executives, most with few, if any, employees reporting to them, met with Trump for every significant decision. He still personally signed every check, sometimes hundreds a week. His burgeoning interest in buying stocks with borrowed money was being handled by a new hire, Susan Heilbron, a Yale Law School graduate whom Trump had bumped into during her years working for the Koch administration and the New York State urban development agency. Slender and elegant in fashionably tailored suits, Heilbron frequently glided in and out of Trump's office at will, as he met with consultants and employees trying to sort out his plans for the West Side rail yards and other projects, to pass him a yellow sticky note on which she had written the recent price fluctuations of a few stocks.

Wall Street investors who believed Trump might take over a large transportation conglomerate did not see the small staff or the yellow sticky notes. They saw the Donald Trump in the media, the one *Forbes* said that year was worth at least $850 million and had just manipulated the stock of two other large companies on rumors he might take them over. As Bear Stearns bought $67.5 million in stock for Trump, again without requiring him to put up much, if any, of his own money, the stock rose in response to his involvement. After two months of driving up the stock price by sounding like he might buy a majority of the shares, he quietly sold. He announced he was out the next day.

The Wall Street Journal reported that available details suggested his gain was "more than $55 million." *The New York Times*, citing "a source close to the New York developer," said he profited by "about $80 million." As Trump walked toward Tavern on the Green in Central Park for a dinner one night that May, a reporter asked him whether that $80 million figure was correct. "I don't comment on what I make," he answered, and then coyly wiggled his hand to indicate the figure was about right. He added that he "was very well compensated" for a few weeks' work.

The actual figure was just under $11 million, and that was the total before he covered the interest on the money he borrowed from Bear Stearns to buy the stocks. Figures about his gains on every deal were inflated, and to great effect. All served as signposts of his wealth, the key factor creating the impression that he was a takeover threat to any company.

Forbes reported that Trump's profits totaled $125 million from his runs on Holiday, Bally, and United, and later included that figure to compute Trump's net worth as more than $1 billion. Casino regulators, with access to his financial records, eventually reported that Trump's gain on those three stocks was actually $33 million before covering expenses on the loans from Bear Stearns. The information we would later obtain from his tax returns showed that he declared $25.4 million that year in short-term capital gains, generally the tax category for such profits.

That July, Dan Dorfman of *USA Today* reported that Trump was rumored to be acquiring stock in Golden Nugget, another company that owned casinos, and was considering a takeover. Dorfman told readers that Trump had a "net worth of more than $1 billion." Dorfman wrote that Trump, reached by telephone in Monte Carlo, had declined to elaborate. But "a source close to Trump" told Dorfman: "It's an investment for now, but let's see what happens," the second part being a phrase that Trump has probably uttered more times that his own mother's name. Dorfman warned, however, that "risk looms for stock players who ride Trump's coattails. Reason: He might unload his block if the stock runs up," as he had done before. He mentioned that Nevada casino regulators were upset with Trump's earlier greenmailing and might reject the license he would need there to complete a takeover. Dorfman, the reporter who first took Trump's takeover moves seriously, was onto him.

Even with those caveats in the public record, the stock still rose on the rumor. This time, Trump sold five days after Dorfman's column ran, for a gain of $103,788.

Aside from the cigarette habit that killed him, James Crosby might have resembled the sort of executive Donald Trump was trying to become. Crosby, a dedicated playboy, took over leadership of a paint manufacturer that his father and other investors had bought in 1958 and shifted it into real estate, hotels, and casinos, with an occasional attempt to take over an airline. Renamed Resorts International, Crosby's company had owned Paradise Island Casino in the Bahamas for almost thirty years and had opened the first casino on the Atlantic City boardwalk in the 1970s. When Crosby died at age fifty-eight in 1986, Resorts was working on what the Crosby family saw as a temple to his legacy, the largest casino in Atlantic City, to be called the Taj Mahal.

Though Resorts was a public corporation, the Crosby family controlled nearly all the voting shares, and they wanted to see the Taj Mahal finished. I. G. "Jack" Davis, who had served as company president under Crosby, set out to find someone with the wherewithal and the construction expertise to finish the job. He soon contacted Donald Trump, who, by reputation at least, met both standards. Before the first anniversary of Crosby's death, Trump and the Crosby family had agreed he would pay $135 a share for the Crosbys' voting stock and offer the same price to holders of all other outstanding shares of the super-voting stock. The total would come to $101.6 million for Trump to control the company, though not own it outright.

Trump again borrowed the funds, and this time he offered his interest in the Grand Hyatt as collateral, in violation of the partnership agreement with the Hyatt company. This put Hyatt's investment at risk as well, but the company would not be aware of what he had done for several years to come.

The purchase, friendly as it was with Davis and the Crosby family, fell in the category of a further debt-fueled acquisition by Trump. But news reports framed it as the latest evidence that Trump had become a corporate raider. Ace Greenberg, who was collecting multimillion-dollar fees for Bear Stearns with most Trump stock purchases, fueled the image of his client as armed and on the hunt. "He has an appetite like a Rocky Mountain vulture," Greenberg told *The Wall Street Journal*. "He'd like to own the world" and has access to "hundreds of millions, including what Bear Stearns can get him." While the page-one article was framed around "Mr. Trump's rise as a raider," it mentioned his penchant for causing a stock price to rise by threatening a takeover and then selling to pocket the easy money.

The Crosbys eased Trump's path because of his expertise in construction. Trump vowed he would finish the casino within one year: "The most immediate problem is to bring in the Taj Mahal as quickly and efficiently as possible."

By the time Trump took over in July 1987, Resorts' budget for the Taj Mahal had swelled to more than $500 million. Yet Trump soon said he had been shocked to learn after the deal that he would need to raise $550 million to complete the project. "I only just came into the Taj Mahal," he said that fall. He expected to raise the money through junk bonds, a process that would delay construction and greatly increase costs.

How could it be that before taking on $100 million in debt of his own and responsibility to shareholders, and believing completion of the Taj Mahal was central to the company's survival, he did not closely scrutinize how much construction would cost? He had access to financial and construction records. But he was shocked by the figures he saw *after* he closed the deal.

By then, Trump's lack of due diligence in major transactions, his belief that his instinct triumphed over in-depth analysis by anyone else, had become a defining characteristic. It was what stood out to Holiday executives when they partnered with him on the Plaza casino. It was what determined the fate of the USFL. It was why his plan to nearly triple the size of the previously approved project at the West Side rail yards had stalled and become increasingly costly.

When Trump took over at Resorts, he kept Davis on as president, and the two became friendly. Trump insisted on a services agreement that would pay him about $108 million over the first five years for managing construction of the Taj Mahal and other oversight tasks at Resorts. Shareholders resisted adding an expensive layer of management to a still failing company, and casino regulators worried that siphoning off so much money would put completion of the casino even more in doubt.

During a hearing near the state capital of Trenton, Greenberg showed up to convince the regulators that Trump would be essential to borrowing money for the project. "Without a Mr. Trump, there will be no Taj Mahal, no financing, and perhaps no Resorts International," Greenberg told the panel. Greenberg believed lenders would not blink at Trump's $108 million contract. "That's the price that this entertainer-impresario wants for his services. I think he's worth it."

TRUMP'S TAKEOVER BLUFFS that year benefited from one of the greatest stock bubbles in history. By late August, the Dow Jones Industrial Average had risen 44 percent in seven months.

Some analysts noted signs of doom, and Trump joined that chorus. On August 24, Dan Dorfman reported in his *USA Today* column that Trump had pulled most of his money out of the stock market because he thought a major correction was coming. "It's not a question of will it happen, but only when it'll happen," Trump told Dorfman. "If you look at our economy, the crazy dollar and world events, such as the Mideast problems, there's no justification for the market being this high."

Trump and the other naysayers were right. On October 19, 1987, the market plunged 22 percent in a few hours, the largest single-day percentage drop since the Great Depression.

At *The Wall Street Journal*'s newsroom in lower Manhattan, the events led to an all-hands-on-deck call for news related to the crash. Reporters phoned every possible source of information. Randall Smith, who cowrote the Heard on the Street column for the *Journal*, felt the pressure. The Dorfman column quoting Trump had stuck in his head, so he left a message for Trump. But he did not expect the call to be returned. They had a history. Trump had stopped speaking to him four years earlier, when Smith wrote an article describing Trump as "no stranger to hyperbole" in selling his apartments.

Then Smith's phone rang. It was Trump, eager to talk. "I sold all my stock over the last month," he said. On a tight deadline, Smith printed Trump's claims. He cited "one market source" who said Trump made $175 million during the market rise. The story got picked up by news organizations across the country. Smith remembers how Norman Pearlstine, the *Journal*'s editor, singled out his story as a bright spot in the day's coverage.

Not long after the story ran, it dawned on Smith that Trump had not sold the stock in Resorts International that he had bought for more than $100 million. He was also certain that Trump still owned millions of dollars of stock in Alexander's, a department store chain with real estate that interested Trump. Both were true. Trump had indeed still been in the market and saw his shares tumble by millions on Black Monday. Decades later, Smith still regretted giving voice to Trump's phony claims, but he sees it as an unfortunate outcome of the "crank out the stories" ethos of the day.

Trump had also told Smith that the worst was yet to come: "I think the market is going to go down further," he said, because "there are just too many things wrong with the country." That time he was wrong. Within two days, the market had gained back more than half of its losses. And Donald did not heed his own advice. He bought a big block of stock in the Hilton Hotel company, again with borrowed money. He sold it four weeks later for a gain of $632,130 before interest.

The agreement to take over Resorts and Ace Greenberg's comments calling him a hungry vulture had momentarily restored his legitimacy as a corporate raider. In the next year, he would temporarily buy, pump, and sell stocks in Federated Department Stores, MCA, and Gillette. His gains on those three stocks would approach $18 million before expenses, even as analysts once again started noting that he had never completed a hostile takeover. Trump's ability to execute a consequential bluff was perhaps unsurpassed. But his ability to bring a consequential project to a profitable conclusion seemed to be failing him.

20

CAMPAIGN OF TRUTH

BY THE TIME he began acting like a corporate raider, Donald Trump's primary identity as a real estate developer was gasping for air in the weedy and rusted railroad yards on the West Side of Manhattan. He had owned the yards now for more than two years. His interest payments and property taxes were approaching $20 million a year, and he had spent millions of dollars more on consultants and planners and enlarging his staff. He needed two challenging elements of the project to come together: a major tenant to lock in enough revenue that lenders would finance his Television City, and the cooperation of City Hall in awarding him a large tax abatement and rezoning the area.

He had made both more challenging with his actions. The prior year, he had drained whatever well of goodwill he may have had with the Koch administration. The mayor had not been a fan of Trump since their dispute over the tax abatement on Trump Tower. But Koch's view of Trump grew darker in 1986, when Trump began making a splash of criticizing city government for not completing reconstruction of the Wollman ice-skating rink in Central Park. Trump offered to finish the work at cost, which Koch accepted. Trump's contribution was convincing HRH Construction, which had handled the Grand Hyatt and Trump Tower for him, to finish the skating rink at their cost, promising that the favorable publicity would provide more than enough profit. HRH handily finished the simple job, a slab of concrete with freon tubes, in six months. Trump held a news conference and took credit without mentioning HRH. He would bad-mouth Ed Koch and the city's inability to finish the job.

So Trump faced an uphill battle one Friday afternoon in the spring of 1987, when he placed an unscheduled call to the City Hall office of Alair Townsend, Mayor Koch's deputy mayor for finance and economic development. As a woman at the highest levels of city government, Townsend was something of a rarity, but she had been that sort of rarity for most of her adult life. Before joining the Koch administration in 1981, she had worked in Washington, D.C., for seventeen years, rising to assistant secretary for management and budget of the Department of Health and Human Services, directing a staff of seven hundred to manage a budget of $250 billion.

Townsend was no one's idea of a pushover. She had not spoken to Trump before, but she picked up the phone when she was told he was on the line that day. Right away, Trump started talking about NBC's plans to leave the city. He framed the threat of losing the network as a crisis that the city government needed to prevent at all costs. He worked her over about how NBC wanted to move to his location, his grand Television City, on the West Side. He argued that the city government should negotiate only with him and waive his property taxes for the next thirty years to keep a major employer like NBC. And he demanded an answer within two hours.

Even from Donald Trump, it was a shocking proposal. By Townsend's rough calculation, Trump's abatement would cost the city $1 billion over the decades, a savings that would go straight to him and the buyers of his luxury apartments. Townsend did not believe the city needed to give up that much revenue to keep NBC. The timing also made no sense to her. Trump wanted a huge tax break now, amid a strong economy and a construction boom, that was far more generous than the tax break he had been given a decade earlier for the Grand Hyatt during a recession and with construction at a standstill.

Townsend had heard NBC making noises about moving when their lease at Rockefeller Center ended. But she knew that negotiations with big companies often played out like a game of chicken. She doubted NBC really wanted to leave the city. Hard to imagine, she thought, turning on the television to hear "Live from Secaucus, New Jersey, it's *Saturday Night Live*!"

She told Trump that his proposal sounded ridiculous. But she assigned Jay Biggins, the city's top economic development official, to meet with him and discuss it further.

Later that afternoon, right at the close of business for the weekend, Trump met with executives at NBC. In trying to lock down the deal right there, Trump assured the network executives that he had the city's support for his abatement. Everything was in place, he told them. It was a bluff on a monumental scale. He left without a commitment.

On Monday morning, an NBC executive called Koch and asked if it was true that the city was fully behind Trump. Koch told the executive no, it was not true, and the city had no reason to offer such a massive benefit to Donald Trump. The bluff had failed. And his reputation at City Hall was in worse shape than ever.

THAT SUMMER, Barbara Res returned to Trump Tower. She had left on good terms in 1984, and Trump hired her back at $200,000 a year, a large salary in 1987, in part to focus on his plans for the West Side rail yards.

There had been changes in personnel since she left. Louise Sunshine, Trump's first key employee, had left after a fight with Trump over money. And Trump had hired Tony Gliedman, the director of housing for the Koch administration, whom he'd called "the Fat Fuck," to also help make something happen on the West Side. He told Gliedman that as a condition of employment, he had to lose one hundred pounds. Gliedman put up with the abuse because, with children entering college, he needed to make more money than he had with the city.

The biggest change Res noticed on the twenty-sixth floor was in Trump himself. In her mind, his first flush of fame had gone to his head. Everywhere he went, Matt Calamari was at his side serving as a bodyguard. He no longer listened to anyone. During Res's first tour with Trump, they had lively disagreements about construction, but always in the spirit of sharing a common goal. Now Trump insisted that his first impulse, which he referred to as his instinct, was always the best course. He only valued people who agreed with him. And he would lose his temper more frequently.

He deemed anyone who opposed him, or even just inconvenienced him, to be fatally dumb. For example, when Trump realized that Mar-a-Lago was three miles from the local airport, and directly under a flight path, he took no personal responsibility for failing to recognize that fact. The noise from jets disturbed his sleep and social life, and that was reason enough, in his mind, to launch a yearslong war of words, calling the management of the airport "tragic and stupid" and "a disgrace." He supported two candidates for the Palm Beach County Commission to fight for his peace and quiet. Both lost.

In the two weeks after Trump first called Townsend, Biggins and half a dozen employees from the city met with Trump and his lawyers several times at Trump Tower. After some of those meetings, Trump would call Townsend to complain. Townsend found him to be demeaning and patronizing, calling her "hon" and behaving as if he thought he could charm her off her high heels, as she later recalled. When she did not go along with whatever bothered him, he would call the reporters at City Hall and complain that she did not know what she was doing. Some of the reporters would then call Townsend, who was well respected, and tell her that Trump was trying to plant stories about her.

Biggins and Townsend knew that Trump had bluffed NBC about city officials promising him a huge tax abatement. But during those meetings, Biggins picked up on a second bluff—Trump was trying to convince them that NBC had committed to moving to his project, and the city better get on board or the network would decamp for New Jersey. He insisted that the city should negotiate with NBC only through him, because the network was only interested in his site and plan.

That second bluff caused Biggins and Townsend to lose all faith in Trump. "We became uncomfortable with the extent to which he was representing his status with NBC," Biggins later recalled. He wrote a memo to Koch at the time telling the mayor, "The kind of brinksmanship and misstatement of the facts we have seen is not the kind of conduct we can tolerate in a partner with so much at stake."

Townsend, Biggins, and Koch recognized that NBC was the prize for the city, not Trump. They decided to negotiate only with NBC and offer the network a movable package. NBC would be eligible for one set of subsidies if it invested heavily in Rockefeller Center and stayed put. There would be a comparable package of incentives should NBC decide to move within the city, whether to Trump's location or elsewhere. That offer would still be lower than what Trump wanted.

During the last of about four meetings at Trump Tower in May 1987, they told Trump their decision and that they had already begun speaking directly with NBC. As Townsend and Biggins remembered it, Trump reacted with a mix of shock and anger, calling them stupid and saying most people would sacrifice a favorite body part to be in a deal with him. They had watched him enough not to be surprised by the anger, or the insults, but they were shocked themselves that he did not expect them to speak directly with NBC executives.

After being briefed by Townsend and Biggins, Koch met with Robert C. Wright, the president and chief executive officer of NBC, and then announced the city's decision. He explained it to reporters in a simple way: "We're saying to NBC, 'Here are the financial incentives. Take them wherever you want to, to any developer, and then squeeze that developer.'"

Knowing what was coming in advance, Trump had time to consider a response, to tamp down his anger in hopes of realizing a better outcome on another day. Instead, he swung for Koch's head. "I am not at all surprised that this is the mayor's response because he has absolutely no sense of economic development. And this is precisely the reason why company after company is leaving New York, and that, as an example, most of New York does not even have cable television, the homeless are unnecessarily wandering the streets, the schools are a disaster and why, after seven years, the city cannot even build a simple skating rink. Koch is incapable of moving anything forward. He should resign from office. He can't hack it anymore."

Trump made the city's decision about him. In his telling, he was being persecuted, again, because he was Donald Trump. "He is more concerned about appearing to give anything to Donald Trump than he is about losing NBC," Trump said.

Koch retorted: "If Donald Trump is squealing like a stuck pig, I must have done something right. Common sense does not allow me to give away the city's treasury to Donald Trump."

Their disagreement played out in the city papers like a celebrity divorce, with little discernible effort to determine who was right. Koch did not roll over. He called Trump "piggy, piggy, piggy" at one point to describe what Trump wanted from the city. But he would not engage blow for verbal blow. Trump continued his tirade for months, as if Koch's refusal to open the city's purse strings for Trump was a proxy for the totality of Koch's mind, soul, and abilities. He would say Koch "has no talent and only moderate intelligence" and is "a moron." He vowed to "do a real number on Koch." He assigned lawyers to explore impeaching Koch, and, after learning that impeachment was not possible under the City Charter, announced he would take down the mayor with a "campaign of truth" revealing all his failures.

It could not have been a more different approach than his father took over the course of his career. Fred Trump had spent his life cultivating friendships with city politicians and party officials, especially Abe Beame and Bunny Lindenbaum, that might someday pay a dividend. As it turned out, the biggest business benefit of those relationships went to his son, when Beame sealed Donald Trump's first deal on the Commodore hotel by vouching for him and his father. But there was also something genuine in Fred's friendship with Beame. They spent significant time together, from the long drive they took to Virginia during the war, well before Beame held any significant power, to attending each other's birthday and anniversary parties long after Beame had retired from politics.

Donald had given $350,000 to city candidates in the prior five years, much of it to Andrew Stein, who had become president of the City Council since helping Trump set up a meeting on the Trump Tower tax abatement (nearly all of it through companies owned by his father, who no longer needed a city official's approval for much of anything). Trump could still count on Stein to make a phone call on his behalf, but Stein would never have the power to push through a major project on his own.

Trump now found himself in a moment of great need, with the burden of monthly costs on the rail yards bearing down on him, and not an ally to be found.

WHILE HIS EFFORTS to move forward with his primary business languished, Trump focused more energy on expanding his public image. In September 1987, he spent $94,801 on full-page advertisements in *The New York Times*, *The Boston Globe*, and *The Washington Post*, with an open letter from Donald J. Trump to "The American People." The ad blew past the grandiosity of his father's full-page advertisement four decades earlier that cast the plain Shore Haven apartments in Brooklyn as a symbol to passing ships of "The American Way of Life." Donald's advertisement argued that Japan and Persian Gulf countries were taking advantage of the United States by not reimbursing the nation for defense expenditures on their behalf. As evidence of the nation's injury, Trump wrote that "the world is laughing" at our politicians and "our great country."

He did not mention Ronald Reagan, the Republican president whose actions he was criticizing. He also ignored the complex geopolitical and economic history that led to those decisions. But he had heard laughter, so he was sure he was right. Trump logic.

That night, Trump appeared on *Larry King Live*, the highly rated CNN evening show, to discuss the advertisement. He mentioned nine times that other nations and their leaders were laughing at the United States and its leaders. He referred repeatedly to "this horrible horrendous deficit" of $200 billion, which he described as losing money.

"The United States is, if it were a corporation, it would be bankrupt," he said. He added that "this could be much, much worse, unfortunately, than recession. This could be a step beyond, hate to, I hate to use the word 'depression.' But if we do not solve the $200 billion a year loss, which is exactly what we have, this country is going to have some very, very serious problems in the early 1990s."

King never challenged Trump's command of the facts or his logic. It was not clear whether Trump was referring to the nation's budget deficit, which would mean spending exceeded revenues, or the trade deficit, which would mean imports exceeded exports. The budget deficit had been $221 billion the year before, but it had fallen to $150 billion by the time Trump was speaking. And Japan, the country Trump said was doing great because it was "ripping off the United States," had a higher budget deficit than the U.S. as a percentage of its gross domestic product, the measure that economists find more meaningful than the raw number. The trade deficit stood at $160 billion.

Trump's only specific complaint referred to the United States' expenditures to help defend Kuwait, Japan, and Saudi Arabia, which would suggest he was referring to a budget deficit. A caller to the show asked whether he was recommending an unconstitutional tax on foreign governments. "You can call it a tax, you can call it whatever you want to call it, but those countries should be paying us major billions of dollars and you won't have any deficits whatsoever," he responded. "And then we'll be able to help the poor and the sick and the homeless and the farmers and everybody else."

A caller from Toronto seemed to think he was referring to the trade deficit and asked whether he thought the solution should be government restrictions on trade or a more entrepreneurial business sector. Trump did not correct the caller to say he was referring to budget deficits. He said only that while he supported free trade, "we don't have free trade," which he knew because "I have many friends. They go over to Japan. They can't open up anything."

Those two points—America being ripped off and laughed at by other countries—would form the foundation, if not the entirety, of Trump's positions on international affairs for decades to come. The attention he drew on the show and from the advertisement led to him briefly being talked about as a possible presidential candidate. At the invitation of a Republican organizer in New Hampshire hoping to recruit Trump to run for president, he spoke at a meeting of the Portsmouth Rotary Club. During his speech to a room packed with Rotary members, local voters, and reporters, Trump announced that he would not run. But he again made a speech about the United States getting ripped off.

One local woman in the crowd, Judy Taylor, said she found Trump to be "very exciting. Money is power, and power is the ultimate aphrodisiac."

It all served as perfect publicity tour for the publication of his book *The Art of the Deal* in November 1987. Howard Rubenstein's team further fueled interest by arranging television appearances for Trump with Johnny Carson, David Letterman, Phil Donahue, and Barbara Walters, all under the agreement that their segments would run on a date agreeable to Rubenstein to maximize the impact on sales. *Vanity Fair* and *New York* magazine ran extensive excerpts. *People* magazine solicited the opinion of its bureaus across the country as to whether Trump was now a national figure with reach and recognition beyond the East Coast. The poll concluded that he was the "ultimate super businessman," and the editors decided to put him on the cover.

Decades later, when we obtained his tax records for those years, the first figure that jumped off the page was the losses he reported at what had seemed to be the height of his power and wealth. For the year *The Art of the Deal* was published, Trump's core businesses reported a negative income of $45.4 million. His stock bluffs and inherited wealth had produced greater results than his business acumen. He reported $25.4 million in short-term capital gains, mostly, if not entirely, from the stocks he sold after letting investors believe he might take over the company. And he reported another $9.3 million in long-term capital gains, which appeared to be almost entirely from his father's efforts. And despite his promise to donate royalties from the book, the records we obtained showed that he reported no charitable contributions through at least 1995.

Trump held book signings at Trump Castle casino for anyone who bought a book, and he bought newspaper advertisements to promote the events. There were rumors of him directing associates to buy large numbers of books to push it onto the bestseller list. It all worked. *The Art of the Deal* became an instant bestseller.

He held a book party in the atrium of Trump Tower. In the crowd of the usual bold-faced names stood a young woman from Georgia with flowing blond hair and a broad smile. Donald had been introduced to her a couple of years earlier by a fellow USFL team owner, who had judged a swimsuit contest that the young woman had entered in Florida. Nothing came from that brief encounter. But the young woman, Marla Maples, had since moved to New York City to pursue an acting career. Their paths crossed again, and this time, something happened. She had just turned twenty-four. Donald was forty-one, married, and with three children ages three to ten. She would soon be showing up at boxing matches and other events that Trump sponsored in Atlantic City, and would go on to change the course of his life.

There would be no depression in the early 1990s, just an eight-month recession that had little to do with any sort of deficit. There would be no fact-based campaign of truth regarding Koch, just more insults. In the years to come, Donald would continue to spend millions a year trying unsuccessfully to launch a large-scale project on the West Side. But he was far from finished taking on costs that he could not support indefinitely.

21

WHITE ELEPHANTS

THE AGING JET was just what Donald Trump had wanted, only not quite enough. It was a 727, a giant in the sky, for which he paid an oil company $8.3 million. The jet burned so much fuel that he would spend more than $1 million a year to use it, often just for trips to and from Mar-a-Lago or for ski trips to Aspen with his family during the holidays. He spent millions more adding a second conference room, two more bathrooms, and emblazing "Trump" on its tail. But he refused to let his casino managers use the jet as a perk to thank high rollers, who Trump considered "slobs" not worthy of using his gold-plated bathrooms.

He found the jet just weeks after spending $2 million on a used Super Puma Aerospatiale helicopter that seated eighteen. He spent more to remodel the helicopter to his tastes. With banks continuing to lend him seemingly limitless amounts of money, Trump's purchases grew increasingly personal and splashy, each geared toward generating publicity, deepening his image as wealthy and therefore successful at everything he touched. And with each acquisition, he took on increasingly risky levels of debt.

He spent millions re-renovating his Trump Tower triplex, ripping out the tasteful décor shortly after it had been completed by designer Angelo Donghia and featured in *Architectural Digest*. Trump, who had never found the Donghia design to be flashy enough, hired Henry Conversano, an eminent designer of casino floors and high-roller suites with a theatrical flair. The "warm modern" look that Trump described was replaced by gold leafing on the ceiling, the tops of white onyx columns, parts of the wall, and the furniture. Everywhere the eye turned, something shone brightly back. Huge crystal chandeliers hung from recessed ceiling panels painted with murals of shirtless heroic men and cherubs floating through the clouds, framed in gold. A waterwall poured across a stretch of rust-colored onyx.

A member of the design team snuck into the apartment of Saudi arms dealer Adnan Khashoggi in Olympic Tower, where Trump and Ivana once lived, and took measurements of Khashoggi's very long living room. Donald wanted something bigger, and so walls were removed to create a living room that some began referring to as "a gilded bowling alley." Others thought "Louis XIV on steroids" better captured the overall effect.

His austere father no longer seemed like a role model. Donald Trump's benchmarks now fell more in line with someone like Khashoggi, who owned hotels, shopping malls, and an oil refinery, and who reveled in showing off his twelve estates and his three extravagantly appointed commercial-size jets. Khashoggi was also, like Trump, among the few people from the business world willing to be featured on *Lifestyles of the Rich and Famous*.

As Trump made a run to attain Khashoggi-like status, Khashoggi himself suffered a major setback. His holding company filed for bankruptcy, and a lender forced the sale of his most ostentatious possession, the 282-foot yacht he had named after his daughter, Nabila. The yacht, which had appeared in a James Bond film, featured a helipad, a three-chair hair salon, a movie screening room, and more than one hundred telephones on a satellite communications system. With five decks of living space, the yacht held a full crew of fifty-two.

Trump negotiated a deal to pay $30 million, until Khashoggi learned that Trump planned to keep the name *Nabila* on the yacht's stern. Khashoggi was so uncomfortable with the thought of someone else traveling on a boat bearing his only daughter's name that he accepted $1 million less for Donald agreeing to rename the yacht. It would become *Trump Princess*. Once again, Trump took out a loan for the full purchase price.

Within Donald's small office, only one person had any experience with boats. Jeff Walker, his old acquaintance from the military academy who had worked on the Grand Hyatt and Trump Tower, had grown up in Connecticut around boats and the ocean. Walker had never owned a boat longer than twelve feet, but he knew port from starboard. Donald put him in charge of the yacht.

Neither Trump nor Walker had seen the *Nabila*. Trump told Walker he wanted to spend about $6 million on upgrades. Walker flew to Italy to see the yacht, then sailed for a shipyard in Maakum, in the Netherlands. Walker specced out the work he thought Trump would want—a new double rudder system, interior modifications that would require cutting through the steel hull, rebuilt engines, onyx installed almost everywhere, and more than a thousand feet of chamois leather. He flew back to New York to meet with Trump and break some potentially bad news. "I saw the boat," he told Trump. "Number one, it's incredible, really incredible. I can get it done for you. But instead of six million, it's going to be ten million."

Trump started screaming. That's what Walker had expected. He knew how this would go, and he liked it. Trump gave him great latitude, which he appreciated. When Trump was unhappy, he would scream, become abusive even. But if you could steel yourself, the anger would pass, so long as you could assure Trump that everything would work out to his liking.

When Trump ran out of gas about the new estimate, Walker said, "Look, you know how well I know you and your tastes and what you're going to want. I know you, probably better than anybody. I know it has to be perfect. If it's not perfect, you're not going to be happy, and I'm going to be in trouble."

Trump calmed down and increased the budget to ten million. Walker began flying to the Netherlands every other week to check on the progress. As the work neared completion, Donald decided to fly over to see the results. He boarded his 727 with his assistant, Norma Foerderer; Ivana; her assistant, Lisa Calandra; and Walker.

Every employee of the shipyard, located on a protected inlet off the North Sea, lined up along the dock to greet their wealthy benefactor from America. Trump proudly strolled through this newest emblem of his wealth. He glowed with pride. Then, in one room, his eye turned toward a table with a telephone, a particularly dated European model, with an ornate receiver sitting in a fussy cradle. Walker watched as Trump turned red. Here it comes, he thought. Trump began raging, cursing, and screaming about how much he hated those phones and wanted them gone. Then he picked up the phone and, *swissssshhhh*, threw it across the room. It zipped past Walker and smashed into a wall. With the yacht crew sheepishly looking on, Ivana stepped in to calm him down. Walker waited for his moment.

"Look, don't worry about it," he finally said. "I made a mistake. I should have had those things taken out. They'll be gone by the time you get out of here. And we'll have all new phones in here within two days."

DURING ONE BUSY WEEK in February 1988, Trump sat through a meeting at Trump Tower trying to convince the owners of the New England Patriots to sell their NFL team to him. He served as a presenter at a film industry award ceremony at Lincoln Center in New York. And he negotiated rights to host a Mike Tyson championship boxing match in Atlantic City. He left it to his brother Robert to attend what seemed likely to be an uneventful hearing that week near Trenton, New Jersey.

The license for Resorts International to operate its casino in Atlantic City was up for renewal, and the Trumps expected the Casino Control Commission would follow its usual course and renew the license without controversy.

At least one commissioner, Valerie H. Armstrong, a former private lawyer and administrative judge who grew up in the Atlantic City area, arrived that day with a different idea. Armstrong had voted to approve Donald Trump's taking control of Resorts the year before. She went along with the position that Trump had the best chance to finish the Taj Mahal, and that completing that casino had become central to the future of gambling in Atlantic City. But since then, Trump had for months used the threat of not completing the Taj Mahal to win concessions from the commission.

Those threats included his $108 million services contract and for him to close Resorts' other Atlantic City casino and operate it only as a hotel, which would solve the problem for him of not being allowed to own more than three casinos in Atlantic City.

Trump then announced that he still could not obtain financing and would only complete the Taj Mahal if he owned the company outright. "If I have the company, I can just put up my own money," he said at the time. The stock had traded at $66 a share before the October stock market crash. Trump had helped drive down the price by suggesting that Resorts might have to seek bankruptcy protection. He offered $15 a share. That figure was quickly rejected, and Trump increased his offer to $22. Shareholders eventually went along, pending settlement of several shareholder lawsuits.

After months of mostly accepting Donald's demands, Armstrong questioned his motives and integrity. She said the "gaping holes" in his representations to the commission "could lead to several conclusions regarding Resorts' business and development strategies. While it might be possible to conclude that the events of the past eight months resulted from happenstance, impulse, fate or events beyond Trump's or Resorts' control, it is also just as easy, perhaps easier, to conclude that many of the events leading to Mr. Trump's current merger proposal have been carefully staged, manipulated and orchestrated." Armstrong wondered out loud whether Trump tried "to drive down the value" of Resorts' stock so he could buy the company at an artificially lower value.

Armstrong said that if the vote were held that day, she would vote against renewing Trump's license to operate the Resorts' casino. Another commissioner, W. David Waters, said he felt the same. Waters had recently said, "I feel that I've been used" by Trump and his manipulations. That put Trump's license in jeopardy. He needed four of five commissioners to prevail.

As Robert Trump listened politely in the audience, the commissioners voted to pause the hearing and seek more information from the Trumps. Robert slipped out of the hearing room and called his brother. He then told waiting reporters that Donald had accepted the commission's invitation to straighten things out. "Any issue can have five different sides," Robert said.

Armstrong had not been alone in her suspicions. Several shareholder lawsuits had already accused Trump of putting his own interests ahead of theirs and the company. Marvin B. Roffman, a prominent casino-industry analyst for brokerage firm Janney Montgomery Scott in Philadelphia, said he thought Trump's threats should not be taken at face value. Trump had spent about $100 million buying up Resorts' super-voting stock—too much money to risk letting the Taj Mahal sit unfinished.

A week after Armstrong's comment, Donald Trump showed up to testify. He swore that the only reason he offered to take the company private was that because of his excellent history borrowing money, he would be able to obtain financing for construction with comparatively low-interest bank loans. "I can borrow money at a very prime rate and borrow it personally, but it would be inappropriate for me to borrow money for a company I only own ten percent of," he told the commission.

He said he was close to a deal with a bank. "Banks would have never loaned the money to Resorts as Resorts," he said. "They're loaning the money—I mean, they're loaning the money to me. They couldn't care less about Resorts, in my opinion. Maybe that's an overstatement, but the banks are essentially doing it because I own the company."

He added that he did not have to resort to junk bonds, which he said crushed companies with high interest rates. "The funny thing with junk bonds is that the junk bonds is what really made the companies junk. That's why they're called junk bonds, the rates are so high on the junk bonds that they make the company, that could have been a very good company, they make them junk, so it's like a self-fulfilling prophecy, almost."

Trump eased Armstrong's mind by no longer threatening to pull the plug on the Taj Mahal, promising to give his "best efforts" to obtain financing and finish the project. The five commissioners voted unanimously to approve the license, opening the door to Trump taking the company private. Smiling broadly in the hearing room after the vote, Trump reiterated that he would do his best to get the Taj Mahal built. "This is like a large-scale Wollman Rink," he said.

A new bidder, with a name bigger than Trump, appeared three weeks later. Merv Griffin, the former talk-show host and singer, had sold his game-show empire, including the timeless hits *Jeopardy!* and *Wheel of Fortune*, for $250 million. When Griffin saw how cheaply Trump might be able to acquire multiple casinos, he made an offer well above Trump's, at $35 a share.

The two battled it out in public for a month before coming to an agreement at Trump Tower in April. Trump would get the partially completed Taj Mahal, and Griffin would take over the rest of Resorts. In addition to buying the outstanding stock, Griffin paid Trump the approximately $102 million that Trump had paid to take control of the company, along with $64 million pursuant to the services contract Trump had recently negotiated. Trump paid Griffin $299.7 million for the unfinished hulk of the Taj Mahal and some other assets, including three helicopters.

Both Trump and Griffin declared victory. That November, Trump did exactly what he had repeatedly said he would not do: he took on $675 million of junk bond debt, at a 14 percent interest rate, to complete construction of the Taj Mahal. He committed to paying nearly $100 million a year in interest, including almost $150 million before he planned to open the casino and generate his first penny in revenue. Part of the junk bond proceeds were earmarked to cover his first two interest payments. He borrowed money from bondholders to pay them their interest.

Roffman, the casino industry analyst, noted that the Taj Mahal would have to record gross receipts of more than $1 million a day just to cover its interest payments, something Roffman thought unlikely after the excitement of the opening passed.

Trump had also buried the Castle casino in expenses. Ivana, in a bid to compete with her husband's other casino, Trump Plaza, had persuaded Donald to spend more than $100 million building Crystal Tower, a fourteen-story hotel with one hundred high-roller suites. The suites were appointed with marble, pure wool carpets, and gold bathroom faucets that cost $1,800 each. He also spent $2 million dredging a path to the Castle for his *Trump Princess* yacht, millions more renovating a marina, and charged the expense for operating the yacht to the Castle. In a town where older suburbanites arrived in buses to sit in front of a slot machine with a paper cup full of coins, Trump had bet a fortune on attracting million-dollar poker players from Monte Carlo and Las Vegas. The Castle would never make money.

At the time, Roffman noted broad challenges ahead for casinos in Atlantic City. More than a decade after gambling had been legalized, in part to bring back the Shore town, most of the city remained run-down. High rollers had grown disenchanted and returned to Las Vegas. Roffman said that looking ahead to 1989 and 1990 is "scaring me to death."

As the national economy slowed, Trump took on costs and debts with breathtaking speed, each time without seriously running the numbers to spec out potential profits. He saw his involvement in any business as likely to produce enough revenue to cover any costs. The only brakes on his spending and acquisition would be lenders, and the lenders were always ready with a green light.

"I mean, the banks call me all the time, can we loan you money, can we this, can we that," Trump told New Jersey casino regulators. "There is tremendous liquidity if you have a good statement and if you're solid. The banks, they want to throw money at you."

He had for years gazed out the window of his Trump Tower office at the iconic Plaza Hotel two blocks north, a stately marquee to a more glamorous era lording over the southeast corner of Central Park. He could see the edges of the mansard roof, with turrets on the corners and patinaed copper detail, topping off the white brick base. It had been the place where crowds once flocked to see heirs to the Vanderbilt fortune sip tea, and decades later, glimpsed at the Beatles during their first United States tour.

While fighting with Merv Griffin in March 1988, Trump bought the twenty-one-story hotel for $407.5 million. Citibank lent him $425 million for the purchase, yet another loan requiring nothing up front. And Trump personally guaranteed $125 million of that total, meaning the bank could go after any of his assets if he defaulted. The 808-room hotel had made a profit of $22 million the year before, not enough to cover even his interest payments.

Trump embarked on an expensive updating of the dowdy and dated hotel. And as he acknowledged in a full-page advertisement he took out in *New York* magazine, he had "purchased a masterpiece—the Mona Lisa," for a price that made no sense. "For the first time in my life, I have knowingly made a deal that was not economic—for I can never justify the price I paid, no matter how successful the Plaza becomes."

Donald Trump made one final debt-fueled purchase, this one for a business in which he had no experience. Eastern Airlines began shedding assets in 1988 to fend off bankruptcy. Trump bid for the airline's crown jewel, its shuttle service between Boston, New York City, and Washington, D.C. That October, he reached a deal to pay $365 million for twenty-one aircraft and the shuttle routes. Once again, Citibank provided the entire amount.

He would call it Trump Shuttle. He held a news conference at the site of his other newest acquisition, the Plaza Hotel. Standing before a model of a jet painted with a Trump Shuttle logo, Trump admitted he knew little about operating an airline, but said, "I want to run it as a diamond, an absolute diamond."

He assigned Jeff Walker, who had just finished the renovation of the *Trump Princess*, to handle the making of Trump Shuttle's 727s into glamorous apartments in the sky. Walker knew less about jets that he did about giant yachts, but he had advised Trump not to buy the airline. He saw too many factors that could not be controlled, especially the powerful labor unions. But once the deal was done, Trump put Walker in charge of renovations. He oversaw the installation of leather seats, high-end carpets, simulated marble in the restrooms. "No plane looked like this at the time," Walker later recalled.

In about a year, Trump had taken on almost $1.7 billion in new debt between the Taj Mahal, the Plaza Hotel, Trump Shuttle, and Trump Palace, and none of them were producing enough profit to cover his interest payments. He was paying more than $20 million a year in carrying costs on the fallow West Side rail yards. He had performed little due diligence on the profit potential of anything he bought. He increasingly substituted his lenders' judgment for his own.

Forbes put the value of Trump's assets above his debts at $1.7 billion in 1989. The magazine would soon realize the error in taking Trump's word on his businesses. But for now, the *Forbes* figure continued to support the invented perception that Trump was among the wealthiest people in America.

An empire of that size should produce some sort of return for its owners. But the tax records that we acquired decades later showed that Trump reported losses of $185 million from his core businesses in that year. He was living off borrowed money, using hundreds of millions of dollars of cash flowing through the casinos to cover his debt payments.

Roffman had posited that Trump must have been bluffing about being willing not to build the Taj Mahal because he would not want to find himself with a white elephant, a term for a business asset that does not produce enough revenue to cover its costs. Now, Donald Trump had a circus tent full of white elephants.

AS HE ACQUIRED PROPERTIES and toys and crushing debt, Trump and Ivana arrived in Manhattan aboard the newly refurbished *Trump Princess*. Trump described his purchase of a yacht as an act of patriotism. "I feel very strongly that America should have the great jewels, and this is one of them." He added that the yacht had been "owned by people in a country that really has taken advantage of the United States," a reference to Khashoggi being from Saudi Arabia.

Meanwhile, he moved the two main women in his life around like figurines on his personal Monopoly board. His relationship with Marla Maples had grown more serious. She showed up at events, and he kept her holed up at the St. Moritz hotel, just a short walk from Trump Tower. Ivana still spent three long days a week at the Castle casino in Atlantic City. When Trump bought the Plaza Hotel, he removed Ivana from her job at the Castle and put her in charge of renovating and running the Plaza Hotel. Marla, in turn, was shipped down to Atlantic City, splitting her time between lounging on the *Trump Princess* and in rooms in the Trump Plaza casino.

He grew short tempered with Ivana, sometimes erupting over differences in decorating choices at the Plaza Hotel. Trump would grow angry, screaming and yelling about something Ivana had bought, and storm out of the building. He would find solace on the short walk back to Trump Tower. Tourists would flock to him, tell him how much they admired his success and wealth, and compliment him on his good looks. Some would ask for photographs or an autograph. With each new rush of adoration from a stranger, the anger would melt away, his posture would straighten again. This benefit of fame served as his elixir.

When Trump moved Ivana back to Manhattan, he put Steve Hyde, who had been his top executive at the Plaza casino, in charge of all his Atlantic City operations. Ivana was crestfallen. It was the job she thought she had earned running the Castle, working selflessly to please her husband. The position made Hyde central to Donald's ability to run three casinos efficiently enough to pay the crushing interest payments he owed to his lenders. Donald had not focused on building an executive team with a bench deep enough to survive change. He counted on his brother Robert to serve as his eyes and ears. He paid Hyde, a devout Mormon and father of seven, more than $1 million a year and put great faith in him. The rest was left to Hyde's number two, Mark Grossinger Etess, another seasoned casino executive.

On October 10, 1989, Hyde and Etess boarded a rented helicopter in Manhattan for the short return flight to Atlantic City. At 1:42 p.m., its main four-blade rotor and the tail rotor broke free and the helicopter plunged 2,800 feet to the wooded median between lanes on the Garden State Parkway. Hyde, forty-three, and Estess, thirty-eight, were killed, as were Jonathan Benanav, thirty-three, an executive vice president of the Trump Plaza casino hotel, and two other men.

Trump expressed condolences for the families and complimented their contributions to his company. He then made their deaths about himself, saying he had intended to be on the helicopter but changed plans at the last minute. But for him, the real import of the crash would be the loss of leadership at a crucial moment. With one of the biggest casinos in the nation under construction, costs approaching $1 billion, and almost $50 million in interest payments coming due every six months on just that one project, Trump had no one he trusted leading his casinos.

He and Ivana had for several years taken a ski trip to Aspen around Christmas. In 1989, she traveled ahead of him with their three children. Donald arrived on his newly acquired jet with Marla. He had her driven to a condominium he had rented for her and a girlfriend. By then, Ivana had heard rumors of a woman named Marla. On the afternoon of New Year's Eve, their paths crossed on a sundeck outside a midmountain restaurant. Accounts of the words exchanged that day have varied but typically go something like this:

"Why don't you leave my husband alone?" Ivana asked.

"Are you happy?" Marla responded, and then professed her love for Ivana's husband.

At that moment, there was no part of Donald Trump's fortunate life that did not sit on the brink of disaster.

22

WILDEST EXPECTATIONS

A WEEK BEFORE THE TRUMP Taj Mahal would finally open, Trump's casino executives organized a pep rally for more than six thousand new employees. In the casino's cavernous new arena, dealers and maids and cocktail waitresses wore glowing neon sticks around their necks and wrists while dancing and singing along to "We Are Family," the 1970s disco hit by Sister Sledge. Hoots and hollers erupted from the darkness. After a few more songs, lasers shot colored light rays across the large room. Theatrical smoke puffed from the stage. On several large projection screens, a man appeared with the bug-eyed stare of a silent movie villain, a satin turban atop his head.

"I am Fabu the Fabulous!" his voice bellowed from loudspeakers. "I am the resident genie of the Trump Taj Mahal . . . the eighth wonder of the world!" Fabu went on to explain that he had not been summoned by "any mere lamp rubbing," but rather it was "your spirit of teamwork, of motivation, and of commitment to success that got me here."

The leadership team that Trump had installed after the helicopter crash the previous fall took the stage and shouted questions to generate excited cheers in response. "When I told you that this building is the most fabulous hotel casino in the world, did I tell you the truth?" asked Walter Haybert, who Trump had named president of the Taj Mahal. "Do we have the most magnificent casino in the world?" asked Willard C. "Bucky" Howard, the casino's executive vice president. Robert joined the executives and kicked up his leather loafers with casino dancers. "We're going to give our customers so much fun they won't want to leave us!" he told the crowd of employees.

More smoke filled the stage. The triumphant song "Eye of the Tiger" from the *Rocky* films blasted from the speakers. Curtains parted, and out into the smoke and thumping music walked Donald Trump. The crowd chanted "Donald! Donald!" in unison. He took the microphone to fire up his staff. "Boy, a lot of payroll," he began, killing the excitement in a flash. "I asked someone, 'Am I paying them today, or does it start Monday?' And I was told it started two weeks ago. That's okay."

He then threw a line of support to his employees—"You really are great people"—before patting himself on the back for once again overcoming naysayers. "You know, the risk with the Taj was getting it built. But the building has come out so well," he said. "It's going to be a lot of fun proving people wrong about it. I love proving people wrong.

"When we took on this project, we made a decision: Do we go first class, or do we go in with paint and glue. And we decided, at great cost, to lay it on the line."

THE PEOPLE TRUMP WANTED to prove wrong were mostly industry analysts who agreed that he had laid everything on the line, but doubted the market in Atlantic City could support his spending. Back in December, *Fortune* had pointed out that Trump had missed two deadlines to complete construction and faced a possible cash crunch. A $47 million interest payment was due on May 15, only a few weeks after he would begin generating revenue. The popular Wall Street publication, *Grant's Interest Rate Observer*, wrote that Trump's overall debt put his financial stability "under suspicion."

It was all the sort of quantitative analysis Trump despised. He produced a letter from the Arthur Andersen accounting firm saying he had hundreds of millions of dollars on hand. "I don't need a lot of cash," he said. Then he began trying to sell his yacht and the Plaza Hotel, but only to have cash for more acquisitions, he insisted.

Analysts believed Trump would simply be taking players away from other casinos, including the two he owned. So did his own executive vice president, Bucky Howard, who remembered telling Trump before the opening that the Taj Mahal was going to fail. "It was doomed way before the start," Howard later recalled.

Marvin Roffman had been saying for more than a year that the Taj Mahal would need on average $1.3 million of revenue every day to meet Trump's debt payments, a level the Atlantic City market could not support. In December 1989, he told the *Miami Herald* that Trump's fame and the spectacle of the huge Taj Mahal would make for a flush spring and summer, but the cold winter months in New Jersey would be a challenge.

Two weeks before the scheduled opening, *The Wall Street Journal* quoted Roffman making the same point: "When this property opens, he will have had so much free publicity he will break every record in the books in April, June, and July. But once the cold winds blow from October to February, it won't make it. The market just isn't there."

Trump could not take it anymore. He sent a letter that day to Roffman's boss, Norman T. Wilde Jr., president and chief executive officer of Janney Montgomery Scott. He called Roffman's comments "an outrage," and added, "I am now planning to institute a major lawsuit against your firm unless Mr. Roffman makes a major public apology or is dismissed." The firm's chairman, Edgar Scott, never addressed whether Roffman had been correct in his assessment. Scott told Roffman that he could no longer speak to the press or testify before the Casino Control Commission, and that he would lose his bonus for the year. Scott called Trump the next day to let him know Roffman had been disciplined and to ask how Trump wished the firm to handle an apology. Trump said he wanted Roffman to write him a contrite letter. After his bosses found Roffman's draft letter to be insufficient, they wrote one for him. "Unquestionably, the Taj's opening will be the grandest and most successful the city has ever seen," the new letter said, and added that Roffman had "every hope that the Taj will ultimately be very profitable." Roffman, still concerned about losing his job, signed the letter.

Trump thought the letter did not go far enough. He wanted Roffman to say he was sure the Taj Mahal would be profitable. Roffman went home and stewed over what had happened. His duty, as he saw it, was to be truthful to investors and potential investors. The next afternoon, he sent a fax to Trump retracting his apology and saying he had not written the letter himself. He was fired the next morning.

Trump also took his war of words to Neil Barsky, the *Wall Street Journal* reporter who quoted Roffman's warning. Since covering real estate for the *New York Daily News*, Barsky had long been one of the few reporters to scrutinize Trump's claims and promises. "Dear Neil," Trump wrote in a letter to Barsky.

"From your first incorrect story on Merv Griffin—to your present Wall Street Journal article, you are a disgrace to your profession! Sincerely, Donald J. Trump."

BY THEN, his problems with Ivana had broken into public view and added another layer to doubts about his finances. He was on a plane returning from Tokyo, having attended a Mike Tyson fight there, when Liz Smith, the lead gossip columnist at the *Daily News*, wrote that Ivana had been devastated to learn "that Donald was betraying her." She had been so busy, Smith wrote, taking care of the family while serving as "her husband's full-time business partner, that she had absolutely no idea that the marriage was in trouble."

The Sunday that he returned, Donald moved out of the Trump Tower triplex and into the smaller apartment that he had bought for his parents to use. He began dishing self-serving insider details to reporters, especially his friend Cindy Adams, the gossip columnist at the *New York Post*. Donald's first line of attack was to argue that he was the one, not Ivana, who instigated the split. But the appetite for tawdry details was endless. An entertainment reporter for the *Post* would later recount sitting in the office with the top editor when Trump called demanding front-page treatment making him look good. After prodding, he offered that Marla always said that Trump provided her the "best sex I've ever had." The quote, which Marla soon disavowed, became one of the most famous front-page headlines in New York City tabloid history.

Eric and Ivanka were still young enough not to be entirely aware of all the attention. But Don Jr., twelve, grew angry with his father and stopped speaking to him. The boy began spending summers with his maternal grandparents in Czechoslovakia, where he learned to hunt and fish from his grandfather.

Around the same time that he took up with Marla, Trump had persuaded his unwitting wife to sign a new prenuptial agreement increasing the cash she would receive in the event of a divorce to $25 million and removing a phrase mentioning "the great love and affection each has for the other." After confronting Marla in Aspen, Ivana came to believe she had been played, that Donald had known he would be leaving her soon and lured her with the increased payout to somehow prevent her from getting even more. She made it clear she would challenge its validity in court, creating another threat to his finances.

Trump had toyed with bringing Marla Maples to the Taj opening events, but aides convinced him otherwise. In an interview on national television, Donald called the split "a horrible thing on a personal basis," but said it had piqued interest in the coming opening of the Taj Mahal. Requests for press credentials jumped from two hundred to more than two thousand, he said. "It brings people maybe for the wrong reasons," he said. "I don't like bringing people for that reason. But nevertheless, the controversy probably is not a negative thing in terms of a building or a business."

At the entrance road to the Taj Mahal, visitors drove between two large concrete arches and matching life-size elephant statues. The casino's exterior was capped by colorful onion domes and seventy-foot-high minarets. The sprawling gambling floor, bigger than two football fields at 120,000 square feet, held more than 3,000 slot machines and 160 gambling tables, all surrounded by gold mirrors, large crystal chandeliers, Carrera marble, and purple carpeting.

At the front door, the "Sultan's Royal Greeters" wore elaborate sparkling turbans, ostrich feathers, gold sashes, and tassels, with lots of purple. Employees worked in character and were referred to as "performers"—Sinbad the Sailor, Ali Baba, or a few of the Forty Thieves. It all created the feel of an Epcot installation at Disney World without much attention to authenticity, a kitschy fantasy detached from history, geography, and certainly from its namesake mausoleum in India. The restaurants danced around continents—a Safari Steakhouse, a Marco Polo Italian restaurant, and a Casbah lounge—and suites bore the names of King Tut, Cleopatra, Michelangelo, and Alexander the Great. Cocktail waitresses wore culture-clashing Turkish fez caps with harem pants. "It's all Hollywood," explained Steve Campbell, the Los Angeles–based interior designer who oversaw such choices. Campbell said he found his inspiration in a 1960s television sitcom. "It's the *I Dream of Jeannie* look."

The architect, Francis X. Dumont, described his guiding vision as "a maharajah's palace." Paul Goldberger, the *New York Times* architecture critic, described the result as a "plain building dressed up to within an inch of its life" and offering no more real joy than "the bleakness of crumbling Atlantic City" outside.

But an architecture critic from the *Times* was most certainly not the target audience. Alma Guicheteau, seventy-six, and Teresa Tamanini, sixty-eight, two self-described "casino buddies," made the hour drive from their homes in Vineland, New Jersey, to survey the big trial opening.

"Ooooh, Alma, look at those chandeliers," Teresa cooed. "They're byoooooo-tiful."

Alma saw a sharp-dressed man and asked him, "How the hell do you get your parking stamped?" She had accidentally hit the jackpot. The man in a suit and tie turned out to be Bucky Howard. "I'll personally initial it for you," Bucky said, "and you know what else? Donald Trump is about to walk through that door."

And so he did. Trump walked over and signed autographs for Alma and Teresa of Vineland. Both were delighted. "Teresa," Alma said as Trump walked away, "he's thinner than he is on TV."

The Taj, as everyone called it, filled that week with gamblers and gawkers, many of them older women who came for a thrill of possibly bumping into Donald Trump. Joanne Jones of Lakewood, New Jersey, scampered a few steps across the floor of the Taj Mahal and slapped Trump lightly on the shoulder, then started screaming. "I *touched* him. I touched Donald!"

She caught her breath for a beat, and then lost it again. "Ooh, I can't stand it," she shouted. "I have to go to the bathroom."

JOANNE AND ALMA AND TERESA could not see that behind those doors, Donald's chances of being saved by a rush of cash from his new casino were dwindling. After a trial opening on Monday, his finance people could not reconcile the cash with the totals from the three thousand slot machines. The numbers were off by almost $2 million. In the push to open, the director of finance at the Taj became so exhausted that he collapsed on the casino floor and was hauled out on a stretcher. As gamblers lined up outside by the thousands, the Casino Control Commission informed Trump that he could not open the doors again until he could show where the money went.

In a panic, Trump called John R. O'Donnell, the experienced casino pro whom Stephen Hyde had put in charge of running Trump Plaza, now Trump's only profitable casino. O'Donnell, who everyone called Jack, was only thirty-two, but he had spent his life in and around casinos. His father had transformed a pinball manufacturer into Bally Manufacturing, the largest maker of slot machines in the world.

O'Donnell's assistant interrupted him during a staff meeting to tell him

Trump was on the line. O'Donnell suspected the boss was not calling with good news. "Jack, I'm at the Taj. . . . I got big fucking problems over here," O'Donnell remembers Trump saying. "I've been in meetings with the state all morning. They're not going to let me open. I've got a bunch of fucking idiots down here."

Trump sent a limousine to pick up O'Donnell. At the Taj, two security guards rushed him past the jeering throngs waiting outside. He remembers one woman screaming out, "Whatsa matter, Donald? Ain't ya got enough money?" As he walked to the gambling floor, O'Donnell saw over a hundred men and women in suits huddled, whispering to one another. He recognized the Casino Commission officials and approached Robert Trump and Harvey Freeman, the lawyer and key Trump adviser. He asked Robert if things were as bad as they looked. Robert, calm as ever, said, "I don't know, Jack. It doesn't look good."

Nearby, Freeman was staring at the purple carpeting and muttering to himself. "Not good . . . This is not good." O'Donnell tried to get him to speak clearly. Freeman mumbled something about the opening representing "a make-it-or-break-it" moment. "You don't know how big this is," Freeman said, as O'Donnell remembers it. "We've been spending like crazy . . . We've got to reverse this."

O'Donnell made his way to Trump, who looked uncharacteristically tired and wrinkled. "Jack, you've got to get me opened," Trump said, and then repeated it, "You've got to get me opened." O'Donnell said he needed time to figure out the problem. "No," Trump said, cutting him off. "That can't be . . . fifteen minutes. You've got to get this place open in fifteen minutes." O'Donnell knew that would not be possible, but he agreed just so he could get to work. By then it was already 1:15 p.m. The day was slipping away.

O'Donnell spent the next two hours diagnosing the problem. Casino regulations required the involvement of two sets of employees in transfers of cash between the main internal bank, known as "the cage," and the change booths placed around the floor. Every transfer had to be documented. The system was designed to prevent employees from skimming cash from the ocean flowing before them. More than $5 million had moved through that process on the first short trial day. But O'Donnell found that massive transfers had not been documented, mostly due to poor planning and training. This was a major problem, a violation of state regulations that carry fines. It couldn't be undone.

O'Donnell thought the only solution would be to count the money accurately, work through the variances with the regulators, and agree to pay whatever fines the state levied. He knew Trump would be impatient. The first day of test runs, with all the excitement of the new building and endless media attention, had yielded a win for the house on the slots of $603,000, about half of what Trump needed every day to make his interest payments.

As he moved through the casino, he crossed paths again with Trump and Walt Haybert, the Taj president. "I want him fired," Trump was screaming at Haybert. Trump was disappointed that the finance executive who had collapsed had not been sacked even before he was released from the hospital. "I don't want to see his fucking face in this building again." From Donald's perspective, the executive had failed and fainted not because of pressure due to poor planning and execution by the management team, but because he was soft. "I'm gonna fire all you assholes," he said to Haybert. "I want pricks in here. I want people in here who are gonna kick some ass."

O'Donnell waited for an opening before explaining his plan to Trump. He spent the next hour with staff counting cash and reaching an agreement with the regulators. Finally, at 4:20 p.m., the state allowed the doors to open, more than six hours after the scheduled start. The crowd had shrunk to a few hundred. News reporters had hung around. Trump assured them the delay was caused by his own success. "It was a lot bigger than everybody anticipated," he said. "The tables were flawless, but the slots did so much business it took longer than expected to reconcile."

The slot machine troubles for the first day had been papered over. But the operational problems remained unresolved. As the crowd and reporters moved on, Trump turned to O'Donnell. "Jack, from now on, you're in charge here," he said, as O'Donnell remembered. "You got carte blanche. You fire whoever you want. . . . Look at these jerk-offs."

Trump took a limousine to the Castle casino, where he boarded his helicopter and headed home to his parents' apartment in Trump Tower. While O'Donnell and Robert Trump oversaw the rest of the work for the grand opening on Thursday night, Trump spent the next two days holed up in his office with lawyers preparing to refuse to revise the prenuptial agreement with Ivana.

THE EVENING OF THE GRAND OPENING, a crowd of more than two thousand gathered near a stage in front of the main entrance, beneath a giant neon sign with the name "Trump" in bright red above the words "Taj Mahal." Merv Griffin showed up to introduce Trump, a sign of how closely their futures had become intertwined with the survival of Atlantic City gaming. By then, the debt that Griffin piled onto Resorts had forced him to put the company in bankruptcy. Griffin took the stage to the sound of his first hit single—"I've Got a Lovely Bunch of Coconuts"—and made light of his reduced finances. "I used to have a lot of coconuts," he said. No longer a foe, Griffin introduced Trump as "America's foremost entrepreneur."

Trump took the stage to a round of cheers. "What has happened here is really beyond my wildest expectations," he told the crowd. "They talked about $1 million a day. I think we did that in the first few hours."

Trump made no mention of the slot machine problems. He pouted, reached out with one hand, and rubbed the top of a three-foot-tall Aladdin's Lamp. Fabu appeared on a large screen. "Good evening, master. I, Fabu, am here at your service," the actor said to Trump. "Is this not a magnificent house? Open sesame!" The casino doors swung open, and a spectacular seven-minute fireworks show lit up the sky above the boardwalk. The patriotic march "Stars and Stripes Forever" blasted from loudspeakers.

Trump went to the ballroom on the second floor for a private party. His public relations people had been leaking the names of major celebrities who would attend. A fashion model and a few professional boxers showed up, but none of the movie stars—Tom Cruise, Jack Nicholson, Melanie Griffith—whose names had been floated. His father, Fred, who was now eighty-four, wearing a reddish toupee, mingled and beamed with pride at the magnitude of his son's latest creation. Donald's sisters, Maryanne and Elizabeth, also made the trip.

Robert Trump would not be relaxing at the party. State regulators summoned Trump's executive team to several rooms in the hotel where they had set up offices to oversee the opening. Robert, John O'Donnell, and Harvey Freeman walked into the rooms at about midnight. Dino Marino and his staff were waiting. Marino, a certified public accountant and Notre Dame graduate, had been in charge of monitoring the finances of casinos in New Jersey since the first one opened in 1978. He told the Trump crew that the slot machine problems had not been fixed, and he could not give them the operating certificate they needed to open.

That set off a high-stakes strategy session between O'Donnell, Freeman, and Robert Trump. They had hired contractors to fix the physical problems with the cage and install more change booths. But they knew that the casino would not handle the cash from three thousand slot machines for several weeks. They decided their best chance was to ask Marino if they could open half the slot machines, with the rest roped off. At about 1:00 a.m. in the morning, Marino agreed.

They did not see Trump before turning in for the night. The next morning, they all received calls to be in Walt Haybert's office by 8:30 a.m. The three of them arrived before Donald. He walked in with his hair still wet, sat down, and crossed his legs. He was clearly agitated. "Am I going to have all my slots open today?" he asked.

O'Donnell and Nick Ribis, Trump's top lawyer in Atlantic City, started to answer. But Trump interrupted to ask Haybert whether he had fired the financial executive who had collapsed. He did not like the answer and began cursing. "Shut the fuck up!" he shouted at Haybert. "I tell you to do something and you don't do it . . . This is the most fucked-up operation I've ever seen!"

Trump grew more animated when he said he had heard that he would not be allowed to open all the slot machines. "You guys are fucking crazy!" he yelled. "I don't want it! I want every machine open this weekend!"

Haybert told Trump that there was no way to change course that fast.

"You!" Trump shouted at Haybert. "I've listened to you long enough. You know what? You're a fucking idiot!"

He screamed that Haybert was "the one who fucked this place up." He complained that just like when he opened the Trump Plaza casino years ago, the slot machines were not working when interest burned brightest. He had blamed the failure at the Plaza on his partners, the Harrah's casino company. This time, he blamed the men sitting before him. "We're going to lose a fortune!" he shouted.

Robert tried to calm his brother, saying there had been no way to see this coming. Donald interrupted. "I'm sure as hell not going to listen to you in this situation," he said. He blamed Robert for convincing him to hire Haybert and not overseeing what was happening. "I'm sick and fucking tired of listening to you."

Donald continued on his tirade. Robert had finally heard enough. He stood up, walked to his office, and told his secretary to find him some boxes. He packed as quickly as he could, then boarded a helicopter for Manhattan. Their days working together were numbered.

Within an hour, Trump demoted Haybert from president of the Taj to chief financial officer. He installed Bucky Howard, who had spent his career focused on marketing casinos but had never run one before, as the new president of the business central to his chances for survival. As he announced the changes to the top managers, Trump blamed them all for the slot machine failure and called them "weak shit" and "a bunch of assholes."

About half of his slot machines would remain closed for the next several weeks, costing him millions of dollars. The existential threat of the coming interest payments was compounding.

Just minutes after he stopped cursing at his top executives, Trump welcomed Michael Jackson for a preplanned tour of the Taj. He and the legendary pop star walked through the casino floor smiling as they were mobbed by entertainment reporters and thousands of rabid Jackson fans. Trump's security team could barely keep them moving through the throngs. Robin Leach, filming a segment about the casino opening for *Lifestyles of the Rich and Famous*, walked with them. They made for an unusual trio—the diminutive pop icon, the large braggart in pinstripes, and the everyman Brit who fetishized ostentatious spending. "To have Michael at the Taj Mahal, he's my friend, he's a tremendous talent, and, ah, it's really my honor," Trump said to the *Lifestyles* camera. "It's, ah, it's a big day for me."

As Hal Gessner, Leach's senior producer, later remembered it, Trump seemed like a "king showing us his fiefdoms." But Gessner soon caught a glimpse of the king's other side. As part of the episode, Gessner spoke with workers in the casino and heard that Trump was not paying the contractors who built the Taj. Gessner worried about the show someday being embarrassed. He spoke with Leach and suggested it might be prudent to stop filming episodes about Trump's wealth. Leach agreed. "I think we kinda milked that cow, and we both knew it was over," Gessner recalled.

Within a month, Trump admitted to withholding $35 million in payments to contractors. His spokesperson described the dispute as typical of the end of big projects. But Trump needed money. He had a $42 million interest payment coming due on the Trump Castle bonds, and another $47 million on the Taj Mahal bonds.

He called O'Donnell at home late one night and told him that he wanted to cut staffing at the casinos by 20 percent. O'Donnell objected, arguing that a staff reduction of that size would slow down operations so much that revenues would drop. "Just do it, Jack," Trump told O'Donnell. "Just do it. It's going to be a positive. Believe me."

In a subsequent conversation, Trump once again blamed his misfortunes on the three casino executives who had died in the helicopter crash. They were more than colleagues to O'Donnell. Steve Hyde and Mark Etess had been his best friends. When Trump went down that road again, O'Donnell told him, "Donald, you can go fuck yourself" and quit. As O'Donnell saw it, Trump knew little about running a hotel and casino, and refused to listen to people who did, so he made unforced errors and then blamed others for his predictably bad outcomes.

Even before the layoffs and withheld payments to contractors, Trump had tried to generate cash by selling the *Trump Princess*, the Trump Shuttle, and part of his interest in the Plaza Hotel, but nothing came of it. He tried to refinance some loans, to no avail.

Trump's bankers, who saw his attacks on Roffman as a sign of distress, began talking about calling his loans. Trump quietly retained an accounting firm, Kenneth Leventhal & Company, to meet with his lenders and negotiate a plan to reduce or suspend his debt payments. As a first step, the Leventhal accountants evaluated Trump's finances. The situation was dire. They estimated that Trump would run out of cash in June. His businesses collectively were not producing enough profit to cover his expenses.

Leventhal set up confidential meetings at Trump Tower with Trump's four biggest lenders. As many as fifty bankers and lawyers were slipping into the building every day for long meetings on the twenty-sixth floor with Trump and his aides.

More evidence emerged that Trump was in trouble. *BusinessWeek* and *Forbes* both reported that Trump would be coming up tens of millions of dollars short on his annual interest payments. *Forbes* estimated that Trump's assets were only worth $500 million more than his debts. Casino regulators concluded at about the same time that his net worth was $205.7 million.

Trump claimed he was suffering under the weight of being himself. "It's Trump bashing week," he told *The Press of Atlantic City*. On the ABC show *Primetime Live*, he told Sam Donaldson that he was being persecuted by *Forbes*, the publication most central to building Trump's fictional image as a self-made billionaire. "*Forbes* has been after me for years, consistently after me," he told Donaldson, adding, "It's a disgrace." He complained that *Forbes* had undervalued his assets. He cited no evidence, only his belief that things he owned must be worth more than what he had paid to buy them.

"What I own is trophies," he told Donaldson. "The Plaza Hotel, which I wouldn't sell, but the Plaza Hotel's a trophy. The Taj Mahal, where it has record earnings, that's a trophy. I own trophies. A trophy doesn't go down."

"Well, now, you can't pay your bills with trophies," Donaldson said.

"I think you can pay your bills with trophies," Trump replied.

A FEW WEEKS LATER, Neil Barsky, the *Wall Street Journal* reporter who had written about the Taj, was playing poker in an Upper East Side apartment with some prominent businessmen. A banker who knew that Barsky had occasionally covered Trump's businesses offered a surprising bit of news: "Donald Trump is driving 100 miles per hour toward a brick wall, and he has no brakes," the banker said. "He is meeting with all the banks right now."

The next morning, Barsky began calling Trump's lenders—Bankers Trust Corp., Chase Manhattan Corp., Citicorp, and Manufacturers Hanover Corp. He learned from his contacts about the secret meetings that had been taking place. Trying to avoid his payments, Trump had offered the banks a share of his ownership in the Plaza Hotel and the Grand Hyatt in New York, if they erased some of his debt. The banks rejected his proposal.

The banks had grown increasingly concerned that Trump's businesses were not producing enough cash to cover his interest payments on $2 billion in bank debt, especially with interest payments also coming due on another $1 billion in bond debt. His only profitable businesses were the first two—the Grand Hyatt and Trump Tower—which he built in tandem with experienced partners.

Barsky's story ran on the front page of the *Journal* on Monday, June 4, 1990, under the headline SHAKY EMPIRE: TRUMP'S BANKERS JOIN TO SEEK RESTRUCTURING OF DEVELOPER'S ASSETS. The banks were hesitant to call their loans and force Trump into bankruptcy because some of his properties were no longer worth enough to cover the money he owed on them, and because in a bankruptcy proceeding a judge would be in control. They discovered also that Trump had cross-collateralized his loans. If one bank forced Trump to repay immediately, it could set off a chain reaction with all of them fighting over the same properties. Most worryingly, they had lent Trump $900 million with nothing but his personal guarantee. If they called his loans due, assets would have to be unloaded at fire sale prices, and they would all be fighting for a place in line to collect.

The banks chose to force Trump to rein in his free spending and sell his biggest losers. "He will have to trim the fat: get rid of the boat, the mansions, the helicopter," one banker involved in the talks told Barsky.

The day before Barsky's story was published, Trump flew to Las Vegas on his personal jet to promote his forthcoming second book, *Trump: Surviving at the Top*, at an annual convention of booksellers. He checked into a suite with its own pool at the Mirage hotel and casino. That evening, Peter Osnos, Trump's editor at Random House, went to pick up Trump and escort him to a reception the publisher was hosting for a thousand people. Osnos was surprised when Marla Maples answered the door, in a bikini. The couple had not appeared in public very much. Her presence would draw whispers and eyeballs.

The next morning, just as Barsky's story was published, Trump spoke to the three thousand book-industry professionals in attendance. As Osnos would recall it, Trump took the stage to a large crowd mostly unaware that his reason for belief in his own excellence had just been pulverized.

He described the inevitably sad fate of someone—his future dead self, it seemed—who had been seen as a "great success, fantastic, fantastic" during his life. "He kicks the bucket. The kids fight over the estate. They say the Plaza Hotel is not a good location. Your ex-wives are all fighting and saying what a bum you are. Their husbands, who they marry, who's living in your room—I've seen this—saying Trump was an idiot, what the hell did he know."

He said some chapters in his book, maybe even the entire tome, might need to end with question marks. He had tried to convince Osnos to delay publication, but Osnos convinced him that this would be a bigger seller than his first book. "He knows how to turn me on, because I want to do that, keep going higher and higher. And then we die, and nobody gives a damn."

ON THAT DAY IN JUNE 1990, Trump owed banks and bondholders $3.4 billion, nearly all of it high-interest debt he used to assemble his eclectic empire in about six years. His casinos alone were teetering under the interest payments on $1.3 billion in borrowed money.

It all came to a head when he missed interest payments totaling $73 million that month. He and the banks struck a deal that suspended some future interest payments and gave him another $65 million loan to cover the coming interest expenses. Having seen the small-time operation on the twenty-sixth floor, the banks required Trump to hire a chief financial officer and stick to a business plan, two measures that would be a starting point for most serious businesses. Trump agreed not to seek any other loans and put nearly everything else he owned on the line as collateral.

One clause in the agreement was surely a bright spot for Trump. He would be placed on a monthly personal expense allowance of $450,000, a number that struck many as too absurdly large to consider a limitation. But considering the hole Trump had dug for himself, it was a pittance, barely enough to cover what he was spending to maintain Mar-a-Lago, only one of his homes.

That allowance, though, would keep his image intact. It meant he could maintain the appearance of wealth, which to him meant the appearance of success. That appearance is what had drawn flocks of regular people to his casinos and to a Republican rally in Vermont, and made talk-show hosts swoon. His businesses were failing, but the appearance was becoming his business.

Newspapers and television stations across the country focused on the extravagant allowance. Many of the articles quoted—who else?—Robin Leach: "Donald Trump has always lived and worked the lifestyle of the rich and famous, and it will continue under the new circumstances."

With the $47 million bond payment on the Taj coming due on November 15, lawyers for Trump and the bondholders engaged in tense days of negotiations at the Plaza Hotel. They could not agree on how big a share of the casino Trump would give up to bondholders in exchange for lowering Trump's 14 percent interest rate. A deal was reached as bondholders threatened to force the Taj into involuntary bankruptcy. Under a prearranged bankruptcy plan, Trump would only own half of the Taj, but he would control the company's board. To hang on, he had agreed to an interest rate reduction of less than three points, a rate still so high that it all but guaranteed he would face more trouble in the future. He would also be paid an annual management fee of $500,000.

In announcing the deal, Trump took no responsibility for saddling the casino with so much costly debt, or for blowing his own construction budget by $160 million, or for creating more casino space than Atlantic City's gamblers could support. He blamed all the Taj's problems on a national recession. "Maybe the word is depression," he told reporters that day.

During a fifteen-year rise, he had paid close attention to aesthetic details, from the waterfall and ficus trees in the lobby of Trump Tower to the angle of the telephone handsets on his yacht for high rollers. He had not paid similar attention to financial details, especially whether his individual businesses could support the payments on the money he borrowed to buy or build them. He glossed over those essential calculations by assuring himself, and anyone who asked, that revenues would rise to whatever was needed simply because the word "Trump" was above the door. It was his singular egocentric *Field of Dreams* business philosophy—if Trump builds it, they will come. It had been enabled by his father's support, a rising economy, and a period of free lending.

But he had been proven wrong. The early results showed the Taj was not bringing more gamblers to Atlantic City, it was only drawing gamblers from the other casinos there, including Trump's other two casinos. His businesses were cannibalizing one another. A moment of reckoning was upon him. It arrived during an economic period when he could not count on a rising tide to make up for his lack of fiscal discipline. He needed access to a deep well of cash.

23

NO INTENTION TO ASK

One Sunday in December 1990, Donald Trump stood near the back of the Venetian Ballroom at the historic Breakers Hotel in Palm Beach, watching as an auctioneer tried to gin up prices on some of the unsold condominiums at Trump Plaza of the Palm Beaches. At his side was Rowanne Brewer, a twenty-six-year-old Miami model who had been Miss Snap-on Tools of 1989 and was the subject of a story in the *National Enquirer* headlined TRUMP DUMPS MARLA FOR SEXY MODEL. A local squad of high school cheerleaders in uniform served as ushers to whisk successful bidders away to sign documents.

The twin white towers had been the first test of Trump's notion that anything with his name on it would increase in value. It had not worked out. In 1986, Trump had paid $43 million for the unfinished 221-unit building in West Palm Beach. He had been spending $2.9 million a year more in interest and operating costs. Less than half of the apartments had sold—only one that entire year—and once the remaining $27 million mortgage balance came due, the bank forced him to begin auctioning off units.

Trump hoped that his celebrity aura would increase interest. Indeed, more than five hundred people packed the historic ballroom. But most were reporters, gawkers, and autograph seekers. Only 137 registered to bid. Some expressed surprise that the units remained unfinished, with cement floors and no interior walls. The units sold above the auction minimum price, but 40 percent below Trump's original asking price, for a total of $8.8 million that day. He paid the auctioneer $500,000 and would be required to hold a second auction.

Ever the salesman, Trump framed the forced sell-off that day as evidence of forward thinking. "Auctions are the wave of the future for real estate," he said.

Still neck deep in a hole, he proceeded with his usual superlative soup: "It's been tremendous, very successful. It's exceeded my expectations. I have never seen anything like this."

But he remained in a mad hunt for cash to meet his obligations. His divorce from Ivana had been finalized the week before, and the settlement further squeezed his finances. Without the approval of his bankers, he handed her a certified check for $10 million, along with the estate in Connecticut and use of Mar-a-Lago for one month each year.

By then, Jeff Walker had sailed the *Trump Princess* into ports around the world trying in vain to find a buyer at the $100 million price point that his boss wanted. Trump had even notified his partners in the Grand Hyatt that he could not spend money on new bed mattresses and other updates, even as AAA downgraded the hotel's rating from four diamonds to three.

"I am no longer in a financial position to spend money on such a project," he added.

With an $18.4 million bond interest payment on the Castle casino coming due the day after the auction, Trump executed a plan to secretly tap into the most reliable well of money in his world. It was almost perfect.

The morning that the Castle payment came due, a man named Howard Snyder walked into the Castle and found his way to the cage, the main cashier area at the casino. Snyder turned over a certified check in the amount of $3.35 million and a letter saying he was acting as an attorney for Fred Trump. The cashiers verified that the check was good and opened an account in Fred's name. Snyder walked over to a blackjack table and requested the entire amount in chips. The dealer stacked 670 gray gambling chips, each worth $5,000, on the green felt. Snyder pushed them all into a small case and, without placing a bet, walked out of the casino to a waiting car. He rode away under police escort.

With that clandestine infusion from his father, Donald Trump made his bond interest payment that Monday, December 17, 1990. He may still have been a little short; Snyder returned to the Castle the following day with a personal check for $150,000 from Fred Trump and walked out with that amount in chips. Donald boasted to reporters that he had made the payment when everyone doubted him. He told the world that his other companies had plenty of money lying around to make up the difference.

"We don't need an outside infusion," he told *The Wall Street Journal*. He told

The Press of Atlantic City that the Trump Organization—his company, not his father's—had "made an infusion in cash."

"It's in the genes, I really believe that," he told *The Wall Street Journal* a month later. "A lot of guys would have gone into a corner and put their thumbs in their mouths. I'm a fighter."

He was not aware that casino regulators had caught wind of Fred's chip purchase the day after Snyder appeared. The entire scheme had been videotaped by security cameras, and those tapes are regularly reviewed by regulators, especially when extremely large transactions take place. That week they quietly opened an investigation. Fred stashed the chips and would carry a loan of $3.5 million on his books for years to come.

THE MONTH AFTER THE CHIP PURCHASE, Donald hosted a fifty-fifth anniversary party for his parents at the Plaza Hotel. His banks had reined in his personal spending and dealmaking, but he still could load up his companies with personal expenses. The entire extended family attended the sit-down dinner on Saturday evening, along with dozens of Fred's and Donald's associates, bankers, and attorneys.

W. Taylor Johnson Jr., who as a boy in Norfolk had befriended Freddy Trump while their fathers built military housing during World War II, flew up to New York for the event with his wife, Rena. Taylor spoke in a thick southern accent and still, at the age of fifty, felt like a fish out of water in the fancier corners of Manhattan.

Mary Trump, at seventy-eight years old, still seemed buoyant and gracious to Taylor. She made him and Rena feel at home. She invited them to breakfast the next morning and then insisted on giving them a ride in a limousine to their next stop. In the car, Taylor asked her whether Fred had given her an anniversary present. He knew the answer would be yes, but he got a kick out of Mary. She played along, smiling and nodding playfully, just how Taylor remembered her. She held out her hand and showed him the ring Fred had bought her at Tiffany's, a bright red ruby, her favorite stone, surrounded by fifty-five diamonds. Taylor asked her the color of her current car, even though he knew the answer. Mary tilted her head of red hair and said, "Red," stretching out the word. He asked her what kind of car it was, again knowing the answer. She affected modesty. "Rolls-Royce," she said.

Fred's spending never rose beyond occasional extravagances for his wife—a ring, a fur coat, and a fancy car. They did not travel abroad. He bought a small house in Florida, but it was for Mary's sister. These days, when he and Mary went to Florida, they stayed at Mar-a-Lago.

Not long after the anniversary party, they took a trip there with all their children except for Donald. Fred arrived with something on his mind. Two of his lawyers had recently sent him an amendment to his own will that he had not requested. The codicil, as such things are called, had been created by an outside lawyer at the direction of his son, Donald, and these lawyers said Donald wanted him to sign it. Fred was now eighty-five and not as sharp as in years past, but he had been reading legal documents for decades, and he thought this one spelled trouble.

On the grounds of Mar-a-Lago, he showed the codicil to the lawyer he trusted most, his daughter, Maryanne, who was then serving as a federal judge.

"This doesn't pass the smell test," he said.

Fred told Maryanne that it looked like Donald was trying to gain more control and access to Fred's fortune, and in doing so could put that fortune at risk. "He was disturbed by what he read," Maryanne later recalled. "Dad was very concerned, as a man who worked hard for his money and never wanted any of it to leave the family, that Donald's creditors could come in and take what Dad had worked so hard to make."

Maryanne herself worried that Donald's maneuver could deplete the family fortune to such a degree that her sister, Elizabeth, who never found her way in a career, could wind up penniless. Fred told Maryanne to have a new will drawn up that would give his four surviving children equal authority and make sure that neither Donald, nor Donald's lenders, could reach freely into his father's bank accounts. "Get it done," he told Maryanne.

Maryanne found a lawyer and had the work finished by the end of April. She did not discuss the change with Donald until after their father had signed his new will. Donald would now have less influence than he had before in the event of their father's death.

By then, Fred was already under investigation by the New Jersey attorney general's Division of Gaming Enforcement for the chips gambit. They forced him to submit extensive financial documents and become qualified as a financial supporter of his son's casinos, a measure designed to keep the mob out of

Atlantic City. Still, Fred did not seem annoyed with Donald. In keeping with the history of their relationship, he laid blame, according to his children, at the feet of the two lawyers—Irwin Durben and Jack Mitnick—who had worked for him for years before doing Donald's bidding.

"My father was quite unhappy that they had not had the courtesy and the professionalism to tell him that they were working on something, truly on his behalf as well as Donald's behalf, and gave it, gave him a document, and said, 'Sign this and we've got to get it fast, sign it,'" Robert later recalled. "So, he was very unhappy with those two individuals, particularly."

THE WORLD LEARNED about Fred and Donald's chip scheme from Neil Barsky. With another $46 million bond interest payment coming due in two weeks, Barsky reported on May 31 that Trump was "considering borrowing money from his father" to avoid being forced to put the casino into bankruptcy. Barksy's 450-word story ran on page nine, but the Associated Press called Trump that morning to follow it. Barsky had struck a nerve. That day, Trump called the *New York Post*. "It's an evil, vicious, false and misleading article," Trump said to the *Post*. "I have no intention to ask or will I ask my father for financial assistance." He went on to allege that six weeks earlier Barsky had squeezed him for three tickets to a championship heavyweight boxing match between Evander Holyfield and George Foreman. The tickets to the fight, sponsored by Trump Plaza casino at the Atlantic City Convention Center, had a face value of $1,000 each. Trump told the *Post* that Barsky should be fired and that he might sue the newspaper. "It's a disgraceful situation and I certainly hope that *The Wall Street Journal* takes appropriate action," he said.

Barsky first heard about Trump's accusations when a *Post* reporter called him. No one had ever questioned his ethics before. Unnerved, he walked outside the *Journal*'s office in lower Manhattan, found a pay phone, and called his wife. He spent a weekend writing a memo explaining what had happened. After Trump's office offered him the tickets, he had asked his editor, Fred Bleakley, if it would be all right to take them because he saw it as a chance to meet more Trump company insiders. Bleakley left it up to him. In retrospect, both saw it as a mistake.

Bleakley and Norman Pearlstine, the *Journal*'s executive editor, initially stood by Barsky. They noted it was probably not good judgment, but also that it seemed odd that Trump had not complained when Barsky was allegedly twisting his arm. Instead, he waited more than a month until an article he did not like was published. The editors saw no evidence of animus or favor in Barksy's coverage.

A little more than a week later, a *Times* media columnist wrote that Pearlstine himself had once accepted a free helicopter ride to Atlantic City and tickets to another heavyweight boxing match from Trump. Pearlstine had also reasoned that the event would be a chance to get to know bankers and others who the paper covered. Once Pearlstine's trip came to light, journalism ethics experts criticized the *Journal*'s poor judgment and seeming lack of internal controls. Barsky felt the pressure increasing. A few weeks later the *Journal* announced that he would no longer cover Trump.

Trump had prevailed, without puncturing the truth of Barsky's criticism. Barsky felt like his bosses had thrown him under the bus to quiet the noise that started with Donald Trump. "Having my integrity questioned was so shattering," he recalled decades later.

Marvin Roffman, the analyst who was fired after Barsky quoted him predicting Trump's Taj Mahal would not cover its debts, was proven correct. An arbitration panel ordered his former employer to pay him $750,000, and Trump settled the $2 million defamation lawsuit that Roffman had filed against him. The settlement with Trump was kept confidential, but the amount was large enough for Roffman to launch his own firm and, decades later, still have money for luxuries. In 2021, Roffman, who had retired, told a reporter: "Today, I bought a new Bentley, or should I say, Trump bought it for me."

THE INTENSITY OF TRUMP'S reaction to Barsky's reporting showed how detached the image he had cultivated was from reality, and how hard he would fight to keep those realities hidden. The reality was that Fred had already given Donald millions of dollars through unrepaid loans, trust funds, and interest paid on loans that existed only on paper.

And the two of them were working together at that moment to accelerate the process of wealth transfer. Fred had lent Donald $15 million early in his career that remained unpaid. In the late 1980s, they agreed to convert that debt into an investment in Donald's latest real estate project, a condominium building in Manhattan he would call Trump Palace.

The project would be a financial failure. Most developers saw the slowdown coming after years of overdevelopment in the city and held on to their cash. Donald pushed forward, even demanding that Blanche Sprague, his director of sales, inflate her analysis of the total anticipated sales from $179.2 million to $265 million so he could convince a bank to lend him $220 million. But sales came in slowly after the building opened. Trump fell behind on the mortgage, and his bank forced him to turn over all unsold units.

Fred Trump wrote off the $15 million he had given his son as a total loss on his tax returns. Decades later, we discovered that fact buried in Fred's income tax returns and audited financial statements. Fred's records showed the cozy nature of the arrangement. His financial statements said he had "sold" his $15 million investment in Trump Palace for $10,000, to his son. The sale took place the same week that he gave Donald his annual cash Christmas gift of twice that amount.

Those kinds of transactions are not allowed to be used as tax write-offs precisely because of the cozy nature of it all. The IRS has no way to tell whether the loss represented a legitimate investment or a disguised gift. Fred's investment certainly served as a gift, one that would have been subject to a federal gift tax of 55 percent. Instead of increasing Fred's taxes, the $15 million write-off on his own taxes *reduced* his tax bill by about $5 million. Fred did not reveal in his tax returns that the losses were attributable to his son's failure, an omission that could rise to the level of tax fraud.

The initial analysis by Sprague, ignored by Trump, proved to be flawless. The 283 apartments at Trump Palace eventually sold for a total of $181 million, within one percentage point of Sprague's estimate.

Fred was still funneling money to his son in a variety of ways. The trusts that Fred had formed decades earlier for his children were producing about $220,000 a year for each. In the late 1980s, he began converting the eight buildings he had given them into condominiums, the sales generating about $1 million a year each for Donald and his siblings. Donald was still collecting more than $100,000 a year from the senior citizen housing complex that his father had given him a share of in the 1970s. Even before the $3.5 million chips "loan" and grabbing for his father's will, Donald was regularly receiving more than $1.5 million a year from his father.

But there was a hint in Fred's records that the support for Donald at his nadir may have been far greater. Before and after 1990, Fred regularly reported taxable income of about $10 million a year. But that year he suddenly reported almost $50 million in taxable income, including a massive distribution from his companies of $31.5 million. Nothing had changed in Fred Trump's world. The rents on his buildings varied little year to year. And he most often left his profits sitting in company accounts to avoid taxes. But for 1990, the large distribution helped produce a federal income tax bill of $12.2 million, and a state and city income tax bill totaling another $5.7 million. Fred clearly felt some immediate need for a huge amount of cash, and he was willing to pay almost $18 million in income taxes to get it. Why? His investments showed no commensurate increase. His bank statements did not show any large purchases. Fred and Mary continued to live as they had for decades in Jamaica Estates.

His favorite son was a black hole for Fred Trump's cash. Donald Trump's tax returns for that year reported that his core businesses lost $263.7 million. He carried over another $154 million in losses from prior years, and overall reported total adjusted income of negative $400.3 million. A comparison with an annual sampling of high-income earners showed that Donald Trump's core business losses in 1990 and 1991 were more than double those of the nearest taxpayers in the IRS information for those years.

About the time that Fred and Donald Trump filed their 1990 tax returns, Donald testified before a congressional task force about exploring potential changes to the tax code. He framed his difficulties as the result of a downturn in the real estate market. "The real estate business—we're in an absolute depression," Trump told the lawmakers, adding: "I see no sign of any kind of upturn at all. There is no incentive to invest. Everyone is doing badly, everyone."

Everyone, perhaps, except his father.

THE MIDDLE OF JUNE had become the worst time of the year for Donald Trump. Just as the days grew longer and warmer in New York and Atlantic City, and he celebrated his birthday, the interest payments on his Trump Castle casino kept coming due, an annual existential crisis.

He had been living under a microscope for more than a year, with casino regulators and his banks closely monitoring his finances. During the prior year, all his businesses combined had come up $36.1 million short of covering expenses, even with the influx from his father. To make up the difference, he had burned through all but $2.9 million of his cash and expected to run out before the end of summer.

He had no chance of coming up with the Castle bond payment due on June 17, 1991. His bankers were no longer willing to gamble on him. He agreed to give up almost everything to reduce his debts and avoid personal bankruptcy. Most of his life's work, a gold-plated jalopy of a conglomerate, would go back to the banks and be sold off for parts. Bankers Trust would have the power to take his share of his first project, the Grand Hyatt he had rebuilt from the old Commodore hotel in Manhattan. Boston Safe & Trust Company would force the sale of the *Trump Princess*. Citibank would off-load the Trump Shuttle, which had never made a profit, and his stock in Alexander's department store chain.

As he had done with the Taj Mahal, he would give up half the equity in his other two casinos, Trump Plaza and Trump Castle, in prepackaged bankruptcy reorganizations to convince bondholders to let him pay a lower interest rate. But those agreements came with a repayment deadline in June 1995.

He had already sold his personal 727 jet. Keeping his head above water still depended on him selling condominiums he owned in Trump Tower for millions of dollars. If those sales did not come through as expected, Trump's "personal bank balance may be insufficient to cover his monthly obligations," casino regulators noted.

THAT YEAR, 1991, had been tough for Fred and Mary Trump. One afternoon, Mary, seventy-nine, drove her Rolls-Royce five minutes from the house in Jamaica Estates to the stores along Union Turnpike. As she walked down the bustling street, a sixteen-year-old boy shoved her into a wall, then to the ground, and ran off with her handbag. Her face was bloodied, and she was hospitalized. At the same time, Fred Trump underwent hip-replacement surgery and emerged foggy and forgetful. A doctor diagnosed him with mild senile dementia. They both returned home from the hospital at about the same time, with the help of a nurse and a therapist.

After he healed, Fred insisted on going to his office every day. But most days he checked in, shuffled some papers, and left for lunch with Amy Luerssen at Gargiulo's, an old-school Italian restaurant in Coney Island. Some days he did not return. His children started to notice. "I think his memory was starting to go," Maryanne would recall. "Occasionally, there would be lapses."

Robert came to the rescue. After Donald had yelled at him over the Taj Mahal slot machine failure, Robert retreated to his father's offices. He had spent the last two decades in the high-octane world of Wall Street and serving as his older brother's number two in Manhattan and the casinos. He began commuting instead each day from Manhattan to the ground floor of the Beach Haven apartments on Avenue Z in Brooklyn. There, among the metal desks and the cigar store Indians, he helped Fred and a small staff manage and maintain Fred's twelve thousand apartments. His father eased the transition with a salary of $500,000 a year.

Donald's attempt to gain control of his father's will, and Fred's and Mary's diminishing health, had focused the family's attention on the inevitable. All of Fred's properties were still entirely owned and controlled by him. If he died with his affairs in that state, the family would likely be forced to sell a chunk of his empire just to pay the estate taxes. Fred's advisers had for several years urged him to shift ownership to his children through a trust in order to minimize the tax hit. But Fred would not budge.

Cash presented the biggest risk. Fred's buildings were worth the equivalent of more than $1 billion today. But in the event of his death, the family's lawyers could play games with the values assigned to each building to reduce the estate tax. Cash, on the other hand, was cash. Every dollar in Fred's accounts would instantly be worth forty-five cents after the federal estate tax took its bite. And New York State would take more. Fred had about $50 million in cash sitting in his business accounts.

A plan was soon devised to funnel some of Fred's cash to Donald and his three siblings. They would accomplish that goal by adding a sham layer to Fred's business, one designed to evade the gift and estate taxes. They would call that extra layer All County Building Supply and Maintenance. It would serve no purpose beyond creating an off-ramp to send cash to his children. The goods and materials that Fred bought for his buildings—tens of millions of dollars a year for everything from cleaning supplies to commercial boilers—would instead now be purchased in the name of All County. Then John Walter, Fred's nephew and loyal employee for years, would create a new bill, padded with an extra 10 or 20 percent, so the goods could be "sold" to Fred's company at the inflated amount.

It was as simple as it was deceptive. Every $20,000 boiler that Fred had been buying would now be bought in the name of All County and billed to Fred at $24,000, and the difference split between the four children and their cousin. Vendors who had negotiated a deal with Fred would sometimes call asking why they received a check from All County Building Supply and Maintenance.

All County worked so well that the family created a second similar entity, Apartment Management Associates, which padded other expenses of Fred's businesses and passed the proceeds along to Donald and his siblings.

John Walter later said that Fred approved of the plan because it meant he could get that money to his children without paying a "death tax," as he called it. "He loved to save taxes," Walter said.

Fred also approved of the scheme because it would mean larger rent increases on his rent-regulated apartments. State laws allowed landlords to apply for rent increases based on the money they spent on certain upgrades and repairs. Fred always thought it was unfair that if he could negotiate lower prices on goods, he would also be allowed a lower rent increase. "I should be able to get the same benefit that it would cost the tenants," Fred complained to his nephew. It was warped logic reminiscent of Fred's belief during his building years that if the government offered to lend him money equal to actual building costs, he should be allowed to submit documents showing what an average builder would pay and pocket the difference. So the Trumps began submitting the padded bills to request rent increases from state officials. Part of the cost of Donald Trump's off-the-books inheritance would be passed along to his father's middle-income tenants.

For the children of Fred Trump, the padding would add up. Within a few years, Donald and his siblings would each be receiving more than $2 million a year. They would be required to pay income taxes, a far smaller tax bite than gift and estate taxes at the time, on that money. But Donald's massive business losses wiped away his tax liability every year. He would keep the full amount.

The invoice padding would remain a family secret for decades until we uncovered it, as would the $15.5 million loan that Fred converted to an investment in Trump Palace and never collected, and the other ways he secretly passed along money to Donald in times of need. We calculated that, by the end of 1992, Fred Trump had provided his favorite son more than $34 million. But Donald's biggest paydays from his father's fortune were still to come.

By late 1992, the remnants of the empire Donald had built, the pieces he fought to keep from lenders and investors, were still teetering. He owned only half of his three casinos, but holding on would require a massive balloon payment in thirty months. Unable to cover the interest payments on the Plaza Hotel, he sought the protection of bankruptcy court for the fourth time. He had hung on to the West Side rail yards, but it was devouring more than $18 million a year. Mar-a-Lago was costing him $3 million a year. His strongest-performing asset remained the commercial space at Trump Tower. But Trump Tower was not producing enough cash to cover his money losses.

At promoting an alternative version of himself, he remained on solid footing. Just as a judge approved the third of his casino bankruptcies, Trump threw himself a party at the Taj Mahal. In front of a crowded ballroom, a screen showed stock prices from a newspaper. As horns blared the first bars of the theme song from *Rocky*, a red boxing glove punched through the screen. Out stepped Donald Trump, wearing a tuxedo under a red satin boxing robe. He held his gloves at his chest and curled his lips upward like an Elvis Presley impersonator.

"Let's hear it for the king!" an announcer shouted.

Trump's parents traveled to the event, and Donald singled out his mother for comforting him when times were tough. Trump had put his lawyer, Nick Ribis, who had never run a casino, in charge of all his Atlantic City operations. Ribis read a poem that ended like this: "Against the odds his opponents buckled with a thump, the winner was Donald J. Trump."

A photograph of Trump stepping through the screen in boxing gear ran in newspapers across the country with headlines touting his self-proclaimed comeback. Trump gave no hint of how much his career and prospects had changed.

24

THE SPY NEXT DOOR

Abraham Wallach took his seat in the studio across from Robert MacNeil, the esteemed coanchor of *The MacNeil/Lehrer NewsHour.* The show's staff had invited Wallach, who had two MBAs from Ivy League universities and a long career as a real estate executive, to appear as an expert analyst for a segment on Donald Trump's collapsing finances. The camera trained on his face, his tightly curled hair and oversized glasses, as MacNeil asked whether Trump was correct to blame the struggling real estate market in New York for his downfall. "Yes, he can blame market conditions to some extent," Wallach answered in a flat tone. "But I think the reality is, if you pay too much for properties and if your ego is as large as his is, and you just buy everything in sight, part of the blame has to squarely rest in your own lap."

It seemed to Wallach like an innocuous analysis. Trump saw things differently. A week later, Wallach was served at his home and office with papers notifying him that he was being sued by Trump for $250 million. Wallach was stunned. He asked for advice from a lawyer who worked with both his firm and Trump. The lawyer spoke with Trump and a few days later told Wallach that Trump would drop the suit if Wallach did not publicly criticize him. The lawyer also said Trump wanted Wallach to come see him. Again, Wallach was stunned.

When he visited Trump's office, he was left sitting in a waiting area for so long that he began to nod off. Trump eventually greeted him. Wallach was surprised at how Trump towered over him and shook his hand so firmly that it hurt. They spoke for a few minutes about Trump's troubles but were repeatedly interrupted by phone calls, people coming into the office, or a thought that popped into Trump's head. Somehow, in those few broken moments, Wallach's answers impressed Trump. After a few more discussions, he offered Wallach a job to help fix his financial problems. The foe had become a friend.

On Wallach's first day in 1990, it looked like a fire drill was in progress on the twenty-sixth floor of Trump Tower. Trump had cut salaries, and his small band of executives could see the coming years of stagnation and headed for the door: Barbara Res, who had a hand in nearly every Trump project since the Commodore; Jeff Walker, who been one of his first employees; Tony Gliedman, the former city official whom Donald Trump called "the Fat Fuck"; Blanche Sprague, the sales manager; Susan Heilbron, who had slipped Trump yellow sticky notes about stocks; and Norm Levin, who had spearheaded the costly West Side rail yards efforts for Trump. All packed up their desks in short order.

Trump would long harbor ill will toward everyone who jumped ship in his time of need. He didn't care that they had families and responsibilities and were seeking stability and opportunity. It was a betrayal. Evidence of insufficient loyalty.

Despite declaring victory in public and privately tapping deeper into his father's wealth, Trump faced a few harrowing years ahead to trim his expenses further, especially his debt payments, before he would be required to pay off the casino bondholders in June 1995. Struggling to keep his lenders from taking everything he owned, he had focused his energies on keeping a few properties: Mar-a-Lago, his greatest emblem of wealth; the Plaza Hotel, the stately but worn old New York hotel; and the West Side rail yards, the large swath of empty land along the Hudson River that he saw as his greatest opportunity to create a legacy. Wallach would take the lead in getting him there.

Trump's ownership of the Plaza Hotel faced an immediate threat. With his loan in default, and Trump owning only 51 percent, Citibank was trying to sell the hotel and push him out. Citi had rehired Patricia Goldstein, who had been one of its real estate lending stars in the 1970s, to work out problems within its $22 billion real estate loan portfolio. Goldstein agreed to let Trump keep the hotel if he found a partner rich enough to pay off the mortgage, but she also hired an international real estate marketing firm to find her own buyer. It would be a race: one of the world's biggest banks squared off against Donald Trump and Abe Wallach.

Trump hoped to convert the hotel into luxury condominium apartments. He needed someone to cover the existing mortgage, which exceeded the building's worth, and construction costs. Wallach spent six weeks crisscrossing Asia—Singapore, Hong Kong, Tokyo, Kuala Lumpur, Jakarta, Bangkok, and Shanghai—meeting with people wealthy enough to bankroll Trump. He found little interest, until he met Walter and Wendy Kwok in Hong Kong. They were members of one of the wealthiest families in the world, with a large real estate and hotel portfolio. About the time that *Forbes* had dropped Trump from its list of the wealthiest, the magazine estimated that the Kwok brothers were worth $6.4 billion. Wallach had dinner with the Kwoks at their mansion overlooking Repulse Bay and went for a ride on their yacht. He convinced them to travel to New York, stay at the Plaza, and meet Donald Trump to hash out a possible agreement.

They dined together at the Four Seasons, with Marla back as Donald's date. Walter and Donald golfed. Abe and Wendy, who had gone to college in New York, shopped at a popular outlet mall north of the city. Everything went well, until one morning, when the Kwoks and their two young sons became trapped in the Plaza's seven-thousand-square-foot Presidential Suite. The suite's heavy old wooden door would not open, even with bodyguards tugging at it. After the hotel's staff busted the door into splinters, the Kwoks told Wallach that the Plaza needed too much work.

Crestfallen, Wallach walked across the street to Trump Tower to break the bad news to the boss. From what he remembers, Trump reacted with a roiling eruption of curses. He stormed out of the office, down the elevator, and across the street. He took one step through the Plaza's front door and started shouting again: "Get the goddamn manager down here!" Workers gathered around. Wallach remembers Trump shouting "You're fired!" at everyone he saw. He walked over to a man standing nearby and asked, "What do you do here?" Before the man could answer, Trump said: "You're fired!"

"I'm a guest at the hotel," the stunned man responded.

Trump eventually found the actual manager and fired him too.

In the race with Citibank to hang on to the Plaza, Trump and Wallach were back in the starting block.

IN OCTOBER 1993, Donald and Marla's on-again, off-again romance produced a baby girl. They named her Tiffany, after the store next door to Trump Tower. They decided to marry.

The engagement would proceed with the speed of any shotgun wedding. On a Thursday evening two months after Tiffany's birth, they informed their families that they would wed before Christmas. The next day, they issued a news release. The wedding and reception would be held at the Plaza Hotel. Marla expected a small and intimate affair. "Of course, it may grow," she told Liz Smith, the gossip columnist, with a laugh. "You know Donald."

They invited fifteen hundred people. He hired a publicist to plan the wedding in about ten days. Caroline Herrera, dress designer to celebrities, who typically spent six months styling the perfect gown, had ten days to create Marla's dress. But after seeing Marla for a fitting, Herrera told a *New York Daily News* reporter that she was not worried. "She wasn't wearing any makeup, and she just had a baby. But she has a fabulous figure. She's tall, too, so whatever she wears is going to look great."

On December 21, dozens of photographers and a thousand onlookers crowded around a red carpet outside the Plaza. Most of the invited A-list celebrities did not attend. Michael Jackson, Arnold Schwarzenegger, and Tony Bennett all took a pass. Howard Stern, the radio shock jock, Susan Lucci, a soap opera star, and O. J. Simpson all mugged for the cameras. Most of the somewhat noteworthy attendees had appeared in Trump's rise and fall. Ace Greenberg had handled the stock trades in Trump's pretend takeover attempts; Robin Leach had helped create the image of Trump as endlessly wealthy; Carl Icahn had convinced the Trump-weary casino bondholders to give him one more chance; and Adnan Khashoggi had been the original owner of the *Trump Princess.*

Trump's children also did not attend. Donald Jr., Eric, and Ivanka stayed in Aspen with their mother on the annual holiday ski trip, where Donald would no longer be welcome. Baby Tiffany stayed at home.

As the crowd took their seats, Donald escorted his father into the ballroom. Fred appeared frail and unsteady. Donald helped him gingerly take his seat in the front row, and returned as the ceremony began to help his father join him at the altar and serve as his best man. Donald clasped his father's hand and several times put his arm around Fred to steady him.

As Caroline Herrera predicted, Marla indeed looked the part of the beautiful bride. She wore a sparkling $2 million tiara studded with 325 diamonds that Trump had borrowed from the jeweler Harry Winston. Opera star Camellia Johnson sang "Somewhere" from *West Side Story.* The Reverend Arthur Caliandro of Marble Collegiate Church, the location of Trump's first wedding to Ivana, led the couple through their vows, ending with the casual line, "I give you my love." Donald kissed Marla, and then turned to his father and kissed him on the cheek.

The reception included a sit-down dinner featuring sushi, lamb, beef, tuna, and turkey, followed by a huge five-layer cake and an orchestra. Abe Wallach also attended and found himself intrigued by the mounting costs he saw in the food and entertainment offerings. He later learned that $500,000 in costs for the wedding went straight to the Plaza Hotel's balance sheets. Wallach anticipated that Patricia Goldstein at Citibank, who was closely monitoring the hotel's bottom line, would not be pleased. But she already had a potential buyer unlikely to care about such a trifling amount.

WHILE WALLACH CRISSCROSSED the globe, Goldstein had connected two extremely wealthy men—Kwek Leng Beng, a Chinese real estate developer who owned a major hotel chain, and Saudi Prince Alwaleed Bin Talal Bin Abdulaziz Al Saud. She convinced them to work on a plan to buy out the Citi mortgage on the Plaza Hotel, leaving Trump at the curb.

Trump and Wallach caught wind of the deal. Trump decided their only option was to play dirty, hoping to buy more time by destroying the Kwek-Alwaleed deal. Wallach morphed into a corporate spy. He learned from an older doorman that everything said in the suite where Kwek and Alwaleed were negotiating could be heard through the wall from an adjoining sitting room. He spent several days sneaking quietly down the hall, past the suite door, and slipping into the sitting room next door. He sat down in a chair with a notepad and listened while two of the world's richest men discussed the old hotel.

He gathered a few actionable tidbits. Wallach learned which bank the pair had lined up for a loan and tried to sour the bank on the deal. But he failed. He also heard the men talk at length about whether the hotel's shabbiness might hint at structural weakness. Not long after, someone reported significant and dangerous structural defects in the hotel to the city's buildings department. Inspectors and fire marshals barged into the Astor suite and told Alwaleed and Kwek to evacuate for safety reasons. Point made. But the pair remained undeterred.

Trump took his shot with Goldstein. He dusted off the playbook he had developed to damage the careers of Marvin Roffman, the casino analyst, and Neil Barsky, the *Wall Street Journal* reporter, after they said truthful but hurtful things about him. Goldstein had mentioned to Trump that her husband, Jack, was dying of cancer, and she was struggling to find end-of-life care for him. Trump got a message to Cardinal John O'Connor, of the Archdiocese of New York, who quickly secured Jack a spot in a hospice run by the church. It was a generous act, had it all ended there. But now seeing his hotel slip away, Trump tried to use his favor as leverage to persuade Goldstein to spike the Kwek-Alwaaleed deal. She declined, letting him know that the two events were unrelated. Trump later tried to damage Goldstein's career, implying she had used the hotel deal to get him to do a personal favor for her. But the ploy he had used against Roffman and Barsky did not work. Goldstein continued in her long and respected career, a pioneer as a woman in the field of real estate.

The Kwek-Alwaleed deal closed, valuing the Plaza at $325 million, which was $100 million less than Trump had borrowed to buy the hotel seven years earlier. Having invested $20 million for the purchase and millions more on renovations and planning, Trump would walk away with nothing. But he would not have to cover the costs of his wedding to Marla. As Wallach remembered it, the buyers just folded the $500,000 wedding costs into the purchase price. "They didn't care about a half a million bucks or so," he would say later.

EVEN BEFORE LOSING the race with Citibank over the Plaza Hotel, Wallach was fighting to save one more of Trump's prize possessions, the West Side rail yards. He spent days at his desk flicking through Trump's Rolodex, searching for someone with deep enough pockets to pick up Trump's $210 million mortgage and finance his $3 billion plan for the site. Wallach and Trump caught word that Chase Manhattan Bank was looking for someone to pick up the mortgage and take over. Trump had also retained two New York real estate brokers with connections in Asia—Susan Cara and Carrie Chiang—with the promise of a $10 million commission, according to Wallach.

Wallach mailed letters, made calls, and took meetings. He struck out every time. In Wallach's telling, he finally received a bit of a welcome from three Chinese real estate executives—Henry Cheng, Vincent Lo, and George Wong—who were in Trump's Rolodex because he had met them during a failed effort to build a casino in Macau. Wallach knew the three and their company, New World, would have the required expertise and access to cash. They agreed to meet in Hong Kong. According to Carrie Chiang, she already knew Henry Cheng and made the connection with Trump. Either way, in short order the two agents were on a plane with Wallach and Roger Roisman, an outside lawyer retained by Trump.

By now, the fantastical vision that Trump unveiled in 1985 for Television City—8,000 apartments, 1.7 million square feet of retail space, more than 3 million square feet of offices, and the world's tallest building—had crumbled without Trump ever signing a tenant, securing a loan, or winning the needed zoning changes. A slightly downsized plan called Trump City also went nowhere. In 1992, at his darkest moment, he gave in to the local civic groups and agreed to fifty-seven hundred apartments in sixteen buildings, along with paying for the improvements to the nearest subway stop. The city approved the plan and zoning changes that year. Trump had a clear runway to land what would still be the biggest project of his life, but his reputation made it impossible for him to obtain financing for the $3 billion plan.

In Hong Kong, New World provided rooms for Trump's people in the Grand Hyatt, an eight-hundred-room hotel owned by the company. The next morning, they took cabs to New World headquarters, a mirrored office tower in the Central district. Wallach presented his market research and financial projections and the challenges of building in Manhattan. Carrie Chiang talked about Trump's power to draw attention to anything, and Susan Cara explained life and culture on the Upper West Side. The Trump team thought the presentation went well. They all adjourned to a multicourse dinner at an elegant restaurant.

Two days later, Wallach was called back to meet again with Cheng and Lo and their team. They sorted out the broad terms of an agreement. Wallach made clear that Trump could not put in more money or guarantee any loans. Cheng's team would negotiate the terms of buying out the Chase mortgage and control all financial and budget decisions. They agreed that Trump, who had spent $30 million so far holding on to the land and developing plans, would receive a 30 percent share but have no voice in decisions. His name, though, would feature prominently on the final project.

Wallach thought all that would go down easily with Trump. But more immediately, Cheng and Lo wanted Trump to fly to Hong Kong, play a round of golf, and sign documents. Wallach knew that Trump was not fond of long flights, especially on short notice. When he called the boss, Trump screamed that he would not go. It would look desperate. They would see it as a sign of weakness. Wallach told him that if this deal fell through, Chase would most certainly foreclose and sell the land to Cheng and Lo without him. Trump acquiesced. He flew on a commercial flight with his bodyguard, Matt Calamari. Henry Cheng reserved a large suite for Trump at the Grand Hyatt. Trump arrived in the evening, showered, and insisted that Wallach help him try to find a hamburger in Hong Kong.

Susan Cara had given Trump several books to help him prepare for the intricacies of Chinese culture. He had not read any of them. But like the classmate who helped him at Fordham University three decades earlier, Cara witnessed how quickly Trump could absorb information that was explained to him in a conversation. Chiang, who was steeped in Chinese culture, advised Trump to "cut the bullshit," resist his usual inclination to exaggerate and boast, because his suitors would walk away if they felt he was not being straight.

Trump met Henry Cheng and several of his friends for a round of golf at 7:00 a.m. As with Walter Kwok, Trump's life had paralleled the broad strokes of Henry Cheng's life. They were of almost identical ages, born one year apart, and Cheng had inherited a real estate company that had been founded by his father. But Cheng had expanded his father's company so much that bankrolling Trump's Manhattan project would not be a heavy lift.

Cheng and his friends suggested playing for a large sum of money, as much as $100,000 a hole, though accounts of the money have varied over the years. Trump refused. Cheng did not take offense. And Trump restrained his boisterous impulses, as Carrie Chiang had suggested. Trump later asked her, "Carrie, did I do all right?" She told him that he had done just fine. They had a deal.

Trump would receive a $1.2 million annual management fee during construction. But buried in the partnership agreement was a secret that would be kept for almost two decades (until Trump's litigious nature resulted in it being revealed in a Manhattan court): Trump had given up control. Henry Cheng's company would have unfettered authority over budgets and all major decisions. Cheng would decide whether his company and Trump would take any money out of the partnership, even in the most profitable years.

Trump's business judgment would be neither an asset nor a burden. And with his diminished ability to obtain bank financing, this model of limited influence over major projects would become his new reality.

For Cheng, the deal offered an opportunity to move money from Hong Kong, where he perceived the market to be peaking, to New York City, where he perceived it to have reached its nadir. "In Hong Kong, China, we've done bigger projects than this, much bigger," he told *The New York Times*.

Trump told a different story.

"I'm building a city within the greatest city, and beyond the financial aspects, from an ego standpoint, that means a lot," he told *New York* magazine. "And this is a deal from which everybody benefits. The civics are going to get their great park. I get the thing done. The Chinese are gonna get a wonderful return on their money. But the biggest beneficiary is New York City. I brought $2.5 billion here, and 25,000 construction workers are actually going to be working instead of sitting home.

"This is the biggest fucking deal in the history of New York real estate. And it's the best deal I've ever made."

The civics would not get their park. Whether it was the biggest deal in the city's history could be debated. But giving Henry Cheng authority over business decisions would eventually make the deal the most financially successful of Donald Trump's career. In the short term, however, he still needed to pay off his casino debts and hang on to his Florida mansion.

After he bought Mar-a-Lago in 1985, Trump told Robin Leach that other potential buyers wanted to do "the wrong things with Mar-a-Lago," like convert it to condominiums or a hotel. But after his brush with financial collapse, and with the deadline to pay off a $12 million mortgage on the property by June 1995 sneaking up, some of those wrong things started looking just right to Trump.

Faced with $3 million a year in costs, including maintaining a staff of twenty-five, Trump sought approval to subdivide the property into nine homes he would call the "Mansions at Mar-a-Lago." The idea sparked a battle on several fronts. When preservationists balked, he threatened to sell the estate to the Reverend Sun Myung Moon, whom he hinted would flood the blue-blooded island with moonies. When Palm Beach rejected his subdivision proposal, Trump filed a $50 million lawsuit against the town for violating his constitutional rights. "I don't usually litigate," Trump said, quite preposterously. "But our constitutional rights were taken away." In his usual fashion, Trump claimed to be persecuted for being himself. "If anyone else but Donald Trump owned it, they would approve it," he told *The Washington Post*.

As Trump tried to figure out how to placate the town's opposition, a friend one day recommended that he call a young lawyer named Paul Rampell, the well-connected son of a Palm Beach accountant. Rampell saw the subdivision plan as too divisive, and he thought a sale to another individual was not likely because of the high maintenance costs, the same reason that Trump had been able to buy it at a bargain price. He suggested that Trump consider converting the estate into a private club. Trump initially balked at the idea, but after nearly a month of telephone conversations, he agreed and hired Rampell to navigate the approval process.

They overcame objections from preservationists by giving away the power over a long list of internal and external modifications. Trump said he would spend $10 million converting the estate into a club. He installed fire suppressant sprinklers. He built a spa in the basement bomb shelter. Everything would be made handicapped accessible. The landscaping, including a nine-hole pitch-and-putt golf course, was upgraded. The library would be converted to a bar.

He had already taken a large step down the status ladder. Since the banks had taken his jet, he and Marla had been taking commercial flights to Palm Beach. He would also have to share his ostentatious second home. It would be initially more akin to a semiprivate boutique hotel, with ten guest rooms, a dining hall that would become a restaurant, and a banquet hall to rent out for weddings and parties. Banquet halls would become to Donald, on a smaller scale, what rental apartments had been for his father: an ongoing source of revenue. "Donald has got a thing about catering. He really loves catering," one former employee remembered. "He likes ballrooms and clubhouses because they're good for catering and events, parties."

As he opened membership to anyone willing to pay a $50,000 initiation fee and annual dues of $3,000, Trump released a list of prominent people he said would be members, including Prince Charles and Princess Diana; Henry Kissinger, the former secretary of state; and the actress Elizabeth Taylor. When reporters checked, they were told Trump had simply sent free and unsolicited membership papers.

Trump also made it sound like a gala opening in April 1995, just before the club closed for the summer, would be jammed with celebrities. But Donald and Marla, and Frank and Kathie Lee Gifford, were the closest to marquee names. The guests were more like Saul Jacobsen, a retired DuPont Chemical executive, who at eighty-two years old said he was ready for a little extravagance: "I had a doctor friend who said, 'You economize all your life, while your kids fly first class.' I want to go first class."

One morning in June 1995, Donald Trump and Marla Maples stood on the floor of the New York Stock Exchange. Wearing his usual dark-blue suit and a burgundy necktie, he craned his neck up to glimpse the board showing trading activity on his first public company, Trump Hotels and Casino Resorts. Marla, wearing a bright red skirt-suit with black trim, craned her neck to look at Donald. "This is a very important day, and it's going to be a great day," he said.

The initial public offering gave investors the chance to buy up to 60 percent of Trump's first casino, the Plaza, at $14 a share. The price never rose much above that baseline. Trump saved the best deal for himself. Taking the company public was the final step to getting his lenders off his back, and he pocketed millions of dollars by piling new debt onto his shareholders. Two years earlier, he had sold $100 million in junk bonds on the Plaza casino, using more than half of the proceeds to pay off his personal loans. Now that debt folded into the public company. The stock offering raised $140 million. That week Trump also sold another $155 million in junk bonds, at a stunning 15.5 percent interest rate, saddling the new company with even more debt.

The public company immediately used some of the almost $300 million it had raised to clear more of Trump's personal debts. During his financial pinch two years earlier, Chemical Bank had forced him to give up his ownership of the Trump Regency, a hotel next to the Trump Plaza. He held an option to buy it back for $60 million, which included debt on the hotel and $35.9 million that he personally owed the bank on the Grand Hyatt in Manhattan. The new public casino company exercised that option, transferring Trump's debt to its own balance sheet. The following year, Trump sold his share of the Grand Hyatt to his partners, the Pritzker family of Chicago, for $140 million. His first major project was no longer his.

He began piling on personal extravagances to the public company's balance sheets. He had leased back the same jet the banks took from him, and began charging much of its costs to the casinos. He paid himself large fees for what was a part-time job, including a $1 million "construction and management" fee for overseeing the demolition of a steel skeleton next to the Trump Plaza casino. But he had finally cleared the last of the loans from banks that had threatened to force him into personal bankruptcy.

He had in the prior decade recorded more than $1.1 billion in business losses on his tax returns, a failure of historical proportions. It would create what is known to tax experts as a "net operating loss" of a slightly lower amount that could carry over for years to wipe away income taxes, should he ever have a profitable year. Net operating losses of that magnitude are rare for individuals.

Trump's losses were also noteworthy because he had not actually lost his own money. The money he lost was borrowed from banks and bondholders who invested in his casinos. When the banks and bondholders agreed to reduce his debt, that money counted as income under tax law, something called cancellation of debt income. But someone in Trump's orbit developed a plan to claim that the debt had been swapped for equity in his partnerships, an aggressive maneuver that the IRS had already banned for corporations. Trump's tax lawyers told him he had a less than 50 percent chance of prevailing if the IRS audited him, but that appears not to have happened. Trump would have it both ways. He did not have to cover the income taxes for $1 billion in income from banks and bondholders that he squandered, and he could use the losses to wipe out any income or profits he made for the next eighteen years.

In May 1995, weeks before he wiped away the last of his threatening debts by fobbing it off on stockholders of the new casino company, Trump and his siblings took a more personal step to begin increasing their wealth.

Fred Trump still owned his entire empire, and still refused to give up control. As he approached his ninetieth birthday, his acuity slipping, his children convinced him to sign power of attorney over to Robert Trump, relinquishing authority over his affairs. Robert, who worked at his father's office in Brooklyn every day, still followed Donald's direction in all business matters. Between the trust funds, the invoice-padding operation, and other devices created to siphon off his father's wealth outside the gift and estate tax system, Donald was already collecting almost $2 million a year from his father's companies. His own business failures meant he kept that money tax-free. With power of attorney, however, Donald and his siblings could begin taking ownership of their father's massive cash machine, and Fred could do nothing to stop them.

It would be a long time before a bank would be willing to loan Donald Trump money to undertake a major real estate project on his own. But despite how much he had lost, he held on to just enough to appear wealthy. This is what mattered most to him. It made him more than just another handsome fellow on the streets of New York City. It gave him credibility. It gave him an air of success. The appearance of extreme wealth, combined with his unique variety of charisma and unquenchable thirst for attention, would persuade companies with very real resources—and excellent credit ratings—to pay him for serving as the face of their projects.

The arc of his comeback, such as it was, had not quite risen above where he had stood when he finished Trump Tower more than a decade prior. He had spent five years shedding assets. To acquire new businesses, the sort to make a splash and boost the public's perception of his wealth, he would have to do so without borrowing much money.

But those were challenges for another day. Within months of taking the Trump Plaza casino public, he began describing himself as bigger than ever, having triumphed, not over his own poor judgment, but over forces beyond his control. Looking out across a room of business leaders in Manhattan that fall, he saw no peers: "I'm the biggest in real estate in New York, and I'm the biggest in the gaming industry," he said.

25

ALWAYS THERE FOR ME

On a summer day, two weeks after taking his casino company public, Donald Trump stood next to Rudy Giuliani, the mayor of New York City, in front of the hulking steel frame of a skyscraper at the southwest corner of Central Park. They were joined by other city and state officials, all lined up in suits and ties while awkwardly holding heavy jackhammers. They joked and smiled for the cameras, a moment that spoke to the importance of a major construction project in the city, with the commensurate jobs and tax revenue.

When reporters asked questions about the plan to convert a decrepit office tower into a gleaming hotel and apartment building, it was Trump who said, "We think this is the best project in New York by a factor of ten." He positioned himself to sound like the man in charge, a real estate developer who owned the land and the building and was taking a multimillion-dollar risk.

The man who was actually in charge and taking the risk did not appear in the photos. Dale Frey, the stocky and bald chief executive of the General Electric Investment Corporation, managed $70 billion in assets, including the old Gulf & Western office tower that had been on this very site. A button-down corporate man with four decades at General Electric, Frey never thought he would be doing business with the likes of Donald Trump. But something had to be done about this underperforming asset, an outdated office building in a prime location that noticeably swayed in the wind. As he evaluated seven proposals, one of which included Trump teamed up with another developer, he spoke with real estate brokers in New York who told him that Manhattan condominiums with the Trump name tended to fetch higher prices than others, especially from foreign buyers.

Trump would be serving essentially as an employee. He partnered with a larger real estate development firm, the Galbreath Company of Ohio, which would take the lead. For advising on the city market and drawing the attention of potential buyers, Trump would receive a fee and the chance to buy the restaurant space and parking lot when the building was completed. His real estate brokerage would sell many of the units. But he would risk no money and receive no share of profits from sales. His history of poor financial projections, based on his belief that a Trump project would generate enough revenue to cover whatever he spent, would not play a role.

He had few options. Banks would not lend him enough money to finance a large-scale project on his own. Nonetheless, he would strive to create the impression that he was calling the shots.

AFTER FIVE YEARS of cleaning up Trump's messes, Abe Wallach was eager to find a way forward for his employer. He adapted his approach to the new realities, which would mean projects requiring little investment. He had for several years thought the financial district around Wall Street represented an opportunity. It had fallen out of favor for office space, compared to midtown. There were high vacancies, but Wallach expected the neighborhood would come back someday.

Trump had little experience with office space—just a few floors within Trump Tower—and had told Wallach he had no interest in downtown. But Wallach thought the struggling area represented his best hope to find a large building at a small price. He spent days walking the narrow streets, until he came upon 40 Wall Street, a seventy-two-story tower that had been the tallest building in the world for the first year after its completion in 1930. The tower rose elegantly from a broad base, narrowing on the upper floors and topping out with a copper pyramidal dome and spire, coated in a green patina. The building had cycled through a string of neglectful owners over the decades, including Ferdinand Marcos, the Philippine dictator. One owner had simply turned the building over to his bank and walked away after occupancy had fallen.

Wallach toured the building. He liked what he saw. Run-down lobby. Creaky elevators. Vacant floors. Rotten windowsills. It all screamed "bargain."

A broker told Wallach the building could probably be had for $1 million, an absurdly low price. He staged a tour for Trump, carefully planning the limousine route to make sure the initial impression would overcome Trump's resistance to downtown. Trump stepped from the car to see the sun-soaked copper tower framed by an opening between buildings at the end of the block. For as much as Trump's original buildings were shiny and modern, classic old New York architecture—like that of the Plaza Hotel—held a power over him. He was sold.

Only one potential obstacle remained. The building and the land under it were not owned by the same person, a fairly common situation in Manhattan. The building leased the land from a wealthy German family, and the current lease was set to expire in thirty-eight years, at which point ownership of the building would revert to the German family. Trump was familiar with this arrangement, known as a ground lease. It was the same mechanism that his father had used to fund Donald's first trust—Fred gave the land under Beach Haven to his children and then leased it back from them for the rest of his life. Wallach and a real estate lawyer whom Trump had recently hired, Bernie Diamond, headed to Hamburg to meet with Walter Hinneberg, the head of the family that owned the land.

Hinneberg had made a fortune in shipping and real estate. He met Wallach and Diamond at the airport in a Mercedes limousine and drove them to his home on a grassy knoll above the Elbe River. Wallach marveled at the classic furnishings and artwork. They sat at the formal dining table for dinner. Hinneberg wanted to know whether Trump was as outrageous as he was portrayed in the media. Wallach told him that Trump saw the media attention he drew as a marketing ploy and often used variations of a quip: "Bad publicity is better than no publicity."

Over several days of bargaining, Hinneberg expressed concern about Trump putting the deal at risk with large loans that he might not repay. Eventually, they all agreed that Trump could take out loans to bring the building up to current standards, but only after signing enough top-flight long-term tenants to cover the debt payments. It was the sort of financial discipline Trump had rarely practiced on his own. Hinneberg also agreed to extend the lease to 250 years, with built-in lease escalations, potentially linking the two families for generations to come.

Wallach and Diamond negotiated a purchase price of $1 million. Diamond recognized that the prior owners had been paying property taxes as if the building were fully occupied, which was definitely not true. Diamond retained an outside lawyer to pursue a property tax refund, which eventually totaled several million dollars. Wallach and Diamond essentially brought Trump a nice payday with a classic piece of New York's skyline thrown in for free, though the costs of keeping the mostly empty building open would run $5 million a year.

Later, three generations of the Hinneberg family traveled to New York on the *Queen Elizabeth 2* ocean liner to visit their new tenant/partner. Trump invited them, and Wallach, to his apartment at Trump Tower for dinner. Wallach, who had become friendly with Walter Hinneberg by then, noticed him looking stunned, if not repulsed, by the garishness of the gold-on-gold motif, the white grand piano, and the waterfall in the living room. But Hinneberg voiced appreciation for Trump's taste in artwork, which would appear to be one of the most important collections in the world. A Matisse. A Cézanne. A Monet. As Hinneberg raised a camera to photograph the works, Trump placed his hand in front of the lens. Please, no photos, he said. The insurance company would not allow photographs. Hinneberg, Wallach, and Trump all exchanged knowing glances. Wallach knew the paintings were cheap reproductions, and Trump's cover story was one of the less clever lies he had ever heard the boss offer. Hinneberg graciously moved on. He later told Wallach that he knew the paintings were fakes because he had seen the original of at least one in a Hamburg museum.

Not long after, Abe Wallach and Bernie Diamond sat in a room on the East Side of Manhattan with most of New York's top real estate development companies. There were executives from Tishman Construction, which had built the original World Trade Center towers, and Related Companies, which Stephen M. Ross had made into one of the largest residential developers in the state. Bernard Spitzer was there as well. He had built or bought many Manhattan buildings, including one on Fifth Avenue where Donald and Ivana once lived and another where Donald set up his first office. They had all come to hear a presentation about an eighteen-story office building across the street from the United Nations headquarters, offered for $60 million. They all knew the real prize would be the right to replace the old building with something very large.

Wallach looked around the room and thought to himself, How do we compete with this? All these companies could easily produce hundreds of millions of dollars in financing. So he bluffed. He raised his hand and asked whether Trump's Asian partner would be able to get back the nonrefundable $10 million deposit, with interest, if community opposition blocked a sale. There was no Asian partner. But since news articles had mentioned Trump's Asian partner on the West Side rail yards, Wallach thought the bluff might sound believable and scare off some bidders.

Later, Wallach walked the neighborhood with Sandy Lindenbaum, son of Fred Trump's real estate lawyer and longtime friend, Bunny. Sandy was now the city's preeminent zoning lawyer. Wallach worked with Sandy to line up the air rights from the neighboring buildings, which would allow them to build higher, while Diamond got Trump excited about the project.

Most of all, Wallach needed a partner with deep pockets. He called his new friend Walter Hinneberg and explained his dilemma. Hinneberg thought the deal sounded like a good fit for Daewoo, a South Korean conglomerate. He suggested that Wallach call Kang Ko, a vice president of Daewoo's real estate group, and offered to put in a good word for Wallach.

Within a few days, Ko returned Wallach's call. Wallach assembled an informational packet and sent it off to Ko. A little more than a week later, Kang Ko and his boss, H. C. Kim, head of Daewoo's real estate group, arrived in New York for a meeting. Wallach gave them a tour of the site before they all sat down with Donald at Trump Tower.

Kim appealed to Trump's vanity, asking him the secrets of his success, how he learned the development business. For a deal that involved several hundred million dollars, it all progressed very fast. They agreed that Trump would run the development process, obtain air rights and zoning approvals, and deal with any community opposition. Trump would also be responsible for obtaining the construction loan, though the Koreans would provide a guarantee to ease discomfort with Trump among banks. But the Koreans wanted to make sure the money worked. They would have approval rights over key financial decisions, the design and height of the building, and power to review all bids. And they would install two of their employees in Trump's offices to monitor everything.

The only sticking point came when they discussed how much money each would contribute to the deal. Trump, as Wallach recalled it, wanted to be able to say he owned half of the project. The Koreans thought that was fine, but it meant that each side would contribute $30 million, which was not possible for Trump.

"Daewoo became concerned," Wallach later recalled. "They were not used to haggling and dealing with someone like Trump. They approached things logically, but logic was not something that had allowed for Trump's success."

The solution was to let Trump put his name on the building—Trump World Tower—and accept a lesser share of profits. Daewoo would put up $55 million while Trump kicked in only $5 million. Trump's tax returns would show that Daewoo received 90 percent of the income for the crucial first years of sales.

The attention, though, would all go to Trump. Even with partners watching over his spending, Trump would have his name on three more Manhattan buildings, two of which he did not own. During the years when Trump's business losses were among the largest in the nation, the appearance of his wealth had been at least partially rehabilitated.

WHILE WALLACH AND DIAMOND FOCUSED on three skyscrapers, Trump pursued something lower and greener: turning the game he had loved since his days at Fordham University into a business. Fashioning himself as a golf impresario would come with a far lower price tag than acquiring skyscrapers, airlines, and mammoth casinos. Without senior partners or Wallach there to moderate him, he embarked on a suburban real estate buying spree that would devour much of his profits from his Manhattan real estate.

He began with several helicopter rides forty miles north of Trump Tower to tour an aging chateau, Seven Springs, which sat on two hundred acres next to a small lake. The fifty-thousand-square-foot Georgian-style mansion had been built in about 1919 for Eugene I. Meyer Jr., the onetime head of the Federal Reserve Board and longtime owner of *The Washington Post*. Meyer's daughter, Katharine Graham, held her wedding at Seven Springs and later became publisher of the *Post*. The family had left the estate and $5 million to Yale University for use as "a place of creative thinking about problems of intellectual and public significance." It was later transferred to Rockefeller University, which offered it for sale in 1994 for the first time in its history.

The $9.75 million listing received the attention of newspapers, but no firm buyers emerged until Trump showed up. He paid $7.5 million in April 1996 and soon announced plans to build a 72-hole golf course surrounded by twenty-five mansions, which he would offer for prices starting at $10 million. He planned to sell only two hundred memberships to keep the course from getting too crowded, a membership base so tiny that it would reinvent the metrics of golf club finances. Trump planned an initiation fee of $200,000, well above any other course in the area. And he told a meeting of local Realtors that he expected to be finished within about twelve months. "We're going to do something spectacular," he told the agents. "I hope you folks have a good time selling them."

Some locals thought he sounded out of touch. "Realistically, given what I know of the complexity and burdens of the Bedford Planning Board right now, one year sounds *highly* optimistic," the lawyer for one realty firm said at the meeting.

The estate straddled three towns in Westchester County, and officials in each would have a hand in approving or denying Trump's request for zoning changes. The lake below the château and its grounds created another sticky problem for Trump—it supplied drinking water for the local town. Officials and residents would not take kindly to surrounding their drinking water with a golf course dripping in fertilizer and pesticides.

Neither Trump nor anyone on his small staff had ever been involved with building or running a golf course. He signed contracts with a bevy of outside consultants to win the necessary approvals and come up with a viable plan. Internally, he hired one man, Dominic Bradlee, to push the process along. Bradlee, whom everyone called Dino, was the son of legendary *Washington Post* editor Ben Bradlee of Watergate fame. He was married to the journalist Leslie Marshall, who had just written a feature on Trump and his apartment for *InStyle* magazine. After the interview ended, she'd mentioned that her husband was building single-family homes in upstate New York. Trump had said he needed a project manager and asked that the husband contact him. Trump eventually extended a job offer.

Handsome and athletic in his late thirties, Bradlee had graduated from Yale

University, dropped out of Harvard Business School, and moved to the Catskills Mountains in upstate New York. He loved being outdoors and taught himself carpentry and then how to build houses. He knew little about golf, and nothing about golf course construction. Trump first put him in charge of overseeing the rehabilitation of 40 Wall Street, where crews were removing asbestos insulation. And then he decided Bradlee could handle golf courses. It became lore around Trump headquarters that every time Trump bought another swath of land, he would show up the next morning in the doorway to Dino Bradlee's office.

"I bought some land," Trump would say enthusiastically. "Let's do another golf course!"

ONE FRIDAY, Trump stood in the back of a meeting room at the InterContinental Hotel in midtown Manhattan, watching silently as the auctioneer, Sheldon Good, worked through bids on suburban houses. Trump had come for a different sort of property, a 97.5-acre undeveloped parcel in Westchester County known as French Hill. He waited for his moment and pounced, with a winning bid of $750,000.

In the coming months, he put down another $2 million for acres of land in an area known as Indian Hills, some of it bought out of foreclosure after other developers had failed. Trump envisioned two courses on the marshy and hilly land.

Trump dropped both projects in Dino Bradlee's lap. Still struggling to overcome the obvious problems at Seven Springs and to rehabilitate 40 Wall Street, Bradlee now took on two more challenging pieces of land. He hired Tim Miller, a planner and environmental consultant, to acquire the necessary approvals.

Miller surveyed the land and realized that Trump had dug himself a deep hole. French Hill was essentially a swamp, with portions of part of New York City's watershed or designated as protected wetlands. Not only would Trump need rezoning approval from several local towns, but he would also need sign-offs from the Army Corps of Engineers, New York City, and the state's Department of Environmental Conservation.

"He wanted to be a golf course guy, and he thought that these were big, cheap, inexpensive pieces of land," Miller later recalled.

Trump agreed to pay Miller between $500,000 and $750,000 for an environmental impact report. The costs would only grow. He also hired Jim Fazio, the less famous and less expensive brother of course designer Tom Fazio, to come up with a design.

As Miller expected, the projects faced opposition on all fronts. Trump had three recent purchases dead or dying. His efforts to reimagine himself as a suburban golf course tycoon were foundering on the shoals of his own impulses.

AT THE TIME, there were about forty golf courses in Westchester County, and not all of them were doing well. The five county-owned courses, all open to the public, were jammed, with tee times filled fifteen minutes after becoming available. But the private courses were fighting for members. One named Briar Hall had gone bankrupt, and its lender had foreclosed in 1994. The club had only 150 members and was offering new memberships with no initiation fee and annual dues as low as $2,750. When an auction was held, no one offered the minimum bid of $9.3 million. Alan Parter, a business consultant who at the time was helping Japanese investors find golf courses to buy in the United States, toured Briar Hall. He and his partner, Tadashi Hattori, who also ran golf courses for a Japan-based company, saw a worn-out clubhouse and an unremarkable course. "We thought, from our knowledge of golf and our knowledge of courses," Parter later remembered, "that this was not a particularly interesting course. You're in an area, Westchester, that has some of the top courses in the country. And this was just not particularly good."

One day not long after, a long black limousine pulled up in front of the clubhouse. Out stepped Donald Trump. A twenty-five-year-old Briar Hall employee named Carolyn Kepcher watched in admiration. She would later write in a memoir that his physical presence and personality filled the entire driveway. Kepcher had been hired by the bankrupt club a year before to bring in new members. It was her first golf course job. She had previously managed a restaurant for a couple of years after college. She considered the restaurant experience to be "her Yale" and selling golf memberships to be "her Harvard." As Trump toured the premises with Kepcher and the club's general manager, he asked Kepcher whether she thought the club could be salvaged. She took a breath, worried she might expose her lack of experience, and told him that she thought the clubhouse should be replaced.

Trump met with the mayor of Briarcliff Manor and other local officials to get a sense of how much opposition he might face to replacing the old clubhouse and building condominiums on the 143-acre site. He left the meeting satisfied enough to pay $8.5 million for the course.

Not long after, Trump visited Dino Bradlee to tell him the plan. And he soon told the young Carolyn Kepcher that she would become the new club's general manager. It was not respectful of her potential talents, but the men in Trump's office noted that aside from being young, she matched his general tastes in women—blonde, tall, and slender.

At the same time Trump had committed money to four prospective golf courses in suburban New York, he pursued a fifth course across Lake Worth from Mar-a-Lago in Florida. He had long talked about building a course near Mar-a-Lago and finally became interested in an undeveloped swath of land, a junglelike stretch surrounded by a strip club, government offices, and a twelve-story jail, and just two blocks from the roar of the local airport.

The land was owned by the county. Trump had for years criticized county officials for directing jets over Mar-a-Lago, threatening to sue for the thunderous noise and fumes. He accepted no blame for his choice to buy a property two miles from an airport and a straight line off the end of a runway.

Bruce Pelly, the manager of the airport, heard that Trump was interested in leasing the barren land next to the county jail. Pelly's first thought was, Fine, but the lease must stipulate that Trump will not sue the county about this silly noise business. Even if the court ultimately agreed that such a complaint was ridiculous, Pelly estimated that the costs to taxpayers of defending the case would approach $1 million.

When Trump caught wind of the demand toward the end of negotiations, he rushed to file a noise-complaint lawsuit. Then he told local reporters that that county offered to lease him the land if he dropped the lawsuit, flipping the script on Pelly and other officials. The county let Trump's phony telling of the negotiations slide and signed a lease starting at $438,000 a year, rising in future years, for the land next to a jail.

Once again, Trump had expenses mounting on a collection of land that was not producing revenue.

Donald, Marla, and Tiffany had settled into the same Trump Tower triplex where he had lived with, fought with, and walked out on Ivana. A self-described country girl, Marla had focused on giving the third floor a feeling of home. She had thirty tons of soil spread on the terrace, topped with grass, a sandbox, and a wooden swing set. She spent her time in the upstairs kitchen, which opened to a playroom. Some nights, she would sleep there with Tiffany. She prided herself on cooking dinners and cherished the time they spent together as a family. During a tour with a reporter, a wistful sadness crept in as she described evenings that often took a different turn. "Donald likes to eat at seven sharp. I like family time around the table, but Donald likes to take dinner down to the bedroom and eat in front of the TV, to decompress."

In May 1997, Trump announced that he and Marla had separated. Anonymous quotes in newspapers from "a person close to Donald"—by then well-known code in the city's newsrooms for Donald himself—said he had split with her now to cap the amount she could receive in a divorce. Their prenuptial agreement, according to this person close to Donald—called for Marla to receive $1 million if they permanently separated before their fifth anniversary, and perhaps more after that date. That day was still nineteen months away.

The prenuptial agreement was tightly held by the couple and their lawyers. We obtained a copy decades later that showed Marla would receive $1 million thirty days after she vacated all of Trump's properties, and another $1 million to buy a home. Tiffany's college expenses would also generally be covered. The agreement included a list of Donald's assets at the time of their marriage, as well as a line that would be at odds with how Donald spoke publicly about his father's wealth: "Donald anticipates significant future inheritances."

What no one outside the immediate family knew at the time was that Donald and his siblings were months away from taking ownership of their father's empire. After they had encouraged their father to sign away power of attorney in 1995, they had immediately begun the process of taking his properties through a trust, a step that their father had long resisted.

They used a mechanism called a grantor retained annuity trust, or GRAT for short. GRATs are a form of trust funds that work like magic, enabling extremely wealthy people to pass assets to heirs outside the onerous gift and estate taxes. They fit squarely within current tax law and, in several respects, well outside the bounds of common sense.

The notion is based on creating an artifice that Fred Trump's children were buying his empire from him at fair market value. Were his assets stocks and bonds, the value of those assets would be established by a marketplace. But because the assets being transferred included only real estate, establishing the value fell to the approximation of property appraisal.

They hired Robert Von Ancken, the same appraiser the family had hired in 1981 to determine the Fred Trump Jr.'s share of the rental apartment buildings that his father had given to him and his siblings. Back then, Von Ancken had put the "highest and best use" value of all seven buildings at $13.2 million, a finding that kept the estate tax very low. The Trumps immediately began converting those buildings to cooperative apartments and offered the units to current residents at a total of $90.4 million.

For the new trust fund, Von Ancken would do even better for the Trumps. He valued the 25 apartment complexes with 6,988 apartments—and twice the floor space of the Empire State Building—at $93.9 million. In 2004, the same buildings would be valued at nearly $900 million by banks issuing mortgages on the properties. The New York City real estate market certainly increased in those years, but not nearly tenfold.

Fred Trump's tax returns, which we later obtained, showed what appeared to be many absurdities in Von Ancken's appraisals, especially when we compared his numbers to recent sales of similar buildings. Von Ancken valued Argyle Hall, a six-story brick Fred Trump building in Brooklyn, at $9.04 per square foot. Six blocks away, another six-story brick building, two decades older, had sold a few months earlier for almost $30 per square foot.

Von Ancken valued Belcrest Hall, a Trump building in Queens, at $8.57 per square foot. A few blocks away, another six-story brick building, four decades older with apartments a third smaller, sold for $25.18 per square foot.

Tax laws allowed for another major reduction to Von Ancken's $93.9 million appraisal. Assets are considered to have less value to anyone who is not a majority owner, which makes perfect sense. Buying a business in which you have no control over decisions would be worth less to most people than having the power to run the business as you see fit. But, for tax purposes, creating the artifice of loss of control is just as effective. The Trumps accomplished that by restructuring Fred's businesses so that he and Mary, his wife of more than sixty years, each controlled 49.8 percent of the corporate entities that owned his buildings and split the remaining 0.4 percent among their four children. It stretched credulity to argue that eighty-five-year-old Mary Trump represented a threat of rebellion to Fred Trump's independent operation of his businesses. But that assertion, combined with another $18.3 million in standard deductions, reduced the taxable value of what was, or would soon be, a nearly $900 million real estate empire, to just $41.4 million. Von Ancken later told us that his working papers, if he still had them, would support his figures.

The IRS audited the transaction and increased the total to $57.1 million. The 38 percent change may have felt like a victory to the IRS agent, but Donald Trump and his siblings surely celebrated. In the end, the transfer of the Trump empire cost Fred and Mary Trump $20.5 million in gift taxes, hundreds of millions of dollars less than they would have paid in gift or estate taxes based on the empire's actual market value. Donald Trump and his siblings were required to make $21 million in annuity payments, but that money did not come out of their pockets. They used their newest asset—their father's empire—to secure a line of credit from M&T Bank for that amount. And they used the revenue from their father's empire to repay the money.

On the day the Trump children finally took ownership of Fred Trump's empire, Donald Trump's net worth instantly increased by tens of millions of dollars. And from then on, the profits from his father's empire would flow directly to him and his siblings. This sudden influx of wealth came only weeks after he had published his third book, *The Art of the Comeback*.

"I learned a lot about myself during these hard times," he wrote. "I learned about handling pressure. I was able to home in, buckle down, get back to the basics, and make things work. I worked much harder, I focused, and I got myself out of a box."

Privately, he had also learned the value of being born rich. Based on the trove of Fred Trump's financial records that we had acquired, we calculated that Donald Trump's share of profits from his father's company averaged about $6 million a year going forward. That flood of new cash came in late 1997, when he was still in the middle of spending to rebuild his image. Two years of his father's profits could have covered his initial investments in Trump

World Tower, 40 Wall Street, and the four properties he bought as possible golf course sites.

His casino businesses, meanwhile, had plummeted again under the weight of his decision-making. A year after the initial public offering, the company issued more stock and sold $1.1 billion in junk bonds. The money paid off $330 million in bonds on the Plaza that had been guaranteed by a company Trump controlled, as well as almost $30 million that Trump personally owed to two banks. The public company also bought the Trump Taj Mahal and Trump Castle, shifting more of Trump's debt to shareholders. The stock market saw the $525 million that the public company had paid for the Castle, a money loser for years, as too much. The stock began a long slide, falling from about $35 a share before the sale, to $12 months later. The company posted losses of $66 million in 1996, $42 million in 1997, and $40 million in 1998, a trend that continued.

For as much as his shareholders suffered, Trump pulled cash out of the struggling businesses. He received a $1 million a year salary for what was a part-time job. In 1996, he was paid a $5 million bonus. Trump casinos reported paying about $300,000 a year in "pilot costs" to transport high rollers in Trump's jet. The casino company leased office space in Trump Tower in Manhattan, and Trump's other businesses were paid to entertain its "high-end customers." Shareholders later alleged in a lawsuit that at least part of the money was paid for big-name performers, including Celine Dion, Tony Bennett, and Billy Joel, to appear at Mar-a-Lago.

One night in the mid-1990s, Alan King, the acerbic comic of television and film, performed to a small crowd at Mar-a-Lago. After the show, Alan Marcus, who worked as a consultant for Trump, came across King sipping a drink in an adjoining room.

"What are you doing here?" Marcus asked the famous comedian.

"Let's face it," King said, "If I want to perform in Atlantic City, I have to perform at Mar-a-Lago."

By the time Donald Trump and his siblings took over their father's empire, Fred and Mary Trump rarely left their house in Jamaica Estates. Fred was ninety-three years old and greatly diminished by dementia and other infirmities. In June 1999, he was taken to Long Island Jewish Medical Center, not far from the house. He died there two weeks later.

His career could serve as a parable for a certain twentieth-century American experience. A son of immigrants, he taught himself home building in the wide-open land of what would become the nation's most densely populated city. He mastered increasingly large projects funded by nascent government programs intended to heal the injuries of the Great Depression, World War II, and the postwar recovery. He pinched pennies, mastered his craft, and twisted those government programs to attain tremendous wealth.

Among the tributes to Fred Trump placed in newspapers following his death, one from an association of his peers captured a quintessential compliment to a man of Fred Trump's generation: "His word was his bond."

Fred didn't crow about his wealth. He lived a mostly private life. His few brushes with notoriety turned sour. Yet he somehow raised a man who, perhaps more than anyone else, thirsted for constant public attention, for himself and his wealth, and turned that need into his greatest commodity.

Fred's funeral was held at Marble Collegiate Church, the site of Donald's first wedding. It was attended by the biggest names in New York real estate and politics. Ivana, who had not instantly warmed to Fred, came and wept at times. Donald brought his latest girlfriend, a tall and steely-eyed model from Slovenia named Melania Knauss.

The siblings each said a few words. Elizabeth Trump read a poem she said her father had liked. Donald offered a eulogy that struck many as more about himself than his father. He rambled through a list of his own projects—Trump Tower, Trump Taj Mahal, the skating rink—to conclude his father "was always there for me."

Mary Trump, who had immigrated from Scotland and cleaned homes before meeting her dashing builder, died the following year after a brief illness. She was eighty-eight.

To DESIGN THE GOLF COURSE next to the West Palm Beach jail, Trump again hired Jim Fazio. Bradlee flew down to Florida for several days a week to oversee the work. Trump said he spent $40 million on the course, which, if true, made it one of the most expensive courses of its era. Bradlee oversaw the clearing of more than two hundred acres of jungle and the construction of a 25,000-square-foot clubhouse. Two million cubic yards of soil were trucked in and shaped into contours atop the pancake-flat parcel. Lakes were dug and filled. Thousands of trees were planted, especially to block the view of inmates at the county jail and muffle their trash-talking at golfers. The main landscaping attraction would be a man-made waterfall.

Florida is not a state known for its waterfalls. Golf course designers generally strive to create courses that evoke a more perfect vision of the natural world. Trump's sense of design tended to evoke a more natural vision of the casino world, and waterfalls had become central to his aesthetic, from the lobby in Trump Tower to his own apartment.

Trump's love of waterfalls led him to Philip di Giacomo, whom the *Los Angeles Times* once referred to as "one of the world's premier creators of faux rock environments." Di Giacomo had traveled the world working with landscape architects. In 1999, he was invited to meet with Dino Bradlee at Trump Tower about constructing a waterfall in Florida. They chatted in Dino's office for just a few minutes before Dino called Trump to join them. Di Giacomo immediately realized that he was not there to share his philosophy of using stones to inspire. Trump took over. Di Giacomo thought to himself, "It took me sixty years to learn how to do rock work, and he learned it in a minute and a half." Still, di Giacomo took the job for a waterfall budgeted at roughly $1 million. During construction, Trump made a habit of wandering out to the site and insisting that certain stones be repositioned.

Di Giacomo's waterfall, with adjustments by Donald Trump, would become the most unique feature of Trump's course in West Palm Beach. It spanned more than fifty feet, curving around the seventeenth green. The beige stones rose in sawtooth angles, bearing an eerie resemblance to the exterior of Trump Tower. Some five thousand gallons of water a minute pump over the precipice of the 101-foot cliff of black granite. "There's never been a waterfall like this on a golf course," Trump said. "It's a seven-million-dollar golf hole. It's probably the most expensive golf hole ever built."

Others saw it differently. Sportswriter Rick Reilly described the waterfall as "so fake looking you're sure you saw it on Fantasy Island." Di Giacomo thought it looked like "a first-class piece of junk" when Trump proudly showed it to him. As Trump stood on the grass waxing semipoetic, the stone man thought, "This guy can look at a pile of dog shit and tell you how wonderful it is."

Jim Fazio entirely redesigned the Westchester course. Trump bought more property adjacent to the course at Fazio's suggestion to allow for a longer reimagined layout. He called the new course Trump National Golf Club Westchester and said he spent $30 million in some interviews and $40 million in others. He predicted the course would host many PGA championships. "This will be the best course in New York," he said.

When the club opened in 2002, Trump told reporters that he had 210 members who had paid initiation fees of $150,000. He said he doubled the fees because of high demand. Company insiders said Trump liked this new business model in part because each new private club brought a rush of cash from member initiation fees, and Trump required them to agree they could not demand the money be returned for thirty years, unless a new member was waiting to join. He used that money as it came in.

Assuming the figures Trump cited were accurate, in Westchester the initiation fees covered the costs of construction to that point. He still had not built the clubhouse. And he postponed the plans to build seventy-one condominiums and sixteen townhouses on the property.

WHILE HE CELEBRATED the opening of the West Palm Beach and Westchester courses, Trump was furious that he still had not won approval to develop courses, or anything else, on the three other pieces of land he'd bought in the area, French Hill, Indian Hills, and Seven Springs. He had spent millions of dollars on consultants and other expenses to maintain those properties.

"Everybody wants to shoot at me because it's me," he told a *Wall Street Journal* reporter as he trimmed a fingernail with a gold clipper. "They're saying, 'Let's fight Trump because it's Trump.' They think it's glamorous. It gives them something to do."

Tim Miller, whose firm had studied the environmental impact of Trump's plans and proposed solutions, had felt the brunt of Trump's frustration over the years. Trump had once screamed at Miller, "I'm not going to give you another penny until this project is approved!" He hesitated for a moment, and then shouted, "No, you're fired!" Trump later changed his mind, and Miller and his employees worked years more for Trump. But in the end, Trump insisted he would only pay Miller by giving him membership at the Westchester course. Miller eventually let the membership lapse because he could not afford the annual dues.

Trump also took his frustration with Seven Springs out on Dino Bradlee, which struck others in the office as unfair. It was Trump who had bought the properties without performing any due diligence. And Trump had pushed Bradlee beyond his comfort zone.

Bradlee had taken on a more personal role for Trump as well. In the late 1990s, a new summer intern showed up on the twenty-sixth floor at Trump Tower. Trump's oldest child, Don Jr., had just finished his first year studying business at the University of Pennsylvania, his father's alma mater. Trump assigned Bradlee to take Don Jr. under his wing for the summer. Pudgy and wearing his hair wavy and long, Don Jr. camped out in Dino's office every day and tagged along as Dino oversaw five potential golf course projects. Donnie, as he was called, would later describe Bradlee as a mentor. Some in the office thought Donnie was more interested in working in the woods somewhere, as a hunting guide or forest fire scout.

Taking the blame for the stalled projects became too much for Dino Bradlee, and he departed around 2002, about the time that the Westchester course opened. He returned to building single-family homes in wooded areas and eventually moved to Greece.

Another key executive on Trump's small staff left around the same time. For years, people around the office had noticed that wallets seemed to occasionally disappear. But Abe Wallach had been keeping a secret. Even before Trump had hired him, he had a problem. It began when he found a credit card in the back of a taxi and decided to buy himself something. The rush he felt gave him a brief escape from the stress of his work, and the stress of masking his private life as a gay man. He never needed the money. But he did need the thrill and escape, and so he would steal from friends, clients, and colleagues. No one around him knew that he had been convicted of theft years before Trump hired him.

By 2002, Wallach had started to feel that his obsession over Trump's bottom line fueled self-destructive behavior. He told Trump he needed to leave and came clean as to why. Trump, according to Wallach, promised to keep the secret. But within a short period of time, Wallach heard that everyone in New York real estate knew about his problems.

By then, Donnie had graduated and joined the company full-time. He would essentially take Dino's place. His early involvement struck some as ham-handed. His father, enamored now by the business of banquets, Bar Mitzvahs, and weddings at Mar-a-Lago, wanted all his golf course clubhouses as big as possible. During a meeting to review plans at the office, Don Jr. demanded that Andrew Tesoro, the architect on the Westchester course, fudge the drawings they were about to submit to the town to make the ballroom look much bigger than was allowed.

"My dad wants it bigger," he insisted, as Tesoro later recalled.

Tesoro told Don Jr. he was not willing to put his license to practice at risk, and Don Jr. eventually gave up. Tesoro's relationship with the Trumps would soon grow more complicated.

Once the clubhouse was completed, Tesoro asked that the remaining $141,000 balance of his bill be paid. After several requests and phone calls, he was told someone from Trump's office would meet with him in the new clubhouse. He entered the large lobby, with its grand sweeping staircase, and felt his heart sink. It looked like a surprise reunion of everyone who had worked on the project. "There was the landscape architect, the tile company president," he recalled later. "There must have been at least fifty people in the lobby waiting to negotiate their final bill."

One by one, the contractors were called into the six-thousand-square-foot grand ballroom that Tesoro had designed. Tesoro was directed to one corner, where more than a dozen of Trump's lawyers and managers waited for him at a round dining table stacked high with papers. There, under the huge crystal chandeliers, Tesoro was offered $50,000, just over a third of what Trump had agreed to pay. "I left," he later recalled. "I was furious."

He consulted a lawyer, who said winning a lawsuit would cost more than Trump was shorting him. Feeling defeated, he agreed to accept the $50,000. But when even that didn't come through, Tesoro called Andrew Weiss, then Trump's widely liked and respected construction manager, for an explanation. "Well, Mr. Trump thinks that he has spent enough on this building, and he doesn't want to pay anymore," Weiss told him. He called Bernie Diamond, with whom Tesoro was friendly. Diamond said his job was to make suing Trump long and expensive.

Exasperated, he called Trump's assistant, Rhona Graff, and asked to see Trump. Tesoro raced to Trump Tower. He recounted the situation to Trump:

You owe me $141,000 and I agreed to accept $50,000, which I now regret, but even that wasn't paid. "What the hell is the trouble?" he asked Trump.

Trump put his arm on Tesoro's shoulder. "You're the most talented architect I've ever met," Trump said, as Tesoro recalls. "And just because you're such a nice guy, I'm going to tell them to give you a check for twenty-five thousand dollars."

Part IV

DRAMALITY

Wealth is like sea-water; the more we drink, the thirstier we become; and the same is true of fame.

—*Arthur Schopenhauer*

We need money. We need hits. Hits bring money, money bring power, power bring fame, fame change the game.

—*Young Thug*

26

THE PRODUCER

IN OCTOBER 1982, a twenty-two-year-old former British paratrooper arrived at Heathrow Airport with his mother. He was holding a ticket to Central America, where he intended to find decent-paying work as a military adviser, a plan he had kept from his mother to avoid further worrying her after his tours of duty in active combat zones. As they said their goodbyes, she made a plea to her only child.

"We've been through a lot in the past few years, between the Falklands and various operations you've been on. Promise me, no more guns."

Mark Burnett made that promise. When his flight landed in Los Angeles for a stopover, he walked off the plane and into the California sunshine. He had six hundred dollars to his name and no ticket home. That day, he called a friend for a ride, answered a classified ad, and was hired to become a live-in nanny for a wealthy Beverly Hills family.

Tall, athletic, with a thick head of hair and a charming accent, Burnett soon took up with a young woman named Kym Gold from a wealthy Malibu family. She had grown up palling around with Sean Penn, Rob Lowe, and Charlie Sheen. She dreamed of designing clothes. Her stepfather was a prominent personal injury lawyer and businessman. Burnett had grown up in the East End of London. His father worked at a Ford Motor factory on the river Thames, and his mother at a battery plant next door. Kym Gold gave him entrée to a world he had seen only on screens.

She started a business named Kymberly Suits You. She bought damaged T-shirts, reimagined them with dye and sewn-on patterns, and sold them from a booth on Venice beach. Burnett joined in and found he enjoyed selling. They made real money, selling hundreds of shirts every weekend at a profit of about fifteen dollars each.

Burnett would later say it was during his time selling T-shirts with Kym that he first read *The Art of the Deal*, which altered the course of his life. Kym Gold doesn't recall Mark ever mentioning the book or reading anything other than an occasional spy novel.

In 1988, Kym and Mark married in a ceremony at her parents' Malibu home. He took a job as vice president of a company her father had founded called Faces International, which charged Hollywood hopefuls to include their photo in a magazine circulated within the industry. The following year, while on a business trip to the company's offices in New York City, Burnett walked into a room while an associate, Dianne Minerva, was convincing a young actor to pay $2,500 to have his black-and-white photo included in the next edition. Burnett began encouraging the man to upgrade to the full color "Publisher's Page" for $7,500. As the actor resisted, Burnett's sales approach shifted toward badgering him, in a polite English manner, to please help himself: "Do you want to make it, or is this just a hobby? Very few people are offered such prestigious placement, and if you don't take it, someone else will. Only an idiot would turn this down."

The actor agreed to up his "investment" to $4,000, and promptly passed out on the floor. Burnett had also made an impression on Minerva. They began an affair. Within months, Burnett quit the company and his marriage.

Kym Gold went on, with her second husband, a fabric salesman, to cofound True Religion Brand Jeans, a fashion sensation that eventually sold for more than $800 million. Burnett founded a credit card telemarketing company and married Dianne. They bought a house in Topanga Canyon, an enclave in the Santa Monica Mountains above Malibu. It was a nice life. But he would later admit that at parties he often felt "unbelievably jealous" of the attention lavished upon people who worked in Hollywood, which to him seemed "exciting, glamorous, and the most creative place on earth."

In 1991, Burnett read a story about Raid Gauloises, a days-long endurance race named after its cigarette company sponsor. Teams of five contestants traveled to a secret, exotic location to navigate their way across hundreds of miles of unforgiving wilderness and conquer a series of skill challenges. Reading that article would change the course of his life.

Later that year, Burnett formed the race's first American team.

In 1994, he acquired the North American television rights to the race from its French creator and convinced MTV to air it as a special. Burnett sold the show, which he would call *Eco Challenge*, to other networks. He had cracked open a side door into the glamorous life he had coveted.

During those years, a British television producer named Charlie Parsons was making the rounds of studios pitching a show he called *Expedition Robinson*. Parsons stranded contestants on a deserted island and forced them to compete in survivalist challenges. First airing in 1997, it became a hit in Sweden and the Netherlands.

Burnett met Parsons during a chance encounter at Fox Studios in Los Angeles and soon after persuaded Parsons to sell him the North American rights to the show. Burnett would call his version *Survivor*, which he imagined being "bigger, more dramatic, and more epic than any nonfiction television ever seen." He pitched the concept to all four broadcast networks, along with the Discovery Channel and the USA Network. But even with the narrow critical success of *Eco Challenge*, and the popularity of Parsons's concept overseas, the prospects for a prime-time show based on survival challenges seemed uncertain. Every sales pitch ended with rejection.

At a holiday party in December 1997, Burnett chatted up a director he knew, Zalman King, best known for erotic dramas like the film *Wild Orchid* and *Red Shoe Dairies*, a long-running series on Showtime. King introduced Burnett to his manager, a lawyer named Conrad Riggs, who had recently left Disney to start his own company. Riggs had years of experience negotiating major deals in Hollywood and had a long list of connections. Burnett hired Riggs to find a deal for *Survivor*. The two would become nearly inseparable over the next decade. Burnett, the consummate salesman, would call Riggs "one of the best dealmakers in the entire entertainment industry."

Sometime around then, CBS called to schedule a second meeting. The network was down in the ratings at the time and needed a hit. Burnett showed Leslie Moonves, the network's head of entertainment, a mock cover of *Newsweek* featuring *Survivor*. Still not sure of the show's potential, Moonves imposed tough terms. To reduce the network's financial risk, Burnett would have to help CBS sell the concept to advertisers. "Burnett's ability to deliver that, because he is such an amazing salesman, was pretty clear," one former executive recalled.

Burnett remembers it as a turning point. "The moment Leslie said yes was one of the most exciting and horrifying of my life. I was finally in the big leagues."

As he had with Raid Gauloises and *Eco Challenge*, Burnett recognized that corporations would pay to have their products appear on the show—what is known as product integration. Riggs told the network that it would have to share the money from traditional advertising and from product integration in order to sign Burnett. It was a provision that would make Burnett—and later, a struggling New York real estate developer—a lot of money.

Survivor debuted on May 31, 2000, becoming an instant cultural phenomenon. Newspapers and television shows covered each week's episode as if it were a sporting event. The show was featured on covers of *Time* and *Newsweek*. As the ratings and reviews came in, the amounts the network charged for the slots they had held back continued to climb, translating into millions of dollars for Burnett and the network. Moonves had a champagne-colored Mercedes convertible delivered to Burnett's home. Upon its arrival, Mark and Dianne came outside in their pajamas, like kids on Christmas morning.

"Oh my God," exclaimed Mark. "Di, I've made it!"

Cultural pundits and professors opined endlessly about what this new breed of television—telegenic people facing off death and conspiring against one another—said about America and its values. Burnett had little use for such debates. He did not even like the term "reality television," preferring "dramality." The important innovation, in his telling, was the realignment of the business model of television that he and Riggs had negotiated—keeping revenue from expanded product integration for themselves. On *Survivor*, contestants bid for a bag of Doritos or competed for a meal from Outback Steakhouse. Logos on the set appeared in strategic framing. Burnett told industry reporters that seamlessly blending brands into a storyline was easy enough. "Does the public care? No. As long as it's done honestly. I'm the first one that's really done product placement on a network. It's an integral part of the plan."

He and Moonves briefly engaged in a public spat over whether Burnett, as he was telling the world, had a revenue-sharing deal with CBS that paid him half of all the show's advertising and product-integration money. Networks typically fund the multitude of shows that fail with the profits from the few that succeed. Other networks were concerned that Moonves had set a new and dangerous precedent. Moonves told *The New York Times* that he would never have signed a fifty-fifty deal with a producer: "It would change the whole model of the network business."

The two settled the profit split from season one and struck a new deal for season two in a confidential arbitration proceeding. Whether Moonves had given away half the store in the first season was not revealed, but, practically, it did not matter. By the end of *Survivor*'s first year, Burnett and Riggs had leveraged the show's success, and the impression that he was getting half of its sponsor revenue, to win that deal for new seasons of *Eco Challenge* and two other new show concepts. Burnett had become a hot Hollywood commodity. Riggs began every negotiation insisting that the long-standing rules no longer applied. "If you want Mark, you've got to split the revenue," he told studios across Los Angeles. Much as Moonves feared, Mark Burnett had already changed the business model of network television.

In the spring of 2002, Burnett rented the Wollman skating rink in Central Park for a *Survivor* season finale. As he warmed up the crowd for a television moment, Burnett noticed the skating rink owner, Donald Trump, and his girlfriend, Melania Knauss, sitting in the front row. Burnett instinctively knew just the show of respect that would win Trump over. The two spoke after the filming. Burnett told Trump about how *The Art of the Deal* had impacted him and said the word "Trump" about a dozen times. Trump told Burnett he was a genius and said, "I'd love to work with you someday."

By the end of 2002, Burnett had shot six seasons of *Survivor*, and an additional season of *Eco Challenge*. He had spent most of those years living in unforgiving landscapes around the world. He began to imagine what might come next. Throughout the years since, he has described different moments that served as inspiration for a new show. A colony of ants swarming a carcass invoked visions of humans fighting for survival in Manhattan. The jaguars circling the crew's tents at night in the Amazon made not dying at work seem appealing. A BBC documentary about disputes in business showed the potential for office-based dramality. But the motivation Burnett has most often cited was a painful conversation with his son.

By then, Mark and Dianne had separated. They had two young sons, James and Cameron. One day, when he was far from home, he had "an agonizing phone call" with James, his oldest. The boy said, "Daddy, I forgot what you look like." Burnett's mind raced. This is not good. I've got to get a normal job in a city. What can I do? How can I make a show like *Survivor* . . . in the city? What do people need? They need jobs. What if I do, like, a twelve-week job interview?

"But it's got to have a hook to it, right?" he thought. "They've got to be working for, like, someone big and special and important."

In February 2003, Donald Trump was once again facing a casino bankruptcy. He had until November to come up with $312 million to pay off a portion of the company's debt. The casinos continued to lose money every year, thanks to interest payments on the $1.7 billion in bonds and loans that Trump had already loaded on the company's back. His plan was to sell almost $500 million in new junk bonds, hopefully at slightly better rates. To persuade potential bond buyers, Trump vowed to pump $30 million of his own money into the casinos. His businesses continued to struggle, with his tax returns showing losses carried forward rising above $300 million.

As usual, Donald Trump had been in the news almost nonstop, at times for completely trivial reasons. One round of stories revealed that Trump was dumping his insurer, AIG, ostensibly because he was unhappy with the cost and service. A few days later, another round of stories revealed that Trump had actually grown angry when AIG refused to buy his new casino junk bonds.

It was an inauspicious start to the year. Then, one day in February 2003, a phone call changed his life. Rhona did not pick up. As Burnett recalled the conversation, Trump answered himself.

"Hello."

"Mr. Trump?" a male voice asked, with a flash of surprise.

"Who's this?"

Mark Burnett almost hung up. I'm not ready for this, he thought. He had just flown in from Los Angeles and was calling from a car on his way to Manhattan. He had run the idea for a new show past Conrad Riggs, who loved it, but he had not yet prepared a complete pitch. He figured he needed two weeks to work out the details. He called because he expected to reach a secretary who would look at the calendar of one of the world's busiest executives and hopefully grant him an appointment later that month. Instead, here was the man himself, answering his own phone.

"It's Mark Burnett."

"Ahhhh, *Survivor* genius. What's up?"

"Well, I've got this . . . you said about doing a show together?"

"Yeah, *Survivor*'s gotten bigger than ever!" Trump responded. "It's the number one show. You wanna do a show with me?"

"Yeah, I do," Burnett said.

"Well, I'm at the office now. Come over right now to Trump Tower and let's talk about it."

This cannot be happening, Burnett thought. He considered calling back and pleading for more time, but he feared it would cost him Trump's respect. He had studied Trump enough to know he had only one shot, and he had to take it. He went straight to Trump Tower and was promptly ushered up to the twenty-sixth floor. He gave his best explanation of the show—*Survivor*, only the jungle is Manhattan. It would be a season-long job interview for the greatest job ever, with regular people battling through business challenges to win a one-year dream apprenticeship with Donald J. Trump, legendary billionaire, the biggest real estate developer in New York City. At the Trump Organization. In the climactic scene of each episode, Trump, the boss, would fire someone. Trump, Trump, Trump.

"Everyone is asking me to do TV shows," Trump said. But he hadn't liked those ideas, because it was all about following him around, watching him make deals and comb his hair. "This is smart. This could work. We'll do it. What's the deal?"

Just like that, without consulting anyone or taking time to reflect, Trump had said yes. Burnett believed he needed Trump. Riggs had contacted several moguls—Jack Welch, Warren Buffett, and Richard Branson—but Burnett and Riggs felt those other moguls would either not be open to the demands of a weekly show or lacked the necessary charisma and good looks. For better or worse, Trump drew eyeballs. He would make for good television and never shy away from a camera. Burnett thought the normal talent fees paid by the network would not be enough to lock in someone of Trump's stature. He knew the deal it would take.

"Fifty-fifty," Burnett said.

"Okay," Trump said, and the two men shook hands.

Riggs drew up a contract. Trump would play himself in this new show for one year and receive half of all the show's profits. Without doing any work off camera, Trump would benefit from Burnett's years of accomplishment, especially from him having taken a battering ram to the business model of television production. With Burnett's growing mastery of product integration, the ceiling was unknowable.

If Burnett wondered whether this fellow with a wide-open schedule who answered his own phone really was the billionaire head of a massive empire, he never let on. He returned to Los Angeles, and Riggs began scheduling pitch meetings with network executives.

After the success of *Survivor*, Burnett was greeted with open arms. Industry insiders saw him as the master of a new domain, one he had almost single-handedly created. All three major networks expressed interest. But NBC was the most motivated. The following year would see the end of *Friends*, one of the most beloved shows in television history and a crown jewel of the network's lineup. NBC had grown envious of CBS's success with *Survivor* and saw itself as behind on reality television. Its early effort—a gross-out fest called *Fear Factor*—was internally seen as unappealing for both the network and advertisers. Jeff Zucker, who had spent his career at NBC, rising to become executive producer of the *Today* show, had been promoted to head of the entertainment division in part to catch up with the reality television wave. He hired Jeff Gaspin to run what was still new enough to call "alternative programming." Zucker and Gaspin had worked together in New York at *Today* in the 1990s before Gaspin left to run original programming at VH1, where he developed *Behind the Music*, an early reimagining of dramatized nonfiction television.

On Monday, March 3, four weeks to the day after Burnett pitched Trump, he and Riggs drove to NBC's studios in Burbank. In a third-floor conference room, they met with Zucker, Gaspin, and Marc Graboff, the network's president of business operations. Graboff had a history with Burnett. He had been at CBS when the network bought *Survivor* and worked with Burnett on that show. Burnett excitedly described the show as "*Survivor* in a different jungle . . . the jungle of Manhattan." He mentioned that he had signed Donald Trump but said he could switch to another mogul in later years. The meeting was short.

"We want to buy it, right now," Zucker told them. "Don't let him leave until we make a deal," he told Graboff.

Burnett let the NBC executives know that he had an offer from ABC. With his hot name and another offer in hand, Zucker and Graboff felt Burnett held all the cards. So when Riggs demanded control of product integration and the revenue it generated, they did not put up a fight. "It was just something that was kind of a deal point that Burnett really insisted on, and he had the leverage to do it at that point," a person briefed on the meeting recalled.

No producer had yet pulled off product integration on a scale large enough to concern Zucker and Graboff. They wanted a hit show on the scale of *Survivor*, which would generate a fortune for the network from traditional thirty-second commercials, regardless of whatever cash Burnett could pull out from making the contestants drink Mountain Dew.

After a deal was worked out, Zucker and Gaspin talked about the Trump factor, and their memories of him from their years in New York. Thinking of Trump as the quintessential businessman made both men laugh. They thought of Trump as "a bit of a joke" and were not enamored with the thought of him serving as something like a mentor. "But it was all about Mark Burnett, one hundred percent about being in business with Mark Burnett."

Zucker told people that he knew of Trump's need for attention and saw that trait as of value to the show's prospects. "If the show didn't work, it wasn't going to be for a lack of publicity," Zucker later recalled. "I knew that Donald Trump was an ego, PR hound, a PR whore, a PR whatever you want to call it. He knew how to generate publicity."

The network agreed to pay Trump an appearance fee of $50,000 per episode, which with the addition of the finale would work out to $750,000 for the season. This was on top of whatever he would make from the profit split he and Burnett had agreed to in February.

ON APRIL 1, 2003, NBC announced that it had bought thirteen episodes of the new show. Zucker, Burnett, and Trump promoted the coming program on the network's *Today* show, shortly after an update on the two-week-old U.S. invasion of Iraq. The morning show would serve as a reliable and powerful house organ for Trump and *The Apprentice* for years to come.

Both men made Trump's involvement sound benevolent. Trump said, "Mentoring up-and-coming executives has been something I've always enjoyed." He told the *New York Post* that the show would not take much of his time or energy. "I'm pretty busy. I'm the biggest developer in New York and I'm not looking for additional work."

"This is Donald Trump giving back," Burnett said. But then he went further, invoking the still-fresh wounds of 9/11 to argue that Trump's entrepreneurial know-how was helping to fund the War on Terror. "What makes the world a safe place right now? I think it's American dollars, which come from taxes, which come because of Donald Trump."

Some tax dollars keeping America safe may have, with a dose of generously contorted logic, come "because" of Donald Trump, but certainly not from him. Neither Trump nor his businesses had paid federal income taxes in years, thanks to his massive business losses. All of that, however, remained secret.

In articles teasing the show, Burnett and Trump sounded as if they were in the thick of a fresh bromance. They attended a Neil Young concert together at Trump's Taj Mahal casino. They visited Seven Springs, the estate in Bedford, New York, that Trump was still trying to turn into a golf course. They attended a private party and concert in Manhattan celebrating the release of Wyclef Jean's new album, *The Preacher's Son*. Burnett told *The New York Times* that he considered Trump to be a "soul mate."

A month after the announcement, Trump joined Burnett and Zucker at what the networks call "the upfronts," the annual ritual of networks seducing major advertisers with the celebrity and glamour of their coming fall shows. Reality programs were largely scorned at the upfront events that year. Zucker said little of the new show in his presentation at Radio City Music Hall.

But something in Zucker's few comments piqued the interest of Richard Linnett, a reporter for *Advertising Age* sitting in the front row. He returned to his office and talked his editor into letting him pursue a longer profile of Trump and the show. He expected the usual delays when trying to arrange an interview with the head of a large business—multiple emails and telephone calls with intermediaries, followed by a wait for approval. In this case it was shockingly fast. "I just got on the phone, called Trump headquarters, and they said Donald would love to talk to you. I am like okay, that's great . . . And Trump invited me into his world."

He saw something that was a loosely held secret within the New York City press corps: Trump worked hard to draw reporters in. His charms in person are very different from the person seen in hundreds of television appearances over the decades. He can make any person in front of him seem like the only person he cares about at that very moment. He can be self-effacing, seem humble even. Trump began calling Linnett almost every day, often extending an invitation to drop by on short notice. He showed Linnett the stack of recent news articles about himself, gave him a tour of the offices, and introduced him to Don Jr. and other employees. Trump was solicitous in mining Linnett for information on how ratings work, and which companies spent the most on commercials. He gave Linnett a tour of the construction at the former Delmonico Hotel.

"I was at his beck and call."

One offer went too far for Linnett's comfort. A friend of Trump's called to extend an invitation for Linnett to fly on Trump's private jet to Florida and spend time with Trump at Mar-a-Lago. Linnett declined for ethical reasons.

During the time they did spend together, Trump boasted about the power of his name on any product. "Trump is the hottest brand out there. I put my name on a building, and I get five thousand dollars a square foot. That's twice what the guy gets across the street. I put my name on a golf course, Trump National in Briarcliff Manor, and I get three hundred thousand dollars per member. Other guys only get twenty-five thousand."

Advertising Age casts an intense light on the industry it covers and takes claims like that seriously. Linnett called Millward Brown, a market research agency, and asked if it would conduct a special survey for the magazine measuring the value of Trump's name compared to other well-known people, or "branded business entrepreneurs." The survey of two thousand people found that only 2 percent of respondents would buy a product associated with Trump, compared to 13 percent for Oprah Winfrey.

Linnett's article, published that August, quoted Ann Green, a vice president of the firm, saying that Trump's brand value was strong among "a younger, male, aspirational audience." But not so much among women. "If you look at older females, he does tend to alienate them. He is not necessarily actively irritating like some of the other names we surveyed, but he has a weakened appeal."

Trump was not pleased with the article, and the same friend who had extended the offer for a free stay at Mar-a-Lago called to let Linnett know. Their friendship was over.

At that very moment, Trump was trying to leverage the announcement of the show to sign licensing deals. He had summoned a consultant named Mark Hager to Trump Tower to discuss getting his name on a line of clothing. They signed an agreement that September. Hager decided to run the idea past Marvin Traub, a trusted friend who had been the chief executive of Bloomingdale's for two decades and now worked as a consultant. At one of their regular breakfast meetings, Hager told Traub that Trump had hired him to pursue a clothing licensing deal and would star in a network show launching in a few months.

"That is advertising value worth hundreds of millions of dollars," Hager told Traub. "While your image right now of Donald Trump is X, I believe it will change after that show."

He asked Traub what he thought, and whether he might want to be involved. Traub dismissed the offer with a laugh.

Even with the bad news from the Millward survey and the consultants, Trump still had a few licensed products hitting the market. But it was small-ball stuff. He let an upstart publisher use his name and likeness to launch a glossy magazine called *Trump World* to be distributed at his properties, and, hopefully someday, newsstands. He debuted his own bottled water, called Trump Ice.

Preparations for the show pushed forward. NBC created a website for candidates to file initial applications. The questions included "How important are scruples in business?" and "Have you ever been caught cheating in school?" Burnett's producers launched a sixteen-city tour to interview applicants. Rob LaPlante, a producer for Burnett, told the *Miami Herald* he was looking for people who "have the desire to be an apprentice of Donald Trump" and had "personalities that grab you."

"People look at Donald Trump as a beacon of opportunity. He has a reputation of whatever he touches turns to gold, and people want to find out how he does it."

Burnett's crew had the summer to make that all look plausible.

27

"I USED MY BRAIN"

After experiencing years of sensory overload in jungles around the world, the first thing Burnett's producers noticed when they arrived on the twenty-sixth floor of Trump Tower was the stink, a musty and moldy carpet smell that seemed to emanate from every corner. As they walked through, with eyes trained to notice small details, they saw the chipped wood on seemingly every piece of furniture. It was the summer of 2003. Trump Tower had just turned thirty. The décor dated back to when Mark Burnett was a nanny.

What the offices did not communicate was success, wealth, or moguldom, the qualities the producers were about to assign to Trump on national television. Bill Pruitt, a producer who had come from *The Amazing Race*, remembered the disconnect between what he expected and what he saw. "When you go into the office and you're hearing billionaire, even recovering billionaire, you don't expect to see chipped furniture, you don't expect to smell carpet that needs to be refreshed in the worst, worst way."

"The whole thing was absurd to all of us," remembered Alan Blum, who had been hired by Burnett from an advertising agency to help produce the show. He and his fellow producers laughed about the "foul smell" and "dingy, shabby, awful" impression the place made.

The smallness of the operation was also hard to reconcile with what Trump described in public. The epicenter of a supposed international empire of golf courses, hotels, office and residential buildings, and assorted other enterprises took up just one floor of not quite ten thousand square feet. Fewer than fifty people worked in the office. Trump's desk showed no signs of real work—no computer, contracts, or files. It was just smothered by newspaper and magazine articles focused on one subject: himself.

The production team realized that they faced a different sort of challenge than they had on *Survivor.* There, as the title suggested, the contestant's goal was to prevail by staying alive amid the jungle creatures and brutal elements on a deserted island. Life (along with $1 million) was a manifestly worthy goal, requiring no dramatic embellishment. On *The Apprentice*, however, the goal would be a one-year work-study program (and a $250,000 prize, paid by NBC). That central conceit would require viewers to believe that Trump was a businessperson of such stature that graduates of prominent law and business schools would battle, connive, and humiliate themselves for a chance to study at his side for one year. That's not how most Americans perceived Trump at the time. He was the billion-dollar talker, known for peddling salacious details of his divorces and affairs to tabloid gossip pages. The bankruptcies. The campy fast-food commercials. In the most recent Gallup poll measuring Trump's reputation at the time, 98 percent of those polled knew his name, but 58 percent viewed him unfavorably. Burnett's team needed to flip that number to make *The Apprentice* believable.

"Our job was to make him look legitimate, to make him look like there was something behind it, even though we pretty much all knew that there wasn't. But that was our job," remembered Jonathon Braun, a producer who had worked on *Survivor.* "We weren't making a documentary . . . Richard Attenborough was not narrating this. This was an entertainment prime-time network show."

One NBC executive involved in *The Apprentice* at the launch would later remember it this way: "The whole thing was a facade. The whole 'I'm a tycoon, I'm a busy man. I'm buying and selling, I am operating, my day is packed full of meetings . . . I am so busy I have to take helicopters to get everywhere.' I mean, no. He was sitting there cutting press clippings, sending them to people."

Compared to changing public perceptions, the easier part of reinventing Trump would be creating a physical space that, unlike his actual offices, exuded power and wealth. Burnett had considered renting space nearby to build a set. Then Trump told him that office space on the fourth floor of Trump Tower was vacant, and he would happily rent it to Burnett for a modest sum. His tax records would show that he billed Burnett more than $440,000 a year in rent, roughly market rates for the best class of office space in the neighborhood.

To build out the space, Burnett brought in Kelly Van Patter, a set designer who had worked for him on five seasons of *Survivor.* She created two sets: a 6,500-square-foot living area, and a 1,520-square-foot boardroom and lobby. Burnett wanted the boardroom design to evoke the feeling of a library at Harvard University.

The living space would become what was referred to on the show as the contestants' suites; Trump's employees called it "the loft." It was a windowless grouping of small rooms, in a space originally built for offices, with cameras in every area. One element of pure theater in each episode would be showing the contestants taking an elevator from their "suites" to the boardroom, often set to dramatically tense music. In reality, the two sets were steps away from each other on the same floor.

Beyond the studio space, the harder work of reinventing Trump had only just begun.

WHILE MOST OF BURNETT'S TEAM was in New York, Jay Bienstock, himself a pioneer of reality television, locked himself in an editing bay at Burnett's headquarters in Los Angeles for six weeks. At his side was Stephen Frederick, a skilled video editor and *Survivor* veteran accustomed to the massive editing requirements of the new genre. The basic ratio was familiar by then: a thousand hours of incongruous video comes in; forty-four minutes of beautiful television goes out.

Bienstock had been a central figure in the visual and storytelling genius of Burnett's dramality. He had won an Emmy as a producer on *Survivor* and produced episodes of *Eco Challenge.* Before that he had worked for Jeff Gaspin at VH1, where they teamed up on *Behind the Music*, the series that perfected the narrative arc of a comeback: musicians rising from obscurity, falling back to obscurity at the hands of their personal demons, only to vanquish those demons and rise again.

Burnett assigned Bienstock and Frederick to apply that magic to Trump, to create a few hypnotic minutes of video portraying his life as a convincing comeback story. It had to flip the audience's view of Trump, make working for him and learning from him seem like a life-altering experience.

Burnett had spent months talking about the Trump comeback story in interviews. It was how Trump saw himself. In his own telling, Trump left out the role of his father's wealth in fueling his original rise and softening his fall. He ignored his own responsibility for the decisions that led to his downfall and exaggerated the degree to which he had made a comeback. There were no personal demons, no unforced errors.

Burnett's plan to remake Trump would be a stark departure from what had become the typical formula for introducing a new show, or season. Rather than first introducing contestant backstories as a narrative cornerstone, the opening moments of the first episode would establish the credentials of the host—the value of the prize—in a three-minute segment called "Meet the Billionaire."

Bienstock would deploy all the moving parts of television production that Burnett had built over the prior decade—the capacity for breathtaking cinematography, the artful crafting of storylines, the original musical scores evoking location and tension, the editing of mountains of tape into moments of poignancy—to make the premise of this new show believable.

The production value of *Survivor*, its sensory magnetism, often gets overlooked for the guilty pleasures of watching telegenic contestants backstab one another to dodge death. Burnett has only occasionally spoken about the style of his shows, of letting shots breathe, of creating a majestic cinematic moment from a drop of water falling from a leaf, or a spider weaving a web. His early shows took viewers on guided tours through menacing wildernesses, the dancing light, the intertwined shapes, and the mingling colors hidden in the undergrowth. On *Eco Challenge*, Burnett pioneered filming from helicopters with gyro-stabilized cameras, an advancement that gave viewers the sense of smoothly gliding like an eagle above oceans and forests.

For *The Apprentice*, Burnett's camera operators, veterans of jungles, would film from helicopters above Manhattan. They would pound the pavement across the Northeast, capturing images of anything bearing the Trump name or the likeness of Trump himself. They would render him tall and consequential, grimacing into the camera or toward the horizon, the very image of wealth and achievement.

Kevin Harris, who had worked for Burnett as a producer on *Eco Challenge*, oversaw the filming of an early scene at the top of Trump Tower that would make Trump appear to be the king of New York. The shot would begin tight on Trump, with a beat to create a mystery as to the location. The camera angle widened to reveal the man standing atop the fifty-eight-story tower, before widening farther to reveal Trump lording above the city's skyline and streets below. It would be shot from a helicopter hovering just above the tower. On the day of filming, as Harris and the crew huddled a few feet away preparing for the shot, Trump suddenly shouted at him.

"KEVIN! Is my hair okay?"

Harris turned around to see that the wind at nearly seven hundred feet above street level and the nearby whirling helicopter blades had levitated Trump's hair, which looked like a cotton candy pancake floating over his head. Harris quickly realized that if he spoke the truth the entire shoot would be lost to vanity.

"Yeah, it looks fine!" Harris shouted above the noise, knowing that the gusts would subside, and Trump's hair would return safely to its natural resting place. They shot some seven takes, with the helicopter going up and down each time, to make sure they had a moment with Trump's hair in place. It took a crew of several people and a helicopter a full day.

"We took the tapes back to the edit bay," Harris later recalled. "We had rented one in New York just to review some of that footage. And when that tape went in and that happened the whole room erupted into laughter."

Harris, who remains fond of Trump, remembered that as the moment when he realized it would be the crew's job to protect their star from embarrassment. Bienstock and Frederick sifted through hundreds of hours of tape, assigned more shoots, and wove it all together with original music and a scripted voice-over for Trump.

The final video opened with a signature Burnett montage from a helicopter, taking viewers soaring across New York Harbor toward Manhattan, past the Statue of Liberty, lights twinkling in her crown, and through the city's skyline. Then onto the bustling streets and the floor of the stock exchange, as Trump uttered words of grace and clarity that sounded like nothing he had ever said before or since. "New York, my city, where the wheels of the global economy never stop turning. A concrete metropolis of unparalleled strength and purpose that drives the business world."

The tone then shifted to a mix of hope and menace, with a nod to *Survivor* and Burnett's original pitch to NBC. "Manhattan is a tough place. This island is the real jungle. If you're not careful, it can chew up and spit you out," Trump said. Just then, the camera showed a shabby male figure lying prone on a street bench.

"But if you work hard, you can really hit it big," Trump continued, as the camera passed over Seven Springs—the aging estate north of the city where Trump was still in the process of failing to build a golf course. "And I mean, really big!"

It was then that Burnett's vision of Trump as a great comeback story was given voice, beginning with Trump using his favorite lie of the era to introduce himself. "I'm the largest real estate developer in New York. I own buildings all over the place, model agencies, the Miss Universe pageant, jetliners, golf courses, casinos, and private resorts like Mar-a-Lago, one of the most spectacular estates anywhere in the world."

The screen filled with neon lights glowing outside the Trump Taj Mahal casino, part of the casino company that had never turned a profit and of which he then owned less than half.

"But it wasn't always so easy. About thirteen years ago, I was seriously in trouble. I was billions of dollars in debt. But I fought back, and I won, big league. I used my brain. I used my negotiating skills, and I worked it all out. Now my company is bigger than it ever was. It's stronger than it ever was. And I'm having more fun than I ever had. I've mastered the art of the deal, and I've turned the name Trump into the highest-quality brand."

As he mentioned the words "highest-quality brand," the screen filled with images of Trump Ice, a bottled water that would fail as a business, and Trump Place, an apartment building bearing Trump's name that had been financed, built, and controlled by other people.

With that, the "comeback" story was complete.

"As the master, I want to pass along my knowledge to somebody else," Trump said. He then briefly explained the parameters of the game. The next shot showed him stepping from a limousine to board a helicopter. "This is the chance to work for me at a huge salary, and more importantly, learn enough so that maybe they, too, can become a billionaire someday. This is going to be the dream job of a lifetime. Who will succeed, and who will fail, and who will be the Apprentice?"

The three-minute masterpiece ended with the opening baseline of "For the

Love of Money," a 1973 soul song by the O'Jays that served as the theme song for the series. The song overlaid a video again portraying Trump as sophisticated, serious, glamorous, and a tad imperial. His name seemed to be on everything. A jet, a helicopter, the Taj Mahal again. And there was slow-motion Trump, walking out of the sunlight and reposing in the lap of luxury. The mix of music and imagery conditioned viewers to associate Trump with the theme song's lyric, "Money, money, money . . . money!"

Repeated week after week, that video would remake Donald Trump in the public's imagination. Contestants endlessly swooned in his presence. Eighteen months after the first episode aired, a Gallup poll found half of Americans held a favorable view of Donald Trump. Burnett had done it.

"We were making him out to be royalty in almost every opportunity," Pruitt said. "It was our mission to make sure that everybody watching understood that to work for him would be a big deal."

Some of Burnett's producers and NBC executives had reservations about portraying Trump as logical, successful, and substantial. But not enough to get in the way of a potential hit show.

"You were casting an actor," Jeff Zucker said. "He was playing a part. We knew that.

"It's called reality television, but it's never real, per se."

ONE DAY IN THE FALL of 2003, Trump took a break from playing a successful billionaire to attend a confidential briefing on the performance of his massive trust funds.

Trump had long kept these periodic meetings secret. Only Allen Weisselberg, his loyal financial adviser, attended from his office. Trump's brother Robert drove in from their father's old headquarters at Beach Haven apartments. Robert arrived with the three executives helping him run Fred Trump's empire—Steve Gurien, Dennis Hasher, and Donald's cousin, John Walter. Maryanne Trump Barry took time off from hearing cases in a federal courthouse in New Jersey for the meeting. Elizabeth Trump also attended.

As they sat around the conference table, Hasher and Gurien ran through the mundane details of the rental apartment buildings that the siblings had received from their father through the trust five years earlier. Gurien covered all the boring stuff: the number of vacancies, the coming maintenance costs, and the financial results for the period.

The sisters, who had never been allowed by their father to have a role in the family business, sat quietly. But they perked up for the main event—the distribution of checks. The buildings remained as profitable as ever. The joyful task fell to Gurien, the chief financial officer. Then, just as Gurien reached for the checks, Donald interrupted to change the course of family history.

"I think now is a good time to sell," he said.

The pronouncement landed with a thud. Robert had heard this before, but still seemed gobsmacked. Since he was in his early forties, after the falling out with Donald over the botched opening of the Taj Mahal, Robert's only work had been running their father's real estate empire, including during the difficult years as their father declined. At fifty-five, Robert would have nothing to do for work after a sale. And selling would create personal complications for him as well. Robert had been married for almost twenty years to Blaine Trump, who was best known in New York for her work as a board member of God's Love We Deliver, a charitable organization that delivers meals to sick people. But Robert had for some time been involved in an affair with Ann Marie Pallan, an employee of his in the Beach Haven office. That office was the home base for their romance.

The order to sell was also a betrayal of Fred Trump's last wishes. Back in 1991, one of his advisers had told a lawyer working on his will that the patriarch was "very adamant on certain aspects—never wants money to leave the Trump family" and "wanted to keep the empire together—not dissipated."

Donald Trump did not mention that he needed, or just wanted, a massive check all at once, though some of those present suspected that as his motivation. Any hopes that *The Apprentice* would greatly improve his finances seemed far off; he still needed to come up with millions of dollars to hang on to control of his casinos. He explained that the real estate market was as high as it would ever be, and they could not substantially increase profits because the buildings were subject to rent regulations.

Donald directed Robert to oversee the solicitation of private bids, and to move forward quickly and quietly. There would be no polished video marketing plans, no public listing of the buildings through real estate brokers. For perhaps the first time in his life, Donald Trump would leave his promotional abilities on the sidelines of this game.

Three potential bidders were quietly contacted. Financial records on thirty-seven apartment projects and several shopping centers were bound into books and distributed to the bidders, after they signed confidentiality agreements. Three bids were submitted, including one from Rubie Schron, an intensely private owner of a large apartment building portfolio in the city. One evening in December 2003, Schron called Donald Trump and won the contest by increasing his offer to $705.6 million. Other buyers were found for a few remaining properties, yielding another $32.3 million. It would all take just a few months to finalize. After paying off the small remaining mortgages, each sibling's share would come to $177.3 million. They still each owned their shares in Starrett City, the large apartment complex that Fred Trump had invested in decades earlier to produce tax deductions.

Donald told his siblings he had struck a great deal for them. The mortgages taken out by the buyers told a different story. Banks typically lend no more than 75 to 80 percent of what they determine to be the value of commercial properties; the 75 percent threshold was explicitly stated in some of Schron's mortgages. Schron and the buyers of the few other buildings borrowed a total of $731 million, putting the banks' valuation of Fred Trump's empire at about $975 million.

Donald Trump, the self-described world's greatest dealmaker, had sold the bulk of his father's empire for almost $250 million less than it was worth. But a big payday was coming, thanks to his father.

28

THE TALENT

DAVID GOULD LOOKED PERPLEXED. Donald Trump had just asked the members of the losing team on the first episode of *The Apprentice* to name the worst leader on their team of contestants. Everyone said Sam Solovey. Except Sam, who said David was the worst. The contestants had battled to make the most money selling lemonade on the streets of Manhattan. Sam had decided his bold stroke would be selling one cup of lemonade for $1,000. He failed. Trump told Sam to "be careful" because "you're a wild man."

All that sounded to David like he would be safe. And then Trump turned to David and uttered the words that would become his calling card.

"You fired."

The producers watching in the windowless control room adjacent to the fake boardroom were shocked, bewildered, and excited. Gould was a licensed medical doctor with an MBA then working as a venture capitalist. The producers had thought Gould would be around for a long time. At least one producer, Katherine Walker, thought he was a genius, the smartest guy in the room by far. But shocked as they were, the moment also brought a tingle of excitement. "Right then we knew that we had a show, because this is not what you expected," Walker recalled later.

Trump's unpredictability, a vice in business, proved to be a virtue on television. The practices behind Trump's worst failures over the decades—demanding brevity over all else, shutting down complicated discussions, ignoring written material and expertise, and, above all else, believing genetic superiority made his gut instinct the best course of action in all situations—had found its perfect home in a pretend boardroom. Trump's confident impetuousness lent a final dramatic twist to the contestant backbiting that filled most of the show. It made for good television.

Unpredictability would become a trend. "He would fire the absolute wrong person," recalled Jonathon Braun. Braun eventually picked up on what he thought was a clue that Trump was about to fire someone without any real reason. He would slam the table.

"That's one where he had no idea what was going on and he would just make something up. He just had to choose a name. And maybe that was the only name he remembered of the people sitting around."

And for those moments when Trump's choice threatened to reflect badly on him, Burnett's producers deployed television magic to save face. "Our job then was to reverse engineer the show and to make him not look like a complete moron," Braun said. They would go back through the tape from the week—the contestants were filmed at nearly every waking moment—and selectively choose snippets "to make the person who he fired look not as good."

When the first episode aired, the boardroom scene included a clip of Trump explaining his decision. "I don't see that you stepped up at all," Trump said to David Gould. Sharp viewers might have noticed that the camera did not show Trump speaking those words, and his voice took on a different quality from the rest of the scene.

Week to week, the criteria for survival could feel like a house of mirrors. In one episode, Trump fired a contestant named Jason, letting Sam slide for taking a nap during the competition and lying about it to Trump. Lying could be fatal, but not necessarily so. Trump fired a team leader, Kwame, for not firing Omarosa Manigault Newman after she lied to him. Then the show itself repeatedly brought Omarosa back for future seasons. *The Apprentice* became an object lesson in how to stand out for the wrong reasons. The female team in the first show sold their lemonade for five dollars, throwing in an ounce of flirt, a kiss on the cheek, and even a phone number. "I was surprised that, yeah, I did use sex to sell lemonade," one female contestant told viewers. George Ross gleefully described it as one dollar for the lemonade and four dollars for the girl. That equation would repeatedly play out in future episodes. Not exactly the sort of advanced business skills the show had promised.

Sam Solovey continued his stunts, at one point offering Trump a suitcase he said was filled with $250,000 in cash to let him stay on the show for another week. Sam mentioned the suitcase was a Samsonite, as if he selected the brand because its name was similar to his own. It later emerged that Sam had made a side deal with the luggage company, and that the suitcase was not stuffed with cash.

This was the golden rule at the Trump school of business: Do nothing boring. That was the unforgivable mistake that David Gould committed in the first episode.

And Trump's two advisers were not quite as they were described to viewers. Trump introduced Carolyn Kepcher as "the chief operating officer of one of my companies, and Carolyn is a killer. There are many men buried in her wake." Killer is high praise in the Trump family, but the meaning is fungible. Kepcher was not quite a major Manhattan macher. At thirty-four, she had worked at Trump's golf course in suburban Westchester County in New York for almost a decade. As the show launched, Trump was paying her a salary of $115,000—roughly the same compensation received by the principal of the public elementary school near the golf course.

Trump introduced George Ross on the show by saying he "has been with me for twenty-five years." It was an artful turn of phrase, suggesting Ross had been an executive in Trump's company for decades. He had not. Ross, seventy-five, had worked exclusively for Trump for seven years before filming began on *The Apprentice*. He had been a prominent real estate lawyer with other firms in the city for fifty years.

Burnett had come up with the idea that Trump should have two sidekicks. But neither he, nor Trump, nor the network paid them extra for their appearances on the show. Because it was a federally licensed game show, *The Apprentice* fell under the same exclusion as news programs from the requirements to pay guild wages to people who appeared on camera. And Trump viewed the pair as compensated to work for him, whatever tasks he assigned. He also insisted that they continue to meet the responsibilities of their existing jobs.

Game show status also forced the producers to abide by regulations, adopted in response to the game show scandals of the 1950s, that prohibited them from telling Trump whom to select. Trump's unpredictability in the boardroom was a product not just of his personality but also the fact that he wasn't involved in strategy, filming, or production. He would not typically see the contestants "working" during the week. He would only appear for the taping of a few brief speaking parts on location, and for the boardroom scene to hear reports on how contestants had performed.

But the facts never really mattered. Drama mattered. Comedy mattered. Entertainment value mattered. And Trump was dramatic, occasionally funny, and always entertaining. Looking at the tape of those early episodes, NBC executives felt a tension in the boardroom that seemed real enough—and entertaining. They wanted more.

"Watching people try to market a lemonade stand wasn't all that interesting to me," said one NBC executive who was involved in the show. "But what was kind of interesting was the boardroom. . . . We asked Mark to extend those scenes a little bit."

THE SHOW'S RATINGS took off. An average of 20.7 million people watched the show that season. Trump became more famous than ever. That March, VH1 aired *The Fabulous Life of Donald Trump*. Two weeks later, on April 3, he hosted *Saturday Night Live* for the first time. "It's great to be here for *Saturday Night Live*," Trump said in opening the show. "But I'll be perfectly honest, it's even better for *Saturday Night Live* that I'm here. Nobody's bigger than me. Nobody's better than me. I'm a ratings machine. I've got the number-one television show, *The Apprentice*. Where after just one season, I'm about to become the highest-paid television personality in America!"

Back in his offices at Trump Tower, when the microphones were turned off, Trump expressed concern that being exposed as a less-than-stellar businessman might hurt the show. As the show flashed dramatic footage week after week of the neon lights of the Taj Mahal casino breaking through the darkness, it became increasingly clear that Trump would not be able to stave off yet another round of bankruptcy at his gambling halls. He asked visitors to his offices whether they thought "the B-word"—his euphemism for bankruptcy—would hurt the show's ratings.

Whatever the business realities, the show served as a weekly promotional tour of Trump's life and business, with the contestants serving as a choir of fawning approval. Trump's apartment in Trump Tower was "Really, really rich!" A truck of Trump's new bottled water was "Cool!" The Taj Mahal casino warranted a "This place is amazing!" The entire twelfth episode was centered around the Taj Mahal. Two weeks later, the finale was framed as a battle between staging a Jessica Simpson concert at the Taj Mahal and a golf tournament at the Trump golf course that Kepcher ran in Westchester.

In the hands of Burnett's production team, everything bearing the Trump name appeared majestic. Even the ultimate prize for the winning contestant was presented with pretaped pieces that played like commercials for the properties themselves. After Trump selected Bill Rancic as the first season winner, he gave Rancic a choice "between overseeing operations at two fabulous locations in my organization." One was the planned tower in Chicago that was then still a hole in the ground, described by Trump in the video as destined to be "among the world's greatest towers. It'll be a shimmering jewel on the Chicago skyline." The other was the Los Angeles golf course he was renovating into "one of the greatest golf courses and clubs anywhere in the world, even superior to Pebble Beach." Both videos included Burnett's signature sweeping helicopter shots and symphonic original music.

By the spring of 2004, the remaking of Donald Trump was complete, and with greater reach than even Burnett's success with *Survivor* could have forecast. It could have ended there. Trump's contract with Burnett to host the show expired at the end of the first season. Burnett and the network had toyed with the idea of using a different mogul for later seasons. But with the success of season one, Burnett and the network wanted Trump back.

NBC offered Trump a raise from $50,000 an episode to $60,000. Trump thought he deserved something more in line with the stars of big network comedies. He went to Burnett and Riggs, who told him they could not afford to pay him more. He was already in line to receive half of Burnett's profits, which had not taken off yet but represented massive potential compensation for the talent on a show.

Not giving up, Trump reached out directly to the network executives. A lunch was scheduled with Zucker and Graboff at Jean-Georges, the four-star restaurant that was his tenant in the commercial space at the Trump condominium hotel on Columbus Circle in Manhattan. Trump arrived alone, carrying a leather folder. After some small talk, Zucker got to the point.

"Look, we really want you to come back for season two," he said.

"I am a very busy man," Trump responded. "You have to make it worth my while."

Trump then placed his leather folder on the table and opened it up. He had brought a pile of newspaper and magazine articles about the show's success. He showed them a document he described as a financial statement that said he was worth $3.5 billion. The network executives saw it differently: "It was definitely a prop."

Trump continued, unfazed. "I know the cast of *Friends* is making, each, one million dollars an episode, and that's only a half-hour show. And there's only one of me, so you should pay me one million dollars an episode."

Zucker and Graboff had been negotiating with big egos for years. This kind of ploy was not likely to induce a quiver. Trump did not seem to realize the nature of his leverage: it was now his star power, his centrality to the show, not whatever he thought his random collection of properties, or his time, was worth.

Zucker asked Trump if he would agree that a big portion of the net worth on his document was based on the goodwill of his brand.

"Oh, absolutely," Trump responded.

"Would you say it's five or ten percent of your brand?" Zucker asked.

"Oh, yes, absolutely," Trump responded.

If that is the case, Zucker said, "You should pay us."

Zucker repeated the $60,000 per episode offer. Trump did not push further, but the lunch ended without a firm agreement. Graboff went back to his office, called Trump's agent, and repeated the offer. The lawyer would not accept, so Graboff said, "Okay, we are out." Trump held out overnight. The next day, his lawyer called Graboff and accepted.

Later that year, Trump released a new book—*Trump: How to Get Rich*—cowritten with Meredith McIver. Trump had by then adopted Zucker's logic regarding his salary. "My pay per episode, while substantial, does not, for me, mean very much. It is nowhere near what the stars of *Friends* rake in. The real value is in the free advertising and publicity The Trump Organization has been receiving. I can't put a monetary value on that."

There was no hint in anything Trump said or did that he realized the magnitude of what was coming. The business model that Burnett had spent the prior decade perfecting—selling corporations on the value of letting him weave their products into his show—was about to make Trump the equivalent of a second inheritance. And as when he was born, other people would do all the work.

INTEGRATING CONSUMER PRODUCTS into filmed entertainment has a history dating back to silent movies. When characters in film and on television ate a candy bar, drank a beer, or smoked a cigarette, the director's choice of brand wasn't necessarily artistic. Commerce led E.T. to munch Reese's Pieces and James Bond to drive a BMW.

With *Eco Challenge* and *Survivor*, Burnett had laid the foundation for increasing the involvement of marketing departments in his shows. But no one on his team recognized the full potential of it when *The Apprentice* launched. As with those earlier shows, the focus was still on finding companies willing to help cover production costs in exchange for their products appearing on the show. Burnett hired Justin Hochberg away from Microsoft's digital television operation to serve as his point person for connecting with sponsors. With the show still unproven and the genre itself still somewhat new, Hochberg was initially received skeptically. He eventually contacted the friend of a friend who had just started a new company called Marquis Jets, which leased blocks of time on private jets.

Marquis Jets had not even hired an advertising agency yet. Hochberg made his pitch to the company president, Ken Austin. Austin recognized that exposure on a prime-time television show, a potential forty-two-minute infomercial, could help kick-start his company, even with the risk of not controlling how the company would be portrayed. But Austin did not think it made sense to pay for the exposure. Instead, Marquis Jets agreed to fly the winning contestants of the second episode to Boston for their "reward," a weekly ritual of the show.

The company's name and services were the focus of nearly every segment. The two teams were tasked with creating an ad campaign for the company. The women's team won with oddly framed photos that made plane parts—a tail assembly, a wing, an engine—appear phallic. The campaign was dead on arrival. "It made us nervous," Austin said. But it paid off. Marquis Jets saw a twentyfold increase in calls the next day, and the company's CEO, who appeared on the episode, suddenly found himself getting recognized in airports.

For most of the first season, only a few consumer products made cameos: a beer here, a bottle of champagne there. Burnett's product-integration team focused its energies on getting stuff for free. "We were just looking at it like . . .

all right, we don't have to buy this so that saves us X, Y, and Z on the budget," Kevin Harris recalled.

But as word spread about the show's ratings and impact on Marquis Jets during season one, marketing professionals at some of the world's largest corporations took notice. A call to Harris from the marketing department at Procter & Gamble changed the game. The company wanted to know if it would be possible for Burnett's team to create a task—an entire episode—around a new toothpaste.

"Toothpaste, that doesn't sound very sexy and glamorous," Harris responded.

"We will give you half a million dollars if you develop a challenge around the launch of the toothpaste," the marketing person responded.

Suddenly, toothpaste sounded quite glamorous. Harris said he would check with Burnett. He presented the offer to the boss, but as they talked it out, they both felt it would amount to selling out the show. Harris delivered the bad news to Procter & Gamble. "We want to keep the integrity of the show. So thanks for the opportunity, but we're going to pass." The woman on the phone barely let him finish the sentence.

"How about a million dollars?" she asked.

Harris was shocked. He told her he would get back to her and called Burnett.

"Mark, I don't know. This is crazy, but they just doubled it without even thinking. Maybe there's something here. We should look at this."

"Okay, I agree," Burnett said. "You've got it. Run with it."

Harris called back again and said Burnett's team would need to retain control of everything about the challenge. The company would have no direct input as to how the toothpaste was presented, and it would need to come up with another $100,000 to fund the teams' efforts.

"Okay, deal," was the answer.

Harris thought to himself, "Oh, shit. That's weird." He could not believe how effortlessly Procter & Gamble had more than doubled their offer, without adding other demands. Since Burnett's team would maintain creative control, they quickly got over the sense that they might be selling out; the involvement of Fortune 500 companies felt like a "shot of steroids" that further legitimized the show.

The first day of filming the episode, Trump descended the escalator into the lobby of Trump Tower to a soundtrack of royal trumpets punctuated with clash cymbals. The contestants were waiting for their briefing.

"Good morning," Trump said. "We're in the lobby of Trump Tower. It's big. I think big. I want you to think big too."

Trump said the goal was "to see who could create the most buzz" for the new vanilla-and-mint-flavored Crest toothpaste, with a budget of $50,000 for each team. The women's team decided to spend $20,000 hiring Mike Piazza, then the catcher for the New York Mets, to make an appearance at an outdoor event in Manhattan and brush his teeth with the new flavor.

"It tastes delicious," Piazza announced through a mouth full of bubbles.

The men's team toyed with creating a $1 million sweepstakes but could not pull it off. Their fallback plan was a circus-themed party.

In the end, both events were attended by only a few dozen people, not much buzz for one of the nation's biggest companies and advertisers, and arguably not even a great value for $100,000. But the show's television ratings took care of those shortcomings. The website that Crest had set up for the new flavor was visited eight hundred thousand times within two hours. More than 4.7 million people eventually hit the site. Major advertisers took notice, and the phone in Burnett's secret production office began ringing off the hook.

Burnett and Riggs needed more staff to turn the show's ratings gold into real gold. One key hire came on a golf course. Riggs often talked about the show while playing rounds with an old friend named Dan Gill, who worked in commercial real estate. Riggs mentioned what he saw as the show's shortcomings, especially the hokey tasks like selling lemonade. Gill came up with a few ideas on the fly—including a home-improvement challenge—that intrigued Riggs. He hired Gill in February 2004.

At thirty-nine years old, Gill was one of the oldest members of Burnett's staff. Sadoux Kim was just twenty-four, and he looked so young that many people assumed he was an intern. Harris was in his early thirties, slender, with a boyish haircut and manner. Gill's relative maturity, and a shock of prematurely white hair, helped ease corporations into writing massive checks. "When the show came on the air in January 2004, Madison Avenue just understood it," Gill later recalled. "This wasn't somebody eating a potato chip or having a beer on *Survivor* and then you never discussed it again. This was actually a forty-three-minute episode where it was all about the brand. It was better than anybody had ever seen."

Alan Blum was a New York advertising executive who wanted to move to Los Angeles and work in show business. A friend arranged a few meetings with Burnett's growing team. "I think Mark knew it all along," Blum later recalled. "Once the show was visible and public it was the easiest thing in the world to sell."

Burnett also hired an outside firm, Madison Road, to chase brand-integration deals. The total that Burnett's team collected for brand integration reached $9.4 million for season two. And it was clear they were just getting started. Burnett's plan to build a popular show and sell everything on every episode to sponsors was quickly becoming real. Half of the profits from that growing fortune were going to Trump, even though he was not involved in any aspect of the business.

Trump sometimes gummed up the product-integration effort by pushing for side deals with sponsors, trading on his new fame from the show. Gill convinced Genworth Financial to pay $4 million to sponsor the season two finale, the highest amount a sponsor would ultimately pay to be on the show for years to come, if not ever. After signing the deal, the company requested that Trump record a message that would be used as a voicemail blast to their employees announcing the company would sponsor the season finale. Trump made clear that he wanted to get paid for the few minutes of work. That didn't sit well with Gill, who knew Trump was already destined to make a fortune on that episode.

"I am like, 'You *are* getting paid to do it.'"

Trump ultimately agreed to record a voicemail blast to Genworth's employees—"Tune in and get ready to be fired up! Not fired . . . but fired up!"—without receiving an extra check. But he would keep pushing for extra money from the show's sponsors outside of his agreement with Burnett.

THE TELEVISION STUDIOS for the QVC network sit on a sprawling campus outside Philadelphia, in West Chester, Pennsylvania. It is a busy place. Every year, thousands of loyal viewers make pilgrimages in buses and cars to tour the birthplace of home shopping. Celebrities and corporate chieftains arrive in helicopters to hawk their wares on air. They typically land at Brandywine Regional Airport, which sits just beyond a row of trees from the QVC campus, and take a limousine, provided by the network, around the runway to the studio entrance. Michael Dell, the billionaire founder of one of the world's largest computer companies, took that drive when he appeared on the show to sell laptops.

In the fall of 2004, the network was notified that a guest scheduled to arrive via helicopter from New York was unwilling to be inconvenienced by that five-minute limousine ride. No, Donald Trump would need to land his helicopter within a short walk of the studio door. The network's security staff was directed to quickly convert a field on the grounds into a makeshift heliport, painting markings on the grass and installing lights nearby just for Donald Trump.

An episode for the second season of *The Apprentice* had recently been filmed at the QVC studios. It was a great success. Trump had not been present for the filming; his scenes were filmed in New York. He scheduled a day to come on his own to sell copies of his new book on air. His helicopter appeared over the trees about thirty minutes late. A few people, including Dan Gill from Burnett's team and QVC's senior vice president, Tim Megaw, had been waiting at Trump's new personal heliport. They watched as the aircraft dropped down toward the painted cross. It hovered briefly, then inexplicably flew off toward the building.

"What the hell is going on?" Megaw said.

The helicopter buzzed toward the employee parking lot, maybe two hundred feet away, and set down, its rotors kicking up hundreds of pebbles and firing them off in all directions. Megaw watched as rocks pelted dozens of cars owned by the network's employees. He wondered whether the landing was legal. It certainly was not safe. More than a few of his coworkers would file insurance claims to cover the damage.

Gill felt "fucking pissed" and "so embarrassed." QVC had paid $900,000 to be on the show and shelled out additional money to transport the production team on helicopters, and the contestants on buses, from Manhattan to Pennsylvania. Now, they had made special accommodations for the star to sell his own book, and stoning a lot full of cars did not feel like a show of gratitude. He asked Trump's pilot and bodyguard why the helicopter had not landed on the customized spot. The answer did not make him feel any better.

"He didn't want to step on the grass and muddy his shoes."

But Trump was the star, and he increasingly behaved like one, a moody and appearance-focused presence with no involvement in, or little concern for, the broader work of producing the show and maintaining relationships with sponsors.

The customary marker on the floor where an on-air personality is expected to stand during a shot is an X. Trump demanded a T. In the production room just offstage from the boardroom set, a monitor hung at an odd height, a little more than six feet above the floor, for one reason: so the tall host could watch playbacks of his scenes without wrinkling his clothes or craning his neck. When he arrived for a location shoot, the production crew's radios would buzz with news of whether he seemed happy or testy.

One regular source of frustration was Trump's attention span. He would accept only the shortest of briefings. Several producers remember him completely losing focus when a woman he found attractive crossed his field of vision. His contribution to editing choices, the most monumental task of reality television, was limited to suggesting which of his boardroom lines he thought worked best.

Harris recalls that Trump had only one question on his mind: "How much are they paying?"

Gill said he would often have no more than four minutes to brief Trump before taping began. "I'm giving him all the stats about this company. And all that he cared about was how much money the integration thing would give to Trump Productions. That's really the only time he would look at me."

After hearing the number from Gill, Trump would typically wax on for a moment about how much he loved the sponsor's product.

Jordan Yospe, a senior lawyer on Burnett's team who briefed Trump on sponsors, came to appreciate Trump's lack of concern with anything other than the size of the check. One day he would film a spot saying a certain razor was the best in the world, and the next he'd be fine saying on camera that its competitor was the best in the world.

"It just did not matter to him, as long as he was getting paid," Yospe later recalled. "Many actors, pro athletes, and the like look at this differently. They don't want to shill for brands unless they believe in the product."

One other set of numbers drew Trump's attention: press accounts of the show's ratings. "Once he was on *The Apprentice*, it was full *Apprentice*," Harris recalled later. "He even joked about going from reading *The Wall Street Journal* to reading *Variety* every day." Trump had for decades inflated his wealth when speaking to reporters. Now he had a new number to artificially pump up. Network executives noticed that Trump was regularly quoted in articles saying the show was rated number one, even when its ratings were strong but not at the top of the list.

But the reality of the ratings figures Trump cited was not important. What was of value to the network was Trump's willingness to speak with any reporter at any time. As one producer recalled: "Anything you can do from a marketing point of view, anything that put him in front of the press, he was super accommodating. I mean, he couldn't have been a better reality star."

Under Trump's and Burnett's original deal in 2003 to split everything, Trump was listed in the credits at the end of every show as an "executive producer." He would later claim to have cocreated or "conceived" the show with Burnett. In reality, Burnett was behind every decision and left nothing to chance. He even hired a group of rejected contestants to serve as secret task testers. Known internally as the Dream Team, they would work with a film crew to test ideas for challenges.

Trump was more focused on monetizing his expanded fame outside of Burnett's reach. Three months after *The Apprentice* debut, Clear Channel radio signed Trump to tape two ninety-second segments from his office each week. One would air the day after *The Apprentice* and would revolve around Trump expanding upon his firing decision the night before. The second would be an open forum for Trump to riff on the events of the day that interested him, including celebrity baby names, how pretentiously the brand "Jaguar" is pronounced in commercials, and whether Kevin Federline was right for Britney Spears.

"It's nice to be loved," Trump told *USA Today* when describing the radio spots. Though the value of radio love was not revealed at the time, Trump's financial records show he collected more than $2 million from a Clear Channel subsidiary during his contract's first two full years. That same year, Hasbro rereleased the Trump board game that had grown dusty on toy store shelves back in 1989, and paid Trump $500,000 for the privilege. After pelting cars in the QVC parking lot, Trump's appearance on the network generated about $500,000 in book sales in one day. That year, the book's publisher paid Trump more than $1 million in royalties, and nearly that much again in 2005. Trump even began selling T-shirts with his *Apprentice* catchphrase—"YOU'RE FIRED!"—emblazoned on the front.

Trump's difficulty keeping his word in business extended to his relationships with Burnett's team. No amount was too small to pocket. Levi's paid $1.1 million to sponsor an episode during season two. Just before the scene in which a Levi's executive would pick the winning team, Kevin Harris heard Trump tell his girlfriend, Melania, to go upstairs and change into her Levi's. The couple's return appeared on the episode. Trump entered the room where the Levi's executives were waiting and opened his palms toward Melania's jeans. "I have my girlfriend. She's wearing your jeans." As Trump spoke, Melania smiled and turned halfway around to reveal the fit from all sides. Robert Hanson, the president of Levi's, said, "Those look fantastic on you."

Melania remained in the room, and remained silent, for the rest of the scene as Hanson announced the winning team. After filming wrapped, Harris spoke with Trump and offered to see if he could get Levi's marketing people to hire Melania for a modeling gig, playing off the episode.

"It's a great idea, Kevin," Trump answered. "Tell you what, I'll give you ten percent of anything you get for Melania."

Harris quickly obtained an offer for Melania to be paid $50,000 for posing for photographs and making a public appearance. About a week later, Harris was in the studio on the fourth floor when Trump called and invited him up to his penthouse apartment.

"I've got something for you," Trump said.

Harris hustled to the elevator, excited to receive his $5,000 check. When he arrived, Trump opened the door and yelled upstairs for Melania. She gracefully descended the staircase carrying a golf putter in a felt sleeve and ceremoniously handed the putter to Trump, who presented it to Harris.

"Thanks for doing the deal," Trump said. He then took the putter back, produced a Sharpie, and added his EKG-like signature to the felt cover. "There you go."

Harris suspected the putter had cost $300 at most. Trump had made it into a power play, almost daring Harris to push back. He thought for a beat: All right, Kevin, you have one second to make a decision. Are you going to say something? "I said to myself, you know what? It's not worth it. It's not worth it to say a word. I'm just going to swallow this. He is my host. The TV show is a bigger deal." Harris accepted the putter, walked away, and "never looked back."

Trump's desire to make additional money from his name began to rub some sponsors the wrong way. He could be so snippy with executives of massive corporations that he seemed to be working against the interests of the show.

Mark-Hans Richer was the chief marketing officer for General Motors. He had just overseen the company's successful sponsorship of a car giveaway on Oprah Winfrey's show. General Motors had agreed to pay $3.5 million to sponsor an episode on *The Apprentice*, which the company would use to introduce a new two-seat roadster, the Pontiac Solstice. It was a stunning amount of money, especially for a midseason episode. Everyone on the product-integration team worked to keep the company comfortable. No one would profit more from that work than Trump, who stood to collect almost $2 million from the episode.

The producers told Richer to show up one morning at Trump's office building at 40 Wall Street for filming of a brief scene. He was waiting in the lobby with Burnett's crew when their radios crackled with an announcement that the host had arrived: "He is in a good mood."

Filming began quickly. Trump exchanged business pleasantries with Richer, asking about Pontiac's business performance, and then wedged in a boast, comparing the made-up value of his office building to the performance of a major automobile brand. "Well, I hope it does as well as this building. I bought it for a million. And it's worth four hundred million. And I'm happy."

The scene cut to a deserted Wall Street in front of the New York Stock Exchange building. The producers told Richer to stand next to Trump and let him take it from there. The contestants arrived for Trump to explain the challenge that week. Before Trump told them that they would be creating a marketing campaign for the new car, he once again reverted to form.

"On my right, I have executives from the Pontiac Motor Division of General Motors. General Motors is valued at twenty-five billion dollars, which by the way is only nineteen billion more than me. So that's not so great. You started a lot earlier than I did."

The comparison was beyond absurd. It was true that GM then had a market capitalization of $25 billion, but Trump made up the size of his own net value, as he would later admit to doing for any purpose that served him in any given moment. GM that year reported revenue of $194 billion and employed 324,000 people worldwide. (And as for timing, General Motors had been founded by William C. Durant in roughly the same decade that Trump's grandfather had begun buying real estate in New York City.) But was Trump joking? There was no sign of facetiousness or mischief in his delivery. Either way, Richer, whose job included protecting the company's image, decided he could not let the jab pass, especially given that the company was paying for the appearance.

"You've got time," he said with a smile.

To which Trump snapped back: "That's right. I'm catching."

At the time, Richer could not help but think, "Wow, this guy is really insecure about his financial standing." Oprah, who was most likely worth considerably more than Trump, had not felt the need to measure herself up to GM. Despite Trump's awkwardness, the episode was a tremendous success for Pontiac. Buyers for the first thousand cars, which were not even fully built yet, registered online within forty-one minutes of the episode's broadcast. All was forgiven. Other potential advertisers took notice.

But Richer still had to deal with a personal pitch that Trump made off camera. He wanted General Motors to create a car named after him. "No offense, I don't think it should be a Pontiac," Trump said to the director of marketing for Pontiac. "It should probably be a Cadillac."

Richer thought maybe Trump was trying to be funny and responded in kind, invoking the name of another General Motors brand: "Why don't we make it a Hummer? We'll call it a Trummer."

The host did not laugh. Getting paid for putting his name on things was no joke to Trump; it was a primary focus of his work off camera. Trump told George Ross to give his business card to Richer and said the two should speak again, which revealed to Richer that Trump was quite serious. After a bit of research, Richer decided there was no point in taking it seriously. "We couldn't really find a compelling case for how a Trump-licensed product had been successful."

A year later, Richer appeared in another episode his company sponsored to introduce a new convertible. He spent several awkward minutes sitting next to

Trump in a car backstage at the theater in the Taj Mahal casino, waiting for the car to roll out in front of the audience. Trump did not say a word, even after Richer reminded him about their previous meeting. Trump only grumbled.

"I realized that maybe he was pissed that we didn't do the car deal."

NOT LONG AFTER the season one finale, a job listing ran deep in the classified advertisements section of *The New York Times*, with a thinly veiled link to Trump and the show.

> Help Wanted
> MARKETING/SALES
> LICENSING EXPERT
> To negotiate and monitor licensing fees for one of
> the country's hottest brands. Must be expd. Call George
> Ross 212-715-7249.

The ad ran again on June 22, right above one seeking a receptionist for a doctor's office in the Bronx. Cathy Hoffman Glosser, who had led licensing efforts at Marvel Comics and consulted for *The New York Times*, called Ross's office. The two met soon after at Trump Tower. Ross scheduled her to come back to meet with Trump. Glosser had grown up on the Upper East Side of Manhattan in a family with a three-generation history of owning and selling commercial real estate. But the topic never came up. Trump wanted his name on consumer products. If Cathy Glosser could get kids around the world to wear Spider-Man pajamas, what could she do for Trump? After a brief interview, he offered her a job.

Donald Trump was on the cusp of a moment he had long pursued: money for nothing more than being Trump. No investment. No financial risk. No significant labor. He had made countless business decisions based on the belief that something with his name attached to it was worth multiples more than the same thing without his name. It allowed him to ignore the losses at golf courses and buildings he bought, to look past larger industry and economic trends. He'd made countless bets on that proposition, some of which went horribly wrong. But the success of the show made it seem likely that corporate America would come around. Other companies would take the risk, and Trump would get his check either way.

There was nothing innovative or particularly entrepreneurial in the effort. In fact, Trump was heading down a path pioneered by earlier celebrities. Jaclyn Smith, a star of the 1970s television hit *Charlie's Angels*, is often credited as a trailblazer in using her television celebrity as a launchpad for a broad licensing operation. After leaving the show, Smith marketed lines of fragrance, clothing, and home furnishings. Later, Kathy Ireland, a supermodel from her appearances in the *Sports Illustrated* swimsuit editions of the 1980s and 1990s, made a fortune licensing apparel and home products, including rugs and window coverings. Paris Hilton, whose reality show *The Simple Life* had debuted one month before *The Apprentice*, would go on to publish a bestselling memoir, host *Saturday Night Live*, and sign licensing deals for clothing, accessories, and fragrances bearing her name.

After fretting all year that another bankruptcy at his casinos could hurt the show and possibly his licensing potential, the moment finally arrived in November 2004. The refinancing of junk bonds the year before had not been enough to ward off collapse. The level of debt Trump had buried them under meant that his Atlantic City casinos and hotels had not been updated for years, falling behind the freshness quotient seen as vital to success in the industry. A flashy new competitor, the Borgata, was drawing an increasing share of the Atlantic City gambling market. But in Trump's telling, it was just a technical matter. He appeared on CNN with Larry King, who repeatedly gave Trump a platform to brush away the significance of failures in his largest single enterprise and letting down his investors. Trump's response was, essentially, that the latest casino bankruptcy was unimportant to him, and so, therefore, unimportant.

"It's really just less than one percent of my net worth," Trump said on the show. "Frankly, without *The Apprentice*, I don't think people would have even talked about Atlantic City."

He had a point. The years of work that Trump had put into the casinos, the investment of $100 million two decades earlier, was now essentially worthless. He was negotiating to have his equity in the company cut in half, to 29 percent, in exchange for giving the company another $55 million in cash—on top of the $15 million he had pumped in the year before. He would step down as chief executive but remain chairman of the board and retain his $2 million a year "services agreement." For Trump, his return on investment in casinos had largely devolved into a tax write-off that paid for him to use his helicopter and jet.

But the reality of Trump as a businessman mattered less than ever to his financial health. On May 4, 2004, he and his siblings spent the day signing documents that finalized the sale of most of their father's empire. Donald would walk away with $177.3 million, a massive watershed inheritance capping a lifetime of parental support.

Another influx of $11.9 million that year came from *The Apprentice*—almost all of it thanks to the work of Burnett's team lining up sponsors. The total was significantly more than his profit that year on the commercial space in Trump Tower.

And thanks to Trump's real-life performance in business and favorable laws governing family trusts, those waves of cash came to him largely tax-free. Losses from prior years on businesses he ran wiped away all his federal income tax liability for the year.

He could see signs that increased fame and the image makeover provided by Burnett's team would change the way corporate marketing departments saw him. After the first season of the show was a certified hit, Mark Hager, the licensing expert whom he had signed the year before, and a colleague, Jeff Danzer, took a run at convincing Phillips-Van Heusen to create a line of Trump-branded shirts and ties. This time he was able to schedule a meeting at Trump Tower with the clothing company's head of marketing. After the meeting, in June 2004, Phillips-Van Heusen agreed to license the Trump name.

Hager and Danzer thought they had accomplished the first step in Trump's goal and would be receiving 10 percent of the deal, per their agreement with Trump. They expected to find a happy new television star when they arrived at Trump Tower in late July. But Trump had no intention of giving them a cut.

"Nobody manages my brand but me," Trump told them. "Everything we do here is under my thumb. I do everything."

Danzer's company sued. Trump testified that he had made the connection to Phillips-Van Heusen on his own. "PVH is the largest shirt manufacturer in the world of shirt and ties, I guess. Regis Philbin is the one who first told me about it, because he had a very successful show also."

Before they parted ways completely, Danzer warned Ross that failing to vet people and companies asking to license the Trump name presented a grave danger. A celebrity brand is little more than the value of a positive public image. Tarnish that image, and a personal brand becomes just a name again. "George, the way I understand it, the reason [our company] was granted the deal was not only to secure the best possible licensees but to manage the brand and the business to get the most out of it and to ensure that the credibility and integrity of the Trump name is kept at the highest level," Danzer wrote in a letter to Ross and copied to Trump. "The easy part is getting the license. . . . The hard part is managing the brand to become a tremendous long-term business for Mr. Trump."

That was not advice Trump would take. But as a brand, "Trump" was no longer the same name that had made the former head of Bloomingdale's laugh, or the head of marketing for Pontiac crack wise about a giant jeep called "Trummer." In his testimony, Trump acknowledged what had changed. "This all happened because of the success of *The Apprentice*."

Glosser reported to work at Trump Tower in August. Trump gave her the title of executive vice president of global licensing and directed her to report to George Ross. At that point, she had no staff, no secretary, and set up shop in a vacant office eleven floors below Trump. She began reaching out to the chief marketing officers of major companies, with an initial focus on men's clothing and accessories. By December, she had locked in deals with Marcraft Group to produce a Donald Trump suit and with Estée Lauder to market "Donald Trump—The Fragrance." The cologne sold for sixty dollars, packaged in a glass bottle with vertical ridges that resembled the exterior of Trump Tower, topped off with a shiny gold cap.

On December 7, Trump flew to Chicago with Glosser and Bill Rancic for an event to promote the new scent at Marshall Field's flagship department store. Rancic's prize apprenticeship for winning season one was supposed to be overseeing construction of Trump's tower in Chicago, which was not yet under construction. Instead, he spent this day lending his newfound celebrity and good looks to increasing the marketing wattage of a Trump-branded product, no hard hat required.

The two men walked down a runway in the store as more than one thousand onlookers cheered. They signed bottles of the scent, and most anything else fans stuck in front of them, including a guitar. A reporter for *Women's Wear Daily* asked Trump about his new fame.

"I've gotten used to it," Trump said. "I've always had it, and now I have it more. Now it's gotten to a point where it's ridiculous. But when I get crazy about it—all of the photographers, all of the people, all of the touching—I remind myself that it probably will not always be this way, and I might as well enjoy it."

And he suggested that contestants in future seasons might be devoting more time to helping him sell a burgeoning portfolio of products named Trump.

"By that time, we should have more for them to promote."

29

THE DANGER OF OVERCOMMERCIALIZATION

IN JANUARY 2005, as the third season of *The Apprentice* aired, Donald Trump and Melania Knauss planned the grandest affair of the coming winter season in Palm Beach, a wedding that would introduce the couple as a new kind of American royalty. There would be a brief ceremony at the Church of Bethesda-by-the-Sea, followed by a gala reception in Mar-a-Lago's newly reconstructed ballroom. The guest list was tailor-made to generate nose-against-the-glass entertainment-media coverage, filled with network talk-show hosts—Katie Couric, Matt Lauer, Regis Philbin, Barbara Walters, Star Jones, Gayle King, and Kelly Ripa—as well as the famous people they talk to and about—Russell Simmons, P. Diddy, Simon Cowell, and Heidi Klum. A few of Trump's famous friends from politics would attend—Rudy Giuliani, Chris Christie, Bill and Hillary Clinton—as well as the Yankee great Derek Jeter and basketball star Shaquille O'Neal. Tony Bennett, Billy Joel, Elton John, and Paul Anka would perform at the reception.

As much as the wedding represented a union of two souls, it also brought together all the underpinnings of Trump's new financial life. The publicity platform that the show gave him. The get-stuff-for-free machinery that Burnett's team had built. The marketing of his own burgeoning celebrity brand. It all came together in fiscal harmony on January 22, 2005.

During the week before the blissful event, Donald and Melania practically took up residence on NBC's *Today* show. Melania was there on Tuesday. Donald showed up on Wednesday. Both Donald and Melania made themselves available on Thursday, which just happened to be the day that the new season of *The Apprentice* would debut. The hosts, Couric and Lauer, gleefully encouraged the couple to wax on about the splendors of their coming wedding while simultaneously promoting their network's prime-time hit.

"Well, we're so happy for both of you," Couric said at the end of the interview. "I know the third time's the charm. And we wish you the very best and much happiness for many years to come."

"Thank you," Trump said. "And make sure you watch *The Apprentice* tonight, Katie."

"Oh my God, do you ever quit?" Couric laughed.

News articles leading up to the event nearly all mentioned that the couple would travel from the ceremony to the reception in a Maybach, a luxury car brand that had recently been reintroduced by Mercedes-Benz and sold for more than $300,000. It was a curious detail for the Trump camp to mention. The 2.9-mile drive typically takes all of eight minutes. But the Trumps dishing of details did not include Donald's financial ties to the brand.

During season two of *The Apprentice,* Dan Gill convinced Mercedes-Benz to let the show use two Maybachs to transport the winning team from a Hamptons heliport to a nearby mansion for a glimpse at how wealthy people live. And just a month before the wedding, Maybach had paid $50,000 to sponsor part of the season two finale. During the same year, Maybach had held a small ceremony at Mar-a-Lago to give Trump the keys to a Maybach. It's not clear whether Trump paid for the car. Mercedes had offered to give Burnett use of a Maybach, but he had turned down the offer to avoid a tax hit. Burnett's get-stuff-for-free squad heard that Trump (perhaps not accustomed to worrying about paying income taxes) accepted.

Numerous news stories that year said Trump owned his Maybach, which would have put him in an elite circle; only 410 were sold in the U.S. during 2003 and 2004 combined. Either way, the publicity lent additional credibility to his place in the pantheon of wealthy American entertainers. The new car, which Mercedes went to great lengths to promote, had its moment in the pop culture spotlight that year. Gossip columns reported that Mariah Carey, Will Smith, Jay-Z and Beyoncé, Jennifer Lopez and Ben Affleck, and Madonna had use of, or owned, new Maybachs.

Some news reports said that suppliers of food, transportation, entertainment, just about everything for the wedding, were working for reduced fees, or for nothing. Just being named by Donald and Melania in the breathless coverage of the day was enough. The *New York Post* reported that Trump had so many endorsements and deals that "some are suggesting" he may have made a profit on his nuptials.

Trump fed that impression. But in at least one case, it appears to have been an effort to mythologize his personal value to high-end brands. Trump obtained Melania's wedding and engagement rings from Graff jewelers, a detail he mentioned repeatedly during interviews. "It's from Graff jewelers, who are terrific," he said on CNN. The company had also been featured on season two of *The Apprentice*, providing a $50,000 shopping spree for the team that won an episode. Citing sources close to Trump, the *Post* and others reported that Trump took possession of the $1.5 million wedding ring for either half of the list price, or nothing, in exchange for the publicity he would generate. Trump left the impression the story was true without saying so directly. "Hey, I bought a ring. I got it from Graff, who negotiated hard. And I said, 'You're going to get a lot of publicity and I want a great price, blah, blah, blah.'"

Graff did not comment on the suggestion of a deal at the time. The company said years later it had not given Trump a break, but the impression had been created. The episode also struck a discordant note with Donald's public criticism of his own son, Don Jr., who had recently accepted a free engagement ring in exchange for staging his proposal to his fiancée in front of the jewelry store in a New Jersey mall.

In an interview on CNN, Trump told Larry King that his son had risked damaging the family's ability to make money from its name. "I guess he's trying to learn from me, Larry. But you know, from a business standpoint, I guess it's sort of cute, but I didn't like it. I certainly don't like it with respect to a wedding ring." Trump said his approach was better—"I don't do a big stunt over it"—and he explained the why to his son: "You have a big obligation. You have a name that's hot as a pistol. You have to be very careful with things like this."

Even Trump's new line of men's clothing got a boost. Reporters were told that Terry Lundgren, the chief executive of Macy's, which had exclusive rights to carry the line, showed up in a Donald Trump tuxedo.

A decade after Trump had opened Mar-a-Lago as a private club, his third wedding would mark the island's transition from the quiet old-money ways of Palm Beach society to Trump's ostentatious flash.

Trump's reception and the ensuing media attention served as the best imaginable ribbon cutting for the centerpiece of another burgeoning line of work—banquet hall operator. After converting Mar-a-Lago to a club, Trump had opened its small existing ballroom to rentals for weddings and other events. The new ballroom—which was said to measure somewhere between eleven thousand and twenty thousand square feet—offered a larger space for bigger-ticket events. It would be dubbed the Donald J. Trump Ballroom. Anyone wanting to hold their wedding reception in the exact same room as Donald and Melania could do so. The new couple honeymooned at the club as well, a decision that Trump used in interviews for months to promote the business.

"Why are we going to leave the gorgeous, beautiful house called Mar-a-Lago and venture out onto some tropical island where things aren't clean?" he told Larry King.

During the year before the wedding, Trump had boasted that he was spending $42 million on the new ballroom. For inspiration, he had looked to Versailles, Louis XIV's fantasy royal residence outside of Paris. Trump said he had installed 24-karat-gold moldings, custom-made crystal chandeliers, and marble floors.

On his tax returns, Trump increased the value of Mar-a-Lago by $4 million the year the ballroom was built. In the years to come, renting out the ballrooms of Mar-a-Lago and his golf courses would become an increasing focus of Trump properties, but one the Trumps would never fully embrace in public.

Burnett arrived for the wedding with his glamorous new girlfriend, the actress Roma Downey, star of *Touched by an Angel*, and his two sons, James and Cameron. He and Trump had come to feel so close that Cameron, age seven, served as ring bearer and wore a page's outfit that Melania had commissioned from Dior.

Don Jr. and Eric served as best men. At the reception, Don Jr. began his toast by saying he thought this wedding would be his father's last. The groom took the microphone to thank Melania for "the best six years of my life, my little Melania" and for "putting on a great show" in planning the day.

Melania had tapped the brakes on fully commercializing her wedding. Networks had wanted to film the ceremony and reception, but Melania demanded some semblance of decorum and privacy. The truce was broken when the new bride caught Katie Couric taking video with a tiny camera. Donald had mistakenly given Couric permission, but NBC agreed never to use their correspondent's bootleg tape of their star's wedding. Still, guests were required to relinquish phones and cameras, because Donald had sold exclusive photography rights to Getty Images.

Melania wore a custom wedding dress from Dior, made from enough white satin to span a football field and with embroidery that took 550 hours to complete. Her shopping trip was featured in the February 2005 issue of *Vogue*, which hit newsstands the week before the wedding.

Pulling away in the Maybach, she waved through the rear window to a crowd of photographers and well-wishers. The smoky model squint Melania had perfected was replaced by a wide, beaming smile and joyful eyes.

KEVIN HARRIS AND HIS WIFE had flown from Los Angeles on a private jet, rented by Burnett, to attend the wedding. Flying private was not a level of luxury to which the Harrises were accustomed. As they sat in the church, his wife realized that the glamorous head of hair immediately in front of them belonged to supermodel Heidi Klum. They later met Bill and Hillary Clinton. At the reception, they sipped Cristal champagne and nibbled on caviar and lobster hors d'oeuvres by Jean-Georges Vongerichten. The opulence, the celebrities, it was all a bit overwhelming. Trump swept up and down the long dinner tables at the reception to exchange a few brief words with his guests.

"Hey, what do you guys think?" Trump asked. "Pretty cool, huh?"

That night, while Barbara Walters and other celebrities enjoyed the suites at Mar-a-Lago, Harris and his wife slept at a nearby hotel. Harris is not inclined to envy. He felt fortunate to be one of the few employees invited. He liked being around Trump and was happy for his financial success, even as he did all the work on the deals. After word spread through marketing departments of the impact of the episode that Crest sponsored, even more corporate marketing officers rushed in. Harris kept a running list of twenty eager companies. The team had not yet found the ceiling of what companies would pay to see a game show built around their products.

For the season three premiere, which aired the evening that Trump made Katie Couric blush by promoting both the show and his wedding, Dan Gill had lined up a deal for Burger King to pay $3.07 million for the sponsorship and an additional $500,000 for being featured on the season debut. That wasn't the end of it. The company also had the option to pay $300,000 to use a few minutes of audio clips "of scenes featuring Donald Trump, in the boardroom and otherwise." Trump would receive $137,500 of that money for letting the company use recordings of things he had already said. Burger King was thrilled with the attention, crediting the exposure for a large sales bump that January.

Burnett's team was finding other ways to monetize the contestants. Hanes paid $1 million to sponsor a season three episode. The task required contestants to design a T-shirt commemorating the company's fiftieth anniversary. After filming, the shirts were shipped to Walmart stores in advance of the episode airing. The day after it was broadcast, Harris sent Burnett and the rest of the team an email saying Hanes had sold out the initial printing of 35,000 shirts by 11:00 a.m. and was printing 100,000 more.

"Do we earn anything on this???" Burnett responded.

Yes, answered Harris: 8 percent of sales would be paid to Burnett's production company. Hanes wanted to make shirts in connection with other Mark Burnett shows, and the company was eager to host another episode. "All in all, a great task and a very satisfied partner."

Production costs ate only a small portion of the cash coming in. The rest was split between Trump and Burnett. Trump was now collecting $1 million or more from each episode just from the product integration. He still showed little interest in how it all worked other than being excited to learn each week during filming how much the sponsor had paid.

For all the financial strength, the new season exposed weaknesses in the basic conceit of the show—that this was a serious business endeavor by people serious about business. Yet even the missteps worked in Trump's favor.

Contestants for the season were split into two teams based on educational attainment—college graduates and high school graduates. "Would you be embarrassed if the high schoolers kicked your ass?" Trump asked the college grads in one episode. Dove paid $2 million for an episode to introduce its new cucumber-infused Cool Moisture Body Wash. The college grad team dreamed up what its leader called a "little vegetable porn creation." Their video showed a man and a woman in a restaurant kitchen passionately washing a cucumber as if it were, well, not a cucumber. The male worker then departs arm in arm with another man, and the female worker is left clutching a very clean cucumber. It was a phallic joke, a gay joke, and a masturbation joke all in one. The high school grads had the common sense to avoid going dirty with a big soap brand. But they did not seem to understand how body wash, or soap, works. Their ad showed a sweaty man using the body wash on his face, and then wiping off the lathery bubbles with a dry towel.

Donny Deutsch, the advertising impresario who served as Trump's marketing expert on the episode, snapped at the teams: "You both sucked." In the boardroom scene, Trump also expressed outrage and did not select a winner for the episode: "You know this is the first time something like this has ever happened. I'm angry with all of you."

Dove was tickled pink. The attention that the new body wash received washed away concern about a clumsy cucumber metaphor. *Advertising Age* reported that following the airing, the Dove website was bombarded with three thousand visitors a second. The company sent out four hundred thousand samples within five days. The term "Dove and Apprentice" became a hot search on Google. The enduring principle of Trump's life—that any attention is better than no attention—was the moral of the show.

Challenging the contestants to develop marketing plans for massive companies had become a fallback task for the show's producers. It was a silly notion on its face. The sponsors all had well-funded professional marketing departments and access to the best advertising agencies in the world. Some episodes exposed that silliness.

Dove, for example, is owned by Unilever, a massive multinational consumer goods company. After firing a contestant at the end of the Dove boardroom scene, Trump said, "Those commercials were just awful. Dove is better off making their own ad." And voilà! Trump and Kepcher introduced a new Dove commercial for the body wash, which had been created by Ogilvy Chicago. Viewers were not told explicitly, but the rollout of the real ad had been planned in advance.

Trump continued to work his own side deals with the show's sponsors. A few months after the Dove episode aired, news crews were summoned to Trump Tower for what turned out to be a marketing stunt unrelated to the show. On cue, Trump appeared and lifted up a laundry basket bearing the name and logo of another Unilever brand, All detergent. Unilever said Trump would wash the clothes so they could be donated to charity. As part of his agreement, Trump called journalists, telling a *Boston Globe* reporter, "Unilever is a great company" and "my mother used this product." He also recorded voice-overs for an online game that showed a digital version of him washing clothes and saying things like, "The Donald can do the work of forty dry cleaners!"

In addition to his share of the $2 million that Dove paid to Burnett for *The Apprentice* episode, Trump received that year another $850,000 from Unilever, and $250,000 from a public relations firm that the company used. In a few hours of hawking soap, Trump had made twice as much money as Mar-a-Lago earned that year.

THE FIRST SIGN THAT DOMINO'S expectations might not be met came on set when Trump defined the challenge for the episode the company would sponsor. "For your next task," Trump told the contestants, "you are going to create an original style of pizza for Domino's using toppings they don't usually offer on a menu. I like meatballs. I like lots of different things on it."

Meatballs. No one expected Trump to mention meatballs. Trump didn't seem to realize that when the umpire says he likes meatballs, the players throw meatballs. Both teams went off to their respective studios to brainstorm. Bren Olswanger, the contestant who had conjured the cucumber fantasy for Dove, suggested something like a cheeseburger pizza. A Domino's executive who was on set, Trisha Drueke-Heusel, told him that the company already had a cheeseburger pizza. That was not entirely true, but within a few minutes, both teams decided to create their own version of a meatball pizza.

This was not ideal television. Burnett had warned his product-integration and creative groups to avoid having two contestant teams doing the same thing because the audience simply could not keep track of which team was doing what. Indeed, the episode felt like a meatball mishmash, with two teams selling the same pizzas from mobile vehicles in Manhattan. The high school grad team sold more of its meatball pizza than the other team and won.

"You called it a meatball pie?" Trump asked the winning team as they shared breakfast in his apartment. "I think they're going with that now. Aren't they going to make what you did? I think they're going with it. No, no, from what I understand. I think it's a great idea."

Except they weren't. After watching the filming, Domino's executives decided the best choice for their menu was . . . anything but meatballs. Behind the scenes, Drueke-Heusel let Dan Gill know the bad news in a letter a month before the episode aired: "Domino's will not be launching the pizzas the teams came up with during the Domino's task."

Drueke-Heusel had made a name for herself at Domino's developing a Philly cheesesteak pizza, which had been a counterintuitive hit. On the second page of her letter to Gill, she came clean about the little white lie she had told Olswanger during filming. Despite what she said, no Domino's stores were selling cheeseburger pizzas. But she had one in the development pipeline at that very moment. It was now ready to go, and the company planned to air commercials promoting it during *The Apprentice*. Drueke-Heusel asked for one tiny editing favor: cut the scene where she said Domino's already had a cheeseburger pizza, just to avoid any "conflicting messaging" between the show and the commercial.

Things were not supposed to turn out this way. The marketing experts at Domino's Pizza had taken great care to figure out what it was worth to sponsor an episode of the show. They had performed an analysis that projected the cost of a thirty-second commercial outward to a full twenty minutes of attention during an episode. But they decided that such a simple multiplier did not quite fit because the brand would not be the focus for that entire period. More importantly, the company had no control over how its products would be portrayed. They landed at first on something in the range of $900,000 to $1.3 million. Then Domino's chief marketing officer, Ken Calwell, called Dan Gill. They chatted about the potential impact, and Domino's decided to offer $2.5 million. Weeks later, the company signed a contract to pay $2.75 million.

For that kind of money, companies expected their interests to be protected by Burnett and the network. But Burnett's team was still making all this up as they went along. There were no models to value the integration of products into storylines.

In her letter, Drueke-Heusel also let Gill know that she had sidestepped the apparatus of *The Apprentice* to hire Trump as the company's new cheeseburger pie spokesman: "We are currently negotiating with Mr. Trump to appear in a commercial for this new pizza and have purchased ad time in our episode to run this new spot." She added that she was excited to see the show on air.

But when the show finally aired, it came with an unpleasant surprise. Somehow, in the time between when the episode was filmed in late 2004 and its airing in early 2005, Papa John's, one of Domino's biggest competitors, had learned key details about the contest. Papa John's went guerrilla, sidestepping Burnett and NBC to buy commercial time in sixty local television markets across the country. During a break in the Domino's episode, Papa John's crashed the party.

"Why eat a pizza made by apprentices when you can call the pros at Papa John's?" the ad inquired. And what flavor of pizza was Papa John's featuring? Yes, the very meatball pie the contestants were conjuring.

Burnett's team did not see it coming. Domino's definitely did not see it coming. At about 3:00 a.m. in Los Angeles, the general counsel for Burnett's production company, Jordan Yospe, awoke to his phone ringing off the hook. It was Domino's chief operating officer and another executive calling to give him an earful. How could this have happened? How could you not watch out for us? Neither he nor Burnett knew such a move was even possible "because, frankly, we were producers, and we didn't know how ad sales worked," Yospe later recalled.

"It was a big deal, but it was not a money issue, it was a PR issue."

It was the sort of mistake that Burnett, the former commando, called "mission failure," letting down a major corporate sponsor who expected the show to look out for its interests. But Trump, detached from responsibility and decision-making, would make money on both the promise and the betrayal.

Trump recorded a voice-over for the following week's episode, which had already been filmed and edited. There would be no meatball ad-lib this time. Nothing was left to chance. Trump was handed a script. In the final cut that aired, only the faces of everyone else in the room—Carolyn, the contestants—were shown as Trump, after introducing the new task, made an awkward transition.

"And speaking of last week's task, here's something you didn't know. Both teams created meatball pizza. But if you had done your market research like Domino's did, you would have discovered that customers don't want meatball pizza. What they want is cheeseburger pizza."

The show had been used to set the table for the new offering, totally separate from any contest or storyline in the show. The sponsor's bruised feelings had been smoothed over. During the commercial breaks, Domino's aired the cheeseburger pizza commercial featuring Trump. There he was, in his office, accepting delivery from a Domino's delivery man. As Trump noshed on the cheeseburger pizza, he blithely told the deliveryman that Domino's should invent a cheeseburger pizza.

"You oughta be paying me for this," Trump deadpanned.

Saturday Night Live spoofed the ad, with Darrell Hammond rendering Trump as a clueless pseudothespian, improvising absurd riffs on the wonders of pizza and mispronouncing Domino's. But the money was no joke. Domino's paid Trump $500,000 that year. That money came directly to him, separate from his share of the $2.75 million the company paid to Burnett's company on the original mission failure episode that his comment inspired.

Burnett's team learned several lessons from the show: Sponsors would let the ridiculousness slide, and they had no concern about the integrity of the show as a business education forum. As long as the ratings held up, the sponsors would keep paying.

Burnett's money team had never dreamed they would see these kinds of numbers. In one year, they had gone from trying to get sponsors to give them things for free to expecting more than $2 million an episode. Jordan Yospe looked at the figures coming in and thought, "unbelievable . . . shocking . . . just unbelievable."

Kevin Harris had a different thought. How much longer is the network going to let Burnett and Trump keep taking all the product-integration money? "Clearly, this isn't going to last forever, because this is a very weird deal that NBC made."

THREE DAYS BEFORE TRUMP'S WEDDING at Mar-a-Lago, Burnett convened his money team at his production offices in Bel-Air. They reviewed what was working and what needed work. A PowerPoint presentation cataloged the observations and ideas. Product-integration deals needed to be signed earlier, to give the creative side more time to develop fresh tasks. There was a risk of becoming "overreliant" on some types of contests, especially creating commercials and publicity campaigns for new products. There was a "danger of overcommercialization" and crossing the "fine line between engaging TV and infomercial."

Much praise for the increase in product-integration revenue was heaped on Dan Gill and Sadoux Kim, "who deliver over and above expectations" despite "both their limited backgrounds in the branded-integration space." A plan was presented to reduce the reliance on outside firms, like Madison Road, and bring more of that in-house to be handled by Gill and Kim, along with Mark Mitten.

Trump was never invited to these sorts of meetings. But he was a topic of discussion. Deep into the presentation appeared what would have seemed like a bombshell to the larger television industry. Burnett directed the team to find ways to cut Trump out of the money from the show. "Explore stand-alone Apprentice properties without Trump's presence (separate what MBP controls vs Trump)." There were ideas to create an Apprentice college curriculum, a speaking tour for the cast, or a version of the show for children. To the crew, it seemed fine for Burnett to propose cutting Trump out of the money the same month that he attended Trump's wedding. This was business. Besides, Trump already had a track record of going around Burnett's production company for deals.

Gill had seen it firsthand. On the streets of New York City one day, he noticed a flyer for a Learning Annex conference. The continuing education company had been founded by a man named Bill Zanker out of his studio apartment decades earlier. Gill cold-called the company to ask if it might want to sponsor an episode during season four. He spoke with Heather Moore, the company's vice president of business operations and product management. Moore loved the idea. She mentioned that Zanker knew Trump. (Trump had spoken at a Learning Annex seminar previously.) At the time, Gill assumed Trump's relationship with Zanker would help seal a deal. Gill and Moore began haggling over price, something upward of $2 million, the range of what had become typical. Then, out of the blue, Moore changed course. She said Trump and Zanker had worked out a side deal on their own. The Learning Annex would pay Trump directly for a series of speeches. Soon after, Zanker issued a press release saying he was going to pay Trump $3 million for three speaking engagements—"That's over $16,000 a minute!" the release said. "I know that a million dollars an hour will get him into the Guinness Book of World Records—but he's worth it!" Zanker said. The relationship would earn Trump a total of more than $7 million for about twenty appearances.

Burnett agreed to let the Learning Annex sponsor an episode for just $50,000, one of the smallest amounts for that season and not even enough to cover production costs. During a production meeting in Los Angeles, with more than twenty people seated around a conference table and the rest of the room packed with people standing, Gill revealed Trump's end run around Burnett's team to sign with the Learning Annex. These discussions always carried the risk of bruising the feelings of the people in the room doing the real work of bringing in money and getting the show made, many of whom were still working for a hundred dollars a day. People doing such deals in other shops were making a 10 percent commission; Burnett's staff was still on wages. But Gill wanted everyone to know why Burnett's company had not collected several million dollars for the episode.

One senior member of Burnett's staff listening to Gill that day thought Trump's side deals sounded "icky" and "slimy" and undermined everyone working to make Trump money under his already generous contract. But he was "the talent," the preening star of the show, and it made no sense to risk making him so angry that he would not show up for shooting and shut down production.

Burnett seemed displeased but willing to let it go as a cost of keeping the talent happy.

"Look, we're in production," Burnett told the staff according to a person who was present. "[Let] the chips fall where they may, and we'll still get a great episode. Trump's going to make some money. What can we do about it?"

30

BETTER THAN REAL ESTATE

During the season two finale of *The Apprentice*, Donald Trump picked Kelly Perdew as his next apprentice. Perdew was not a typical intern. He was thirty-seven years old and a graduate of the United States Military Academy at West Point, with graduate degrees in law and business from the University of California Los Angeles. He had already founded and sold a successful software company.

As Perdew stood next to Trump on a stage before a packed audience at Lincoln Center in Manhattan, he watched two videos presenting projects he could work on for Trump: a coming Trump hotel in Las Vegas; or a stretch of apartment buildings under construction on the old West Side rail yards in Manhattan.

"When I build, I build big," Trump said in the second video. "And Trump Place, my four-billion-dollar project on Manhattan's West Side, is one of the largest land developments anywhere in the world. When completed, seventeen new buildings will stretch across eight million square feet of prime real estate. It'll also include a twenty-one-acre park that's my gift to the city of New York. When finished, Trump Place will be the crown jewel of modern living and urban planning. New York City will be very, very proud."

Trump's description of the project—filled with misleading invocations of "I" and "my"—sounded great to Perdew. "Mr. Trump," he said, "as much as I love Vegas, I actually took this challenge and came to be your apprentice so that I could learn from you. And I think I can do that much better close to you, here in New York. So I'll take New York."

Trump made no mention of the fact that he did not control the West Side project, a power he had given away a decade earlier to help avoid being forced into personal bankruptcy. His Hong Kong partners owned 70 percent and controlled all major decisions, including whether Trump ever received any portion of the profits. They had hired a prominent construction manager. Trump's role was to bring attention to the project, a responsibility he certainly fulfilled on television that day in December 2004.

The promise Trump made to Perdew did not survive his first day on the job. Perdew reported for work at Trump Tower at 9:00 a.m. As he waited, Trump walked out of his office with several men. They all exchanged greetings and small talk with Perdew. One of the men had been a former wrestler. Another was a dentist. A couple of them had developed smaller apartment buildings. They had been speaking with Trump about using his name on a fifty-two-story apartment building they planned to build in downtown Tampa. Perdew mentioned that he had lived in Tampa and attended elementary school nearby, in Sarasota. Trump listened for a few minutes before interrupting.

"Kelly's going to come down and help you guys," he blurted out.

After months of triumphing over televised backstabbing and minor humiliations, Perdew would not be exposed to the world of big real estate development. But he would be directly involved in the most profitable business in which Donald Trump ever engaged. The Tampa crew arrived at Trump Tower as part of a parade of suitors seeking to capitalize on Trump's new fame from *The Apprentice.* They came bearing checks, very large checks, simply for the use of his name. The core product of the Trump Organization would no longer be expertise in site selection, construction, or golf course or casino operations. The core product would be five letters.

Led by the former professional wrestler Jody Simon, the Tampa crew paid Trump $125,000 when he agreed to let them use his name in 2004, another $775,000 in 2005, almost $1 million in 2006, and committed to paying him at least $2 million more. Whether or not the tower was ever built would not change those figures. He would receive more money if condos sold at profitable prices. Trump required that they followed standards he had created—mostly ceiling height and window size—and not tell anyone that this was only a licensing deal.

His employees noticed how eagerly Trump took this easy money without performing any due diligence on the people paying him. Did they have a viable business plan? Could they finish the project? Would a failure tarnish the value that Mark Burnett had created for the Trump name? Those sorts of questions rarely came up in early 2005. Trump liked to say he followed his instincts, but his instincts seemed to be driven by the number of commas on a check.

"It's always a vetting problem," said one longtime employee. "Let's just say that the biggest enemy to the Trump licensing program was Trump, in his lack of desire or interest to do anything but take a check."

Trump joined Perdew at an office building in Tampa to promote sales. Police partially blocked the usually busy intersection and watched over the scene from horseback and on foot. Sixteen valets parked the cars of wealthy potential buyers. Trump stepped from a black limousine wearing a dark suit and a bright purple tie, with Melania at his side. They joined a private reception for fifty, with a harpist playing and cocktails flowing. Trump eventually addressed the crowd of six hundred waiting in a tent on the vacant lot, many of whom had already turned over $100,000. He said the units were selling like gangbusters.

"We can't do much better than we're doing here," he told the crowd, adding that he wished he could say the building was completely reserved, "But I'm getting modest in my old age."

Buyers had to come up with a 20 percent nonrefundable deposit to lock in a unit. Trump was there to close the deal. Trump also said he and Melania were likely to buy a unit, because it would be "cool" to stay there when they came to watch the Yankees spring training games. And Don Jr. would be buying a unit as well. Trump told the potential buyers that he owned "a substantial stake" in the building. "I recently said, 'I'd like to increase my stake,'" he told the crowd. "But when they're selling that well, they don't let you do that."

That was entirely untrue. Trump had invested nothing in the project. And the project still did not have financing for construction. A member of the development team told a local reporter: "We have indeed spent in the millions. But you'll be amazed how fast we go from here."

As the crowd of buyers stood in the tent next to the river, no one on the development team had thought to test the soft soil they stood on to see if it could support a fifty-two-story building.

A YEAR LATER, the developers still did not have financing when they held a ceremonial groundbreaking on March 2, 2006. Trump sent Kendra Todd, winner of the third season of *The Apprentice*, in his stead, and expressed his regrets that he could not attend because Melania was about to give birth. Eight days later, though, he appeared in Los Angeles at a contestant audition for *The Apprentice*. And eight days after that, he spent the weekend at Mar-a-Lago with talk show host Regis Philbin and Philbin's wife. On Monday, March 20, he claimed to be shocked that Melania had given birth to a boy a week earlier than expected.

"I continue to stay young, right? I produce children, I stay young," Trump, then fifty-nine, said during a call in to *The Don Imus Show* on MSNBC about twenty minutes after the birth.

He and Melania named the boy Barron—Trump's longtime pseudonym with reporters. In an appearance on CNN's *Larry King Live* the next day, Trump said he had considered giving his son Eric the name but "just didn't have the courage to do it. And now I just went for it. And I just like the name. I've always liked the name, and Melania loved the name."

The year would become perhaps the most frantic of Trump's life. His company had two ongoing construction projects—the Chicago tower and another in Las Vegas with a partner—and he was trying to win approval to build a golf course in Scotland. Those projects would normally max out the capacity of Trump's small staff. But fueled by his newfound fame, he continued to sign real estate licensing deals with developers across the country and beyond. In 2006 alone, he announced construction projects in Atlanta, Dallas, Delaware, two in Florida, Hawaii, Philadelphia, New York City, and White Plains, along with Panama, Mexico, and Israel. Trump typically lied or fuzzed the fact that he did not own the projects and was not the developer, creating the illusion that he was everywhere, buying properties, taking on risk, and pouring concrete.

And the illusion expanded beyond real estate. He announced a line of furniture, an online travel agency, and a mortgage brokerage. He peddled vitamins, get-rich-quick schemes, and made numerous paid speeches. He published and promoted two books with coauthors: *Trump 1010: The Way to Success* and *Why We Want You to Be Rich*. He squeezed in the filming of two seasons of *The Apprentice* in 2006.

As a full-fledged television celebrity, he found entertainment news outlets ready to broadcast his every comment—the more outrageous, the better. He called Rosie O'Donnell "fat" and "a loser" after she called him a snake-oil salesman and a disloyal husband, and said he was not self-made and had bankruptcies in his past. He attacked Martha Stewart because she had accepted an offer to host a spinoff of *The Apprentice* that did not gain traction with viewers. He sued the journalist Tim O'Brien for reporting in his 2005 book, *TrumpNation: The Art of Being the Donald*, that Trump's assets were worth only $250 million (a suit that was dismissed). He fired Carolyn Kepcher from *The Apprentice* after she became independently popular.

As Trump turned sixty that June, his personal life grew as complicated as his public life, in ways that may have damaged his value as a celebrity endorser had the details become public. While Melania was home with baby Barron, Trump filmed part of an episode of *The Apprentice* at Hugh Hefner's Playboy Mansion in Los Angeles. He met a thirty-five-year-old former Playmate of the Year named Karen McDougal and, she would later say, began a sexual affair. The following month, Trump played in a celebrity golf tournament at Lake Tahoe. He finished sixty-second in a field of eighty. But after a round, he met a twenty-seven-year-old adult film actress who went by the stage name Stormy Daniels. She would later say they had sex that day and kept in touch as Trump promised to help her appear on his television show.

Even in public, his propensity to describe women as inanimate objects occasionally broke into view. During an appearance on a talk show, Trump was asked how he would feel about Ivanka, then twenty-four, appearing in *Playboy*. With Ivanka sitting next to him, Trump said it would depend upon the photos, then added: "She does have a very nice figure. I've said if Ivanka weren't my daughter, perhaps I'd be dating her." He later said he was joking.

He announced one thing that he would not do, and it became a topic of news coverage for months. "I'm not going to run for governor because I'm having too much fun doing what I'm doing now. I'm the largest builder in New York, I'm building things all over the country, I have one of the top shows on television. It's a little hard to leave all of that."

ON VALENTINE'S DAY 2006, four men from Michigan, the founders of a multilevel marketing company called American Communications Network, joined the parade of people seeking an endorsement at Trump Tower. They arrived two days after a major snowstorm and would say their bond with Trump was forged by his admiration that they had triumphed over the city's damp streets.

"You made it!" they would quote him saying when they arrived, words they would say he uttered "with clear admiration."

"Trump puts a lot of stock into keeping commitments and going the extra mile—and so do the ACN founders," they later said in a promotional magazine.

Trump no doubt also put stock in the contract he had signed the week before with ACN. They agreed to pay him at least $2 million to "endorse ACN as a celebrity." That total would include $1 million to spend no more than two hours taping a promotional video and another $1 million to speak for one hour at each of three rallies of people recruited to the ACN marketing program.

The four men—Robert Stevanovski, Greg Provenzano, and twin brothers Tony and Mike Cupisz—had worked in other multilevel marketing companies that failed. They formed ACN in 1993, after energy deregulation opened the door to companies selling access to the power grid, and later the more sweeping energy deregulation in California that gave rise to Enron. They expanded into selling long-distance telephone plans following the deregulation of that sector.

The four had neither graduated from college nor worked in telecommunications or energy. They saw themselves as selling dreams, the promise of freedom from monotonous jobs. They crisscrossed the country holding rallies in packed auditoriums and arenas, preaching their gospel of financial independence. For the bargain price of $499, anyone could buy the privilege of selling their energy and telephone plans. Their rallies took on the air of evangelicalism. "Life is God's gift to you, and what you do with that life is your gift to God," an announcer said in a video they showed at some rallies.

"They are dissatisfied with something in their lives," one of the founders, Tony Cupisz, told a reporter while backstage at a rally in Columbus, Ohio. "They're dissatisfied with work, or with the glass ceiling, or by the feeling that they should have something better."

Trump would become the motivational general to ACN's army of the dissatisfied. He had for years toed at the edge of the dodgy world of get-rich-quick schemes. His books since *The Art of the Deal* had been billed as not-so-subtle ways to become as rich as he claimed to be. Published the year of his debut on *The Apprentice*, *How to Get Rich* gave up the veneer of subtlety. He would openly embrace using his fame, and the aspirational lift of *The Apprentice*, to reach into the wallets of disenchanted people.

Trump appeared at some ACN rallies. Videos of him were shown at others, as well as in living rooms across the country as reps tried to convince their friends and relatives to join. "The two things I've mastered over the years is understanding the importance of timing in business and the ability to recognize great opportunities," Trump said in one such video. "So, I'm here to tell you about a company that provides these two essential components for success."

"I like real estate," Trump added. "But this is probably better."

ACN's deal with Trump entered a heightened phase when the company began selling desk phones with the ability to make video calls. They did not always make clear that the ACN video phones could connect only with other ACN phones. Around the same time, cell phones began allowing video connections to other cell phones, making the ACN phone nearly obsolete at birth.

ACN became the center of two episodes of *The Apprentice*. "I think the ACN video phone is amazing," Trump said before one of the ACN episodes. "I simply can't imagine anybody using this phone and not loving it."

The company's revenues had grown in the 1990s to almost $500 million a year. But few of their reps made more than a few hundred dollars a year. Their income came mostly from taking a percentage of the $499 fee paid by new recruits. Many would say they bought into the program because they trusted Trump.

ACN had long combated allegations that it was a pyramid scheme. In the video Trump made for $1 million, he assured potential reps that the company was solid. "We do a lot of research on companies before we agree to do something like I am doing for you," Trump said. "And ACN is a great company."

It is unclear whether Trump's research included reading a seven-thousand-word article about ACN in *The New Yorker.* Published in 2001, the article described the plight of sales representatives struggling to make more money than they were spending to recruit new sales reps and attend ACN conventions. Everyone involved knew the prices they were offering for electricity and phone services were higher than competitors, but the reps were told to view people who raised such issues as "rotten apples" and to search out crisp red apples instead. More than power and phone lines, they were selling Opportunity, always spelled with a capital *O*.

Trump's income tax returns, which we later obtained, showed that he collected $8.8 million from the company, the last check coming the year he ran for president. At that point, after years of assuring potential recruits that he had thoroughly vetted the company, he demanded that ACN scrub his name from its website and promotional materials. And he developed amnesia about his research into the company.

"I do not know the company," he told *The Wall Street Journal*. "I know nothing about the company other than the people who run the company. I'm not familiar with what they do or how they go about doing that, and I make that clear in my speeches."

He performed another about-face when he was forced to testify under oath in a lawsuit filed by ACN sales reps. "I think it was George Ross, who worked for me," Trump testified. "I think he did research. He was a smart person, and he was just one of many people that liked it. They liked the company."

ANOTHER MULTILEVEL MARKETING COMPANY that joined the parade of suitors to Trump Tower sold vitamins and supplements. "We hit it off," Trump recalled in an interview about himself and the company's founders. "I checked into their past, and they were solid people. They had a nice track record, but even more importantly they had a lot of people who thought highly of them."

The company, Ideal Health, had been founded in 1997 by three veterans of other multilevel marketing businesses: Scott and Todd Stanwood, who are brothers, and Lou DeCaprio, all of Boston. The business focused on a multivitamin costing $69.95 a month and supposedly tailored for each buyer based on a urine test that cost $139.95. Follow-up urine tests sold for $99.95 every six months.

Looking into the company would have revealed that Ideal Health was barely staying afloat. The company's chief executive was so desperate for cash that he persuaded a credit card processing company to reduce the amount he was required to hold in reserve just to free up $400,000. Complaints against the company were piling up at the Federal Trade Commission. Representatives said they paid thousands of dollars for classes and materials with the promise of big paydays that never came.

Ideal Health was rebranded as Trump Network. Trump riled up a convention in Miami of people trying to convince their friends and relatives to buy vitamins and weight-loss supplements bearing his name. "When I did *The Apprentice*, it was a long shot," Trump told the crowd. "This is not a long shot."

It was not a long shot for Trump. The licensing deal paid him $2.6 million during the two years before Trump Network folded. The Stanwood brothers and DeCaprio filed for bankruptcy and a bank foreclosed on the 8,300-square-foot house they shared. With Trump's promotions, the network had grown from about five thousand reps to more than twenty thousand. But few of them accomplished more than lining Trump's pockets.

"They changed us to the Trump Network, so we thought we were his company, he was invested in us," Jenna Knudsen, once a high-ranking saleswoman with the company, told *The Washington Post*. "But we were just an endorsement. We were just paying to rent his name." She was not sure whether Trump was to blame for the collapse. "But he certainly did not do what he said. He did not support us. He did not make this company his baby company. And somewhere between [the owners] and Donald Trump, they devastated thousands of people. And no one ever apologized."

THE PARADE OF CHECK-BEARING suitors to Trump Tower continued, but Trump rarely put his own money into their enterprises. He made an exception when a man in his late thirties with an impressive business pedigree showed up. Michael Wang Sexton had graduated from Tufts University and earned an MBA from Dartmouth University's Tuck School of Business. He had worked for Andersen Consulting before launching a small firm with a couple of colleagues. Looking for new opportunities, he focused on online educational programs, and he thought television's newest business celebrity would be the vehicle to give him a leg up.

"It was my concept," Sexton later said. "The idea of attaching the Trump brand to it was very much inspired by *The Apprentice* show."

Sexton had never worked in education or in real estate. But he was able to get an appointment at Trump Tower. He pitched Trump on a licensing deal for use of his name and likeness to create a business selling Donald Trump's secrets to success. He did not have a printed business plan, but he told Trump that using his fame from the show would give the new company an immediate presence in the marketplace. They would sell recorded lectures to owners of small and midsize businesses.

That meeting lasted ten minutes. Trump embraced the concept and assigned an in-house lawyer to hash out the details with Sexton. The day they presented the terms to Trump, he changed direction and said he wanted to own the company. He agreed to provide Sexton with up to $3 million to get started in exchange for what became about 93 percent ownership. It would be called Trump University, though it would not be licensed as an institution of higher learning or issue degrees.

Sexton initially contracted with a few business professors from universities to prerecord lectures that could be viewed for a fee online. The lectures were priced at $300 each. Trump said that he would record some sessions himself. They sold printed material at Barnes & Noble bookstores. Trump and Sexton announced the venture in a press conference in the marbled lobby of Trump Tower. Trump said his goal was "to help a lot of people."

"I love the concept of starting what I think will be a great university," he said.

New York officials almost immediately notified Trump that calling his business a "university" required meeting specific standards and acquiring a state license. Trump ignored the directive for years to come.

Larry King once again invited Trump, as well as Sexton, to discuss the new venture on his show. "We teach people how to become rich," Sexton told King. "Whether it's investing successfully in real estate or starting or launching or growing a company. We teach people how to succeed."

"Michael is a fantastic guy," Trump said. "He knows more about education than just about anybody I've met. And I went to the Wharton School of Finance. I've seen great educators. I've had a great education. I'm a great believer in education. That's why I love doing this, and I love working with people like Michael."

Before too long, Sexton met with Allen Weisselberg, Trump's finance chief. Weisselberg grilled him about when the company would start making money. With Sexton collecting $250,000 a year and other expenses mounting, Trump's $3 million would not last long. Sexton suggested adding in-person seminars.

To make the shift, Sexton and Trump contracted with Mike and Irene Milin of Boca Raton, a married couple who had peddled get-rich-quick programs since the 1980s. The Milins had operated National Grants Conferences, live seminars during which they promised to reveal "hundreds of billions" of dollars in "free" government grants. They had been accused of fraud and deceptive marketing in numerous states, including settling allegations in Texas in 1993 and Florida in 2001. But the complaints continued.

The Milins began advertising "The Donald Trump Way to Wealth Seminar" in cities across the country, at prices of more than $1,000. Attendees were encouraged to spend even more on course materials and coaching. When Trump and Sexton saw the Milins opening the wallets of seminar attendees, they switched the business model of Trump University to live seminars. The two businesses became indistinguishable, sharing publications and promotional materials.

Thousands of "exclusive" seminar invitations were mailed to get people to show up. After a free ninety-minute teaser, the hopefuls would face a hard sell to buy additional packages ranging from $1,495 for a "Profit from Real Estate" workshop to $34,995 for the "Trump Elite Gold" program, with sessions on wealth preservation, how to incorporate a business, buying foreclosed properties, and investing in real estate investment trusts.

Marketing materials played off *The Apprentice*, with Trump asking, "Are you my next apprentice? Learn from the master." Trump sent the winners of *The Apprentice* on the road to promote his get-rich-quick seminars. Randal Pinkett, the season four winner, and Sean Yazbeck, the season five winner, appeared at seminars in Salt Lake City, Austin, New York City, Tampa Bay, and San Diego. They spoke with reporters in still more cities, including Memphis, Wichita, and Pasadena.

Trump did not appear at the seminars or review the printed or recorded material shown at them. He also did not meet the instructors, though promotional material said the teachers were "handpicked" by Trump. Sexton led the recruitment of new instructors, most of whom had a background in sales. Years later, the Associated Press would discover that more than thirty of Trump's experts on wealth had bankruptcies, credit card defaults, or other histories of financial problems. At least four of them had prior felony convictions, including the professor who was at the top of his class.

James Aubrey Harris had pled guilty to aggravated assault in Georgia in 2001. He was sentenced to sixty days in the Gwinnett County Jail and five years of probation. By 2008, Harris had become Trump University's top earning professor. He often opened his presentations saying that his father had left him and his siblings with their drug-abusing mother in New Jersey when he was young. At nineteen, he slept on the streets of New York City before meeting a man who taught him real estate.

At a seminar in Tampa that year, Harris bounded across the stage in a Tommy Bahama shirt to rile the crowd with a cheerleader's passion. He repeatedly asked the crowd how they were doing until the response reached a deafening volume. "Write this down," he said as his first bit of advice. "Your license plate, when I'm done with you, is gonna say 'PAID FOR.' Got that?"

Over the ninety minutes, his lesson stuck to the obvious. Start with small deals. Buy property in the name of a corporate entity. Borrow money. Hunt for foreclosures.

"Are you with me class?" he shouted. "Give me a big YES!"

Sweaty but still energetic, Harris implored the group to buy the $1,495 three-day seminar package, without telling them that if they did, they would be taken into a room and badgered to max out their credit cards to buy the Trump Elite Gold program for $34,995. He had several lines to separate the room into winners and losers, and to separate the winners from their money. At one point, he said the room was full of "gonna-bes and wanna-bes" and no one should want to be a wanna-be. "There are three groups of people," he said at another point. "People who make things happen; people who wait for things to happen; and people who wonder, 'What happened?' Which one are you?"

Harris had such success selling the packages that Sexton's team sent transcripts of his pitches to other instructors. In some years, he earned about $500,000 from Trump University. He bought expensive cars—a Range Rover and a Cadillac Escalade—and lived in a gated community outside Atlanta with his wife and two children.

John C. Brown succumbed to Harris in 2009. He made his way from his studio apartment in uptown Manhattan to a midtown Marriott Hotel because he thought Donald Trump would speak and help him learn about real estate. He committed to the $1,495 three-day program, led by Harris. Brown later recalled how Harris seemed "very motivational."

"He made me feel like if I did not buy the program, I would not succeed," Brown later recalled. "Mr. Harris said that we would be able to make our tuition money back after our first few real estate deals."

Brown could not afford the complete "Trump Gold Elite" for $34,995. So he used multiple credit cards to pay $24,995 for a three-day field mentorship program that did not include the classroom seminars. Internal records Trump University kept about students, which later emerged in litigation, showed that its employees realized that John Brown was digging himself a hole. "This student is maxing himself out and I did indicate to him that because of this he will not be able to qualify for traditional financing," one Trump University worker noted. Others mentioned that he had pulled money from his retirement accounts and the total cost would "spread him pretty thin."

His mentor was Steve Gilpin, whom Brown was told was "one of Trump's top mentors." He was allotted ten brief phone calls with Gilpin and a two-day tour of properties for sale in Philadelphia, at his own cost. Brown was not impressed. "Because the program was called a university, I expected live training in a classroom setting." After the tour finished, Trump University employees badgered him in repeated phone calls to give positive marks on an evaluation form. "I kept refusing, but after several calls I said that I no longer cared and that I just wanted them to stop calling me. Trump, then, as far as I know, changed my lower rating to higher ratings for Mr. Gilpin. But on a scale from one to ten, Trump Elite, for me, was a three or four. The information they provided was basic and mediocre." Brown asked for a refund, but he was rejected. Years later, he was still struggling with credit card bills.

His mentor, Gilpin, had been hired after he failed to make the cut in an audition to be a contestant on *The Apprentice*. Not long after, he received a call to meet with Sexton about joining Trump University. He had found himself sitting in an office at 40 Wall Street talking to Sexton and others about teaching people the Trump way in real estate. Gilpin didn't know Trump or the Trump way, and his experience in real estate was limited to a few years working as a mortgage broker. But he realized right away that while he had limited knowledge about the real estate business, everyone else in the room had less. They were not interviewing him so much as milking him for information. He was the expert.

Gilpin took the job, and soon came to regret it. He later wrote a memoir about his experiences. "From 2007 until 2010, it seemed the focus for Trump University was purely on separating suckers from their money," he wrote. He recalled sitting in on an interview with one prospective instructor and thinking that if they hired him, "We're all going to jail."

James Harris's years as Trump University's top instructor would be the peak of his life. He and his wife went through an acrimonious divorce in which she accused him of physical and psychological abuse. A judge granted a restraining order that included banning him from being close to his children's school. A few years later, reporters for the *Daily Mail* found him on a beach in Mexico posing for pictures as the "naked Caribbean cowboy" while trying to sell his expertise in how to get rich for a few hundred dollars. He wrote on a social media post that he could not return to the U.S. because the judge in his divorce case had issued a warrant for his arrest after he repeatedly failed to pay his wife's legal bills.

It seems the only person who did well with Trump University was Donald Trump. He pulled $5 million from the enterprise. But a growing storm of complaints and investigations in several states soon began to run up large legal costs.

DONALD TRUMP HAD WORKED for his father as a young man performing menial tasks on the Trump Village construction site and at an unglamorous apartment complex in Cincinnati. He saw enough of his father, even at that late stage in his career, to know that to Fred Trump, running a successful business meant precisely calculating expected revenue, zealously controlling costs, and never taking on more projects at one time than he could closely monitor.

Donald's children began working at Trump Tower at a time when running the business mostly meant flying to ceremonial ribbon cuttings for construction projects being built by someone else. Little work was required beyond sifting through the hundreds of licensing offers flowing through the door every month and making sure certain design thresholds would be met. Compared to Fred's bricks and concrete, this was a paint-and-pillows operation.

Trump's adult children occasionally branched out on their own, taking advantage of the massive free attention that every endeavor with the Trump name now attracted.

Don Jr. had become friendly with a mortgage broker named E. J. Ridings, who suggested starting a mortgage brokerage under the Trump name. He seemed like the right guy to Don. He said he had worked in the financial industry for fifteen years, including as a top executive at Morgan Stanley, and was currently a leader of a mortgage firm. Don took the idea and that information to his father, who signed off.

The news conference to launch Trump Mortgage drew more attention than any new mortgage brokerage could reasonably expect. The lobby at Trump Tower filled with entertainment reporters, business reporters, and photographers. Jennifer McGovern, who worked for the new company, only saw flashing cameras and reporters. She looked out across the crowd and thought, "Where are our clients? Where are the people we're trying to woo? All I see are photographers."

"The brand has never been stronger," Trump told *The Wall Street Journal.* "This was just a good time to utilize the name and have a really good mortgage company."

Don Jr. could not have been more pleased. "This one's really my baby," he told *Forbes.*

Eight months after the official launch, *Money* magazine reported that Ridings's background was not what he had told Don Jr. and what the Trumps had told the world. Ridings had worked in the nutritional supplement business and was the owner of a cleaning service. He had worked at Morgan Stanley's stock brokerage subsidiary Dean Witter Reynolds for less than three months. When he befriended Don Jr., he had only recently entered the mortgage business.

Don Jr.'s baby was shut down before it learned to walk. His father expressed a lack of disappointment at the failure of what he dismissed as only a licensing deal. "The mortgage business is not a business I particularly liked or wanted to be part of in a very big way," he told a reporter.

After she joined the regular cast of *The Apprentice*, Ivanka entered into her own licensing deals for jewelry and other products. She also chose an endorsement deal that looked to the outside world like a charitable act. She appeared at a launch event to help raise money for the nonprofit Cookies for Kids' Cancer in the lobby of Trump Tower and made herself available for a few media interviews. During one interview, Ivanka said she was very excited when the Glad Products Company, known for its plastic wrap, and the nonprofit Cookies for Kids' Cancer approached her.

"Obviously it's the holidays," she continued. "Everyone should try to philanthropically give back what they can around the holidays. But most importantly, they're raising money for pediatric cancer research. And, you know, this is something that resonates with everyone. But especially as a new mom, I thank God every day for having a healthy little girl."

There was not much of a hint in her comments that Ivanka was being handsomely paid for her endorsement, a point that we found fifteen years later buried in an unrelated court filing. Glad paid her $285,000 for a few hours of appearances and media interviews spread over four days, plus $4,500 for hair and makeup. She did use the power of her new fame to draw attention to the charity.

THE BOOM FROM LICENSING and endorsements, in tandem with a rush of cash from *The Apprentice*, immediately improved Trump's finances more than any business he had created himself.

He had made almost nothing from licensing or endorsements before *The Apprentice* launched in 2004—a net of $46,000 in 2003. Then came $3.3 million in 2004; $6.2 million in 2005; $12.7 million in 2006; $15.5 million in 2007; $16.6 million in 2008; $18.5 million in 2009; and $30.6 million in 2010. That's a total of $103.2 million in pure profit over seven years. And that windfall arrived in addition to $135.2 million during the same period as his share from the television show. The cash would allow Trump to buy more businesses and paper over failures at others he already ran.

But the way he had managed his licensing business all but ensured that the river of cash would slow and the value of his name to other businesses would shrivel.

Forty of the real estate licensing deals Trump announced were never completed. Trump would testify in some lawsuits that he correctly represented himself as a partner in some of those failures because he was to receive a percentage of sales. But he knew the difference between being a partner and leasing his name, the primary one being the risk of losing money. Following the norms of celebrity licensing and endorsement, Trump would be paid handsomely regardless of the outcome.

In Tampa, the developers discovered in August 2006 that their site next to the river could not support a fifty-two-story tower without expensive supports. The development team Trump had publicly endorsed had no background with such difficulties. Unable to secure financing through traditional channels, the Tampa developers tried to borrow money from a convicted fraudster whose access to cash, it turned out, came from payroll companies through which he withheld taxes from checks but did not immediately turn over to the government. At a criminal trial later, his defense included testimony he suffered from a mental illness that caused delusions. The Tampa crew tried again, paying $150,000 to the "very Reverend Father Barney" of South Bend, Indiana, in the hopes of securing a $200 million loan from the faith-based lender that he ran.

The not-so-very reverend turned out to be Barney Canada, an ex-con who had served time in another loan scheme.

After collecting $2 million from the developers before they ran out of money, Trump sued them in 2007 for the next $2 million, revealing the existence of the licensing deal he had insisted be kept secret. Apartment buyers sued to get their deposits back. Then the buyers sued Trump. The project had died in 2007, but in a pretrial deposition, Trump blamed the 2008 financial crisis. He said that by his calculus the buyers who made nonrefundable deposits believing in him should consider themselves lucky because they would have been worse off if the building had been completed and the condos had fallen in value.

A similar pattern played out in numerous Trump licensing deals.

Trump described a project in Fort Lauderdale as "my latest development" in marketing material. The project died, leaving buyers without their deposits. Alex Davis, one buyer in the failed building, told *The New York Times* that he bought in because he believed Trump would make sure it worked out: "The last thing you ever expect is that somebody you revere will mislead you."

A planned beach resort in the Dominican Republic, Trump at Cap Cana, shows more than any other how detached Trump's licensing income had become from business success. A press release said Trump had signed a "partnership agreement."

"I am excited to be building Trump at Cap Cana for several reasons," the announcement quoted Trump as saying. "We look forward to developing thousands of spectacular acres into an elite destination that will be known worldwide in the years to come. I look forward to visiting often with my family."

Trump and Ivanka and Eric all traveled to Cap Cana for a large sales event, posing for pictures with the actual developers and stirring the crowd. Adding to the buzz, the project had been featured on the season six finale of *The Apprentice* as one of two choices for the winner to pick to work with Trump. (The other choice, a planned tower in Atlanta, was also a licensing deal that never happened.) Eric and Ivanka greeted buyers at a tropical restaurant with tables of gourmet food and champagne. The Trumps helped sell $300 million worth of lots that day. Construction never began. Buyers lost most of their money. The tax returns that we later obtained would show that Trump went on to collect $15.9 million on the project.

Licensing and endorsements monetized the traits that set Trump apart during his lifetime, especially the singular innate charisma that enabled him to draw attention to himself and his endeavors, real or imagined. *The Apprentice* amplified that gift, transmitting a cleaned-up version of Donald Trump into living rooms across the country.

Trump played it all for the short term, risking the reputational damage that could wreck the value of his name to other businesses. He faced waves of lawsuits. Years later, he would pay $25 million to settle lawsuits over Trump University. But the short-term gain brought him a second lucky stroke in a very lucky life, a rush of cash matched only by the money he inherited from his father.

31

REAL ESTATE

When NBC announced its fall lineup in May 2007, *The Apprentice* was nowhere to be found. Ratings had tumbled as the format grew stale, and the network had quietly decided to cancel the show. Before network executives made a formal announcement, Trump beat them to the punch, announcing he would leave the show to launch a "major new TV venture."

A few days later, Trump—along with Ivanka, Don Jr., and Eric—held a press conference in front of their Chicago tower, still under construction six years after Trump announced the project. They celebrated partial completion of the exterior work and made clear they were still trying to sell units. One reporter asked why sales had slowed in recent months. But questions from reporters quickly turned to the show.

"NBC wants very much for me to do *The Apprentice*," Trump answered. "It's been an amazing experience for me, but it's very hard. I'm building this job, and we've got jobs—with Ivanka, Don, Eric—we've got jobs all over the world that are going up. It's very, very hard for me to find the time to do another season of *The Apprentice*, as much as I love doing it, and as much as I love the show, and as much as I love NBC."

At about that time, Ben Silverman, a producer behind the hit shows *Ugly Betty*, *The Office*, and *The Biggest Loser*, took over the NBC division responsible for *The Apprentice*. Silverman learned the show had been canceled, but he also knew that he had adopted a looming problem: a writer's strike only months away. He wanted a guarantee of fresh shows even if all his scripted shows went dark.

A celebrity version of *The Apprentice* in England had done well months earlier.

That seemed like an easy option to Silverman. Other network executives warned him that Trump would not accept being overshadowed by bigger celebrities. Silverman called Mark Burnett, who accepted the idea, but also said he expected Trump to balk. Silverman felt he knew how to win Trump over, so he called.

"All I know is there's more in *The Apprentice*," he later recalled saying, "but I want to make it about celebrity."

"Really?" Trump said.

"Because you, Donald, are the biggest celebrity in the world," Silverman told his star. "And you will be the decision-maker of the other celebrities."

"You're right!" Trump responded.

With that, the show abandoned any pretense of a job interview to join Trump's company for a year and learn business from a master. The celebrity contestants would compete for a donation to a charity of their choice. The new version would frequently devolve into embarrassing train wrecks between washed-up stars and long-retired athletes. NBC insiders began calling the show *Celebrity Screaming*. Well past their prime, most contestants desperately needed, or wanted, the exposure of appearing on a prime-time show. "They were playing for fame," Silverman later recalled.

Most importantly for Trump, the television show would remain the engine that fueled his licensing and endorsement deals, by far his largest source of income and still growing at that point. The Trump family controlled and owned two ongoing construction projects—the Chicago tower and a new golf course in Scotland—and half of a third, a hotel in Las Vegas. All were costing Trump millions a year. And the public casino company bearing his name, of which Trump remained chairman of the board, looked to be hurtling toward yet another bankruptcy.

But it was Chicago, a ninety-two-story tower with debts approaching $770 million, that posed the greatest threat to Trump's finances, greater than any risk he had faced in decades.

In 2003, when Trump unveiled his design for a tower on the site of the Chicago Sun-Times Building, he said it would be finished in 2007. He began taking deposits for units in late 2003, before he tore down the Sun-Times Building. *The Apprentice* debuted in January 2004, and as Trump's notoriety rose with the show's ratings, he announced that he had contracts to sell three quarters of the condominiums in the planned building for a total of $515 million.

With those contracts in hand, Trump secured two loans. Fortress Investment Group LLC, a hedge fund and private equity company based in New York, agreed to lend him $130 million to finance the purchase of the Sun-Times Building and the cost of razing it. And Deutsche Bank, a German bank that was one of the few willing to do business with Trump, agreed to lend him another $640 million.

In part because of Trump's past performances with lenders, the money would not come cheap. Deutsche Bank's real estate lending division got over its qualms by requiring Trump to personally guarantee $40 million of the total, meaning he would be on the hook to pay that amount even if he never finished the building or sales fell short. The bank also vetted Trump's list of buyers who had made deposits to make sure they were real and could close the sale when their unit was finished. Deutsche bankers reviewed Trump's income tax returns and were shocked by what they saw. "The vast majority of his income was from NBC for *The Apprentice*," one person familiar with the process later recalled.

For taking those measures, Deutsche kept $13 million of the loan total in fees, according to a bank executive familiar with the loan.

For its part, Fortress extracted a very high interest rate—one person involved said the rate was at least 12 percent—and a required $49 million "exit fee" at the end of the loan. Both lenders then sold off parts of the debt to other banks and investment firms, spreading both the risk and the reward.

Trump fell behind his 2007 completion schedule with dreadful consequences. His budget increased, in part because he decided to shrink the spa to add more hotel condominiums. He filled that hole with $65.1 million of his own money.

He planned to stagger the opening and sales of the condominium units so he would have enough money to pay down the construction loan before it came due in May 2008. But contracts for sales never budged much past the 75 percent he announced in 2004, and some buyers who had signed contracts years earlier did not close when the units were finished.

In addition to the traditional retail space and residential condominiums, there would also be 339 hotel condominiums, a newer concept. The hotel condominium buyers could stay in their units for part of the year and let the units be operated as a hotel room by Trump for the rest of the year. The hotel condominiums did not sell well. Trump said publicly that he did not mind owning more than one hundred of them, because he wanted the profits from the hotel operation. But even assuming the rooms would be full enough, and at high enough rates, to turn a profit, that money would arrive in small amounts over many years compared to the rush of hundreds of millions of dollars from selling units. Not much help with his loan deadline fast approaching.

Trump backed out of two promises he had made to increase money coming to him. He canceled most of the reduced-rate sales contracts he had signed with "friends and family." And he withdrew a commitment to give the hotel condo owners a share of the proceeds from rentals of meeting rooms and ballrooms. One person familiar with Trump's views at the time said he was "pissed off about the fact that the sales of the hotel condos had stalled."

Then, in March 2008, a rating service downgraded mortgage-backed securities held by Bear Stearns, accelerating the worst financial crisis in the U.S. since the Great Depression. Banks drastically slowed down issuing loans.

Trump had not generated sufficient sales to pay off his construction loans by the May deadline, and his chances of finding another bank willing to lend him hundreds of millions of dollars to refinance those loans had vanished.

EVEN IN THE CRISIS, Trump and his three grown children only came to Chicago once every few months. They would typically schedule their visits around an interim step in construction. The people working at the site every day for outside contractors and others divided people on the job into workhorses and show horses. All four Trumps were seen as show horses. "Donald and Eric and Don and Ivanka—that was all just bullshit," one professional involved in the project later recalled. "Whenever they were in a meeting you sort of nod your head and smile and then they leave, and then you start getting the work done."

Trump was busy filming back-to-back seasons of *The Celebrity Apprentice*, making paid speeches and appearances at ribbon cuttings for licensing deals, periodically flying to Scotland to deal with problems getting his golf course there approved, and occasionally focusing on the plummeting performance of the Atlantic City casinos bearing his name.

At the end of April, Trump held another event to mark the opening of the hotel portion of the Chicago building with a ribbon-cutting ceremony. He was asked about the growing financial crisis. He said that his project had benefited from "old financing" received long before the crisis and encouraged people to buy now.

"This is a great time for people to start buying, looking at buying, and buying," Trump said. "This is the time, because all of a sudden they're going to wake up and they'll see prices have gone up twenty-five, thirty percent. Then they're going to say, 'Ohhhh.' No different than a stock. They're going to say, 'I missed our opportunity.' So, this is an amazing time to buy, throughout certain parts of the country, but in particular in Chicago."

He mentioned that he had sold "hundreds of millions of dollars" worth of units and then levied his forecast for real estate prices. "I think the market is now going to start going up."

Following Trump's advice that day would have been a costly mistake. Housing prices nationally would continue to fall for almost three more years, and the recovery in Illinois would lag the national market for at least seven years beyond that.

Trump's "old financing" would not save him. Two days later, Trump's team talked through the project's status with his lenders again in a conference call. Deutsche Bank's printed agenda for that discussion, which we later obtained, showed that the project's cost had ballooned to $858.9 million. Trump's loans totaled a maximum of $770 million, and he had committed to putting in $88.9 million of his own cash, most of which had been spent. Trump expected closings on some residential units under contract to take place between July and October 2008, and the rest during the first half of 2009, long past the due date on the loans. So far, 63 percent of units were in contract or had closed, for total expected proceeds of $564 million.

Trump asked for a six-month extension on the loan. Deutsche Bank noted in its presentation that "the Trump name instantly drives attention in every major electronic and print medium" and "the Trump family holds celebrity cachet which further promotes interest for the brand." In short, Trump argued that his family's status as television celebrities would drive up sales prices.

His lenders granted the extension.

Over the summer, dozens of the buyers who had bought their units early at lower prices put them up for sale at costs as much as 30 percent below what Trump was asking for his unsold units. That flood of cheaper units further slowed Trump's sales and put downward pressure on his asking prices. And then the financial crisis worsened with the bankruptcy of Lehman Brothers.

On September 24, the Trump team met in the new Grand Ballroom of the Chicago tower with twelve of its lenders to request another six-month extension past the current November 7 deadline. The presentation packet given to lenders showed there had been no new sales. Since May, eleven hotel unit buyers and thirty-three residential buyers backed out of their contracts before closing. Sales on the residential condos could not close until the units were completed, which was not going to happen until 2009. The retail space would not help before the November deadline, but it might if the deadline was extended. Eric Trump told the lenders that the first retail spaces should be completed by the end of the year, and the commercial real estate firm of CBRE had been hired to lease out the spaces and explore the possibility of Trump selling the entire 83,000 square feet of retail space.

In exchange for another extension, Trump offered to pay millions of dollars in additional interest and one-time fees. That offer began weeks of meetings to hash out terms. By the Friday before the November deadline, Deutsche bankers believed they had reached an agreement with Trump on the terms for another extension.

Trump, though, wanted to find a way out of the loans altogether. As the condos had sold, he had paid down the Deutsche loan to about $334 million. During a brainstorming session, one of his lawyers suggested finding a way to exercise the force majeure clause in the mortgage, which allowed exceptions in the case of a natural disaster that could not be anticipated. One of Trump's lawyers, Steve Schlesinger, mentioned that Alan Greenspan, chairman of the Federal Reserve, recently called the financial crisis a "credit tsunami," which seemed to fit the definition of a natural disaster.

Schlesinger mentioned the idea to Trump.

"It's worth a shot," Schlesinger remembered Trump saying. Schlesinger also remembered Jason Greenblatt, Trump's in-house lawyer, seeming to think he was "full of shit" for suggesting such a thing. But papers were drawn up and served on Deutsche Bank the following Tuesday, the day after the loan had come due.

Deutsche executives who thought they had reached terms for Trump to extend the loan were shocked to find "a bunch of shit signed by Donald" waiting for them at the office, one banker recalled. "People were pissed," the banker said. "You had a faction there, understandably, who were like, 'I told you this was going to happen.'"

Deutsche Bank countersued to force Trump to pay the $40 million that he had personally guaranteed, and Fortress sued as well. Trump kept selling condos. The lenders worried that Trump might pull his name off the building and walk away, leaving them owning a building they did not want without the Trump name to attract condominium buyers.

The cases were settled in July 2010. The terms were confidential. But we later learned that Fortress settled for $48 million, which Trump paid in 2012, and Deutsche Bank agreed to take just $99 million. Trump got out of repaying $286 million that he had received from lenders and spent on the building.

Trump still owed $99 million to Deutsche, and the bank had vowed not to do business with him again. His son-in-law, Jared Kushner, made an introduction that served as a lifeline.

Deutsche Bank, which did not have a major presence in the U.S., was building a division to lend to high-net-worth individuals. Kushner knew the head of that division, Rosemary Vrablic, through his father's real estate business and introduced Vrablic to Trump.

Vrablic's division soon made two loans to Trump, personally guaranteed by him, for $99 million so he could pay off another division of Deutsche Bank that would no longer lend to him.

To issue the loan, the bank required Trump to maintain a net worth of at least $2.5 billion and cash on hand of at least $50 million, and to submit to an annual review to ensure he still met those thresholds. The bank's first analysis of the figures Trump provided showed the potential for trouble ahead. The analysis estimated that Trump's entire operation generated $13.4 million in extra cash during the first six months of 2012. That total included $19.8 million from his television show, and $32.4 million from licensing deals, meaning that without that $52.2 million, his core businesses would put him deep in the red. He would need his income from television and a constant flow of new licensing deals—the payments from which were typically front-loaded—to keep the lights on.

By then, Trump had secretly made an audacious claim on his tax returns. For the year 2008, he declared to the IRS that his investment in the Chicago tower was worthless. His tax return showed total losses from businesses he ran of $678,005,977. Trump's accountants used that stunning figure to eliminate Trump's entire tax bill that year. He paid no federal income taxes during a year in which he collected $14.8 million from *The Apprentice* and $18.5 million from celebrity endorsements and licensing deals.

When we, working with Paul Kiel of *ProPublica*, discovered Trump's remarkable savings from the worthlessness deduction fifteen years later, tax experts we consulted were shocked that the IRS had not audited the claim, especially because a large chunk of the money seemed to be based on borrowed money. But Trump went a step further.

Trump had, in essence, taken a total loss on the project before ever knowing how the numbers would ultimately work out, and he still was able to keep the portion of the tower he had not yet sold. He and his tax advisers, though, executed a maneuver to claim that he, in essence, lost the same money again. Trump merged the partnership through which he owned the tower into another partnership, then used that new structure as a fig leaf to declare another $168 million in losses on the tower over the next decade. It was if he had shifted his coins from one pocket to the other, and the IRS eventually caught on.

The resulting audit remained active through at least 2022, and an adverse outcome could cost Trump more than $100 million in additional taxes, plus interest and possible penalties.

The massive retail space in the Chicago tower remained empty, and Trump continued to lose money on the property. After declaring it worthless on his 2008 tax returns, Trump's accountant removed the Chicago tower from his annual "statements of financial condition" to avoid a discrepancy. Trump provided those statements to banks and reporters to demonstrate his wealth. In Trump's telling, it was as if the largest building he ever constructed never existed.

In Atlantic City, analysts noted that the crippling debt he had loaded on the company years ago had left nothing to renovate the casinos and hotels, or even keep them looking fresh. His longtime investment bankers at Donaldson, Lufkin & Jenrette had noted the same. In a court filing, the firm noted: "The Trump name does not connote high-quality amenities and first-class service in the casino industry . . . Rather, the Trump name is associated with the failure to pay one's debts, a company that has lost money every year, and properties in need of significant deferred maintenance and lagging behind their competitors."

Randal Pinkett, the winner of season four of *The Apprentice*, showed up not long after to work on what Trump had billed as major renovation of the casinos. Trump then directed him to spend much of his yearlong apprenticeship appearing at press conferences and Trump University events, using his fame from the show to draw attention to Trump's latest licensing deals. What time he spent with the casinos gave him a window into the world of businesses that Donald Trump controlled and ran.

Pinkett, who had earned master's degrees in business and electrical engineering from MIT, recognized right away that the $110 million budget would not go far enough. Everything in the three large casinos looked like the 1970s to Pinkett. Purple carpeting. Gold all over the walls. "It was just a retro throwback," he later recalled. When the renovations were complete, the effect remained incomplete. "You see shades of modernity over there, and I look over here and I still see shades of 1970."

Trump dispatched Pinkett to serve as an ambassador in Philadelphia, where his casino operation had pinned its hopes for the future on winning community approval for a new casino in a predominantly African American neighborhood. Pinkett, who is Black, attended a few community meetings and heard nothing but opposition, mostly because of the perception that Trump's casinos in Atlantic City had not been good for residents there. One night, the Trump team was booed off the stage and left dejected. On the drive back to Atlantic City, Pinkett sensed that Trump's executives realized the company could not survive without that project.

In early 2009, as Trump casinos lurched toward bankruptcy for the fourth time, Trump was still trying to hang on to control of the company. At loggerheads with board members who had been selected by bondholders after the 2004 bankruptcy, he offered to buy all or a part of the casino company bearing his name. He was rebuffed.

Trump announced in February 2009 that he was quitting the board of directors. "If I'm not going to run it, I don't want to be involved in it," he told the Associated Press. "I'm one of the largest developers in the world. I have a lot of cash and plenty of places I can go."

As a result of the bankruptcy, Trump would lose the $2 million a year he had been receiving under a services agreement with the casino company. But his tax lawyers had a plan to make his failure even more lucrative.

The same day Trump quit the casino company board, he notified the board, and then the Securities and Exchange Commission, that he had "determined that his partnership interests are worthless and lack potential to regain value" and was "hereby abandoning" his stake. The language was crucial—the precise wording of IRS rules governing the most beneficial, and perhaps aggressive, method for business owners to avoid taxes when separating from a business.

A partner who walks away from a business with nothing can declare all the losses on the business that he could not use in prior years—known as suspended losses—to wipe away tax liability on income from other sources. The partner can then request a refund of previously paid income taxes. Prior to 2009, that refund request could only go back two years. But that November, the window was more than doubled by a little-noticed provision in a bill that President Barack Obama signed as part of the Great Recession recovery effort. Now business owners could request full refunds of taxes paid in the prior four years, and 50 percent of those from the year before that.

For 2009, Trump declared what appear to be suspended losses of $777.2 million. The recession recovery bill allowed him to use those losses to request a refund of every dime in federal income taxes he had paid on the rush of cash from *The Apprentice* and related licensing deals for 2005 through 2007—a total of $70.1 million, plus $2,733,184 in interest. Following its usual procedures, the IRS issued those refunds and began an audit after the fact of its appropriateness. Trump also received $21.2 million in state and local refunds, which often piggyback on federal filings.

It was the second year in a row that Trump declared losses exceeding $700 million, a combined total of more than $1.5 billion. In the years ahead, he would use the remaining balances of those losses to wipe away income taxes on future profits, almost entirely from *The Apprentice* and licensing deals.

Thanks to his tax lawyers and accountants, and an assist from President Obama, Trump had essentially collected more than $90 million for failing. The IRS audit would remain open for years to come, posing a potential threat if the final decision went against him. But for the foreseeable future, the cash was his.

Years later, Michael D. Cohen, one of Trump's lawyers from that era, recalled Trump beaming with delight at a massive refund check he had just received from the IRS and saying, "He could not believe how stupid the government was for giving someone like him that much money back."

In 2016, when we asked Trump about his three decades of failure in Atlantic City ending with being pushed out of the company bearing his name, he said the timing worked out well for him because things went further downhill from there.

"Sometimes you're better off lucky than good," he said.

In June 2008, Trump's 727 landed on the Isle of Lewis, part of the Outer Hebrides archipelago off the western coast of mainland Scotland. His mother had grown up there, in the village of Tong, before she left for America at age eighteen. Trump made his way to an airport building where several second cousins still living in the area waited to meet him. At this homecoming of a sort, the cousins handed him babies, and he handed them autographed copies of his latest books on how to get rich.

After a brief exchange with his cousins, Trump's motorcade proceeded to his mother's childhood home. His sister, Maryanne, accompanied him. She had visited the island and their relatives there twenty-four times over the years. Donald had been once, when his mother brought him as a toddler. One reporter asked whether the visit was designed to help him finally win approval to build a golf course on land he had bought two years earlier. Trump insisted it was not. He just had been so busy "building jobs all over the world."

"You reach a certain point in life where you like to think [about] where you came from, where your parents are from," Trump said.

Trump said he selected Scotland for a golf course because his mother was "Scotch," a term Scots use to describe their whiskey and pie, but not so much themselves. "If it weren't for my mother, would I have walked away from the site?" he asked rhetorically. "I think I probably would have, yes. The reason I got involved was because of the feeling I have for Scotland."

He stayed inside his ancestral home for not quite two minutes, according to a local paper, before returning to the airport for a quick flight to mainland Scotland for the latest hearing on his proposal to build a golf course near the town of Aberdeen, on Scotland's northeastern coast.

He had made the decision to buy the eighty acres in a snap. Two men, Neil Hobday, who worked as a project manager building golf courses, and Ashley Cooper, who ran Trump's golf course in Bedminster, New Jersey, both remember him saying "buy it" after they independently described the land and its potential as a world-class links-style golf course. Trump paid $12.6 million cash for Menie Estate in March 2006.

Trump had for years been trying in vain to create a course that would attract major professional tournaments and hoped this would be the place. "His number one, two, and three goal was those major championships," Cooper later recalled.

He had spent no time pondering the possibility that locals might put up a fight. He publicly said they would bend to his will, or he would build his course in another part of Europe. "This development will either happen very quickly or not at all," he said at the time. "I never like to get disappointed. I'm going to get a course in Europe, but I would prefer to build in Scotland because of my mother."

When he heard about a plan to build electricity-generating windmills off the coast, he fired the opening salvo in what would become his forever war on windmills. "I would have no interest in proceeding," he said. "If they were to ruin Aberdeenshire and Aberdeen with that, then I would walk away. We would sell the site and go elsewhere."

As it would turn out, Trump would not win approval quickly. The windmills would be installed. And Trump would continue to push his case for years, in the process making a local dairy farmer into a folk hero.

Trump pushed Hobday to buy the adjoining properties from the families who lived on them, including Michael Forbes, who owned twenty acres near what was to become the fairway of Trump's first hole. Goats wandered his grassy pasture. Ramshackle sheds and rusted farm equipment surrounded his small home. His mother, Molly, lived in a separate house on the land. They had been there for nearly four decades and rebuffed Hobday's offers.

Frustrated, Trump pushed the local Aberdeenshire council to take some of the properties against the will of the owners through a process known as a compulsory purchase order. As much as Trump professed his great feeling for Scotland and its people, his aggression sparked the formation of a group that called itself "Tripping Up Trump." Forbes eventually sold an acre of his land to the group as part of its effort to undermine any attempt by the local government to take the properties.

Over the years of their standoff, Trump referred to Forbes as a "village idiot" and suggested he knew enough about "Scotch" people to question Forbes's background. "His property is a pigsty. It's terrible. His barn is all rotted and rusted and falling down. I mean, it's terrible," Trump said at one point. "My mother was born in Stornoway, and she was so meticulous. And if I dropped a little piece of paper on the floor as a baby she said: 'pick up that paper.' She was the most clean woman I've ever seen. She was immaculate. The people of Scotland are that way.

"I don't know where he comes from," Trump continued. "Maybe his heritage is from somewhere other than Scotland."

Forbes repeatedly said he did not want money. He wanted his home and to be left alone. He offered a succinct message to Trump: "Go back to hell, where you came from."

Their battle became the subject of a documentary film, which gained attention when Brian May, the guitarist for the band Queen, gave the filmmaker permission to use "Bohemian Rhapsody" in the soundtrack. The rock classic includes the line:

He's just a poor boy from a poor family,
Spare him his life from this monstrosity

Environmental concerns raised another obstacle for Trump. The dunes on the land had received Scotland's most sensitive environmental designation. The constantly shifting mounds of sand and earth, blown by the persistent North Sea winds and pushed by its tides, are seen as living things by scientists. Block them in on one side and they begin a slow death. They were also home to seven species of endangered rare birds.

At a hearing in late 2007, a local council found the risk to the dunes to be too great. Trump had spent time over the prior two years entertaining Jack McConnell and Alex Salmond, successive first ministers of Scotland with the power to overrule the local council. Both officials believed the project would be a win for Scotland. Trump next took his case to them.

At the June 2008 hearing, Trump remained defiant. "If you reject this, there will be a terrible blow to Scotland," he told the officials. Snickers emerged from the audience when Trump said he knew more about the environment than his consultants. "I would consider myself an environmentalist in the true sense of the word," he said.

Martin Ford, a local legislator who had voted against the plan the year before, blamed Trump for creating his own problems by not performing due diligence on the site before opening his wallet. "You have little understanding of the property you bought or the environmental status of it," Ford said.

That failure, the tendency toward snap decisions, the belief that local officials would bend to his will, had frustrated Trump's development goals for decades. At Indian Hills, French Hill, and Seven Springs in Westchester County, New York. At Mar-a-Lago in Florida. At the old West Side rail yards in Manhattan. It was the same pattern of practice that led him to put his name to dozens of licensing projects that failed, many of which landed him in court. But as he sat there being criticized, Trump expressed confidence that he had never made a misstep.

"You know, nobody has ever told me before I don't know how to buy property," he said. "You're the first one. I have done very well buying property. Thanks for the advice."

The panel eventually approved Trump's proposal, but added the requirements that he build a school, shops, and low-cost housing on land provided by the government. Salmond, one of the officials who had been criticized for seeming too close to Trump, said the potential impact to the local economy was too large to reject the plan. "Six thousand jobs, including 1,400 which will be local and permanent, is a powerful argument," he said.

It would be two more years before Trump met every requirement to begin construction, and two more after that before he opened one golf course. For the foreseeable future, there would be no second course, no vacation homes, and no large hotel. Trump converted an old castle on the property into a small hotel and restaurant and would employ fewer than a hundred people there.

Hobday marveled at Trump's endless energy, especially on his trips to Scotland, when he seemed to move and talk around the clock. "He could say some crazy things, but he is a workaholic," Hobday later recalled. He caught a different glimpse of Trump's complicated life on one trip to New York during those years. One day in the office at Trump Tower, Trump introduced him to a tall buxomly woman with blond hair. After she left, Trump showed Hobday playing cards with nude images of the woman and said she had pitched him on creating a pornographic evangelical television show. Hobday was bewildered. He only later realized the woman was Stormy Daniels, the adult film actress with whom Trump has denied having an affair. Daniels told us that she recalled the meeting. She did not recall talking about a church-porno television show and assumed that if she did it was in jest.

When Trump announced his plans for Aberdeen, he gave voice to the *Field of Dreams* business philosophy that for three decades had guided his decisions, justifying any expense to build to his personal tastes. "In my history, if I build something, then people come," Trump said.

He built it; they did not come. Trump has said he spent $60 million on Aberdeen "out of my back pocket." There have been no major golf tournaments there. The course regularly offers discounted rounds. Trump's tax returns, which we later obtained, show that he pumps an average of $6 million a year into the course to cover operating losses.

DURING ONE OF THE CEREMONIAL events at the Chicago tower, Trump answered a question that no one had asked. "I know how to build," he said. "What I really know how to do is build. Somebody said, 'Oh, you know how to sell.' I said, 'I don't know how to sell. I know how to build.'"

He ran through a few achievements and ended with this: "I just built a city along the West Side of Manhattan. I know how to build."

In some ways, it harkened back to a concern his father had expressed that people might refer to him as "a promoter" instead of his chosen identity as "a builder." Like so many phrases that flow from Donald Trump, the claim he made to support his contention that he was a builder, not a salesman, flew by without anyone seeming to realize that it was not true. On the West Side, he had been mostly a salesman, not a builder.

As the businesses he ran floundered after 2010, having given away control of the West Side under duress turned out to be one of the luckiest strokes in Donald Trump's lucky life.

In 2005, the Hong Kong investors sold the project, known variously as Riverside South and Trump Place, to the Extell Development Company and the Carlyle Group for $1.76 billion. Because of the agreement Trump had signed years ago, they did not need his permission.

Trump sued the Hong Kong partners, contending they had wrongly sold the project without consulting him and that the sale price should have been closer to $3 billion. He charged they had sold at a low price because they were using "their control over the disposition of Trump Place to extract kickbacks and other compensation." He offered no proof of that allegation.

The Hong Kong team then used the proceeds from the sale to buy two large office towers, 1290 Avenue of the Americas in Manhattan and 555 California Street in San Francisco, for $1.76 billion. The deal was orchestrated with a complex tax strategy, known as a 1031 exchange, to avoid paying taxes on the gain from the West Side project.

Trump went to court again seeking to scuttle the deal, and a judge again ruled against him.

The following year, the Hong Kong partners sold their 70 percent share in the two buildings to Vornado Realty Trust. Once again, Trump was just along for the ride. He had no voice in the sale, and he was now a minority partner to Vornado in the two buildings. Vornado was headed by Steven Roth, a contemporary of Trump's who had founded and built his company into one of the largest of its kind. Whether Trump ever received a dime more from the project, even if it was hugely profitable, would be entirely at the discretion of Roth's company.

Trump sued a third time to block the sales. To his great fortune, that lawsuit was also dismissed.

In 2012, Roth refinanced the San Francisco building. After paying off the old mortgage, Roth had $522 million left over. Refinancing is one of the most splendid aspects of real estate ownership. As far as tax laws are concerned, the proceeds are not taxable as profit or income, because the money must be paid back. In reality, it will almost certainly someday be rolled into another mortgage or building. So most developers treat that money as tax-free income.

Though he was under no obligation to do so, Roth passed along more than $100 million of that cash to Trump. Despite Trump's efforts, much of his losses on businesses he ran would be covered by a windfall from a business that was not subject to his judgment.

Similarly, thanks to the reinvention of *The Apprentice* as *The Celebrity Apprentice*, the show's ratings and the licensing deals from Trump's fame had risen again. For appearing on the show and letting other businesses use his name and promotional abilities, Trump received a total, after nominal expenses, of $51.3 million in 2011 and $37.5 million in 2012. That came on top of his $100 million-plus distribution from Vornado. But thanks to his losses on businesses he ran, he paid no federal income tax in either year.

By then, after decades of appearing on national television and being asked his opinion as a successful businessman on international affairs, he had interjected himself into the 2012 presidential campaign. He appeared frequently on television, especially Fox News, to accuse President Obama of not releasing his full birth certificate to hide that he had been born in another country, making him ineligible to be president. Trump never offered a glimmer of evidence, but his accusations and prominence made him the father of what became known as the birther movement.

In April 2011, Obama called his bluff and released his long form birth certificate. They appeared face-to-face at the White House Correspondents' Dinner. Obama took wry aim at Trump. He joked that Trump was pleased because now he could focus on issues that matter, such as whether the moon landing had been fake. He mock-complimented Trump for his "credentials and breadth of experience" and cited a recent episode of *The Celebrity Apprentice* in which Trump had to decide whom to fire after a contest at a steakhouse.

"There was a lot of blame to go around," Obama said. "But you, Mr. Trump, recognized that the real problem was a lack of leadership. And so ultimately you didn't blame Little John or Meatloaf. You fired Gary Busey. And these are the kind of decisions that would keep me up at night."

As the ballroom erupted in laughter, Trump sat stone-faced.

32

DON'T DO THIS FOR THE MONEY

In April 2012, Dan Tangherlini sat down in his new office as administrator at the federal General Services Administration, which oversees most federal contracts. He had just been transferred over from the Treasury Department after several GSA executives had been caught using taxpayer money to pay for lavish parties during a conference in Las Vegas.

As Tangherlini settled into his new role, several colleagues and friends asked whether he would spike an offer from Donald Trump to lease and redevelop the Old Post Office building in Washington, D.C. They mentioned Trump's long history of bankruptcies, which can allow a contractor to get out of almost any ongoing obligation. But those inquisitors also rumbled about the wisdom of signing a deal with a guy who had been making unsupported accusations about President Obama being a Muslim born in another country.

"I remember people asking me, 'He's been so critical of the president. He's had all these bankruptcies. Why would you agree to do a deal with that person?' And I said, 'It's not my personal choice. It's not the General Dan Administration. It's the General Services Administration.'"

Then Tangherlini looked at the size of Trump's offer. There had been ten bids, and he saw a wide gap between Trump's $200 million offer and the second highest one.

Tangherlini saw only reasons to move forward. The Old Post Office had been a chain around the taxpayers' necks for decades. It had not functioned as a post office since the 1930s, and efforts over the years to repurpose the interior of the grand building had failed. It was operating as an office building with a shopping mall, but the government spent $7 million a year more on the building than it collected in rent. His primary concern was that taxpayers would not be left holding a half-finished building if Trump failed. If he finished construction, the government would own everything Trump put into the building. Tangherlini required that Trump put up $50 million in cash to disincentivize him from walking away if things got tough. Like others monitoring the bidding process, though, he wondered how Trump could ever make the numbers work.

"They were proposing room rates at seven hundred dollars a night, and no one pays that kind of money for a room in D.C.," he later recalled.

Other bidders agreed. One bidding team that included Hilton Hotels and Resorts bid $140 million and faulted the GSA for not conducting a "price reasonableness analysis" of Trump's bid. That analysis, according to the group, would have shown that Trump's figures were based on "hotel room revenues which are simply not obtainable in this location."

Tangherlini understood the concerns. "But ultimately, we just made sure that the agreement said that if they made a mistake, that it was their mistake, not ours."

Trump answered the criticism during an interview with *The Washington Post* in his office at Trump Tower. He grinned at the question. "In a way, we are paying too much for the Old Post Office," he said. "I mean, we are paying too much for the Old Post Office. But we will make that so amazing that at some point in the future it'll be very nice."

Trump would repeatedly say that cost was no object in his plans for the new luxury hotel, which included 261 rooms, 3 restaurants, a spa, and banquet facilities. He let Ivanka take the lead on the project, both during the bidding process and the publicity tour after the announcement. During one presentation, she described the renovation as a legacy project for the Trump family, a business that her recently born daughter might someday run. "We are not cutting corners," she said at the event unveiling the architectural plans. "And we take our mandate of creating the finest hotel in the country, if not the world, very, very seriously."

"The thing I do best is build, believe it or not," Trump said when he took the microphone. "Better than *The Apprentice*, better than politics. I build. That's what I do best." He then turned toward his eldest daughter and playfully reenacted his signature line from the show: "You better do a good job, or you're fired."

Trump's initial financier for the project backed out in 2013. He went back to Deutsche Bank's personal wealth lender, Rosemary Vrablic, who offered a $170 million loan, if Trump would personally guarantee repayment.

By then, ratings for *The Celebrity Apprentice* were in decline. His ability to plug deficits in businesses he ran with cash from the show and licensing deals was slipping away, just as he took on large debts in a late-life acquisition phase.

THE BUSINESS OF GOLF can be particularly tough. There are high fixed costs to maintain courses, no matter how many golfers play, and the number of rounds played can be greatly impacted by weather. Larger demographic, economic, and cultural trends present other challenges. The second decade of the twenty-first century was no exception. One industry analyst reported that privately owned courses on average lost money every year after the 2008 recession. Losing just two cents on every dollar of revenue would have been considered a banner year.

But Trump often said that his interest in golf was not about profits and losses. "I don't do this for the money," Trump once said of his golf courses. "I do it for the fun. I get pride out of shaping land. I think it's really special. I make my money on Manhattan real estate, and that's wonderful, so I'm in a position where I can do things like this that other people can't do."

Trump was flush with cash from his success on television and in avoiding income taxes when one of his lawyers, Michael D. Cohen, heard that Doral Country Club near Miami had gone into bankruptcy. Trump did not take the course's failure as a warning sign. He still believed that any business with his name would bring in enough money to cover expenses.

Once again, he put Ivanka in charge of the Doral project. The Trumps began pursuing another low-interest mortgage from Rosemary Vrablic. Ivanka noted in internal emails that current rates through normal banking channels would be too high for a golf resort, given the risks involved in the business. But when she received the numbers from Vrablic, she saw her problem as solved.

"It doesn't get better than this," she wrote to Jason Greenblatt, an in-house Trump Organization lawyer.

Greenblatt responded that someone should make sure her father would be okay with the increased wealth requirements that Deutsche Bank placed on the loan offer: a net worth of $3 billion and cash on hand of $50 million. "The net worth covenants and DJT indebtedness limitations would seem to be a problem?" Greenblatt wrote. And Trump would need to personally guarantee repayment.

"That we have known from day one," Ivanka wrote in response.

The Trumps accepted the terms and closed on the Doral purchase in June 2012. Trump paid $150 million for four courses at Doral, the most famous being the "Blue Monster" and announced he would spend a stunning $250 million on renovations, including all seven hundred rooms in the worn hotel. Ivanka would head up the project.

"I'll spend more than a Wall Street guy," Trump said. "We're going to make it the top tournament course on the tour."

After the renovations were complete, Trump sought to have his property taxes lowered on Doral. He was required to submit financial statements proving the course was not generating enough profit to warrant the value assigned to it by property assessors. Only $104 million of Trump's purchase price was included in the assessment. At one point during the hearing, the special magistrate, Leonardo Delgado, stared down at Trump's documents showing that Doral had lost $2.4 million in 2014, a number that did not include millions of dollars in mortgage payments. Delgado began to chuckle and turned to the county property assessor, Murry Harris.

"So, he spent $104 million to lose two and a half million dollars a year?" Delgado said. "I know how to lose that money without having to spend $104 million. How 'bout you, Murry?"

THE NATIONAL GOLF FOUNDATION had been tracking the ups and downs of the golf business since the Great Depression. From its two-story headquarters in Jupiter, Florida, the nonprofit group collected data on rounds played at courses across the country and reported its findings in the hopes of helping grow the sport and the business. Those findings had not been very positive for several years. In 2008, the foundation reported that for two consecutive years the number of courses closing had been greater than the number of courses opening for the first time since the end of World War II.

In 2014, the foundation reported that the number of players in the U.S. had fallen by five million during the prior decade. And 20 percent of the current 25 million active golfers were likely to quit within a few years. Those findings tracked the falloff in golf gear sales at one of the nation's largest sporting goods retailers. "We really don't know what the bottom is in golf," Edward Stack, the chief executive of Dick's Sporting Goods, said in a conference call. "We anticipated softness, but instead we saw significant decline. We underestimated how significant a decline this would be."

As he continued to expand his purchase of golf courses, Trump took great offense at any suggestion of the sport's decline. He gave the chief executive of Dick's a pass, but he personalized his criticism of the National Golf Foundation and its longtime president, Joe Beditz, who had gone to work at the foundation as director of research in 1984 after earning his PhD in educational research and measurement.

In 2014, a reporter for *Sports Illustrated* asked Trump, in light of the foundation's findings on declining interest in golf, why he was investing so heavily in golf courses.

"I think the National Golf Foundation is run by a person who is incompetent, virtually incompetent," Trump answered. "I would say you're fired."

He added that he thought the foundation "should be a positive force and it's really a negative force."

While the industry contracted, Trump expanded.

Don Jr. had played a course called Doonbeg Golf Club, a links-style course on the Atlantic coast of Ireland, in County Clare. Upon visiting more than a dozen courses, only Doonbeg impressed him. Designed by retired professional golf champion Greg Norman, Doonbeg opened in 2002 under the ownership of Charles P. "Buddy" Darby III. Darby has one overarching recollection of the golf course: "It never made me any money." He hung on as long as he could. But by 2013, he still "couldn't see the light at the end of the tunnel." He sold the course to a hedge fund, which then lost the course in receivership.

Trump bought it out of receivership in 2014 for $11.9 million and vowed to spend millions to renovate the course and the 218-suite lodge. Through 2018, Trump spent $38.5 million at Doonbeg on renovations and covering operating losses, according to his tax returns.

A few months later, Trump bought Turnberry, a course with more name recognition than any other he had built or bought, on the southwest coast of Scotland. The first course there opened in 1901, and a lodge followed in 1906. Its three links courses are considered among the most beautiful in the world, with views opening to the Atlantic Ocean, a lighthouse on the property, and

Ailsa Craig, a volcanic island ten miles away. The courses there have been home to many major tournaments, including the famed battle between Jack Nicklaus and Tom Watson at the 1977 Open Championship.

Turnberry also had a history of financial difficulties. Starwood Hotel and Resorts bought it in 1997, then sold it to Leisurecorp, a subsidiary of the Dubai government, in 2008, and the following year Leisurecorp put the course up for sale.

Trump came on the scene in 2014. He did little in the way of due diligence before buying the property for between $63 million and $70 million. He soon announced he would spend as much as $200 million more to update its neglected elements. Ralph Porciani, Trump's general manager at the course, said the scope of needed repairs came as a surprise to Trump: "Did he realize that it needed as much spent on it? No, because when it's a heart purchase you want to get the deal through as quick as possible."

The course closed for renovations, which included adding a new Donald J. Trump Ballroom with seating for five hundred, and reopened in June 2016. Like many of Trump's golf courses, banquet facilities to host weddings and other events occupy a central role in Turnberry's finances. Food and beverage makes up 59 percent of Turnberry's revenue. Porciani said less than a third of its hotel guests are there to play golf.

Years later, Porciani remained focused on making Turnberry sustainable as a business "because it hasn't been for decades."

Trump's tax returns show that he never turned the course around financially. He had invested $153 million in Turnberry through 2018 to cover losses and other expenses. He reported making a small profit for the first time in 2022.

By 2015, the entertainment money spigot that had kept cash flowing to Trump without requiring any expertise in buying, building, or running a business had begun to dry up. His income from *The Celebrity Apprentice* and the licensing and endorsement deals that moved in tandem with the show's ratings plummeted from $51 million in 2011 to $22 million in 2015. The trend would continue downward, cutting into Trump's ability to prop up his businesses with his celebrity riches.

With many of his businesses losing money, he partially filled the hole left on his balance sheet by selling off his stocks and bonds. He unloaded $98 million in stocks in just one month, January 2014, and sold $54 million more in 2015, and another $68.2 million in 2016. He held almost no stocks at that point. During those same years, cash reported by his businesses on tax returns fell 40 percent.

In its annual reviews of Trump's finances, Deutsche Bank noted in 2016 that he had reported negative cash flow for four of the last five years. But the bank thought the picture would improve as he completed construction projects. During one of those years, he met Deutsche Bank's requirement that he maintain $50 million in cash available by claiming that he had access to the cash on hand in the partnership through which he owned 30 percent of two office buildings with Vornado Realty. He could beg Steven Roth, the head of Vornado, for that money, but he had no right to it.

In the spring of 2015, Trump invited the two NBC executives in charge of *The Celebrity Apprentice* to meet with him at Trump Tower. As soon as they all sat down, Trump made it clear that he had made a very important decision.

"I'm running" for president, Trump told them. "I'm going to win, especially if I'm running against Hillary. I'm going to win the race."

Trump said he had seen numbers that proved his point. He did not cite any. But both the NBC men knew it was possible. The network did its own polling on its television stars, with a rigor that they believed would make political pollsters look like amateurs, and they knew that Trump remained immensely popular across many demographics. Even among African Americans. Even when he belittled President Obama.

Trump had hinted to the same two men in 2011 that he might run. They talked him out of it. But this was clearly different. As Trump walked with them down through the lobby, he stopped at a kiosk with Trump-branded neckties. He pointed out that they were made of lovely silk. Then he said he liked these extra-long ties "because they point to your dick." Trump scooped up a handful of the ties. The two network executives walked back to Rockefeller Center carrying a shopping bag of very long neckties and secretly planning to replace their host.

On June 16, 2015, Trump finally and fully emerged from behind the carefully crafted visage of competence that had been crafted of him by Mark Burnett's editors more than a decade earlier. He descended the brass escalator into the marble lobby of Trump Tower that he had obsessed over as a young man. His third wife, Melania, followed behind and his grown children waited below. A crowd of apparent supporters wearing Trump T-shirts and holding signs, many of whom had been quietly paid to do so, cheered him on. A horde of reporters and photographers packed the lobby, just as others had for countless other Trump announcements over the decades. But this was not about the purchase, real or hopeful, of a building, a football team, an airline, or a casino.

"So, ladies and gentlemen, I am officially running for president of the United States, and we are going to make our country great again," Trump told the crowd.

He soon launched into a dystopian description of modern American life, as if speaking directly to the same army of the disaffected who had been the target audience of his get-rich-quick programs a decade earlier. He used the same proof of failed policy as he had on television news shows since the 1980s—unnamed others are laughing at us.

"When do we beat Mexico at the border?" he asked. "They're laughing at us, at our stupidity. And now they are beating us economically. They are not our friend, believe me. But they're killing us economically. The U.S. has become a dumping ground for everybody else's problems. . . . When Mexico sends its people, they're not sending their best. . . . They're sending people that have lots of problems, and they're bringing those problems with us. They're bringing drugs. They're bringing crime. They're rapists. And some, I assume, are good people."

His words landed hard in offices across the country that marketed products under Trump's name to a wide audience.

Paul Telegdy, then the head of unscripted television at NBC, had thought he might be replacing Trump to avoid equal-time issues in a presidential race. But now he saw the problem as more immediate. He called within an hour and told Trump that he had a few days to retract those statements or "things are going to go very wrong for you here."

"What are you saying?" Trump asked.

"I am saying we won't be able to be in businesses with someone who is outrageous," Telegdy responded.

Trump called Telegdy "a pussy" and threatened to sue.

Network executives joined several conference calls to discuss how to proceed. NBCUniversal had two relationships with Trump: *The Celebrity Apprentice* and the Miss Universe pageant, which the network televised and Trump co-owned. The sense that Trump had become too toxic for a general audience seemed clear. They decided to cut all ties with Trump, dropping both the pageant and *The Celebrity Apprentice*.

On June 29, Telegdy and Steve Burke, NBCUniversal's chief executive, called Trump to let him know. Trump grew angry, accusing them of buckling to a "Hispanic lobby" and criticizing them for not honoring their contracts. They ultimately agreed to soften the public statement about *The Celebrity Apprentice* by suggesting the host spot would be his if he decided to return. Trump claimed he had not been fired but had quit and announced he would sue the network over the pageant. He issued a statement calling the network "weak and so foolish to not understand the serious illegal immigration problem in the United States."

One of the biggest sources of income in Trump's life, the show that paid him nearly $200 million over thirteen years, was gone forever. The licensing deals fell next.

The next day, Macy's announced it would drop all Trump products. Bottles of a fragrance called Empire by Trump were pulled off the shelves and immediately shipped back to Parlux, the company that made the scent. Muriel Gonzalez, a cosmetics executive at Macy's, told Parlux president Donald Loftus that the unusual decision had been made at the highest levels of the company. She told Loftus that Macy's had a large Hispanic clientele and "couldn't tolerate" Trump's comments.

And the day after that, Serta, which had paid Trump $15.3 million for use of his name over the prior six years, dropped him as well. A week later, the PGA canceled a scheduled tournament at a Trump golf course. Then Phillips-Van Heusen, which had sold Trump-labeled men's clothes for a decade and paid him more than $10 million, announced it would wind down the brand.

Trump's value as a brand for licensing, especially for consumer products, had been diminishing for years, relegated increasingly to dicey real estate projects in developing nations. Suddenly, his income from licensing and endorsement deals, a category that had paid him $230 million since the launch of *The Apprentice*, came to a near complete halt.

Trump's hotel in Washington, D.C., opened shortly before the 2016 election. He mentioned it in his first debate with the Democratic nominee, Hillary Clinton, and took a break from his campaign the week before the election to make an appearance there. In its first two years of operations, he would pump almost $17 million more of his own cash into the hotel to cover losses. He faced similar trouble at his other projects from the prior decade, especially losses at his Chicago tower and the three golf courses in Scotland and Ireland. But he was no longer receiving enough money from show business to fill in the holes.

On his way to defeating Clinton that November, Trump often repeated a line on the campaign trail—"I'm really rich"—to argue that his experiences in business made him uniquely suited to be president. He certainly appeared rich. That he had received the equivalent of a half billion dollars from his father, another half billion as a reality television star, and lost much of that money creating an illusion of success, never came up.

EPILOGUE

On the morning of January 20, 2021, Donald and Melania Trump walked out of the White House toward a crowd of waiting reporters and photographers. Speaking over the hissing engine of the nearby military helicopter, Trump said, "it's been a great honor, the honor of a lifetime" and "an amazing four years.

"And I just want to say goodbye, but hopefully, it's not a long-term goodbye. We'll see each other again. Thank you all very much. Thank you."

The couple then walked slowly across the South Lawn and up the steps to Marine One, where Trump turned and double-pumped a clenched fist before stepping aboard. The helicopter circled the Capitol before heading to Joint Base Andrews for a formal ceremony. From a stage on the tarmac, Trump looked to his grown children and said they had sacrificed "a much easier life" to assist his presidency.

"So, just a goodbye," he said. "We love you. We will be back in some form."

He boarded Air Force One, which lifted into the hazy blue sky while the small audience on the ground heard a recording of Frank Sinatra singing "My Way."

And now, the end is near
And so, I face the final curtain . . .

As Trump made clear, he did not intend for that day to mark the end of his time as president. He had spent the prior ten weeks fueling a lie that he had won the 2020 election, a lie that had inspired throngs of his supporters to storm the U.S. Capitol on January 6. He became the first president since 1869 to refuse to attend his successor's inauguration.

In the final fog of untruths and pettiness that defined so much of his presidency, it seemed, for a moment at least, that he and his grown children would return to the world of the Trump Organization, the easier life he said they had sacrificed. Hidden behind the veil of a chaotic presidency, that world had been shrinking for years.

After a lifetime devoted to announcing his latest notion of a new venture with great frequency, Donald Trump and his family went notably silent. Plans by Don Jr., Ivanka, and Eric to launch a less-expensive line of hotels called Scion and a three-star hotel chain called American Idea both died without a shovel being turned.

Needing cash, as his annual income from television and licensing his name dried up, the Trumps had sold off bits and pieces of the company's assets: the land around his golf course near Los Angeles, condominiums in buildings he built decades ago, and a mansion in Beverly Hills. Though mostly symbolic, apartment buildings, some of which he built and some to which he licensed use of his name, pulled down the brassy five letters above their front doors.

Trump's tax returns, looked at in total, show the hole left by his dwindling value as a brand endorser. He burned through cash and sold off his stocks as his annual windfall from licensing and *The Apprentice* tumbled from a high of $51 million in 2011 to $2.9 million in 2018. The pain continued. In late 2023, the owner of the most lucrative licensing agreement of Trump's *Apprentice*-era career, a hotel in Honolulu that paid Trump $31.3 million from 2009 through 2018, ended the deal and dropped the Trump name.

Facing what appeared to be a worsening cash crunch after leaving office, Trump unloaded two high-profile businesses: his licenses to operate a golf course in the Bronx and the hotel in Washington, D.C.'s Old Post Office that devoured cash.

Trump's tax returns showed that he had been pumping $7 million to $10 million a year into the Old Post Office hotel to cover losses. He sold the lease to operate the hotel in 2022 to CGI Merchant Group, a small private equity firm in Miami that had said it specialized in buying hotels at distressed prices. Contrary to that mission, analysts noted the extraordinarily high price that

CGI paid Trump for the hotel. CGI did not make it to the two-year anniversary of the deal before defaulting on its primary loan.

The sale price was high enough to more than cover Trump's mortgage. He received $126 million from the sale after paying off his debt. That sounds like a windfall. But based on our calculations, he owed at least $40 million in taxes on the gain. He had invested $73 million in cash in the project through 2020. And at that rate, he would have put at least another $15 million into the building prior to the sale. That would make his post-tax return on investment over a decade somewhere around zero.

The last two major developments of his career, his apartment and hotel tower in Chicago and the hotel in Washington, as well as his three most recent golf courses in the United Kingdom, had all been financial failures that required constant infusions of cash. Trump moved those businesses and most of his other golf courses into one company, DJT Holdings LLC, and pumped $589 million dollars into that company from 2010 through 2020. He never had one year when he took more money out than what he put into it to cover losses.

As he entered the White House, Trump had initially promised to deal with potential conflicts of interest by placing his businesses in a trust run by Don Jr. and Eric. Analysts at the time said only a blind trust would create a meaningful wall between Trump and his businesses, a step Trump would not take. His tax returns revealed the trust to be a narrow fig leaf. It operated under Trump's social security number—Trump's trust was Trump. He may as well have called it the John Baron trust.

Though it was not known at the time, we found on his tax returns suggestions that his wallet received a boost from his presidency. At Mar-a-Lago, revenue from new membership fees rose sharply after Trump declared his candidacy, from $664,000 in 2014 to just under $6 million in 2016. Trump doubled the cost of initiation in January 2017. That money went straight into his pocket. He withdrew from the business nearly the exact amount of his increased revenue from initiation fees, a total of $26 million from 2015 through 2018, a rate almost three times higher than what he had been extracting from the club. The names of new members remained secret.

Our colleagues at the *Times* uncovered evidence that hundreds of people with interests before the federal government rented rooms at Trump's hotel in Washington, D.C., during his presidency. Overnight, anyone could funnel the money to the president of the United States by renting a block of rooms at one of his hotels or booking a few hundred tee times at a money-losing golf course. A federal system based on curtailing even the appearance of a conflict of interest had been turned on its head.

But whatever additional money he received from those interested in currying favor with, or just being close to, a U.S. president appears in hindsight to have only kept his company from shrinking even faster.

As of this writing, Trump faces substantial threats to his finances. A longstanding IRS audit, which appears to include claimed losses on his Chicago tower and his casinos, could cost Trump more than $100 million to resolve. In 2024, a Manhattan jury ordered Trump to pay $83.3 million to the writer E. Jean Carroll for defaming her after she accused him of raping her decades ago. And a New York judge ordered Trump to pay $454 million, including interest, in a fraud case brought by the current New York attorney general, Letitia James. Trump has vowed to appeal both judgments.

Donald Trump has faced these moments before, periods when it seemed his failures could not be saved only by aggressive tax maneuvers or not paying his debts. But there always came a new windfall from plain old luck. The luck of his birth. The luck of being made into a television celebrity. And the luck of being pushed into the best deal of his life against his will.

Those lucky breaks paid off again in recent years.

The luckiest deal of his life, the one Trump was pushed into and tried to kill with three lawsuits—the one in which a partner swapped Trump's thirty percent interest in the development on the West Side for the same share in two office buildings run by Vornado Realty—delivered another lifeline in 2021. Vornado refinanced one of the buildings with a larger mortgage. Donald had no involvement in the transaction, but he may have received a tax-free windfall of as much as $185 million.

Trump's lucky birth paid off one more time as well. Starrett City, the middle-income housing project his father invested in fifty years earlier and passed along to his children, was sold in 2017. His share of the proceeds totaled $18 million, another piece of an inherited fortune to a septuagenarian who claims his father only gave him "peanuts."

None of that seems likely to meet the demands he faces. Trump's stake in his upstart social media company may offer salvation. When the parent company of Truth Social went public in March 2024, a buying frenzy pushed the value of Trump's shares to more than $4 billion, though he could not yet sell. That valuation put the small company, which had recently reported quarterly revenues of about $1 million, on par with large corporations like U.S. Steel. Many market professionals expected the stock price to plummet at some point.

As he continues to burn through cash and tries to pay court judgments, will Trump be forced to sell some of his money-losing golf courses, especially his three cash-devouring alligators in the United Kingdom? Will the downturn in demand for office space push his one office building, 40 Wall Street, permanently into the red after decades of unreliable profitability? Will the same problem, along with reduced demand for retail space, damage the prospects for the asset he built first, and was always his best performer, Trump Tower? From what we saw on his tax returns, any hit to the profitability of Trump's passive investment in the Vornado-owned office towers alone could threaten his overall financial viability.

Here's the part that may sting most in a country that sees itself as history's greatest meritocracy: Good things happened to Donald Trump. He did not earn most of those good things. He was born. He was discovered by a revolutionary television producer. And he was pushed into an investment against his will. And from those three bits of good luck came the equivalent today of more than $1.5 billion. That sort of tailwind could paper over a litany of failure and still fund a lavish life. And there is no evidence that in fifty years of labor Donald Trump added to his lucky fortunes. He would have been better off betting on the stock market than on himself.

Five decades before Trump pumped his fist on the steps of Marine One, President Richard M. Nixon struck a similarly defiant pose at the same spot. He turned before entering the helicopter, flashed an awkwardly broad smile, and raised both arms in his signature victory sign—the two-finger salute that came to symbolize peace to younger Americans. But the courses of their presidencies leading up to their forced departures differed in at least one distinct way.

Nixon had spent the prior two years denying that his administration had any involvement with a break-in at Democratic party headquarters at the Watergate complex in Washington. Republicans stood by him. Three impeachment votes failed. But then the U.S. Supreme Court rejected Nixon's claims of executive privilege and forced him to release recordings of White House meetings, including one of him orchestrating a cover-up. Congressional Republicans visited him at the White House to tell him that he had lost public support and the support of his own party, and would be thrown from office. With nowhere left to turn, Nixon announced his resignation the next day.

Trump had been repeatedly caught making demands that would have likely ended prior presidencies. He told a Ukrainian president that military aid to help ward off Russian aggression might not be coming unless the Ukrainian government announced an investigation of Joe Biden and his son. After he had lost the 2020 election, Trump was recorded telling a Republican official in Georgia to "find me the votes" that would flip the election in his direction. Even out of office, he was recorded showing a classified document to a journalist to cast aspersions on a former cabinet official Trump perceived as disloyal.

But unlike Nixon, Trump did have somewhere to turn. During his lifetime, a new media ecosystem had come into existence, one eager to explain away evidence of any Republican president's wrongs and endlessly magnify the thinnest assertion of any Democrat's missteps. That ecosystem evolved from talk radio in the 1980s and gained dominance on cable television in the 1990s with the launch of Fox News.

Trump was the most perfectly imperfect vessel for the realm of Fox News. He had been telling self-serving lies and fantastical exaggerations to journalists for his entire adult life: He had taken over his father's large company; his father's company was small; he was independently worth billions; and he was John Baron. Through it all, he showed no fear of shame at being caught in a lie.

Fox and Trump found a common purpose during the Obama presidency, when Fox amplified Trump's racist fantasy that Obama had been born in Africa and was therefore not eligible to be president.

During Trump's presidency, Fox gave his supporters safe harbor from confronting his most craven acts. They would hear talking points, thought bubbles, for why their support of Trump made them superior patriots. In this virtual world, no criticism or finding of fault against Trump could be based on merit. It was all part of an orchestrated attack by bad actors—sufferers of Trump Derangement Syndrome, deep state bureaucrats, woke liberals, courts working under the secret orders of Democrats, or the liberal-controlled mass media. Trump and his media allies had installed a boogeyman under every Republican bed, mobilizing and sanctifying legions of the scared and angry. Most beneficial to Fox, scared and angry viewers do not change the channel.

By the end of Trump's presidency, even more reliable defenders than Fox had cropped up on cable television and the internet. The battle for viewers became a contest of supplication. The day Trump left office hinting that he planned to return, Chanel Rion, the White House correspondent for One America News, a niche station seeking to out-Fox Fox, picked up where Trump left off. Rion looked past the complete defeat of Trump's court challenges of the election and his campaign's inability to cite any evidence that Trump won the election. She called Trump's farewell comments "a temporary goodbye."

"The fight has only just begun," she said.

For those living in the Fox News information biosphere, support for Trump appeared endless and self-evident. It was all viewers saw all day, every day. It would seem impossible to believe Trump lost the vote when the television constantly tells you that everyone loves him. In that world, there would be no credence given to polls showing Trump left office with the lowest approval ratings of any president in the history of polling.

There have been moments when the ecosystem showed signs of strain. Fox paid $787 million to settle a lawsuit filed by the voting machine company that Trump's representatives and Tucker Carlson said had flipped votes to Biden. The network also fired Carlson, its top-rated host, who had led the charge in pushing Trump's insistence that he won the 2020 election. Will Fox and other outlets show more hesitancy to promote Trump's self-serving lies? Could it be that his shameless mendacity and lack of concern with defaming others will be the factors that ultimately cow the media ecosystem that helped make him viable as a candidate?

Either way, the rise of that ecosystem was perhaps the final lucky stroke of Trump's very lucky life. The man who became famous thanks to the rise of celebrity business journalism and "wealth porn" in the 1980s, the man who was discovered as a midlife ingenue at the birth of reality television, now enters any dispute with an unquestioning megaphone at his disposal. Nixon should have been so lucky.

THE FACT-FREE BUBBLE Fox News created around Donald Trump as president must have felt familiar. He had spent his adult life in a similar bubble financed by his father. In this comfortable place, he could hide his failures, pay for them with his father's money, and, later, a celebrity's fortune. There would be no metrics measuring his success, just the impression of self-created wealth that he willed into existence.

From the moment he left his father's careful planning practices behind, he protected his bubble by waging war on the fact-based world that might pop it. The first reporters to glimpse inside his failing businesses. The first former employees to say Trump was not what he seemed. The first analyst to show why Trump's biggest casino would fail. The public officials who opposed the scope of his development proposals over the decades. He typically dispatched them with a lie and an assigned motive—they were out to get him, the persecuted Trump. "Everybody wants to shoot at me because it's me," he said almost thirty years ago.

Then Mark Burnett's *The Apprentice* fortified Trump's fact-free bubble, while also making it national and bankable in ways that Trump never did on his own.

Trump first emerged from his bubble when he announced his candidacy for president in 2015. He would be held up to real metrics and historical norms, his claims of accomplishment examined with a level of seriousness commensurate with the job he sought. That process remains ongoing, and, we hope, has been advanced by the creation of this book. But one of Trump's primary missions since 2015 can be reasonably described as an effort to destroy public confidence in the historical pillars of fact in America so that only his pronouncements would hold credibility.

He began his campaign seeking to undermine all journalism beyond Fox News. He told the television journalist Lesley Stahl, as she recalled, that he had made attacking the media a centerpiece of his campaign—calling reporters "enemies of the state"—to "discredit you all and demean you all so that when you write negative stories about me no one will believe you."

He took the same tack with the entire executive branch of the federal government. He would find no competency in the Pentagon, the Department of State, agencies that enforce regulations, or, eventually, his own cabinet and vice president. In Trump's hands, these were the realms of deep state bureaucrats, the swamp, a place Trump alone could purge but most assuredly a place where no one questioning him could be trusted.

With a wave of civil and criminal cases that to many read like a predictable outcome of Trump's actions, he set out to destroy credibility in the judicial branch.

During the 2016 campaign, as a mountain of evidence of Trump's deceptions emerged in three lawsuits against Trump University, Trump took to Twitter to call the federal judge in two of the cases, Gonzalo P. Curiel, "very unfair. An Obama pick. Totally biased—hates Trump." Trump said Curiel, whose parents emigrated from Mexico before his birth, came from a "very pro-Mexico" society and so hated Trump. As a legal strategy, the bias allegation failed. Trump agreed to pay $25 million to settle the two class action lawsuits and a civil case brought by New York's attorney general at the time, Eric T. Schneiderman.

Yet that strategy appears to remain Trump's legal tactic, with similar success within the legal system. Consider how he has characterized judicial and law enforcement officials involved in recent cases against him: the judge in the New York fraud trial is a "Radical Left Trump Hating Judge" with a "Trump Hating Clerk"; the New York attorney general who brought the fraud case is a "racist" and "Trump hating"; the federal judge who oversaw E. Jean Carroll's defamation lawsuit is a "Crazed, Trump hating Judge"; and special counsel Jack Smith, a lifelong Republican who oversaw the investigation that led to Trump's federal indictment in the January 6 case, is "deranged" and, of course, a "Trump hater."

Trump has said those sorts of things long enough that we should accept it is not a contrived strategy but how he sees the world: Anyone who questions or opposes him on any issue, large or small, is only another Trump hater, out to get him for impure reasons. It is a worldview that allows him to claim he has never made a mistake, in business or politics, a key feature of the protective bubble he seems to need to feel good about himself.

And it also now animates a significant number of his political supporters. As much as the illusion of success was the ultimate creation of Trump's first seventy years, the illusion of his persecution may be his final masterpiece.

It is too soon to tell whether Trump's rise has been singular to him or has revealed a shift in America's culture and politics that will last. But this version of America—a place with no agreed-upon facts, where being a person of one's word no longer matters, where one man's self-created problems serve as a proxy for a nation under attack—this is the world as Donald Trump wants it to be.

American voters now face a third chance to decide whether it is the world they want.

ACKNOWLEDGMENTS

We are forever grateful, first and foremost, to the people who have trusted us with records and their personal experiences, sometimes at great personal risk. That trust is what made this project possible. They asked nothing of us beyond a promise to pursue the truth. We owe them our gratitude for helping us explore the claims most central to Donald Trump's argument for why he should be president. In eight years of trying to lift the veil on a family business that keeps even its employees in the dark, we have met wonderful, brilliant, and engaging people. There are too many to mention here, and some we cannot mention. But some we must.

Mary Trump was a courageous truth-teller who never wavered in her enthusiastic support of our mission. She risked further ostracization from her family as well as public insults and legal action from her famous uncle.

Chaz Littlejohn, an earnest and brilliant young man, came to us willing to risk his liberty to help us inform the public about the truth behind Donald Trump as a businessman. He has paid a steep price. Like Mary Trump, he never suggested anything beyond our pursuit of the truth. We will never forget.

Dan Gill, who worked on the set of *The Apprentice*, provided us with boxes of records from the show and spent countless hours explaining them. Neil Hobday was a generous tour guide through the world of Trump's golf business.

Jack O'Donnell and Barbara Res caught on to the real Donald Trump early and have been generous ever since helping the rest of us understand. Others who deserve mention and our thanks include Neil Barsky, Brad Borden, Steve Rosenthal, Jeff Walker, Abe Wallach, Annamaria Forcier, and Sandy McIntosh.

In coming to terms with the highly technical areas of tax law, we would have been lost in the weeds without the generous help of several experts. We hold a special place in our hearts for Jim Ledley, one of the most prominent estate and trust lawyers in New York, who was endlessly patient and exceptionally generous with his time. Jim made arcane work fun.

Joel Rosenfeld, an accountant who has specialized and taught real estate accounting for decades, served as our numbers shaman, able to explain the big concept and the line-level details from general ledgers and tax returns. From responding to our weekend texts and inviting us for backyard consultations during the COVID lockdown, every minute was an enlightening joy. We took no offense to your suggestion that one of us was now prepared to sit for the CPA exam.

Our editors at *The New York Times* were integral to our reporting on Trump's finances over the years, which provided the starting point and backbone for this project. Matthew Purdy and Paul Fishleder are gold-standard shepherds of investigative reporting, a humble and easygoing powerhouse duo who have led reporting teams at the *Times* to many Pulitzer Prizes. They made us better.

Our work on Trump's finances spanned the tenures of two executive editors at the *Times*, Dean Baquet and Joseph Kahn. Both were intricately involved in our reporting through the years, devoting their considerable talents and wisdom to our work. Their support and excitement for getting to the truth made all the difference. Both encouraged us to pursue this project and supported us taking time away from the newspaper to complete it. We thank you for all of it.

David McCraw, chief counsel of the *Times*'s newsroom, has the eye of a skilled editor and has been on the front lines of fighting to protect the First Amendment for decades. He was in the trenches with us year after year as we worked to shed light on Trump's finances. He is without peer, and we are thankful for his advice and friendship. (And, of course, for prevailing in Trump's lawsuit against us, including winning that check for $392,638.69 from him as reimbursement for the *Times*'s legal expenses.)

Our reporting on Trump's finances also spanned the tenures of two publishers, Arthur Sulzberger Jr. and his son A.G. Sulzberger. Both have been incredibly courageous and supportive, often in ways that did not show. We owe a debt of gratitude to the extended Sulzberger family, who, as the information-wants-to-be-free edict of the internet threatened the business model of every newspaper, risked their family fortune and legacy on a bet that people would pay for quality journalism. Some other media companies and families folded, sold, or cut toward irrelevance while chasing plummeting revenue trends. We are forever grateful for their courage, selflessness, and belief in the mission of this inspiring place.

Ann Godoff, a legendary book editor, rolled the dice on us, two newspaper reporters who had never written a book. For first-time authors, reading a list of books and authors Ann has published can induce sweaty shakes. She was, at every step over a very long journey, brilliant, warm, and encouraging. Notes from Ann describing what works and what needs adjustment in a batch of chapters arrive so beautifully written and frighteningly intelligent that they feel suitable for framing. And they keep you charging ahead, smarter and more confident for having benefited from her endless talent. We will always be grateful.

Ann's team at Penguin Press also deserves notice and our gratitude, including Casey Denis, who gracefully answered our endless first-timer questions, as well as Liz Calamari and Sarah Hutson for introducing the world to this book, Christopher Brian King for designing the stunning and provocative book jacket, and Victoria Laboz.

We cannot fully express our gratitude to our agent, Elyse Cheney. She was an invaluable asset to us and this project—a tireless advocate, hand-holder, educator, friend, and thoughtful reader. Her excitement for books in general and this project in particular brightened moments when it all seemed too overwhelming. She has somehow assembled a team that shares her infectious spirit. Thank you to Grace Johnson, Claire Gillespie, and Beniamino Ambrosi.

Julie Tate, a brilliant researcher for the *Times*'s investigative team, was a joy and a tremendous asset in helping us button down what felt like a few million facts in this project.

We have been fortunate to work with colleagues who surprise and delight and made vital contributions to our work in the *Times* that set us down the path to this project. Mike McIntire, one of the most accomplished investigative reporters in the country, greatly advanced everything he touched during the several years that we worked with him on aspects of Trump's finances. A finer colleague could not exist.

Gabriel Dance, a creative and brainy genius on the investigative team, oversaw the creation of vivid multimedia additions—including films, interactive graphics, and animated images—that left indelible impressions. If that work sounds glamorous, and it can be, we would like to place in your mind's eye a vision of Gabe and two other *Times* colleagues launching a small motorboat into a polluted New York City waterway in hopes of capturing a few seconds of drone footage over a Fred Trump project.

Rory Tolan and Lanie Shapiro, copy editors on the investigative team, have been treasured and tireless compatriots in everything we have done leading up to this project. Susan Beachy and Kitty Bennett are researchers who can find anything. Other *Times* colleagues who were important in the work leading up to this project include Megan Twohey, Steve Eder, Rebecca Corbett, and Dean Murphy.

The Trump era has presented unique challenges to journalism. We feel fortunate to have spent those years surrounded by the finest collection of journalists anyone could imagine. And we expand our admiration to colleagues at other news organizations to have regularly surprised, impressed, and challenged us.

Buettner:

I have had more good fortune than anyone has a right to expect, and the biggest blessing of all has been spending my life with Stacey Chiavetta, my wife, my love, my partner in all things. Your support and our laughter keep me going. Sometimes I think all I need is one more chance to bring you coffee and see you smile. I literally could not have gotten through this project without you (including converting our no-longer-needed nursery into an office, with the coolest Gentleman's Grey wall color). Thank you for never letting me know how exhausting it must have been to listen to me ramble about this project for three years.

And to our wonderful daughter, Emma, you are the light of our lives. Between this book and the COVID-19 shutdowns, we three spent much of your high school years in the house together all day. Seeing you that much, hearing your stories and thoughts, created memories I will treasure forever. You'll never know how much your words of encouragement meant to me. I'm so proud of the person you have become.

My mother, Bonnie Lowes, always an insatiable reader and joyful storyteller, put the bug in me to do this kind of work without either of us knowing it. Thank you, Mom. Your love and endless optimism have saved me many times throughout my life, and it still lifts my day to speak with you.

Not many people in my inner circle knew I was working on this project. Some friends propped me up with a laugh and words of support when I needed it most, especially Chris Gibbons and Lisa Nicosia, Joe Schram and Kate Keough, and Emma's best buddies, Tess and Olivia. And a thanks to all the softball parents on the sidelines and in the dugouts, especially Mike Poli, Dan Secor, and Doug Sasfi. I never told you all how much those days meant to me, of the value to this project of a head- and heart-clearing diversion.

Thanks, as always, to Jeanne Abbott, who patiently showed me how college-level journalism can be made into professional-quality work. Those small moments, your generosity and encouragement, made me believe I could do this work. And that changed everything.

Thanks to Elliot Jaspin for showing me more than thirty years ago how to handle large data sets and write SQL queries. All these years later, those skills are still vital to what I do.

Thanks will always be due to the editors who took fliers on me over the years, especially Tom Curran, Arthur Browne, and Joe Sexton. You gave me a chance and made me better.

Charles Bagli, the finest real estate reporter of his generation, gave me scores of free master's classes over the years on the intricacies and personalities of real estate in New York City. You're an excellent friend and I miss seeing you every day.

And there are colleagues who have impacted my life with their friendship and my career by exemplifying the best of our profession, including Jim Dwyer, Kevin Flynn, Joe Calderone, Willy Rashbaum, Joel Siegel, Paul Schwartzman, Juan González, Jerry Capeci, Gene Mustain, Dean Chang, Dan Barry, Danny Hakim, Walt Bogdanich, and Michael Luo.

A special thanks to Daniel Heneghan, a former reporter who went on to a career at the New Jersey Casino Control Commission, for generously explaining the ways of Atlantic City over the years.

I am certainly lucky to have thrown in my lot with Susanne Craig, an indefatigable and whip-smart reporter, as well as the most generous of colleagues. We have worked together every day on thorny and stressful research for the last eight years, a chunk of that becoming too familiar with each other's lunch preferences while locked in a secret room at *Times* headquarters. We had hundreds of aha! moments and a million laughs. We are great friends and a formidable team. I will always be grateful. Thank you for all of it.

Craig:

I am grateful for the support from a bunch of pretty amazing people.

Gary Park at the *Calgary Herald*, who took a chance on me years ago and remains a great friend. Bill Hickey in Windsor and Tim Pritchard and Mike Babad in Toronto. The incomparable Mike Siconolfi, who edited me for years at *The Wall Street Journal*. And thank you to Larry Ingrassia, for hiring me not once, but twice, at the *Journal* and the *Times*.

My friends at the *Times* are awesome—and among the most talented reporters there are. Yes, Willy Rashbaum, I am talking about you. And Rachel Abrams, Grace Ashford, Kim Barker, Walt Bogdanich, Dean Chang, Rebecca Corbett, Gabe Dance, Kirsten Danis, Mike McIntire, Ellen Pollock, Rebecca Ruiz, Carolyn Ryan, Jessica Silver-Greenberg, and James Stewart. Bojan Vukadinovic is one of the best bartenders in New York City and has served most of us on our best, and worst, days.

Thanks to my friends Shawna Richer, Kirsten Grind, Nick Devlin, Elaine Park, Jenny Liberto, and Theo Francis and his family, notably his parents George and Bettina. Also Karin Riedl, Lisa Ferrari, Pat Ferrari, Kannan Sundaram, Artemis Anninos, Emily Flitter, Chris Reese, Lorie Hearn, Barry Meier, Lorna and Pete Prediger, and David Langdon. You listened to my stories, sometimes over and over, with patience and a sense of humor, and I am forever thankful.

My family has always been there for me. Thank you, David Craig and Heather Sutherland, her husband, Ward, and their daughters, my nieces, Sam and Hanna, as well as Karsten Thacker, Rob Welsh, and Patti, my stepmom. My folks passed away a long time ago, but I try to channel the best of them every day.

When Russ and I started this project, my friend Kirsten Grind gave me some sound advice about writing a book with someone. It's like being at sea in a rowboat with another person, she said. If you don't both keep rowing, you will drown. Russ and I are first-time authors, and this book was trial by fire. Russ is a relentless reporter, brilliant writer, and someone I am proud to call a friend. We had our fair share of late nights and contentious debates over thorny tax issues during this project. But we made it. Russ, it was an honor to write this book with you.

NOTES

We have benefited from the work of many other authors and reporters who were early to break through the wall of secrecy around Donald Trump's finances and life. We credit their work in the notes below, but several deserve special recognition.

Neil Barsky broke through that wall early. Wayne Barrett and Gwenda Blair set the template for the Trump family history and Donald Trump's challenges as a businessman. Books by Tim O'Brien, David Enrich, and David Cay Johnston also stand out. Marie Brenner's early reporting on Trump's life provided a level of gorgeous detail about events that now seem historic.

Patrick Radden Keefe's piece for *The New Yorker* caught our eye, and his books on other topics served as a general inspiration.

We note here that Trump, through spokesman Jason Miller, did not respond to requests for comment.

Introduction

1 **The Trump offer was so:** Author interview with Dan Tangherlini.

2 **At the time, Trump:** Jonathan O'Connell, "How the Trumps landed the Old Post Office Pavilion," *Washington Post*, August 17, 2012, https://www.washingtonpost.com/business/how-the-trumps-landed-the-old-post-office-pavilion/2012/08/17/54cbf1da-bbdd-11e1-9134-f33232e6dafa_story.html.

2 **"Today is a metaphor":** "Trump International Hotel Ribbon Cutting Ceremony," C-SPAN, October 26, 2016, accessed on February 28, 2024, https://www.c-span.org/video/?417489-1/trump-international-hotel-ribbon-cutting-ceremony.

8 **In his telling:** Donald Trump to Howard Kurtz, *Media Buzz*, Fox News, October 11, 2015, accessed on March 1, 2024, https://www.foxnews.com/transcript/donald-trump-punches-back; Donald Trump to Anderson Cooper, CNN, March 29, 2016, accessed on March 1, 2024, https://cnnpressroom.blogs.cnn.com/2016/03/29/full-rush-transcript-donald-trump-cnn-milwaukee-republican-presidential-town-hall/.

8 **"It has not been":** NBC, "Donald Trump's TODAY town hall," October 26, 2015, accessed on March 1, 2024, https://www.today.com/news/donald-trump-joins-today-town-hall-follow-it-live-t52111.

1: A Natural Virgin Market

11 **He would become:** "Helps Build Queens," *Brooklyn Daily Eagle*, May 9, 1923, Long Island Section.

11 **His alma mater:** "Ryan Expected at Big School Meeting Friday," *Brooklyn Daily Eagle*, February 1, 1923.

11 **Students waited in line:** "A Seat for Every Child," *New York Tribune*, October 13, 1921.

11 **He ignored his school's:** "Helps Build Queens."

11 **He delivered building supplies:** Gerald S. Snyder, "'Village' Is Trump Card in His Game of Life," United Press International, July 27, 1964.

11 **He took a job:** "Helps Build Queens."

12 He eventually built: Alden Whitman, "A Builder Looks Back—and Moves Forward," *New York Times*, January 28, 1973.

12 his choice of childhood toys: Snyder, "'Village' Is Trump Card in His Game of Life."

12 His parents, Frederick and Elizabeth: Ancestry .com, s.v. "Fred Trump" (born 1869), Department of Commerce and Labor—Bureau of the Census, "Thirteenth Census of the United States: 1910."

12 Frederick traveled to: Gwenda Blair, *The Trumps: Three Generations of Builders and a Presidential Candidate* (New York: Simon & Schuster, 2015), 48–49.

12 He returned to New York City: Blair, *The Trumps*; Ancestry.com, s.v. "Fred Trump" (born 1869). "Enumeration of the Inhabitants," New York State, 1915.

12 He bought his young family: Ancestry.com, s.v. "Fred Trump" (born 1869), "Thirteenth Census of the United States: 1910."

12 Their neighbors mostly rented: Ancestry.com, s.v. "Fred Trump" (born 1869), "Thirteenth Census of the United States: 1910."

12 struck down by the Spanish flu: Richard J. Roth, "Trump the Builder Plays Mothers as Ace Cards," *Brooklyn Daily Eagle*, May 14, 1950; death certificate of Frederick Trump, obtained by authors.

12 Frederick left his wife: Will of Frederick Trump, 1918, obtained by authors.

12 While Fred was still: Snyder, "'Village' Is Trump Card in His Game of Life."

12 She had designs: Blair, *The Trumps*; Ancestry.com, s.v. "Fred Trump" (born 1869). "Enumeration of the Inhabitants," New York State, 1915. Authors' note: Job descriptions for her three children in the 1925 census reflected her plan, with John listed as a draftsman, young Elizabeth as a stenographer, and Fred as a carpenter.

12 She formed the first: "Development in Coney Is Peak of a 40-Year Building Career," *New York Times*, January 5, 1964.

12 He took classes: Snyder, "'Village' Is Trump Card in His Game of Life"; Roth, "Trump the Builder Plays Mothers as Ace Cards."

12 They would pay cash: Blair, *The Trumps*, 120.

13 classified advertisements to sell homes: Classified advertisement, "BEFORE YOU BUY / SEE / E. TRUMP & SON / DISTINCTIVE COLONIAL HOUSES / IN BEAUTIFUL HOLLIS," *The Chat* (Brooklyn, New York), October 2, 1926, 35. Fred Trump would continue to use the same phone number, Jamaica 10199, in classified ads through at least 1934.

13 By 1925, Elizabeth and her children: Carl Ballenas with the Aquinas Honor Society of the Immaculate Conception School, *Jamaica Estates* (Mount Pleasant, SC: Arcadia Publishing, 2010), 9.

13 The Trumps bought a house: State of New York, "Enumeration of Inhabitants," 1925.

13 The best known: "The Rise of Felix Isman," *New York Times*, February 10, 1907; "Profits in Real Estate," *The Sun* (New York), July 7, 1912.

13 Another Jamaica Estates founder: "Degnon Terminal Add 1,000,000 SQ. FT," *New York Times*, June 11, 1922.

13 He commissioned a stone mansion: "Jamaica Estates, a Home Park in the City," *Brooklyn Times*, May 27, 1911; "The New Hill Section," *Daily Long Island Democrat*, September 20, 1911.

13 Isman, Degnon, and the other: Ballenas, *Jamaica Estates*, 51.

13 To the right: Ballenas, *Jamaica Estates*, 54.

13 They hired a famous: "To Develop 8,000 Lots," *New York Times*, August 11, 1907, 8. The landscape architect was Charles Wellford Leavitt Jr., whose landscape design works included estates, country clubs, and universities. A civil engineer, Leavitt also designed the racetracks at Belmont and Saratoga, and the grandstands of Forbes Field, the baseball stadium in Pittsburgh.

14 The original partnership: "Ask Felix Isman for Figures in Jamaica Estates," *Brooklyn Daily Times*, January 21, 1914.

14 More than fourteen hundred potential: "Jamaica Lot Auction," *New York Times*, June 13, 1920.

14 they placed an advertisement: Classified advertisement, *The Chat*, October 9, 1926.

14 Fred built them: Blair, *The Trumps*, 149.

14 John headed to college: "Poly Gets New School Building," *Brooklyn Daily Eagle*, March 14, 1929; "John Trump Dies," *New York Times*, February 26, 1985.

14 Their sister, Elizabeth: "Walter-Trump," *Brooklyn Daily Eagle*, June 18, 1929; Ancestry.com, s.v. "Elizabeth Walter" (born 1904), Department of Commerce—Bureau of the Census, "Fourteenth Census of the United States: 1930."

14 He built sixteen homes: "Small Home Plans Increase Building Outlook in Queens," *Brooklyn Times Union*, July 2, 1930, Home Edition with Long Island News.

14 Then twenty-five years old: "F.C. Trump Plans More Model Homes," *Brooklyn Daily Times*, Long Island Edition, March 8, 1931, 21.

15 "Stroll around this parklike": Display advertisement, *Brooklyn Daily Eagle*, March 15, 1931, D3.

15 Nearly one-quarter: Universities-National Bureau Committee for Economic Research, "The Measurement and Behavior of Unemployment," National Bureau of Economic Research, 215, https://www.nber .org/system/files/chapters/c2644/c2644.pdf.

15 Roughly half of all construction: Congressional Research Service, "The Labor Market During the Great Depression and the Current Recession," 6, https:// crsreports.congress.gov/product/pdf/R/R40655/4.

15 He hung a sign outside: Trump Markets advertisement, https://www.boweryboyshistory.com/2020/11 /a-grocery-story-americas-first-supermarket-opens -in-queens-1930.html.

15 It was a concept created: Ballenas, *Jamaica Estates*, 96.

15 After proudly advocating: Trump Markets advertisement.

15 A decades-old financial house: "Lehrenkrauss Receivers Are Picked in Court," *Brooklyn Daily Eagle*, December 7, 1933.

15 Fred bid in bankruptcy court: "Lehrenkrauss Sale Approved by Referee," *Brooklyn Daily Eagle*, March 27, 1934.

16 During the process: Author interview with Milton Hyman, 2022; Ancestry.com, s.v. "William Hyman" (born 1903), Department of Commerce and Labor—Bureau of the Census, "Thirteenth Census of the United States: 1910."

16 Nominally back in real estate: Snyder, "'Village' Is Trump Card in His Game of Life."

16 He thought kick-starting: Dialogue in this section was drawn from Franklin D. Roosevelt, "CONFIDENTIAL Press Conference #160," Warm Springs, Georgia, Georgia Warm Springs Foundation, November 23, 1934, Franklin D. Roosevelt Library and Museum, https://www.fdrlibrary.org, 238–46.

17 National Housing Act: Kenneth T. Jackson, *Crabgrass Frontier: The Suburbanization of the United States* (New York: Oxford University Press, 1985), 203–9; "First Annual Report of the Federal Housing Administration" (Washington, D.C.: United States Government Printing Office, January 29, 1935).

17 the FHA would refuse: Jackson, *Crabgrass Frontier*, 207–9.

17 He and a partner purchased: "Circus Grounds Acquired as Site for 450 Homes," *New York Herald Tribune*, July 4, 1936.

17 Beyond them, as far as the eye could see: Advertisement, "Trump Scores Again in Flatbush," *Brooklyn Daily Eagle*, February 26, 1939, 4E.

17 He would dig holes: Joseph B. Mason, "Biggest One-Man Show," *American Builder*, December 1940, 25.

18 The homes would sell: "Plans 400 Homes for New Colony in East Flatbush," *Brooklyn Daily Eagle*, May 9, 1937.

18 When the model home: "Builders Get Plaque," *New York Times*, August 12, 1936.

18 After the ceremony: "Night Force Employed to Rush Houses," *Brooklyn Daily Eagle*, May 23, 1937.

18 As a teenager: Mary Anne MacLeod listed her occupation as "domestic" on "List or Manifest of Alien Passengers to the United States," on the SS *Cameronia*, September 12, 1934; Blair, *The Trumps*, 47.

18 Fred Trump, thirty: Marriage announcement, *Brooklyn Daily Eagle*, January 20, 1936.

18 Her hometown newspaper: Nina Burleigh, "Mary Trump: The Lucky Lass from Stornoway," *American Heritage*, September 2020, https://www.americanheritage.com/mary-trump-lucky-lass-stornoway.

18 The ceremony was followed: Wedding dinner menu, Harold P. Bock, the Carlyle, to Miss M. MacLoud, December 23, 1935, obtained by authors.

18 After a brief trip to Atlantic City: Blair, *The Trumps*, 148.

18 His mother, Elizabeth: Ancestry.com, s.v. "Elizabeth Trump" (born 1880), Department of Commerce—U.S. Bureau of the Census, "Sixteenth Census of the United States: 1940."

18 He did not have an office: Mason, "Biggest One-Man Show," 25.

18 He did not borrow money: Mason, "Biggest One-Man Show," 24.

19 water down paint: Blair, *The Trumps*, 160, 296.

19 At the cost of nails: Numerous newspaper advertisements from across the country show standard 16d framing nails—roughly 50 nails—offered at no more than four cents per pound.

19 He generally did not hire: Mason, "Biggest One-Man Show"; Ancestry.com, s.v. "Amy Celentano" (born 1912), "Charles H. Luerssen" (born 1872), Department of Commerce—U.S. Bureau of the Census, "Fourteenth Census of the United States: 1930."

19 Many would refer to her: Deposition of Robert Trump, probate proceeding for the will of Fred C. Trump, obtained by authors.

19 Hyman's son, Milton, recalled: Author interview with Milton Hyman, 2022.

19 A feature article in *American Builder*: Mason, "Biggest One-Man Show," 24.

19 Builders could readily: "New FHA Financing Greatest Building Aid, Vannemann Says," *Brooklyn Daily Eagle*, January 15, 1939, 1E, 2E.

20 Fred liked to say: "New Flatbush Homes Attract Many Visitors," *Brooklyn Daily Eagle*, January 15, 1939, 1E, 2E.

20 "When the big crowds arrived": "New Flatbush Homes Attract Many Visitors."

20 After one of his new buyers: Abe Greenberg, "Real Estate," *New York Daily News*, August 10, 1940.

20 He advocated for New York: "Seek 'Home' Slogan for Motor Plates," *New York Times*, May 14, 1939.

20 The fair featured: Jackson, *Crabgrass Frontier*, 187.

20 Fred sent five hundred: "Trump Staff Visits Fair for Original Ideas," *Brooklyn Eagle*, October 1, 1939; "Trump Accepts Worker Ideas for Dwellings," *Brooklyn Daily Eagle*, October 22, 1939.

20 Fred offered to cover: "Builder Urges Free Entry to Fair for Poor," *Brooklyn Daily Eagle*, August 20, 1939.

20 "I refer to the vast": "Builder Urges Free Entry to Fair for Poor."

21 He continued to find: "War Conditions Creating Problems for Appraisers," *Brooklyn Daily Eagle*, April 20, 1941, 27.

21 The seller was Joseph P. Day: "Trump Plans to Rebuild Area in Bensonhurst," *New York Herald Tribune*, April 20, 1941, C1.

21 He would spend $500,000: "Trump Plans to Rebuild Area in Bensonhurst."

21 "There is a natural virgin": "Trump Plans 700 homes in Bensonhurst," *Brooklyn Daily Eagle*, April 20, 1941, 27.

21 A writer for *The Brooklyn Daily Eagle*: "Trump Home Operation Opens for Inspection," *Brooklyn Daily Eagle*, December 12, 1941.

21 Fred touted the value: "Trump Home Operation Opens for Inspection."

2: The American Way of Life

22 The coastal area: The Hampton Roads-Peninsula War Studies Committee, College of William and Mary, Charles F. Marsh, ed., *The Hampton Roads Communities in World War II* (Chapel Hill, NC: University of North Carolina Press, 1951), 3–9; Thomas J. Wertenbaker and Marvin W. Schlegel, *Norfolk: Historic Southern Port* (Durham, NC: Duke University Press, 1962), 27–47.

22 Tranquil as the waters: Marsh, ed., *The Hampton Roads Communities in World War II*, 61.

22 There were not enough: Information in this section was drawn from Marvin W. Schlegel, *The Norfolk Virginian-Pilot*, and *The Ledger-Star*, *Conscripted City: Norfolk in World War II* (Norfolk War History Commission, 1951; repr., Norfolk, VA: Hampton Road Publishing 1991), 51–60, 171–85.

23 His latest Brooklyn project: "800-Lot Donation Spurs Victory Garden Drive," *Brooklyn Daily Eagle*, February 27, 1943.

23 "Rents are still soaring": "Here's How They're Building Houses in Busy Norfolk Va.," *Berkshire Eagle*, May 9, 1942.

23 The new program: "F.H.A. Plan Is Liberalized," *New York Times*, May 31, 1942.

23 But the law did not require: F.H.A. Investigation Report, "Report of the Senate Committee on Banking and Currency," 84th Congress, 1st Session, January 6, 1955, 1–4.

24 "Dividends or rates of return": "Plans Norfolk Housing," *New York Times*, April 18, 1943.

24 He had been beaten: "East Hilton Plans Pushed," *Daily Press* (Newport News), December 25, 1940; "Willard Park Tract Is Sold," *Norfolk Ledger Dispatch*, July 18, 1941.

24 By the summer of 1942: Authors' note: Known as "garden apartments" for the grass and walkways between buildings, the form of building would become ubiquitous across the country thanks to Section 608. See "Garden Apartments Converted," *New York Times*, November 26, 1978.

24 Fred occasionally stayed: Blair, *The Trumps*, 158.

24 The Trump and Hyman kids: Author interview with Milton David Hyman, 2022.

24 They were listed as partners: "County Brings Suit Against Southampton Apts., Inc., to Collect $7,595 in Tap Fees," *Daily Press* (Newport News), November 15, 1944; "'Minor Dispute' Causes Unions to Pull Workers," *Daily Press* (Newport News), December 15, 1944.

25 Taylor Jr. was shocked: Author interview with W. Taylor Johnson Jr., 2022.

25 his two closest acquaintances: Blair, *The Trumps*, 493, 503.

25 During one drive: Blair, *The Trumps*, 503.

25 Forty-two warships: Thomas J. Wertenbaker, *Norfolk: Historic Southern Port* (Durham, NC: Duke University Press, 1962), 359.

25 Fred Trump had built: "Talbot Park Apartment Project to Be Completed, Filled Shortly," *Norfolk Virginian-Pilot*, June 20, 1943; "Apartment Unit Nearly Finished," *Daily Press* (Newport News), March 2, 1944; "Build New War Homes," *New York Times*, June 21, 1942.

26 use as Victory gardens: "800-Lot Donation Spurs Victory Garden Drive," *Brooklyn Daily Eagle*, February 27, 1943.

26 "Nails are impossible": "Building in Borough Is Nearly at Standstill as Home Need Grows," *Brooklyn Daily Eagle*, June 16, 1946, 1, 34.

26 A recent government study: Wilson Wyatt, Veterans Emergency Housing Program, Report to the President, February 7, 1946 (Washington, D.C.: U.S. Government Printing Office, 1946), 4.

26 To support the building: "Ceiling Prices Set to Speed Building," *New York Times*, December 18, 1945; Al. Case, "End Controls to Aid Housing, Avery Advises," *Chicago Daily Tribune*, March 7, 1946; "Reports Home Building Black Market," *Chicago Daily Tribune*, March 7, 1946.

26 a lot of metal: "Lack of Supplies Hampers Builder," *New York Times*, April 14, 1946.

26 A neighbor, a jewelry maker: "Organize to Keep Business Building Out of Jamaica Estates," *New York Times*, August 2, 1929; Ancestry.com, s.v. "Edward Abel" (born April 7, 1879), Department of Commerce—U.S. Bureau of the Census, "Sixteenth Census of the United States: 1940"; Blair, *The Trumps*, 230.

26 Fred bought Abel's lot: Blair, *The Trumps*, 230.

26 Fred Trump, son: The Degnon mansion still stood, but it was now used as a monastic retreat. Degnon, a devout Catholic, had sold the estate to the Passionist Fathers, who founded the Immaculate Conception Church and a school on the grounds.

27 Three weeks before Donald Trump: Congressional Research Service Report, "A Chronology of Housing Legislation and Selected Executive Actions, 1892–1992," December 1993, 23, https://www.huduser.gov/portal/publications/commdevl/Chronology_1892_1992.html.

27 The amendment sweetened: Congressional Research Service Report, "A Chronology of Housing Legislation and Selected Executive Actions, 1892–1992," 22.

27 More significantly, the FHA: F.H.A. Investigation, "Report of the Senate Committee on Banking and Currency," 1955, 43–44.

27 To oversee that huge pot: F.H.A. Investigation, "Report of the Senate Committee on Banking and Currency," 1955, 127–28.

27 He was a fireplug: F.H.A. Investigation, "Report of the Senate Committee on Banking and Currency," 1955, 19–20.

27 Powell dispatched personnel: "Builders and FHA Arrange 60 Clinics on Housing Law," *Chicago Tribune*, September 19, 1948.

27 He crisscrossed the country: "FHA Allots Billion for Rental Homes," *New York Times*, April 15, 1947, 43.

28 He would call the project: From the air, Shore Haven would appear to be ten buildings, but Fred would apply for building permits and market it as thirty-two separate structures, perhaps ensuring he could apply for as many five-million-dollar mortgages as possible.

28 The 1946 changes: F.H.A. Investigation, Report of the Senate Committee on Banking and Currency," 1955, 1–4, 43.

28 To maximize his loan amount: Federal Housing Administration, Project Analysis forms, filed by Fred Trump, January 1949, in James P. McGranery and Regina Clark McGranery papers, Manuscript Division, Library of Congress.

28 Grace and Powell signed: "Gets FHA Commitment on $9,125,500 Housing," *New York Times*, August 30, 1947, 23; "1,344-Family Project to Rise in Bensonhurst," *Brooklyn Daily Eagle*, June 22, 1947, 1.

28 *The Brooklyn Daily Eagle* ran a photograph: "Early Tenants Applications," *Brooklyn Daily Eagle*, July 13, 1947, 28.

28 By August, another three thousand: "Gets FHA Commitment on $9,125,000 Housing."

28 He made an impassioned plea: "1,344-Family Project to Rise in Bensonhurst."

28 "I have now adopted": "High House Prices Seen Benefit to Earlier Buyer," *New Herald Tribune*, February 7, 1948, 22.

29 A purchase in December 1947: "Trump Plans Apartments for 2,000 Families," *New York Times*, December 21, 1947.

29 For less than $200,000: F.H.A. Investigation, Hearings Before the Committee on Banking and Currency, United States Senate, 83rd Congress, 2nd Session, pursuant to S. Res. 229, 1954, Part 1, 396.

29 Based on the cost estimates: "Trump Will Build Brighton Housing with 1,860 Suites," *New York Times*, September 11, 1949.

29 He would not have to start: F.H.A. Investigation, Hearings Before the Committee on Banking and Currency, United States Senate, Part 1, 52.

29 To raise the construction money: F.H.A. Investigation, Hearings Before the Committee on Banking and Currency, United States Senate, Part 1, 419.

29 He still did not feel: F.H.A. Investigation, Hearings Before the Committee on Banking and Currency, United States Senate, 1954, Part 1, 419.

29 Tomasello's father, James: "J. V. Tomasello, 56, Contractor, Dies," *Brooklyn Daily Eagle*, April 22, 1937.

29 He would become a 25 percent: F.H.A. Investigation, Hearings Before the Committee on Banking and Currency, United States Senate, Part 1, 419.

29 By the time the first $4.1 million: Executive Session, Special Interview to Investigate Federal Housing Administration, Washington, D.C., June 18, 1954, 296; F.H.A. Investigation, Hearings Before the Committee on Banking and Currency, United States Senate, Part 1, 293.

30 Maryanne, only eleven: Maryanne Trump speaking to her niece Mary Trump in 2018, recorded by Mary Trump and reviewed by the authors.

30 Some months later: Mary Trump, *Too Much and Never Enough: How My Family Created the World's Most Dangerous Man* (New York: Simon & Schuster, 2020), 21.

30 The procedures led to: Maryanne Trump speaking to Mary Trump.

30 With his final child born: Information in this section about the trusts Fred Trump created in 1949 was drawn from New York City property records; Fred Trump's federal IRS gift-tax returns, obtained by authors; and David Barstow, Susanne Craig, and Russ Buettner, "Trump Engaged in Suspect Tax Schemes as He Reaped Riches from His Father," *New York Times*, October 2, 2018.

31 Fred also began giving: Fred Trump's federal IRS gift-tax returns, obtained by authors.

31 only 3 percent: U.S. Department of the Commerce, Bureau of the Census, "Income of Families and Persons in the United States: 1950," March 25, 1952, 1.

31 Physicians earned an average: William Weinfeld, "Income of Physicians, 1929–49," July 1951, https://fraser.stlouisfed.org/files/docs/publications/SCB/pages/1950-1954/4374_1950-1954.pdf.

31 The Cadillac now bore: "Of Kings and Queens," *New York Daily News*, August 10, 1950.

31 Fred directed subcontractors: Richard J. Roth, "Trump the Builder Plays Mothers as Ace Cards," *Brooklyn Daily Eagle*, May 14, 1950.

31 It was the largest project: Executive Session, Special Interview to Investigate Federal Housing Administration; F.H.A. Investigation, Hearings Before the Committee on Banking and Currency, United States Senate, Part 1, 413.

31 He staggered tasks: "Large Brighton Apartment Project Near Completion," *New York Herald Tribune*, September 17, 1950; Roth, "Trump the Builder Plays Mothers as Ace Cards."

31 FHA rules governing costs: Author tabulation from FHA questionnaires, filed by Fred Trump in January 1956, in McGranery Papers.

31 But Fred decided that: F.H.A. Investigation, Hearings Before the Committee on Banking and Currency, United States Senate, 1954, Part 1, 410–11.

32 Since Fred handled: Author tabulation from FHA questionnaires.

32 By the time he finished: Author tabulation of FHA forms filed by Fred Trump, in McGranery papers.

32 Before he could take: Memorandum from Fred C. Trump to William C. Warren, April 21, 1959, in McGranery papers.

32 But Clyde Powell: Blair, *The Trumps*, 188.

32 The next day, Charles wrote: Letter from Richard P. Charles to Commissioner of Internal Revenue, December 22, 1950, in McGranery papers.

32 Within one week: Letter from E. I. McLarney to Shore Haven Apartments No. 2, Inc., December 29, 1950, in McGranery papers.

32 Fred wrote himself two checks: Memorandum, "re: Fred C. and Mary Trump—Federal Income Tax for the Calendar Year 1950," in McGranery papers.

33 He had already taken: Matthew J. Tosti, memorandum, September 14, 1955, in McGranery papers.

33 A large chunk of that money: F.H.A. Investigation, Hearings Before the Committee on Banking and Currency, United States Senate, 1954, Part 1, 52.

33 He and Tomasello: F.H.A. Investigation, Hearings Before the Committee on Banking and Currency, United States Senate, 1954, Part 1, 52; Executive Session, Special Interview to Investigate Federal Housing Administration, 301–2, 307.

33 And the money Fred kept: Author tabulation of FHA forms filed by Fred Trump in McGranery papers; FHA Investigation, Hearings Before the Committee on Banking and Currency, United States Senate, 1954, Part 4, 3582, 3586.

33 During construction of Fred Trump's: F.H.A. Investigation, Hearings Before the Committee on Banking and Currency, United States Senate, 1954, Part 1, 400; property records creating ground leases filed with the New York City Department of Finance, Office of the City Register, by William Hyman, sample: 1948, Reel 7278, 130.

33 Before he finished that task: The dialogue and description of events regarding the death of Bill Hyman and his son's subsequent decision to take a summer job with Fred Trump were drawn from the authors' interview with Milton Hyman.

34 "For generations, the Statue of Liberty": Display advertisement, "The American Way of Life," *New York Times*, January 16, 1949, R2.

3: They Just Went Wild

36 One summer day: Except where otherwise noted, this account of Powell in Norfolk for the opening of the Mayflower and the events that followed is drawn from testimony by William Taylor Johnson and Frederick Alfred Van Patten; F.H.A. Investigation, Hearings Before the Committee on Banking and Currency, United States Senate, 83rd Congress, 2nd session, pursuant to S. Res. 229, 1954, Part 4, 3229–33, Part 3, 2116–31, https://catalog.hathitrust.org/Record/100672141.

36 He preferred racehorses: "Ex-FHA Chief Before Tax Court," *Pasadena Independent*, November 15, 1957.

36 Also there to mark the occasion: "Mayflower Cornerstone," *Norfolk Virginian-Pilot*, August 19, 1950.

36 They all posed: "Collins Speaks as Cornerstone Laid at Beach," *Norfolk Virginian-Pilot*, August 19, 1950.

38 *Architectural Forum* published: "Apartment Boom," *Architectural Forum*, January 1950, 97.

38 In 1952, he received notice: Memorandum from Fred C. Trump to William C. Warren, April 21, 1959, attached to a letter from William C. Warren to Commissioner of Internal Revenue, May 15, 1959, in James P. McGranery and Regina Clark McGranery papers, Manuscript Division, Library of Congress.

38 In correspondence not made public: Memorandum from Fred C. Trump, April 21, 1959, in McGranery papers.

39 The new administration: William C. Warren to Commissioner of Internal, May 15, 1959, in McGranery papers.

39 He called the Gross matter: F.H.A. Investigation, Hearings Before the Committee on Banking and Currency, United States Senate, 1954, Part 4, 3469, 3470, 3474.

39 As the investigation progressed: "F.H.A. Head Out in Probe of Housing Loan Scandals," *Boston Globe*, April 13, 1954.

40 But his boss, Albert Cole: "F.H.A. Head Out in Probe of Housing Loan Scandals."

40 Cole hired William F. McKenna: Francis Stephenson, "Chief Resigns in FHA Scandal," *New York Daily News*, April 13, 1954.

40 He had been charged: F.H.A. Investigation, Hearings Before the Committee on Banking and Currency, United States Senate, 1954, 79.

40 McKenna also discovered: F.H.A. Investigation, Hearings Before the Committee on Banking and Currency, United States Senate, 1954, 33–37.

40 "There are certain allegations": F.H.A. Investigation, Hearings Before the Committee on Banking and Currency, United States Senate, 1954, 2079.

41 When he appeared: Homer E. Capehart interview, *Longines Chronoscope*, CBS, 1954.

41 "We certainly are going": Homer E. Capehart interview.

41 On April 19, 1954, he sat: Anthony Leviero, "F.H.A. Aide Invokes Fifth Amendment in Housing Inquiry," *New York Times*, April 20, 1954.

41 He provided the same answer: Leviero, "F.H.A. Aide Invokes Fifth Amendment in Housing Inquiry."

41 He added that Taylor: F.H.A. Investigation Report, "Report of the Senate Committee on Banking and Currency," 84th Congress, 1st Session, January 6, 1955, 20–21.

41 He left the hearing room: Author interview with W. Taylor Johnson Jr.

41 In the spring of 1954: "Andrews Asserts Housing Windfall was 65.5 Million," *New York Times*, April 21, 1954.

42 Fred entered the Capitol building: Dialogue in this section was drawn from the testimony of Fred Trump before the Senate Banking Committee during executive session, June 18, 1954.

43 Three weeks later: "Housing Probers Call New Yorker," *New York Daily News*, July 10, 1954.

43 "That means I drew it out": Except where noted, dialogue in this section was drawn from F.H.A. Investigation, Hearings Before the Committee on Currency and Banking, United States Senate, pursuant to S. Res. 229, 1954.

44 Fred had made the same point: Testimony of Fred Trump before the Senate Banking Committee, June 18, 1954, 326.

45 "That is unpardonable": Congressional Record, July 28, 1954, Housing Act of 1954, Conference Report, 12, 353.

45 "FHA people just went wild": Congressional Record, July 28, 1954, 12, 353.

46 "ashamed of and embarrassed by": "Ex-FHA Chief Before Tax Court," *Pasadena Independent*, November 15, 1957.

46 Maryanne later said the hearings: Gwenda Blair, *The Trumps: Three Generations of Builders and a Presidential Candidate* (New York: Simon & Schuster, 2015), 197.

46 Freddy joked to his high school pals: Author interview with James Nolan, 2022.

46 Fred saw those changes: Draft Complaint and Prayer for Judgment, *Fred C. Trump v. Norman P. Mason*, 1958, 3, in McGranery papers.

46 When the FHA refused: Thomas S. Gray to Matthew J. Tosti, November 16, 1959, in McGranery papers. Trump sold the land back to the city at what appeared to be a $500,000 profit, but he later asserted in court papers that after paying the carrying costs on the land for several years he lost $15,770.28. Defendants Memorandum in Opposition to Motion for the Appointment of a Receiver and for an Injunction, at 7, *William Tomasello v. Fred C. Trump*, in New York State Supreme Court, Queens County (Civil Action 10700-1959).

46 the FHA was a preferred stockholder: F.H.A. Investigation, Hearings Before the Committee on Banking and Currency, United States Senate, 1954, 16.

47 In July 1955, a full year: Letter to Fred Trump from Norman Mason, in McGranery papers.

47 Two of Powell's former: *Thomas Gray v. Joseph J. Brunetti Construction Co., Inc.*, Appellant, 266 F.2d 809 (3d Cir. 1959), https://law.justia.com/cases/federal/appellate-courts/F2/266/809/185672/.

47 Perce had frustrated senators: Housing Act of 1954, Hearings Before the Committee on Banking and Currency, United States Senate, 83rd Congress, 2nd Session, on S. 2889, S. 2938, S. 2949, April 1954, Part 3, 1733–1767, https://catalog.hathitrust.org/Record/100672141.

47 Gray and Perce typically: *Thomas Gray v. Joseph J. Brunetti Construction Co., Inc.*

47 They impressed at least one: *Thomas Gray v. Joseph J. Brunetti Construction Co., Inc.*

47 "The situation was not so bad": Memorandum of telephone conversation, September 22, 1955, in McGranery papers.

47 After some back and forth: Memorandum for Judge McGranery, May 7, 1956, in McGranery papers.

48 When the FHA came after: Fred C. Trump to James McGranery, June 29, 1959, in McGranery papers.

48 The FHA had demanded: Letter from Matthew J. Tosti to James P. McGranery, May 29, 1959, in McGranery papers.

48 But someone at the FHA: Notice to Take Depositions, at 1, *The United States of America v. Ash Corporation, et al*, in United States District Court, Eastern District of Virginia, Norfolk Division (Civil Action No. 59 C 2325), in McGranery papers.

48 "Dear Judge: Taylor Johnson": Fred C. Trump to James McGranery, June 29, 1959, in McGranery papers.

48 Taylor wrote to McGranery: W. Taylor Johnson to James P. McGranery, June 24, 1959, in McGranery papers.

48 After negotiating with the agency: Matthew J. Tosti to James P. McGranery, May 29, 1959, in McGranery papers.

49 As a result, Fred took over: James P. McGranery and Regina Clark McGranery papers, Manuscript Division, Library of Congress.

49 As Fred's efforts: Thomas S. Gray to James P. McGranery, August 22, 1960, in McGranery papers.

49 the commissioner's resignation: Associated Press, "Zimmerman Resigns Federal Housing Post," *Poughkeepsie Journal*, October 10, 1960; Marsh Cunningham to James P. McGranery, undated, in McGranery papers.

49 But Fred waited: Marsh Cunningham to Matthew J. Tosti, March 30, 1959; David Fuss to James P. McGranery, July 1, 1959; David Fuss to Green Park Sussex, July 7, 1959, in McGranery papers.

49 "It is Fred's idea": Matthew J. Tosti to James P. McGranery, October 7, 1955, in McGranery papers.

49 The FHA predictably objected: Legrand Perce and Thomas Gray to James P. McGranery, undated handwritten letter, 3, in McGranery papers.

50 Section 608 had increased: F.H.A. Investigation," Report of the Senate Committee on Banking and Currency, 1955, 99.

50 When the FHA finally foreclosed: Fred Trump to Judge McGranery, December 15, 1960, in McGranery papers.

50 He devised what he thought to be: Memorandum decision dated January 30, 1961, at 2, *Fred C. Trump v. Norman P. Mason*, in United States District Court, District of Columbia (Civil Action No. 60 C 4147), in McGranery papers.

50 The FHA saw through: Lemuel Showell to Fred C. Trump, December 21, 1960, in McGranery papers.

50 "As a taxpayer": Fred Trump to Judge McGranery, December 21, 1960.

50 He sent a memo: Fred Trump to Judge McGranery, December 15, 1960.

50 Fred sued to challenge: Memorandum decision dated January 30, 1961.

51 By the end of the decade: Defendants Memorandum in Opposition to Motion for the Appointment of a Receiver and for an Injunction, at 2, *William Tomasello v. Fred C. Trump.*

4: In His Father's Sights

52 Mark Golding, a friend: The description of events in this paragraph is based on an author interview with Mark Golding, 2022.

52 Friends who were around: Author interview with Jan VanHeiningen, 2022.

52 the garage door opened: Author interview with Jan VanHeiningen.

52 If Freddy and his friends: Author interview with Louis Droesch, 2022.

53 "We'd go to some candy store": Author interview with Louis Droesch.

53 On some weekends: The dialogue and description of events about Fred Trump's old sofa were drawn from an author interview with Louis Droesch.

54 He left the customary check: Author interview with Paul Onish, 2022; Marc Fisher, "Growing Up Trump," *Moment*, May 16, 2017.

54 The check in the name: Author interview with Paul Onish.

54 He splurged on cars: Fred Trump's general ledgers and banking records, obtained by authors; author interviews with confidential sources.

54 She considered attending: The quotes in this paragraph attributed to Maryanne Trump were drawn from a recording of Maryanne Trump speaking to her niece Mary Trump in 2018, recorded by Mary Trump and reviewed by the authors.

54 For tenth grade: Author interview with James Nolan, 2022.

55 flip one seat: Author interview with Jan VanHeiningen.

55 Their fathers were not poor: Author interview with Jan VanHeiningen.

55 It was the setting: Author interviews with James Nolan and Jan VanHeiningen.

55 "It was a total cacophony": Author interview with James Nolan.

55 Freddy acquired his first boat: Author interview with Jan VanHeiningen.

55 Fred would sit silently: Author interview with Jan VanHeiningen.

55 He played only one sport: St. Paul's School 1956 yearbook.

55 He joined the Sacristans Guild: St. Paul's School 1956 yearbook, 44.

55 VanHeiningen remembers thinking: Author interview with Jan VanHeiningen.

55 He liked to parrot one-liners: Interviews with high school and university friends of Freddy Trump.

56 "He certainly admired": Author interview with James Nolan.

56 "a solid C": Author interview with James Nolan.

56 The two friends both applied: Author interview with James Nolan.

56 Freddy told his friends: Author interview with Jan VanHeiningen.

56 "He would walk into a room": Maryanne Trump speaking to her niece Mary Trump in 2018.

56 He rolled onto campus: Author interviews with Stuart Oltchick and Sol Magid, 2022.

57 Freddy nonetheless conjured up: Author interview with David Miller, 2022.

57 David Miller, a fraternity: Author interview with David Miller.

57 A wide porch spanned: The dialogue and description of events about Freddy's time at the Sigma Alpha Mu fraternity house was drawn from author interviews with Sol Magrid, David Miller, and Stuart Oltchick.

57 He parked it safely: Author interview with Sol Magrid.

57 All three survived: "Boy Faces Auto Crash Charges," *Morning Call* (Paterson, N.J.), July 31, 1959.

57 It had existed before: Ray Farkas, "Flying Club Revived, Wants to Buy P-26," *Brown and White* (Lehigh University), February 22, 1955.

58 A new group of students: "New $525 Plane Purchased by Students Air Enthusiasts," *Brown and White*, January 14, 1955.

58 Renting the plane: "Flying Group Buys 'Almost New' Plane," *Brown and White*, March 6, 1959, 4.

58 He listed his height as: Fred Trump's 1957 application for student pilot license, FAA records, obtained by authors.

58 The Aeronca, a two-seater: "Aeronca 7AC Champion," *Plane and Pilot*, updated November 20, 2017, https://www.planeandpilotmag.com/article/aeronca-7ac-champion/.

58 a club member crashed: "Crash Reports Stir Conflict," *Brown and White*, April 8, 1960.

58 Members acquired a replacement: "Flying Group Buys 'Almost New' Plane."

58 As he approached the grass airfield: Author interview with Stuart Oltchick.

58 Sol Magrid twisted: Author interview with Sol Magrid.

58 small plane to the Bahamas: Mary Trump, *Too Much and Never Enough: How My Family Created the World's Most Dangerous Man* (New York: Simon & Schuster, 2020), 52.

59 She had competed: "Local Girls Are Stewardesses," *Fort Lauderdale News and Sun Sentinel*, November 27, 1960.

59 Linda, whose father: Trump, *Too Much and Never Enough*, 55.

59 he ordered his son: The dialogue and description of events in this section are based on accounts of the events written by Vincent Abramo and provided to the authors in 2021.

5: Toy Soldier Academy

61 Elizabeth, four years older: Author interview with Annamaria Forcier, 2022.

61 Donald and his mother: Interview with Mary Trump on *Selina Scott Meets Donald Trump* (Aberdeen, Grampian Television, 1995), TV movie.

61 Donald saw the story: Donald J. Trump with Tony Schwartz, *Trump: The Art of the Deal* (New York: Ballantine Books, 1987), 62.

61 He was the tallest: Author interview Mark Golding, 2022.

61 On the soccer field: Author interview with Paul Onish, 2022.

61 A neighbor said he once: Author interview with confidential source, 2022.

61 At the Atlantic Beach Club: The dialogue and description of events regarding the Atlantic Beach Club was drawn from an author interview with Sandy McIntosh, 2022.

62 In seventh grade, Brant: "Blotter," Kew-Forest School 1957 yearbook, 44.

62 they collected baseball: Transcript of an interview with Peter Brant by Michael E. Miller, *Washington Post*, 2016.

62 "I like to see": Kew-Forest School 1958 yearbook, 93.

62 in sixth or seventh grade: The description of events about Donald Trump's friendship with Peter Brant was drawn from transcript of an interview with Brant by Michael E. Miller.

63 "That was it": Author interview with Paul Onish.

63 He was issued an M1 rifle: Details about Donald Trump's daily routine at the New York Military Academy were drawn from interviews with several of his classmates, many of whom are quoted in the book.

63 During one visit: Michael Hirsh, "Trump Has Mocked the U.S. Military His Whole Life," *Foreign Policy*, September 8, 2020. Authors' note: George Michael Witek changed his last name to White after attending the New York Military Academy. Recent stories mentioning him sometimes refer to him as George White.

64 Theodore Dobias, a stout man: NPR interview of Theodore Dobias that aired on WLRN on September 1, 2016.

63 He lived in a house: Author interview with Michael Scadron, 2022.

64 He was taught how: NPR interview of Theodore Dobias.

64 When he failed: Michael Kranish and Marc Fisher, *Trump Revealed: An American Journey of Ambition, Ego, Money and Power* (New York: Scribner, 2016), 39.

64 His days were ruled: The description of Donald Trump's routine at the New York Military Academy was drawn from interviews with Douglas Reichel and Sandy McIntosh.

64 "Conditions are such": Advertisement, *New York Times*, September 8, 1906.

65 management of younger cadets: The description of the power structure at New York Military Academy was drawn from interviews with various former NYMA cadets, 2022, and Peter Ticktin, *What Makes Trump Tick: My Years with Donald Trump from the New York Military Academy to the President* (Herndon, Va.: Mascot Books, 2020), 12.

65 He had never held a firearm: The dialogue and description of events in this paragraph was drawn from an author interview with Douglas Reichel.

66 Donald excelled at the domestic: Paul Schwartzman and Michael E. Miller, "Confident. Incorrigible. Bully: Little Donny Was a Lot Like Candidate Donald Trump," *Washington Post*, June 22, 2016.

66 The cadet, Theodore Levine: Ailsa Chang, "This Is Where Donald Trump Played by the Rules and Learned to Beat the Game," *Morning Edition*, NPR, November 10, 2015.

66 He played one year: Shrapnel, New York Military Academy 1964 yearbook, 105. Authors' note: Trump also played sports on the junior varsity level.

66 The baseball team played: Shrapnel,146.

66 The results show Trump: *Poughkeepsie Journal*, April 19, 1964 (Trump 0 for 3); *Journal News*, April 23,

1964 (Trump 1 for 3); *Daily Item*, May 7, 1964 (Trump 0 for 2); *Morning Call*, May 11, 1964 (Trump 0 for 4); *Daily Item*, May 12, 1965 (Trump 0 for 3); *Journal News*, May 21, 1964 (Trump 0 for 3).

66 **the academy's soccer team:** Author interviews with Douglas Reichel and William Specht.

67 **"He's got to learn":** Maureen Seaberg, "Young Donald's Reality Show," *New York Daily News*, February 6, 2005.

67 **He was put in charge:** Author interview with Sandy McIntosh.

67 **Sandy McIntosh, who attended:** Author interview with Sandy McIntosh.

67 **Trump would be promoted:** Interviews with former New York Military Academy classmates of Donald Trump; Michael E. Miller, "50 Years Later, Disagreements over Young Trump's Military Academy Record," *Washington Post*, January 9, 2016.

67 **They noticed that:** Author interview with Sandy McIntosh.

67 **During his first month:** The description of events regarding Lee Raoul Ains and Donald Trump's reassignment was drawn for author interviews with Sandy McIntosh and William Specht, and from Miller, "50 Years Later, Disagreements over Young Trump's Military Academy Record."

67 **"His father was rich":** Hirsh, "Trump Has Mocked the U.S. Military His Whole Life."

68 **Witek was surprised:** George Witek's reaction to the decision to put Donald Trump at the front of the Columbus Day Parade is based on comments he made in a 2018 email exchange with Sandy McIntosh, obtained by authors.

68 **Donald would always claim:** Transcript of a 2014 interview with Donald Trump conducted by Michael D'Antonio, author of *The Truth About Trump* (New York: St. Martin's Press, 2015).

68 **Witek assembled his staff:** The description of events in this paragraph is drawn from Hirsh, "Trump Has Mocked the U.S. Military His Whole Life," author interviews with NYMA cadets, and a 2018 email exchange between George Witek and Sandy McIntosh, reviewed by authors.

68 **All except Trump:** Shrapnel, 120.

68 **On the day yearbook portraits:** The dialogue, description of events, and biographical information in this section were drawn from an interview with Michael Scadron.

69 **Scadron was expelled:** "Head of Academy Resigns," *New York Times*, March 8, 1964.

69 **He graduated from another high school:** Author interview with Michael Scadron.

69 **Scadron would lose track:** Author interview with Michael Scadron. Donald Trump hired Scadron for a short period in the 1970s.

70 **In Donald's mind:** Interview with Donald Trump conducted by Michael D'Antonio.

70 **There were the top ten:** Information in this section on the 1964 graduating class of the New York Military Academy was drawn from the 1964 school yearbook.

71 **"When I got into basic training":** Hirsh, "Trump Has Mocked the U.S. Military His Whole Life."

71 **at least two other captains:** "Robert J. Ayling," obituary, *Gouverneur Tribune-Press* (N.Y.), October 15, 1997; "Wins Wings," *Hartford Courant*, May 26, 1970.

71 **"I was in the military":** Interview with Donald Trump conducted by Michael D'Antonio.

71 **"always the best athlete":** Interview with Donald Trump conducted by Michael D'Antonio.

71 **In reality he was outbatted:** Shrapnel, 62, 104, 207.

71 **Donald also claimed:** Interview with Donald Trump conducted by Michael D'Antonio.

71 **Singleton would be:** "Ken Singleton," MLB.com, https://www.mlb.com/player/ken-singleton-122272.

71 **He once identified the scout:** Marie Brenner, "Trumping the Town," *New York*, November 17, 1980; Paul Solotaroff, "Trump Seriously: On the Trail with the GOP's Tough Guy," *Rolling Stone*, September 9, 2015; Daniel Bates, "Exclusive: Donald Trump pictured in uniform as a cadet captain," DailyMail.com, July 21, 2015; Greg Boeck, "Playing to Win, Trump Finds Sport in Every Deal," *USA Today*, May 30, 1990.

72 **"if he worked at it":** Boeck, "Playing to Win, Trump Finds Sport in Every Deal."

72 **"I was supposed":** Brian Kilmeade, *The Games Do Count: America's Best and Brightest on the Power of Sports* (New York: ReganBooks, 2004).

72 **"He singled out the $100,000":** Kilmeade, *The Games Do Count.*

72 **He would settle:** Mary Trump, *Too Much and Never Enough: How My Family Created the World's Most Dangerous Man* (New York: Simon & Schuster, 2020), 52.

6: March the Line

73 **In the summer of 1957:** Testimony of Fred Trump before the State of New York Commission of Investigation, January 26, 1966, 303.

73 **Following state laws:** The Redevelopment Companies Law, as described in Thomas W. Ennis, "Group Offers Aid on Cooperatives," *New York Times*, March 31, 1957.

73 **Fred was enraged:** Testimony of Fred Trump before the State of New York Commission of Investigation.

73 **He was paying a property tax bill:** Television interview with Fred Trump, January 1966, https://www.youtube.com/watch?v=hfWSNwNP3aA.

73 **"competition right across the way":** Testimony of Fred Trump before the State of New York Commission of Investigation.

73 **Cashmore's best friend:** Gwenda Blair, *The Trumps: Three Generations of Builders and a Presidential Candidate* (New York: Simon & Schuster, 2015), 173.

74 **Music Under the Stars:** "Fund for Israel Near End of Drive; 2 Music Events to Be Staged Here in Campaign to Raise $1,934,000 for Institutions," *New York Times*, June 1, 1952.

74 **an unfair "giveaway":** Testimony of Fred Trump before the State of New York Commission of Investigation, 305.

74 **a private chat with Cashmore:** Testimony of Fred Trump before the State of New York Commission of Investigation, 304–5.

74 **"I knew John Cashmore":** Television interview with Fred Trump, January 1966.

74 **Cashmore, born the youngest:** "Arthur D. Cashmore Dies," *New York Times*, October 11, 1951.

74 **He and his wife:** List of outbound passengers on the

Andrea Doria, American Export Lines, March 23, 1954, Ancestry.com.

74 Though he was never charged: Wayne Barrett, *Trump: The Greatest Show on Earth* (New York: Regan Arts, 2016), 101.

75 failed to keep the Dodgers: Dick Young, "Phils Seek Gilliam-'Nix' Says Buz," *New York Daily News*, March 1, 1956; Charlie Vackner, "Fernandez in Shape If Pee Wee Isn't," *Brooklyn Daily*, March 6, 1956; passenger manifest, Brooklyn Dodgers private air charter to Havana from Miami, March 6, 1956, Ancestry.com, s.v. "John Cashmore."

75 Kazan had moved: "Abraham E. Kazan Dies at 82; Master Co-op Housing Builder," *New York Times*, December 22, 1971.

75 Kazan came to see: Abraham E. Kazan, "Coöperative Housing in the United States," *Annals of the American Academy of Political and Social Science* 191, Consumers' Coöperation (May 1937): 137–43, https://www.jstor.org/stable/1019871; "Abraham E. Kazan Dies at 82; Master Co-op Housing Builder.

75 He led the International Ladies Garment Workers Union: "Abraham E. Kazan dies at 82; Master Co-op Housing Builder."

76 "Friendliness didn't help": Barrett, *Trump: The Greatest Show on Earth*, 123.

76 "The only way we can": The information in this section is based on Charles Grutzner, "Co-op Developer Fights Opposition," *New York Times*, December 10, 1958.

76 "John Cashmore was interested": Television interview with Fred Trump, January 1966.

76 Kazan and Trump were summoned: The quotes and description of events in this paragraph were drawn from the testimony of Abraham Kazan before the State of New York Commission of Investigation.

77 He died of a heart attack: "Cashmore Dies; Brooklyn Chief," *New York Times*, May 8, 1961.

77 Initially reluctant, he went along: Gerald S. Snyder, "Village' Is Trump Card in His Game of Life," United Press International, July 27, 1964.

77 "It took a long time": Gerald S. Snyder, "Village' Is Trump Card in His Game of Life."

77 Two state programs: "Trump Homes Hope to Get State Financing," *Coney Island Times*, August 9, 1963.

77 One program would allow him: "Trump Homes Hope to Get State Financing."

77 The other program: "Trump Homes Hope to Get State Financing."

77 He got started with: Ninth Annual Report of the Temporary Commission of Investigation of the State of New York to the Governor and the Legislature of the State of New York, 1967, 96.

78 Fred Trump would charge: Ninth Annual Report of the Temporary Commission of Investigation of the State of New York, 96.

78 As soon as the plans: The Temporary Commission of Investigation of the State of New York, "An Investigation Concerning the Limited-Profit Housing Program," 1966, 149–57.

78 that section of Coney Island: Michael T. Kaufman, "Housing and Amusements Give Coney Island a Dual Place in the Sun," *New York Times*, March 19, 1964.

78 The city, which under Mitchell-Lama: The Temporary Commission of Investigation of the State of New York, "An Investigation Concerning the Limited-Profit Housing Program," 149–157.

78 But still he directed: Transcript of Public Hearing of the State of New York Commission of Investigation, January 26, 1966, 270.

78 Lindenbaum had recently: Martin Tolchin, "$520,000 Legal Fee Involving a Co-op Blocked by 3 City and State Agencies," *New York Times*, October 10, 1972.

78 Fred had Matthew Tosi: Tolchin, "$520,000 Legal Fee Involving a Co-op Blocked by 3 City and State Agencies."

78 But just to be sure: Transcript of Public Hearing of the State of New York Commission of Investigation, 272.

78 "I don't do lobbies!": Alan Lapidus, *Everything by Design: My Life as an Architect* (New York: St. Martin's Press, 2007), 9.

78 "They had to be plain": Lapidus, *Everything by Design*, 10.

79 He told reporters: "Trump Village Oversubscribed," *Kings Courier*, July 28, 1962, 1.

79 Fred directed the real estate: "Record Number Seek Trump Apartments," *Kings Courier*, July 14, 1962, 1.

79 The state had demanded: Testimony of Fred Trump before the State of New York Commission of Investigation.

79 "I saw that this was growing": Testimony of Fred Trump before the State of New York Commission of Investigation.

79 Donald, home from the military academy: Blair, *The Trumps*, 239.

79 If tenants complained: Mary Trump, *Too Much and Never Enough: How My Family Created the World's Most Dangerous Man* (New York: Simon & Schuster, 2020), 54.

80 At one older building: Blair, *The Trumps*, 244.

80 "One of the tenants": Author interview with Sol Magrid.

80 his father made him deliver: Author interview with Sol Magrid.

80 Taylor grew up: The dialogue and description of events in this section regarding Taylor Johnson Jr.'s friendship with Freddy Trump was drawn from author interviews with Taylor Johnson Jr.

81 She had just been hired: Trump, *Too Much and Never Enough*, 55.

81 Flying was so glamorous: "Local Girls Are Stewardesses," *Fort Lauderdale News and Sun Sentinel*, November 27, 1960.

81 Freddy proposed within the next year: Trump, *Too Much and Never Enough*, 55.

81 Taylor Johnson served: "Trump-Clapp," *Fort Lauderdale News and Sun Sentinel*, January 21, 1962.

81 Fred and Mary attended: Author interview with W. Taylor Johnson Jr.

81 Linda's father worked: Trump, *Too Much and Never Enough*, 55; property records for 823 SW 14th Court, Fort Lauderdale, Florida.

81 Maybe they felt: Author interview with David Miller, 2022.

82 From what Annamaria saw: Author interview with Annamaria Forcier.

82 He logged hundreds of hours: Information in this section is based on FAA records, obtained by the authors.
82 She had quit the airline: Trump, *Too Much and Never Enough*, 58.
82 He alluded to "a rift": Author interview with Taylor Johnson Jr.
82 He was soon accepted: Author interview with Bob Kavula; Trump, *Too Much and Never Enough*, 61.
82 With the last buildings: Trump, *Too Much and Never Enough*, 61.
82 Classmates in the training: Michael Kranish, "Trump Pressured His Alcoholic Brother About His Career. Now He Says He Has Regrets," *Washington Post*, August 8, 2019.
82 "It was very prestigious": Author interview with Annamaria Forcier.
82 "When he was a pilot": Author interview with Annamaria Forcier.
83 When he thought: The information in this section about Taylor Johnson Jr.'s wedding was drawn from an author interview with Taylor Johnson Jr.
83 Donald drove up: Trump, *Too Much and Never Enough*, 62; author interviews with Roger Gedgard and Bob McMahon; "Presidential Candidates Report Their First Cars," The Associated Press State and Local Wire, January 14, 2004.
83 Robert Trump, barely a teenager: The wading pool scene is based on a photo, obtained by the authors.
83 "Dad's right about you": Marie Brenner, "After the Gold Rush," *Vanity Fair*, September 1990.
83 At the age of twenty-six: Author interview with Bob Kavula, 2022.
83 "He had problems": Author interview with Bob Kavula.
83 TWA encouraged Freddy: Trump, *Too Much and Never Enough*, 66–67.
84 fly with two smaller airlines: Trump, *Too Much and Never Enough*, 67.
84 Taylor Johnson remembers: Author interview with W. Taylor Johnson Jr.
84 His weight plummeted: Freddy Trump's FAA records, obtained by the authors.
84 They took an apartment: Trump, *Too Much and Never Enough*, 67.
84 He rented a small weekend place: Trump, *Too Much and Never Enough*, 73; Author interview with W. Taylor Johnson Jr.
84 He would put up: Author interview with Annamaria Forcier.
84 In her mind: Author interview with Annamaria Forcier.
84 held a small ceremony: "About the Coney B'd of Trade," *Coney Island Times*, December 27, 1963.
84 When applications were being: Author interview with Susan Shavitz, 2018.
84 But only Jews seemed: "About the Coney B'd of Trade."
84 Al Sinrod, the president: "About the Coney B'd of Trade."
84 "While we are basically": Ralph Weiskittel, "Fred Trump on the Go: Landlord's Lost Without Wings," *Cincinnati Enquirer*, October 2, 1966.
85 Swifton Village in Cincinnati: Associated Press, "Brooklyn Builder Buys Cincinnati Home Colony," *New York Times*, January 16, 1964.
85 Patio Gardens in Flatbush: "Suites on View at Patio Gardens," *New York Daily News*, June 20, 1964.
85 A profile in *The New York Times*: "Development in Coney Is Peak of a 40-Year Building Career," *New York Times*, January 5, 1964.
85 "I don't consider it work": Snyder, "'Village' Is Trump Card in His Game of Life."
85 He still signed every check: Author interview with W. Taylor Johnson Jr.; Probate Proceeding, Will of Fred C. Trump, Surrogate's Court, Queens County (Index No. 1999-3949), sealed deposition of Robert S. Trump on February 24, 2000, obtained by authors. Authors' note: Robert Trump testified that his father still signed almost all his business checks into the early 1990s, with his nephew being the only other signatory.
85 He personally visited Virginia: Author interview with W. Taylor Johnson Jr.
85 He traveled to Maryland: Karen DeYoung, "N.Y. Owner of P.G. Units Seized in Code Violations," *Washington Post*, September 30, 1976.
85 And now he began flying: "Swifton Village a Loser, But No Worry to Tycoon," *Cincinnati Enquirer*, January 6, 1965.
85 his secret to success: Weiskittel, "Fred Trump on the Go: Landlord's Lost Without Wings."

7: It's All Over Now

86 flags outside Steeplechase Park: "Son of Park Founder Dies. Steeplechase Mourns Death of Frank Tilyou," *Coney Island Times*, May 15, 1964.
86 The land was zoned: Lou Powsner, "Shore Enough!," *Coney Island Times*, May 28, 1965.
86 James Onorato, who had managed: Steeplechase Park: Sale and Closure, 1965–1966; Michael P. Onorato, ed., Diary and Papers of James J. Onorato, 1998.
87 Fred offered the Tilyous: Steeplechase Park: Sale and Closure, 1965–1966; Diary and Papers of James J. Onorato.
87 He agreed to let: Steeplechase Park: Sale and Closure, 1965–1966; Diary and Papers of James J. Onorato.
87 On the morning of July 1, 1965: Unless otherwise noted information about the Steeplechase closing was drawn from Steeplechase Park: Sale and Closure, 1965–1966; Diary and Papers of James J. Onorato.
87 "If we can make it pay": McCandlish Phillips, "Return of Coney Island: Amusement Area, Badly Hurt Last Year, Is Attempting to Win Back Customers," *New York Times*, April 13, 1966.
87 Lindsay's incoming parks: Barrett McGurn, "Lindsay Park Boss Fights Coney Housing," *New York Herald Tribune*, December 2, 1965, 11.
87 "They turned it down": "Coney Hopes of Revival Dashed by N.J. Fun Lord," *Daily News*, July 28, 1965.
87 "The fact is that": McGurn, "Lindsay Park Boss Fights Coney Housing."
88 On the evening of Monday: Author interview with confidential source.
88 the Boeing 727 crashed: David S. Broder, "58 Feared Dead as Jet Crashes Near Cincinnati; Plane Hits a Hill," *New York Times*, November 9, 1965.
88 Fred told some family: Author interview with confidential source.
88 Robert Strauss, a field auditor: Information in this

section regarding Robert Strauss's visit to Trump Village was drawn from the testimony of Fred Trump before the State of New York Commission of Investigation, January 26, 1966.

88 **the rental rates Fred was paying:** Testimony of Leo V. Silverman, an assistant director of the Bureau of Finance and Audits, New York State Division of Housing and Community Renewal, before the State of New York Commission of Investigation, January 26, 1966.

88 **They checked the form:** Testimony of Leo V. Silverman.

89 **A young investigator there:** "Ninth Annual Report of the Temporary Commission of Investigation of the State of New York to the Governor and the Legislature of the State of New York," February 1967, 116–17.

89 **From the state-supplied mortgage:** "Ninth Annual Report of the Temporary Commission of Investigation," 118.

89 **Fred pocketed thirty extra dollars:** "Ninth Annual Report of the Temporary Commission of Investigation," 118.

89 **One commissioner, Jacob B. Grumet:** Testimony of Leo V. Silverman.

89 **"This is peanuts":** The dialogue and description of events in this section were drawn from the testimony of Fred Trump before the State of New York Commission of Investigation.

90 **The commissioners drew:** Except where noted the information and dialogue in this paragraph were drawn from the testimony of Abraham Kazan before the State of New York Commission of Investigation, 246–47 and 254.

91 **The rentals were larger:** Ninth Annual Report of the Temporary Commission of Investigation, 109.

91 **Silverman told the commissioners:** Dialogue and information in this section was drawn from the testimony of Leo V. Silverman before the State of New York Commission of Investigation.

91 **Fisch knew the city had done:** Ninth Annual Report of the Temporary Commission of Investigation, 149–57; author interview with Joseph Fisch, 2022.

92 **Fisch grilled Bunny:** Testimony of Abraham M. Lindenbaum before the State of New York Commission of Investigation, 373.

92 **It would be charged:** Martin Tolchin, "$520,000 Legal Fee Involving a Co-op Blocked by 3 City and State Agencies," *New York Times*, October 10, 1972.

92 **He referred the facts:** Author interview with Joseph Fisch, 2022.

92 **"Today, prosecutors would fight":** Author interview with Joseph Fisch.

93 **"Never heard of that":** Television interview with Fred Trump, January 1966, https://www.youtube.com/watch?v=hfWSNwNP3aA.

93 **He had Freddy hire:** "Tiger Seals Big Deal to Make Steeplechase Animal Heaven," *New York Daily News*, February 26, 1966.

93 **As he signed:** "Tiger Seals Big Deal to Make Steeplechase Animal Heaven."

93 **The City Planning Commission:** Phillips, "Return of Coney Island; Amusement Area, Badly Hurt Last Year, Is Attempting to Win Back Customers."

93 **Another planning official:** Phillips, "Return of Coney Island; Amusement Area, Badly Hurt Last Year, Is Attempting to Win Back Customers."

93 **He proposed developing:** "Coney Island Mulls an All-Weather Pleasuredome," *New York Daily News*, July 21, 1966.

93 **"Mr. Trump is stuck":** "A 160-Foot-High Pleasure Dome Is Proposed for Coney Island," *New York Times*, July 24, 1966.

93 **He promised that six:** "Steeplechase Hits Dust Wednesday," *New York Daily News*, September 17, 1966.

94 **He showed up one day:** Steeplechase Park: Sale and Closure, 1965–1966; Diary and Papers of James J. Onorato.

94 **"You are cordially invited":** Steeplechase Park: Sale and Closure, 1965–1966; Diary and Papers of James J. Onorato.

94 **Onorato saw the event:** Steeplechase Park: Sale and Closure, 1965–1966; Diary and Papers of James J. Onorato.

94 **Bulldozers arrived on:** "Steeplechase Hits Dust Wednesday."

94 **The day of the event:** Photo of Fred Trump at the demolition party.

94 **He encouraged guests:** David Behrens, "The Coney Island of His Mind," *Newsday* (Long Island, N.Y.), June 4, 2003.

94 **The city eventually:** Charles G. Bennett, "Park Usage Voted for Steeplechase," *New York Times*, May 23, 1968.

94 **He wrote a letter:** Fred Trump, "Park Peeve," *New York Daily News*, March 20, 1967.

95 **collect more than $65 million a year:** Confidential financial statements of various Fred Trump entities, obtained by authors.

95 **He would make clear:** Confidential will drafting notes from Fred Trump's attorney, Robert Sheehan, written in 1991 and obtained by authors.

95 **He would cast about:** Author interviews with Stuart Oltchick and David Miller.

95 **She graduated with honors:** "Maryanne Trump Is Betrothed to David Desmond," *Herald Statesman*, July 13, 1959.

95 **She was pursuing:** "Maryanne Trump Is Betrothed to David Desmond."

96 **They had a son:** Maryanne Trump Barry commencement address, "Fairfield University Commencement Address," C-SPAN, May 22, 2011, https://www.c-span.org/video/?299640-1/fairfield-university-commencement-address.

96 **Desmond had graduated:** "Maryanne Trump Is Betrothed to David Desmond"; Mary Trump, *Too Much and Never Enough: How My Family Created the World's Most Dangerous Man* (New York: Simon & Schuster, 2020), 81.

96 **"My husband was a deadbeat":** Maryanne Trump speaking to her niece Mary Trump in 2018, recorded by Mary Trump and reviewed by the authors.

96 **They lived in a Fred:** Trump, *Too Much and Never Enough*, 81.

96 **"They never knew":** Maryanne Trump speaking to her niece Mary Trump in 2018.

96 **From her mother:** Trump, *Too Much and Never Enough*, 82.

96 Several family members: Author interview with confidential source.

96 she paid for food: Trump, *Too Much and Never Enough*, 82.

96 Her younger sister, Elizabeth: Author interview with confidential source.

96 Elizabeth took a job: "Elizabeth Trump Weds James Grau," *New York Times*, March 27, 1989.

96 He became captain: "Robert Trump, BU Alum and President's Brother, Dies," *BU Today*, August 16, 2020.

8: All Show

97 "He'd get in there": Christine Wolff, "From Swifton Village to Trump Tower," *Cincinnati Enquirer*, June 28, 1990.

97 After four years: Author interview with John Malnati, 2022.

97 He enrolled in the business school: Author interviews with Donald Trump's Fordham classmates Bob McMahon and John Malnati, 2022.

97 On the Monday of orientation: "University Freshman Class Survives Orientation Week," *Fordham Ram*, September 18, 1964.

97 The four of them: Author interviews with Bob McMahon and John Malnati.

98 Donald drove the Austin-Healey: Author interview with John Malnati.

98 "Son, deliveries are made": Author interview with John Malnati.

98 He did join the school's: "Squashers Season Squelched: 3–9," *Fordham Ram*, March 3, 1966.

98 McMahon and Gedgard introduced: Information in this section on Donald Trump's interest in golf at Fordham is based on author interviews with Bob McMahon and John Malnati.

98 C-plus to B-minus range: Author interviews with Bob McMahon and John Malnati.

98 Pacia quickly recognized: Author interview with Georgette Pacia.

98 "He picked it up as quickly": Author interview with Georgette Pacia.

98 "He golfed every opportunity": Author interview with Georgette Pacia.

99 Reserve Officers' Training Corps: Author interviews with Bob McMahon and John Malnati.

99 But with the United States': Author interviews with Bob McMahon and John Malnati.

99 paid cadets forty dollars: "Army ROTC Enrollment Decline," *Fordham Ram*, December 4, 1964.

99 Students at Fordham were told: John A. Nolan, "Rose Hill Hit by Draft; Students to Be Tested," *Fordham Ram*, March 3, 1966.

99 "had to do well": Author interview with Georgette Pacia.

99 he did not excel: "Dean's List," *Fordham Ram*, September 23 and 30, 1965.

99 "Because where I'm going": Author interview with Steve Lesko, 2022.

99 Donald's brother Freddy: The dialogue and description of events in this section on Donald Trump's application to Wharton were drawn from author interview with Jim Nolan.

100 "I got in quickly": Matt Viser, "Even in College, Donald Trump Was Brash," *Boston Globe*, August 28, 2015.

100 "I realized then": Howard Blum, "Trump: The Development of a Manhattan Developer," *New York Times*, August 26, 1980.

100 He was introduced by Robert Moses: Gay Talese, "New Landmark Greeted with Fanfare in Harbor," *New York Times*, November 22, 1964.

100 Two days later: "Verrazano Architect Receives Honorary Science Doctorate," *Fordham Ram*, November 24, 1964.

101 later that week: Associated Press, "11 to Receive Science Honor," *Courier-News* (Bridgewater, N.J.), November 28, 1964.

101 Back in the 1950s: David Barstow, Susanne Craig, and Russ Buettner, "Trump Engaged in Suspect Tax Schemes as He Reaped Riches from His Father," *New York Times*, October 2, 2018.

101 He gave them each: Fred Trump's federal IRS gift-tax returns, obtained by authors.

101 In 1962, he gave: Barstow, Craig, and Buettner, "Trump Engaged in Suspect Tax Schemes as He Reaped Riches from His Father."

101 He filed a gift-tax return: Information in this paragraph is based on a review of Fred Trump's federal IRS gift-tax returns, obtained by authors.

102 Donald didn't do anything: Fred Trump financial and tax records, obtained by authors.

102 "I'm buying apartments": Author interview with William Specht.

102 "I never saw him": Author interview with Jim Nolan.

102 Classmate Candice Bergen: Viser, "Even in College, Donald Trump Was Brash."

103 "He was Fred's bill collector": Rebecca Tan and Alex Rabin, "Many of Trump's Wharton Classmates Don't Remember Him," *Daily Pennsylvanian*, February 20, 2017.

103 He also claimed for years: Rebecca Tan and Alex Rabin, "Was Trump Really a Top Student at Wharton? His Classmates Say Not So Much," *Daily Pennsylvanian*, February 15, 2017.

103 top of his class: Michael Kranish, "Trump Has Referred to His Wharton Degree as 'Super Genius Stuff.' An Admissions Officer Recalls It Differently," *Washington Post*, July 8, 2019.

103 They smiled for a photo: Photo of Donald Trump's graduation from Wharton.

103 That doctor found: Steve Eder, "Did a Queens Podiatrist Help Donald Trump Avoid Vietnam?," *New York Times*, December 26, 2018.

9: By No Means Standing Still

107 "Emphasis on BUTCHER": During the early years of Donald Trump's tenure with his father's company, classified advertisements listing the Trump phone numbers and a contact of "Mr. Baron" appeared in *The New York Times* on the following dates: July 21, 1968; August 18, 1968; September 5, 1968; October 25, 1968; November 2, 1968; February 5, 1969; February 21, 1969; March 2, 1969; March 5, 1969; March 19, 1969; March 30, 1969; December 26, 1969; January 1, 1970; and February 7, 1970. The list is an incomplete sampling of such ads.

108 the Palace Theatre: *George M!*, a musical biography produced by Black of Broadway legend George M.

Cohan, was awarded for choreography and received a best performance nomination for its star, Joel Grey.

108 Donald arrived without: Michael Paulson, "For Trump, Broadway Held Sway," *New York Times*, March 7, 2016. Further details of the Trump-Black meeting generously provided by Mr. Paulson from his unpublished notes.

108 The interior of the stately: Ruth Selden-Sturgill, "Metropolitan Club Building," New York City Landmark Preservation Commission, September 11, 1979. Further details from the Metropolitan Club website, https://www.metropolitanclubnyc.org.

108 He played violin: Patrick Clark, "Old Broadway Hand Made His Debut at 11," *New York Daily News*, April 19, 1970.

109 "He had done his homework": Paulson, "For Trump, Broadway Held Sway," *New York Times*, March 7, 2016.

109 Donald seemed earnestly interested: The description of events in this paragraph was drawn from Paulson, "For Trump, Broadway Held Sway," and author interview with Richard Seff, 2022.

109 Black expected most critics: Hobe Morrison, "No 'Debut' for 'Paris Is Out,'" *Rockland County Journal-News*, December 5, 1969.

109 Instead of a one-day tidal wave: Clive Barnes, "Theater: 'Paris Is Out!'" *New York Times*, February 3, 1970; George Oppenheimer, "'Paris Is Out' Has a Very Familiar Ring," *Newsday*, February 3, 1970; Hobe Morrison, "Broadway Beat," *Herald-News* (Passaic, New Jersey), January 20, 1970 (Morrison was the *Variety* theater critic who also wrote a syndicated column).

109 The *Playbill* for *Paris*: Oddly enough, given Donald's older brother's comedic obsession, the show would have been a musical based on the life of W. C. Fields. Black produced the show on tour, with Mickey Rooney and Bernadette Peters in the starring roles, but the production fell apart before its scheduled debut on Broadway in the fall of 1971.

110 "All cash!" the ads screamed: Classified advertisement, *New York Times*, March 19, 1972.

110 But the insurance company: State of New Jersey, Department of Law and Public Safety, Division of Gaming Enforcement, "Report to the Casino Control Commission," October 16, 1981, 36.

110 Fred paid $862,752: Division of Gaming Enforcement, "Report to the Casino Control Commission," 37.

110 His siblings received: Division of Gaming Enforcement, "Report to the Casino Control Commission," 36.

111 After the building opened: Division of Gaming Enforcement, "Report to the Casino Control Commission,", 40.

111 The drab building began: David Barstow, Susanne Craig, and Russ Buettner, "Trump Engaged in Suspect Tax Schemes as He Reaped Riches from His Father," *New York Times*, October 2, 2018.

111 Donald would later suggest: Judy Klemesrud, "Donald Trump, Real Estate Promoter, Builds Image as He Buys Buildings," *New York Times*, November 1, 1976.

111 "Cincinnati to us": "Swifton Village a Loser, But No Worry to Tycoon," *Cincinnati Enquirer*, January 6, 1965.

111 Fred accepted the $6.75 million: "Swifton Village Purchased," *Cincinnati Enquirer*, December 23, 1972, and Gwenda Blair, *The Trumps: Three Generations of Builders and a Presidential Candidate* (New York: Simon & Schuster, 2015), 247.

111 In 1957, Fred had bought: Deed for 22 Bayfield Lane, June 24, 1957, obtained by authors. Fred Trump purchased the property in the name of Edgerton Hall, Inc., the entity through which he owned an apartment building by the same name.

111 The four-bedroom house: Numerous classified advertisements in *The New York Times*, including on July 3, 1971, listing the office phone number in Brooklyn.

111 Fred sold it: Deed for 22 Bayfield Lane, dated February 18, 1972. At the time of the sale, Fred Trump owned the property in the name of Beach Haven Apartments No. 4, an entity through which he owned part of his Beach Haven Apartments.

111 Muggings had grown: "Queens Residents Hire a Private Security Patrol," *New York Times*, December 5, 1971, A6.

112 A local state senator: "Housing Proposal Disputed in Queens: Residents Express Doubts," *New York Times*, November 11, 1973.

113 Robert Olnick, a lawyer: CUNY TV, *BuildingNY*, Michael Stoler interview of Leonard Boxer, May 9, 2011, https://www.youtube.com/watch?app=desktop&v=wBtQAE4NIFA.

113 The apartment project: Author interview with Robert Rosenberg, 2017.

113 The state of New York: Owen Moritz, "Starrett City Okayed; Housing for 20,000," *New York Daily News*, July 28, 1972.

113 "They weren't investing for gains": Author interview with Robert Rosenberg.

113 A dozen or so Lazard: Details regarding partners from "Starrett City Associates, Second Limited and Restated Agreement of Limited Partnership," January 1, 1973, Docket No. 403, *Harvey Rudman and Harold Kuplesky v. Carol Gram Dean, Disque D. Deane, et al.*, in Supreme Court of the State of New York, County of New York, (Index No. 650159-2010).

113 He invested another $1 million: Details regarding partners from "Starrett City Associates, Second Limited and Restated Agreement of Limited Partnership," January 1, 1973, Docket No. 403, *Harvey Rudman and Harold Kuplesky v. Carol Gram Dean, Disque D. Deane, et al.*

114 "It's one of the best investments": William Sherman, "Real Estate vs. Real People," *New York Daily News*, August 5, 2007.

114 He would call: Klemesrud, "Donald Trump, Real Estate Promoter, Builds Image as He Buys Buildings"; and as evidence of his expertise with affordable housing: Transcript of testimony by Donald J. Trump to the New Jersey Casino Control Commission, April 20, 1987, 142–43.

114 Donald Trump, having escaped: Steve Eder, "Did a Queens Podiatrist Help Donald Trump Avoid Vietnam?," *New York Times*, December 26, 2018.

114 Also inside that day's newspaper: Alden Whitman, "A Builder Looks Back—and Moves Forward," *New York Times*, January 28, 1973.

116 Fred was the opposite: Author interview with Richard Kahan, 2023.

10: Shadowboxing

117 On the morning of October 15: Memorandum of the United States in Response to the Affidavits of Donald Trump and Roy Cohn, at 10, *United States of America v. Fred C. Trump, Donald J. Trump, and Trump Management, Inc.*, in United States District Court, Eastern District of New York (Civil Action No. 73 C 1529).

117 Wolf had already notified: Memorandum of the United States in Response to the Affidavits of Donald Trump and Roy Cohn, at 10.

117 Following normal procedures: Memorandum of the United States in Response to the Affidavits of Donald Trump and Roy Cohn, at 11.

117 "They are absolutely ridiculous": Morris Kaplan, "Major Landlord Accused of Antiblack Bias in City," *New York Times*, October 16, 1973, 1.

117 Over the prior year: FBI Field Office memorandum dated November 6, 1972; FBI 302 dated November 24, 1972; FBI Field Office memorandum dated April 16, 1973.

117 The investigation had begun: Memorandum of the United States in Response to the Affidavits of Donald Trump and Roy Cohn, at exhibit 3.

117 A trend emerged: Plaintiff's Answers and Objections to Defendants' First Interrogatories, at 1–6.

118 For this new challenge: Memorandum of the United States in Response to the Affidavits of Donald Trump and Roy Cohn, at 7.

118 The man who spent his life: Memorandum of the United States in Response to the Affidavits of Donald Trump and Roy Cohn, at exhibit 1.

118 Within a couple of weeks: Memorandum of the United States in Response to the Affidavits of Donald Trump and Roy Cohn, at exhibit 1.

119 It had been founded: Peter Braunstein, "Disco," *American Heritage*, November 1999, vol. 50, no 7; Judy Klemesrud, "A New Retreat for the Rich—Surrounded by Tumbledown Shacks," *New York Times*, January 6, 1974, 60.

119 Le Club had been called: Ernest Leogrande, "The Genesis of Murray the K's World," *New York Daily News*, May 1, 1966, 17–18; Peter Benchley, "Five In Spots for the Midnight Chic," *New York Times*, November 8, 1970.

119 The initial membership: Benchley, "Five In Spots For the Midnight Chic."

119 where a brother-in-law: Patrick Doyle and William McFadden, "Kennedy In-Law in a Taxi Fracas," *New York Daily News*, July 2, 1974.

119 In Donald's telling: Donald Trump with Tony Schwartz, *The Art of the Deal* (New York: Random House, 1987). chapter 5; Ivy Meeropol, director, *Bully. Coward. Victim. The Story of Roy Cohn* (New York, HBO Documentary and Motto Pictures, 2020), interview with Roy Cohn.

119 "I'm just not built that way": Trump, *The Art of the Deal*, 79.

119 "My view is": Trump, *The Art of the Deal*, 79. Authors' note: Cohn recounted a similar version of their conversation *in Bully. Coward. Victim. The Story of Roy Cohn.*

120 Cohn filed a motion to dismiss: Motion to Dismiss, at 1, *United States of America v. Fred C. Trump, Donald J. Trump, and Trump Management, Inc.*.

120 The filing included an affidavit: Affidavit in Support of Defendants' Motion to Dismiss or for a More Definite Statement, at 1–2.

120 Instead, he had relied on: Memorandum of the United States in Response to the Affidavits of Donald Trump and Roy Cohn, at 11.

120 Cohn also filed a countersuit: As and for a First Defense and by Way of a Counterclaim, at 1.

121 "That would be reverse discrimination": Jesse Brodey, "Landlord Trump Retaliates, Sues U.S. for $100 Million," *New York Daily News*, December 13, 1973.

121 Asked what evidence: Barbara Campbell, "Realty Company Asks $100-Million 'Bias' Damages," *New York Times*, December 13, 1973, 34.

121 In a related filing: Memorandum of the United States in Opposition to Defendant's Motion to Dismiss, Motion for More Definite Statement and in Support of Plaintiff's Motion to Dismiss the Counterclaim, at 15.

121 Six weeks later: Order, February 5, 1974, *United States of America v. Fred C. Trump, Donald J. Trump, and Trump Management, Inc.*

121 She was one year: Ancestry.com, s.v. "Abraham Finkelstein," 1950 United States Census of Population and Housing, Queens County, Flushing, New York.

121 Her paternal grandparents: Ancestry.com, s.v. "Abraham Finkelstein," 1930 United States Census, Population Schedule, New York County, New York.

121 They opened a laundry: Ancestry.com, s.v. "Abraham Finkelstein," 1930 United States Census, New York County, New York; U.S., World War II Draft Cards Young Men, 1940–1947, Bronx, New York.

121 She went on to Beaver College: Beaver College, "Log 1968," Glenside, Pa., 1968, 171, Scholarworks@Arcadia, https://scholarworks.arcadia.edu/college_yearbooks/; Donna Fields Goldstein, "About," LinkedIn, https://www.linkedin.com/in/donnafieldsgoldstein/. (Beaver College was renamed Arcadia University in 2001 and has accepted male students since 1973.)

122 After being assigned: Reporter's Transcript of Proceedings, October 24, 1974, at 12 and 41–42, *United States of America v. Fred C. Trump, Donald J. Trump, and Trump Management, Inc.*

122 One day that July: Reporter's Transcript of Proceedings, October 24, 1974, at 51.

122 Miranda had said: Affidavit of Elyse S. Goldweber, August 5, 1974, at 2.

122 He concluded his first interview: Affidavit of Elyse S. Goldweber, August 5, 1974, at 2.

122 But he invited Goldstein: Reporter's Transcript of Proceedings, October 24, 1974, at 89.

122 Within a day, Miranda visited: Reporter's Transcript of Proceedings, October 24, 1974, at 85.

122 He spoke with Donald: Reporter's Transcript of Proceedings, October 24, 1974, at 86.

122 The Trumps had a brief affidavit: Reporter's Transcript of Proceedings, October 24, 1974, at 83.

122 The affidavit was notarized: Affidavit of Roy M. Cohn, July 26, 1974, Exhibit 2, at 1.

122 "I can no longer tolerate": Affidavit of Roy M. Cohn, July 26, 1974, Exhibit 2, at 1.

122 Ten days after Goldstein: Affidavit of Roy M. Cohn, July 26, 1974, Exhibit 2, at 3.

122 "Commencing with her entry": Affidavit of Roy M. Cohn, July 26, 1974, Exhibit 2, at 1.

122 He said former employees: Affidavit of Roy M. Cohn, July 24, 1974, Exhibit 2, at 1–2.

122 The motion also complained: Affidavit of Roy M. Cohn, July 24, 1974, Exhibit 2, at 2.

123 Goldstein's bosses worried: Reporter's Transcript of Proceedings, October 24, 1974, at 110.

123 He testified that when: Reporter's Transcript of Proceedings, October 24, 1974, at 5.

123 Miranda acknowledged inviting: Reporter's Transcript of Proceedings, October 24, 1974, at 89.

123 "A nice girl": Reporter's Transcript of Proceedings, October 24, 1974, at 89.

123 Cohn, who had terrorized: Reporter's Transcript of Proceedings, October 24, 1974, at 110.

123 Neaher reminded Cohn: Reporter's Transcript of Proceedings, October 24, 1974, at 110–11.

123 "This is the first time": Reporter's Transcript of Proceedings, October 24, 1974, at 111.

123 They reached an agreement: Memorandum in Support of Plaintiff's Request to Enforce a Settlement Agreement, June 4, 1974, at 1.

124 That June, Goldstein and her boss: Memorandum in Support of Plaintiff's Request to Enforce a Settlement Agreement, June 4, 1974, at 1.

124 They also turned the tables: Affidavit of Donna Goldstein, June 6, 1975, at 1–2, and Affidavit of Frank E. Schwelb, June 6, 1975, at 1–2.

124 "Off the record, Judge": Reporter's Transcript of Proceedings, June 10, 1975, at 6.

124 Judge Neaher started to say: Reporter's Transcript of Proceedings, June 10, 1975, at 9.

124 "One hour, judge": Reporter's Transcript of Proceedings, June 10, 1975, at 10.

124 "I think it is discriminatory": Reporter's Transcript of Proceedings, June 10, 1975, at 33.

124 Donald repeatedly complained: Reporter's Transcript of Proceedings, June 10, 1975, at 32, 33, 37, 61.

124 Though it was not said: "Place Your Classified Apartments Advertising in The New York Times," display advertisement, *New York Times*, October 3, 1976.

124 Goldstein tried to strike: Reporter's Transcript of Proceedings, June 10, 1975, at 41.

124 Donald snapped back: Reporter's Transcript of Proceedings, June 10, 1975, at 42.

124 Goldstein reminded them: Reporter's Transcript of Proceedings, June 10, 1975, at 45.

124 "We deny that": Reporter's Transcript of Proceedings, June 10, 1975, at 45.

124 Donald insisted that Goldstein: Reporter's Transcript of Proceedings, June 10, 1975, at 45.

125 "We were not convicted": Reporter's Transcript of Proceedings, June 10, 1975, at 34.

125 "Don't be too sure": Reporter's Transcript of Proceedings, June 10, 1975, at 34.

125 The judge had initially said: Reporter's Transcript of Proceedings, June 10, 1975, at 34.

125 Fred insisted that Tysens: Reporter's Transcript of Proceedings, June 10, 1975, at 13.

125 Donald added, "I can attest": Reporter's Transcript of Proceedings, June 10, 1975, at 32.

125 But when the Trumps: Drew S. Days to Betty Hoeber, July 12, 19773, Civil Rights Litigation Clearinghouse, https://clearinghouse.net/doc/83443/.

125 The Trumps would agree: Reporter's Transcript of Proceedings, June 10, 1975, at 47.

125 He declared "full satisfaction": Joseph P. Fried, "Trump Promises to End Race Bias," *New York Times*, June 11, 1975.

126 His publisher removed: Edwin McDowell, "LeFrak Passage out of Trump Book," *New York Times*, May 11, 1988.

126 Two decades after his sister: Paul Schwartzman, "Star War for the Empire," *New York Daily News*, March 28, 1999.

126 A judge threw out: Salvatore Arena, "Leona Aces Trump in Landmark Battle," *New York Daily News*, December 17, 1999.

127 "To make it in this city": Ken McKenna, "Weaving City Rents: The Pattern Is Crazy," *New York Daily News*, January 24, 1975.

11: Whatever the Trumps Want

128 A young female aide: Video of inauguration, reviewed by authors.

128 Always affable but rarely inspiring: Sam Roberts, "An Old Generation Takes Over at City Hall," *New York Daily News*, January 2, 1974.

128 He alluded to the Watergate scandal: "Text of Beame's Address," *New York Times*, January 2, 1974.

129 Beame took the oath: Murray Schumach, "Beame Inaugurated, Vows Integrity and Efficiency," *New York Times*, January 2, 1974.

129 During World War II: Gwenda Blair, *The Trumps: Three Generations of Builders and a Presidential Candidate* (New York: Simon & Schuster, 2015), 493, 503.

129 With declining revenues: Ken Auletta, *The Streets Were Paved with Gold* (New York: Random House, 1979), chapter 2.

129 Beame hosted a reception: "4,000 Throng Lobby of the Met for Reception Honoring Beame," *New York Times*, January 2, 1974.

129 He drew the line: "4,000 Throng Lobby of the Met for Reception Honoring Beame."

129 The market for commercial: Shirley L. Benzer, "The Long-Range Outlook for Builders," *New York Times*, January 19, 1975; "State of New York City Housing and Neighborhoods 2008," Furman Center for Real Estate and Urban Policy, New York University, 9–12, https://furmancenter.org/files/sotc/State_of_the_City_2008.pdf.

130 Penn Central Transportation Company: Associated Press, "Profit Keeps the Throttle Open," *New York Times*, February 4, 1968.

130 The merger only: Philip Shabecoff, "Collapse of Penn Central Reflects Ills of Railroads," *New York Times*, February 11, 1973; Staff Report of the Securities and Exchange Commission to the Special Subcommittee on Investigations, "The Financial Collapse of the Penn Central Company," (Washington, D.C.: U.S. Government Printing Office, 1972), https://fraser.stlouisfed.org/files/docs/historical/house/1972house_fincolpenncentral.pdf.

130 In 1970, Penn Central: "Penn Central Bankruptcy Sends Shock Waves Through Commercial Paper Market," Goldman Sachs, https://www.goldmansachs.com/our-firm/history/moments/1970-penn-central-bankruptcy.html.

130 the bankruptcy court appointed: Mike Leary, "Pennsy Trustees Ask Court to OK Realty Manager," *Philadelphia Inquirer*, July 5, 1973.

130 Koskinen, the younger: "John A. Koskinen, Deputy Director of the Office of Management and Budget," U.S. Office of Management and Budget, https://clintonwhitehouse1.archives.gov/White_House/EOP/OMB/html/jakbio.html.

130 Eichler, then about forty-three: Ned Eichler, *Fame or Fortune: Giants of the Housing Industry Revealed* (Indiana: iUniverse, 2005), vii.

130 But Eichler had ventured: Eichler, *Fame or Fortune*, viii.

130 They spent months: Eichler, *Fame or Fortune*, 24.

130 They decided to focus: Eichler, *Fame or Fortune*, 25; interviews with John Koskinen, 2022 and 2023.

131 Eichler and Koskinen calculated: Author interviews with John Koskinen.

131 Months after he started: The dialogue and description of events about Ned Eichler's initial contact with Donald Trump were drawn from *Fame or Fortune*, 27.

132 Donald Trump, Eichler thought: Eichler, *Fame or Fortune*, 28.

132 "I guess you should ask": Eichler, *Fame or Fortune*, 29.

132 "The limo will pick you up": Eichler, *Fame or Fortune*, 29.

132 "Whatever the Trumps want": Eichler, *Fame or Fortune*, 29.

132 Eichler could also see: Blair, *The Trumps*, 258–59

133 "Many very successful fathers": Blair, *The Trumps*, 259.

133 He sent Eichler: Blair, *The Trumps*, 261.

133 Eichler and Koskinen rejected: Author interviews with John Koskinen.

133 "I don't drink or smoke": Eichler, *Fame or Fortune*, 28.

133 Late that July: Joseph P. Fried, "2 West Side Rail Yards Are Sought for Housing," *New York Times*, July 30, 1974, and Frank Mazza, "Penn C to Sell Midtown Yards," *New York Daily News*, July 30, 1974.

134 In reality, he had offered: *Reorganization Court Proceedings, The Penn Central Transportation Company, Debtor*, vol. 7 (Washington D.C.: CRR Publishing Company, 1981), Doc. No. 8301, 7–9.

134 *The New York Times* called Donald: Fried, "2 West Side Rail Yards Are Sought for Housing."

134 He also told reporters: "Buy 100-Acre Landfill Next to Offerman Park," *New York Daily News*, January 16, 1974.

134 The Trumps had not: New York City property records for BBLs 3-6944-80, 3-6944-480, 3-6491-207, and 3-6491-292.

134 Three months later, the city: "U.S. Slips in with 150G for Uplift of Ferry Terminals," *New York Daily News*, April 22, 1974.

134 He quickly announced: "Asks $55M Ferry Center," *New York Daily News*, May 13, 1974.

135 Eichler expected that: Eichler, *Fame or Fortune*, 30.

135 First, he scheduled: Eichler, *Fame or Fortune*, 31.

135 Not long after: Wayne Barrett, *Trump: The Greatest Show on Earth* (New York: Regan Arts, 2016), 146–67.

135 As Donald said about Starrett: Hearing transcript, June 10, 1975, at 46, *United States of America v. Fred C. Trump, Donald J. Trump, and Trump Management, Inc.*

136 But not long before: Memorandum and Order No. 1807, *Reorganization Court Proceedings, The Penn Central Transportation Company, Debtor*, vol. 7, Document No. 8651.

136 He filed an analysis: *Reorganization Court Proceedings, The Penn Central Transportation Company, Debtor*, vol. 7, Doc. No. 8301, 268–69, "Supplementary Affidavit of Edward P. Eichler in Support of the Petition of the Trustees for Authority to Enter into and Implement Agreements with Trump Enterprises, Inc., Relating to 60th Street Yard and 30th Street Yard in New York, New York," dated November 12, 1974, per summary vol. 17, 599.

136 Eichler raised what: "Supplementary Affidavit of Edward P. Eichler."

136 "Trump has no projects": "Supplementary Affidavit of Edward P. Eichler."

136 If he ever built anything: Memorandum and Order No. 1807, *Reorganization Court Proceedings, The Penn Central Transportation Company, Debtor.*

12: Everything He Touches

137 The first few floors: "The Commodore: A New Hotel on Pershing Square New York," *American Architect and Architecture* 115 (January–June 1919), 337–38.

137 Its kitchens and ballrooms: "Commodore Hotel Started," *The Sun* (New York), October 22, 1916; "10,000 Meals a Day Will Be Served in Hotel Commodore," *New York Tribune*, July 15, 1917.

137 *The New York Times Magazine*: "42nd Street Viaduct and the Commodore Hotel," *New York Times Magazine*, November 26, 1916.

137 The hotel was built: "The Real Estate Field," *New York Times*, September 13, 1961.

137 More than half: Ned Eichler, *Fame or Fortune: Giants of the Housing Industry Revealed* (Indiana: iUniverse, 2005), 32.

137 One store space: "Justice Delayed," *New York Daily News*, May 26, 1976.

138 Eichler obtained an appraisal: "Supplementary Affidavit of Edward P. Eichler in Support of the Petition of the Trustees for Authority to Enter into and Implement Agreements with Trump Enterprises, Inc., Relating to 60th Street Yard and 30th Street Yard in New York, New York," dated November 12, 1974, per summary vol. 17, 599.

138 In a vacuum: "Commodore Hotel Started."

138 Every real estate professional: Carter B. Horsley, "Foreclosure Action Is Begun Against the Chrysler Building," *New York Times*, August 30, 1975.

138 "You guys should pay me": Eichler, *Fame or Fortune*, 33.

138 The end of the conversations: Author interviews with Mike Bailkin, 2022.

138 Shostal told Bailkin: Author interview with Claude Shostal, 2022.

139 Trump also often arrived: Author interviews with Mike Bailkin.

139 "Hey, you got to help": Author interviews with Mike Bailkin.

139 He recognized that: Wayne Barrett, "The Dirty Deal That Helped Make Donald Trump," *Village Voice*, originally published February 26, 1979, republished in February 28, 2019; Author interviews with

Mike Bailkin: "The city had no option except to deal with Trump. He had site control."

139 In truth, Trump did not: Barrett, "The Dirty Deal That Helped Make Donald Trump."

140 Trump told Bailkin: Author interviews with Mike Bailkin.

140 On the fly: Author interviews with Mike Bailkin.

140 "I'm going to watch": Meeting and substance from author interviews with Mike Bailkin.

140 He finally turned to Bailkin: Author interviews with Mike Bailkin.

140 Their flagship company: Marilyn Bender, "The Very Private Pritzkers," *New York Times*, October 14, 1973.

141 Amoroso had been looking: Robert E. Tomasson, "Deal Negotiated for Commodore," *New York Times*, May 4, 1975; Gwenda Blair, *The Trumps: Three Generations of Builders and a Presidential Candidate* (New York: Simon & Schuster, 2015), 280.

141 Pritzker's company and the Trumps: Tomasson, "Deal Negotiated for Commodore."

141 "Nobody wants to loan": Author interview with John Koskinen.

141 Koskinen and Eichler understood: Author interview with John Koskinen.

141 He offered few parameters: Michael Sterne, "City Offers Incentive Plan to Increase Employment," *New York Times*, January 10, 1976.

142 A managing director: Carter B. Horsley, "Commodore Plan Is Key to the City's Tax-Aid Strategy," *New York Times*, March 28, 1976.

142 When news of the abatement: Randall Smith, "Ace Developer: Donald Trump Builds a Real-Estate Empire Using Loans, Contacts," *Wall Street Journal*, January 14, 1982.

142 Now he said it would close: Charles Kaiser, "The Commodore Closing Tuesday," *New York Times*, May 12, 1976.

142 Either way, the special tax abatement: Glenn Fowler, "Tax Plan Voted to Permit Rebuilding of Commodore," *New York Times*, May 21, 1976.

143 "He was this spoiled kid": Rene Rodriguez, "Real Estate Veteran Louise Sunshine Reflects on Storied Career and Challenges Ahead," *Miami Herald*, November 8, 2019.

143 "After I had obtained": CUNY TV, *BuildingNY*: "New York Stories, Michael Stoller interview of Louise M. Sunshine: LMS Consulting LLC," May 31, 2016, https://www.youtube.com/watch?v=RfDvmPk0Pko, at 12:38.

143 In her first year: Rodriguez, "Real Estate Veteran Louise Sunshine Reflects on Storied Career and Challenges Ahead."

143 "I knew their reputations": Author interview with John Koskinen.

144 The city drew more visitors: Ken Auletta, *The Streets Were Paved with Gold* (New York: Random House, 1979), 254.

144 He moved into: Blair, *The Trumps*, 340.

144 He held season tickets: Judy Klemesrud, "Donald Trump, Real Estate Promoter, Builds Image as He Buys Buildings," *New York Times*, November 1, 1976; State of New Jersey, Department of Law and Public Safety, Division of Gaming Enforcement, "Report to the Casino Control Commission," October 16, 1981, 23.

144 Bailkin recalls Donald speaking: Author interviews with Mike Bailkin.

144 One in particular: Ivana Trump, *Raising Trump* (New York: Gallery Books, 2017), 40.

144 "I noticed that you": Trump, *Raising Trump*, 41.

145 They walked out of Maxwell's: Trump, *Raising Trump*, 42.

145 The next day: Trump, *Raising Trump*, 42.

145 The day after that: "Lunch Queen Tries Rival Diner," *Baltimore Sun*, July 23, 1976; United States Department of Energy, "Historical Gasoline Prices," https://www.energy.gov/eere/vehicles/fact-741-august-20-2012-historical-gasoline-prices-1929-2011.

145 She caught a flight: Trump, *Raising Trump*, 42.

145 One evening, he called Jeffrey Walker: The dialogue and description of events in the paragraph regarding Jeffrey Walker's double date with Donald and Ivana Trump is based on an author interview with Jeffrey Walker.

146 Fred did not drink alcohol: Author interview with confidential source.

146 Fred Trump had a house account: Mary Trump, *Too Much and Never Enough: How My Family Created the World's Most Dangerous Man* (New York: Simon & Schuster, 2020), 161.

145 The Trumps' table: Trump, *Too Much and Never Enough*, 162.

146 Around that time: Klemesrud, "Donald Trump, Real Estate Promoter, Builds Image as He Buys Buildings."

148 "Washington is going": Associated Press, "$125 million D.C. Convention Center Proposal Unveiled," *Danville Register* (Virginia), July 8, 1976.

148 "This is ridiculous": Michael E. Miller and Michael Kranish, "Donald Trump First Swept into the Nation's Capital 40 Years Ago. It Didn't Go Well," *Washington Post*, October 21, 2016.

148 He had recently used: Classified advertisements: *New York Daily News*, June 12, 1974; *New York Times*, March 24, 1974.

148 As Mr. Baron: Classified advertisement, *New York Times*, May 29, 1975.

148 They staged what they called: Mike Smith, "High-Rise Tenants Protest Facilities," *Norfolk Virginian-Pilot*, May 31, 1975.

148 "This has never happened": Smith, "High-Rise Tenants Protest Facilities."

148 He hired a local property: "High-Rise Tenants Take Case to Court," *Norfolk Virginian-Pilot*, June 10, 1975.

148 The tenants dropped: "Towers Suit Dropped," *Norfolk Virginian-Pilot*, July 2, 1975.

148 "We are going to make": "Trump Vows Towers' Upgrade," *Norfolk Virginian-Pilot*, July 12, 1975.

149 "We're going to have": Mike Smith, "A Watery Tower Adds to Woes of Residents," *Norfolk Virginian-Pilot*, July 12, 1975.

149 Unable to get the Trumps: Karen DeYoung, "N.Y. Owner of P.G. Units Seized in Code Violations," *Washington Post*, September 30, 1976.

149 The local chief: DeYoung, "N.Y. Owner of P.G. Units Seized in Code Violations."

149 But Fred pled no contest: Elizabeth Becker, "Apartment Rentals Halted Until Repairs Are Made," *Washington Post*, October 29, 1976.

149 Donald also claimed: Klemesrud, "Donald Trump,

Real Estate Promoter, Builds Image as He Buys Buildings."

149 For that year: State of New Jersey, Department of Law and Public Safety, Division of Gaming Enforcement, "Report to the Casino Control Commission," 33.

150 As 1976 ended: State of New Jersey, Department of Law and Public Safety, Division of Gaming Enforcement, "Report to the Casino Control Commission," 29.

150 She knew almost no one: Trump, *Raising Trump*, 57.

150 Roy Cohn attended: Wayne Barrett, *Trump: The Greatest Show on Earth* (New York: Regan Arts, 2016), 197–98.

151 "This was a political event": Author interviews with Mike Bailkin.

151 The newlyweds headed: Trump, *Raising Trump*, 58. Authors' note: The option to redevelop the hotel that Donald had claimed to control for two years had been finally signed shortly before his wedding.

151 It would take another: Leasehold Mortgage Between Regency-Lexington Partners and Manufacturers Hanover Trust Company, May 19, 1978, filed with New York City Department of Finance, Office of the City Register, reel 439, p. 1781.

151 Manufacturers Hanover, a bank: Blair, *The Trumps*, 295, citing Michael Stone, "Clash of the Titans: Business Tycoons Donald Trump and Jay Pritzker," *Chicago magazine*, October 1994.

13: The Latest Jewel

152: Beame was not given: John Lewis, "Work Starts on Hyatt Hotel, Replacing Commodore," *New York Daily News*, June 29, 1978.

152 He struck Steinglass: Author interview with Ralph Steinglass, 2022.

153 "I hate granite" Author interview with Peter Samton, 2022.

153 They had met after: Lindsy Van Gelder, "Architect Der Scutt," *New York Daily News*, September 29, 1980.

153 He would call Scutt: Van Gelder, "Architect Der Scutt."

154 Before demolition began: Author interview with Jeffrey Walker.

154 People lined up: Compiled by Wes Rehberg from Press wire services, "Hotel Trimmings for Sale," *Press and Sun Bulletin* (Binghamton, N.Y.), January 4, 1978.

154 But Walker appreciated: Author interview with Jeffrey Walker.

155 "Read this, memorize it": Barbara A. Res, *Tower of Lies* (Los Angeles: Graymalkin Media, 2020), 13.

155 Res suspected that would: Author interviews with Barbara Res, 2021 and 2022.

155 When an expensive piece: Barbara Res, *All Alone on the 68th Floor: How One Woman Changed the Face of Construction* (self-published manuscript, 2013), 87.

156 But he paid: Author interviews with Jeffrey Walker.

156 "There were a number of issues": Author interview with John Nicolls, 2022.

156 "He would sit down": Author interview with Ralph Steinglass.

156 Ivana, who was pregnant: Ivana Trump, *Raising Trump* (New York: Gallery Books, 2017), 61.

156 Ivana told him: Trump, *Raising Trump*, 61.

156 He could now claim: Author interview with Paul Goldberger, 2022.

156 They were still living: Patricia Lynden, "Where the Donald Trumps Rent," *New York Times*, August 30, 1979.

157 She hired an interior: Lynden, "Where the Donald Trumps Rent."

157 She occasionally made good: Author interview with Ralph Steinglass.

157 "Every single decision": Trump, *Raising Trump*, 60.

157 Res became convinced: Res, *All Alone on the 68th Floor*, 80.

157 All of it added up: Author interview with Ralph Steinglass.

158 Koskinen thought it was: Author interview with John Koskinen.

158 Shortly after, Donald expanded: Owen Moritz, "Casino Fever—Is It Catching?," *New York Daily News*, May 13, 1979.

158 The extra costs: Author interview with Ralph Steinglass.

158 As word reached Chicago: Confidential author interview with former Hyatt executive.

158 Though it was not known: Ivana Trump application for casino license filed with the New Jersey Casino Control Commission, May 13, 1985, 38(f) to 38 (j).

158 Stephenson arranged a $35 million: State of New Jersey, Department of Law and Public Safety, Division of Gaming Enforcement, "Report to the Casino Control Commission," October 16, 1981, 27.

159 In the fall of 1978: Associated Press, "PA Reports 2nd Inquiry for World Trade Center," *Newsday*, September 1, 1978.

159 Soon after, Goldmark received a call: Author interview with Peter Goldmark, 2022.

159 Goldmark told Donald to leave: Author interview with Peter Goldmark.

160 "I don't like to talk about a deal": Joseph Egethof, "Big Deals Are Easy for Top N.Y. Broker," *Chicago Tribune*, February 20, 1979.

160 The winning bid: Jay Weiner, "LI-Linked Group Purchases Mets for $21.1 Million," *Newsday*, January 25, 1980.

160 When Donald read a magazine: Donald Trump with Tony Schwartz, *The Art of the Deal* (New York: Random House, 1987), 107.

160 He set up a meeting: Randall Smith, "Donald Trump Builds a Real Estate Empire Using Loans, Contacts," *Wall Street Journal*, January 14, 1982.

160 On a cold day: Gwenda Blair, *The Trumps: Three Generations of Builders and a Presidential Candidate* (New York: Simon & Schuster, 2015), 338.

161 Calls were placed: Blair, *The Trumps*, 340.

162 The biggest real estate families: David Samuels, "The Real-Estate Royals. End of the Line?," *New York Times Magazine*, August 10, 1997.

162 But Donald, who had spent: Frank Lombardi, "Pick W. 34th for 257M Center," *New York Daily News*, April 29, 1978.

162 "The city really needs": Vincent Cosgrove, "Center's Developer Trump Offers Good Deal, if City Plays Rights Cards," *New York Daily News*, November 22, 1978.

162 Koch shot him down: Cosgrove, "Center's Developer Trump Offers Good Deal, if City Plays Rights Cards."

162 John Koskinen, who with Eichler: Author interview with John Koskinen.

162 Residents and prominent businessmen: Vincent Cosgrove, "Skyscrapers in Midtown Too Tall a Story for Panel," *New York Daily News*, September 3, 1979.

162 "Anyone else proposing": Ken Auletta, "Complexes, Persecution and Otherwise," *New York Daily News*, September 23, 1979.

163 While he lamented: Auletta, "Complexes, Persecution and Otherwise."

163 One month later: Glenn Fowler, "Tower Approved for Bonwit Site," *New York Times*, October 20, 1979.

163 Harry Helmsley, a contemporary of Fred's: Res, *All Alone on the 68th Floor*, 105.

163 Blond waitresses fanned out: Marie Brenner, "Trumping the Town," *New York*, November 17, 1980.

163 A waterfall, shiny bronze: Paul Goldberger, "42nd Street Is About to Add Something New and Pleasant: The Grand Hyatt," *New York Times*, September 22, 1980.

163 Ivana, glamorous in a white: Brenner, "Trumping the Town."

163 He paid his respects: "Grand Hyatt Opens on 42nd Street," *Newsday* (Long Island, N.Y.), September 26, 1980.

163 Mayor Ed Koch said: "Grand Hyatt Opens on 42nd Street."

163 As the evening: Res, *All Alone on the 68th Floor*, 105.

164 He said he had been: Gail Collins, "New York's Golden Boy," *The Democrat and Chronicle* (Rochester, N.Y.), September 28, 1980.

164 "When you went into": Collins, "New York's Golden Boy."

164 The tide of companies: Carter B. Horsley, "In Environs of Grand Central, New Strength," *New York Times*, April 30, 1978.

164 During those four years: Winston Williams, "Penn Central to Ask Permission for Sale of 3 New York Hotels," *New York Times*, April 7, 1978.

164 In 1979, hotel occupancy: Randy Smith, "New Hotels Losing Millions," *New York Daily News*, May 19, 1981.

165 "I think it may be: Interviews with John Koskinen. Authors' note: Koskinen, who was later named commissioner of the Internal Revenue Service by President Barack Obama, suspects he was kept on in that role by President Trump because he "has always had a fond spot in his heart for me" due to the Commodore deal.

165 On NBC, Tom Brokaw: NBC News, *Today Show*, August 21, 1980, https://vimeo.com/389032761.

166 For 1979, the year: State of New Jersey, Department of Law and Public Safety, Division of Gaming Enforcement, "Report to the Casino Control Commission," 33.

166 Yet he lived: Howard Blum, "Trump: Development of a Manhattan Developer," *New York Times*, August 26, 1980.

166 "That was my idea": Claudia Cohen, "Trump Empire Strikes Back," *New York Daily News*, September 17, 1980.

166 "Because of the magnitude": Cohen, "Trump Empire Strikes Back."

167 City workers eventually: Author interview with Jeffrey Walker.

167 The next day, someone: Claudia Cohen, "Trump Banner Disappears," *New York Daily News*, October 2, 1980.

167 Indeed, Walker and a couple of men: Author interviews with Jeffrey Walker.

14: Mr. Baron's Tower

168 He paused to chat: Kenneth C. Crowe, "Trump Work No Luxury for Unpaid Illegal Aliens," *Newsday*, January 15, 1984.

168 They were known as: *Diduck v. Kaszycki & Sons Contractors, Inc.*, 774 F. Supp. 802 (S.D.N.Y. 1991).

168 As the foreman: Crowe, "Trump Work No Luxury for Unpaid Illegal Aliens."

168 Kaszycki changed his company's name: *Diduck v. Kaszycki & Sons Contractors, Inc.*, 874 F.2d 912, 1989, U.S. App. LEXIS 6527 (decided May 10, 1989).

169 While planning to close: Author interview with Barbara Res.

169 Kaszycki kept no records: *Diduck v. Kaszycki & Sons Contractors, Inc.*, 774 F. Supp. 802 (S.D.N.Y. 1991), 5.

169 Thirty to forty men: *Diduck v. Kaszycki & Sons Contractors, Inc.*, 774 F. Supp. 802 (S.D.N.Y. 1991), 6.

169 Often working without hard hats: Selwyn Raab, "After 15 Years in Court, Workers' Lawsuit Against Trump Faces Yet Another Delay," *New York Times*, June 14, 1998.

169 After pressuring Kaszycki: *Diduck v. Kaszycki & Sons Contractors, Inc.*, 774 F. Supp. 802 (S.D.N.Y. 1991).

169 But after an article: Suzanne Daley, "Bonwit Building Set for the Ultimate Sale," *New York Times*, March 16, 1980.

170 From the windows of his art gallery: The accounts of Robert Miller and Penelope Hunter-Stiebel drawn from Jonathan Mandell, *Trump Tower* (New Jersey: Lyle Stuart Inc., 1984), 41–44.

171 Hawkins told a reporter: Robert D. McFadden, "Builder Orders Bonwit Art Deco Sculptures Destroyed," *New York Times*, June 6, 1980.

171 "I contribute that much": Robert D. McFadden, "Builder Says Costs Forced Scrapping of Bonwit Art," *New York Times*, June 9, 1980.

172 That summer, Donald Trump: Wayne Barrett, *Trump: The Greatest Show on Earth* (New York: Regan Arts, 2016), 222.

172 One of Fred's corporations: General ledger for Trump Village Construction Corp., obtained by the authors.

172 Donald took the corner: Barbara A. Res, *Tower of Lies* (Los Angeles: Graymalkin Media, 2020), 31.

172 Norma sat in the open: Barbara Res, *All Alone on the 68th Floor: How One Woman Changed the Face of Construction* (self-published manuscript, 2013), 114.

172 As the pay problems: *Diduck v. Kaszycki & Sons Contractors, Inc.*, 774 F. Supp. 802 (S.D.N.Y. 1991).

172 Over the months: *Diduck v. Kaszycki & Sons Contractors, Inc.*, 874 F.2d 912, 1989 U.S. App. LEXIS 6527.

172 During one phone conversation: Kenneth C. Crowe, "Trump's Hardball Tactics Are Revealed in Court Documents," *Newsday* (Long Island, N.Y.), August 29, 1988.

173 Within an hour: Crowe, "Trump's Hardball Tactics Are Revealed in Court Documents."
173 Two weeks later: Tom Robbins, "The Art of the Don Deal," *New York Daily News*, April 15, 1990.
173 The real Irwin Durben: Robbins, "The Art of the Don Deal."
173 "I suspect whoever spoke": Crowe, "Trump's Hardball Tactics Are Revealed in Court Documents."
173 "I want you to build": Res, *All Alone on the 68th Floor*, 106.
174 He convinced her: Res, *All Alone on the 68th Floor*, 107.
174 So he would pay her: Barbara Res, drawn from an early manuscript of *Tower of Lies*, reviewed by authors.
174 He watched in disgust: The dialogue and description of events in this section about the U.S. Open was drawn from interviews with Barbara Res and from her book *Tower of Lies*, 29 onward.
175 It was located: Carter B. Horsley, "Olympic Tower Dedicated Here," *New York Times*, September 6, 1974.
176 "It was all legal": Author interview with John Barie, 2022.
176 "Young man, you may be": George Ross, *Trump-Style Negotiation* (New York: John Wiley & Sons, 2006), 226–27. Authors' note: When Donald told the story of that meeting in *The Art of the Deal*, his father was not present, and it was Hoving who refused to sign a contract that day because he believed his handshake should suffice.
177 He insisted that: Res, *All Alone on the 68th Floor*, 123.
177 "No, no!" he would scream: Res, *All Alone on the 68th Floor*, 102.
177 "You gotta take him off my back": Author interview with Barbara Res.
178 "I don't understand it": Randy Smith, "Housing Chief Bows to 'Politics,' Trump Charges," *New York Daily News*, April 21, 1981.
178 *New York* magazine wrote: Joe Klein, "Has Andy Stein Finally Grown Up?," *New York*, August 24, 1981.
178 Even when he did well: Klein, "Has Andy Stein Finally Grown Up?"
179 "Trump requested to see you": Smith, "Housing Chief Bows to 'Politics,' Trump Charges."
179 But here he was being: *Trump Equitable v. Gliedman*, Appellate Division of the Supreme Court of New York, May 20, 1982.
179 Tony agreed to look: *Trump Equitable v. Gliedman*, 1982.
179 "I don't know whether": Edward I. Koch, *Mayor: An Autobiography* (New York: Simon & Schuster, 1984), 401.
180 "I am entitled": Koch, *Mayor*, 401.
180 He won an interim: Clyde Haberman, "Ruling Supports Tax Abatement Asked by Trump," *New York Times*, July 22, 1981.
180 "Aristotle Onassis was": Randy Smith and Katherine Schaffer, "Judge Oks Trump Tax Break," *New York Daily News*, July 22, 1981.
180 The next day, he filed: "Trump Suing City and Housing Chief," *New York Times*, July 23, 1981; Department of Gaming Enforcement report, March 15, 1982, 54.
180 In private, Donald: Author interview with Barbara Res.
180 One reporter wrote: Roger Director, "Thanks for the $3.5 Million Condos, Don," *New York Daily News*, July 27, 1981.
180 "This 350-pound commissioner": Roger Director, "Thanks for the $3.5 Million Condos, Don.
181 Three weeks later: Randy Smith, "Posh Condo Wins $10M Tax Cut," *New York Daily News*, August 13, 1981.
181 "It does seem": August 17, 1981 letter to Ed Koch from Donald Trump, reviewed by authors.
181 "It seems incredible": "No Abatement for Trump," *Newsday* (Long Island, N.Y.), May 21, 1982.

15: So Much Hoopla

182 They found him: Author interviews with James Nolan and Jan VanHeiningen.
182 Freddy moved back home: Mary Trump, *Too Much and Never Enough: How My Family Created the World's Most Dangerous Man* (New York: Simon & Schuster, 2020), 57.
182 During the summer: Trump, *Too Much and Never Enough*, 115.
182 Donald came to the house: Trump, *Too Much and Never Enough*, 121.
182 Word spread among: Trump, *Too Much and Never Enough* 121; interviews with former fraternity friends of Freddy Trump.
183 "That's not going to happen": Trump, *Too Much and Never Enough*, 125–26.
183 Paperwork filed in court: Paperwork filed in Queens Surrogate Court associated with the estate of Fred C. Trump Jr.
183 Other trusts loaned: David Barstow, Susanne Craig, and Russ Buettner, "Trump Engaged in Suspect Tax Schemes as He Reaped Riches from His Father," *New York Times*, October 2, 2018.
183 And following their grandfather's: Trump, *Too Much and Never Enough*, 127–128.
184 Though it all went: Barstow, Craig, and Buettner, "Trump Engaged in Suspect Tax Schemes as He Reaped Riches from His Father."
184 That figure would have: Barstow, Craig and Buettner, "Trump Engaged in Suspect Tax Schemes As He Reaped Riches From His Father."
184 Mary would later be told: Trump, *Too Much and Never Enough*, 172.
184 In October 1980: Jack O'Brian, "Voice of Broadway," *Jersey Journal*, October 29, 1980.
184 In 1981, *New York Daily News*: Claudia Cohen, "Donald Trump Buys Barbizon-Plaza Hotel," *New York Daily News*, March 17, 1981.
185 He invited Greenberg: Jonathan Greenberg, "Trump Lied to Me About His Wealth to Get onto the Forbes 400. Here Are the Tapes," *Washington Post*, April 20, 2018.
185 "Okay, then $20,000 each": Greenberg, "Trump Lied to Me About His Wealth to Get onto the Forbes 400."
185 Even using Donald's round: Greenberg, "Trump Lied to Me About His Wealth to Get onto the Forbes 400."

186 Donald would be among: UPI, "People," *Troy Daily News*, January 16, 1984.

187 He's worth more": Greenberg. "Trump Lied to Me About His Wealth to Get onto the Forbes 400."

187 "My best deals": Marie Brenner, "Trumping the Town," *New York*, November 17, 1980.

187 Jeff Walker, who had always: Except where noted, details regarding the purchase of the Connecticut house were drawn from an author interview with Jeffrey Walker.

188 Donald took a little persuading: Author interview with Jeffrey Walker; "Trump's Former Greenwich Mansion Up for Grabs," *The Real Deal*, August 22, 2022; Ivanka Trump Casino Control Commission license application, May 13, 1985, 49.

188 In the grand two-story foyer: Author interview with Jeffrey Walker.

188 Louise Sunshine caught wind: Donald J. Trump with Tony Schwartz, *Trump: The Art of the Deal* (New York: Ballantine Books: 1987), 190.

188 Donald paid $65 million: State of New Jersey, Department of Law and Public Safety, Division of Gaming Enforcement, "Report to the Casino Control Commission," October 16, 1981, 61–64.

188 He dispatched Macari: Author interview with Barbara Res.

189 He had already spent: Michael A. Hiltzik, "Battle over Operations in Atlantic City; Trump-Harrah's Partnership in Casino Erupts into a Bitter Feud," *Los Angeles Times*, July 28, 1985.

189 Lapidus, typically wearing: Alan Lapidus, *Everything by Design: My Life as an Architect* (New York: St. Martin's Press, 2007), 145, 147.

189 He paid a visit: Gwenda Blair, *The Trumps: Three Generations of Builders and a Presidential Candidate* (New York: Simon & Schuster, 2015), 344.

189 He flew to New York: Trump, *Trump: The Art of the Deal*, 167; "Holiday Inns Joins Trump in Casino," *Press of Atlantic City*, July 1, 1982.

189 Ultimately, Harrah's would: William E. Geist, "About New York: On Being a Billionaire at 40," *New York Times*, June 14, 1986.

190 Phil Satre, a top executive: Author interview with Phil Satre, 2022.

190 "I think I'm probably": Author interview with Phil Satre.

190 "I want my name on it": Author interview with Phil Satre.

191 Satre left Trump Tower: Author interview with Phil Satre.

191 "The building is on fire": Res, *All Alone on the 68th Floor*, 136.

191 The entire twenty-eighth floor: Associated Press, "Fire Damages Top Floors of Unfinished Building," *Daily Item* (Port Chester, N.Y.), January 29, 1982.

191 Whether intentional or not: "Fire at 5th Ave. Tower Traps Worker in Crane," *Newsday*, January 29, 1982.

191 Eddie Bispo, the concrete superintendent: Jonathan Mandell, "Scraping the Sky," *New York Sunday News Magazine*, February 13, 1983.

191 "It didn't give anybody": Mandell, "Scraping the Sky."

192 He ordered commemorative: Res, *All Alone on the 68th Floor*, 139.

192 But he extended invitations: "Postings; Tower Topped Off," *New York Times*, July 11, 1982.

192 "There's nothing wrong": Robert Carroll, "Tower Hits the Top," *New York Daily News*, July 27, 1982.

192 Koch patted Fred: Daniel Bogado and Natasha Zinni, directors, *Trump: An American Dream*, episode 1, "Manhattan," (Los Gatos, CA: Netflix, 2017).

192 "Ah, well, I have nothing": *Trump: An American Dream*, episode 1.

192 "So have a good time": *Trump: An American Dream*, episode 1, at 45:30.

192 "I've never been to a topping-off": Mandell, "Scraping the Sky."

193 Tom Balsley sat: The dialogue and description of events in this section about Tom Balsley's waterfall pitch are based on an author interview with Tom Balsley, 2022.

194 Barbara Res, John Barie: Author interview with Barbara Res.

194 The water would fall: Author interview with Tom Balsley.

194 Balsley made several trips: The dialogue and description of events in this section regarding Donald Trump's decision to cut down the ficus trees were drawn from author interviews with Tom Balsley, Barbara Res, and Jeff Walker.

196 The lawyer warned: New York Department of City Planning, Charles E. Tennant letter to Donald Trump, March 7, 1984. Authors' note: These letters were provided to us by Kristine Miller, professor, Department of Landscape Architecture, University of Minnesota.

196 "The missing trees": Donald Trump letter to Philip Schneider, April 16, 1984. Letter provided to authors by Kristine Miller.

196 "It's his tower": Author interview with Tom Balsley.

197 *The New York Times* architectural: Paul Goldberger, "Architecture: Atrium of Trump Tower Is a Pleasant Surprise," *New York Times*, April 4, 1983.

197 One of the first assignments: Author interview with Barbara Res.

197 Donald had cut his costs: Author interviews with Ross MacTaggart and Barbara Res.

197 "They expected to just": Author interview with Ross MacTaggart.

198 He added a conference room: Marylin Bender, "The Empire and Ego of Donald Trump," *New York Times*, August 7, 1983.

198 One of several lengthy: Bender, The Empire and Ego of Donald Trump."

199 "The day we opened": Patrick Reilly, "Trump Tower . . . Donald's Trump?" *Women's Wear Daily*, June 2, 1983.

16: Almost Rational

203 He hired a market research firm: Associated Press, "New Football League Gets ABC Contract," *Orlando Sentinel*, May 27, 1982; Michael Janofsky, "U.S.F.L. on ABC Again in '85," *New York Times*, April 25, 1984.

203 Dixon went on the road: Jeff Pearlman, *Football for a Buck* (New York: HarperCollins, 2019), 1–7.

204 Dixon hired a media broker: Barry Stanton, "Football Season Invades Spring," *Daily Item* (Port Chester, N.Y.), May 27, 1982.

204 ESPN soon followed: Janofsky, "U.S.F.L. on ABC Again in '85."

204 He pushed the Generals: Phil Pepe, "General Walker," *New York Daily News*, February 24, 1983.

204 "Get to New York": Paul Reeths, *The United States Football League, 1982–1986* (Jefferson, NC: McFarland & Company, Inc., 2017), 148.

205 "We're really not doing this": Ken Auletta, "Donald J. Money, Sportsman," *New York Daily News*, September 25, 1983.

205 "What I like": Ira Berkow, "Trump Building the Generals in His Own Style," *New York Times*, January 1, 1984.

205 "When I want something": Robert H. Boyle, "The U.S.F.L.'s Trump Card," *Sports Illustrated*, February 13, 1984.

205 "War is not a good thing": Richard Gutwillig, "Trump Plays Hand, Tabs Walt Michaels," *Journal News*, December 16, 1983.

206 "Donald Trump can say": Gutwillig, "Trump Plays Hand, Tabs Walt Michaels."

206 Breaking with Dixon's plan: William N. Wallace, "Barbaro Signs Pact with the Generals," *New York Times*, November 8, 1983.

206 Sipe's new two-year contract: Jane Gross, "Sipe Signed by the Generals," *New York Times*, December 27, 1983.

206 Before the year ended: Bryan Burwell, "Michaels Is in . . . but Martin Is Out," *New York Daily News*, December 16, 1983.

206 He quickly set the upstart league: Michael Janofsky, "U.S.F.L. Owners' Merger Strategy in '84 Revealed," *New York Times*, June 8, 1986.

206 "If we expect": Janofsky, "U.S.F.L. Owners' Merger Strategy in '84 Revealed."

207 "People don't want to watch:" Michael Kranish and Marc Fisher, *Trump Revealed* (New York: Scribner, 2016), 174.

207 "I guarantee you folks": Craig Stock, "NFL Waits Its Turn in Lawsuit," *Philadelphia Inquirer*, June 10, 1986.

207: "I don't want to be a loser": Kranish and Fisher, *Trump Revealed*, 174.

207 She worked with: Karen Croke, "Go-Go Generals," *New York Daily News*, March 9, 1984.

208 On the Sunday: Carla Cantor, "Move Over Cowgirls, Here Come the Generals," *Daily Record*, January 16, 1984.

208 The judges added: Drew Jubera, "How Donald Trump Destroyed a Football League," *Esquire*, January 13, 2016.

208 Waiters served caviar: Sally Wilson, "All This and the Generals," *Press and Sun Bulletin*, February 21, 1984.

208 "This is a natural place": Wilson, "All This and the Generals."

209 "warm modern": Steven M. Aronson, "New York Apogee," *Architectural Digest*, July 1985, 106.

209 There was a separate bedroom: Ivana Trump, *Raising Trump* (New York: Gallery Books, 2017), 63.

209 He would soon order: Author interview with Tim Macdonald, an interior designer who worked with Angelo Donghia.

209 The opening sequence: The description of the *Lifestyles of the Rich and Famous* episode in the paragraph is based on an author review of the show, obtained from Robin Leach Lifestyles of the Rich and Famous Audiovisual Collection, 1984–1999, MS-01102_006, Special Collections and Archives, University Libraries, University of Nevada, Las Vegas.

210 "Trump made great TV": Author interview with Leellen Patchen, 2023.

210 "I believe in spending extra": The description of the *Lifestyles of the Rich and Famous* episode in the paragraph is based on an author review of the show.

210 The payroll of his entire: Hubert Mizell, "Bassett an Anxious Father as Bandits Take First Steps," *Tampa Bay Times*, March 6, 1983.

210 In October 1983: Manny Topol, "NFL Points to USFL's Letters," *Newsday* (Suffolk Edition), June 27, 1986.

211 "If we are not successful": Topol, "NFL Points to USFL's Letters."

211 An article on the front: Michael Janofsky, "U.S.F.L. Envisions Fall Schedule Beginning in 1987," *New York Times*, April 15, 1984.

211 "*The New York Times* is": Paul Domowitch, "Bandits Bassett: Switch Story Trump Up," *Sporting News*, April 30, 1984.

211 Around that time: Michael Janofsky, "Rozelle Contradicts Trump," *New York Times*, July 18, 1986.

212 It was Rozelle who offered: Bryan Burwell, "USFL Deals Its Trump Card," June 24, 1985.

212 In August 1984: Jim Byrne, *The $1 League: The Rise and Fall of the USFL* (New York: Prentice Hall Press, 1986), 197; Pearlman, *Football for a Buck*, 206–7.

212 "We don't think": Dave Anderson, "U.S.F.L. at the Crossroads," *New York Times*, July 1, 1984.

213 The NFL had been sued: Michael Janofsky, "Charges Fly from U.S.F.L.," *New York Times*, October 19, 1984.

213 NFL was "petrified": Janofsky, "Charges Fly from U.S.F.L."

213 "If you are going to play": *30 for 30*, season 1, episode 3, "*Small Potatoes—Who Killed the USFL?*," directed and written by Michael Tollin, aired October 20, 2009, on ESPN.

213 But Trump signed him: Doug Flutie, "Small Potatoes—Who Killed the U.S.F.L."

213 "When a guy goes out": UPI, "Trump Asks Help in Paying Flutie," *New York Times*, April 2, 1985.

214 Donald called reporters again: George Usher, "Trump Says Flutie Deserves His Pay," *Newsday* (Suffolk Edition), April 4, 1985.

214 After hiding behind: Bob Sansevere, "Is Generals' Baron an Alias of Trump?" *Minneapolis Star-Tribune*, June 3, 1985.

214 Sansevere wrote a brief story: Sansevere, "Is Generals' Baron an Alias of Trump?"

214 The day he first saw: Lapidus, *Everything by Design*, 139.

214 He chose a big construction: Contractor advertisement, *Press of Atlantic City*, April 5, 1990.

215 Harrah's executives began: Daniel Heneghan, "Set to Bet," *Press of Atlantic City*, May 8, 1984.

215 He opened with "America": David J. Spatz, "Diamond Keeps Fans Dancing," *Press of Atlantic City*, June 17, 1984.

215 Holmes Hendricksen, Harrah's: The dialogue and

description of events about Holmes Hendricksen's interaction with Donald Trump is based on an author interview with Phil Satre.

215 **Regulators would not let:** Fen Montaigne, "Trump and Harrah's Patch Things Up," *Philadelphia Inquirer*, January 20, 1985.

216 **Satre, Harrah's gaming executive:** Author interview with Phil Satre.

216 **Darrell Luery, Harrah's general manager:** Author interview with Darrell Luery, 2022.

216 **He would even complain:** John R. O'Donnell with James Rutherford, *Trumped!: The Inside Story of the Real Donald Trump—His Cunning Rise and Spectacular Fall* (n.p.: Crossroad Press, 2016).

216 **"That caused a lot of":** Author interview with Phil Satre.

217 **But ultimately, Robert:** Author interview with Darrell Luery.

217 **The slot machines would:** Steve Swartz, "Holiday, Trump Drafting Terms to End Rocky Alliance Over Atlantic City Casino," *Wall Street Journal*, November 11, 1985.

217 **Someone identified only as:** Montaigne, "Trump and Harrah's Patch Things Up."

217 **With staff members watching:** Author interview with Phil Satre.

217 **He still refused:** Author interview with Phil Satre.

218 **Government reports had described:** Al Delugach, "N.J. Regulators Cite Ties with Korshak: Atlantic City Hilton's Casino License Denied," *Los Angeles Times*, March 1, 1985.

218 **Some other casino operators:** Bob McHugh, "Investment at Resort Looks Bleak," *Asbury Park Press*, March 8, 1985.

218 **The Hilton company:** Jim Perskie, "Hilton Postpones License Hearings," *Press of Atlantic City*, April 29, 1985.

218 **He funded the purchase:** New Jersey Casino Control Commission, "Report on Trump's Castle Associates' Application for Renewal of Its Casino License," May 9, 1986, 10.

219 **"I wouldn't do that":** Michael A. Hiltzik, "Towering Presence in New York; Donald Trump Stirs Controversy with Grandiose Structures," *Los Angeles Times*, April 7, 1985.

219 **"The Trump name has been":** Fen Montaigne, "Casino Partners' Court Dispute Turns Bitter," *Philadelphia Inquirer*, July 15, 1985.

219 **"I have created":** Montaigne, "Casino Partners' Court Dispute Turns Bitter."

17: Risk and Reward

220 **She reluctantly found:** Barbara A. Res, *Tower of Lies* (Los Angeles: Graymalkin Media, 2020), 138.

220 **He gave her a Cartier:** Res, *Tower of Lies*, photo section.

220 **Trump insisted, with no evidence:** Michael A. Hiltzik, "Towering Presence in New York: Donald Trump Stirs Controversy with Grandiose Structures," *Los Angeles Times*, April 7, 1985.

220 **He called it:** Donald Trump interview, "Trump's the Name, Donald Trump," *60 Minutes*, CBS News, November 17, 1985.

221 **out of touch with the realities:** Hiltzik, "Towering Presence in New York."

221 **The critic, Paul Gapp:** Paul Gapp, "Will New York Get New 'Tallest Building': Don't Bet on It," *Chicago Tribune*, August 12, 1984.

221 **He had also proposed:** Owen Moritz, "Trump Deals an Ace: He'll Scrape Sky," *New York Daily News*, November 18, 1985.

221 **"It was easier":** Hiltzik, "Towering Presence in New York."

221 **The current holder:** Martin Gottlieb, "Trump Planning 66th St. Tower, Tallest in World," *New York Times*, November 19, 1985.

222 **He had won:** Jesus Rangel, "Estimate Board Gives Extension to Lincoln West," *New York Times*, October 5, 1984.

222 **In mid-1984, Stephenson:** Martin Gottlieb, "Trump Set to Buy Lincoln West Site," *New York Times*, December 1, 1984.

222 **Around that time:** Author interview with Norman Levin, 2022.

222 **After growing up:** Ken Gross, "Trump's View from Above," *Newsday*, November 19, 1985.

222 **"He had started":** Author interview with Norman Levin.

222 **Donald assumed a $115 million:** Ivana Trump application for casino license filed with the New Jersey Casino Control Commission, May 13, 1985, note 2.

222 **renderings on a wall:** Fred A. Bernstein, "Rafael Viñoly, Global Architect of Landmark Buildings, Dies at 78," *New York Times*, March 3, 2023.

223 **Trump said something:** Author interview with Norman Levin.

223 **"I like big better than small":** Thomas Hine, "An Architect Who Fills Tall Orders," *Philadelphia Inquirer*, September 4, 1985.

223 **"I wanted the ultimate":** Susan Heller Anderson and David W. Dunlap, "An Architect Is Named for Trump City," *New York Times*, January 23, 1985.

223 **He asked them if he could report:** Author interview with Norman Levin.

224 **"Why hasn't the site":** Author interview with Norman Levin.

224 **"That explosion absolutely":** Author interview with Norman Levin.

224 **Trump arranged for:** Author interview with Norman Levin; Owen Moritz, "Apple Sauce," *New York Daily News*, October 12, 1987.

224 **Jahn's design called for:** Paul Goldberger, "Television City Project: Tempered, But Still Big," *New York Times*, October 24, 1986.

224 **the Federal Aviation Administration:** Author interview with Norman Levin.

224 **There were concerns:** *Trump: What's the Deal?*, directed by Libby Handros (1991), at 1:11:10.

225 **"I think people were mesmerized":** Author interview with Norman Levin.

225 **Earlier that year:** Video of Fred Trump accepting the Horatio Alger Award in New York City in 1985, https://www.youtube.com/watch?v=KNJLzxHwENo.

226 **After Fred left:** Author interview with Norman Levin.

226 **When the fourth annual:** "The Forbes Four Hundred," *Forbes*, October 28, 1985.

227 **A producer on the show:** Author interview with *60 Minutes* producer Grace Diekhaus, 2023.

227 As the segment ended: Moritz, "Trump Deals an Ace: He'll Scrape Sky."
228 Donald described the 7,900: Martin Gottlieb, "Trump Planning 66th St. Tower, Tallest in World," *New York Times*, November 19, 1985.
228 "The world's tallest building": Joe Starita, "No. 1 Cty to Get No. 1 Building?," *Miami Herald*, November 19, 1985.
228 "Prepare yourself for": Owen Moritz and Thomas Hanrahan, "Tall Order by Trump," *New York Daily News*, November 19, 1985.
228 "It looks like the quintessential": Moritz and Hanrahan, "Tall Order by Trump."
228 "Of all the neighborhoods": Moritz and Hanrahan, "Tall Order by Trump."
229 "I always told Donald": Robert H. Boyle, "The USFL's Trump Card," *Sports Illustrated*, February 13, 1984.

18: All of Life Is a Stage
230 In the 1920s: Michael Luongo, "The Ironic History of Mar-a-Lago," *Smithsonian*, November 2017.
230 Steel magnate Henry Phipps: Barbara Marshall, "Ghost Mansions of Palm Beach," *Palm Beach Post*, March 5, 2017.
231 One by one, wrecking balls: Marshall, "Ghost Mansions of Palm Beach."
231 President Richard M. Nixon: John McDermott, "Nixon Tours Estate at Palm Beach," *Miami Herald*, July 8, 1974.
231 the costs were too high: Patricia Bellew, "Mar-a-Lago: Even Uncle Sam Couldn't Afford to Keep Her," *Miami Herald*, August 3, 1981.
231 Four brokers, including Sotheby's: Patricia Bellew, "Palm Beach Estate of Heiress Post Is Put Up for Sale," *Miami Herald*, April 23, 1981.
231 "Well, maybe Mar-a-Lago": "The Chart of the Deal: An Annotated Guide to the Sale of Mar-a-Lago," *Palm Beach Post*, June 18, 1989.
231 The Marriott Corporation explored: Nick Ravo, "Developer Trump to Buy Mar-a-Lago for Private Home," *Miami Herald*, October 11, 1985.
232 For the $10 million note: Multiple sources including Frank Cerabino, "'Art of Deal' May Haunt Trump in Tax Fight; County Views Book as Mar-a-Lago Artful Dodge," *Palm Beach Post*, June 18, 1989.
232 "He's bought a winter house": Robin Leach Lifestyles of the Rich and Famous Audiovisual Collection, 1984–1999, MS-01102_006, Special Collections and Archives, University Libraries, University of Nevada, Las Vegas.
233 Trump was soon spending: Kenneth Leventhal & Company, "The Trump Organization and the Relationship Bank Group (Consisting of: Bankers Trust Company, Citibank, N.A., Manufacturers Hanover Trust) Agreed Upon Procedures Report," June 14, 1990, 41.
233 "You care very much": Robin Leach Lifestyles of the Rich and Famous Audiovisual Collection, 1984–1999.
233 Soon after, Trump bought: State of New Jersey, Department of Law and Public Safety, Division of Gaming Enforcement to Members of the Casino Control Commission, April 7, 1987, 52.
233 He took on a $60 million: Mortgage and Security Agreement, Trump Palm Beaches Corporation to Marine Midland Bank, October 22, 1986.
233 He paid Fugazy: State of New Jersey, Department of Law and Public Safety, Division of Gaming Enforcement to Members of the Casino Control Commission, 53–54.
233 More broadly, the Florida: Ava Van de Water, "Condo Market Cools, Crawls," *Palm Beach Post*, September 8, 1986.
233 "We changed the name": Christopher Boyd, "'Boy Builder' Trump Keeps Wealth, Reputation, Skyscrapers on the Rise," *Miami Herald*, December 21, 1986.
234 Trump made Iacocca: State of New Jersey, Department of Law and Public Safety, Division of Gaming Enforcement to Members of the Casino Control Commission, 54.
234 "People think that": Boyd, "'Boy Builder' Trump Keeps Wealth, Reputation, Skyscrapers on the Rise."
234 Around the same time: Ivana Trump application for casino license filed with the New Jersey Casino Control Commission, Note 1, May 13, 1985.
234 Bankers Trust issued him: State of New Jersey Casino Control Commission, "Report on Trump Plaza Associates' Application for Renewal of its Casino License," April 20, 1987, 23.
234 Not long after: New York City property records.
235 Harrah's executives came: Michael A. Hiltzik, "Battle over Operations in Atlantic City: Trump-Harrah's Partnership in Casino Erupts into a Bitter Feud," *Los Angeles Times*, July 28, 1985.
235 In the spring of 1986: Daniel Heneghan, "Trump Buys Out Harrah's for Full Control of Casino," *Press of Atlantic City*, May 16, 1986.
235 Donald took on yet another: State of New Jersey, Department of Law and Public Safety, Division of Gaming Enforcement to Members of the Casino Control Commission, 8–9.
235 Donald also agreed: State of New Jersey, Department of Law and Public Safety, Division of Gaming Enforcement to Members of the Casino Control Commission, 6.
235 Though small by comparison: Fred Trump financial records obtained by the authors.
235 For Donald's fortieth birthday: William E. Geist, "About New York: On Being a Billionaire at 40," *New York Times*, June 14, 1986.
236 "Who else could play": Larry Sutton, "Trump Plays His Ace," *New York Daily News*, July 11, 1986.
236 People stopped him: Geist, "About New York: On Being a Billionaire at 40."
236 He may not have had: Wendy Keeler, "Bits & People," *Palm Beach Daily News*, April 20, 1986.
236 In the few weeks before: Daniel F. Cuff, "Exploring Strategies That Work; Leverage, a 2-Edged Sword," *New York Times*, June 1, 1986; William K. Stevens, "Downtown Developer: Willard G. Rouse 3d; Reshaping Philadelphia's Skyline," *New York Times*, May 4, 1986.
236 The *Times* name-checked: N. R. Kleinfield, "Executive Fun and Games," *New York Times*, June 8, 1986.
236 "We're also damn good": Laurence Shames, "Wharton Reaches for the Stars," *New York Times*, June 8, 1986.
236 Four years earlier, there had been: Edwin Mc-

Dowell, "The Rush to Write 'Son of Iacocca,'" *New York Times*, May 11, 1986.

237 As publishers searched: Peter Osnos, "Editing Donald Trump," *New Yorker*, November 3, 2019; Jane Mayer, "Donald Trump's Ghostwriter Tells All," *New Yorker*, July 25, 2016.

237 Schwartz, who had written: Mayer, "Donald Trump's Ghostwriter Tells All."

237 "This book could very well": Liz Smith, "Random House to Play Its Trump," *New York Daily News*, March 5, 1986.

237 Schwartz quickly grew frustrated: Mayer, "Donald Trump's Ghostwriter Tells All."

238 Schwartz, who had earned: Mayer, "Donald Trump's Ghostwriter Tells All."

238 Rozelle had taken notes: Bryan Burwell, "Pete: Didn't Offer Trump Franchise," *New York Daily News*, July 18, 1986.

238 In his closing arguments: Richard Hoffer, "Football Jury Gets Ball Today," *Los Angeles Times*, July 24, 1986.

238 He said the USFL: Hoffer, "Football Jury Gets Ball Today."

238 And he quoted Bassett: Manny Topol, "Final Pleas to Jury in NFL-USFL Trial," *Newsday* (Long Island, N.Y.), July 24, 1986.

239 He began his summation: Topol, "Final Pleas to Jury in NFL-USFL Trial."

239 "Without damages," Myerson continued: Topol, "Final Pleas to Jury in NFL-USFL Trial."

239 The mere fact that: Manny Topol, "USFL-NFL Case Up to Jury," *Newsday*, July 25, 1986.

239 "Thus, you should infer no": Michael Janofsky, "N.F.L. Found Liable on Only One Charge—Confusion on Award," *New York Times*, July 30, 1986; Manny Topol, "USFL-NFL Case Up to Jury."

239 "Yes," replied Patricia McCabe: Manny Topol, "Jeru Says NFL's a Monopoly, but Awards USFL Only $1," *Newsday*, July 30, 1986.

240 He said in court: Wayne Barrett, *Trump: The Greatest Show on Earth* (New York: Regan Arts, 2016), 262.

240 Because the jury had ruled: UPI, "Court Ruling Means NFL Must Pay Attorneys' Fees," February 20, 1990.

240 For his part, Trump: George Usher, "Losers Are Stunned," *Newsday*, July 30, 1986.

240 "It was small potatoes": *30 for 30*, season 1, episode 3, "Small Potatoes—Who Killed the USFL?," directed and written by Michael Tollin, aired October 20, 2009, on ESPN.

240 In 1986, when Barbara Res: Res, *Tower of Lies*, photo section.

240 In 1986, the year Donald turned forty: *The People of the State of New York v. The Trump Corporation, Trump Payroll Corporation*, Supreme Court, Criminal Term, New York County, N.Y., Indictment No. 1473-21, Trial Testimony of Allen Weisselberg, November 15, 2022, beginning on 1603.

241 For 1986, Trump reported: Donald J. Trump I.R.S. Tax Transcript, Schedules C and E, tax year 1985, obtained by authors.

19: Entertainer-Impresario

243 A fast-talking son: Randall Smith, "News Hound," *Jackson Sun* (Tennessee), March 6, 1988; "Dan Dorfman Q&A," History of Business Journalism, School of Media and Journalism at the University of North Carolina at Chapel Hill, http://www.bizjournalismhistory.org/history_dorfman.htm.

244 In an article: Dan Dorfman, "Will New York Get a New Hotel," *New York*, April 26, 1976.

244 His pronouncements in print: Margalit Fox, "Dan Dorfman, 82, Dies; His Tips Moved Markets," *New York Times*, June 19, 2012.

244 In early September 1986: Dan Dorfman, "Trump Acquires Stake in Holiday Corp.," *Minneapolis Star-Tribune*, September 3, 1986.

245 As recently as one year before: Casino Control Commission document, signed May 3, 1985.

245 Within a month: New Jersey Division of Gaming Enforcement, April 7, 1987, 32–34.

245 Trump called Rose: New Jersey Division of Gaming Enforcement, 36.

245 He quickly came to believe: John Crudele, "Holiday Corp. Plans Restructuring," *New York Times*, November 13, 1986.

246 Not quite four weeks: Laurie P. Cohen, "Holiday Corp.'s Stock Trades Actively on Possible Bid from Donald Trump," *Wall Street Journal*, September 29, 1986.

246 "At the very best": Laurie P. Cohen, "Holiday Corp.'s Stock Trades Actively on Possible Bid from Donald Trump," *Wall Street Journal*, September 29, 1986.

246 Casino regulators with access: Casino Control Commission report, April 7, 1987, 34.

246 Suspicion spread on Wall Street: Susan Voyles, "More Bally Stock Traded; Company Denies Trump Rumors," *Reno Gazette-Journal*, November 15, 1986.

246 Trump did not make: Laurie P. Cohen, "Trump Holds Stake in Bally Equal to 9.5%," *Wall Street Journal*, November 21, 1986.

246 Within a week after: Charles Storch, "Takeover Talk Lifts Bally Stock," *Chicago Tribune*, November 14, 1986; Cohen, "Trump Holds Stake in Bally Equal to 9.5%."

246 He took what was: "In His Own Words: Attorney Paul Bible of Lewis and Roca," *Northern Nevada Business Weekly*, January 8, 2012.

247 He called a reporter: Ken Miller, "Gaming Chief Fears Trump 'Greenmailing' Casino Corporations," *Reno Gazette-Journal*, December 5, 1986.

247 "It appears what Donald": Miller, Chief Fears Trump 'Greenmailing' Casino Corporations."

247 "I was very surprised": Ken Miller and Laura Myers, "Trump Denies Bally 'Greenmail' but He'll Likely Buy More Stock," *Reno Gazette-Journal*, December 20, 1986.

248 In late February: Casino Commission Control report, 43.

248 In another ninety days: Casino Commission Control report, 45.

248 He would later say: Casino Commission Control report, 63.

248 "I assume Bear Stearns": Glenn Kessler, "Trump to Pay $750,000 to Settle Antitrust Suit," *Newsday*, April 6, 1988.

248 One source was familiar: Laurie P. Cohen, "Donald Trump Is Said to Acquire Holding in UAL," *Wall Street Journal*, March 13, 1987.

248 "In real estate he's": John Crudele, "Talking Deals; Trump Forays on Wall Street," *New York Times*, March 5, 1987.

249 Trump personally called: Robert J. Cole, "Takeover Talk Lifts UAL Stock," *New York Times*, April 9, 1987.

249 He said the company's new name: Cole, "Takeover Talk Lifts UAL Stock."

249 "To fend off an earlier": Cole, "Takeover Talk Lifts UAL Stock."

249 Slender and elegant: Author interview with Barbara Res.

250 *The Wall Street Journal* reported: Laurie P. Cohen, "Trump Sells UAL Stake, Sources Say; Gain May Be More Than $55 Million," *Wall Street Journal*, April 30, 1987.

250 *The New York Times*, citing: "Trump Sale of UAL Stake," *New York Times*, April 30, 1987.

250 "I don't comment": Micheline Maynard, "Trump Makes a 'Killing,'" *Newsday*, May 7, 1987.

250 *Forbes* reported that Trump's profits: "The Forbes Four Hundred; Billionaires," *Forbes*, October 24, 1988, 174.

250 Casino regulators, with access: 1987-05-28—Trump Castle renewal (for United); 1987-04-07—Trump Plaza Renewal (for Bally and Holiday).

250 That July, Dan Dorfman: Dan Dorfman, "Trump Digs Nugget," *USA Today*, July 9, 1987.

251 Even with those caveats: State of New Jersey, Department of Law and Public Safety, Division of Gaming Enforcement, to Members of the Casino Control Commission, in the Matter of the Application of Trump Plaza Associates and Trump's Castle Associates, April 14, 1988, 67.

251 He soon contacted Donald Trump: Julie Amparano, "Trump Matches Pratt Proposal to Control Resorts, and His Prospects Seem Stronger," *Wall Street Journal*, March 9, 1987; Daniel Heneghan, "Trump New Owner, Resorts Chairman," *Press of Atlantic City*, July 22, 1987.

251 This put Hyatt's investment: *Refco Properties, Inc. v Donald Trump et al.*, 1994 complaint, 14.

252 "He has an appetite": Linda Sandler, "Donald Trump's Raids on Public Companies Have Some Thinking He Depicts a New Breed," *Wall Street Journal*, April 1, 1987.

252 "The most immediate": Heneghan, "Trump New Owner, Resorts Chairman."

252 "I only just came": John Froonjian, "Trump Likens A.C. Challenge to Earlier Triumph," *Press of Atlantic City*, November 19, 1987.

252 Trump insisted on: Donald Janson, "Trump Wins Approval to Shift Resorts License," *New York Times*, December 17, 1987.

253 During a hearing near: Daniel Heneghan, "Banker: No Trump; No Taj," *Press of Atlantic City*, December 1, 1987.

253 Randall Smith, who cowrote: Author interview with Randall Smith, 2022.

253 "I sold all my stock": Randall Smith, "Big Investors Say They Knew Better Than to Overstay: Trump and Others Who Sold Have Small Expectations of Any Turnaround Soon," *Wall Street Journal*, October 20, 1987.

254 Not long after the story: Randall Smith, "Wall Street Crash," *Phillips Exeter Bulletin*, Winter 1988.

254 Decades later, Smith still: Author interview with Randall Smith.

254 "I think the market": Randall Smith, "Big Investors Say They Knew Better Than to Overstay."

254 His gains on those three: State of New Jersey, Department of Law and Public Safety, Division of Gaming Enforcement, to Members of the Casino Control Commission, in the Matter of the Application of Trump Plaza Associates and Trump's Castle Associates, April 14, 1988, 68, 69.

20: Campaign of Truth

255 His interest payments: Kenneth Leventhal & Company, "The Trump Organization and the Relationship Bank Group (Consisting of: Bankers Trust Company, Citibank, N.A., Manufacturers Hanover Trust) Agreed Upon Procedures Report," June 14, 1990, 12.

255 But Koch's view: Author interviews with Alair Townsend, 2022, and George Arzt, 2021.

255 Trump offered to finish: Joyce Purnick, "Trump Offers to Rebuild Skating Rink," *New York Times*, May 31, 1986.

255 Trump's contribution was convincing: Janet Babin, "Is Donald Trump Saving NYC Millions, or Making Millions Off Taxpayers," WNYC News, October 19, 2016, https://www.wnyc.org/story/donald-trump-saving-nyc-millions-or-making-millions-taxpayers.

255 So Trump faced: Author interview with Alair Townsend.

256 Before joining the Koch: Joy Allen, "Koch Names New Budget Chief," *Newsday*, July 31, 1981.

256 She had not spoken to Trump: Author interview with Alair Townsend.

256 Townsend did not believe: Author interview with Alair Townsend.

257 On Monday morning: Thomas J. Lueck, "Keeping NBC in New York: Saga of Deals, Rhetoric and Risks," *New York Times*, December 14, 1987; author interview with Alair Townsend.

257 She had left on good terms: Barbara Res, *All Alone on the 68th Floor: How One Woman Changed the Face of Construction* (self-published manuscript, 2013), 193.

257 The noise from jets: Neely Tucker, "Trump: Airport Location Should Be 10 Miles South," *Miami Herald*, February 2, 1987.

258 He supported two candidates: Jose De Cordoba, "Airplane Noise Plagues Jet Set," *St. Petersburg Times*, March 5, 1989.

258 In the two weeks: Author interview with Alair Townsend and Jay Biggins.

258 "We became uncomfortable": Author interview with Jay Biggins.

258 "The kind of brinksmanship": Memo to Ed Koch from Jay Biggins, dated June 1, 1987, reviewed by authors.

259 He explained it to reporters: Alan Finder, "Koch Rejects Tax Break for Trump TV City Site," *New York Times*, May 29, 1987.

259 "I am not at all surprised": Bill Murphy, "The Brawl at the Hall," *Newsday* (Long Island, N.Y.), May 29, 1987.

259 "He is more concerned": Finder, "Koch Rejects Tax Break for Trump TV City Site."

259 He would say Koch: Bob Drury, "Latest Battle in a War of Words," *Newsday*, September 11, 1987.

259 He vowed to: Marcia Kramer, "Peacock Throne Is Trump's," *New York Daily News*, June 10, 1987.

259 He assigned lawyers: Marcia Kramer, "Trump: Let's Dismantle Ed," *New York Daily News*, June 19, 1987.

260 They spent significant time: Abraham D. Beame Collection, LaGuardia and Wagner Archives, LaGuardia Community College.

260 Donald had given: Marcia Kramer, "Contributing to Temptation," *New York Daily News*, December 23, 1986; Frank Lombardi, "A Money-Spendered Thing," *New York Daily News*, December 15, 1985; Frank Lombardi, "He's Bucking for a Fight," *New York Daily News*, November 27, 1985.

260 In September 1987: Michael Oreskes, "Trump Gives a Vague Hint of Candidacy," *New York Times*, September 2, 1987.

261 That night, Trump appeared: The dialogue in this section is based on a Donald Trump interview with Larry King, *Larry King Live*, CNN, September 2, 1987.

262 One local woman: Fox Butterfield, "New Hampshire Speech Earns Praise for Trump," *New York Times*, October 23, 1987.

262 Howard Rubenstein's team: Tony Burton, "Trump's Clarion Call," *New York Daily News*, December 6, 1987; Michael Fleming, Karen Freifeld, and Susan Mulcahy, "Trump's Kind Word for Nearly Everyone," *Newsday*, November 11, 1987.

262 *People* magazine solicited: Burton, "Trump's Clarion Call."

263 In the crowd of the usual: Michael D'Antonio, *The Truth About Trump* (New York: St. Martin's Press, 2016), 175–77, 186–188; Marie Brenner, "After the Gold Rush," *Vanity Fair*, September 1990; John R. O'Donnell with James Rutherford, *Trumped!: The Inside Story of the Real Donald Trump—His Cunning Rise and Spectacular Fall* (n.p.: Crossroad Press, 2016), 60, 63–66; Phile Roura and Daniel Hays, ". . . and in the Middle Is Maples the Model," *New York Daily News*, February 14, 1990.

21: White Elephants

264 It was a 727: State of New Jersey, Department of Law and Public Safety, Division of Gaming Enforcement to Members of the Casino Control Commission, April 7, 1987, 55.

264 The jet burned so much: John R. O'Donnell with James Rutherford, *Trumped!: The Inside Story of the Real Donald Trump—His Cunning Rise and Spectacular Fall* (n.p.: Crossroad Press, 2016), 47.

264 He spent millions more: O'Donnell, *Trumped!*, 47.

264 But he refused: O'Donnell, *Trumped!*, 47.

264 He found the jet: State of New Jersey, Department of Law and Public Safety, Division of Gaming Enforcement to Members of the Casino Control Commission, 55.

264 Trump, who had never found: Patricia Leigh Brown, "Designed to Dazzle: Casino Hotel Suites," *New York Times*, September 3, 1987.

265 A member of the design team: Author interview with Ross MacTaggart.

265 Donald wanted something: Author interview with Ross MacTaggart.

265 Others thought "Louis XIV": Timothy L. O'Brien, *TrumpNation: The Art of Being the Donald* (New York: Open Road Media, 2005), 43.

265 His holding company filed: Michael Isikoff and Jay Mathews, "Khashoggi's U.S. Company Files for Bankruptcy," *Washington Post*, January 29, 1987; State of New Jersey, Department of Law and Public Safety, Division of Gaming Enforcement to Members of the Casino Control Commission, April 25, 1988, 41–42.

265 The yacht, which had appeared: John Taylor, "Trump Princess: Inside Donald Trump's Lavish 86m Superyacht," *Boat International*, December 1, 2021.

265 Walker had never owned: Author interview with Jeffrey Walker.

265 Trump told Walker: The dialogue and description of events about the *Trump Princess* are based on an author interview with Jeffrey Walker.

267 During one busy week: Paul Harber and Mark Blaudschun, "Donald Trump Negotiating to Purchase the Patriots," *Boston Globe*, February 17, 1988.

267 He served as a presenter: Patricia O'Haire, "This Just in . . . ," *New York Daily News*, February 16, 1988.

267 And he negotiated: Bill Gallo, "Trump Offered Tyson-Spinks," *New York Daily News*, February 20, 1988.

267 At least one commissioner: Daniel Heneghan, "State Delays License Vote for Resorts," *Press of Altantic City*, February 19, 1988.

267 Those threats included: Heneghan, "State Delays License Vote for Resorts."

267 Trump then announced: Joseph Tanfani, "Trump Bids for All of Resorts," *Press of Altantic City*, December 22, 1987.

267 "If I have the company": Tanfani, "Trump Bids for All of Resorts."

267 He offered $15: Tanfani, "Trump Bids for All of Resorts."

267 That figure was quickly rejected: Daniel Heneghan, "Adviser Calls Taj Overruns Exaggerated," *Press of Altantic City*, February 19, 1988.

268 She said the "gaping holes": Donald Janson, "Jersey Balks at Renewal of Trump Casino Permit," *New York Times*, February 5, 1988.

268 Another commissioner, W. David Waters: Donald Janson, "Trump Appears Before Casino Panel," *New York Times*, February 14, 1988.

268 "Any issue can have": Associated Press, "Queries on Trump Delay Resorts Vote," *Asbury Park Press*, February 19, 1988.

268 Several shareholder lawsuits: Stipulation in the matter of the application of Trump Taj Mahal Associates limited partnership for a casino license, March 23, 1990, 88–89.

268 Trump had spent about: Isadore Barmash, "Trump Hints at Federated Stake," *New York Times*, January 14, 1988.

268 "I can borrow money": Casino Control Commission hearing testimony, February 8, 1988, 273–274.

268 "Banks would have never": Casino Control Commission hearing testimony, 234.

269 "The funny thing": Casino Control Commission hearing testimony, 277.

269 "This is like a large-scale": Neil Barsky, "Trump Wins in Court of Last Resorts," *New York Daily News*, February 25, 1988.

269 Trump paid Griffin $299.7 million: Stipulation in the matter of the application of Trump Taj Mahal Associates limited partnership for a casino license, 9–10.

269 That November, Trump did: Stipulation in the matter of the application of Trump Taj Mahal Associates limited partnership for a casino license, 12.

270 Roffman, the casino industry analyst: David Johnston, "A.C. Casino Owners Reported 'Petrified' at Wynn Plan," *Philadelphia Inquirer*, October 7, 1988; Dave Von Drehle, "Donald Trump's Last Resort?," *Miami Herald*, December 28, 1989.

270 The suites were appointed: O'Donnell, *Trumped!*, 81.

270 More than a decade: Von Drehle, "Donald Trump's Last Resort?"

270 Roffman said that looking: Daniel Heneghan, "Analyst Predicts Dire Times for Casino Industry," *Press of Atlantic City*, June 2, 1988.

270 "I mean, the banks": Casino Control Commission hearing testimony, February 8, 1988, 273–74.

271 Citibank lent him $425 million: State of New Jersey, Department of Law and Public Safety, Division of Gaming Enforcement, "Preliminary Report on the Financial Condition of the Donald J. Trump Organization Post-Restructuring," August 13, 1990, 98–99.

271 And as he acknowledged: Advertisement in *New York*, September 12, 1988, 27.

271 That October, he reached a deal: State of New Jersey, Department of Law and Public Safety, Division of Gaming Enforcement, "Preliminary Report on the Financial Condition of the Donald J. Trump Organization Post-Restructuring," August 13, 1990, 99–100.

271 Standing before a model: "Trump Buys Shuttle Line from Eastern," *Los Angeles Times*, October 12, 1988.

271 Walker knew less: Author interview with Jeffrey Walker.

271 "No plane looked like this": Author interview with Jeffrey Walker.

271 In about a year: Leventhal & Company, "The Trump Organization," Schedule II.

272 He was paying: Leventhal & Company, "The Trump Organization," 12.

272 The magazine would soon: Richard L. Stern and John Connolly, "Manhattan's Favorite Guessing Game: How Rich Is Donald," *Forbes*, May 14, 1990.

272 "I feel very strongly": Daniel Hays, "Nabob's Landing: 38M 'Boat,'" *New York Daily News*, July 5, 1988.

273 He grew short tempered: Author interview with Barbara Res.

273 He paid Hyde: Harry Berkowitz, "Inside Team Trump," *Newsday*, September 18, 1989; O'Donnell, *Trumped!*, 15.

273 Hyde, forty-three, and Estess, thirty-eight, were: Robert Hanley, "Copter Crash Kills 3 Aides of Trump," *New York Times*, October 11, 1989.

273 Trump expressed condolences: Carolyn Colwell and Barbara Whitaker, "Foul Play, Blast Ruled Out in Copter Crash," *Newsday*, October 12, 1989.

274 "Why don't you leave": Maureen Orth, "The Heart of the Deal," *Vanity Fair*, November 1990; Ivana Trump, *Raising Trump* (New York: Gallery Books, 2017), 147; Susan Brenna, "Ivana's Volley at Trump," *Newsday*, February 13, 1990.

22: Wildest Expectations

275 "I am Fabu the Fabulous!": Rob Laymon, "At the Taj, a Really Peppy Rally," *Press of Atlantic City*, March 30, 1990.

275 "When I told you": Laymon, "At the Taj, a Really Peppy Rally."

275 "Do we have the most": Laymon, "At the Taj, a Really Peppy Rally."

275 The triumphant song: David Johnston, "Taj Mahal Workers in High Spirits," *Philadelphia Inquirer*, March 30, 1990.

276 He then threw a line: Laymon, "At the Taj, a Really Peppy Rally."

276 A $47 million interest payment: Monci Jo Williams, "Trump's Troubles," *Fortune*, December 18, 1989.

276 The popular Wall Street: David Vis, "Publication Predicts Trouble for Trump," *Press of Atlantic City*, February 7, 1990.

276 "I don't need a lot of cash": Williams, "Trump's Troubles."

276 "It was doomed": Russ Buettner and Charles Bagli, "How Donald Trump Bankrupted His Atlantic City Casinos, but Still Earned Millions," *New York Times*, June 11, 2016.

277 In December 1989, he told: Dave Von Drehle, "Donald Trump's Last Resort?," *Miami Herald*, December 28, 1989.

277 "When this property opens": Neil Barsky and Pauline Yoshihashi, "Trump Is Betting That Taj Mahal Casino Will Hit Golden Jackpot in Atlantic City," *Wall Street Journal*, March 20, 1990.

277 After his bosses found: Daniel Heneghan, "Apology Retraction Costs Trump Critic Casino-Analysis Job," *Press of Atlantic City*, March 24, 1990.

277 "Unquestionably, the Taj's opening": Ann Hagedorn, "Philadelphia Analyst Fired After Trump Threatened to Sue," *Wall Street Journal*, March 26, 1990.

277 He wanted Roffman: Hagedorn, "Philadelphia Analyst Fired After Trump Threatened to Sue."

277 The next afternoon: Heneghan, "Apology Retraction Costs Trump Critic Casino-Analysis Job."

277 He was fired: Hagedorn, "Philadelphia Analyst Fired After Trump Threatened to Sue."

278 "From your first incorrect": Neil Barsky, "Trump, the Bad, Bad Businessman," *New York Times*, August 5, 2016; author interview with Neil Barsky.

278 He was on a plane: Liz Smith, "Splitsville?," *New York Daily News*, February 11, 1990.

278 On the Sunday that he returned: Liz Smith, "Marla Hidden Right Under Ivana's Nose," *New York Daily News*, March 23, 1990.

278 An entertainment reporter: Jill Brooke, "The Real Story Behind Donald Trump's Infamous 'Best Sex I've Ever Had' Headline," *Hollywood Reporter*, April 12, 2018, https://www.hollywoodreporter.com/movies/movie-features/i-wrote-donald-trumps-infamous-best-sex-i-ever-had-story-guest-column-1101246/.

278 The boy began spending: Laura Holson, "Donald Trump Jr. Is His Own Kind of Trump," *New York Times*, March 18, 2017.

278 Around the same time: Copy of prenuptial agreement obtained by authors.

278 After confronting Marla: Tony Burton, "Uh, What

Pre-Nup, Donald?," *New York Daily News*, February 13, 1990.

279 In an interview: "Trump Split Good for Business," *Los Angeles Times*, March 29, 1990.

279 "It brings people maybe": "Trump Split Good for Business."

279 At the entrance road: Paul Goldberger, "It's 'Themed,' It's Kitschy, It's Trump's Taj," *New York Times*, April 6, 1990.

279 At the front door: Laura Italiano, "'Hodge-Podge Taj: Casino Décor May Be Inaccurate, but Eclectic," *Press of Atlantic City*, April 5, 1990.

279 "It's all Hollywood": Italiano, "Hodge-Podge Taj: Casino Décor May Be Inaccurate, but Electric."

279 Paul Goldberger, the *New York Times*: Goldberger, "It's 'Themed,' It's Kitschy, It's Trump's Taj."

279 Alma Guicheteau, seventy-six: Laura Italiano, "Taj: Rambling Gambling Hall Has Its Ups—and Its Downs," *Press of Atlantic City*, April 6, 1990.

280 "I *touched* him": Laura Italiano, "'Donald' the Biggest Attraction of Day," *Press of Atlantic City*, April 3, 1990.

280 The numbers were off: Daniel Heneghan, "Taj Starts Late on Second Day," *Press of Atlantic City*, April 4, 1990; John R. O'Donnell with James Rutherford, *Trumped!: The Inside Story of the Real Donald Trump—His Cunning Rise and Spectacular Fall* (n.p.: Crossroad Press, 2016), 220.

281 "Jack, I'm at the Taj": Except where noted the dialogue and description of events in this section regarding the opening of the casino were drawn from O'Donnell, *Trumped!*, 218–21.

282 The first day: Heneghan, "Taj Starts Late on Second Day."

282 "It was a lot bigger": Heneghan, "Taj Starts Late on Second Day."

283 "I used to have a lot of coconuts": Daniel Heneghan, "Trump Opens Taj with a Flourish," *Press of Atlantic City*, April 6, 1990.

283 "What has happened here": Heneghan, "Trump Opens Taj with a Flourish."

283 "Good evening, master": David Johnston, "Taj Opens for Business with a Bang," *Philadelphia Inquirer*, April 6, 1990.

283 State regulators summoned: Except where noted the dialogue and description of events in this section about the night of the grand opening of the Taj Mahal are drawn from O'Donnell, *Trumped!*, 233–39.

285 As Hal Gessner: Author interview with Hal Gessner, 2023.

285 "I think we kinda": Author interview with Hal Gessner.

285 Within a month: Elaine Finn, "Trump Confirms Contractor Fund Withholding," *Press of Atlantic City*, May 4, 1990.

286 "Just do it, Jack": O'Donnell, *Trumped!*, 253.

286 When Trump went down: O'Donnell, *Trumped!*, 263.

286 He tried to refinance: State of New Jersey, Department of Law and Public Safety, Division of Gaming Enforcement, "Preliminary Report on the Financial Condition of the Donald J. Trump Organization Post-Restructuring," August 13, 1990, 14.

286 Trump quietly retained: Kenneth Leventhal & Company, "The Trump Organization and the Relationship Bank Group (Consisting of: Bankers Trust Company, Citibank, N.A., Manufacturers Hanover Trust) Agreed Upon Procedures Report," June 14, 1990, 2.

286 They estimated that Trump: Leventhal & Company, "The Trump Organization and the Relationship Bank Group," Exhibit I.

286 *BusinessWeek* and *Forbes*: Daniel Heneghan, "Trump Defends Finances," *Press of Atlantic City*, May 5, 1990; Richard L. Stern and John Connolly, "Manhattan's Favorite Guessing Game: How Rich Is Donald," *Forbes*, May 14, 1990, 92.

286 Casino regulators concluded: New Jersey Casino Control Commission, "Report on the Financial Position of Donald J. Trump," April 11, 1991, 5.

287 "It's Trump bashing week": Heneghan, "Trump Defends Finances."

287 On the ABC show: *Primetime Live*, May 3, 1990, transcript.

287 A few weeks later: Author interview with Neil Barsky, 2022.

287 "Donald Trump is driving": Neil Barsky, "Trump, the Bad, Bad Businessman," *New York Times*, August 5, 2016.

287 Trying to avoid: Neil Barsky, "Trump's Bankers Join to Seek Restructuring of Developer's Assets," *Wall Street Journal*, June 4, 1990.

288 The day before Barsky's story: Jocelyn McClurg, "Publishers to Bank on Big-Name Books This Fall," *Hartford Courant*, June 4, 1990.

288 That evening, Peter Osnos: Peter Osnos, "What I Saw as the Editor of *The Art of the Deal*, the Book That Made the Future President Millions of Dollars and Turned Him into a National Figure," *New Yorker*, November 3, 2019.

288 As Osnos would recall: Osnos, "What I Saw."

288 He described the inevitably sad: Harry Berkowitz and Karen Freifeld, "Trump Admits Cash-Flow Problem," *Newsday* (Long Island, N.Y.), June 5, 1990.

288 "He knows how to": Berkowitz and Freifeld, "Trump Admits Cash-Flow Problem."

289 On that day in June: New Jersey Casino Control Commission, "Petition No. 211003 of Trump Plaza Associates, Trump's Castle Associates, L.P., Trump Taj Mahal Associates, L.P., and Trump Hotel Management Corporation," August 13, 1990, 2.

289 His casinos alone: New Jersey Casino Control Commission, 2.

289 It all came to a head: Diana B. Henriques, "Payment Deadline Missed by Trump, but Talks Go On," *New York Times*, June 16, 1990.

289 He would be placed: State of New Jersey, Department of Law and Public Safety, Division of Gaming Enforcement, "Preliminary Report on the Financial Condition of the Donald J. Trump Organization Post-Restructuring," August 13, 1990, 15.

289 "Donald Trump has always": Associated Press, "Getting by on $14,794.52 a Day," *Bismarck Tribune*, June 27, 1990.

289 With the $47 million bond: Neil Barsky, "Trump Resumes Talks with Holders of Casino's Bonds," *Wall Street Journal*, November 15, 1990.

289 Trump would only own: State of New Jersey, Department of Law and Public Safety, Division of Gaming Enforcement, "Supplemental Report on the Financial Condition of Trump Taj Mahal Associates Limited Partnership," January 23, 1991, 5–6.

289 To hang on: State of New Jersey, Department of Law and Public Safety, Division of Gaming Enforcement, "Supplemental Report on the Financial Condition of Trump," January 23, 1991, 3.

290 "Maybe the word": Brendan Murphy, "Trump's Taj Mahal Casino to Enter 'Consensual' Bankruptcy," UPI, November 16, 1990.

290 He glossed over: Bruce Chadwick, "Trump's Taj Mahal," *New York Daily News*, March 5, 1988.

23: No Intention to Ask

291 One Sunday in December: A. Engler Anderson, "Trump Auction Sells 35 Condos for $8.5 Million," *Palm Beach Daily News*, December 17, 1990.

291 He had been spending: Kenneth Leventhal & Company, "The Trump Organization and the Relationship Bank Group (Consisting of: Bankers Trust Company, Citibank, N.A., Manufacturers Hanover Trust) Agreed Upon Procedures Report," June 14, 1990, 21.

291 "Auctions are the wave": Jane Victoria Smith, "Trump Auction Raises $8 Million," *Palm Beach Post*, December 17, 1990.

292 Without the approval: Larry McShane, "Trumps Cross the Ts on Divorce Settlement," Associated Press, March 20, 1991; Richard D. Hylton, "Trump Discussing Empire's Breakup to Pay Off Banks," *New York Times*, April 25, 1991.

292 "I am no longer": Donald Trump to Edward W. Rabin, November 7, 1990.

292 The morning that the Castle: *State of New Jersey et al v. Trump's Castle Associates Limited Partnership*, Stipulation of Facts and Settlement Agreement, 4.

292 He may still have been: *State of New Jersey et al Trump's Castle Associates Limited Partnership* 5.

292 "We don't need an outside infusion": Neil Barksy, "Trump Makes Interest Payment on Castle Bonds," *Wall Street Journal*, December 18, 1990.

293 "made an infusion in cash": Daniel Heneghan, "The Donald's Dad Bails Him Out," *Press of Atlantic City*, January 22, 1991.

293 "It's in the genes, I really believe that": Neil Barsky, "Trump Waxes Confident as Funds Wane," *Wall Street Journal*, December 27, 1990.

293 Fred stashed the chips: Fred Trump general ledgers, 1992 and 1993, obtained by authors.

293 Taylor Johnson Jr., who as: Author interview with Taylor Johnson Jr.

293 Taylor spoke with a thick: Author interview with Taylor Johnson Jr.

294 "This doesn't pass the smell test": Deposition of Maryanne Trump Barry, probate proceeding for the will of Fred C. Trump, obtained by authors.

294 "He was disturbed": Deposition of Maryanne Trump Barry.

294 Maryanne herself worried: Tape recording of Maryanne Trump speaking with Mary Trump, her niece, obtained by authors.

294 "Get it done": Deposition of Maryanne Trump Barry.

295 "My father was quite": Deposition of Robert Trump, probate proceeding for the will of Fred C. Trump, obtained by authors.

295 With another $46 million: Neil Barsky, "Trump May Have to Borrow Funds from His Father," *Wall Street Journal*, May 31, 1991.

295 "It's an evil, vicious, false": Jane Furse, "Trump Rips Journal Scribe as Freeloader," *New York Post*, June 1, 1991.

295 Barsky first heard: Author interview with Neil Barsky.

296 A little more than: Alex S. Jones, "Maxwell Fights Murdoch on a New Front: Coupons," *New York Times*, June 10, 1991.

296 "Having my integrity questioned": Author interview with Neil Barsky.

296 In 2021, Roffman: Jim Walsh, "After Plaza Falls, Only Trump's Legacy Will Remain in Atlantic City," *The (Bergen) Record*, February 16, 2021.

297 Donald pushed forward: Wayne Barrett, *Trump: The Deals and the Downfall* (New York: Regan Arts, 2020), 431.

297 The sale took place: Financial ledgers of Fred Trump, obtained by authors.

297 The 283 apartments: Author tabulation of all 283 first-time sales in Trump Palace, drawn from deeds posted on NYC ACRIS.

297 Fred was still funneling: Figures in this paragraph come from the author's analysis of Fred C. Trump's confidential financial records, obtained by authors.

298 But that year: Fred Trump's 1990 tax return, obtained by authors.

298 His bank statements: Fred Trump's bank statements, obtained by authors.

298 Donald Trump's tax returns: Donald Trump's IRS transcript, 1985–1994, obtained by authors.

298 "The real estate business": Testimony of Donald Trump at 1991 House hearing on U.S. Economic Recovery: Depression vs. Recession, November 22, 1991.

298 During the prior year: State of New Jersey, Casino Control Commission, "Supplement to the Report on the Financial Condition of Donald. J. Trump," June 14, 1991, 2.

299 To make up the difference: State of New Jersey Casino Control Commission, "Supplement to the Report," 2; "Donald J. Trump Projected Cash Flow for the Years Ended December 31, 1991, 1992, 1993," January 25, 1991.

299 He agreed to give up: "Report of the Division of Gaming Enforcement Regarding Trump Taj Mahal Associates, Trump's Castle Associates, Trump Plaza Associates, and Donald J. Trump," Trenton, New Jersey, June 13, 1991, 23–28.

299 If those sales did not: "Report of the Division of Gaming Enforcement," June 13, 1991, 29.

299 A doctor diagnosed him: Probate proceedings for the will of Fred C. Trump, October 3, 1991, doctor's diagnosis, obtained by authors.

300 "I think his memory was: Deposition of Maryanne Trump.

300 His father eased: Deposition of Robert Trump.

300 Fred's advisers had: David Barstow, Susanne Craig, and Russ Buettner, "Trump Engaged in Suspect Tax Schemes as He Reaped Riches from His Father," *New York Times*, October 2, 2018.

300 Fred had about $50 million: Financial records for Fred C. Trump's businesses, obtained by authors.

300 It would serve no purpose: Barstow, Craig, and Buettner, "Trump Engaged in Suspect Tax Schemes as He Reaped Riches from His Father."

301 Every $20,000 boiler that: Barstow, Craig, and Buettner, "Trump Engaged in Suspect Tax Schemes as He Reaped Riches from His Father."

301 All County worked: Barstow, Craig, and Buettner, "Trump Engaged in Suspect Tax Schemes as He Reaped Riches from His Father."

301 "He loved to save taxes": Deposition of John Walter, probate proceeding for the will of Fred C. Trump, obtained by authors.

301 State laws allowed: Barstow, Craig, and Buettner, "Trump Engaged in Suspect Tax Schemes as He Reaped Riches from His Father."

301 "I should be able to": Deposition of John Walter, probate proceeding for the will of Fred C. Trump.

301 Within a few years: Confidential Trump business and tax records obtained by authors.

302 He held his gloves: Associated Press photograph, "Trump Shows His Fighting Spirit," *Journal News* (New Jersey), November 9, 1992.

302 "Let's hear it for the king!": William H. Sokolic, "Trump Celebrates Rebound from Financial Pummeling," *Philadelphia Inquirer*, November 9, 1992.

302 "Against the odds": Associated Press, "Trump Shows His Fighting Spirit,"

24: The Spy Next Door

303 The camera trained: Abraham Wallach, interview by Robert MacNeil, *MacNeil/Lehrer NewsHour*, PBS, June 19, 1990, https://www.youtube.com/watch?v=7TAhk0xxOMY.

303 A week later: Author interview with Abraham Wallach, 2021.

304 Struggling to keep his lenders: Author interview with Abraham Wallach and confidential source.

304 Goldstein agreed to let: Abraham Wallach, unpublished memoir, provided to authors.

305 Wallach spent six weeks: Abraham Wallach, unpublished memoir.

305 About the time: "The Billionaires; Asia," *Forbes*, July 18, 1994.

305 "Get the goddamn manager": Author interview with Abraham Wallach.

306 On a Thursday evening: Michael Shain, "A Groom's Best Man Is—His Dad," *New York Newsday*, December 11, 1993.

306 "Of course, it may grow": Liz Smith, "Legal Tender," *New York Newsday*, December 11, 1993.

306 They invited fifteen hundred: Larry Sutton, "Alter Egos," *New York Daily News*, December 19, 1993.

306 He hired a publicist: Todd S. Purdum, "Trump Pledge: In This Plaza, I Thee Wed," *New York Times*, December 18, 1993; Associated Press, "For Richer, for Poorer . . . ," *Newsday*, December 21, 1993.

306 Caroline Herrera, dress designer: Joseph Steuer, "The Dress," *New York Daily News*, December 19, 1993.

306 Howard Stern, the radio shock jock: "Best Guest List—a Select 1,100," *New York Daily News*, December 21, 1993; Rob Speyer, George Rush, and Jane Furse, "Some Big Names on 'No Show' List," *New York Daily News*, December 21, 1993.

306 Trump's children also did not attend: Ivana Trump, *Raising Trump* (New York: Gallery Books, 2017), 193.

306 As the crowd took: Liz Smith, "My Wedding Notebook," *New York Newsday*, December 26, 1993.

306 She wore a sparkling $2 million: Anthony Scaduto and Liz Smith, "The Art of the Wedding," *New York Daily News*, December 21, 1993.

307 "Somewhere" from *West Side Story*: Scaduto and Smith, "The Art of the Wedding."

307 The Reverend Arthur Caliandro: Smith, "My Wedding Notebook."

307 He later learned that $500,000: Author interview with Abraham Wallach.

307 While Wallach crisscrossed: The account of this episode is drawn from Abraham Wallach's unpublished memoir; author interview with Abraham Wallach; Peter Grant and Alexandra Berzon, "Trump and His Debts: A Narrow Escape," *Wall Street Journal*, January 4, 2016.

307 He learned from: Abraham Wallach unpublished memoir and author interview with him.

308 Goldstein had mentioned to Trump: Grant and Berzon, "Trump and His Debts: A Narrow Escape"; Richard T. Pienciak, K. S. Baker, George Rush, and Paul Schwartzman, "Don's Disses from 2 Ex-Mrs." *New York Daily News*, October 18, 1997.

308 The Kwek-Alwaleed deal: David Stout with Kenneth N. Gilpin, "Trump Is Selling Plaza Hotel to Saudi and Asian Investors," *New York Times*, April 12, 1995.

308 "They didn't care": Author interview with Abraham Wallach.

308 Trump had also retained two: Author interview with Abraham Wallach.

309 In Hong Kong, New World: Author interview with Abraham Wallach.

310 Cheng and Lo wanted Trump: Craig Horowitz, "Trump Gets Lucky," *New York*, August 15, 1994.

310 Henry Cheng reserved: Abraham Wallach unpublished memoir and author interview with him.

310 Susan Cara had given: Horowitz, "Trump Gets Lucky."

310 Chiang, who was steeped: Horowitz, "Trump Gets Lucky."

310 Trump met Henry Cheng: Horowitz, "Trump Gets Lucky."

310 Trump asked her: Horowitz, "Trump Gets Lucky."

310 Trump would receive: Plaintiff's Memorandum of Law in Opposition to the Defendant's Motions to Dismiss, Exhibit G-1, Hudson Waterfront Partnerships Notes to Unaudited Financial Statements, A-4961, *Donald J. Trump v The Carlyle Group*, Supreme Court of the State of New York, County of New York (Civil Action No. 2008-603097).

310 But buried in the partnership agreement: Brief of Defendants-Respondents Hudson Waterfront I, II, III, IV and V Corporations, at 1 and 6–7, *Donald J. Trump et al v Henry Cheng et al.*, New York Supreme Court, Appellate Division, First Department, (Civil Action: 2005-602877).

311 "In Hong Kong, China": Edward A. Gargan, "How the Chengs Finessed Trump," *New York Times*, July 15, 1994.

311 "This is the biggest fucking": Horowitz, "Trump Gets Lucky."

311 **Faced with $3 million:** Ava Van de Water, "What Fate Awaits Mar-a-Lago?" *Palm Beach Post*, May 9, 1993.

312 **"I don't usually litigate":** Cynthia Washam, "Trump Mulling Alternative for Mar-a-Lago," *Palm Beach Daily News*, November 8, 1992.

312 **"If anyone else":** Mary Jordan, "Trump Sees Vendetta in Castle Uprising," *Washington Post*, August 6, 1991.

312 **Trump initially balked:** Casey O'Connor, "Palm Beach: 'Like Any Other Town, Only More So!'" *Palm Beach Daily News*, March 15, 2002.

312 **Everything would be made:** Martha Gross, "The Ace of Clubs," *South Florida Sun-Sentinel*, January 22, 1995.

312 **Since the banks:** Author interview with Bruce Pelly, 2021.

312 **"Donald has got a thing":** Author interview with confidential source, 2021.

313 **"I had a doctor friend":** Stephanie Smith, "Trumped-Up Affair," *South Florida Sun-Sentinel*, April 23, 1995.

313 **"This is a very important day":** Kate Sprague, "Watch Trump's Casino Company IPO on the NYSE in 1995 . . . Then File for Bankruptcy," MSNBC, November 30, 2018, https://www.cnbc.com/video/2018/11/30/watch-trumps-casino-company-ipo-nyse-1995-file-for-bankruptcy.html.

313 **That week Trump also:** Russ Buettner and Charles Bagli, "How Donald Trump Bankrupted His Atlantic City Casinos, but Still Earned Millions," *New York Times*, June 11, 2016.

313 **The public company immediately:** Buettner and Bagli, "How Donald Trump Bankrupted His Atlantic City Casinos, but Still Earned Millions."

313 **He held an option:** Buettner and Bagli, "How Donald Trump Bankrupted His Atlantic City Casinos, but Still Earned Millions"; State of New Jersey, Department of Law and Public Safety, Division of Gaming Enforcement, "Reports of Division of Gaming Enforcement on the Application of Trump Taj Mahal Associates for Renewal of a Casino License (Prn 003501) and the Financial Stability of Donald J. Trump," March 1, 1995, 21.

313 **The following year:** Charles V. Bagli, "Trump Sells Hyatt Share to Pritzkers," *New York Times*, October 8, 1996.

314 **He had leased back:** State of New Jersey, Department of Law and Public Safety, Division of Gaming Enforcement, "Reports of Division of Gaming Enforcement on the Application of Trump Taj Mahal Associates for Renewal of a Casino License (Prn 003501) and the Financial Stability of Donald J. Trump," 32; Trump Entertainment Resorts, Inc., Form 10-K, for the year ending December 31, 1999 (filed March 31, 2000), 45.

314 **He had in the prior decade:** Donald Trump's IRS transcript, 1985–1994, obtained by authors.

314 **But someone in Trump's orbit:** David Barstow, Mike McIntire, Patricia Cohen, Susanne Craig, and Russ Buettner, "Donald Trump Used Legally Dubious Method to Avoid Paying Taxes," *New York Times*, October 31, 2016.

314 **As he approached his ninetieth birthday:** David Barstow, Susanne Craig, and Russ Buettner, "Trump Engaged in Suspect Tax Schemes as He Reaped Riches from His Father," *New York Times*, October 2, 2018."

315 **"I'm the biggest":** Bret Pulley, "Crowning the Comeback King," *New York Times*, October 25, 1995.

25: Always There for Me

316 **When reporters asked:** Tim Sullivan, "Trump Unveils Latest Hotel Plans," *The Times* (Munster, Indiana), June 25, 1995.

316 **A button-down corporate man:** Associated Press, "Trump Finds Respect Elusive Despite Renewed Success," *Asbury Park Press*, July 12, 1995.

317 **But Wallach thought:** Author interview with Abraham Wallach.

318 **A broker told Wallach:** Author interview with Abraham Wallach.

318 **Wallach and a real estate lawyer:** The account of Wallach and Diamond's dealings with the Hinneberg family is drawn from Wallach's unpublished memoir, interviews with him, and with another confidential source familiar with the matter.

319 **There were executives from Tishman:** This account was drawn from Wallach's unpublished memoir, interviews with him, and with another confidential source familiar with the matter.

320 **Kim appealed to Trump's vanity:** Author interview with Abraham Wallach.

321 **"Daewoo became concerned":** Author interview with Abraham Wallach.

320 **Trump's tax returns:** Donald Trump's tax return information, obtained by authors.

321 **The family had left:** "$5-Million and Publisher's Estate Are Left to Yale," *New York Times*, June 1, 1973.

322 **Trump planned an initiation fee:** Bob Kappstatter, "200G'S the Link to Trump Golf Plan," *New York Daily News*, January 25, 1996.

322 **"We're going to do something":** Karen Tensa, "Trump Expects to Get Approval for Seven Springs Within a Year," *Mount Vernon Argus*, March 12, 1996.

322 **"Realistically, given what":** Tensa, Trump Expects to Get Approval for Seven Springs Within a Year."

323 **One Friday, Trump stood:** Randi Feigenbaum, "Bidding High for Trophy Homes," *New York Newsday*, September 18, 1997.

323 **Miller surveyed the land:** Author interview with Tim Miller, 2021.

323 **"He wanted to be a golf course guy":** Author interview with Tim Miller.

324 **At the time:** Rick Remsnyder, "County Should Be Briar Buyer," *Citizen Register*, November 28, 1993.

324 **The club had only:** Advertisement, *Standard Star*, July 7, 1995.

324 **When an auction was held:** David Talbot, "Auction of Country Club Draws Bidders but No Takers," *Daily Argus*, December 15, 1993.

324 **"We thought, from our knowledge:** Author interview with Alan Parter, 2021.

324 **A twenty-five-year-old:** Carolyn Kepcher, *Carolyn 101: Business Lessons from "The Apprentice's" Straight Shooter* (New York: Touchstone, 2004).

325 **Trump met with the mayor:** Ken Valenti, "Briarcliff

Manor Mayor Has Meeting with Trump," *Putnam Reporter Dispatch*, March 7, 1996.

325 Pelly's first thought was: Author interview with Bruce Pelly.

325 When Trump caught wind: Author interview with Bruce Pelly.

326 She had thirty tons: Leslie Marshall, "Breakfast Above Tiffany's," *InStyle*, December 1995.

326 "Donald likes to eat": Marshall, "Breakfast Above Tiffany's."

326 They used a mechanism: The information in this section about the trusts set up to transfer Fred Trump's wealth to his children was drawn from David Barstow, Susanne Craig, and Russ Buettner, "Trump Engaged in Suspect Tax Schemes as He Reaped Riches from His Father," *New York Times*, October 2, 2018.

329 The money paid off $330 million: Russ Buettner and Charles Bagli, "How Donald Trump Bankrupted His Atlantic City Casinos, but Still Earned Millions," *New York Times*, June 11, 2016.

329 In 1996, he was paid: Buettner and Bagli, "How Donald Trump Bankrupted His Atlantic City Casinos, but Still Earned Millions."

329 Shareholders later alleged: Buettner and Bagli, "How Donald Trump Bankrupted His Atlantic City Casinos, but Still Earned Millions."

329 "What are you doing here?": Author interview with Alan Marcus, 2022.

330 Among the tributes: Associated Builders and Owners of Greater New York, paid death notice, *New York Times*, June 27, 1999.

330 He rambled through a list: Angela Mosconi, "Trump Patriarch Eulogized as Great Builder," *New York Post*, June 30, 1999.

331 In 1999, he was invited: Author interview with Philip di Giacomo, 2021.

331 Some five thousand gallons: Corey Kilgannon, "The Course That Trump Built," *New York Times*, June 20, 2002.

331 "There's never been a waterfall like this": Rick Remsnyder, "Trump 'Couldn't Be Happier' with His New Course," *Journal News* (Westchester County, N.Y.), July 28, 2002.

331 Sportswriter Rick Reilly: Rick Reilly, *Commander in Cheat: How Golf Explains Trump* (New York: Hachette Books, 2019).

331 Di Giacomo thought it: Author interview with Philip di Giacomo.

332 He called the new course: Rick Remsnyder, "Trump 'Couldn't Be Happier' with His New Course; "Kilgannon, "The Course That Trump Built."

332 When the club opened: Kilgannon, "The Course That Trump Built."

332 "Everybody wants to shoot": Amy Stevens, "Latest Trump Project Is Making Genteel Town Downright Uncivil," *Wall Street Journal*, October 18, 1996.

332 Trump had once screamed: Author interview with Tim Miller.

333 Donnie, as he was called: Deposition of Donald Trump Jr, *Steve Aaron et al v. The Trump Organization, Inc., Aa New York Corporation, and Donald J. Trump, an individual*, Case No. 8:09-cv-2493-SDM-TGW, 2010.

333 He returned to building: Adam Bernstein, "Former Wife of Prominent Post Editor," *Washington Post*, November 14, 2011.

333 Even before Trump: Author interview with Abraham Wallach.

334 "My dad wants it bigger: The dialogue and description of events in the section regarding Andrew Tesoro's attempts to get Donald Trump to pay his bill was drawn from author interview with Andrew Tesoro, 2022.

26: The Producer

339 In October 1982: Mark Burnett, *Dare to Succeed: How to Survive and Thrive in the Game of Life* (New York: Hyperion, 2001), 17.

339 "We've been through": Scott Raab, "Mark Burnett: The ESQ&A," *Esquire*, March 3, 2013.

339 That day, he called a friend: Mark Burnett, *Jump In! Even if You Don't Know How to Swim* (New York: Ballantine Books, 2005), 15.

339 She had grown up: Kym Gold with Sharon Soboil, *Gold Standard: How to Rock the World and Run an Empire* (New York, Skyhorse Publishing, 2015), 27; interview with Kym Gold, *The Bryan Kreuzberger Show*, podcast, February 1, 2019.

339 His father worked: Burnett, *Jump In!*, 17.

339 She bought damaged: Gold, *Gold Standard*, 36 and 38.

340 made real money: Gold, *Gold Standard*, 38.

340 Kym Gold doesn't recall: Author interview with Kym Gold, 2021.

340 In 1988, Kym and Mark: Author Interview with Kym Gold.

340 He took a job: The dialogue and description in the section regarding how Mark Burnett met Dianne Minerva was drawn from Dianne Burnett, *The Road to Reality: Voted Off the Island* (Culver City, Ca.: Agape Media International, 2012), 82.

340 Kym Gold went on: Tiffany Hsu, "True Religion Board Accepts $835-Million Takeover Bid," *Los Angeles Times*, May 10, 2013.

340 That part of his life: David Haldane, "Endurance Race Started Badly, Ended Worse," *Los Angeles Times*, April 4, 1993.

340 Burnett by then: Articles of Incorporation, Burnett Financial Group, obtained by authors.

340 He married Dianne: Burnett, *The Road to Reality*, 82; and property records.

341 In 1994, he acquired: Gary Klein, "Topanga Man Seeking to Stage Race of Endurance," *Los Angeles Times*, March 5, 1994.

341 During those years: Bill Carter, "Exporting 'Millionaire' and 'Survivor' Was a Hard Sell with Cross-cultural Allies and a Detour to Sweden," *New York Times*, July 18, 2000.

341 Burnett met Parsons: Burnett, *Jump In!*, 83.

341 He pitched the concept: Burnett, *Jump In!*, 84.

341 At a holiday party: *James Mark Burnett, et al. v. Conrad Riggs, et al.*, Determination of the Labor Commissioner, May 2011, and confidential source interview, 2021.

341 Burnett, the consummate salesman: Burnett, *Jump In!*, 190.

341 Burnett showed Leslie: Burnett, *Jump In!*, 85.

342 To reduce the network's: Burnett, *Jump In!*, 86.

342 "Burnett's ability to deliver": Author interview with confidential source.

342 "The moment Leslie said": Burnett, *Jump In!*, 85.

342 Riggs told the network: Author interview with confidential source, 2021.

342 Moonves had a champagne-colored: Burnett, *The Road to Reality*, 205.

342 "Oh my God": Burnett, *The Road to Reality*, 205.

342 He did not even like: Bill Carter, "Survival of the Pushiest," *New York Times*, January 28, 2001.

342 "Does the public care?": Carter, "Survival of the Pushiest."

342 He and Moonves briefly: Carter, "Survival of the Pushiest."

343 "It would change": Carter, "Survival of the Pushiest."

343 The two settled: Author interview with confidential source, 2021.

343 "If you want Mark": Burnett, *Dare to Succeed*, 197.

343 In the spring of 2002: Donna Petrozzello, "Survivor' & the City: South Pacific Contest Ends in Central Park," *New York Daily News*, May 19, 2002.

343 As he warmed up: Mark Burnett, keynote presentation at the Entrepreneurial Leaders Conference, Vancouver, 2013, https://www.youtube.com/watch?v=DlfVJL4mSfI.

343 "Trump, Trump, Trump": Burnett, keynote presentation at the Entrepreneurial Leaders Conference.

343 Burnett told Trump: Burnett, keynote presentation at the Entrepreneurial Leaders Conference.

344 One day, when he was: Burnett, keynote presentation at the Entrepreneurial Leaders Conference.

344 "But it's got to have: Burnett, keynote presentation at the Entrepreneurial Leaders Conference.

344 He had until November: Trump Entertainment Resorts, Inc., Form 10-K, for the year ending December 31, 2002 (filed March 31, 2003), 5, 94–95.

344 The casinos continued to lose: Trump Entertainment Resorts, Inc., Form 10-K, 27–28, 41.

344 His plan was to sell: Trump Entertainment Resorts, Inc., Form 10-K, 5.

344 To persuade potential bond buyers: Trump Hotels & Casino Resorts, Inc., "Trump Hotels & Casino Resorts, Inc. Announces Pricing of $490 Million Note Issues by Trump Casino Holdings, LLC," *Business Wire*, March 13, 2003.

344 His businesses continued: Donald Trump's tax return information, obtained by authors.

344 A few years earlier: Inmate booking information, Orleans Parish Sheriff's Office, February 25, 2001, public drunkenness; Larry Celona, "Don Jr. in Stitches: Trump Son Hurt in Comedy-Club Fight," *New York Post*, December 29, 2002.

344 He had just turned twenty-six: Donald Trump Jr.'s W2 employment tax information from the Trump Organization, obtained by authors.

344 One round of stories: Braden Keil, "Trump May Fire Insurance Carrier AIG," *New York Post*, February 21, 2003.

344 A few days later: "Bids & Offers: Hank vs. The Donald," *Wall Street Journal*, February 28, 2003.

344 Trump answered himself: The dialogue in this section between Mark Burnett and Donald Trump is drawn from Mark Burnett's keynote presentation at the Entrepreneurial Leaders Conference, Vancouver.

345 But he hadn't liked those: Donald J. Trump with Meredith McIver, *Trump: How to Get Rich* (New York: Simon & Schuster, 2004), 122.

345 "This is smart": Burnett, keynote presentation at the Entrepreneurial Leaders Conference.

345 Riggs had contacted several moguls: Allen Salkin, "Donald Trump's Hustle," *Los Angeles Magazine*, September 1, 2019.

346 "Fifty-fifty," Burnett said: Burnett, keynote presentation at the Entrepreneurial Leaders Conference.

346 Trump would play himself: Author interview with multiple confidential sources, 2021.

346 Zucker and Gaspin: Biographical information on Jeff Gaspin was drawn from a 2016 press release, "Jeff Gaspin Joins Primary Wave Entertainment as President."

346 In a third-floor conference room: The dialogue and description of events regarding Burnett's March 3 meet at NBC is based on author interviews with Jeff Zucker and Marc Graboff, 2021.

347 "If the show didn't work": Author interview with Jeff Zucker.

347 The network agreed: Author interview with confidential source, 2021.

347 On April 1, 2003: Cynthia Littleton, "Trump, Burnett, NBC in Business with 'Apprentice,'" *Hollywood Reporter*, April 2, 2003.

348 Trump said, "Mentoring": Lynn Smith, "Trump Reality TV: Execs Will Get the Gong," *Los Angeles Times*, April 3, 2003.

348 "I'm pretty busy": Michael Starr, "From the Man Who Dreamed Up 'Survivor' . . . The Donald Does Reality," *New York Post*, April 2, 2003.

348 "This is Donald Trump": Abby Ellin, "Business; 'Survivor' Meets Millionaire, and a Show Is Born," *New York Times*, October 19, 2003.

348 Neither Trump nor his businesses: Donald Trump's tax return information, obtained by authors.

348 They attended a Neil Young: Abby Ellin, "Business; 'Survivor' Meets Millionaire, and a Show Is Born," *New York Times*, October 19, 2003.

348 They visited Seven Springs: Abby Ellin, "Business; 'Survivor' Meets Millionaire."

348 They attended a private party: Abby Ellin, "Business; 'Survivor' Meets Millionaire."

348 Burnett told *The New York Times*: Abby Ellin, "Business; 'Survivor' Meets Millionaire."

348 But something in Zucker's: Except where noted the dialogue and description of events in this section were drawn from an author interview with Richard Linnett, 2021.

349 "Trump is the hottest": Richard Linnett, "'Human Logo': Reconstructing the Trump Brand," *Advertising Age*, August 18, 2003.

349 The survey of two thousand: Richard Linnett, "Assessing Donald Trump as Reality Show and Celebrity Brand," *Advertising Age*, August 19, 2003.

350 Their friendship was over: Author interview with Richard Linnett.

350 He had summoned: Testimony of Mark Hager, in *ALM Unlimited v Donald Trump*, April 17, 2013.

350 "That is advertising value": Testimony of Mark Hager, in *ALM Unlimited, Inc. v Donald J. Trump.*

350 The questions included: "Trump the Competition;

NBC Is Searching for Mogul Wannabes Who Want to Work for The Donald," *Chicago Tribune*, April 28, 2003.

351 "People look at Donald Trump": Christina Hoag, "To Be or Not to Be the Trump's Chump," *Miami Herald*, June 27, 2003.

27: "I Used My Brain"

352 After experiencing years: Author interviews with several *Apprentice* producers and Patrick Radden Keefe, "How Mark Burnett Resurrected Donald Trump as an Icon of American Success," *New Yorker*, December 27, 2018.

352 "When you go into the office": Author interview with Bill Pruitt, 2021.

352 "The whole thing": Author interview with Alan Blum, 2021.

352 Fewer than fifty people: Author interview with confidential source.

353 "Someone big and special": Burnett, keynote presentation at the Entrepreneurial Leaders Conference.

353 In the most recent Gallup: Results from a Gallup poll conducted October 8–10, 1999, "Favorability: People in the News."

353 "Our job was to make him look": Author interview with Jonathon Braun, 2021.

353 One NBC executive involved: Author interview with confidential source, 2021.

353 His tax records would show: Donald Trump's tax return information, obtained by authors.

354 She created two sets: Edie Cohen, "The Real Deal; Reality TV Is True Genius, Thanks to Sets by Kelly Van Patter," *Interior Design*, September 1, 2005.

354 Burnett wanted the boardroom: Civil litigation, *Conrad Riggs. An Individual; and Cloudbreak Entertainment v Mark Burnett et al.*

354 The living space would: Author interview with Bill Pruitt.

354 In reality, the two: Author interview with Bill Pruitt.

354 While most of Burnett's: Author interviews with several *Apprentice* producers, 2021.

355 Kevin Harris, who had worked: Author interview with Kevin Harris, 2021.

356 "KEVIN! Is my hair okay?": The dialogue and description of events in this section were drawn from an author interview with Kevin Harris.

358 Eighteen months after: Results from a Gallup poll conducted June 16–19, 2005, "Favorability: People in the News," https://news.gallup.com/poll/1618/Favorability-People-News.aspx.

358 "We were making him": Author interview with Bill Pruitt.

358 "You were casting": Author interview with Jeff Zucker, 2021.

358 Trump's brother, Robert drove: The description of events in the section about the meeting on Donald Trump's trust funds was drawn from author interviews with confidential sources.

359 Robert had been married: Author interviews with confidential sources.

359 Back in 1991: Confidential will-drafting notes from Fred Trump's attorney, Robert Sheehan, written in 1991 and obtained by authors.

360 Three bids were submitted: David Barstow, Susanne Craig, and Russ Buettner, "Trump Engaged in Suspect Tax Schemes as He Reaped Riches from His Father," *New York Times*, October 2, 2018.

360 One evening in December: Barstow, Craig, and Buettner, "Trump Engaged in Suspect Tax Schemes as He Reaped Riches from His Father."

360 It would all take: Barstow, Craig, and Buettner, "Trump Engaged in Suspect Tax Schemes as He Reaped Riches from His Father."

360 Schron and the buyers: Barstow, Craig, and Buettner, "Trump Engaged in Suspect Tax Schemes as He Reaped Riches from His Father."

28: The Talent

361 "Right then we knew": Author interview with Katherine Walker, 2021.

362 "He would fire the absolute": Author interview with Jonathon Braun.

362 "Our job then was to reverse engineer": Author interview with Jonathon Braun.

363 It later emerged that Sam: Tom Sykes, "Suitcase Sam Traveling Light," *New York Post*, April 17, 2004.

363 Trump introduced Carolyn: Donald Trump on *The Apprentice*, season 1, episode 1.

262 As the show launched: Carolyn Kepcher's W2 employment tax information from the Trump Organization, obtained by authors.

363 Burnett had come up: Civil litigation, *Conrad Riggs. An Individual; and Cloudbreak Entertainment v Mark Burnett et al.*

363 But neither he, nor Trump: Trump Organization payroll information, obtained by authors; author interviews.

363 He would not typically: Author interview with Katherine Walker.

364 "Watching people try to": Author interview with confidential source, 2021.

364 An average of 20.7 million: Gail Schiller, "'Apprentice' Lures Sponsors Despite Ratings Slide," Reuters, December 5, 2007.

364 He asked visitors: Maureen Tkacik, "Where's Donald," *Philadelphia*, May 16, 2006.

365 NBC offered Trump a raise: Author interviews with confidential sources, 2021.

365 Trump arrived alone: The dialogue in this section about Donald Trump's lunch at Jean-Georges is based on author interviews with Jeff Zucker and Marc Graboff.

367 As with those earlier shows: Author interviews with multiple sources.

367 Burnett hired Justin Hochberg: Justin Hochberg's LinkedIn résumé.

367 Hochberg made his pitch: The dialogue in this section was drawn from an author interview with Ken Austin, 2021.

367 Marquis Jets saw a twentyfold: Melinda Ligos, "Business People; Bring on the Reruns," *New York Times*, March 14, 2004.

367 "were just looking": Author interview with Kevin Harris.

368 "Toothpaste, that doesn't sound": The dialogue in this section about Crest toothpaste was drawn from an author interview with Kevin Harris.

369 The website that Crest: Internal *Apprentice* placement/task integration statistics, obtained by authors.

369 Riggs often talked: Author interview with Dan Gill, 2021.

369 Gill came up with: Author interview with Dan Gill.

369 "When the show came": Author interview with Dan Gill.

370 A friend arranged: Author interview with Alan Blum, 2021.

370 Burnett also hired: Author interviews with multiple *Apprentice* staffers.

370 The total that Burnett's team: Financial records from Mark Burnett Productions, obtained by authors.

370 Gill convinced Genworth Financial: Financial records from Mark Burnett Productions.

370 "I am like": Author interview with Dan Gill.

370 Trump ultimately agreed: Voicemail recording, obtained by authors.

371 Michael Dell, the billionaire: Author interview with Tim Megaw, 2021.

371 In the fall of 2004: The information and dialogue in this section involving QVC was drawn from interviews with Tim Megaw and Dan Gill.

372 Trump demanded a T: Author interviews and a photograph of Trump in front a T floor marker, obtained by authors.

372 In the production room: Author interview with Alan Blum.

372 When he arrived: Multiple interviews with *Apprentice* producers by authors, 2021.

372 Harris recalls that Trump: Author interview with Kevin Harris.

372 "I'm giving him": Author interview with Dan Gill.

372 "Once he was on": Author interview with Kevin Harris.

373 As one producer recalled: Author interview with confidential source, 2021.

373 He would later claim: Donald Trump, Twitter, December 10, 2016, 6:27:22 AM EST, https://www.thetrumparchive.com/?searchbox=%22apprentice+conceived%22.

373 He even hired a group: Multiple interviews with *Apprentice* producers by authors, 2021.

373 "It's nice to be loved": Peter Johnson, "Trump Dials Up Radio Deal," *USA Today*, April 29, 2004.

373 Though the value: Donald Trump's tax return information, obtained by authors.

373 That same year: Donald Trump's tax return information, obtained by authors.

373 That year, the book's publisher: Donald Trump's tax return information, obtained by authors.

374 Trump even began selling: Donald Trump, *Think Like a Billionaire: Everything You Need to Know About Success, Real Estate, and Life* (New York: Ballantine Books, 2005), 171.

374 Levi's paid $1.1 million: Financial records from Mark Burnett Productions, obtained by authors.

374 Just before the scene: Author interview with Kevin Harris.

374 "It's a great idea, Kevin": The dialogue and description of events in this section regarding Melania Trump's modeling spot with Levi's was drawn from author interview with Kevin Harris.

375 General Motors had agreed: Financial records from Mark Burnett Productions, obtained by authors.

375 The producers told Richer: Author interview with Mark Hans Richer, 2021.

376 GM that year reported: General Motors 2004 annual report.

376 "Wow, this guy": Except where noted the dialogue and description of events about Mark Hans Richer's two appearances on *The Apprentice* were drawn from an author interview with Mark Hans Richer.

376 Buyers for the first thousand cars: Jean Halliday, "Pontiac's 'Apprentice' Placement Stampedes Viewers to Web," *Advertising Age*, April 20, 2005.

377 Cathy Hoffman Glosser, who had led: Information in this paragraph was drawn from a March 2011 deposition of Cathy Glosser, who testified in *ALM Unlimited v. Donald J. Trump*, Supreme Court of the State of New York, New York County (Index No. 603491–2008).

378 "It's really just less": Donald Trump to Larry King, *Larry King Live*, CNN, November 24, 2004.

378 He was negotiating: Trump Entertainment Resorts, Inc., Form 10-K, for the year ending December 31, 2003 (filed March 30, 2004), 107, 15; Trump Entertainment Resorts, Inc., Form 10-K, for the year ending December 31, 2004 (filed March 31, 2005), 20, 7.

379 On May 4, 2004: David Barstow, Susanne Craig, and Russ Buettner, "Trump Engaged in Suspect Tax Schemes as He Reaped Riches from His Father," *New York Times*, October 2, 2018.

379 The total was significantly: Donald Trump's tax return information, obtained by authors.

379 After the meeting: Trial Transcript at 732–733 and 832, *ALM Unlimited, Inc. v. Donald J. Trump*.

379 "Nobody manages my brand": Trial Transcript, April 15, 2013, at 640, 643, *ALM Unlimited, Inc. v. Donald J. Trump*.

379 "PVH is the largest": Trial Transcript, April 12, 2013, at 389, *ALM Unlimited, Inc. v. Donald J. Trump*.

379 "George, the way I understand": Letter from Jeff Danzer to George Ross, June 8, 2004, filed in *ALM Unlimited, Inc. v. Donald J. Trump*.

380 "This all happened": April 2013 testimony of Donald Trump in *ALM Unlimited, Inc. v. Donald J. Trump*.

380 Trump gave her the title: March 2011 deposition of Cathy Glosser filed in *ALM Unlimited, Inc. v. Donald J. Trump*.

380 On December 7, Trump flew: Julie Naughton, "Building Trumpland: The Donald Flies High in Licensing Blitz," *Women's Wear Daily*, December 16, 2004.

381 "I've gotten used to it": Naughton, "Building Trumpland: The Donald Flies High in Licensing Blitz."

29: The Danger of Overcommercialization

383 "Well, we're so happy": Donald Trump interview with Katie Couric, *Today Show*, NBC, January 25, 2005.

383 During season two: Author interview with Dan Gill.

383 And just a month: Financial records of Mark Burnett Productions, obtained by authors.

383 During the same year: Darrell Hofheinz, "A Brand Reborn," *Palm Beach Daily News*, December 18, 2003.

383 Burnett's get-stuff-for-free: Author interview with Kevin Harris.

383 Numerous news stories: Mercedes-Benz USA, "Highest Year on Record for Mercedes-Benz USA," *PR Newswire US*, January 4, 2005.

384 The *New York Post* reported: Jennifer Fermino, Braden Keil, Rich Alder, and Bridget Harrison, "Trump Rings Up Number 3; Weds Melania in Celeb-Filled Seaside $How," *New York Post*, January 23, 2005.

384 "It's from Graff jewelers": Donald Trump's dialogue in this paragraph was drawn from an interview he had with Larry King, *Larry King Live*, CNN, December 2005.

384 The company said: Susan Adams, "Trump Lied About What He Paid for Melania's Engagement Ring," *Forbes*, February 8, 2018.

384 The episode also struck: Orla Healy, "Trump Jr. Is the Cheapest Gazillionaire—Heirhead Proposes with Free 100G Ring," *New York Post*, November 12, 2004.

384 "I guess he's trying": Larry King, *Larry King Live*, CNN, November 24, 2004.

385 "Why are we going to leave": Donald Trump interview with Larry King, *Larry King Live*, CNN, May 17, 2005.

385 During the year before: Charles Passy, "Palm Beach's Wedding of the Century (So Far)," *Palm Beach Post*, January 16, 2005.

385 For inspiration, he had looked: Jose Martinez, Richard Huff, and Tracy Connor, "Well Aisle Be! Donald & Melania Wed in Ritzy Fla. Bash," *New York Daily News*, January 23, 2005.

385 On his tax returns: Donald Trump's tax return information, obtained by authors.

385 He and Trump had: Fermino, Keil, Alder, and Harrison, "Trump Rings Up Number 3; Weds Melania in Celeb-Filled Seaside $How," *New York Post*.

385 The groom took the microphone: Fermino, Keil, Alder, and Harrison, "Trump Rings Up Number 3; Weds Melania in Celeb-Filled Seaside $How."

385 Donald had mistakenly: Donald and Melania Trump discuss wedding with Katie Couric, *Today Show* transcripts, NBC News, January 27, 2005.

386 Still, guests were required: Fermino, Keil, Alder, and Harrison, "Trump Rings Up Number 3; Weds Melania in Celeb-Filled Seaside $How."

386 Her shopping trip was featured: "Trump Wedding Watch; Melania's Gown: 50 Pounds of Dior Glory," *Palm Beach Post*, January 23, 2005.

386 Kevin Harris and his wife: Author interview with Kevin Harris.

386 "Hey, what do you guys think": Author interview with Kevin Harris.

386 For the season three premiere: Financial records from Mark Burnett Productions, obtained by authors; author interview with Dan Gill.

387 Burger King was thrilled: Agreement dated as of November 1, 2004, by and between Mark Burnett Productions, Inc., and Burger King Corporation, obtained by authors.

387 Hanes paid $1 million: Financial records from Mark Burnett Productions, obtained by authors.

387 "Do we earn anything": Email exchange, obtained by authors.

387 Dove paid $2 million: Financial records from Mark Burnett Productions, obtained by authors.

388 The term "Dove and Apprentice": Jack Neff, "Madison + Vine: 'Veggie Porn' Aside, Dove OK with Fake Ads; Marketer's Turn on 'Apprentice' Creates Big Buzz," *Advertising Age*, February 21, 2005.

388 As part of his agreement: Mark Shanahan, "The Donald Is Cleaning Up His Act," *Boston Globe*, July 21, 2005.

389 In a few hours: Donald Trump's tax return information, obtained by authors.

389 Behind the scenes: Letter to Rob Rohrbach at Mark Burnett from Trish Drueke, copying Dan Gill, February 28, 2005, obtained by authors.

390 Drueke-Heusel had made: "Trisha Drueke-Heusel, 38," *Crain's Detroit Business*, September 26, 2005.

390 They landed at first: The information on Domino's cost analysis was drawn from a September 3, 2004, memo between Ken Calwell at Domino's and Dan Gill, obtained by the authors.

390 They chatted about: Author interview with Dan Gill.

390 Weeks later, the company: September 10, 2004, agreement between Domino's Pizza and a Mark Burnett affiliated company, obtained by authors.

390 "We are currently negotiating": Letter to Rob Rohrbach at Mark Burnett from Trish Drueke, February 28, 2005, obtained by authors.

391 Papa John's went guerrilla: "Trump Tackles Pizza," *CNN Money*, accessed on January 22, 2024, https://money.cnn.com/2005/04/01/news/newsmakers/dominos_apprentice/.

391 "Why eat a pizza": "Trump Tackles Pizza."

391 At about 3:00 a.m.: Author interview with Jordan Yospe.

391 It was the sort: Author interview with Dan Gill.

391 Trump was handed a script: Author interview with Dan Gill.

392 Domino's paid Trump: Donald Trump's tax return information, obtained by authors.

392 Jordan Yospe looked: Author interview with Jordan Yospe.

392 "Clearly, this isn't going to": Author interview with Kevin Harris.

392 A PowerPoint presentation: Mark Burnett Productions confidential January 2005 PowerPoint presentation, obtained by authors.

393 "Explore stand-alone": Mark Burnett Productions confidential January 2005 PowerPoint presentation.

393 Gill cold-called the company: Author interview with Dan Gill.

393 She said Trump: Author interview with Dan Gill.

393 Soon after, Zanker issued: "Donald Trump Signs for Record Speaking Fee—$1,000,000 an Hour; Agrees to Speak for Learning Annex in Three Cities," *PR Newswire US*, January 14, 2005.

393 The relationship would earn: Donald Trump's tax return information, obtained by authors.

393 Burnett agreed to let: Financial records from Mark Burnett Productions, obtained by authors.

393 During a production meeting: Author interview with Dan Gill.

394 But he was "the talent": Author interview with confidential source.

394 "Look, we're in production": Author interview with Dan Gill.

30: Better Than Real Estate

395 He was thirty-seven years: Kelly Perdew's LinkedIn profile.

396 His Hong Kong partners: Brief of Defendants-

Respondents Hudson Waterfront I, II, III, IV and V Corporations, at 1 and 6–7, *Donald J. Trump et al v Henry Cheng et al.*, New York Supreme Court, Appellate Division, First Department (Civil Action: 2005-602877).

396 Perdew reported for work: Jeff Harrington, "Perdew Learning Reality of Trump," *St. Petersburg Times*, February 11, 2005.

396 "Kelly's going to come down": Harrington, "Perdew Learning Reality of Trump."

396 Led by the former: Donald Trump's tax return information, obtained by authors; Examination Before Trial of Donald J. Trump on September 20, 2010, at 131, *Steve Aaron v The Trump Organization, Inc., a New York Corporation, and Donald J. Trump, an Individual*, U.S. District Court, Middle District of Florida, Tampa Division (Civil Action No. 09-CV-2493).

397 "It's always a vetting problem": Author interview with confidential source.

397 Trump joined Perdew: Kris Hundley and Jeff Harrington, "Mogul Holds Court in Tampa," *Tampa Bay Times*, February 1, 2005.

397 "We can't do much": Hundley and Harrington, "Mogul Holds Court in Tampa."

397 Trump told the potential buyers: Hundley and Harrington, "Mogul Holds Court in Tampa."

397 Trump sent Kendra: "FameBot Appearance in Tampa," *Business Journal* (Tampa Bay, Fla.), March 2, 2006.

398 Eight days later: Photos of the event from Getty Images, reviewed by authors.

398 And eight days: Julia C. Nelson, "Trump Announces Son Only Minutes After Wife Gives Birth," *Orange County Register*, March 21, 2006.

398 "I continue to stay young": Nelson, "Trump Announces Son Only Minutes After Wife Gives Birth."

398 He called Rosie O'Donnell: *Larry King Live*, December 23, 2006.

399 He met a thirty-five-year-old: Ronan Farrow, "Donald Trump, a Playboy Model, and a System for Concealing Infidelity," *New Yorker*, February 16, 2018.

399 He finished sixty-second: Randy Youngman, "Back of the Pack: It's a Slam Dunk That Golfers Will Feel Better About Their Games After Watching Charles Barkley and Chris Webber Play a Round," *Orange County Register*, July 20, 2006.

399 With Ivanka sitting: Donald Trump on *The View*, March 6, 2006, as reported by the Associated Press, "Trump Jokes About Dating His Daughter," March 7, 2006.

399 "I'm not going to run": Fredric U. Dicker, "Say What? Now Trump Hints at Prez Run," *New York Post*, January 3, 2006.

399 "You made it!": Anne Archer, "Thinking Big with Donald Trump and ACN," *Success from Home* magazine, September 2014.

399 "Trump puts a lot of stock": Archer, "Thinking Big with Donald Trump and ACN."

400 They agreed to pay him: Endorsement agreement between Donald Trump and ACN, 2006, filed as part of a lawsuit.

400 They formed ACN: David Samuels, "The Golden Pyramid: Building a Fortune on Faith, Phone Bills, and the Patience of Your Friends," *New Yorker*, April 23, 2001.

400 "Life is God's gift": Valerie Lawton, "Phone Service Sold Amway Way," *Toronto Star*, September 20, 1997.

400 "They are dissatisfied": Samuels, "The Golden Pyramid: Building a Fortune on Faith, Phone Bills, and the Patience of Your Friends."

401 "The two things I've mastered": Joe Miller, "The Donald Trump Scandal He Wants You to Forget: Inside His Despicable Scheme to Prey on the Poor & Make Himself Richer," *Salon*, September 15, 2015.

401 "I think the ACN video phone": "ACN Goes Primetime with Encore Appearance on Donald J. Trump's *The Celebrity Apprentice*," press release, March 2011.

401 The company's revenues: Eric Young, "New Marketing Trend Brings Opportunities, Pitfalls," *Sacramento Bee*, May 2, 1997.

401 "We do a lot of research": Yelena Dzhanova, "Inside Trump's Ties to the Multi-Level Marketing Company That Gave Him $8.8 Million When He Was Approaching Financial Ruin," *Business Insider*, October 21, 2020, https://www.businessinsider.com/trump-relationship-acn-mlm-company-lawsuit-2020-10.

401 Published in 2001: Samuels, "The Golden Pyramid: Building a Fortune on Faith, Phone Bills, and the Patience of Your Friends."

402 "I do not know": James V. Grimaldi and Mark Maremont, "Donald Trump Made Millions from Multilevel Marketing Firm," *Wall Street Journal*, August 13, 2015.

402 "I think it was George Ross": Videotaped deposition of Donald Trump, Document 534-27, at 90–91, *Catherine McKoy et al v The Trump Organization et al.*, United States District Court, Southern District of New York (Civil Action No. 18 C 09936).

402 "We hit it off": Erin Ailworth, "Firm's New Moniker May Be Its Trump Card," *Boston Globe*, December 7, 2010.

402 The company, Ideal Health: Ana Swanson, "The Trump Network Sought to Make People Rich, But Left Behind Disappointment," *Washington Post*, March 23, 2016.

402 The business focused: Swanson, "The Trump Network Sought to Make People Rich, But Left Behind Disappointment."

402 The company's chief executive: Affidavit of Plaintiff Blechman in Opposition to Motion to Dismiss, *Dean Blechman v Ideal Health*, Document 30-5, at 7–8, U.S. District Court, Eastern District of New York (Civil Action No. 09 cv 10791).

402 Complaints against the company: Complaints filed with the Federal Trade Commission made public because of a freedom of information request by Charles A. Horowitz, an attorney based in Minneapolis, and posted on the Center for Inquiry website.

402 "When I did": Video remarks of Donald Trump speaking at a Trump Network event in Miami, 2009, https://www.youtube.com/watch?v=XyRE5MN8jrA.

402 The licensing deal paid: Donald Trump's tax return information, obtained by authors.

403 The Stanwood brothers: Bankruptcy petitions filed in U.S. Bankruptcy Court, District of Massachusetts, Eastern Division, by Scott Stanwood (2013 BK 10403), Todd Stanwood (2013 BK 14003), Louis P. DeCaprio (2013 BK 12437); property appraisal of

4 Illsley Road, West Newbury, Massachusetts, filed in Scott Stanwood bankruptcy, Docket 36, at 19.

403 "They changed us": Swanson, "The Trump Network Sought to Make People Rich, But Left Behind Disappointment."

403 Michael Wang Sexton: Wedding announcement for Michael W. Sexton and Julie J. Chanchien, *New York Times*, October 9, 1994.

403 "It was my concept": Videotaped deposition of Michael W. Sexton, Document 220-2, at 26, *Art Cohen v Donald J. Trump*, U.S. District Court, Southern District of California (Civil Action No. 13 C 2519).

403 He pitched Trump: Exhibits to the Affirmation of Assistant Attorney General Tristan C. Snell in Support of the Verified Petition Volume 1 of 9—Exhibits A-G2, Examination of Michael Sexton under oath, at Exhibit B., *The People of the State of New York v Trump Entrepreneur Initiative LLC*, in Supreme Court of the State of New York, County of New York (Index No. 451463-2013).

403 That meeting lasted: Examination of Michael Sexton under oath, *The People of the State of New York v Trump Entrepreneur Initiative LLC.*

404 He agreed to provide: Examination of Michael Sexton under oath, *The People of the State of New York v Trump Entrepreneur Initiative LLC.*

404 Trump said that he would: Patrick Cole, Bloomberg News, "Trump Unveils Online University Venture Bearing His Name Will Start Offering Classes This Week," *Orlando Sentinel*, May 24, 2005.

404 Trump said his goal: Karen Matthews, "Trump Unveils Launch of Trump University," Associated Press Online, May 23, 2005.

404 "I love the concept": *Showbiz Tonight*, CNN, transcript, May 23, 2005.

404 New York officials: Affirmation in Opposition to Respondents' Motions for Partial Summary Judgment, Exhibit AA, Affidavit of Carole Yates, Doc. No. 219, *The People of the State of New York v Trump Entrepreneur Initiative LLC*, in Supreme Court of the State of New York, County of New York (Index No. 451463-2013).

404 "We teach people": *Larry King Live*, CNN, transcript, March 9, 2006.

404 "Michael is a fantastic guy": *Larry King Live*, CNN, March 9, 2006.

404 Before too long: Examination of Michael Sexton under oath, *The People of the State of New York v Trump Entrepreneur Initiative LLC.*

404 To make the shift: Examination of Michael Sexton under oath, *The People of the State of New York v Trump Entrepreneur Initiative LLC.*

404 They had been accused: Alex Leary, "How Trump Institute Failed," *Tampa Bay Times*, July 3, 2016.

405 The Milins began advertising: Leary, "How Trump Institute Failed."

405 After a free ninety-minute: Exhibit FF, Document No. 224, "Trump University 2010 Playbook," *The People of the State of New York v Trump Entrepreneur Initiative LLC*, in Supreme Court of the State of New York, County of New York (Index No. 451463-2013); Multiple affidavits of former Trump University Instructors, including Declaration of Ronald Schnackenburg in Support of Plaintiff's Motion for Class Action, Document No. 48-9, Exhibit 37, *Tarla Makaeff v Trump University, LLC*, U.S. District Court, Southern District of California (Index No. 10 CV 940).

405 Marketing materials played off: Exhibit FF, Document No. 224, *The People of the State of New York v Trump Entrepreneur Initiative LLC*, in Supreme Court of the State of New York, County of New York) (Index No. 451463-2013).

405 Randal Pinkett, the season four: Author interview with Randal Pinkett.

405 Trump did not appear: Examination of Michael Sexton under oath, *The People of the State of New York v Trump Entrepreneur Initiative LLC.*

405 He also did not meet: Examination of Michael Sexton under oath, *The People of the State of New York v Trump Entrepreneur Initiative LLC.*

405 Years later, the Associated Press: Michael Blesecker, "Trump University Staff Included Drug Trafficker, Child Molester," *Sante Fe New Mexican*, October 28, 2016.

405 He was sentenced: *Low v. Trump University, LLC et al*, Southern District of California (San Diego), 10-cv-00940, Document 462-3, Exhibit 5, 2.

406 At a seminar: Information in this section about James Aubrey Harris speaking at a seminar in Tampa was drawn from Ben Montgomery, "Trump U: The Art of the Spiel," *Tampa Bay Times*, June 15, 2008.

406 In some years, he earned: Olivia Nuzzi and Kate Briquelet, "Trump University Hired Motivational Speakers and a Felon as Faculty," *Daily Beast*, March 8, 2016.

406 He bought expensive cars: *Low v. Trump University, LLC et al*, Southern District of California (San Diego), 10-cv-00940, Document 462-3, Exhibit 5, pp. 10 and 13; Nuzzi and Briquelet, "Trump University Hired Motivational Speakers and a Felon as Faculty."

406 John C. Brown succumbed: Account of John C. Brown's experience drawn from Affidavit of John Brown, Document No. 195, Exhibit J-1, *The People of the State of New York v Trump Entrepreneur Initiative LLC*, in Supreme Court of the State of New York, County of New York (Index No. 451463-2013).

407 His mentor, Gilpin: Stephen Gilpin, *The Inside Story of Trump University* (New York: OR Books, 2018).

408 He pulled $5 million: Author analysis of Donald J. Trump tax returns.

408 Don Jr. had become friendly: "Trump Mortgage Unit Plots Aggressive Growth," *Real Estate Finance and Investment*, March 3, 2006.

408 He said he had worked: Stephen Gandel, "Trump Mortgage Chief Inflated Resume," *Money*, December 26, 2006.

409 Jennifer McGovern, who worked: Author interview with Jennifer McGovern, 2021.

409 "The brand has never been stronger": Christine Haughney, "You're Approved: Trump Presents Mortgage Firm," *Wall Street Journal*, April 5, 2006.

409 "This one's really": Stephane Fitch, "The Real Apprentices," *Forbes*, Sep 22, 2006.

409 Eight months after the official launch: Gandel, "Trump Mortgage Chief Inflated Resume."

409 "The mortgage business": Tom Fredrickson, "Undoing of Trump Mortgage," *Crain's New York Business*, August 6, 2007.

409 "Obviously it's the holidays": NYCSingleMom.com, "Chatting with Ivanka Trump at Cookies for Kids' Cancer Charity Event," videotaped interview, December 11, 2011, https://www.nycsinglemom.com/chatting-with-ivanka-trump-at-cookies-for-kids-cancer-charity-event/.

409 Glad paid her $285,000: Trial exhibit PX-01278, at 69–70, *People of the State of New York, by Letitia James, Attorney General of the State of New York v. Donald J. Trump, et al*, Supreme Court of the State of New York, County of New York (Civil Term, No. 452564-2022).

410 He had made almost: Donald Trump's tax return information, obtained by authors.

410 And that windfall: Donald Trump's tax return information, obtained by authors.

410 Forty of the real estate: Author tabulation of failed Trump licensing announcements.

410 In Tampa, the developers discovered: James Thorner, "Troubles for Trump Site," *Tampa Bay Times*, August 26, 2006.

410 Unable to secure financing: James Thorner, "Knight Rides to the Rescue of Trump Tower," *Tampa Bay Times*, November 23, 2006; "Dealmaker Pleads Guilty to Tax Charge," *Tampa Bay Times*, September 24, 2008.

410 At a criminal trial later: "Dealmaker Pleads Guilty to Tax Charge."

410 The Tampa crew tried again: James Thorner, "Ex-Con Sued by Trump Builders," *Tampa Bay Times*, November 8, 2008.

411 After collecting $2 million: Donald Trump's tax return information, obtained by authors; James Thorner, "Trump Cuts Ties," *Tampa Bay Times*, October 1, 2008.

411 The project had died: Examination Before Trial of Donald J. Trump on September 20, 2010, at 61–63, *Steve Aaron v The Trump Organization, Inc., a New York Corporation, and Donald J. Trump, an Individual*, U.S. District Court, Middle District of Florida, Tampa Division (Civil Action No. 09-CV-2493).

411 Trump described a project: Michael Barbaro, "Buying a Trump Property, or So They Thought," *New York Times*, May 12, 2011.

411 "The last thing": Barbaro, "Buying a Trump Property, or So They Thought."

411 Trump and Ivanka: Matthew Mosk, Brian Epstein, and Cho Park, "As Trumps Return to Dormant Dominican Development, Original Buyers and Watchdogs Cry Foul," ABCNews.go.com, June 11, 2018.

411 Eric and Ivanka greeted: Mosk, Epstein, and Park, "As Trumps Return to Dormant Dominican Development, Original Buyers and Watchdogs Cry Foul."

31: Real Estate

413 Before network executives: Reuters, "'You Can't Fire Me, I Quit,' Says Trump to NBC," Today.com, May 18, 2007, https://www.today.com/popculture/you-can-t-fire-me-i-quit-says-trump-nbc-wbna18746527.

413 "NBC wants very much": Video of press conference in Chicago, May 24, 2007, https://www.youtube.com/watch?v=xFbr8-bzKis.

413 Silverman learned the show: Author interview with Ben Silverman, 2023.

413 A celebrity version: Author interview with Ben Silverman.

414 "All I know is there's more": The dialogue and description of events about Donald Trump signing on to *Celebrity Apprentice* is based on author interview with Ben Silverman.

414 In 2003, when Trump unveiled: Mary Umberger and Thomas A. Corfman, "Trump Unwraps Building Plan," *Chicago Tribune*, September 24, 2003.

414 *The Apprentice* debuted: "Ceremony Marks Demolition Work for Trump Tower," *Chicago Tribune*, October 29, 2004.

415 Fortress Investment Group: Verified complaint, at 13, *Donald J. Trump et al v. Deutsche Bank Trust Company Americas et al*, verified complaint, Supreme Court of the State of New York, County of Queens (Civil Action No. 2008-26841).

415 And Deutsche Bank: Verified complaint, at 13, *Donald J. Trump et al v. Deutsche Bank Trust Company Americas et al.*

415 Deutsche Bank's real estate lending: David Enrich, Russ Buettner, Mike McIntire, and Susanne Craig, "How Trump Maneuvered His Way Out of Trouble in Chicago," *New York Times*, October 27, 2020.

415 "The vast majority": Author interview with confidential source, 2022.

415 For taking those measures: Author interview with confidential source, 2022.

415 For its part, Fortress: Author interview with confidential source; Enrich, Buettner, McIntire, and Craig, "How Trump Maneuvered His Way Out of Trouble in Chicago."

415 He filled that hole: Nathan Nelson to William C. Mott Jr., June 2, 2008, attached to verified complaint, at 13, *Donald J. Trump et al v. Deutsche Bank Trust Company Americas et al.*

415 He planned to stagger: Louis R. Carlozo, "How Trump Tower Opened While Still Adding on Floors," *Chicago Tribune*, June 12, 2008.

416 Trump said publicly: Video of press conference in Chicago, May 24, 2007.

416 He canceled most: Alby Gallun, "Dumped by Trump; At The Donald's Tower, 'Friends and Family' Buyers See Deals Nixed," *Crain's Chicago Business*, January 15, 2007.

416 And he pulled: Annie Sweeney, "Evanston Grandma Versus The Donald," *Chicago Tribune*, May 21, 2013.

416 One person familiar with: Author interview with confidential source, 2022.

416 "Donald and Eric": Author interview with confidential source, 2023.

417 "This is a great time": Video of April 28, 2008, news conference, https://www.youtube.com/watch?v=LbjXdvX8Zss.

417 Following Trump's advice: CoreLogic, "Special Report, Evaluating the Housing Market Since the Great Recession," February 2018, accessed on February 2, 2024, https://www.corelogic.com/wp-content/uploads/sites/4/2021/06/report-special-report-evaluating-the-housing-market-since-the-great-recession.pdf.

417 Deutsche Bank's printed agenda: Data in this paragraph was drawn from Trump International Hotel and Tower, lender's conference call agenda, April 30, 2008, obtained by authors.

417 Over the summer: Alby Gallun and Thomas A. Coffman, "Condo Buyers Flip Off Trump," *Crain's Chicago Business*, July 28, 2008.

418 On September 24: Trump International Hotel and Tower, lender meeting agenda, September 24, 2008, obtained by authors.

418 Eric Trump told the lenders: Trump International Hotel and Tower, lender meeting agenda.

418 In exchange for another extension: Trump International Hotel and Tower, lender meeting agenda.

418 By the Friday before: Author interview with confidential source, 2022.

418 As the condos had sold: Affidavit of William C. Mott Jr., November 24, 2008, in the matter of *Donald J. Trump et al v. Deutsche Bank Trust ComAmericas et al.*

418 One of Trump's lawyers: Author interview with Steve Schlesinger, 2023.

418 Deutsche executives who: Author interview with confidential source, 2023.

419 The lenders worried: Author interview with confidential source, 2023.

419 But we later learned: Enrich, Buettner, McIntire, and Craig, "How Trump Maneuvered His Way Out of Trouble in Chicago."

419 Kushner knew the head: Enrich, Buettner, McIntire, and Craig, "How Trump Maneuvered His Way Out of Trouble in Chicago"; Jesse Drucker and David Enrich, "Deutsche Bank Investigates Personal Banker to Trump and Kushner," *New York Times*, August 3, 2020.

419 Vrablic's division soon: Enrich, Buettner, McIntire, and Craig, "How Trump Maneuvered His Way Out of Trouble in Chicago."

419 To issue the loan: Verified Complaint, at 153, *People of the State of New York, by Letitia James, Attorney General of the State of New York v. Donald J. Trump, et al*, Supreme Court of the State of New York, County of New York (Civil Term, No. 452564-2022).

419 The bank's first analysis: Trial exhibit PX-00291, at 10, *People of the State of New York, by Letitia James, Attorney General of the State of New York v. Donald J. Trump, et al.*

419 For the year 2008: Verified complaint, at 21, *People of the State of New York, by Letitia James, Attorney General of the State of New York v. Donald J. Trump.*

420 He paid no federal income taxes: Donald Trump's tax return information, obtained by authors.

420 He filed his tax returns: Donald Trump's tax return information, obtained by authors.

420 The IRS did, however: IRS audit records, obtained by authors.

420 After declaring it worthless: Office of the New York State Attorney General, "Background on Trump Organization Properties and Fraudulent Schemes," 7, https://ag.ny.gov/sites/default/files/tto_release_properties_addendum_-_final.pdf.

420 In a court filing: Russ Buettner and Charles V. Bagli, "How Donald Trump Bankrupted His Atlantic City Casinos, but Still Earned Millions," *New York Times*, June 11, 2016.

421 Pinkett, who had earned: Author interview with Randal Pinkett.

421 On the drive back: Author interview with Randal Pinkett.

421 he offered to buy: Buettner and Bagli, "How Donald Trump Bankrupted His Atlantic City Casinos, but Still Earned Millions."

421 "If I'm not going to run it": Wayne Parry, "Trump Quits Casino Company's Board," Associated Press State & Local Wire, February 13, 2009.

422 As a result of the bankruptcy: Trump Entertainment Resorts, Inc., Form 10-K, for the year ending December 31, 2010 (filed March 31, 2011), 84.

422 The same day Trump quit: Donald J. Trump to Trump Entertainment Resorts, Inc., February 13, 2009, filed with the Securities and Exchange Commission, Accession Number: 0000899140-09-000469.

422 But that November: Russ Buettner, Susanne Craig, and Mike McIntire, "Long-Concealed Records Show Trump's Chronic Losses and Years of Tax Avoidance," *New York Times*, September 27, 2020.

422 For 2009, Trump declared: Donald Trump's tax return information, obtained by authors.

422 Following its usual procedures: Buettner, Craig, and McIntire, "Long-Concealed Records Show Trump's Chronic Losses and Years of Tax Avoidance."

423 Years later, Michael D. Cohen: Michael D. Cohen's testimony before Congress, February 27, 2019.

423 "Sometimes you're better off": Buettner and Bagli, "How Donald Trump Bankrupted His Atlantic City Casinos, but Still Earned Millions."

423 At this homecoming: Severin Carrell, "'I Feel Scottish,' Says Donald Trump on Flying Visit to Mother's Cottage," *The Guardian*, June 9, 2008.

423 She had visited: Carrell, "'I Feel Scottish,' Says Donald Trump on Flying Visit to Mother's Cottage."

423 Donald had been once: Carrell, "'I Feel Scottish,' Says Donald Trump on Flying Visit to Mother's Cottage."

423 He just had been: David Leask, "Mum's the Word: Trump Returns to Lewis as Family Takes Centre Stage," *The Herald* (Glasgow), June 10, 2008.

423 Trump said he selected: Leask, "Mum's the Word: Trump Returns to Lewis as Family Takes Centre Stage."

423 He stayed inside: Carrell, "'I Feel Scottish,' Says Donald Trump on Flying Visit to Mother's Cottage."

424 Two men, Neil Hobday: Author interviews with Neil Hobday and Ashley Cooper, 2022.

424 Trump paid $12.6 million: *People of the State of New York, by Letitia James v. The Trump Organization, Inc., et al.*, supplemental verified petition, Index No. 451685 /2020, 18.

424 "His number one": Author interview with Ashley Cooper.

424 "This development will": Jenifer Johnston and Graeme Smith, "Wind May Be Hazard in Trump's Plans to Build GBP300m Golf Resort; US Tycoon Warns He Will Accept No Delays to Vision," *Herald* (Glasgow), April 1, 2006.

424 "I never like to get": Tom Kirk and Claire Elliot, "Trump Tells Scots: It Was Love at First Sight," *Aberdeen Press and Journal*, April 1, 2006.

424 "I would have no interest": Johnston and Smith, "Wind May Be Hazard in Trump's Plans to Build GBP300m Golf Resort."

424 Trump pushed Hobday: Author interview with Neil Hobday.

424 Ramshackle sheds and rusted farm equipment: Anthony Baxter, director, *You've Been Trumped* 2016.

424 Forbes eventually sold: "Trump Faces Protests over Scotland Plans," UPI, May 26, 2010.

425 Over the years of their standoff: Frank Urquhart, "Donald Trump Jets in and Fires Off 'Slum and Pigsty' Slur," *Scotsman*, May 27, 2010.

425 "His property is a pigsty": Urquhart, "Donald Trump Jets in and Fires Off 'Slum and Pigsty' Slur."

425 "Go back to hell": Urquhart, "Donald Trump Jets in and Fires Off 'Slum and Pigsty' Slur."

425 Their battle became: Frank Urquhart, "Queen Legend Brian May Backs Donald Trump Protest," *Scotland on Sunday*, January 30, 2011.

425 Trump had spent time: Eddie Barnes and Jeremy Watson, "How Jack of Clubs Came Up Trumps for Donald," *Scotland on Sunday*, May 14, 2006; Severin Carroll, "Salmond Steps in to Save Trump's Billion-Dollar Scottish Golf Course," *Guardian*, December 5, 2007.

425 "If you reject this": Ben McConville, "Donald Trump Argues His Case for Contentious Golf Development in Scotland," *Canadian Press*, June 10, 2008.

426 "I would consider myself": McConville, "Donald Trump Argues His Case for Contentious Golf Development in Scotland."

426 Martin Ford, a local: McConville, "Donald Trump Argues His Case for Contentious Golf Development in Scotland."

426 "You know, nobody has ever": McConville, "Donald Trump Argues His Case for Contentious Golf Development in Scotland."

426 "Six thousand jobs": "Scotland Gives Donald Trump Go Ahead for 'World's Biggest Golf Course,'" *Guardian*, November 3, 2008.

427 Trump converted the old: Trump International Golf Club Scotland Limited, Directors' report and financial statements, 2008 through 2022.

427 "He could say some crazy things": The description of events about Stormy Daniels's visit to Trump Tower was drawn from an interview with Neil Hobday.

427 "In my history": Graeme Smith, "Donald Aims to Trump the World with Plan for GBP300m Golf Resort," *Herald* (Glasgow), April 29, 2006.

427 Trump has said he spent: David Ewen, "'I've Already Spent £40m on Golfing Masterpiece," *Aberdeen Evening Express*, May 26, 2010.

427 "I know how to build": Video of news conference on May 24, 2007, https://www.youtube.com/watch?v=G6dm3QAeCvQ.

428 Trump sued the Hong Kong: Complaint, at 3, *Donald J. Trump v Henry Cheng et al*, Supreme Court of the State of New York, County of New York (Civil Action No. 2005-602877).

428 He charged that they had sold: Terry Pristin, "Vornado Goes Both East and West for a Deal," *New York Times*, May 16, 2007.

428 Though he was under no: Donald Trump's tax return information, obtained by authors.

429 Trump received a total: Donald Trump's tax return information, obtained by authors.

429 He joked that Trump: Amy B. Wang, "Trump Was Mocked at the 2011 White House Correspondents' Dinner. He Insists It's Not Why He Ran," *Washington Post*, April 29, 2018.

429 "There was a lot": Wang, "Trump Was Mocked at the 2011 White House Correspondents' Dinner."

32: Don't Do This for the Money

430 In April 2012, Dan: Except where noted the dialogue and description of events in this section about Dan Tangherlini's initial assessment of Donald Trump's offer bid to lease and redevelop the Old Post Office is based on an author interview with Dan Tangherlini, 2023.

431 One bidding team: April 16, 2012, letter to Kevin M. Terry, Contracting Office, United States General Services Administration, from Stephen M. Ryan and Jason W. Kim, Counsel for B.P.-Metropolitan Investors, LLC.

431 "In a way, we are": Jonathan O'Connell, "How the Trumps Landed the Old Post Office Pavilion," *Washington Post*, August 17, 2022.

431 "We are not cutting corners": Trump Organization promotional video, September 18, 2013, https://www.youtube.com/watch?v=PqdfpV47Mu4.

432 He went back to Deutsche Bank's: Trial exhibit PX-00294, at 3, *People of the State of New York, by Letitia James, Attorney General of the State of New York v. Donald J. Trump, et al.*, Supreme Court of the State of New York, County of New York, Civil Term, No. 452564-2022); David Enrich, Russ Buettner, Mike McIntire, and Susanne Craig, "How Trump Maneuvered His Way Out of Trouble in Chicago," *New York Times*, October 27, 2020.

432 One industry analyst: Russ Buettner, "Donald Trump's Income Isn't Always What He Says It Is, Records Suggest," *New York Times*, November 3, 2016.

432 "I don't do this": Rick Remsnyder, "Trump in Golf 'for the Fun,'" *Journal News* (Westchester County, N.Y.), May 27, 2001.

432 "It doesn't get better": December 15, 2011, email to Jason Greenblatt et al from Ivanka Trump, submitted in the New York Attorney General's civil lawsuit against Donald Trump.

433 "I'll spend more": Linda Robertson, "Trump Plans to Make Doral 'Finest Golf Resort,'" *Miami Herald*, March 8, 2012.

433 After the renovations: Buettner, "Donald Trump's Income Isn't Always What He Says. It Is, Records Suggest."

433 "So, he spent": Buettner, "Donald Trump's Income Isn't Always What He Says It Is, Records Suggest,"

433 In 2008, the foundation reported: Gerry Dulac, "Golf Clubs Struggling to Stay in Bounds," *Pittsburgh Post-Gazette*, February 19, 2008.

433 In 2014, the foundation reported: Courtney Trenwith, "Second Time Lucky for Donald Trump in Dubai?," ArabianBusiness.com, May 30, 2014.

434 "We really don't know": Brad Tuttle, "Fore! No, Make That Five! 5 Reasons Golf Is in a Hole," *Money*, June 13, 2014.

434 "I think the National Golf": Interview between Michael Bamberger, a senior writer for *Sports Illustrated*, and Donald Trump, Golf.com, May 15, 2014.

434 Don Jr. had played: Kate Holmquist and Tom Lyons, "Trump Lays Out Ambitious Plans for Doonbeg Golf Resort After EUR 15m Deal; Flamboyant Billionaire Says Investment Shows Ireland's Economy Is Recovering," *Irish Times*, February 12, 2014.

434 "It never made me": Author interview with Charles P. "Buddy" Darby III, 2022.

434 Trump bought it out: Irish corporate records, reviewed by authors.

435 Starwood Hotel and Resorts: James Corrigan, "Trump in the Hunt to Buy £36m Turnberry; American Billionaire Wants Open Course in His Portfolio, Selling Price Is £16m Less Than Dubai Paid in 2008," *Daily Telegraph*, April 28, 2014.

435 He soon announced: "Donald Trump Planning to Spend £120m on Turnberry Resort," *Carrick Gazette* (Scotland), May 24, 2014.

435 Ralph Porciani, Trump's general manager: Interview with Ralph Porciani on *Scottish Chefs Podcast*, 2020.

435 Food and beverage: Interview with Ralph Porciani on *Scottish Chefs Podcast*.

435 He reported losses: Alex Banks, "Trump Golf Course Loses Cash for 10th Straight Year," *Aberdeen Evening Express*, January 15, 2024.

435 Years later, Porciani remained: Interview with Ralph Porciani on *Scottish Chefs Podcast*.

435 His income from *The Celebrity Apprentice*: Donald Trump's tax return information, obtained by authors.

436 He unloaded $98 million: Donald Trump's tax return information, obtained by authors.

436 In its annual reviews: Trial exhibit PX-03137, at 13-14, *People of the State of New York, by Letitia James, Attorney General of the State of New York v. Donald J. Trump, et al.*, Supreme Court of the State of New York, County of New York, Civil Term, No. 452564-202.

436 In the spring of 2015: The dialogue and description of events in this section on the spring 2015 meeting at Trump Tower is based on interviews with confidential sources familiar with the meeting.

437 He called within an hour: The dialogue and description of events in this section about NBC's decision to sever ties with Donald Trump is based on an author interview with Paul Telegdy, 2023.

438 Muriel Gonzalez, a cosmetics executive: Author interview with Diana Espino, an executive at Parlux Fragrances, and a confidential source.

438 And the day after that: "Serta Mattress Maker Latest to Dump Trump," NBCNews.com, July 2, 2015; Donald Trump's tax return information, obtained by authors.

438 A week later, the PGA: "The Companies That Have Dumped Donald Trump," ABCNews.com, July 4, 2015.

500 Then Phillips-Van Heusen: "PVH's Apparel Deal with Trump Ends as Macy's Cuts Ties with Tycoon," Reuters, July 7, 2015; Donald Trump's tax return information, obtained by authors.

Epilogue

441 Speaking over the hissing: C-SPAN, accessed on March 14, 2024, at https://www.c-span.org/video/?508150-1/president-trump-final-white-house-departure; transcript accessed on March 14, 2024, at https://www.govinfo.gov/content/pkg/DCPD-202100046/html/DCPD-202100046.htm.

442 He became the first: Jacey Fortin, "Trump Is Not the First President to Snub an Inauguration," *New York Times*, January 19, 2021.

442 Contrary to that mission: Dan Alexander, "Why Would Anyone in Their Right Mind Pay $370 Million for Trump's D.C. Hotel?," *Forbes*, October 13, 2021.

443 Our colleagues at the *Times*: Nicholas Confessore et al., "The Swamp That Trump Built," *New York Times*, October 10, 2020.

447 She called Trump's farewell: Jeremy W. Peters, "'They Have Not Legitimately Won': Pro-Trump Media Keeps the Disinformation Flowing," *New York Times*, January 20, 2021.

447 In that world: Peter Baker, "Copying Roosevelt, Biden Wanted a Fast Start. Now Comes the Hard Part," *New York Times*, January 30, 2021.

447 Fox paid $787 million: Jeremy W. Peters and Katie Robertson, "Fox Will Pay $787.5 Million to Settle Defamation Suit," *New York Times*, April 18, 2023.

448 He told the television journalist: Eli Rosenberg, "Trump Admitted He Attacks Press to Shield Himself from Negative Coverage, Lesley Stahl Says," *Washington Post*, May 22, 2018.

449 Consider how he has characterized: Lauren Irwin, "Trump Knocks Prosecutor, 'Radical Left Lunatics' in Thanksgiving Message," The Hill, November 23, 2023, https://thehill.com/blogs/blog-briefing-room/4324656-trump-thanksgiving-prosecutor-radical-left-lunatics/; Jack Queen, "Trump Lashes Out at Court Clerk after NY Gag Order Paused," Reuters, November 17, 2023, https://www.reuters.com/legal/trump-lashes-out-court-clerk-after-ny-gag-order-paused-2023-11-17/; Sarah Fortinsky, "Trump Hits New York AG for 'Smirking All Day Long' Amid Fraud Trial," The Hill, November, 14, 2023, https://thehill.com/regulation/court-battles/4308673-trump-james-new-york-smirking-fraud-trial/; Benjamin Weiser, Maggie Haberman, and Maria Cramer, "As Trump Continues to Insult E. Jean Carroll, 2nd Defamation Trial Opens," *New York Times*, January 15, 2024; Jonathan Swan, Maggie Haberman, and Nicholas Nehamas, "'This Is the Final Battle': Trump Casts His Campaign as an Existential Fight Against His Critics," *New York Times*, June 10, 2023.

CREDITS PAGE

6: John Pedin/NY Daily News Archive via Getty Images

7: Dustin Pittman/Penske Media via Getty Images

8: Black River Productions, Ltd. / Mitch Epstein. Courtesy of Sikkema Jenkins & Co., New York. Used with permission. All rights reserved.

9: Bettmann Archive via Getty Images

10: LaGuardia and Wagner Archives

11: Ron Galella/Ron Galella Collection via Getty Images

12: Bettman Archive via Getty Images

13: Ron Galella /Ron Galella Collection via Getty Images

14: Chester Higgins. © 2020 THE NEW YORK TIMES COMPANY

15: Ezio Petersen via UPI/Alamy Stock Photo

16: Jemal Countess/WireImage via Getty Images

17: The Associated Press/Charles Rex Arbogast

18: The Associated Press

19: Jonathan Ernst/ Reuters News & Media

INDEX